Extensively revised Chapter 3, "Developing Higher-Order Thinking Skills Through Programming, Projects, and Research," illustrates how using technology can encourage the development of problem-solving skills.

...NG RESOURCES
...rnsley, S7

... scientist must find a way to create mean-
...ng numerical data into a graphic represen-
... the scientist to contemplate the data in a
... ay also be necessary to find what is a "typ-
... ...mples. For example, the biologist we have
... ...ts from several locations. Calculating a
... te from each location would likely be part
... ...derstand differences across the locations.
... see Chapter 5) to create graphs or calculate
... have gathered.

...ally, the research process is not complete until scientists and student sci-
...ent... communicate what they have discovered. For students, communication
...requires interpretation and the use of existing knowledge. Generating a prod-

Focus

Using a Data Logger to Measure Stress

Laurie Tweeton, a health and physical education teacher, engages her students in projects that require the collection and analysis of data. Some of her projects use a device that records heart rate data. The device, which consists of a strap worn around the chest and a data recorder worn like a wrist watch, allows complete freedom of activity. The data recorder holds more than 8 hours of information and is easily connected to a computer for data transfer.

One of Laurie's favorite projects involves... middle school students. She asks... volunteers with three different... who are willing to wear the heart... ng their workday. When they can... volunteers are asked to push a... recorder when they change ac-... keep notes identifying the differ-... The data logger marks the time... ansitions occur. Students bring... nitor back to school, offload the

data, and enter labels on the chart corresponding to the activities that the parents report. Students then compare the heart rate patterns of each subject and discuss which activities seemed to create the greatest stress.

Having actual data to consider may help you understand the types of investigations that are possible. Laurie allowed us to use the heart rate monitor, and we tried to generate our own authentic investigation. Here is what we came up with. We recently purchased a hot tub (called a spa in some locations) and in reading the operating instructions noted some health warnings. Individuals with certain medical conditions are cautioned against using the hot tub. The heart rate monitor seemed a possible way to measure the stress generated by sitting in 104°F water. The design of our experiment was simple: Establish a 20-minute baseline, sit in the hot tub for 20 minutes, and conclude with a 20-minute

Now that you have had a brief exposure to the kinds of programming that younger students might do, the question becomes what these experiences accomplish. The remainder of this chapter addresses this question.

WAYS TO TEACH HIGHER-ORDER THINKING

It is time to return to the focus of this chapter—higher-order thinking— present a structure that outlines some of the options educators have for h... ing students become better thinkers. We use this structure to consider the... vantages and disadvantages that programming and other applications... technology involving manipulation and measurement offer in develop... higher-order thinking skills.

Classroom approaches to
higher-order thinking

There are three distinct approaches to the instruction of higher-or... thinking skills within a classroom setting, defined by the manner in wh... this instruction relates to the instruction of other areas of the curricul... (Wakefield, 1996):

◆ **Stand-alone approach.** Class activities are focused on the developmen... of higher-order thinking skills. Instruction in thinking skills and conte... area skills and knowledge is independent.

◆ **Dual-agenda approach.** Instruction in higher-order thinking is com... bined with instruction in another area of the curriculum. Instruction i... both areas may be provided independently within the course, but the... content-area learning tasks provide an opportunity for practicing thin... ing skills.

◆ **Authentic task approach.** This approach requires the application of... higher-order thinking in performing activities that lead to the develop... ment of both thinking and content-area skills and knowledge. Rather... than being developed independently, thinking skills are learned throug... the application within domain-appropriate activities.

The debate over which approach is best could be approached in a nu... ber of ways. One issue concerns whether it is reasonable to isolate and le... very general thinking skills so they can then be applied in many areas (Sim... & Anderson, 1989) or whether it is necessary to learn thinking skills wit... the areas in which they are to be applied (Brown et al., 1989). You will... counter comments on this distinction as you continue, but we regard the... sue as unresolved at this point. If it can be assumed that all three approac... have the potential to develop higher-order thinking skills, efficiency may... be an issue to consider. How many schools will be willing or able to off... course dedicated to thinking skills? Is it reasonable to involve students in... gramming, a course that probably is not central to the standard curricul... because it provides a good opportunity to practice higher-level thinking?

Table 3.3 summarizes some key points about the different approache... developing higher-order thinking skills. At the bottom of the table we h...

THE NORTHERN ~~CANCELLED~~ COLLEGE
LIBRARY
BARNSLEY

Chapter 3

Developing Higher-Order Thinking Skills Through Programming, Projects, and Research

ORIENTATION

Chapter 2 was intended to help you develop an understanding of meaningful learning and to challenge you to consider how school experiences might facilitate or inhibit optimal achievement on the part of students. Concerns with how and what students learn have prompted suggestions for school reform. Here, we extend this discussion by focusing on higher-order thinking skills. These skills are valued in society, but they are frequently perceived to be underemphasized in educational settings. We will help you understand what higher-order thinking skills are and consider several strategies for their development in schools.

This chapter also begins our direct consideration of how technology can be involved in student learning. We evaluate the benefits of programming experience as a way to develop student problem-solving skills. We also consider how activities involving various data-gathering devices can contribute to the curriculum. As you make your way through this book, you will find that although we cover many strategies for classroom learning with technology, we do emphasize a particular approach. We have prioritized authentic and collaborative content-area projects. This priority does not imply support for an exclusive focus on projects, but for a change in the frequency with which students encounter this type of learning activity. Authentic projects fit perfectly with the desire to encourage higher-order thinking and emphasize applications of technology that place students in an active role.

80

Northern College
Library

NC02460

CANCELLED
BERKELEY

Integrating Technology for Meaningful Learning

Third Edition

MARK GRABE

University of North Dakota

CINDY GRABE

Technology Facilitator, Grand Forks Schools

HOUGHTON MIFFLIN COMPANY

BOSTON   NEW YORK

EDITOR IN CHIEF: Patricia Coryell

SENIOR SPONSORING EDITOR: Loretta Wolozin

DEVELOPMENT EDITOR: Lisa Mafrici

SENIOR PROJECT EDITOR: Aileen Mason

ASSOCIATE PRODUCTION/DESIGN COORDINATOR: Lisa Jelly

SENIOR MANUFACTURING COORDINATOR: Florence Cadran

MARKETING ASSOCIATE: Caroline Guy

COVER DESIGN: Diana Coe / ko Design
COVER ART: Diana Ong / SuperStock

Copyright © 2001 by Houghton Mifflin Company. All rights reserved.

No part of this work may be reproduced or transmitted in any form or by any means, electronic or mechanical, including photocopying and recording, or by any information storage or retrieval system without prior written permission of the copyright owner unless such copying is expressly permitted by federal copyright law. With the exception of nonprofit transcription in Braille, Houghton Mifflin is not authorized to grant permission for further uses of copyrighted selections reprinted in this text without the permission of their owners. Permission must be obtained from the individual copyright owners as identified herein. Address requests for permission to make copies of Houghton Mifflin material to College Permissions, Houghton Mifflin Company, 222 Berkeley St., Boston, MA 02116-3764.

Printed in the U.S.A.

Library of Congress Catalog Number: 00-133885

ISBN: 0-618-04291-1

123456789–QUF–04 03 02 01 00

Acknowledgment is made to the following sources for permission to reprint selections from copyrighted material:
Preface figure: Copyright © 1993 and published by Weekly Reader Corporation. All rights reserved. Used by permission. **Photo of Len Zabilansky (p. 7):** Used by permission of Leonard J. Zabilansky. **Photo of Charlie Clark (p. 7):** Used by permission of Charles Clark. **Focus box, pp. 38–39:** Reprinted with permission from *National Educational Technology Standards for Students—Connecting Curriculum and Technology,* Copyright © 2000. ISTE (the International Society for Technology in Education), 800.336.5191 (U.S. and Canada) or 541.302.3777 (International). iste@iste.org, www.iste.org. All rights reserved. Reprint permission does not constitute an endorsement by ISTE. **Focus box, pp. 40–42:** Reprinted by permission of National Council for Accreditation of Teacher Education. **Figure 3.5:** Used courtesy of Stagecast. **Figure 4.5:** Used by permission of Sunburst Communications. **Figures 4.8, 4.9, 4.10:** From *Exploring the Nardoo.* Used by permission of The Learning Team. **Figure 6.1:** AOL Instant Messenger screenshot © 1999 America Online, Inc. Used with permission. **Figure 6.2:** Used by permission of Lori Swinney. **Figure 6.8:** Used by permission of North Dakota Game & Fish. **Figure 9.9:** Used courtesy of Interactive Solutions, Inc. **Figure 10.7:** Used by permission of Knowledge Adventure, Torrance, CA. **Figure 11.1:** Reprinted by permission of Netscape Communications Corporation.

Dedication

Allow me to tell a brief story. I remember a trip my wife and I took to my parents' home during the later stages of Cindy's and my education as graduate students. I happened to awake about six in the morning and went down to the kitchen of our old farm house because I was thirsty and needed a drink of water. When I walked into the kitchen, I was surprised to see that the lights were already on and my mother was busy working at the kitchen table preparing her lessons for the day. For some reason, the image has always stayed with me. My mother had taught Home Economics since I was in junior high school, and although I was also preparing for a career in education I had never really thought much about her dedication to what she did. My mother used hardware and software too. She had a shallow tray containing a substance that looked like Jell-O, and with this equipment and typed or hand-drawn spirit masters she would turn out dittoed pages about nutrition, sewing, childcare, or whatever she was intending to discuss. It was a slow process. First, the master had to be pressed against the "Jell-O" for a few minutes. It was important to align the master carefully or the final product would be crooked. Then, blank sheets of paper were individually pressed against the Jell-O–like material and carefully peeled away to create the handouts. Try to keep my mom's use of technology in mind as you read about the techniques we describe in this book. The contrast is amazing and provides just one indication of the tremendous change that has occurred in a relatively brief period of time. This story is intended to get you to think about more than the pace of change in our world. While Cindy and I believe strongly that technology can have a profound impact on our schools, our confidence in technology is justified only in classrooms led by dedicated and skillful teachers. We should be amazed and excited by the power of modern technology, but we should remain impressed by the teachers who begin work at six because last year's lesson may not be good enough. This book is dedicated to Frances Grabe and to all teachers like her.

Brief Contents

Contents

PART 3   Looking at Issues and Looking Ahead   407

CHAPTER 11   Responsible Use of Technology   408

Preface

Sophisticated technology has become so pervasive and intertwined with so many aspects of our private and professional lives that we seldom notice it. We watch movies on DVD and listen to music from CDs. Most magazine and television advertisements include e-mail addresses. Video games, ATM machines, fax machines, cellular phones, caller ID, voice mail, personal satellite dishes—the list of technology innovations we have accepted as commonplace goes on and on.

TECHNOLOGY IN CLASSROOMS

We wrote this book because technology seldom plays the same natural role in classrooms that it does in other areas of our daily lives. A recent survey of new teachers (Market Data Retrieval, 1999a) reports that only one third feel either "very well prepared" or "well prepared" to integrate technology in their classrooms. Many new teachers simply are not ready to take advantage of the resources already available in most K–12 classrooms. We realize that some teachers are uncertain and anxious about computer hardware, software selection, and which technology-supported learning activities are likely to be useful and productive for their students. If you feel that way, we hope the information and suggestions we provide in this book will move you from apprehension to excitement.

THIS TEXT'S PRIORITIES AND GOALS

The title of this book is intended to clearly state our commitment to some specific priorities. First, our emphasis is on *integrating technology*. This phrase is our way of saying our focus is on preparing you to use technology as a powerful tool in helping your students acquire the knowledge and skills of the content area or areas you will teach. If you end up feeling focused on how to use computers, video cameras, and the Internet rather than how to use technology resources to teach reading, mathematics, history, biology, or whatever content area you will teach, we have somehow failed to get our most basic message across. Second, our emphasis is on *meaningful (student) learning*. We focus primarily on what students can do with technology and argue that some experiences are probably more valuable than others. We do not ignore your own technology skills, but we emphasize preparing you to provide effective learning experiences to students.

This book is both about technology *and* about teaching and learning. We feel it is important to consider and discuss both areas together. Our primary goals are to

◆ present the different roles technology might play in your classrooms
◆ provide specific examples of each type of role
◆ link proposed classroom uses of technology with content area and technology standards
◆ inform you of the necessary technical ins and outs of some applications you might use in implementing each role
◆ suggest how teachers might initiate and guide particular technology-supported learning activities in classrooms
◆ promote your thinking and reflection about the best uses of technology

As you think about this information, we hope that you will also consider why you and your future students should spend time using technology in the ways we propose. As a teacher, you function in the important role of decision maker. The discussion of classroom learning and how learning is influenced by classroom tasks and activities should help you make decisions about whether or not you want to devote precious school time to a specific use of technology.

We also hope that as you read this book, you will not assume that school experiences as you know them must remain fixed, with technology somehow finding a way to fit within the existing framework. Some educational leaders are urging both a restructuring of schools and serious consideration of what schools do. *Technology is functioning as a catalyst* in some of these considerations, and it may serve the same role for you. As you think about how to use technology in your classroom, you will likely find yourself examining broad educational issues. We do not attempt to avoid criticisms of technology. Just remember: In most cases effective teaching with technology is effective teaching by any means. Criticisms of the way technology has been used may also alert you to more traditional practices that should also be criticized. For example, if many experts put down an overemphasis on drill-and-practice computer software, what do you think these same experts would say if asked to address the heavy use of traditional worksheets? If some advocates of technology suggest that teachers use technology to encourage a more active and personal form of learning, why not examine how active student learning is when no technology is involved? *We want you to think carefully about teaching and learning with and without technology.*

THE COGNITIVE PERSPECTIVE ON LEARNING

Our intent is to emphasize technology-facilitated classroom activities in an active learning environment—*one that strongly engages the thinking, decision-making, problem-solving, and reasoning behaviors of students.* We use the term *cognitive* to refer to these behaviors. To implement effective classroom activities, it is critical that teachers understand the connection between learning tasks and the mental activities of students.

Chapter 2, "Meaningful Learning in an Information Age," establishes the foundation for this connection. Chapter 2 focuses on developing your understanding of cognitive behaviors and explains how cognitive behaviors are influenced by learning tasks. We continue to emphasize this connection between learning and meaningful learning activities in nearly every chapter. Chapter 6, "Learning with Internet Tools," provides a special emphasis on what are often called higher-level thinking skills—decision making, problem solving, and reasoning. We use the discussion of the Internet as the context for asking you to think about higher-order thinking. Learning from Internet resources, like other "primary sources," requires learners to go beyond reception of information to cognitive skills involving judgment, interpretation, and application. Meaningful tasks taking advantage of the Internet and the immediate access to the information it provides should begin to shift the emphasis of educators away from information storage to other important skills. This is also part of what we mean by meaningful learning in an information age.

Finally, several of the later chapters focus on computer tools that allow students to create multimedia projects and culminate in Chapter 10, "Learning from Student Projects: Knowledge as Design and the Design of Hypermedia." Chapter 10 integrates several important topics—technology tools, cooperative learning, and learning from the construction of authentic content-area projects. The projects discussed in Chapter 10 and throughout the book represent practical examples of classroom tasks that encourage meaningful learning.

FEATURES OF THE REVISION

The first edition of *Integrating Technology for Meaningful Learning* appeared in 1996—and here we are, only five years later, introducing the third edition. The rapid transitions between editions have been a necessary consequence of the rapid pace of development and change in technology and some new possibilities for how technology can be applied in classrooms. What has pleased us as we have worked on the second and third editions has been just how well our original priorities have held up. If anything, themes such as (1) the integration of technology in content-area instruction, (2) authentic technology-supported student projects, and (3) the use of technology to support a more cognitively active approach to learning have become more widely accepted and promoted.

New Features

◆ *Standards Coverage:* This edition has added a description of ISTE, AECT, NCATE, and other major standards that have outlined expectations for K–12 students, preservice teachers, advanced professionals in educational computing, and colleges of education. Standards are one focus of Chapter 2 and are revisited as they apply to other topics throughout the book.

◆ *New Chapter on Problem Solving:* Our original chapter on programming has been recast as a more general chapter on problem solving with technology tools. In this new approach (see Chapter 3), programming is but one type of activity that encourages the development of problem-solving skills.

◆ *Coverage of Video Production:* Video production has been included as a new method for capturing community-based experiences and reflecting on these experiences through the processes involved in preparing video documentaries (see Chapter 9, "Learning to Work with Image, Sound, and Video"). Video production is presented as another possibility for authentic student projects.

◆ *Greater Internet Coverage:* The rapidity and enthusiasm with which K–12 institutions have committed to the Internet have prompted us to provide a much broader description of the ways in which Internet tools and resources can be involved in classrooms and a deeper analysis of some of the challenges of learning from Internet resources and experiences. Chapter 6 now includes a section on the advantages and disadvantages of computer-mediated communication and the proposal that teachers think of web resources as "primary sources." Interpreting most Internet resources as primary sources rather than instructional material provides an important shift in perspective that urges the development of new learning skills and provides needed opportunities for higher-order thinking. The Internet is discussed in several other chapters. Web page authoring is considered as an outlet for student projects in Chapter 10, and Chaptewr 11 ("Responsible Use of Technology") contains an extended description of methods for providing safe access to Internet resources.

A much larger proportion of the references included in the end-of-chapter "Resources to Expand Your Knowledge Base" are addresses for Internet sites. These resources have also been collected into a convenient new "Teacher's Handy Reference," which appears at the end of the book.

Updates and Revisions

◆ *Statistics and Research:* All chapters have been upgraded to include more current descriptive statistics to provide a realistic picture of what resources are available in schools and how teachers are using these resources with students. In addition, all chapters include more recent references to the professional literature and new examples of hardware, software, and instructional activities. We have included many new classroom examples to illustrate what these resources and activities look like in practice.

◆ *Coverage of Reform:* We continue to explore the connection between technology and educational reform. Although the basic goals of educational reform (Chapter 1) do not require computers or other forms of technology, many connections have emerged. Teachers who make greater use of what are described as "constructivist teaching methods" also make greater use of technology (Chapter 2). Technology tools provide many opportunities for engaging students in learning tasks that allow for collaborative work, authentic student-centered exploration, and performance-based assessment.

◆ *Equity Issues:* What has become known as the *Digital Divide* has emerged as a prominent political issue since the publication of the second edition of this book. Our discussion of equity has been modified to reflect new data and new concerns. Great strides have been made in addressing some equity issues, but new concerns have also surfaced. For example, as computers and the Internet play a more prominent role in the completion of class assignments, those students who cannot continue their work at home are at a significant disadvantage. Educators now must be concerned not only with the resources they can make available in schools, but with the other resources students can access within the community. Our discussion of equity in Chapter 11 considers how and why gender, socioeconomic status, aptitude, and physical or learning disabilities may influence opportunities to learn with technology.

OUR APPROACH IS ANCHORED IN EVERYDAY CLASSROOM LIFE

We want very much to assure you that what we propose would be practical for you to implement. Our strategy for doing this has been to rely primarily on our own experiences within our local school district. We decided that it would be unfair for us to piece together a picture of computer and Internet use originating in grant-subsidized schools, high-tech demonstration sites, or what we have gleaned about the latest and greatest applications from the conferences we attend and the journals we read. Yes, the theory, research, and general instructional strategies we describe in this book draw on contributions from a wide range of educational researchers, policy advocates, and demonstration sites. In contrast, however, most of the classroom examples we include come from teachers we know personally.

We both work and live in Grand Forks, North Dakota, and we anticipate that few of our readers have ever visited our community or have more than a vague notion of where it is located. What might be more relevant is that the technology in our schools is present largely because of the investment of local taxpayers. Thus the applications of technology we describe result from the decision making of the school board, local administrators, and teachers. Our resources for technology exceed the averages you will find described in this book, but how and whether teachers make use of these resources is up to them. Our district is certainly not at the extremely sophisticated level of a demonstration site, nor are specific classroom applications of technology mandated.

What we have done in writing this book is draw on examples from some of the more involved and creative teachers we know. We do not claim that these teachers are typical, but rather that they work in fairly typical schools under typical conditions.

THE AUTHORS' COMPLEMENTARY EXPERIENCES

A few comments about our own backgrounds may provide a context for what we emphasize. The topics and theoretical perspective of this book result from a blend of the orientations, experiences, and individual interests of the two authors.

Mark Grabe's background is in educational psychology—he is a professor in the Psychology Department and the Instructional Design and Technology program at the University of North Dakota. He brings to this collaboration the theoretical perspectives and research experiences more typical of a university faculty member. Mark has been developing instructional software for approximately fourteen years in support of his own research activities. Originally trained to teach high school biology, he continues to pursue his interest in science education. Some of his first Internet activities involved designing instructional web sites to promote the outdoor educational programs of the North Dakota Department of Game and Fish. This work, which you will catch glimpses of throughout this book, has encouraged an interest in hands-on science and the role technology might play in it.

Cindy Grabe's original certification was as an elementary school teacher; she later earned a master's degree as a learning disability specialist. After she had worked for many years as a reading specialist, her interest and experience in the use of technology in instruction led her to a full-time technology position with the Grand Forks school district. She has been a technology facilitator, a position that in some districts may be described as a computer coordinator, for ten years. Her position requires that she provide training to district teachers, administrators, and staff members, collaborate on curriculum projects, and conduct demonstration activities with students. She is involved in providing continuing educational experiences for teachers in area schools, and she teaches courses for undergraduate preservice teachers at the University of North Dakota. Cindy deals directly and continuously with the very practical issues of integrating technology in classrooms. Her own work with students and her associations with many gifted classroom teachers are responsible for most of the classroom examples we provide in this book. Cindy has been recognized as an Apple Distinguished Educator by the Apple Computer Corporation.

Cindy and Mark Grabe are the authors of a related book, *Integrating the Internet for Meaningful Learning* (Houghton Mifflin, © 2000), applying many of the themes of this book to classroom applications of the Internet.

LEARNING FEATURES OF THE TEXT

Embedded in the chapter content are special features to help you better understand important concepts and use them in your own classroom.

Scenes from Real Classrooms

Descriptions of actual classroom events can provide a powerful way to "see" in action many of the ideas we present. *Stories* of classroom events and descriptions of actual student *projects* are embedded in many chapters as demonstrations of teacher or student behavior.

Screen Images and Program Examples

The graphics in this book are mostly images captured as they appear on the computer monitor. You may not always have immediate access to the computer tools or the Internet resources we describe, so these images are a convenient way to help you understand what the text explains. Visual examples are one of the best ways to explain topics such as web page design and to present samples from student projects.

Special Features: Focus Boxes, Spotlight on Assessment Boxes, Keeping Current Boxes, and Emerging Technology Boxes

The features that appear under the general titles "Focus," "Spotlight on Assessment," "Keeping Current," and "Emerging Technology" allow us freedom to break away from the main thrust of a presentation and consider a topic in more detail. The topic might involve an extended discussion of an important issue or theory, a suggestion for how a teacher might evaluate a student project, or the description of a new type of application that has promise for classroom use. Setting these discussions apart allows the reader to consider the topics independently from the main discussion.

Activities and Projects for Your Classroom Boxes

We have included a large number of application ideas in this book, but we also recognize that teachers work in many disciplines with students of different ages. Writing activity boxes allow us to list variations of applications that might be more discipline- or age-specific. The combination of the extended examples and the variations provided within the activity boxes is a reasonable way to acquaint you with classroom applications.

End-of-Chapter Activities

Following the text of each chapter, we include several activities we suggest you try. These activities are our attempt to get you to think more actively about important issues presented in the chapters or to try out an application we have described. We have attempted to generate activities that can be accomplished with and without direct access to computer resources, so you should be able to complete at least some of the brief tasks no matter what your circumstances. It would clearly be inconsistent for us to suggest that you can learn meaningfully using only a textbook. We trust that this book will not be the only resource at your disposal and that you will also learn a great deal from teachers and colleagues.

End-of-Chapter Resources to Expand Your Knowledge Base

Each chapter ends with annotated lists of resources that offer further information about the topics, software, and hardware covered in the chapter. We include a variety of resource types, but we have made a decision to emphasize a greater number of web sites than in previous editions. A summary of these web sites has been organized as the "Teacher's Handy Reference" that appears at the end of the book.

ACCOMPANYING TEACHING AND LEARNING RESOURCES

In addition, the complimentary **Real Deal UpGrade CD-ROM** contains convenient links to sites mentioned in the text, as well as chapter outlines, learning objectives, chapter summaries, a glossary of terms, software demos, and video clips.

Listing web sites has one limitation: web addresses may change or disappear. Our solution is to host our own **web site** so that you can keep up with changes that come to our attention. Please visit us at **http://ndwild.psych .und.nodak.edu/book** or connect to our site via the main Houghton Mifflin web page (**http://college.hmco.com** and select "Education"). Our web site is intended as a resource for students. We use the web site to bring information provided in the book up to date and to provide resources that we could not practically include in a book. We urge you to take advantage of this resource.

ACKNOWLEDGMENTS

We owe many individuals our gratitude for helping us bring this book to you. Loretta Wolozin, senior sponsoring editor at Houghton Mifflin, saw in our original proposal the germ of a unique idea and made the trip to North Dakota to talk with us and examine student projects. Putting students in control of powerful tools was not typical, and yet Loretta has supported our belief that this theme should be at the core of what teachers learn about the classroom applications of technology. We were assisted in preparing this edition by the guidance of developmental editor Elaine Silverstein. We hope you will find our arguments and explanations clear and our style friendly. Aileen Mason, senior production editor, was responsible for the tedious tasks associated with page and chapter layout, matching hundreds of citations and references, and polishing our prose. Lisa Mafrici, development editor, has worked with us now for several years. She helped organize our efforts and kept us focused on deadlines and our revision goals. We would also like to thank Seung Jin of Cleveland State University and Shirley F. Yamashita of the University of Hawaii at Manao for their insightful reviews and feedback that informed the development of this edition. No book really results from the work of the authors alone, and this book is no exception.

Finally, we owe a giant debt to the many teachers and students who pro-

Kim's Original Multimedia Project (Converted to Gray Scale)

vided the authentic examples we have included. The quality and creativity of the products and the enthusiasm of the individuals who created them impressed us. We hope these examples will inspire your own work, too.

A FINAL WORD

It is not always possible to determine where ideas originate, but we know exactly how we began working with student-authored multimedia. Nearly nine years ago we were preparing for a workshop in which Cindy planned to introduce Kid Pix to a group of teachers. The teachers were involved in the decision-making process to decide what equipment and software the district would purchase, and we were attempting to develop a convincing argument for the value of tool applications and student-authored multimedia. We were just learning Kid Pix ourselves and were searching for something that would get the teachers excited. Our daughter Kim (then in first grade, now in high school) had been studying dinosaurs, so we scanned a picture of a dinosaur. We asked Kim to use Kid Pix to color the picture and then record a song she had learned about dinosaurs. We were pleased with the result and decided to use the product as part of our presentation. As we continued to work on other parts of the workshop, Kim remained at the computer, singing the dinosaur song over and over. It turned out she was singing as she typed in the lyrics. We saved her picture and still listen to her song from time to time. Because we have thanked many people in this preface, we should also thank Kim, who is owed some recognition simply for being so tolerant of the work habits of her parents. Her own creative talents and her enthusiasm for learning have served to inspire us for what have now been quite a few years. We know students enjoy working in the ways we describe partly because we have had the opportunity to watch and work with them.

A Teaching and Learning Framework for Integrating Technology in Classrooms

Part One *introduces you to the roles that technology now plays in education and the roles it is likely to play in the future. The opening chapters introduce you to this text's major themes: the "tools approach," activity-based approaches to learning, active roles for students, integrated or multidisciplinary approaches to learning, cooperative learning, and the role of teachers as facilitators. You will also explore some major ideas about meaningful learning and find out how educational technology fits among these ideas.*

Chapter 1

Key Themes and Issues for Using Technology in Your Classroom

ORIENTATION

In new fields of study, there should always be opportunities to demonstrate vision and encourage optimism and to dream about, imagine, and even predict the future. Thinking about the future is important for educators. And preparing students for that future requires some consideration of the skills that students will need and the rapidly evolving role of technology in educational practice. As educators, you will participate in shaping an era of dramatic change. We open this chapter with a description of a project that highlights some of the themes and applications that figure prominently in this book. As you read, look for answers to the following questions:

Focus Questions

◆ How does the role of the teacher as facilitator differ from more traditional teachers' roles?
◆ What are the most common inequities in computer use?
◆ Why are students not actively involved with the technology that is already in schools?
◆ What are the characteristics of activity-based approaches to learning?
◆ What experiences are influential in preparing future teachers to make use of technology in their classrooms?

USES OF TECHNOLOGY IN TEACHING AND LEARNING

Although we have written this book as a well-balanced introduction to the many uses of technology in teaching and learning, several themes and suggested applications play more prominent roles than others. The following example, which we describe as involving "authentic tasks" because learners are engaged with tasks that approximate the work of real world practitioners, illustrates some of our priorities.

Ice Dusting: An Introductory Example of Learning Through Authentic Tasks

When we first met Charlie and Len, they were trudging through knee-deep snow pulling a plastic children's sled across the frozen Goose River in Hillsboro, North Dakota. The sled contained some of the tools of their trade: a chain saw, a heavy wooden beam, chains, an ice auger, wooden stakes, a measuring tape, a camera, a pressure meter, and a pneumatic jack. They were dressed in heavy coveralls and looked very much like construction workers.

While you might not guess from their appearance or the setting, Charlie and Len are scientists, and we were visiting their research laboratory. Charlie Clark and Len Zabilansky are associated with the U.S. Army Cold Regions Research and Engineering Laboratory. They were in North Dakota to investigate the potential of ice dusting as a way to manipulate the break-up of river ice. Ice dusting involves spreading some type of substance on ice to increase the rate at which the ice melts. During the spring thaw, large chunks of river ice often pile up against each other and create dams, which increase the likelihood of flooding. This problem of flooding has brought Charlie and Len to North Dakota.

We live in Grand Forks, North Dakota, and our entire community was flooded in the spring of 1997. The winter of 1999 was also harsh, and the snow banks were high. An article in the local paper described the National Guard's involvement in an ice dusting project. Because the entire community shared an interest in flood control, local teachers contacted the National Guard to learn more. Information from Guard personnel led these teachers to the Massachusetts-based Army Cold Regions Research and Engineering Laboratory and the initial conversations with Len Zabilansky. As a result of these conversations, the teachers received an open invitation to observe the research to be conducted on the Goose River.

The middle-school curriculum team first met Charlie and Len as the scientists were preparing the river site for the ice dusting experiment. We were working with the teachers to identify some way in which technology might help students understand what the scientists were doing. The long section of river that Len and Charlie had identified allowed for a comparison of a dusted section and an untreated section of the river. In a science class, the untreated section of the river would probably be called the "control" and the dusted section the "treatment condition."

Charlie was using a hand auger to drill holes in the ice into which he inserted wooden stakes marked with paint rings at 1-inch intervals. The stakes would gradually be exposed as the snow and ice melted. The rings around the stake allow the amount of change to be observed even at a distance as the weakening ice became too dangerous to walk on. Len had fired up the chain saw and was cutting what he called "tongues"—segments of ice about 4 feet wide and 12 feet long joined to the main ice sheet on only one end. The purpose of the tongues of ice was to allow a measurement of ice strength. The wooden beam, chains, and pneumatic jack that the scientists had been dragging through the snow are used to create a lever, which could exert great force on the end of a tongue. The pressure meter was used to measure exactly how much pressure was being applied. The amount of pressure required to break the tongue was used as the measure of ice strength. The data gathered on the thickness of the river ice and the strength of the river ice were the experiment's "dependent variables," and because these measurements were being taken before the river was dusted, the scientists were establishing a "baseline."

Charlie also set up a portable weather station on the bank of the river. Various sensors gathered and recorded digital data on air and water temperature, precipitation, and the amount of direct and reflected light. The scientists were aware that the existing published work relating to their work (primary sources) indicates that the success of dusting may depend on such factors as the temperature, amount of sunlight, and precipitation that falls during the experiment. The weather station allowed the scientists to gather some additional data (moderating variables) in order to interpret their results. Now everything was ready for the treatment to be applied.

We made the trip back to the river the next day to observe the dusting process. A helicopter from the National Guard hovered over the surface of the river with an airborne sand spreader and applied a dusting of sand. Len and Charlie moved back out onto the ice, laid down a ruler, and took some close-up pictures of the ice surface with their camera. The pictures were sent back to their headquarters so that the distribution of the sand particles could be measured. The scientists wished the sand had been scattered more widely, but wind conditions dictated the approach the helicopter was able to take.

We made one final trip to observe Len and Charlie. On this day, they were out in a boat trying to retrieve their weather station. A sudden change in the weather brought a premature end to the research. The ice melted, and the river came up so quickly that some final measurements were not possible. The scientists were in the process of trying to salvage their equipment.

The arguments they would be able to make from their weeks of work would have to be made on the basis of only part of the data they had hoped to gather. Sometimes real science does not work out exactly as planned.

The School Projects

The teachers and technology staff spent time with Charlie and Len taking videos and taking notes. The goal of their efforts was to generate ideas for classroom activities that they and other teachers could use. To accomplish this goal, the curriculum team had to acquire a rudimentary understanding of the "science of ice" and the research questions that were important to the scientists. As the ice dusting research unfolded, the curriculum team shared their experiences with other teachers to generate interest and encourage suggestions for classroom projects. A group of middle-school teachers had students who were taking a physical science course propose to evaluate the effectiveness of various substances for melting ice.

A number of resources were prepared to assist these teachers and their students. The first was a twenty-minute video to acquaint students with the ice dusting research and with the scientists because the Goose River site was too far away for students to visit. The video was intended to build student interest by connecting the work that students would do with issues related to their community and also to the work of scientists. The curriculum team wanted students to appreciate the work that scientists do from a more personal perspective, so they asked Charlie and Len to talk on video about their training and personal interests in addition to describing the Goose River project. Video segments from these interviews and from the activities on the river were edited together to prepare an introduction for classroom use. The video was distributed on tape for classroom presentation and was also available on the project web site.

The team also generated a list of Internet resources that provided information related to the ice dusting project and made the list available to students. Learning to search for Internet resources is an important skill, but there are also times when it is more efficient to direct students to specific online resources for review. Providing some suggestions allowed teachers the option of having students conduct their own online research or immediately focusing student attention on relevant web pages. The number of sites relevant to this specific project was surprising. For example, it was possible to link students to the following sites:

◆ The home page for the Army Cold Regions Research and Engineering Laboratory
◆ A history of flooding on the Goose River
◆ The National Weather Service Ultraviolet Index (an explanation and current map of sunlight intensity)

◆ History of Calendars (related to the importance of the Julian calendar, which the scientists used when recording data at the weather station)

HyperStudio, a multimedia authoring program (see Chapter 8), was used to prepare instructional content to accompany the videotape and explain the process by which the scientists tested ice strength. This stack used illustrations (see Figure 1.1) and images captured from the videotape to explain the method the scientists used to test the strength of the ice and why the experimental methodology required that the scientists repeat this test several times within the "control" and "experimental" sections of the river.

Finally, the curriculum team created a web site (see Figure 1.2) devoted to the ice dusting project. The web site offered:

◆ A pictorial description of the ice dusting research
◆ The original proposal written to gain funding for the Cold Regions Research and Engineering Laboratory project
◆ Project ideas for classroom teachers

FIGURE 1.1
HyperStudio Stack Screen Image. This card explains how the equipment used to break the ice tongues operates as a lever.

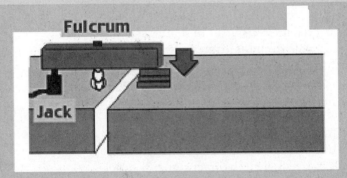

Fulcrum

Jack

A chain connected to the middle of the lever stops the upward movement and causes the other end of the lever to press down on the beam of ice. The point at which the lever is connected to the chain is the fulcrum.

FIGURE 1.2   Home Page for the Ice Dusting Curriculum Project. The small pictures surrounding the central image are "rollovers," which change to text when pointed at with the mouse and serve as links to other material (the same links are listed in text at the bottom of the page). The two men pictured are Charlie Clark (left) and Len Zabilansky (right).

- Links to relevant web sites
- An online version of the ice dusting movie
- The HyperStudio tutorial
- An invitation for students to share their research through the web site

South Middle School Ice Dusting Research Project

Teachers at South Middle School are organized in multidisciplinary teams and are regularly on the lookout for curriculum activities allowing a multidisciplinary approach. The ice dusting project seemed like an interesting opportunity. Although the focus of the project was on physical science, there were also options for developing skills in other areas. The data collection and analysis involved mathematics. The project would require that students gather information in the library and from the Internet. The generation of program reports would require that students write. Issues regarding the environmental suitability of various dusting compounds related to topics covered in social studies. Technology tools would be emphasized throughout, providing the opportunity to acquire new skills in using technology. The multidisciplinary, hands-on nature of the project and connection with the community offered the type of challenge these teachers wanted to present to students from time to time.

Students began by viewing the videotape. The teachers then engaged them in a number of tasks related to the scientific principles and research procedures employed at the Goose River research site. For example, the unique crystalline structure of natural ice results from impurities in the water that are pushed to the boundaries of individual crystals as ice freezes. River ice thus consists of long, vertical ice crystals "cemented" together by frozen water with a high concentration of impurities. When the ice warms, the impure ice melts first, causing the pure ice crystals to separate and the entire sheet of ice to lose strength. Understanding the process by which freezing water causes the concentration of impurities is thus critical to understanding how river ice disintegrates.

When Len had explained ice strength, he suggested a simple experiment that students could try to demonstrate the migration of impurities as water freezes. One of the teachers from South was a member of the curriculum team and decided to give the simple experiment a try. Students mixed food coloring in water and then froze the colored water in Styrofoam cups. What should students observe in this demonstration, and why were they asked to use Styrofoam cups? Styrofoam cups were suggested as a way to prevent the ice from freezing from the outside toward the middle. When the water cools throughout, the food coloring, which is an impurity, is pushed outward, and the middle of the chunk should be clear.

Although the unit on ice consisted of a number of components and interrelated assignments, the main activity was a student research project to find the answer to this challenge: Find the best substance for melting ice. Each two-student team was given a block of ice and allowed to select its own dusting compound. In part, the instructional goals for this project related to understanding the methods of science. Students were asked to define two equal areas on their ice block and to treat one area with a dusting compound. The students were then to develop a method for measuring the melt rate.

The initial plan was to duplicate the procedure that the scientists had used: drill holes in the ice and insert marked stakes. Unfortunately, drilling the holes caused the blocks of ice to crack, so the students had to devise another approach. The simple solution was to place a ruler next to the blocks of ice every 30 minutes and record the height.

The substances applied to the ice covered a wide range and reflected both careful thought and whimsy; among them were sand, black soil, kitty litter, chocolate chips, sugar cubes, and coffee grounds. Besides spreading these substances on the ice blocks, students also filled a glass cylinder with their dusting substance. They placed these cylinders in the sun and periodically used a digital thermometer to determine if the substances differed in the degree to which they were warmed by the sun. The idea was to determine if the substances absorbing the most heat would be the same substances responsible for melting the ice most quickly.

Because several classes participated in the research, experiments were started over an extended period of time. Different starting times brought some different variables into play. The factor of greatest interest was the intensity of sunlight, which would vary over the day and across days. To determine how the intensity of sunlight might influence the melt rate, students used a data grabber designed to record changes in light intensity. A data grabber is a simple digital device consisting of a sensor and data storage mechanism. The device can be connected to a computer to download the data for analysis.

Technology was involved in other ways too. A web cam was set up so that students and anyone else following the project could take a look at the experiment as it was under way. The web cam was not essential, but it did introduce students to some of the basics of remote sensing, and it was a great deal of fun. Data gathered throughout the course of the student research were entered into a spreadsheet as a way of organizing the information and for the purpose of generating charts for visualizing various comparisons. Finally, project conclusions were summarized as web pages. Students created summary pages that presented their research question, the research method they applied in investigating this issue, the results obtained, and unanswered questions or possible ways to improve the research. Students included images in these web pages that they had initially captured using a video camera and then converted to digital images on one of their classroom computers (see Figure 1.3). These pages and also traditional classroom examinations were used in assessing what students had learned.

What did students conclude from their efforts? They determined that kitty litter and possibly a combination of kitty litter and salt melted ice most quickly. They also concluded that research often leads to more questions

FIGURE 1.3   Selected Images from Classroom Web Pages

Measuring Melt Rate

Light Intensity Data Grabber

View from Ice Cam

Heat Absorption Experiment

than it resolves. Spreading salt on the river would probably not be a good idea, they realized.

During his final trip to the Goose River site, Len met with the students who had conducted their own ice research and made presentations to several classes. The students were probably as impressed by Len's enthusiasm for the science of ice as by any facts he provided. Len reviewed the student projects, asked the students some questions, and left the students his e-mail address in case they thought of any more questions.

This was not your typical science lesson.

Did our choice of an introductory example surprise you? We ask this question because we want you to examine your own expectations for how students should work with technology *and* for the type of learning tasks that students should experience. Although technology was involved in the students' work in our example and in the work of the scientists, it was not the focus. Our example also describes students as they learn by doing. The emphasis is not on learning from textbooks, teacher presentations, or computer-based instructional programs. You will find that we discuss a wide variety of classroom applications of technology in this book, and we find potential value in most of it. We think that it is important for teachers to have an understanding of the strengths and weaknesses of many types of learning experiences and that they select a variety of experiences to ensure that students learn in a meaningful way. We will help you understand how technology can contribute to this general goal and help you develop the personal skills necessary to assist students in using technology in a variety of ways.

THEMES OF TECHNOLOGY USE IN THE CLASSROOM

The ice dusting project illustrates many of the themes we emphasize in this book. Here are some of those themes. As you read these introductions to them, focus on understanding how they relate to the ice dusting project.

Spotlight on Assessment

Relating Learning and Assessment

In practice, learning and assessment are being interrelated in complex ways. Assessment methods do more than provide information on the quantity and quality of learning. Student experiences with assessment methods carry over into new learning situations, and the types of assessment anticipated appear to influence how and what they learn.

You probably know this from your own experiences. Do you study differently when you are anticipating a multiple-choice examination than, say, an essay examination? Do you review information differently when intending to demonstrate your understanding through a paper in contrast to an examination? If you are a typical student, the way you think about course content is likely to be heavily influenced by how you think your learning will be assessed (Crooks, 1988). Some researchers

have claimed that the quickest way to change how students learn is to change the way learning is assessed (Elton & Laurillard, 1979). Others believe that students are more influenced by the method of assessment than by classroom experiences and stated instructional goals (Snyder, 1971).

So what does the research on assessment and learning suggest that teachers should do? The answer, but not necessarily its implementation, is fairly simple: Teachers should think carefully about the knowledge and skills they would like students to develop and make certain that those are emphasized in the assessment process. The research suggests that although some learning outcomes may seem difficult to assess, it is very important that we strive nevertheless to find ways to assess them (Crooks, 1988).✴

TECHNOLOGY INTEGRATED INTO CONTENT-AREA INSTRUCTION

Applying skills and extending learning goals

Two points might be raised here. First, the example explored learning about ice and about the methods of science. Whatever the students learned about how to operate the hardware and software systems was secondary to this focus. Moreover, although the students certainly learned a great deal about technology during the project, many of their skills associated with hardware and software manipulation can be applied to new content very efficiently. Second, the technology fit comfortably with the teachers' instructional plans and philosophy and represented more an extension of them than an alternative or addition to them.

A TOOLS APPROACH

Applying software tools to learn

Technology can play various instructional roles. A tools approach assumes that learners can flexibly apply general-purpose software, such as word processing, spreadsheet, or an Internet World Wide Web browser, to various topics. This approach can be contrasted with the use of software developed specifically to teach a particular topic.

AN ACTIVE ROLE FOR STUDENTS

Students' constructive mental behavior

The word *active* as used here does not refer directly to the physical activity of the learner, as might be involved in operating the video camera or measuring the blocks of ice. Rather, *active* describes the mental behavior of the students. In the example, the information to be learned was not presented to students in some kind of final, distilled form. Students had to dig for what they learned. They had to pull together bits and pieces of information from several sources, gather data, generate personal interpretations and summaries, and make decisions. In later chapters, you will see this type of student activity described as "constructive learning" or "learning by design."

A FACILITATIVE ROLE FOR THE TEACHER

Why take a cognitive approach?

When students play a more active role in their own learning, the teacher's role shifts from "dispenser of knowledge" to "facilitator of learning." One assumption behind such a shift is that the student accomplishes learning, and the teacher's role is to consider how to assist the students. A second assumption is that academic work extends beyond the mere storage of information.

This book takes a cognitive approach because the cognitive perspective fits so well with assumptions like these. The focus in a cognitive approach is on mental activity. Consider for a moment the challenge of teaching a behavior that cannot be directly viewed. How would you explain to a young scientist how to be a critical thinker or a problem solver? One promising approach might be to share critical thinking and problem-solving tasks with students, externalize your own thinking while in such situations, and use the externalized product as a way to interact with your students. The science experiments associated with the ice dusting project were not taken from a laboratory manual. The procedures were based on general principles of research methodology, and the students and teachers generated the specifics. As facilitators and participants, teachers had the opportunity to externalize their own thinking as the project evolved.

AN INTEGRATED OR MULTIDISCIPLINARY APPROACH

Using a wide range of skills

It would be difficult to say that the ice dusting project fell within one content area and inappropriate to claim that it had a single objective. Certainly students acquired scientific knowledge; more important, they were involved as practitioners using the methods of science. They used technology tools to acquire information from the physical environment and the Internet, analyze the data they gathered, and present their conclusions. As they worked with the tools, they developed their technology literacy. Working with the data called on their mathematical skills. The multimedia product that they generated required that they use reading, writing, speaking, artistic expression, and library research skills.

COOPERATIVE LEARNING

Technology can enhance interaction among students

One charge that is consistently leveled against using technology in academia is that it isolates students from each other and from the teacher. Nothing could be further from the truth. Technology is a tool and has no inherent or required mode of application. The role of technology in education is always under the control of the teacher and is isolating only if teachers require that students work on projects or assignments alone. In some cases, independent work is appropriate, and in other cases, cooperative work is desirable. As the ice dusting project illustrates, technology can enhance interaction. Students were collaborating *because* of the technology and had an opportunity to meet and interact with Len. Blaming technology for isolating students or engaging them in passive activity is like blaming heavy reliance on worksheets on the No. 2 pencil.

INSTRUCTION BASED ON STANDARDS

How should teachers select the specific learning experiences they will use with their students? A logical response to this question might be that they should

What are standards?

identify experiences that are likely to help students acquire important knowledge and skills. One way that teachers can identify important knowledge and skills is to pay attention to what are called *standards.* Formally established standards list goals that groups of experts have identified. Local curriculum committees might then convert the more general standards into grade-specific expectations and even assessment guidelines. Standards are a way to establish priorities.

One of the science and technology standards that Grand Forks teachers are asked to address states, "Students use the process of scientific inquiry." At the eighth-grade level, students are expected to:

◆ Design and carry out scientific investigations.
◆ Use appropriate tools and techniques to gather, analyze, and interpret data.
◆ Review, summarize, and use the data from a simple experiment to form a logical argument about cause and effect.

The ice dusting project was attractive to some teachers because it provided students with the opportunity to acquire and demonstrate these expected skills.

TECHNOLOGY IN TODAY'S CLASSROOM

What uses of technology are typical today?

Whether you are already a teacher or plan to become one, you are probably interested in what typical schools and classrooms are like. What technological resources—hardware and software—are available to teachers? How does the typical student use technology at the grade level or within the subject area you plan to teach, and how much time each day or week does the student spend learning this way? If you already teach, you are probably interested in how common your own experiences are. The media sometimes focus on glamorous but atypical examples, and it is easy to assume that things are different from your own experiences in other schools or other states. In addition to examining the current state of affairs, it is intriguing to speculate about the future. Will classrooms change drastically during the next ten years because of technology, or will interest in technology wane?

STUDENTS' ACCESS TO TECHNOLOGY

Increasing number of computers in schools

The number of computers in schools is increasing rapidly, and these computers are being interconnected so that students can communicate with each other and access information sources available through the Internet. The trend for the eight-year span ending in 1999 saw the ratio of students to computers change from 13:1 to 5:1. Over the five-year span ending in 1999, the proportion of schools connected to the Internet jumped from 35 percent to 90 percent. In fact, in 1999 over 50 percent of individual classrooms had Internet access (Anderson & Ronnkvist, 1999).

One problem with statistics like these is that they may create false assumptions about what can be done in classrooms or what any given classroom may look like. Schools have been investing in computers for many years, and the capabilities of computers and the capabilities required by newer software applications and even Internet applications have changed drastically. Only 45 percent of school computers are considered "high end"—that is, Pentium or Power Macintosh (actually these categories are really the low end of the computers on the market today) (Anderson & Ronnkvist, 1999). Many of the applications discussed in this book are not possible unless students have access to the more powerful kinds of computers. The data may also create false assumptions about what any given school may look like. At the level of individual states, the student-to-computer ratio for high-end machines varies from 7:1 up to 15:1. The student-to-computer ratio for computers connected to the Internet varies from 7:1 to 30:1. Individual school districts are even more variable (Jerald & Orlofsky, 1999). Teachers working in schools at the extremes of this range likely view the potential of technology for their classrooms very differently.

As we attempt to address the different circumstances that exist in different classrooms, it is important to recognize that the availability of equipment does not totally determine whether students actually work with the equipment. It is possible that equipment could sit unused in the back of the classroom or computer laboratory.

How much time do students spend with computers?

Let's approach this matter in the following way. Do students use school computers? When students were asked to report if they used computers at least once or twice a week, 49 percent of twelfth graders, 38 percent of eighth graders, and 29 percent of fourth graders said they used computers at least this frequently (Jerald & Orlofsky, 1999). When teachers were asked if their students made frequent use of computers (more than twenty times during the year), 25 percent of teachers responded positively. Use varied greatly by content area: 42 percent of elementary teachers, 32 percent of English/language arts teachers, 15 percent of science teachers, and 5 percent foreign language teachers met this criteria (Ravitz, Wong, & Becker, 1999). Your own definition of frequent use may differ from the criterion used in this research.

Where are computers located?

Aside from Internet access, probably one of the most significant recent changes that has influenced general student use of technology is where the computers are located. In 1992, 10 percent of school computers were located in individual classrooms; by 1999, 50 percent of school computers were located in individual classrooms (Anderson & Ronnkvist, 1999). Students working in classrooms with immediate access to at least four computers are two and a half times more likely to be classified as heavy users (at least twenty times per year) than if they have to use computers located somewhere else in the school (Ravitz, Wong, & Becker, 1999).

WHAT STUDENTS DO WITH COMPUTERS

Computers can play a variety of roles in school. They can be used to teach, facilitate the study of traditional content-area topics, provide opportunities for students to learn how to use technology, or give students general-purpose tools for performing academic tasks more efficiently.

The tutor, tool, tutee model

These distinctions are similar to what was originally called the tutor, tool, tutee model (Taylor, 1980). In the role of *tutor,* a computer application could be designed to teach students (for example, a tutorial program explains how to use a photospectrometer, and a drill-and-practice program helps an elementary school student become more proficient with number facts). Computer *tools* are more general-purpose applications designed to help users function more productively—for example, word processing programs used to write reports and database programs used to organize and search for information. Applications that allow students to search for information on the Internet are also considered tools. When functioning in the *tutee* role, the student programs (or teaches) the computer.

Applying technology as a tool

Recent teacher surveys indicate a shift in how students are using technology. In earlier editions of this book, we reported that the most common experiences involved content-area drill activity and learning about the computer and common computer applications—that is, computer literacy. Now it appears that students are most likely to be applying technology as a tool in their own learning. When researchers asked teachers to identify the categories of computer use that applied to their students on at least three occasions during the past year, word processing was the most widely used application (50 percent of teachers). This was the most frequent category of use not only for English/language arts teachers, but also for science, social studies, and elementary teachers. For elementary teachers, drill and basic tutorial applications represented the second most general application. For middle-school and high school teachers, the next most common categories of use were CD reference materials and World Wide Web searches and applications focused on information location and retrieval (Ravitz, Wong, & Becker, 1999).

RESOURCES, EQUITY, AND STUDENT ACTIVITY

It may seem that schools are spending a great deal of money on computers and other forms of technology and that the investment is escalating year by year. In a way this is true. In 1996, the annual investment was $90 per student

(Quality Educational Data, 1996); by 1999, the annual level of expenditure had grown to $120 per student (Market Data Retrieval, 1999b). But when we put these numbers in the perspective of the total annual investment per student, which is in excess of $5,600, the amount is modest (Panel on Educational Technology, 1997).

It might be argued that technology is too expensive only if it is seldom used, has limited impact on learning, or is substituted for other important and productive learning experiences. Certainly these negative arguments have been promoted (Oppenheimer, 1997). In rebuttal, we demonstrate in the following chapters that there are many practical and efficient ways to use technology and that these classroom applications are consistent with what is currently known about effective learning experiences.

How is the money spent? While we are on the topic of expenditures, there are some issues related to how the money set aside for technology is spent. On average, the $120 that schools spend per student is divided up such that 69 percent is spent on hardware, 17 percent on software, and 14 percent on training and support (Market Data Retrieval, 1999b). School-based training and support has long been a concern. Business and industry, in contrast, spend a much higher percentage of their technology on support, and experts have recommended that schools double the present percentage of funding for support and training (Panel on Educational Technology, 1977). Training and support are necessary to develop the skills necessary to take advantage of technology. A high proportion of college graduates (60 percent) say they do not feel well prepared to take advantage of technology in their classrooms. Once they are working in schools, only 20 percent of teachers receive ten or more hours of technology training per year, and less than 30 percent received five hours of training showing them how to use technology in the curriculum areas they teach. Full-time personnel (e.g., computer coordinator, technology integration specialist) are available to help teachers with technology and technology integration in only approximately 30 percent of schools (Fatemi, 1999; Jerald & Orlofsky, 1999; Market Data Retrieval, 1999a).

Recognizing differences in experiences and opportunities Not all students have the same opportunities to learn with technology. We tend to be most concerned with inequities when differences in school opportunities compound existing disadvantages, such as low socioeconomic status (SES), and when differences in student experiences within the same school are associated with a student characteristic (gender, for example) that we feel should not influence educational opportunities. We are alerting you to inequities at this point to provide a foundation for some of the recommendations that follow. The topic of inequities—both the nature of them and possible remedies—is discussed in detail in Chapter 11.

Because the socioeconomic makeup of schools relates to some of the resource variables we have been considering, we will provide an overview of some of the SES equity issues at this point. In several ways, the SES equity situation has improved a great deal. For example, programs such as Title I have helped schools with higher proportions of students from low-income families achieve a similar student-to-computer ratio as wealthier schools, and the e-rate, a subsidy helping schools connect to the Internet, has narrowed the gap in Internet access. Differences nevertheless remain. Wealthier schools have more powerful equipment. For example, in schools with less than 10 percent of the student body receiving subsidized lunches (the variable commonly used to establish SES differences), the ratio of students to Internet computer is 10:1. The same ratio in schools with more than 71 percent of students receiving reduced price lunches is 17:1. These same schools are significantly less likely to have a full-time computer coordinator. Inequities represent missed opportunities for students needing positive experiences. But even when schools in poor and wealthy neighborhoods offer the same experiences, the schools are not compensating for large differences for technology opportunities that exist in students' homes. Our efforts are directed toward acquainting you with the opportunities available in typical schools and some of the inequities, providing you with strategies for using technology efficiently and solid arguments so that you can become an advocate for technology wherever you work.

Inequities are missed opportunities

Computer tasks provide meaningful learning activities for all students. Here a diverse group works with a computer and a CD-ROM. *(© Michael Zide)*

ACCEPTING THE INFORMATION AGE: A DIFFERENT ARGUMENT FOR CHANGE

Tools and skills for a changing world

One perspective urging change in the way we function as educators is based on the belief that students are encountering a rapidly changing world and need the right intellectual tools and skills to function effectively in this new environment. Several characteristics of the future are particularly relevant to educational planning.

LEARNING TO THINK AND LEARNING TO LEARN

Why tomorrow's employees must learn to learn

We are told that employees of the future—our students of today—will experience four or five different occupations during their lifetimes. Because they cannot hope to learn the specific skills required for all these occupations—and that is assuming that those occupations even exist now—it seems most appropriate to alter the orientation of education somewhat, so that more attention is paid to helping students learn how to think and how to learn. Naisbitt (1984) claims that we will have to move away from the training of specialists whose skills are soon obsolete to the development of generalists who can adapt. To be successful, people will have to have periods of learning and work that are less differentiated as distinct time periods in life. Adults will spend more time learning, and much of this learning will occur outside the traditional classroom. You may have heard the phrase "lifelong learners" used to describe individuals who function in this fashion. Although instruction will be available in new forms, learners must be more self-reliant to profit from these opportunities.

THE GROWING BODY OF INFORMATION

The amount of available information

The World Wide Web adds new information resources

Another characteristic of the future that already seems to be here is that learners will face an ever-increasing body of information. For some time now, futurists (Naisbitt, 1984; Toffler, 1980) have delighted in startling us with just how much information is available and how the pace of information generation is accelerating. Six to seven thousand scientific articles are authored daily in the United States alone, for example, and the amount of information available in the world doubles every five and a half years. The World Wide Web, an Internet application we believe offers tremendous potential for learning (see Chapter 6), is beginning to make its own contribution to the information glut. Statistics available at the time this book was written estimated the number of searchable web pages at 800 million (Lawrence & Giles, 1999).

You might be wondering how students can be expected to learn more and more material in the same amount of time—and what classroom teachers

Why learning huge amounts of information may be unnecessary

should be expected to do in this situation. A possible answer is to realize that attempting to learn huge amounts of information may be unnecessary. Learning more information is unnecessary because it is becoming increasingly possible to retrieve specific information as it is needed. Procedures for searching huge bodies of information are becoming both more powerful and more readily available. Libraries are increasingly turning to technology to allow the location of material specifically related to a patron's interests. The Internet allows access to an ever-expanding array of information resources, and services are available to anyone with a computer and a modem. Making productive use of these new resources requires that we all learn new skills. The point is that students can substitute learning to find what they need to know for the impossible task of learning everything they may need to know.

Students can learn to find information

Attempting to learn huge amounts of information may be more than impossible; it may also be unwise. Information is not the same as useful knowledge, and the time spent accumulating huge amounts of factual information might be better spent working with information to generate knowledge of personal significance. New skills are necessary.

RESTRUCTURING SCHOOLS

Educators are talking more and more about the need to restructure schools. Although restructuring means different things to different people, the basic challenge is to think carefully about what we want schools to do and then to consider how we might most successfully accomplish these goals. Strong advocates of restructuring are concerned either that schools are stressing the wrong things or that the methods schools employ are ineffective. We explain some of their concerns in more detail in Chapter 2. Many of the nontraditional learning activities we suggest in this book turn out to be good examples of the types of learning experiences that advocates of restructuring recommend. At this time, we take a moderate position on the issue of restructuring. We value providing more student-centered learning experiences than tend to be commonly available, but we do not see such experiences completely dominating the day-to-day routine in classrooms.

Changing the learning environment

Providing student-centered learning experiences

CHANGING THE WAY TECHNOLOGY IS USED IN SCHOOLS

Although the 1990s were a time of rapid technological growth—when many computers were brought into schools, connected with each other, and connected to the Internet—classroom access to technology is not universal, technology is not always used extensively even when it is available, and the

Focus

The Big Six Research Process

The Big Six process was developed by Eisenberg and Berkowitz as a practical approach to the instruction of the interrelated skills required in using information to solve problems (1990). At one time, such skills might have been called library skills, but with ready access to online resources such as the World Wide Web, this description seems too narrow; "information processing skills" might now be a more accurate description.

These are the six interrelated information processing skills:

1. Task definition. Define the problem, and identify information resources needed to solve it.

2. Information-seeking strategies. Identify the range of possible information resources, and prioritize those resources for investigation.

3. Location and access. Find the information sources and the relevant information within them.

4. Use of information. Process (read, view) the information, and extract relevant ideas.

5. Synthesis. Organize and create a product (e.g., a decision, a paper) from the ideas.

6. Evaluation. Consider the product and the effectiveness of the problem-solving process.

The Big Six skills can also be expressed as a series of questions (Jansen & Culpepper, 1996):

1. What needs to be done?
2. What can I use to find what I need?
3. Where can I find what I need?
4. What information can I use?
5. How can I put my information together?
6. How will I know if I did my job well?

You might already have some experience in applying these skills at your college library and in many of your college classes. How would you find a book that might contain information about the possible relationship between the destruction of the rain forests and global warming? How would you use this information as part of a paper advocating international subsidies for alternative economic ventures in countries likely to resort to massive deforestation? Would you be able to find this same information if you were asked to use the World Wide Web instead of the library? Would you be able to create a multimedia product as a way to present your point of view on this topic?

Although developing information skills has always been part of a solid education, technology provides new opportunities for access, manipulation, and expression that should increase the attention paid to these skills and broaden how educators think about them. (Source: Adapted from Eisenberg & Berkowitz, 1990. Reprinted by permission of the publisher.)✳

consequences of using technology are still hotly debated. What else needs to be done to realize what many see as the tremendous potential of technology? The following sections present some answers to this question.

TEACHER PREPARATION AND TEACHER TRAINING

Are new teachers prepared to use the equipment and software tools that schools can now provide to involve students in effective learning experiences (Moursund & Bielefeldt, 1999; Barksdale, 1996)? The assumption might be that teachers just completing their undergraduate programs would be prepared to use new tools and model new instructional approaches. In fact, new and practicing teachers say that this is not the case (Market Data Retrieval, 1999a; Moursund & Bielefeldt, 1999).

Are new teachers prepared to use technology?

There are three primary reasons for this lack of preparation. First, colleges of education frequently have no better equipment than K–12 institutions do and only a limited inventory of the types of instructional software used in K–12 classrooms. Second, a large number of college faculty members are unable to make appropriate use of technology in their own classrooms or are unwilling to try because of their own lack of preparation, anxiety, or disinterest. And third, the teacher preparation curriculum typically confines experiences with technology to a single course, and one that concentrates on learning to use the technology rather than how to facilitate learning *with* technology (Panel on Educational Technology, 1997).

Integrating technology into diverse teacher-preparation courses

In 1999, the U.S. Department of Education attempted to encourage change by initiating a new grant program, Preparing Tomorrow's Teachers to Use Technology Grant, and in the first year made nearly 225 awards. One of the unique emphases of this program when funding colleges of education is the focus on integrating technology in a *diversity* of courses taken by future teachers. Learning with technology should be experienced in content courses (biology courses for biology majors, history courses for history majors), content-specific instructional applications should be included in methods courses, and education students should practice teaching with technology during field placements and student teaching. A course providing broad coverage of the instructional uses of technology—the type of course we have in mind—might occur early in teacher training to establish a general background or occur late to provide an integrative perspective.

We deal with many of the questions of what it takes to integrate technology throughout this book, but our focus is on how teachers in elementary and secondary schools can do a better job using technology with their own students. It is ironic that the educators of educators persist in employing practices and modeling attitudes that many consider barriers to the effective use of technology in elementary and secondary classrooms. There is probably a positive message for all of us in recognizing this irony, and this message is clearly not limited to the use of technology: Change at all levels of education, which does not come easily, starts with each of us.

Changing how teachers are trained will not have an immediate impact on school practice. It will take years to place a majority of teachers with extensive college-based technology training into the workforce. Even if teachers have had a college technology course within the past year or so, the field advances very rapidly, and new equipment, programs, and ideas for classroom practice are always emerging. There are many practicing teachers who may have had some exposure to computers but have not worked with videodiscs, direct connections to the Internet, video production, digital data probes, or video-capture products (we discuss all of these products in later chapters). The World Wide Web has emerged as a powerful and widely used Internet application in an extremely short period of time. While some may find this situation discouraging, we think it is exciting. The tools of many professions are changing at an incredible rate. Why would we as teachers want to be excluded from this progress?

It is easy to be glib about the excitement of new opportunities. It is another matter to deal with the uncertainty teachers face when they suddenly confront sophisticated new equipment in their classroom. Teachers are used to being in control of their environments and in command of the content they teach. It is not uncommon or even surprising to find them nervous and reluctant to learn how to use technology, particularly when they might be expected to work on it with their students *before* they feel secure in their own mastery. One of us works full-time in helping classroom teachers learn to use technology. During a session designed to introduce teachers to the four new computers that had just been installed in their classrooms, one of the teachers asked if it would be possible to exchange her four computers for a piano.

Once teachers work with the equipment and experience different applications, their enthusiasm usually grows, and they begin to develop ideas of their own that they can implement with the new resources. Probably not all teachers would get to this stage if they had to work completely on their own. This is why ongoing training of teachers already working in classrooms is so important.

We also try to encourage teachers to recognize that technology can represent a unique situation in which they can learn with their students. When new equipment and software show up in your classroom, you have a tremendous opportunity to model problem solving, persistence when things go wrong, and the joy of developing a new skill!

So what do you say when someone wants to trade in computers for a piano? How about, "No, I think you and your students will really enjoy working with these computers once you learn a little more about them"? In the case of this particular teacher, this turned out to be true.

The challenge of keeping current

How teachers respond to new technology

Technology offers unique opportunities

The Emerging Importance of the Computer Coordinator

Do you remember the party scene in *The Graduate* in which Dustin Hoffman receives advice about future vocational opportunities in a single word: plastics? We have similar advice for you: computer coordinator. Schools are hiring staff members to assist teachers, administrators, and sometimes students in making use of technology resources. Initially some administrators assumed that coordinators would work themselves out of their jobs once teachers were trained and began making heavy use of technology. This assumption now seems silly. Technology is a moving target, and it is not cost-effective for teachers to try to keep up on their own.

If anything, there are now more opportunities as staff members in larger districts specialize as network administrators, elementary or secondary specialists, and others who might work with the business and record-keeping applications that provide administrative support to schools. Sometimes such an individual has a primary background as an educator and sometimes not. Even computer coordinators, who usually need to have education backgrounds because of the importance of curriculum awareness and familiarity with the

realities of classroom work, can have very different preparatory experiences. The coordinator job might require graduate training, or some specialized undergraduate training might be sufficient. Some coordinators work full-time as support staff, and some split their time between regular classroom teaching assignments and staff development activities. Their job may require certification of some type, but sometimes employment is merely a matter of convincing an administrator that you can do the job.

We see the ideal computer coordinator as an individual with fairly advanced technical skills who can find ways to use these skills in the service of instructional and learning needs. An understanding of curriculum issues is essential because the priority is curriculum needs, not the technology. Finally, working as a computer coordinator requires advanced social skills. Knowledge of technology and curriculum is of little value unless the coordinator is capable of motivating and supporting teachers as they move out of their comfort zones to try integrating technology into the classroom routine.✳

THE ACTIVITY-BASED OR DESIGN MODEL OF TECHNOLOGY USE

This book explores the classroom use of technology from a range of perspectives. We do, however, make a special effort to have you consider one particular way of using technology. This approach has been described in a number of ways: activity-based learning (Laboratory of Comparative Human Cognition,

1989), the project approach (Katz & Chard, 1989); using computer activities as mindtools (Jonassen, 1996; Jonassen, Peck, & Wilson, 1999), and design projects (Carver, Lehrer, Connell, & Erickson, 1992; Perkins, 1986). We use the term *activity-based learning* throughout this book.

EARLY USE OF ACTIVITY-BASED APPROACHES

Hands-on, student-centered activities

When activity-based approaches were introduced in the 1960s as a way to reform science and math education (Laboratory of Comparative Human Cognition, 1989), most learning and instruction was based in larger groups and was dominated by teacher presentations. This new approach recommended that at least part of the time available for instruction be shifted to hands-on, student-centered activities and that students collaborate in small groups to work on these projects. The teacher thus became responsible for the following:

◆ Selecting the activity and providing the materials
◆ Introducing the activity so that the students' task was set in a meaningful context and had clear goals
◆ Facilitating the students' work as it proceeded
◆ Helping the students see the connections between their observations and associated principles or theory

The teacher's role

Without the careful consideration of what the teacher actually must accomplish in this approach, it might appear that the teacher just presents the assignment and then sits at the desk until the students are ready to turn in their work. As you might expect, this is not at all what was intended. Instead, the teacher moves from group to group, participating, probing, and suggesting. A fundamental goal is to help students shift back and forth between theory, principles, and their own observations and experiences. Many kinds of questions are possible. The teacher might ask if what the students have read about is what they are now observing. What is a good way to explain why this happened?

Positive attitudes and better understanding

When evaluations of activity-based learning were made, the results were impressive: Students had more positive attitudes toward science, demonstrated better understanding of the concepts, and were more advanced in using creative and higher-level thinking skills. Yet more than twenty years later, fewer than 10 percent of science classrooms use what was demonstrated to be a motivating and effective curriculum model. As external funds and professional support were withdrawn, teachers were unable to locate the resources necessary for hands-on activities and did not have the time and often the expertise necessary to develop productive learning activities themselves. The explanation for this situation is a good lesson in some of the realities of implementing change in schools.

TODAY'S USE OF ACTIVITY-BASED APPROACHES AND TECHNOLOGY

The role of technology in activity-based learning

Technology may represent the critical element in reintroducing these ideas in a sustainable way and in allowing activity-based learning to play a more prominent role in K–12 education. The hardware and software that many schools already have or that they can acquire at a reasonable cost can be used to involve students in active learning tasks focused on many of the same topics they would otherwise encounter by listening to teacher presentations or reading textbooks.

Tool applications

The activity-based or project-centered approach that this book explores makes heavy use of computer tools: word processing, graphics programs, database programs, spreadsheets, telecommunications software, sound capture and editing software, hardware and software for capturing images and video segments from a variety of sources, and software for authoring hypermedia. Applying these tools to carefully selected tasks encourages the active mental behaviors so necessary for meaningful learning and critical thinking. The same tool can be applied over and over in new ways and in the processing of new information. This flexibility and reusability overcome some of the preparation difficulties inherent in the activity-based approach of the 1960s. Both teachers and students become adept at using the tools, and projects become easier to implement.

WAYS TO USE COMPUTER TOOLS

Using software tools in student projects

The variety of ways in which software tools can be used in student projects is endless, and new ideas seem to emerge daily. The following categories of use will help you get started thinking about the possibilities.

Authoring

From simple text documents to complex hypermedia

Students author presentations to inform or persuade others. Presentations, which can range from simple text documents to complex hypermedia, can be based on academic information or skills that are already emphasized in existing course work. The audience may consist of classmates or, if the presentation is created in the form of World Wide Web pages, anyone in the world with access to the Internet. The development of presentations requires students to locate relevant information, evaluate and organize the information, and communicate it effectively. If the presentation is a group project, students also practice a number of social skills.

Telecommunications

Students communicate with others at distant sites. The process of communication can be used to obtain information, to develop communication skills, or as an incentive to encourage some other type of academic work. Consider each of these applications. Telecommunications can be used to learn about lifestyles or daily experiences very different from those of the students. A common application is to set up regular interaction with another class in a different part of the country or even in another country. This interaction may even occur in real time and unlike a telephone conversation can include video images. Imagine the experiences that can be shared as students from a farming district discuss their daily lives with students in a major metropolitan area. In addition, consider what students might learn about the French language by corresponding with a "key pal" in Québec or France. Finally, telecommunications can be used to encourage other academic activity. For example, students might exchange book reviews as a way to encourage reading.

What teachers can use telecommunications for

Data Organization and Manipulation

Tools such as spreadsheets and databases can be used to organize and manipulate quantitative and factual data. For example, a spreadsheet can be used to record and perform simple statistics on data obtained from science experiments (as in the ice dusting example). A database could be used to categorize library books along a number of dimensions (author, topic, literary style); store a short description of each book; serve as a way for the readers who are generating the summary data to think about what they have read; and allow readers to search for books that might appeal to them.

Organizing and manipulating information

COMPUTER TOOLS AND STUDENT PROJECTS AS A SOLUTION

Teachers can use computer tools and projects involving authority, telecommunications, or data gathering and manipulation to solve some of the problems inherent in many current applications of technology.

Integration of Technology into the Curriculum

The primary focus of this book is on helping teachers improve student learning opportunities in the traditional content areas. Appropriate projects can provide the opportunity to use technology more extensively in all content areas.

More Effective Use of Existing Resources

The goal in all educational settings is to get the most from existing resources. Technology can be applied creatively to a nearly unlimited number of projects. Students can make minimal or extensive use of technology depending on what is available. Group-based activities make efficient use of available, reasonably priced software. Students do not—and probably should not—

work on projects only when they have access to the technology. In fact, a great deal of the associated planning, information acquisition, and information interpretation can be done offline. Constructing a technology-based product, such as a hypermedia presentation, or engaging in a technology-facilitated experience, such as a telecommunications link with another classroom, serves to direct, encourage, and organize these other learning experiences.

More Active Learning

Existing applications of technology have often focused on fact acquisition and rote memory-oriented learning tasks. Activity-oriented uses of technology emphasize other important learning goals and thus expand the uses of technology and the experiences for students. The emphasis in activity-based learning shifts from the transmission of information to asking critical questions, finding goal-relevant information, evaluating and integrating information to create personal knowledge, and communicating effectively.

Greater Equity of Involvement

Drawing girls and disadvantaged students toward math and the sciences

Using technology as the focal point of group projects puts it in a somewhat different role and seems to involve students who in the past have been less interested in the tasks to which technology has traditionally been assigned. When technology is used to provide opportunities for collaboration and to address self-selected problems in math and science, female and disadvantaged students are more likely to be drawn toward these content areas (Laboratory of Comparative Human Cognition, 1989).

SUMMARY

Classroom use of technology is growing and may be changing in its orientation. Many schools are investing in new equipment, purchasing new software, and encouraging faculty participation in training and innovation. The situation is not without limitations and concerns, however. Growth and enthusiasm are not universal. Technology is expensive, and schools have to consider carefully how resources are to be spent.

Many of the applications identified in this chapter make efficient use of technology. Technology is proposed as a focal point for activities that engage students actively in collaborative, multidisciplinary learning projects in traditional areas of instruction. We argue that such activities are consistent with the goal of developing learners who have the need to store information, but who must also be more capable of processing information to construct useful, personal knowledge. Teachers will need new skills to help students achieve this goal. There will be due emphasis on presenting information and a greater need to model and encourage skills involved in decision making and problem solving.

Although individual teachers can have only an indirect impact on the amount of technology available, they can determine how technology is applied. There are concerns here too. The applications common in classrooms now appear to have created some inequities and have overemphasized fact-oriented learning. The focus on fact-based learning may relate to the more obvious availability of this type of software and the widely held belief that basic skill learning must be accomplished before higher-order skills can be attempted.

General-purpose tool software is widely available, relatively inexpensive because of its reusability, and easily applied in the context of content-area tasks. Tool applications are especially well suited to the gathering, understanding, and application of information. A more holistic approach, in which the learning context motivates and anchors the learning of factual knowledge and basic skills within meaningful tasks, is one alternative. The more holistic approach also seems an effective way to involve all students on a more equal basis.

REFLECTING ON CHAPTER 1

Activities

◆ You can investigate some of the equity issues discussed in this chapter. Check out a general-purpose computer magazine from the library, and make a tally sheet to evaluate the advertisements. How many white males appear in the ads? How many women? How many members of minority groups? You may also be able to classify the role that each person in the ads plays. Is one group consistently more active or more in control than others? Be prepared to compare your observations with those of your classmates.

◆ Consider how technology has influenced you as a college student. A recent argument is that future teachers experience few applications of technology as learners and thus lack the experience and insights necessary to make use of technology when they graduate and move into the teaching profession. Have you used technology as a tutor, tool, or tutee? Have you used technology at all? Write a summary of the ways in which you have used technology as a learner during the past year.

◆ Do you accept the reality of an "information glut"? Generate a list of examples demonstrating changes in the quantity of information available to you. For example, it is possible to watch a television channel solely devoted to providing information about the weather.

◆ Think of a course you have taken recently that seems especially well suited to preparing you for the Information Age. What specific skills were stressed in this course?

Resources to Expand Your Knowledge Base

Many of the topics in this chapter are expanded in later chapters, and additional readings are provided at those points. If you find the idea that technology may change the basic nature of education exciting, you may want to examine the following sources:

Jones, B., & Malay, R. (1996). *Schools for an information age.* Westport, CT: Praeger.

Means, B. (Ed.). (1994). *Technology and education reform: The reality behind the promise.* San Francisco: Jossey-Bass.

Computer magazines for educators do not limit themselves to discussing hardware and software; they also include articles focused on more general ed for K–12 educators, now subtitles its publication *The Magazine for Technology and School Change.* A list of magazines and journals focused on educational applications of technology appears in Resources to Expand Your Knowledge Base at the end of Chapter 3.

Chapter **2**

Meaningful Learning in an Information Age

ORIENTATION

This chapter considers some key ideas related to the goals of education and the nature of learning. How you use technology in your classroom will be determined by the goals you have for your students and your understanding of how students learn.

There is now, as there has always been, considerable controversy focused on our schools. Some are suggesting that schools should make fundamental changes in the knowledge and skills students are expected to develop and in the methods schools use to support student learning. An analysis of the suggestions for school reform and school restructuring provides an opportunity to raise and evaluate issues related to the goals of education.

Content experts suggest educational goals in the form of **standards.** Our intent in familiarizing you with standards and the purposes to which content standards are to be applied is (1) to help you develop a deeper understanding of what experts believe students should learn and (2) to examine the role that activities that use technology can play in facilitating or inhibiting desirable classroom outcomes. We will attend most closely to standards that directly address the knowledge and skills students need to apply technology in their learning.

Finally, it is our intent to help you develop a deeper understanding of how students learn and how technology might contribute to this process. We emphasize a cognitive approach in an effort to help you understand the mental activities of learners and how learning tasks influence student thinking. Theoretical models based within the cognitive tradition suggest that educators can establish learning environments that help students learn more effectively, apply what they have learned, and become more excited about learning. In keeping with some of the goals of school reform, certain learning experiences also appear important in developing the skills necessary to become autonomous and lifelong learners. We believe technology can play a prominent role in providing these productive experiences.

As you read, look for answers to the following questions:

Focus Questions

- ◆ What are the types of change advocated by those promoting educational reform?
- ◆ What are educational standards, and how do they get translated into classroom practice?
- ◆ What do assumptions about the structure of long-term memory imply for the successful storage and use of knowledge?
- ◆ How do external tasks influence internal mental processes?
- ◆ What are authentic tasks, and what is necessary for classroom experiences to be more authentic?
- ◆ Why does existing research not demonstrate the general positive educational benefits of technology that some think to be necessary to justify the money that is spent?

SCHOOL REFORM IN AN INFORMATION AGE

What should schools do?

Think about what we ask our schools to do. First, students must acquire the basic knowledge and skills we expect of an educated person, prepare for work or more advanced education, learn to function as responsible citizens, and develop personal interests that bring richness and meaning to life. As if that were not enough, we also expect schools to "fix things." That is, schools must somehow play a role in addressing the inequities in society, help future citizens appreciate the rising diversity of cultures and languages they are likely to encounter, reduce the slippage in our international economic dominance, head off new health risks, and generally help citizens adjust as the world changes around them. This is a great deal to ask of schools; in fact, given the amount of time students spend in classrooms, it is probably an unrealistic set of expectations.

We view the debate over what schools should be asked to accomplish as an opportunity. That is, the discussions generated by advocation of reform and restructuring provide opportunities to consider and possibly readjust goals and priorities. We see thinking seriously about the purposes of education as important and encourage you to ask questions about whether existing learning experiences are likely to achieve these goals.

As this chapter shows, we believe that technology can play a prominent role in responding to the priorities that school reformers are raising. It is also true, though, that technology is partially responsible for some of the *need* for school reform. Information and communication technologies have helped to create new types of jobs and demands for new skills, which have led educa-

The need for lifelong learning

tional critics to ask how schools can be more effective in meeting these needs. Moreover, the rapid change of technology means that we cannot master a subject once and then simply apply that knowledge for the rest of our lives. As a basic condition of employment, not to mention social and cultural awareness, we must engage in **lifelong learning**.

Another characteristic of our age for which technology—especially the Internet—is partly responsible is the information explosion. The information available on the World Wide Web is mounting so fast that any statistic attempting to quantify how much is available would be seriously out of date before we printed it. With so much raw information available, the question of what and how students should learn—and how teachers should attempt to teach—becomes ever more pressing.

KEY THEMES IN REFORM: ACTIVE LEARNING AND MEANINGFUL EXPERIENCES

Despite the many disagreements among educational reformers, some proposals have drawn a great deal of support. Often you will see a summary table, such as Table 2.1, that contrasts "conventional" or "traditional" education with a "reformed" or "restructured" school setting (for instance, Brown, 1992;

TABLE 2.1

A Comparison of Traditional and Restructured Schools

	CONVENTIONAL SETTING	RESTRUCTURED SETTING
Student role	Learn facts and skills by absorbing the content presented by teachers and media resources.	Create personal knowledge by acting on content provided by teachers, media resources, and personal experiences.
Curriculum characteristics	Fragmented knowledge and disciplinary separation. Basic literacy established before high-level inquiry is encouraged. Focus on breadth of knowledge.	Multidisciplinary themes, knowledge integration, and application. Emphasis on thinking skills and application. Emphasis on depth of understanding.
Social characteristics	Teacher-controlled setting with students working independently. Some competition.	Teacher functions as facilitator and learner. Students work collaboratively and make some decisions.
Assessment	Measurement of fact knowledge and discrete skill. Traditional tests.	Assessment of knowledge application. Performance of tasks to demonstrate understanding.
Teacher role	Present information and manage the classroom.	Guide student inquiry and model active learning.
Possible use of technology	Source of information for absorption.	Source of information for interpretation and knowledge creation. Outlet for original work.

Knapp & Glenn, 1996; Means et al., 1993). Although such tables oversimplify complex issues, they help us identify critical dimensions. Look at the table carefully. What do you think are the common themes of the restructured school setting as opposed to the conventional setting?

If educational institutions must move in a different direction, one source of guidance may come from national curriculum standards. These goals, which summarize the opinions of content experts, are intended to focus classroom learning and the assessment of student competence on essential knowledge and skills. The deliberate process of recommending essential knowledge and skills and the related discussion of how best to help students learn in a meaningful way have served as important factors encouraging educational reform.

NATIONAL STANDARDS, EDUCATIONAL REFORM, AND TECHNOLOGY IN THE CLASSROOM

In 1994, Congress passed the Goals 2000: Educate America Act (House of Representatives 1804, 1994). The paragraph introducing this legislation states that its purpose is

> to improve learning and teaching by providing a national framework for education reform; to promote the research, consensus building, and systemic changes needed to ensure equitable educational opportunities and high levels of educational achievement for all students; to provide a framework for reauthorization of all Federal education programs; to promote the development and adoption of a voluntary national system of skill standards and certifications; and for other purposes.

The year 2000 was selected as the target date by which the nation's schools would be systematically reformed to address concerns summarized in the landmark report *A Nation at Risk* (National Commission on Excellence in Education, 1983). This report argued that large numbers of students were passing through the educational system without gaining the knowledge and skills necessary to contribute in a modern technological society. The lost potential of these citizens was presented as a threat to the economic well-being of the nation. Although the year 2000 has come without the complete realization of goals expressed in the 1994 legislation, activities supported by this legislation continue to be important and continue to promote the general debate about quality education. An important component that is still emerging out of this general initiative concerns the attempt to define standards. These expectations for what students should learn are important in shaping the role that technology ultimately will play in classrooms.

The attempt to define standards

Here is what we want you to know about standards:

◆ Become familiar with what standards are and how standards might influence what you do in your classroom.

◆ Recognize that the emphasis in content-area standards is consistent with the learning theory and the learning activities we emphasize throughout this book.

◆ Become familiar with the specific standards that apply to what students should know about and be able to do with technology.

What Are Standards?

Standards seek to define what students should learn and thus what teachers should teach. Many practicing teachers are likely to be aware of standards and related concepts such as benchmarks and frameworks. They have probably spent recent summers working on curriculum projects to prepare documents summarizing how state and national standards will be implemented in their schools. You may not have had such experiences, so we begin with a description of what standards are and how they are intended to shape learning activity. We then discuss how standards are related to efforts to reform schools and also acquaint you with standards that propose what students should learn about technology and how students should learn with technology. Finally, we review standards that propose what you as a preservice or practicing teacher should know and be able to do in order to help your students use technology effectively.

Standards and school reform

The word *standard* is used in several ways. **Content standards** define what every student should know and be able to do. **Performance standards** explain how students will demonstrate their proficiency in order to establish that a standard has been achieved. Both are important because while performance standards might seem more specific, it is important to understand that the specific demonstrations of proficiency are indicators of more general goals and not goals in themselves.

Standards are written on many levels of detail. In reading the literature on standards, you would come across the phrase *grain size* used in reference to this issue. Here is one way to understand how grain size works in practice. On the national level, professional organizations work to establish general educational goals—the general concepts and skills students should acquire. For example, one current mathematics standard requires that students "demonstrate number sense and an understanding of number theory." Immediately you might wonder how this general standard might apply at the grade level you intend to teach. Does this standard define a single expectation, or could it be interpreted as identifying several different levels of accomplishment? **Benchmarks** define a general standard according to a system describing what should be accomplished by the end of several grade-level intervals, say, K–2, 6–8, and 9–12. Benchmarks for our mathematics standard example include "Understand the relationship of fractions to decimals and whole numbers" (grades 6–8) and "Understand characteristics of the real number system and its subsystems" (grades 9–12) (Kendall & Marzano, 1996).

Standards and benchmarks

Even when standards are defined in terms of benchmarks, the level of detail—that is, grain size—is not sufficient to specify learning experiences and assessment procedures. In part, this vagueness is purposeful. Telling teachers specifically what and how to teach is a touchy matter that professional organizations formulating standards at the national level have tried to avoid. These organizations have instead tried to establish general goals. Then states and individual school districts are encouraged to interpret these national standards and benchmarks. Here is where curriculum frameworks are developed. A curriculum **framework** further specifies and organizes the knowledge and skills to be acquired and relates these goals to general instructional processes and assessment techniques (Laboratory Network Program Frameworks Task Force, 1998). Our previous reference to groups of teachers working on standards during the summer encompassed this process of creating frameworks to guide local efforts. Teacher plans, sometimes called lesson plans, could represent a continuation of this planning process. Teachers take frameworks established locally and decide exactly what activities to implement. The classroom teacher takes what began as general standards at the national level and then were expressed as topical units contributing to a suggested sequence of instruction at the local level, and translates them into specific lesson procedures based on specific learning resources. And sample progress indicators at the national level end up moving through a process requiring greater and greater specificity, resulting in the development of learning objectives and related assessment techniques at the classroom level. The teacher usually determines the specific learning activities that students work on and how student understanding will be evaluated (Bartz & Singer, 1996).

Curriculum frameworks and lesson plans

Standards and Reform

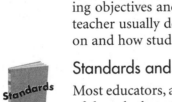

Most educators, and certainly most preservice teachers, are probably unaware of the role that standards or at least the discussion of standards has played in educational reform. We hope that the translation process we have just described has helped you understand how national standards may end up influencing classroom practice. You might wonder if what could appear to be the creation of a common curriculum is the major contribution of standards to educational reform. The term **alignment** is sometimes used to promote the benefits of bringing many partners—classroom teachers, those who prepare teachers, companies responsible for the development of instructional materials, and organizations responsible for creating evaluation instruments—together around a common vision. While some would urge an agreement on some very specific content goals (Hirsch, 1988), the standards and the process of implementing standards as we have described them clearly leave room for interpreting goals within a regional and local context. We think alignment and reform are best understood as operating on this more general level.

Alignment means a common vision.

You might not make the connection between standards and reform with only a quick examination of standards that apply to your own content and grade-level interests. Understanding some of the fundamental changes that are being proposed requires a broader look at standards, assumptions about how they are to be applied, and beliefs about how student accomplishments should be evaluated. Standards emphasize many aspects of the reform agenda.

STANDARDS FOR LEARNING WITH TECHNOLOGY

The International Society for Technology in Education (ISTE) has established standards and benchmarks that define general expectations for what students should know about and be able to do with technology. The list of standards is short enough that we can provide it here (see Focus: ISTE Technology Standards). We have provided benchmarks for one standard to help you understand how the standards might be interpreted across grade levels (International Society for Technology in Education, 1998).

Once you have examined the ISTE standards ask yourself how such expectations might influence your classroom. There are probably some standards you may not have thought to be your responsibility or perhaps do not see as essential. This book should be helpful in preparing you to address many of these standards, but there are some we ignore. As we have suggested, the translation of standards into classroom practice or, in our case, into what is emphasized in our contribution to the professional development of teachers involves professional judgment, prioritizing, and an understanding of how the learning experiences each of us provides fit within a larger scheme.

Standards prompt discussion and reflection.

If nothing else, standards have prompted discussions among classroom teachers, college of education faculty members, professional bodies advocating for their disciplines (e.g., American Association for the Advancement of Science, National Council of Teachers of English), textbook publishers, local, state, and federal politicians, and many other special interest groups. These discussions concern some fundamental and difficult topics: What are the purposes of education? What should all educated citizens know and be able to do? We encourage you to reflect on these questions and how they apply to your own teaching.

ENCOURAGING EQUITY: STANDARDS

Standards promote equity. The standards that apply to K–12 students emphasize what all students should know and be able to do. Consider this observation. You frequently find the word *literacy* used in connection with standards (e.g., science literacy, computer literacy). The implication is that there are certain skills and knowledge that are essential for the productive functioning of all citizens, and at a minimum schools must help students achieve these goals. Standards imply that educators are to have similar

Literacy and basic skills

Focus

ISTE Technology Standards

Foundation Standards for Students

1. Basic operations and concepts
   - Students demonstrate a sound understanding of the nature and operation of technology systems.
   - Students are proficient in the use of technology.

2. Social, ethical, and human issues
   - Students understand the ethical, cultural, and societal issues related to technology.
   - Students practice responsible use of technology systems, information, and software.
   - Students develop positive attitudes toward technology uses that support life-long learning, collaboration, personal pursuits, and productivity.

3. Technology productivity tools
   - Students use technology tools to enhance learning, increase productivity, and promote creativity.
   - Students use productivity tools to collaborate in constructing technology-enhanced models, preparing publications, and producing other creative works.

4. Technology communications tools
   - Students use telecommunications to collaborate, publish, and interact with peers, experts, and other audiences.
   - Students use a variety of media and formats to communicate information and ideas effectively to multiple audiences.

5. Technology research tools
   - Students use technology to locate, evaluate, and collect information from a variety of sources.
   - Students use technology tools to process data and report results.
   - Students evaluate and select new information resources and technological innovations based on the appropriateness to specific tasks.

6. Technology problem-solving and decision-making tools
   - Students use technology resources for solving problems and making informed decisions.
   - Students employ technology in the development of strategies for solving problems in the real world.

Communication Tools (Benchmarks)

Grades 3–5

- Use technology tools (e.g., multimedia authoring, presentation, Web tools, digital cameras, scanners) for individual and collaborative writing, communication, and publishing activities to create knowledge products for audiences inside and outside the classroom.
- Use telecommunications efficiently and effectively to access remote information, communicate with others in support of direct and independent learning, and pursue personal interests.

Grades 6–8

- Design, develop, publish, and present products (e.g., Web pages, videotapes) using technology resources that demonstrate and communicate curriculum concepts to audiences inside and outside the classroom.

◆ Collaborate with peers, experts, and others using telecommunications and collaborative tools to investigate curriculum-related problems, issues, and information, and to develop solutions or products for audiences inside and outside the classroom.

Grades 9–12

◆ Use technology tools and resources for managing and communicating personal/professional information (e.g., fi-

nances, schedules, addresses, purchases, correspondence).

◆ Routinely and efficiently use online information resources to meet needs for collaboration, research, publications, communications, and productivity.

◆ Select and apply technology tools for research, information analysis, problem solving, and decision making in content learning.✳

expectations of students without regard for gender, socioeconomic status, ethnicity, or region of the country. In addition, standards imply the development of useful knowledge. For example, the science standards are promoted as important in the development of a workforce capable of competing in an open world economy and of preparing citizens to deal with individual, family, and community decisions (e.g., health issues, environmental issues) in an informed way (Raizen, 1998).

Equity is also emphasized in the NCATE/ISTE standards that apply to the preparation of teachers. Here are some examples presented from the NCATE Program Standards for Educational Computing and Technology that were approved in 1997:

1.2.5 Demonstrate awareness of resources for adaptive assistive devices for students with special needs.

1.2.6 Demonstrate knowledge of equity, ethics, legal, and human issues concerning use of computers and technology

1.3.3 Design, deliver, and assess student learning activities that integrate computers/technology for a variety of student grouping strategies and for diverse student populations

1.3.4 Design student learning activities that foster equitable, ethical, and legal use of technology by students.

To us—and you will see this idea emphasized throughout the book—one all-important theme promoted by standards and the reformed school is that students have greater experience with learning tasks that are *active* and *meaningful.* You may wonder exactly what those terms mean. That is what we are about to explore. Our goal is to get you to think about the student's mental behavior as a learner and how, as a teacher, you can influence this behavior.

Focus

How Standards May Be Shaping What You Learn About the Application of Technology

You may be using this book in a course that is part of a teacher certification program or an advanced program to prepare technology specialists. If so, there are standards that have been developed to guide the education that you receive. Many institutions preparing K–12 educators in the United States seek accreditation from the National Council for Accreditation of Teacher Education (NCATE). An accrediting agency promotes and monitors quality educational experiences, and standards are an important component of this process. Institutions wanting to list programs as NCATE accredited are required to demonstrate through documentation and periodic discussions with a visiting team of reviewers that established standards have been implemented.

Here are some ways in which NCATE standards shape the preparation of educators to teach with and about technology. As you examine this list, you will note that NCATE sometimes adopts standards prepared by other professional organizations with more focused content-area interests.

- Standards provided by the International Society for Technology in Education (ISTE) or the Association for Educational Communication and Technology (AECT) are used to evaluate advanced programs preparing candidates for computing and technology coordinators, library media specialists, and similar leadership positions.
- ISTE standards provide guidance to programs preparing candidates to teach computer literacy courses and secondary computer science courses.
- ISTE standards can also apply to the general preparation of teachers to integrate technology in content-area instruction and define what is necessary to receive **endorsement.**
- Standards that apply to the preparation of candidates to teach specific content areas (e.g., math, social studies) are also relevant because these standards establish implications for how technology might best be used in classroom settings.

To give you some idea of how standards are presented, we will use some examples from the NCATE/ISTE standards for Initial Endorsement in Educational Computing and Technology Literacy. NCATE/ISTE expectations are presented as a combination of content standards and performance indicators. Because there are more than sixty performance indicators, our examples include the content standards and one related performance indicator. We have selected indicators we think that you will likely be capable of satisfying upon completion of the course in which you are enrolled. Although some of the terms may be unfamiliar to you, think about the indicators that you do understand and establish what you think you and other students in your class should be able to do to demonstrate satisfactory skill or knowledge.

Foundations

1.1 Basic Computer/Technology Operations and Concepts: Candidates will use computer systems and run software; access, generate, and manipulate data; and publish results. They will also evaluate performance of hardware and software components of computer systems and apply basic troubleshooting strategies as needed.

1.1.4 Use imaging devices such as scanners, digital cameras, and/or video cameras with computer systems and software.

1.2 Personal and Professional Use of Technology: Candidates will apply tools for enhancing their own professional growth and productivity. They will use technology in communicating, collaborating, conducting research, and solving problems. In addition, they will plan and participate in activities that encourage lifelong learning and will promote equitable, ethical, and legal use of computer/technology resources.

1.2.1 Use productivity tools for word processing, database management, and spreadsheet applications.

1.3 Applications of Technology in Instruction: Candidates will apply computers and related technologies to support instruction in their grade level and subject areas. They must plan and deliver instructional units that integrate a variety of software, applications, and learning tools. Lessons developed must reflect effective grouping and assessment strategies for diverse populations.

1.3.2 Describe current instructional principles, research, and appropriate assessment practices as related to the use of computers and technology resources in the curriculum.

Specialty Content Preparation in Educational Computing and Technology Literacy

2.1 Social, Ethical, and Human Issues: Candidates will apply concepts and skills in making decisions concerning social, ethical, and human issues related to computing and technology.

2.1.2 Describe strategies for facilitating consideration of ethical, legal, and human issues involving school purchasing and policy decisions.

2.2 Productivity Tools: Candidates integrate advanced features of technology-based productivity tools to support instruction.

2.2.6 Apply specific-purpose electronic devices (such as graphing calculator, language translator, scientific probeware, or electronic thesaurus) in appropriate content areas.

2.3 Telecommunication and Information Access: Candidates will use telecommunications and information access resources to support instruction.

2.3.3 Use automated online search tools and intelligent agents to identify and index desired information resources.

2.4 Research, Problem Solving, and Product Development: Candidates will use computers and other technologies in research, problem solving, and product development. Candidates use a variety of media, presentation, and authoring packages; plan and participate in team and collaborative projects that require critical analysis and evaluation; and present products developed.

2.4.8 Design and publish simple online documents that present information and include links to critical resources.

Professional Preparation

3.1 Teaching Methodology: Candidates will effectively plan, deliver, and assess concepts and skills relevant to educational computing and technology literacy across the curriculum.

3.1.4 Design and practice methods and strategies for teaching problem-solving principles and skills using technology resources.

3.2 Hardware/Software Selection, Installation, and Maintenance: Candidates will demonstrate knowledge of selection, installation, management, and maintenance of the infrastructure in a classroom setting.

3.2.2 Research, evaluate, and develop recommendations for purchasing instructional software to support and enhance the school curriculum.

We suggest that you use these standards to think about your existing knowledge and skills and what else would be important for you to learn.

Source: NCATE Program Standards for Educational Computing and Technology Approved in 1997 (International Society for Technology in Education, 1997). See Resources to Expand Your Knowledge Base at the end of this chapter for information on how to locate the NCATE standards online.✳

COGNITIVE MODELS OF SCHOOL LEARNING

As you read about the instructional strategies and learning activities in this book, you will note that we frequently speculate about how an experience influences a learner's mental activities. We believe that understanding how classroom experiences influence mental behaviors can be invaluable to the decisions teachers make about using technology in the classroom. Attempting to understand the mental behaviors involved in thinking and learning represents a *cognitive perspective.*

A cognitive perspective

Cognitive models emphasize how students acquire information and skills, solve problems, and engage in such academic tasks as reading, writing, and mathematical reasoning. Understanding how such tasks are accomplished, the barriers to be overcome, and sources of individual variability can help you recognize differences in performance and propose modifications to your students' instructional environment. In addition, understanding how different learning tasks encourage or discourage specific mental behaviors can help you assign more effective tasks and create a more productive learning environment for your students.

TWO APPROACHES TO DESCRIBING LEARNING AND THINKING ACTIVITIES

How these two approaches differ

In this chapter we take two approaches to describing learning and thinking activities. The first approach explores some of the fundamental properties of mental activity. The second approach explores important issues of school learning at a more conceptual level. By conceptual, we are referring to a level of description classroom teachers may use more commonly to discuss how students learn. The major distinction between these approaches is in the amount of specificity they use to describe learning and thinking activities.

We present this discussion of school learning because we want you to examine how applications of technology might influence student thinking and learning. You will revisit many of these principles in later chapters as we discuss specific applications of technology and describe strategies for using them in your classroom. We encourage you to consider the material in this and the following chapters actively. Discuss the assumptions and proposals with your classmates and instructor.

FUNDAMENTAL PROPERTIES OF MENTAL ACTIVITY

Implications of characteristics of mental behavior

Learning and thinking activities can be described in terms of multiple *memory stores,* the *processes* or mental actions that we use as we think and learn, and some *executive mechanisms* that oversee and control the processes and determine whether the processes have accomplished what we as learners have intended. We will not spend a great deal of time exploring classroom learning and thinking at the most fundamental level. However, we do want to familiarize you with some of the most important characteristics of mental behavior and show you some important implications of these characteristics for specific classroom situations involving technology.

MEMORY STORES

Two memory stores

Memory stores function within the cognitive system to hold information. Once information is taken in through our sensory receptors (e.g., eyes, ears), memory stores come into play. This discussion considers two memory stores: short- and long-term memory.

Short-Term Memory

The most effective way to describe **short-term memory** (STM) is as consciousness: the thoughts, ideas, and images of which a person is aware at any point in time. A moment of reflection will give you some insight into the contents of your short-term memory right now. What ideas are you aware of? These ideas are available in your short-term memory (we hope they include the ideas presented here).

Working memory

Time and capacity limits

Short-term memory is also frequently called **working memory**. Learning and thinking activities occur in working memory. Again, a bit of reflection will suggest some important characteristics of working memory. Experience should suggest that working memory operates within time and capacity limits. That is, there is a limit to how much information we can be aware of and how much mental activity we can engage in at any one time. There is also a limit to how long information will be maintained in working memory without continued attention. How often have you found yourself repeating something or concentrating on it to keep the thought available? Mental rehearsal is a way we all attempt to respond to the time limits of working memory.

Many of the characteristics of working memory have implications for explaining learning or thinking difficulties and, as a result, how specific task performance might be improved. Using what you now know about the characteristics of working memory, think about the following classroom scenario:

Jack and his seventh-grade classmates have been receiving keyboarding instruction for several years. Jack can find most of the keys without looking, and he uses the computer to type papers he has already handwritten. However, he is not an accomplished typist. His English teacher has assigned an in-class theme and decides it is important for students to learn to compose at the keyboard. The teacher takes the class to the computer lab and tells the students they must complete their papers by the end of the class period. Jack has great difficulty with this task. Although his typing proficiency clearly limits how quickly he can work, his problems go beyond his ability to get his ideas down on paper. He has an unusual amount of difficulty thinking of what he wants to say and how he wants to organize his paper. The paper he writes is atypically poor.

What does short-term or working memory have to do with Jack's poor English paper? One very likely explanation for Jack's writing problems involves the time and capacity limitations of working memory. If Jack must think to recall the keyboard position of individual letters, the thinking behavior he must employ in order to type competes for working memory capacity with the various thinking behaviors required to write the paper. The slow speed at which he works only makes matters worse. He is forced to expend his limited cognitive resources to keep thoughts active for a longer period of time.

There are some ways this situation can be improved. An improvement in typing proficiency is a long-term solution, but it has little immediate value. If the teacher insists that the paper be typed in class, Jack might improve his performance by first generating an outline of his ideas and referring to this outline as he works. In this manner, Jack would decrease what he has to accomplish and retain in working memory.

The teacher might also want to think carefully about the goals of the assignment. There may be other ways to accomplish the same ends. If both developing writing skills and composing at the computer are important, imposing a severe time limitation is probably not a good idea for novice typists. Either less demanding assignments should be given, or students should have an extended period of time to complete the assignment.

The relationship between word processing and writing is one example of a situation in which the student uses technology as a tool to perform some other academic task. It is helpful for teachers to recognize that in situations like this, an inexperienced student really faces several cognitive tasks. First, the student needs to learn to use a particular computer program. Second, the student needs to perform some academic task using the technology. Composing at the keyboard draws on both the motor skills of typing and the thinking and problem-solving skills used in writing. Under certain circumstances, the combination of these tasks can strain working memory.

The need for well-developed computer skills

The story about Jack provides a worst-case scenario of a student who is still an unskilled typist trying to complete a difficult writing assignment. Both the use of the technology and the academic task are difficult for him and compete for his limited working memory resources. The story also illustrates that challenging classroom assignments become unnecessarily difficult when the computer skills needed to perform them are not well developed. Teachers may fail to see that the opposite relationship between classroom tasks and technology also holds. Students may have difficulty learning to take full advantage of the power of computer programs when they apply the programs only to challenging classroom problems. When the task to be accomplished is difficult or must be completed under time pressure, the student is less likely to explore the potential of the technology and, as a consequence, never gets beyond using the technology in the most mundane fashion.

A play phase

To ease the burden of learning to use new programs, students might first be asked to apply programs to very easy or familiar tasks. In other words, it is often useful to allow for a *play phase*. A play phase is valuable because it allows students to explore the capabilities of new software in low-stress settings with low-stress tasks. For example, when students are first learning the features of a word processing program, they should write on a topic such as their families or themselves. This kind of topic allows information to flow freely while the student focuses on features such as fonts, cutting and pasting, and saving the document to disk. Hurrying the process of learning a new program is not always the best long-term solution.

In Chapter 4 we discuss a type of computer software called *drill and practice*. Drill-and-practice activities are relevant when certain skills (such as typing) need to be learned to the point that executing them takes little working memory capacity so the student's attention can be devoted to other mental tasks (such as writing).

Long-Term Memory

Permanent store of knowledge and skills

Long-term memory (LTM) contains a person's permanent store of knowledge and skills—that is, all the stored products of learning—from both formal education and everyday experiences.

Memory components

Contents of Long-Term Memory.   Because we all have some sense of what we know, we all have some insight into what LTM contains. How would you describe all the different things you have learned? Different theorists (Anderson, 1983; Gagne & Glaser, 1987) categorize the contents of LTM in different ways. The memory components we discuss here are imagery, episodic memory, and declarative and procedural knowledge.

Imagery

Remembering textbooks thirty years later

◆ Experience tells us that we have the capacity to store imagery of different types (smells, sounds, visual representations). We are capable of recalling very specific smells (Mom's kitchen when she made chicken dinner on Sundays) or visual images (the house you grew up in) from long ago. Researchers, working mostly with visual images, have demonstrated just how remarkable our long-term storage is. In one creative experiment, researchers (Read & Barnsley, 1977) presented pages from elementary school reading textbooks to adults. The adults, who had not seen these books for as long as thirty years, viewed entire pages, the text portions of pages, or just the illustrations originally on the pages. The adults could recognize all versions above the level of chance and were most accurate when a picture was included.

Episodic Memory

Examples of episodic memories

◆ An **episodic memory** is a stored representation of something you have experienced (Tulving, 1972)—for example, a filmstrip on butterflies viewed in an elementary school science class, a marketing field trip to a local shopping mall to view store window displays, or a conversation with a friend about today's lunch. Episodic memories are rich in detail, much of which may be of no great significance. They can also be related to a particular time and place. In fact, we often use time and place to help us recall the details of a specific event we have experienced. For example, during a quiz, a student may attempt to recall last Thursday's lecture to locate information relevant to a particular question.

In education, episodic memories can be a mixed blessing. Certainly it is important for students to have a rich store of experiences to draw on. In some circumstances, we want students to use experiences from their lives either to discover principles or as a route to a richer understanding of the principles we present as teachers. For example, a psychology instructor might ask, "Did your mother ever tell you that you couldn't have dessert until you'd finished your vegetables? Why do you think she said that?" The instructor hopes that you have had an experience like this and that recalling it might help you understand psychological concepts such as contingency and reinforcement. Life stories also play a very important role in thinking and problem solving outside of schools. We often also use such stories, rather than more abstract principles or rules, to convey knowledge to our daily acquaintances. The recollection of what we or someone else did in a particular situation can be recalled and adapted as a solution to a new problem (McLellan, 1996).

Encouraging students to create knowledge

It is important, however, for teachers to appreciate the limitations of episodic representations. Teachers also do not usually want students to store their academic experiences as episodes. They want students to think about a lecture and store the major ideas rather than the verbatim comments. Much of what we present in this book is focused on this issue: *How do teachers get students to create knowledge and not be satisfied with simply storing information?* Students need to take an active role in working with the information they receive.

Declarative and Procedural Knowledge

◆ Many memory theorists have drawn a distinction between verbally based factual knowledge and know-how (Anderson, 1976, 1983; Gagne, 1985). This distinction is often described as the difference between knowing *that* something is the case and knowing *how* to perform a certain cognitive process or action. **Declarative knowledge** represents our factual knowledge base, and **procedural knowledge** represents the stored methods we use to do things.

Much of school learning has to do with the storage of declarative knowledge. We learn the names of things, significant dates, terms, definitions, number facts, theories of this and that, and many similar categories of facts and concepts. We are also taught to do things: tie our shoes and button our coat, add and subtract, write, solve algebra problems, and argue for a position. In reality, most accomplishments require both declarative and procedural knowledge. It is, for example, difficult to write without having something to say. To engage in an argument, we need the skills of logic and effective communication, as well as factual knowledge.

One final point of clarification: procedural knowledge is not the same as a verbal account of how to do something. Procedural knowledge is demonstrated by actual performance, not by a description of how something should be done. The stored description of where the letter q appears on a keyboard is declarative knowledge. Pressing the q key when desired is procedural knowledge.

Applying several categories of memory contents

A Network Model of Long-Term Memory.   Most academic and life tasks require the use of several categories of memory contents. Consequently, the various elements of memory are most likely meaningfully organized rather than isolated by category of memory unit. Effective educational experiences must result in both the accumulation and the organization of memory units. We call this organized structure of memory units a *network*.

The network is a useful way to conceptualize how what we know (our memory) is stored and the ways memory works. **Network models** represent memory in terms of **nodes**, which are cognitive units, and **links**, which establish the relationships among nodes (Anderson, 1983; Collins & Quillian, 1969; Gagne, 1985; Gagne, Yekovich, & Yekovich, 1993).

Figure 2.1 is a graphic representation of what such models attempt to describe. This representation portrays a small part of a high school biology student's knowledge. Included are examples of the four categories of LTM contents:

FIGURE 2.1   Network of Biological Knowledge Stored in LTM

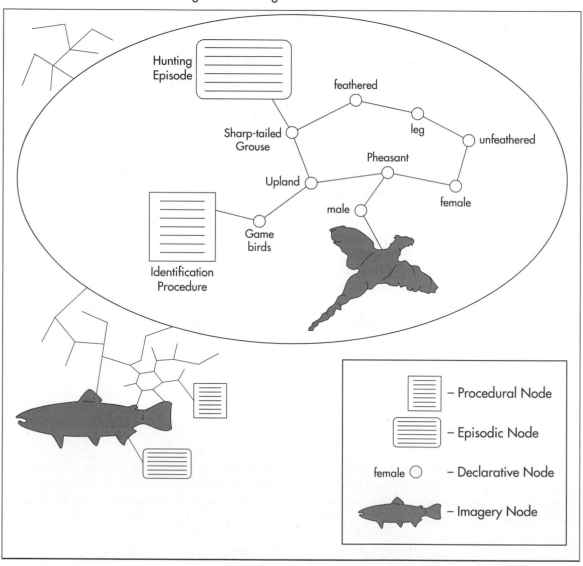

Meaningful links

(1) imagery (recollections of animals the student has seen), (2) episodic knowledge (the recollection of a hunting trip), (3) declarative knowledge (conceptual knowledge about pheasants and grouse), and (4) procedural knowledge (the stored strategy for identifying particular game birds). As you can see from the figure, these elements are linked in meaningful ways. For example, the image of a male pheasant is connected with the concept "male" and "pheasant." (What would you guess is one way to distinguish a female pheasant from a sharp-tailed grouse? One difference is whether the leg is feathered or unfeathered.)

Organized and unorganized elements of memory

The network-like structure of memory explains an important characteristic of human thought. We seldom recall isolated thoughts. One idea seems to make us aware of other ideas, images, or stored experiences. The related nodes that are first activated or brought into our awareness are those that are the most directly linked. Many important kinds of mental performance depend on more than whether relevant ideas, images, events, and procedures exist in LTM. Performance may depend instead on *how* individual nodes of memory are linked or organized. Organized elements of memory are more likely to be available to our awareness at any given point than are unorganized elements. Mental tasks will go much more successfully when the elements required to accomplish a particular task exist in memory and are well organized.

A major goal of education

If LTM consists of a network of nodes, then a major goal of education is to construct and modify this network. One important way to modify the network is to add new nodes (ideas, events, images, or procedures). However, it is also important to organize nodes by adding new links and possibly eliminating other, inappropriate links. The least valuable learning experiences add few nodes or add nodes linked to few existing nodes. The most valuable learning experiences encourage students to create rich interconnections among stored elements of knowledge. Creating links is not an automatic process. Students must activate stored experiences and find appropriate connections with new ideas. How all this happens is not fully understood, but we provide further insights as we discuss cognitive processes.

PROCESSES: MENTAL TOOLS FOR DOING THE WORK OF THINKING AND LEARNING

Something very important is still missing in our consideration of what is necessary for learning. Thinking and learning are active. Students acquire information from the world around them and generate personal knowledge; they solve problems; they create new ideas and new things. The cognitive system we have described to this point just sits there. If teachers want to search for more effective learning experiences for their students, they will need to have some general ideas about the mental actions that productive learning experiences should encourage.

The basic actions of the information processing system are often referred to as *processes.* Instead of an extended discussion of the volumes of research

Tool categories

on cognitive processes, permit the substitution of a simplifying idea based on this research: that of a *mental tool*. Assume that students have at their disposal mental tools they can use to accomplish a variety of cognitive tasks. Here are four general hypothetical tool categories:

1. **Attend to:** Maintains certain ideas in consciousness for an extended period of time.
2. **Link/Associate/Organize:** Establishes connections between information units stored in LTM or active in working memory.
3. **Elaborate/Extend/Exemplify/Infer:** Creates or discovers new knowledge from the logical and purposeful combination of active or stored memory components.
4. **Test/Evaluate/Question:** Determines whether a situation is as desired or expected.

We have organized the descriptive verbs in groups to indicate that all verbs in a group describe similar functions. Certainly it would be possible to propose more tools or to explain these phenomena in different terms. The point is, within the cognitive system, there seem to exist mechanisms—mental tools—for operating on the raw information fed into the system from the world and for managing and continually modifying what the system has stored previously. These tools accomplish the work of cognitive activity.

METACOGNITION

Knowing how to use mental tools

In evaluating the utility of the mental tool metaphor, Paris and Winograd (1990) note that having a collection of tools is not enough. A good craftsperson knows how to use the appropriate tools wisely and independently to complete desired projects. The same is true of effective learners. Effective tool use requires insights into task demands, awareness of personal strengths and weaknesses, and ongoing analysis of whether progress on the task is proceeding well or poorly. The skilled learner can plan to avoid difficulties or compensate for problems. Perhaps a different tool must be used. Perhaps the action of a tool already employed must be repeated until the desired outcome is achieved.

Metacognition and strategic use of cognitive tools

Any model of reading, writing, problem solving, or general study must propose some mechanism to account for the adaptive and strategic nature of actual student thinking and learning behavior. What prominent researchers and theorists have come up with to account for strategic behavior is the admittedly fuzzy and rather poorly operationalized construct of **metacognition** (Brown, 1981, 1987; Flavell, 1987; Garner, 1987; Paris & Winograd, 1990). Metacognition, which is responsible for guiding cognitive behavior, accounts for the strategic use of cognitive tools and for our ability to evaluate the success of our mental behaviors. Metacognition is usually described in terms of a combination of *metacognitive knowledge* and *metacognitive control functions*.

Metacognitive Knowledge

What metacognitive knowledge consists of

Metacognitive knowledge consists of personal insights into how cognitive tasks such as memory or writing are accomplished, about what makes particular tasks difficult or easy, and about personal cognitive characteristics and capabilities. We all have such knowledge, accurate or not. Students may realize, for instance, that information stored in an organized fashion is easier to retrieve than information stored haphazardly. They may realize that when they can't remember something, they should try to think of related things.

Metacognitive knowledge covers the skills of both academic and professional life. In some cases, this knowledge is the intended result of direct instruction. We are expected to learn strategies for figuring out the meaning of an unfamiliar word, to learn how to research and write a position paper, and to learn how to study for an essay examination. Other metacognitive knowledge is picked up less directly. Some students may realize that math is a particularly difficult subject for them. Students may also figure out that instructors are more likely to ask examination questions on topics covered in class than on textbook topics that were not discussed.

Metacognitive Control Functions

Metacognitive control functions are demonstrated in planning, regulating, and evaluating behaviors (Paris & Lindauer, 1982). Planning concerns decision making before beginning a project; regulating involves adjustments made while working on the task; and evaluating has to do with decisions made once the project has been completed.

Educational significance of metacognitive control functions

Metacognitive control functions have great educational significance. Consider the roles of planning, evaluating, and regulating as they might apply to some of the research and writing tasks involved in a student's preparation of a paper for a history class. The student might begin by outlining a rough set of issues to investigate and identifying some sources of information about these issues. As the student examines the sources, she must locate specific information about the issues and determine if enough information is available to attempt writing the paper. If no information turns up related to some key issue, she may decide to find additional sources, modify the initial topic of the paper, or abandon the original idea entirely. As the student writes the paper, she must determine whether the text meets acceptable standards for spelling and grammar and whether she is presenting the intended ideas in an organized and persuasive manner.

Metacognitive control functions also play a major role in self-directed learning. Thomas and Rohwer (1986) describe study behavior as effortful, private, self-managed activities, often operating with little in the way of external guidance regarding what is to be accomplished or what level of mastery is required. If you think carefully about what is (or was) expected of you as a college student, you will note just how much responsibility advanced students

Metacognitive control functions and self-directed learning

must accept. Usually much more material is presented than would be practical to master. Consequently, you must decide what is essential to master and what you can cover more superficially. The nature of future examinations is also vague, and you must make decisions about how your understanding will likely be evaluated. Finally, as you prepare for these examinations, there are few or no concrete ways for you to judge how adequately you have prepared. Do I understand this chapter well enough to go on to the next? Will I be able to solve this type of problem if it appears on the test? You must develop study plans, evaluate the adequacy of your understanding, and continually regulate study methods and your allocation of time and attention.

Metacognitive skills related to academic performance often need improvement. Study behavior, for example, is often passive (rereading textbook assignments) and relies on less powerful systems for organizing and emphasizing important content (note taking and highlighting). Students frequently use a single study approach, even when course material and evaluation procedures vary considerably. Regulatory functions, the mechanisms that allow learners to adjust their cognitive behavior "on-the-fly," are also suspect. Students frequently are unaware that they have failed to comprehend material they have read (Baker, 1985; Markman & Gorin, 1981). They also seem unable to predict accurately how they will do on tests covering the material that they are studying (Pressley, Snyder, Levin, Murray, & Ghatala, 1987). When students are unable to detect comprehension failures or test preparation difficulties, they are unlikely to use remediation strategies—even simple activities such as rereading or asking the teacher or a classmate for assistance.

Improving study behavior

Using Technology to Improve Metacognitive Skills

Technology may offer several ways to address metacognitive weakness. As the following example illustrates, which of these approaches is to be preferred is controversial. When technology is used for presenting course content, it is possible that certain decisions about learning—for example, about pacing, the sequence of instruction, and the specific content to be covered—can be made by either the learner or the computer (Milheim & Martin, 1991).

Traditional computer-based instruction

The tutorial, a form of traditional computer-based instruction (see Chapter 4), makes heavy use of questions. Students are presented with several screens of information and then are asked questions about the information just covered. If the student does poorly on the questions, a program using *computer control* might automatically move the student into some material attempting to explain the same information in a different way. A program allowing *learner control* would likely allow the learner the option of selecting the review material or continuing to the next section. Empirical studies of computer-based instruction frequently demonstrate an advantage for computer control over learner control (Milheim & Martin, 1991; Steinberg, 1989). Such findings are frustrating to those who advocate what they believe are motivational and learning advantages of allowing the learner to fine-tune instruction to personal needs. However, allowing the learner a great deal of control does not seem to work in practice.

There may be a productive compromise. *Learner control with advisement* is a technique that allows the student to make decisions after considering information or suggestions provided by the computer. In a study evaluating the effectiveness of computer advisement (Tennyson, 1980), students were learning the physics concepts of force, power, velocity, and speed. They first learned formal definitions for each concept. They were then provided with examples and asked to determine which of the four concepts would explain each example. In the learner control condition, students worked with the examples until they felt prepared for the posttest. In the computer control condition, the computer made decisions about how many examples were required, using a mathematical model based on pretest performance and performance on the examples. In the third condition, the learner made the decision to take the posttest but was provided with the same information used in the computer control condition. This study and others have demonstrated that learner control with advisement is superior to unaided learner control (Tennyson, 1980; Tennyson & Buttrey, 1980). Without advisement, students tended to terminate study of the lessons more quickly, possibly indicating that they had overestimated their level of mastery.

Developing metacognitive skills

A possible advantage of learner control with advisement is that this combination of computer monitoring and learner decision making potentially allows for the development of metacognitive and "learning-to-learn" skills. Students are put in the situation of thinking about the decisions they make as they attempt to master the assigned material. This situation is clearly different from the more common situation, in which feedback follows instruction and is likely to be perceived by the student as useful only for determining the grade. Heightened sensitivity to the processes and the successes and failures of learning may allow the student to develop new planning, regulating, and evaluating skills.

A SUMMARY AND TRANSITION

The way that students think about their own behaviors and the way teachers tend to discuss student behaviors are not likely to rely on the fundamental language or concepts of information processing. Classroom concepts of mental behavior tend to involve a more global level of description. We will adopt this global level of analysis as we consider the general topic of active learning.

Before launching into this new discussion, we want to provide ways to connect to what you now know about the fundamentals of how learners process information. We also want to summarize some of the central ideas covered in the first part of this chapter. Figure 2.2 addresses both of these needs. The portion of the diagram labeled "the student" depicts the important components of the information processing system and identifies some of

FIGURE 2.2   Connections Among the Teacher, Learning Environment, and Student

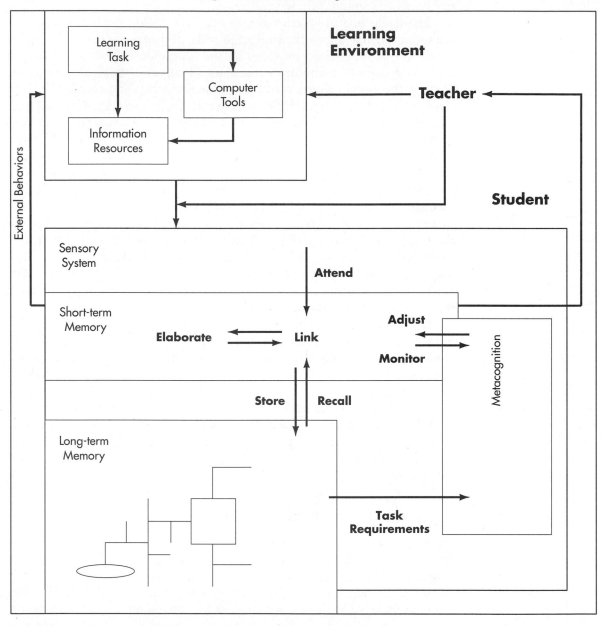

the more important cognitive activities involving these components. This combination of components and basic cognitive activities represents a simple summary of what is addressed by fundamental models of cognitive behavior. Our discussion of conceptual models will focus much more heavily on how effective teachers tend to interact with students and how they involve students in valuable learning activities. Of course, the activities we emphasize in this book use technology. The diagram is intended to suggest that the mental activities a student engages in are strongly influenced by interactions with the classroom teacher and the learning environment that the teacher establishes. You will note that in this diagram, the information a student encounters is not shown in a dominant position. The conceptual models you will encounter next suggest that active learning concerns what students do with information, not how much information the teacher and learning environment can provide.

Linking the fundamental and conceptual models of thinking

Following is a brief review of cognitive information processing. Thinking and learning are represented as the movement and generation of information within short- and long-term memory. The concept of cognitive tools is a useful way to represent how the actions of thinking and learning are accomplished. Many of the cognitive tools we identified are included in the diagram as arrows. Depending on the task, individual students use these tools in a variety of ways and with different degrees of success. A good teacher and an effective learning environment will increase the probability that more desirable outcomes will occur, but the teacher and the environment can only provide information to the learner (see Figure 2.2). Once information about what to know or how to think has been taken in by the student, what actually happens to this information and the content information to which this advice applies is the responsibility of the student. This is where issues of skill, motivation, and existing knowledge come into play. Metacognition, the capacity of a student to evaluate and adjust personal behaviors, also plays an important role in adapting thinking and learning behaviors for success.

How technology can play a role

How is technology involved in this diagram? First, technology can present information to students. Mostly this information will be ideas or concepts the student is to master or perhaps experiences the student is to think about to produce learning. Second, students may use computers and other forms of technology to complete learning tasks. Technology is not a direct source of information. Instead, the student manipulates information using technology as a tool, and the experiences resulting from this manipulation are what the student thinks about and learns from.

Teacher, student, and learning tasks interact.

There are two arrows in the diagram that are easy to overlook but are very important: the arrows leading back from the student to the teacher and to the learning environment. For effective learning, all of these components are intended to be interactive. The student can produce a product—something as simple as the answer to a question or as complex as a multimedia project—for the teacher to evaluate. The teacher's response becomes new information for the student to process. The student also acts on the learning environment. In a simple form of action, the student might select an option within a computer-learning activity, and the computer might then inform the student whether the response was correct. In a more complex action, the results of student thinking behavior may take form in the paper being created on a classroom computer. This half-written composition then becomes another information resource for the student to think about. Does this paper make sense? Will I convince a future reader of my point of view?

While the details of mental behavior can be related to classroom practice, you will find only occasional mention of memory stores and cognitive tools in the chapters that follow. The depth allowed by such an analysis is necessary only in certain situations. For the most part, our discussion of effective classroom use of technology will rely on conceptual models of learning and thinking.

CONCEPTUAL MODELS OF SCHOOL LEARNING

Several useful models of school learning outline instructional goals, preferred instructional practices, and ideal student behaviors.

MEANINGFUL LEARNING

Meaningful learning versus rote learning

According to Ausubel (1963), **meaningful learning** occurs when new experiences are related to what a learner already knows. It can be contrasted with **rote learning**, which Ausubel describes as the learning of a sequence of words with little attention to meaning, as in simple memorization. In both cases learners are processing information, but their mental activities are quite different. Meaningful learning assumes that:

◆ Students already have some knowledge that is relevant to their new learning.
◆ Students are willing to do the mental work required to find connections with what they already know.

Learning tasks can contribute to the establishment of these connections by encouraging the student to recognize personal experiences that are relevant or even by providing new life experiences as part of the learning activity.

Meaningful learning requires motivation.

Because meaningful learning takes work, student motivation is important. Student motivation can be subverted by a reward structure that provides too many incentives for rote learning, a lack of confidence in the ability to learn meaningfully, or disinterest. The teacher's role is to provide an optimal environment that makes the learner feel capable and presents the learner with tasks he or she regards as personally relevant. The student should feel there is some payoff for learning rather than merely memorizing. At a practical level, this might mean that the assessment of learning should require the learner to demonstrate understanding and the ability to apply knowledge as well as recall facts.

Reception Versus Discovery

In addition to meaningful and rote learning, Ausubel differentiated between reception and discovery learning. In **reception learning**, the ideas to be learned are presented directly to students, ideally in a well-organized fashion. In **discovery learning**, in contrast, the student must work to uncover, or discover, what is to be learned. Typically, a large proportion of what is learned in school is acquired through reception learning, and much of what is learned through everyday living is acquired through discovery learning.

Ausubel warned educators not to equate reception with rote learning or meaningful learning with discovery learning. We agree with this warning. The activities connected with discovery are more concerned with generating the ideas to be learned than with relating these ideas to existing knowledge. Rote discovery learning is quite possible, and you can find it in the "cookbook" activities used in some science laboratories. In such activities, a student follows a detailed set of instructions to complete an experiment or task. Technically, the student is using a discovery framework, but because the student makes few decisions and does not have to understand the processes to move from one part of the activity to the next, meaningful learning may not occur. To raise this issue, we sometimes ask the question, "How much chemistry do you learn from baking bread?" The point is that physically manipulating objects and completing activities does not necessarily mean a student is mentally manipulating ideas. This is one of the dangers when teachers think only in terms of classroom activities and not in terms of how effectively and efficiently the assignments engage the learner.

Characterizing Typical Learning Activities

How technology applications fit in this framework

Various instructional applications of technology (for examples, see Chapter 4) fit nicely within this framework of categorizing learning experience. In a computer **tutorial,** technology presents the critical concepts and rules to be learned in a direct manner, and students working with it are engaging in reception learning. In a computer **simulation,** the student attempts to identify key concepts or rules by interacting with a simulated responsive environment presented by the computer. The student has to discover the concepts or rules from the experiences that the environment provides.

Performance Assessment

Students usually take tests alone and under intense time pressure. Unlike classroom tests, many of the problems of life are complex, requiring collaboration with colleagues and coordination of a variety of resources and tools over an extended period of time. Inconsistencies between the way we ask students to use their knowledge and skills in class and the way we believe they will use the same knowledge and skills outside the classrooms trouble many educators and have led to the search for alternative approaches. Many educators have begun to consider performance assessment methods as ways to assess knowledge and skills more authentically.

Performance assessment relies on a variety of methods, all of which require students to demonstrate what they know or can do by creating an answer or a product (Office of Technology Assessment, 1992). One situation in which educators have traditionally relied on performance assessment is the culminating task in graduate education: a thesis or dissertation, which is a formal written presentation of the graduate student's original research. Students must use what they have learned throughout their graduate education to plan and implement a research project, interpret and communicate the results of their research as a written product, and defend the written interpretation of their findings in a public forum. Graduate education is intended to prepare advanced students to function as independent scholars; the production and defense of a scholarly product assesses their ability to perform in this capacity.

Performance assessment covers a continuum of tasks, ranging from essay examinations to collections of work accumulated over time. You are probably already familiar with essay examinations and have had the opportunity to write descriptions, analyses, or summaries to demonstrate your understanding. Research and writing tasks conducted outside class represent a further step along the continuum. Original research and a related exhibition closely resemble the thesis model used with advanced students. A science fair project is a good example. Exhibitions are culminating experiences in which the knowledge or skill gained over many hours of work is displayed. The public nature of the exhibition requires careful consideration of how best to communicate what has been learned; this additional processing has other cognitive benefits. Portfolios anchor the end of the continuum that reflects more inclusive summaries of student performance. You are probably familiar with the term *portfolio* as the collection an artist or architect might put together to demonstrate his or her skills. Student portfolios are similar, containing samples of the student's best work collected over time. Unlike the items in the portfolio of an artist, those in a student portfolio, such as writing samples, are intended to document improvement.

Technology-supported activities can provide many opportunities for performance assessment. Throughout this book are examples and ideas demonstrating how students can use technology as a tool both to learn and to demonstrate what they have learned. The final products are ideal for performance assessment. Thinking of technology in this way is not the most common perspective, but it is clearly one that is gaining attention and credibility.✷

FIGURE 2.3
Learning Activities Categorized by Two Dimensions: Rote Learning Versus
Meaningful Learning and Reception Learning Versus Discovery Learning.
Technology activities appear in parentheses. Descriptions of the technology
activities listed here are provided in later chapters.

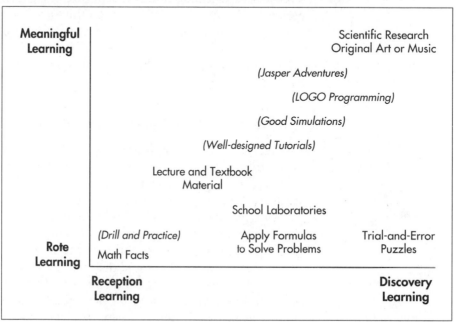

The dual dimensions of rote-meaningful learning and reception-discovery
learning provide an informative framework for categorizing school learning
experiences of all types (see Figure 2.3). The classification of learning activities
in this figure requires assumptions about how the typical student will respond
to the activities. It is always possible that students will react to any given learning task in very different ways. The school tasks not involving technology are
positioned as proposed by Ausubel (1963). We have added technology-related
activities, in parentheses, based on our own perceptions of how these activities
engage learners. If you want to draw your own conclusions, you might look up
the activities in the index and spend a brief amount of time learning what students do as they engage in these activities. You may also want to test your understanding of this figure by considering where other learning activities would
be located. We believe that thinking about tasks and their relationship to student mental behavior is important. You might wonder whether there are some
learning activities that should be avoided. A simple answer would be that all
types of learning may be appropriate under some circumstances. Concern
would probably be appropriate if rote learning were overemphasized or if an

*A framework for
categorizing*

instructional activity resulted in a different type of learning experience than was intended. For example, rote learning may be a reasonable way to approach the learning of basic number facts, but not the historical antecedents of World War II. It is also unlikely that school science laboratories are intended as rote-discovery experiences, and if students are in fact responding to laboratory experiences in a mindless fashion, then this is cause for concern. So part of the task in decision making is to determine what types of mental activities are desired in specific learning situations, and another part is to determine if learning activities used to produce these mental behaviors do result in the intended behaviors.

WHEN TO USE DISCOVERY TECHNIQUES

Discovery techniques are most appropriate when reception methods are unlikely to bring about a high degree of cognitive involvement (Howe, 1972). Such situations include work with younger children and with concepts that are abstract because of unfamiliarity.

Motivation to learn

Motivation can be highly individualistic. An experienced computer programmer might prefer to consult a reference book about a new technique or command rather than work through a tutorial to learn about the technique, which may be unnecessary and distracting. On the other hand, students less interested in programming would likely find a book that lists command after command very boring. Instead, they might become quite wrapped up in a book that involved them in using the commands to create an interesting product. The difference here is motivation to perform the necessary mental work. The programmer is already motivated to learn and will process the new information meaningfully as soon as the ideas have been received. The student may need to be motivated by some exciting task before processing the information. When students are motivated and have adequate background knowledge, reception learning can be quite adequate for meaningful learning.

GENERATIVE LEARNING

Generating meaning for experiences

Like Ausubel, Wittrock (1974a, 1974b, 1989, 1992) argues that students should establish connections with their existing knowledge rather than store isolated elements of information. In Wittrock's model of **generative learning**, a student selectively attends to events and generates meaning for these experiences by relating them to existing knowledge or by drawing inferences. That is, the *active learner* creates a personal model or explanation to account for new experiences within the context of existing knowledge.

In some cases, old ideas can assist a student in interpreting new experiences. In other cases, new experiences require the student to modify existing beliefs. In either case, the process of forming connections is distinct from simple storage of information. The generative model also assumes a motivated commitment from the student. The student must assume responsibility for expending the effort necessary to construct meaning.

Value of generative activities

Although the generative activity Wittrock describes is mental and internal, it appears that external tasks can play a role. The area of reading comprehension offers many examples of improving understanding through the use of generative activities: writing paragraph summaries, developing and answering questions, creating paragraph headings, drawing pictures, or creating analogies or metaphors to encourage interpretation, organization, and storage (Wittrock, 1989). Generative activities have been consistently found to improve comprehension and retention.

The basic idea that internal processing can be influenced by external tasks is quite consistent with our approach. In discussing technology-supported activities throughout this book, we emphasize the importance of what is done with information, not just how to access information.

COMPUTER TOOLS AND THINKING BEHAVIOR

Technology and active learning

Computer tools such as word processors, spreadsheets, databases, and multimedia authoring programs may help students learn actively. Computer tools were designed to facilitate certain activities or to create certain products, and these activities or the construction of these products has great potential for generating meaningful learning. Daiute (1983; Daiute & Taylor, 1981) makes such a proposal in discussing the impact of a computer-based word processing environment on the process of learning to write.

Certain word processor features and the way a word processor stores and manipulates text (easy insertion or deletion, moving blocks of text with cut-and-paste functions, alternative edits without time-consuming rewrites) encourage students to revise their work and thus lead to the development of writing skills. It appears that technology seems to encourage students to write more and to revise more frequently (Pea & Kurland, 1987). If you have used word processing software, this claim may ring true to you. Did you rewrite more frequently and try out several approaches rather than attempt to get by with a single, painfully constructed final draft? If the revision power of the computer encouraged you to write differently, perhaps to experiment with different ways of saying something, then it might be said that the external tool (the computer and word processing software) influenced the thinking processes you employed while you wrote. Perkins (1985) describes this second potential value of many computer tools in terms of the "opportunities get taken" hypothesis. His argument is that powerful tools encourage thinking and exploration because learners are presented with realistic opportunities that involve minimal risks. (Chapter 5 presents a more complete discussion of word processing and learning to write.)

HYPERMEDIA

We devote a substantial portion of this book to the proposal that students can benefit from projects incorporating the production of hypermedia. A hypermedia product might be thought of as a computer-based presentation potentially using some combination of text, pictures, sound, and video. Developing this kind of presentation involves generating the elements of information (text segments, pictures) and creating meaningful links among the elements. Hypermedia authoring offers many of the same benefits as writing to learn. In fact, it has been argued that writing has a privileged status in education that is not entirely deserved and that other means of representation or combinations of representational systems might be better suited to the content of some disciplines (Smagorinsky, 1995). This would certainly seem possible when the content emphasizes visual elements (e.g., biology, art), quantitative forms of representation (e.g., mathematics), or sounds (e.g., music).

Writing not the only form of authoring

We believe that the construction of a hypermedia product and associated activities (research, collaborative interaction with others working on the same product) encourages many of the desirable learning processes presented in this chapter. If we concentrate just on the processes in creating a hypermedia product, students will represent what they have learned in multiple formats (images, text) and organize information and establish links to demonstrate relationships of various types. To produce a hypermedia product, students must understand what they are presenting and think about how they can best represent these ideas to others. Creating the hypermedia product involves several external behaviors that require internal behaviors conducive to meaningful learning. You will encounter strategies for involving students in the creation of content-area hypermedia projects in the later chapters of this book.

It has even been claimed (Jonassen, 1986) that hypermedia may represent a superior learning environment because it is similar in structure to human memory (nonlinear presentation of ideas, multiple linkages among ideas, potential to represent ideas using several different formats). A variation on this theme suggests that having students create hypermedia materials requires them to relate images, ideas, and units of meaning similarly to the actual organization of long-term memory. In other words, the creation of hypermedia is also a useful way to encourage students to search out appropriate relationships among the units of information they are studying.

Long-term memory and hypermedia

CONSTRUCTIVISM

Even a cursory reading of proposals for school reform will quickly acquaint you with the term *constructivism* (see, for instance, APA/BEA, 1995; Knapp & Glenn, 1996; Means et al., 1993). Like Ausubel's meaningful learning and Wittrock's generative learning, **constructivism** generally argues that learners build personal understanding and that this constructive process can be facili-

Learning is the building of useful personal knowledge.

tated by appropriate learning activities and a good learning environment. (There is, however, no single, official explanation for what constructivism represents. The term has been used to address a wide range of issues, from the psychology of individual learning to philosophical reflections on science as a mechanism for pursuing knowledge [Loving, 1997]. Some extreme constructivist positions may be disruptive to those of us attempting to bring practical suggestions to classroom teachers, and we are in agreement with those, such as Loving, who advocate a balanced approach.)

Probably the most generally accepted principle of constructivism is that what a person knows is not passively received, but *actively assembled* by the learner (Jonassen, 1991; Wheatley, 1991). A second principle is that in most circumstances, learning serves an *adaptive* function. That is, the role of learning is to help the individual operate within his or her personal world.

Practical Implications

Students are responsible for learning.

These two principles of constructive learning lead to a couple of significant practical implications. The first concerns the responsibility for learning. The student accomplishes learning, and learning is the result of mental work. Learners must mentally act on the information they receive in order to create personal understanding and transform information into knowledge. Teachers must recognize that the presentation of information by itself may not result in the generation of knowledge. Teachers cannot directly control the mental behaviors that result in learning, but they may be able to model effective learning behaviors for students, and they may assist students by engaging them in activities that facilitate or encourage productive mental activity. Teachers play an important but indirect role.

Learning is context specific.

A second practical implication focuses attention on the context of learning. Context has a lot to do with what the learner perceives as useful knowledge and how she or he integrates new experiences with existing knowledge. In the most critical sense, does the student see connections between the part of his or her world identified as "school" and the part sometimes referred to as "real life"? A student who perceives little or no connection, constructivists argue, will not build much personal knowledge. (Later, we discuss authentic tasks as one way to establish a meaningful context for learning.)

A third implication contends that the primary purpose of education is not the acquisition of universal truths. Because each person has different experiences and is assumed to construct an individual interpretation of these experiences, each person's reality is slightly different. Learning means acquiring not abstract general truths but useful personal knowledge.

REVIEWING THE COMMON THEMES

Rather than get caught up in one particular theory or another, we prefer to focus on the common themes of these various educational theories—themes

Focus

Are We Abandoning Truth?

You may be concerned by the constructivist suggestion that universal truths are not the goal of student learning. But before making up your mind, consider a couple of additional points.

First, most of us have held beliefs that we eventually learned were not truths. Some of these beliefs resulted from faulty information, but some were the official truths taught as part of a particular discipline, such as chemistry, physics, or history. Our ideas that passed for knowledge had to be modified later to handle new findings. Can you think of any such examples from your own education? Science "facts" or theories? Historical interpretations?

Second, we obviously do not end up with widely different views of our world. Education is pretty much a social process, and one adaptive purpose of the social context is to confront and negotiate differences in personal perspectives. When others explain their beliefs, we have new information to test against our personal views. Throughout this book, you'll see that we emphasize both learning tasks involving collaboration and tasks that require learners to represent their understanding in ways that allow others to react. Both types of activity are important.✳

Active learning

that have been frequently emphasized by educational reformers. Let's reiterate these key ideas. First, all of the theories that we have discussed describe the fundamental nature of the learner as *active*. Active learners seek to build an understanding of their personal worlds that will allow them to function productively. This process requires that learners make the effort to build on what they know in order to interpret and respond to new experiences.

True active learners function in a purposeful manner. They are capable of establishing personal goals, developing strategies for addressing these goals, and monitoring whether the strategies have been successful. By taking such a purposeful, active approach, students make their learning experiences meaningful. That is, their new learning relates to their previous knowledge and is relevant to their personal lives. It is deeper than mere rote learning or memorization, and it can be applied not just in school but in "real life."

Now let's turn to the question of what these theories mean for your classroom practice and how technology can help you apply them.

FROM THEORY TO PRACTICE: TEACHING, LEARNING, AND THE ROLE OF TECHNOLOGY

Although educators approach school reform in many different ways, their ideas tend to converge in recommendations for classroom practice. Consider the following general suggestions (Duffy & Bednar, 1991; Means et al., 1993):

1. The catalyst for changing the learning experience at a fundamental level will be centering more of the learner's time on *authentic, challenging tasks*. Students need rich contexts for learning that reduce the emphasis on fact mastery and isolated, discrete component skills and increase the emphasis on *multidisciplinary* tasks that require students to apply and create personal understanding.

2. The social environment should support learning in different ways. Students should have *access to domain experts* who model the skills appropriate to the domain and provide insights into the culture of the domain within what has been described as an *apprenticeship* relationship. Teachers should view their roles differently. The facilitation of thinking and problem solving must accompany the transfer of information. Teachers may guide student work related to unfamiliar content and acquire new knowledge along with their students. Students should spend a greater amount of time working in *cooperative relationships* with other students to explore alternative perspectives and evaluate ideas. These relationships will help provide learning experiences that encourage communication and access to real-world examples. The collective application of these changes in the social context of learning might be said to establish learning communities.

3. A greater emphasis should be placed on *reflective thinking* and *productivity*. The fundamental goal should be the ability to perform relevant tasks with the understanding that not every student will perform the tasks in the same way or acquire the same task-relevant skills.

We see technology as providing an extremely useful set of tools for addressing these goals. Later chapters explore particular uses of technology in greater depth. Here, we isolate a few of the important ideas for more detailed consideration.

AUTHENTIC ACTIVITIES

Research shows that when learning is accomplished as part of an authentic activity, it is more relevant and more likely to be used in future situations (Brown, Collins, and Duguid, 1989). But what, then, are **authentic activities**? According to one interesting perspective, they are the ordinary practices of a

Authentic activities are everyday acts.

culture (Brown et al., 1989). The term *culture* here refers to what might best be understood as ordinary people doing the ordinary things that readers or writers, biologists, users of mathematics, or speakers of Spanish do. Language makes a good example that we can understand from personal experience. Users of a language apply their knowledge as a tool to complete tasks within their everyday environment. By this definition, our use of language is authentic because it has great utility in our daily lives.

Searching for authentic activities in classrooms reveals an interesting insight. In each room there is a recognizable classroom culture, and there are identifiable authentic activities at work within this culture. The problem is that authentic classroom tasks may not be what teachers really intend. The goals, values, and activities of the school culture and the subject matter of culture can be very different (Brown et al., 1989). The student functioning in the culture of a fairly typical classroom uses knowledge to solve problems relevant to the school domain, such as getting the most points possible on the next quiz or pleasing the teacher. But knowledge the student acquires for the school domain may not transfer to any domain beyond the school walls. To state the problem another way, the knowledge students acquire in school is too often inert.

Inert Knowledge

Inert knowledge is knowledge that students have learned but fail to use (Whitehead, 1929). More exactly, it is knowledge that is available in a restricted set of contexts rather than in all of the contexts in which it might apply. Often the restricted context is extremely narrow. Students may activate knowledge for classroom examinations and then fail to recognize the valuable role the same knowledge could play in other situations. For instance, a student who does well on an arithmetic test may have little practical understanding of prices in a supermarket.

Naive theories

An interesting example of inert knowledge can be found in naive science conceptions. We all function somewhat like scientists in our everyday lives as we develop a wealth of knowledge from our unsystematic and uncontrolled daily observations of the world around us (Bruning, Schraw, & Ronning, 1999). We form opinions, or *naive theories,* about all kinds of things based on our observation of daily phenomena. Sometimes these naive theories are simply incorrect and contradict more appropriate theories we have learned through formal education. Yet we can maintain incompatible academic and naive theories at the same time (Champagne, Gunstone, & Klopfer, 1985; Champagne, Klopfer, & Anderson, 1980; Clement, 1983; McCloskey, 1983). For example, education students learn about the value of distributed practice, but many still cram for their examinations. The academic theories seem to be applied in the classroom, and the naive theories in the real world. The presence of incompatible knowledge requires that, at any given time, one knowledge source or the other must be inert. To put these ideas into perspective, recognize that the conditions for naive theory and inert knowledge would seem well suited to apply to a profession like teaching. As educators, we have been both formally prepared to apply principles of effective instruction and informally prepared by what we have observed during years of being in classrooms.

How can naive theories be changed? For change to occur, students need to confront the discrepancies between their naive theories and school models of the world. They must be made aware of both ideas at the same time. Hands-on projects conducted in the school environment seem to be a powerful way to activate both naive theories and school models (Shipstone, 1988). Hands-on projects can provide an element of realism that prevents the student from escaping to a purely hypothetical way of thinking. The student sees not just the academic relevance of certain ideas but also their relevance to other aspects of life. When they serve this function, these projects meet our definition of authentic activities, and these are the types of projects this book emphasizes.

Authentic Activities

Technology provides authentic activities.

Technology can provide many of the resources necessary for authentic activities. We describe the fundamental requirements for authentic activities as the culture of practice and primary information sources.

The *culture of practice* provides the social contact and the purpose for authentic tasks. We have already described authentic tasks as the ordinary practices of a culture and asked you to consider the activities of the culture of biologists, historians, and Spanish speakers. When used as a model for a productive learning environment, a culture of practice would urge the application of content-area knowledge to the practice of tasks appropriate to the content domain. Students would benefit from occasional opportunities to take on some of the tasks of biologists, historians, and Spanish speakers (see Focus: Using the Internet for Authentic Activities).

The Internet can help establish or provide access to such a culture by connecting interested teachers, students, parents, and practitioners who might rally around a particular project. These individuals might be active partners in implementing projects; sources of information, guidance, and feedback; or the audience for whom projects are developed.

Primary sources represent information or data that learners act on to produce personal knowledge. The Internet offers a vast amount of such information. The sources may exist in digital form (documents, images, sounds), in the form of people willing to provide their opinions or knowledge, or in some cases in the form of equipment that provides a stream of data (such as weather data or images from remote cameras). With its connections to a wealth and variety of sources, the Internet can provide an excellent resource for constructing challenging projects that lead students to confront their own preconceptions and modify their thinking.

Focus

Using the Internet for Authentic Activities

We provide examples of authentic activities throughout this book. However, since we explain that such activities might allow students to take on some of the tasks of biologists, historians, or speakers of Spanish and might provide students the opportunity to work with primary sources, here are a few examples to get you thinking about classroom applications.

◆ *Winter bird feeder study.* Students in a sophomore biology class position a bird feeder outside their classroom window and make periodic observations of the birds that visit the feeder each Friday. These data are entered into a web form and submitted to the Cornell Laboratory of Ornithology. The students have joined Project FeederWatch, a group of thirteen thousand amateur scientists who are gathering and sharing data in an effort to understand changes in bird populations (**http://birdsource.cornell. edu/features/pfw/**).

◆ *Life of a one-room-school teacher.* Eighth-grade students are asked to develop a description of what it was like to teach in a northern prairie one-room school in the late nineteenth century. This description should provide some insights into who these teachers were and what their working conditions were like. For primary source materials, students are asked to use the searchable document and image collection provided by the Library of Congress American Memory Digital Library (**http:// memory.loc.gov/ammem/**).

◆ *Spanish-speaking key pal.* Students in a freshman Spanish class are exchanging e-mail with students from Spain to develop their written language skills. The teacher spent a semester in Madrid during college and was particularly interested in locating a companion class from that city. She has a lot of pictures and stories to help her class learn a little more about where their key pals live. The teacher is able to locate a companion classroom using Keypals International (**http://www.collegebound.com/ keypals/**).✷

THE SOCIAL CONTEXT OF LEARNING

Learning, particularly learning within educational institutions, is a social phenomenon. Although the learning theories we have emphasized assume individual responsibility for learning, the social environment in which learners function can be essential in modeling, encouraging, and providing opportunities for essential learning and problem-solving behaviors.

Cognitive Apprenticeship

Educational reformers who want to increase the emphasis on thinking or inquiry skills have tried to develop strategies for teaching such complex mental

Teaching students to comprehend

behaviors. The notion of **cognitive apprenticeship** is one such strategy. Probably the most frequently cited example of cognitive apprenticeship is *reciprocal teaching,* which was designed to teach students how to comprehend written material (Palincsar & Brown, 1984). In this approach, the teacher works with a small number of students. Initially the teacher takes the most active role and models important cognitive behaviors. Because cognitive behaviors (mental processes) cannot be observed directly, important behaviors are defined in terms of behaviors that can be demonstrated: asking questions, summarizing content, identifying and clarifying difficulties, and making predictions.

In reciprocal teaching, the group reads a paragraph together. The teacher then models the target behaviors: asks the students a question, comments about something that seemed difficult to understand, or makes a prediction. Individual students then attempt these activities under the teacher's supervision. Eventually the individual is expected to get to the point of performing all external behaviors and then only the internal equivalents.

The goal of cognitive apprenticeship is to help inexperienced practitioners acquire essential thinking skills. A social environment provides the opportunity to learn from more skilled colleagues and to share responsibility so that a demanding task does not overwhelm the learner. Critical to the approach are opportunities to externalize mental behaviors. Teachers and students describe what they are trying to do as they work on tasks that involve the essential thinking behaviors. The descriptions provide less experienced learners something to consider and model. At the same time, they allow the more skilled practitioners to evaluate and offer advice. The group projects described in Chapter 10 provide great opportunities for this kind of interaction. We also believe that authentic projects allow teachers frequent occasions to model learning and problem-solving behaviors. By their very nature, authentic technology projects are less predictable and more exploratory. Teachers need to be flexible and open to new experiences.

Cooperative Learning

Technology provides many opportunities for cooperative learning.

In **cooperative learning**, students work together to accomplish a learning task. They may accomplish this goal by motivating, teaching, evaluating, or engaging each other in discussions that encourage reflection. When all students contribute, cooperative approaches encourage active learning. Cooperative learning may also be used to accomplish other goals. The methods typically encourage inclusion and are a way to promote heterogeneity of participation with respect to ability, gender, ethnic group, and various disabilities. The nature of the task can vary from working together to prepare for an examination, to serving as a tutor to younger or less experienced peers, to completing a classroom project.

We use the phrase *cooperative learning* in a formal way. Our interest is in the methods of student collaboration that have been purposefully structured

Cooperative multimedia projects require students to work together to explain content-area topics. *(© Michael Zide)*

according to specific and clearly identified principles and have been thoroughly evaluated (e.g., Johnson & Johnson, 1999; Slavin, 1991, 1996). Because not every situation in which small groups of students work together will be productive, we believe the details of how cooperation is structured and proceeds are important.

Experts in classroom cooperation (Johnson & Johnson, 1989; Johnson, Johnson, & Holubec, 1991) suggest that three tasks must be accomplished to ensure productive groups. First, teachers need to help students understand what the desired skill would look or sound like. For example, the teacher may need to explain that a basic principle of working together is learning to criticize ideas and not people. Second, students need the opportunity to practice the skill. Role playing is an effective way to learn social skills. Finally, students new to cooperative projects need to reflect on their use of cooperative skills. Students can benefit from the opportunity to discuss process skills. Did the group encounter conflicts as they worked on the project? Were anyone's feelings hurt because someone misinterpreted the intent of an e-mail message?

There is no single cooperative learning method. Some methods are designed to help students master a body of factual material. There are certainly classroom situations in which this is an important goal, and cooperative methods that use group competition to push all group members to achieve have demonstrated value (Slavin, 1991). The cooperative methods of greatest relevance for this book are those that involve students in group tasks requir-

Three activities for mastering social skills

Methods of cooperative learning

ing both the acquisition and the application of knowledge and skill. **Group investigation,** a task specialization method that results in the production of group projects, is discussed in greater detail in Chapter 10. As students work together on a project, they must discuss course content related to the project. As they interact, they acquire knowledge from each other, and they learn from the process of trying to put their ideas into words in order to allow someone else to understand them. Others in the group may see a problem differently or have a different explanation in mind for some phenomenon. The group process naturally produces a level of cognitive conflict that challenges the personal understanding of group members and encourages more active, **self-regulated learning.**

Learning Communities

We might define a community as a social organization created by people who share common goals, values, and practices. If you try to apply this description to the city or town in which you live, you might find it excessively idealistic. We would agree that most cities and towns fail miserably in meeting this standard. But a functional community can be any collection of people who have identified themselves with a set of goals, values, and practices. Our interests are in understanding how such communities are formed and in using these mechanisms to build learning communities.

Select authentic and challenging tasks.

Communities come together when some form of search process acquaints people who share goals, values, and practices *and* this group begins to act on their common interests. School-based **learning communities** are formed when teachers and students join together to work on long-term projects. The idea is to select authentic and challenging tasks that can be productively approached in a collaborative fashion. The social environment surrounding the project encourages learners of all ages to learn from and teach one another. The task goals of the project shape what knowledge and skills must be acquired, and the nature of authentic tasks usually requires that the learning experiences will cross disciplinary boundaries (Gordin, Gomez, Pea, & Fishman, 1997).

Educators do not have to limit themselves to learning communities formed within school walls. Some have argued, in fact, that schools have become distanced physically, emotionally, and intellectually from the core of our traditional communities (Riel, 1997). Students have few experiences directly connecting what they learn with the world outside the school. Moreover, by focusing on the learning needs of citizens of a narrow age range, schools fail to support lifelong learning. For these reasons, many educators are beginning to create work-based learning communities, which allow students to participate in the practices of a discipline or profession.

This brings us back to what we described earlier as the culture of practice surrounding authentic activities. For a student, it is the essential difference between learning about what biologists or historians have produced as information and having the opportunity at some meaningful level to *function* as a biologist or historian in order to construct personal knowledge (Gordin et al., 1997).

PROJECT-BASED LEARNING

Student projects provide a practical method for combining many of the elements of authentic activities and collaborative learning. Technology provides many opportunities for classroom projects. Examples of projects and descriptions of how they were developed appear throughout this book. The examples in Activities and Projects for Your Classroom: Ideas for Content Area Projects give you the idea. In all cases, small groups of students use some combination of the computer, printer, various programs, and computer peripherals, such as a scanner or video digitizer, to complete the project. In most cases, field or library research is also required.

Activities should require active learning.

Project-based learning is based on tasks, groups, and sharing (Wheatley, 1991). The ideal task should confront each student with a problem for which that student has no immediate solution. The task should also be chosen to focus on key concepts from the desired domain of study. The idea is to engage students in an activity requiring them to work with course content that might otherwise be treated more passively. For example, the general curriculum might specify that students should acquire a basic vocabulary associated with space, learn programming techniques, and observe plants during a field trip. The projects are intended to allow groups of students to meet these general goals in ways that are mentally challenging and motivating. In addition, good projects should (1) encourage students to make decisions, (2) encourage "what-if" questions, (3) require discussion and communication, (4) allow a final product or solution, and (5) be extendible to allow students to move beyond the specific charge they have been given.

Projects seem to be an ideal setting for cooperative approaches. Working with others requires greater attention to understanding. When students work together, they confront the ideas of others and are forced to voice and defend their own beliefs. Trying to explain what you know to someone else, perhaps in several different ways, is a very active way to think through important ideas.

Finally, Wheatley (1991) believes that teachers must allocate time for students to present their ideas, methods, and products. This is important not only at the conclusion of a project, but also as the project evolves. Presenting work is an authentic activity that provides an important source of motivation. Presentation also allows groups to gather ideas from other groups and have their own work critiqued. Initial presentations are likely to be made before the teacher and classmates. Later presentations might be made to students from other classes, parents, and even the general public.

Focus

Lev Vygotsky

Lev Vygotsky, a Russian developmental psychologist working in the early 1900s, is a classic example of a scholar whose ideas were much more influential after his death than during his lifetime. Here is a brief summary of some of Vygotsky's central ideas (Harley, 1996; Vygotsky, 1978):

Private speech. We have all seen children and even adults talk to themselves as they perform a difficult task. Vygotsky believed this externalized speech was quite functional as an "external" guidance mechanism. Vygotsky also proposed that learners use the speech of others as they solve problems. Gradually these forms of guidance become internalized as silent "inner speech."

Zone of proximal development. Think of a set of related educational tasks positioned along a continuum. At one end of the continuum are tasks the learner can perform with ease. At the other end are tasks that are far beyond the capability of the learner. Between these areas are tasks that the learner can perform with the proper support. This area, called the **zone of proximal development**, defines the tasks where instruction is likely to be most productive. Support usually implies adult guidance or perhaps the cooperation of a more experienced peer. There may be other forms of support that

also allow learners to achieve success. With experience, learners become capable of independent functioning.

Scaffolding. **Scaffolding** is doing some of the work for students until they develop the capability or capacity to do it for themselves. Such mechanisms might include reminders, pronouncing or explaining words students do not understand, clear step-by-step instructions, and demonstrations of tasks to be performed. Unlike behavioral approaches, which help less skilled learners by creating a simplified version of the task, scaffolding proposes simplifying the learner's role in accomplishing the actual task.

Reciprocal teaching is regarded as a good example of the application of Vygotsky's ideas. We did not use private speech, the zone of proximal development, or scaffolding in our discussion of reciprocal teaching. See if you can pick out aspects of reciprocal teaching that would illustrate what each of these terms implies. Vygotsky's theoretical ideas are illustrated in several other ideas emphasized in this book—for example, emphasizing the teacher's role as supporting learning rather than dispensing knowledge, the value of learning in cooperative groups, and the importance of engaging students with authentic tasks. ✳

Activities and Projects for Your Classroom

Ideas for Content-Area Projects

We want to make sure that you understand that using technology in content-area instruction can mean something other than learning from the computer in the same way that a student might learn from a book. The student can use the computer to learn by doing. Here are just a few examples to get you thinking about using the computer in this role:

◆ Second-grade students create alphabet books based on a space theme.

◆ Junior high school programmers write a LOGO program to draw a dream catcher.

(A Native American dream catcher is a hoop enclosing an intricate, weblike pattern. The dream catcher is intended to keep bad dreams away from infants. Dream catchers are worn as jewelry or given as presents to new parents.)

◆ High school students develop a multimedia presentation to display wildflowers they observed and videotaped during a nature walk. Special attention is given to a discussion of the habitat within which each species was observed. ✳

WHAT DOES THE RESEARCH TELL US ABOUT LEARNING WITH TECHNOLOGY?

In Chapter 1, we provided some descriptive data on the commitment that educational institutions are making to provide students access to technology. Clearly, the trend is toward an accelerating use of technology and, as you might expect, a corresponding increase in spending for the hardware, software, Internet access fees, staff development, and support staff. In this chapter, we have developed the theoretical framework for the ideas we address in the rest of the book. Has this money dedicated to technological innovations been spent wisely? Has student academic performance improved because of these investments and the new learning experiences they allow? We typically turn to the research literature to answer such questions.

There are literally hundreds of K–12 studies, dating back to the late 1970s, involving computer-based instruction. When a large number of research studies have addressed a topic, a special statistical procedure called *meta-analysis* is frequently used to combine the data from many studies to achieve a general conclusion. These meta-analyses have consistently found benefits for computer-based instruction (Christmann, Badgett, & Lucking, 1997; Fletcher-Flinn & Gravatt, 1995; Kulik & Kulik, 1991). Nevertheless, critics continue to argue that the value of instructional applications of technology

Meta-analyses show benefits.

has yet to be demonstrated (Oppenheimer, 1997). They cite various reasons for their pessimistic position: research showing either no advantage or a negative effect is less likely to be published; studies have tended to involve only a few classes and supportive teachers; and studies are most frequently short in duration and rely on narrow outcome measures prepared by the researchers rather than long-term studies using a general standardized achievement test.

While the general educational use of technology has some relevance, this book really has a narrower focus. First, most of the classroom activities we describe fall within a constructivist tradition rather than the direct instruction tradition of computer-based drill and practice or tutorials. While the basic ideas for constructivist activities have been studied for some time in such fields as cognitive and developmental psychology, few actual classroom applications have been thoroughly evaluated using sound research techniques (Panel on Educational Technology, 1997). There are some promising exceptions (Cognition and Technology Group, 1992; Wenglinsky, 1998), but no body of research that would allow a valid general conclusion.

Here is a simple summary of the research related to technology applications in schools. The issues are complex, the research methods are controversial, and the data are sparse. There is a difference of opinion regarding what should be done in this situation. One position is to stop spending so much money until the studies exist to support particular applications of technology (Oppenheimer, 1997). This position argues that the federal government, many state governments, and many schools should back away from programs they have already initiated. A different position (Panel on Educational Technology, 1997) is to continue the commitment to technology and the Internet, relying on general theory and smaller-scale studies to guide development and expenditures. This second approach also recognizes the need for additional research and argues that only a major commitment at the federal level will allow the type of research needed to provide definitive answers.

Where does this leave you? At least for the time being, it probably leaves you with access to a moderate collection of resources, local expectations that you use these resources productively, and personal responsibility and considerable flexibility for what will happen in your classroom. Specific recommendations for what you should do may be lacking.

The purpose of this chapter has been to provide you with a theoretical foundation for technology-based activities in your classroom. As we discuss each example, we will continue to present a combination of theory, research, and suggestions for classroom activities. Our intent is to help you explore options for the use of technology so that you can make decisions and feel comfortable implementing them.

SUMMARY

Educators should consider what they want classroom applications of technology to accomplish before they invest heavily in hardware, software, Internet access, and support services. This chapter asks you to contemplate instructional goals from several potentially interrelated perspectives.

Advocates of educational reform provide the first perspective. We do not necessarily assume that educators must adopt what reformers recommend, but the agenda for reform does allow a way to identify some critical issues concerning what students should learn, what role teachers and students should play in the education process, and how technology might support these goals and methods. Among the challenges for the educational system are the increasing pace at which new information resources are produced and the rapid pace of change in many disciplines, making necessary a commitment to lifelong learning.

National curriculum experts who have established standards for what K–12 students should learn provide the second perspective. Standards attempt to focus instruction and assessment on essential knowledge and skills. Standards can help define how technology should be used in content-area instruction and what should be learned about technology.

The third perspective is based on theoretical models of learning with many overlapping features. Our presentation differentiates two levels on which these models describe learning. At the microlevel, the information processing model describes cognitive behavior in fine detail. At the macrolevel, classroom learning is defined in ways more likely to be recognized by teachers. Both meaningful and generative learning, both macrolevel models, stress the active role of the learner in creating personal knowledge by establishing links between new ideas and what is already known. Current constructivist models also place the learner in the role of creating personal understanding of experience. These theoretical perspectives have the potential for guiding the use of technology as a way to engage learners in the active mental work valued by these theoretical models.

The final perspective asks that you consider the social context of learning. Learning in schools is a social phenomenon, and concepts such as cognitive apprenticeship, cooperative learning, and the learning community offer insights into the characteristics of a productive social environment for learning.

This chapter concludes with a brief examination of the body of research concerning the effectiveness of technology in education. Many studies exist, but the generally positive tone of this research has been questioned. Critics argue for an evaluation standard based on large-scale studies using general indicators such as standardized achievement tests. Such a demonstration may be impractical to implement.

REFLECTING ON CHAPTER 2

Activities

◆ Provide an example of inert knowledge. What knowledge or skill was involved? Under what circumstances was this knowledge or skill available, and when was it not available?

◆ Generate an example of an activity for your content area of interest that satisfies the definition of an authentic activity. Explain what makes this activity authentic.

◆ Students are sometimes surprised by the scores they earn on course examinations. Propose a practical method that students might use to evaluate their strengths and weaknesses before taking a test.

◆ Locate a recent research study evaluating the influence of technology on student learning. Conduct your own evaluation of the methodology and conclusions of this study. Does the study actually determine that a particular use of technology can benefit students?

Key Terms

alignment *(p. 36)*
authentic activity *(p. 65)*
benchmarks *(p. 35)*
cognitive apprenticeship *(p. 69)*
constructivism *(p. 62)*
content standard *(p. 35)*
cooperative learning *(p. 69)*
declarative knowledge *(p. 47)*
discovery learning *(p. 57)*
endorsement *(p. 40)*
episodic memory *(p. 46)*
frameworks *(p. 36)*
generative learning *(p. 60)*
group investigation *(p. 71)*
inert knowledge *(p. 66)*
learning community *(p. 71)*
lifelong learning *(p. 33)*
link *(p. 47)*
long-term memory *(p. 45)*

meaningful learning *(p. 56)*
metacognition *(p. 50)*
metacognitive control functions *(p. 51)*
metacognitive knowledge *(p. 51)*
network module *(p. 47)*
node *(p. 47)*
performance standard *(p. 35)*
procedural knowledge *(p. 47)*
reception learning *(p. 57)*
rote learning *(p. 56)*
scaffolding *(p. 73)*
self-regulated learning *(p. 71)*
short-term memory *(p. 43)*
simulation *(p. 57)*
standards *(p. 37)*
tutorial *(p. 57)*
working memory *(p. 43)*
zone of proximal development *(p. 73)*

Resources to Expand Your Knowledge Base

NCATE Standards

The National Council for Accreditation of Teacher Education standards are available online at **http://www.ncate.org.**

Books on Key Chapter Topics

Hogan, K., & Pressley, M. (1997). *Scaffolding student learning.* Cambridge, MA: Brookline Books.

Johnson, D., & Johnson, R. (1999). *Learning together and along* (5th ed.). Boston: Allyn and Bacon.

Jones, B., & Maloy, R. (1996). *Schools for an information age.* Westport, CT: Praeger.

McCaleb, S. (1997). *Building communities of learners.* Mahwah, NJ: Erlbaum.

Meichenbaum, D., & Biemiller, A. (1998). *Nurturing independent learners.* Cambridge, MA: Brookline Books.

Wilson, B. (Ed.). (1996). *Constructivist learning environments.* Englewood Cliffs, NJ: Educational Technology Publications.

Learning How to Integrate Technology with Your Teaching

Part Two *introduces you to categories of software, the most frequently applied computer tool applications (word processors, databases, spreadsheets, e-mail, and World Wide Web browsers), multimedia tools, and the ways these applications support students in meaningful learning. You will learn about educational benefits associated with teaching students to program and how to take advantage of the potential of the Internet. You will look at the advantages of hypermedia and multimedia and how they support students in meaningful learning. We will discuss types of multimedia projects you can have your students create and some of the tools and techniques used to produce the sounds and images described in multimedia applications throughout the book. Finally, you will explore the concept of design and the learning opportunities that students have when they design and present projects.*

Chapter 3

Developing Higher-Order Thinking Skills Through Programming, Projects, and Research

ORIENTATION

Chapter 2 was intended to help you develop an understanding of meaningful learning and to challenge you to consider how school experiences might facilitate or inhibit optimal achievement on the part of students. Concerns with how and what students learn have prompted suggestions for school reform. Here, we extend this discussion by focusing on higher-order thinking skills. These skills are valued in society, but they are frequently perceived to be underemphasized in educational settings. We will help you understand what higher-order thinking skills are and consider several strategies for their development in schools.

This chapter also begins our direct consideration of how technology can be involved in student learning. We evaluate the benefits of programming experience as a way to develop student problem-solving skills. We also consider how activities involving various data-gathering devices can contribute to the curriculum. As you make your way through this book, you will find that although we cover many strategies for classroom learning with technology, we do emphasize a particular approach. We have prioritized authentic and collaborative content-area projects. This priority does not imply support for an exclusive focus on projects, but for a change in the frequency with which students encounter this type of learning activity. Authentic projects fit perfectly with the desire to encourage higher-order thinking and emphasize applications of technology that place students in an active role.

As you read, look for answers to the following questions:

◆ What is higher-order thinking, and what are the ways in which the development of higher-order thinking skills might appear in the curriculum?

◆ What are three ways students may benefit from the combination of high-quality programming experiences and thoughtful instruction?

◆ What are the major characteristics of the LOGO programming language?

◆ What is the educational significance of the concept of transfer?

◆ How might the use of data loggers contribute to authentic research projects?

◆ Why might authentic research projects provide an educationally efficient approach to the development of both content-area knowledge and higher-order thinking skills?

WHAT IS HIGHER-ORDER THINKING?

We bet that most educators would say they support the development of higher-order thinking skills, but if they were pressed, many would find that their understanding of what they were advocating for was pretty vague. This lack of clarity is understandable. Higher-order thinking is not a single process (such as word identification) or even a complex skill that has been designated as a focus of the curriculum at a particular grade level (such as learning to read). It involves many cognitive skills and is potentially involved in every content area. To be successful, teachers must accept responsibility for assisting students in the acquisition of higher-order thinking skills, understand the nature of the skills they are helping students to develop, and recognize productive options for helping students learn these skills.

Higher-order thinking involves many cognitive skills.

It is not easy to provide a simple definition of higher-order thinking, but it is possible to list some of the attributes of these behaviors. **Higher-order thinking** is *complex* (tasks can often be accomplished in several ways, and the entire process often unfolds in stages without a complete course of action being evident from the beginning), is *effortful* (tasks require conscious effort), is *self-regulated* (metacognitive planning and monitoring are necessary), and frequently involves *judgment* (the evaluation of conflicting information) (Resnick, 1987). These attributes are characteristic of problem solving and critical thinking, two categories of thinking skill that educators frequently emphasize with their students. **Problem solving** and **critical thinking** are thinking processes with identifiable subskills; some of these are outlined in Table 3.1. Many theorists have summarized the subskills and the sequence in which the subskills in the problem-solving process are executed. Critical thinking can also be described as a series of stages encompassing information

TABLE 3.1

Problem Solving, Critical Thinking, and Related Subskills

HIGHER-ORDER SKILL	PURPOSE	SUBSKILLS
Problem solving	Processes involved in overcoming an obstacle to reach a goal	• Recognize problem exists
		• Represent situation
		• Select strategy
		• Implement strategy
		• Evaluate and repeat if necessary
Critical thinking	Processes involving evaluation—in some applications to make a reasoned choice	• Locate information appropriate to a purpose
		• Analyze arguments
		• Differentiate verifiable facts from personal beliefs
		• Evaluate information source credibility
		• Identify unstated assumptions
		• Evaluate the logic used in reaching a conclusion
		• Weigh evidence or options

Problem solving and critical thinking are interdependent.

gathering, evaluation, and usually decision making. The evaluative component of critical thinking varies with the task to be accomplished.

In many situations, problem solving and critical thinking operate in an interdependent fashion. For example, information problem-solving tasks require students to gather and interpret information to solve a problem and thus draw on both problem-solving and critical thinking skills. As a student, you face an information problem-solving task when your instructor assigns a research paper. You have to locate credible information sources relevant to the assignment, interpret this information, and then integrate the information in a way that satisfies the goals of the assignment. We face many information problem-solving tasks in daily life. For example, we frequently gather and interpret information to achieve a goal when we make major purchases (e.g., buy a car) or navigate about our world (e.g., determine how to make use of the bus or subway system to get to an unfamiliar destination). (We provide an extended discussion of information problem solving in Chapter 6.)

We have a particular interest in the information problem-solving activities of biologists, historians, writers, and anyone else who might be commonly labeled as active practitioners of content-area skills (i.e., biology, history, English). These activities provide one way of defining the authentic tasks that educators might attempt to adapt as learning activities (see Chapter 2). For example, in conducting research, scientists are engaged in information problem solving. They gather information through experimentation or careful observation in order to understand some phenomenon or natural process. Learning tasks that involve authentic scientific inquiry require problem solving and critical thinking. Later we argue that educators should take advantage of the common co-occurrence of these skills in authentic tasks as an opportunity for developing both content knowledge and general higher-order thinking skills.

WHAT IS PROGRAMMING?

A definition of programming

Programming is the process of instructing the computer to perform some desired action. The learner manipulates the computer. Think of it as teaching a student with perfect memory but very limited capacity to interpret what you say. Unless your instructions are explicit, accurate, and detailed, the computer will be unable to understand what you would like it to do. If you are familiar with the classes that computer science majors take, you might equate programming with some image you have of a programmer sitting at a computer terminal typing in code in BASIC, FORTRAN, Pascal, C+, or some other recognizable high-level programming language. It is useful to take a somewhat broader perspective.

Higher-level programming

Programming has not always involved the specialized languages we recognize today. Early programmers did not type in programming instructions using keyboards, but used a series of toggle switches to enter commands in **binary** (1's and 0's); that is, each unique combination of 1's and 0's told the computer to take a very specific action. The world of technology has changed a great deal since then. Higher-level languages now allow programmers to work with commands and ways of combining commands that are easier to learn and easier to enter into the computer than the binary coding. Still, learning these commands and what they do and learning the rules that define how the commands can be combined according to the grammatical rules of the language take a considerable amount of time. The programming techniques of the future may also be very different from today's techniques. Already, some programming environments take a visual approach and allow the "programmer" to arrange **icons** (miniature pictures) representing different computer actions. Later in this chapter, we show you a type of programming in which the computer can be "taught" through a form of demonstration. The programmer "shows" instead of "tells" the computer how to act in a specific situation.

So it is useful to take the perspective that programming can take many forms and different types of programming are evolving to meet different purposes. Once programmers get past the challenge of providing instructions to the computer, either because they have mastered a programming language or because the technology has been adapted to allow some other form of input, manipulating the computer or a device controlled by the computer is a matter of explaining exactly what it is the computer is to do. The challenge at this point is easily underestimated and is much more a matter of higher-order thinking than memorizing the factual information of programming commands and rules.

WHY LEARN TO PROGRAM?

Functions of programming experiences in schools

Programming experiences in schools serve three functions. First, programming is a skill that some believe is important to learn; it provides an understanding of the functioning of the computer and computer software and thus is one way to develop certain aspects of general computer literacy. And for a few students, it may eventually become a profession. Second, programming has been advocated as a powerful environment within which problem solving or some other general cognitive skills can be developed. A great deal of work is in progress to test this claim and to create classroom environments in which the overall benefits of learning general problem-solving skills through programming might best be realized. Finally, programming may allow students to learn the content of some other discipline, such as geometry. It appears possible that programming can provide an active way to explore and construct a personal understanding of content within certain disciplines.

As this chapter proceeds, we explore these final two claims. We emphasize these issues because we see them as important to decisions that educators must make about how students will spend school time. Will students have programming experiences or not? Before this discussion will make much sense, you will need to gain some insight into the programming experiences that students might encounter.

WHY EMPHASIZE LOGO?

Strengths of LOGO

In this chapter we emphasize the LOGO programming language because it allows discussion of the whole range of potential programming benefits. LOGO is a language for developing programming skill and possibly for developing content-area knowledge and general problem-solving ability. It is somewhat unique because it is frequently taught at several grade levels and usually with students of a range of aptitudes. In comparison, other popular programming languages (BASIC and Pascal) seem frequently to be applied primarily as a way to develop programming skill. These languages are more likely to be taught in specialized courses for students with specialized interests.

Focus

Seymour Papert and LOGO

At first glance, Seymour Papert might seem an unusual person to be advocating radically different approaches to elementary education. Proposing new ways children can use technology is not something you might expect from an individual who has earned two doctorates in mathematics and cofounded, with Marvin Minsky, the Artificial Intelligence Laboratory at MIT. However, there is a good deal more to Papert's story.

Before the AI Lab, Papert studied with psychologist Jean Piaget for five years. The view that children construct their own understanding of the world in response to personal experiences in their environment is strongly Piagetian. In 1968, Papert proposed the concept of Mathland. The basic idea was to develop a learning environment for mathematics that provided an experience equivalent to immersing a foreign language student in a foreign country. This general objective, together with the goal of developing a computer language suitable for children, produced the design guidelines for LOGO.

The LOGO programming language first used with junior high students in 1968 contained no graphics and no turtle. Students used the language to accomplish tasks such as translating English to pig Latin and designing strategy games. Papert added the turtle and graphics later to provide a more interesting environment for younger children.

The early work with LOGO was not focused entirely on screen-based experiences. An early version of the turtle was a robot-like device resembling an inverted salad bowl with wheels for legs and a pen for a tail. This device could be programmed to roll around on a sheet of paper and draw designs as it went. Papert believed in putting powerful resources in the hands of children. Early LOGO activities required computational power that did not exist in schools, and the salad bowl turtle cost about $4,000 (without computer). Now the computational power of LOGO can be implemented with computers commonly available in schools, and LOGO is being used to control a variety of machines that students build themselves (see "LEGO-LOGO" beginning on page 100; Papert, 1980; Turkle, 1984).✷

The turtle

PROGRAMMING IN LOGO

The customary method for introducing students or teachers to the LOGO language is through experiences with **turtlegraphics**. The most common version of turtlegraphics relies on a small-screen turtle that moves and draws on the computer screen. The screen turtle's actions are controlled directly by commands issued from the keyboard or indirectly by programs constructed by a programmer. Examples of drawings created with turtlegraphics are scattered throughout this chapter.

TABLE 3.2

Some LOGO
Primitives

PRIMITIVE	EXAMPLE	ACTION
cleargraphics	CG	Clear the screen
forward	FD 10	Move ahead 10 steps
back	BK 10	Move back 10 steps
right	RT 90	Turn right 90 degrees
left	LT 90	Turn left 90 degrees
penup	PU	Leave no trail
pendown	PD	Leave trail
home	Home	Return to center screen
hideturtle	HT	No turtle in graphic
showturtle	ST	Turtle

Different versions of LOGO may use slightly different commands. This list of primitives is from the LogoWriter version of LOGO. If you are using LogoWriter to try out some of these commands, you can obtain a complete list of primitives by entering .primitives.

The individual commands in LOGO are called **primitives** (see Table 3.2). As is true with commands in all other programming languages, LOGO commands must follow an established syntax. The **syntax** for individual commands consists of rules for combining keywords, punctuation, and arguments. In LOGO, commands follow the format *keyword* [space] *argument* (Fay & Mayer, 1988). For example, if you wanted the turtle to move ahead thirty turtle steps, you would issue the command *forward 30* (abbreviated as FD 30). (See Figure 3.1.) In this example, the keyword is *forward* (or FD), the punctuation is a space, and the argument is the number *30*. Expressions such as 30FD, 30 FD, or FD30 are incorrect and will not work. If all of this seems unnecessarily complex for young children, just stop to think about the rules

Commands must follow an established syntax.

FIGURE 3.1
Result of Some LOGO Primitives

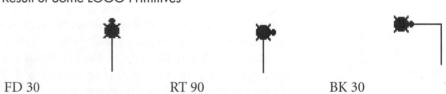

FD 30   RT 90   BK 30

they follow in writing English. Whereas young students would probably be unable to apply appropriate terms to the components of a LOGO command, they are quite capable of learning and following the rules necessary for constructing commands the computer can interpret.

Importance of hands-on experience

We strongly encourage you to take the time to experience programming. The best way to appreciate LOGO is to spend some time at a terminal exploring the features of the language. As you begin, contemplate your own thinking. Insights you have about your own thinking might be helpful when you work later with other beginners. You might want to consider the following questions. What about your experiences do you find frustrating or exciting? What approach do you take when something does not work as expected? How do you feel when you finally solve a problem that has stumped you for some time? (One of us has been known to cheer and punch his fist in the air!)

In the following pages, we provide a brief overview of selected LOGO (LogoWriter) features. For more detail, we suggest that you consult a textbook or manual written to provide a more complete account of LOGO (Muller, 1997).

PROGRAMMING IN DIRECT MODE

LOGO allows the keyboard input and execution of commands in direct mode. **Direct mode** means that each time you press the return key, the command or commands that you have typed are executed. Working in direct mode is a good way to explore the early stages of learning to program and is also a way to work out the details of sophisticated programs after you have become more proficient. Try some of the individual commands (primitives) from Table 3.2. If you type the commands shown in Figure 3.1, you should see the turtle move as indicated. By the way, if you don't want the effect of your commands to accumulate on the screen, enter CG (cleargraphics) at any point to clear the display.

Now, instead of individual commands, try entering the following sequence of commands before pressing the return key:
FD 30 RT 90 FD 30 RT 90 FD 30 RT 90 FD 30 RT 90
Figure 3.2 shows what you will see on your screen.

FIGURE 3.2
Square Resulting from LOGO Commands

PROGRAMMING IN INDIRECT MODE: WRITING PROCEDURES

When working in **indirect mode,** the programmer constructs a set of instructions to be stored for execution at a later time. Because the programmer has to anticipate mentally the effect of each command, this approach makes some new demands. Often the programmer makes an error in thinking through what will happen when the entire sequence of commands is executed, and unexpected consequences occur (computer programmers refer to the errors in their programs as **bugs;** see Focus: The Original Bug). One very nice feature about a stored program is that if the programmer can determine the cause of the flaw in the program, he or she can locate the bug in the stored program and change the offending command or commands. In a way, this is similar to using a word processing program to edit a written document. Editing requires the writer to correct only the offending statement, not redo the entire document.

In LOGO, a set of stored instructions is called a **procedure.** The general format for a procedure is:

TO   *procedurename*
             commands
END

To generate a square as a procedure, you might enter the following list of commands:

TO SQUARE
    FD 30
    RT 90
    FD 30
    RT 90
    FD 30
    RT 90
    FD 30
    RT 90
END

The advantage of a stored program

In direct mode, the entire sequence of commands can now be executed by simply entering SQUARE (then press Return). The procedure SQUARE has been added to the LOGO vocabulary. In a way, the programmer increases the power of LOGO by contributing to what LOGO knows how to do. This is what we mean by describing programming as "instructing the computer."

What if you made a mistake—say, you incorrectly entered 3 instead of 30 for one of the sides? The figure drawn by the procedure would not be what you anticipated (see Figure 3.3)!

However, the process of correcting the error is relatively easy. You simply return to indirect mode, examine the procedure to find the error, and make

FIGURE 3.3
Result of Flawed Square Procedure

the necessary correction. You can now execute the procedure again. If your modification fixes the actual bug, your program should execute as intended.

ADDITIONAL FEATURES OF LOGO

The procedure SQUARE is written in a manner that is not particularly elegant because the two primitives FD and RT are repeated over and over again. What if the procedure involved some cyclical process that had to be repeated hundreds or thousands of times? It would be rather impractical to enter any set of commands that many times. The command REPEAT *number* [*commands*] tells LOGO to repeat the commands within brackets the designated number of times. You could rewrite the procedure SQUARE as follows:

    TO SQUARE
        REPEAT 4 [FD 30 RT 90]
    END

Use of variables
Powerful programming languages also make use of **variables**. The value of a procedure such as SQUARE would be limited if you had to rewrite the procedure every time you wanted the turtle to draw a square of a different

Focus

The Original Bug

The term *bug,* which is so familiar to computer programmers today, has an interesting origin. The term is usually attributed to Grace Hopper, a famous computer pioneer who worked for the U.S. Navy in the 1940s–1960s. Computers used to contain many moving parts and as a result generated heat. Because air-conditioning was not always available, the windows were sometimes left open to contend with the unpleasant temperatures and also to keep the computer cool. On one occasion, the machine that Grace Hopper was working on quit, and workers painstakingly searched for the failed component. The problem turned out to be a moth that had probably flown in through an open window. Hopper reported that she had to "debug" the machine, and this expression for fixing a computer problem has been used ever since. ✶

size. In a way, variables allow you to establish the sequence of actions to be taken when the program is written and to defer assigning specific arguments to these actions. To write a more flexible version of the square procedure, you could establish the length of a side when the procedure is actually executed. You could write this more flexible version of the square procedure this way:

```
TO SQUARE :SIDE
    REPEAT 4 [FD :SIDE RT 90]
END
```

Once you have created the square procedure, you execute the procedure by entering SQUARE followed by the length of the side you want (for example, SQUARE 40). If you forget and enter only the procedure name, LOGO will ask you for the missing value.

Variables as storage boxes

The way LOGO designates and uses variables might be a bit confusing at first. SIDE is a variable name. When a variable name is preceded by a colon (as in :SIDE), this means the value of a variable. When the REPEAT command encounters FD :SIDE, it substitutes the value of SIDE. To establish the value of a variable, you can also use the primitive MAKE "*variablename value* (as in MAKE "SIDE 40). Instead of entering SQUARE 40 to draw a square 40 turtlesteps on a side, you could also enter the command MAKE "SIDE 40 and then the command SQUARE :SIDE to accomplish the same thing. To keep these different ideas straight, you might think of a variable name as a storage place, like a box somewhere in the computer's memory. The MAKE command attaches the variable name to a storage location and allows you to put information in this storage place. When the value of a variable is requested (as in :SIDE), LOGO will check the designated storage location to obtain the needed information. If LOGO finds an empty storage location, LOGO will generate an error message and ask for the needed information (in LogoWriter, SQUARE NEEDS MORE INPUTS).

BUILDING A PROGRAM WITH PROCEDURES

LOGO allows one procedure to "call" another procedure. That is, once a procedure has been written, the action it generates can be called by inserting the name of the procedure within a second procedure. Sometimes the main program or procedure is called a **superprocedure,** and the building block procedures are called **subprocedures**. Often the superprocedure is very simple, consisting of only a series of procedure names (subprocedures). This method is efficient because it allows the programmer to isolate tasks and work on them as manageable units. As we point out later, the ability to identify problem subgoals is also an important general problem-solving skill. Experience with programs that use subprocedures may help students develop this technique for handling complex problems.

Superprocedures and subprocedures

A procedure in LOGO can even call itself. This is accomplished by inserting the name of the procedure within the procedure. When the procedure is activated, the computer executes each command it encounters until it reaches the procedure name. When the computer encounters the name of any procedure, it begins to execute that procedure. In this case, this amounts to starting the sequence of actions generated by the procedure all over again. This special method is called **recursion**. Recursion is an idea that students find extremely intriguing and love to explore (Papert, 1980). The idea of a self-perpetuating process is just fascinating. For example, consider the childhood riddle: If you have two wishes, what would your second wish be? The answer is: Two more wishes (or make one wish and then wish for two more wishes). If you could express the riddle as a procedure, it would look something like this:

Students love to explore recursion.

```
TO WISH
    MAKE WISH1
    WISH
END
```

Recursion can also be demonstrated as a way to extend and produce some interesting effects with procedures that have already been written. The procedure that follows uses SQUARE. There are no repeats in this procedure, but many squares of decreasing size have been drawn. In fact, an IF statement was included to stop the program from going on and on. The results are shown in Figure 3.4.

Extending and producing interesting effects

```
TO BLACKHOLE :SIDE
    SQUARE :SIDE
    RT 12
    Make "SIDE :SIDE*.985
    IF :SIDE.5 [STOP]
    BLACKHOLE :SIDE
END
```

FIGURE 3.4
Results of Blackhole
Procedure

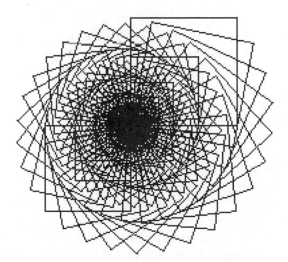

Now that you have had a brief exposure to the kinds of programming that younger students might do, the question becomes what these experiences accomplish. The remainder of this chapter addresses this question.

WAYS TO TEACH HIGHER-ORDER THINKING

It is time to return to the focus of this chapter—higher-order thinking—and present a structure that outlines some of the options educators have for helping students become better thinkers. We use this structure to consider the advantages and disadvantages that programming and other applications of technology involving manipulation and measurement offer in developing higher-order thinking skills.

Classroom approaches to higher-order thinking

There are three distinct approaches to the instruction of higher-order thinking skills within a classroom setting, defined by the manner in which this instruction relates to the instruction of other areas of the curriculum (Wakefield, 1996):

◆ **Stand-alone approach.** Class activities are focused on the development of higher-order thinking skills. Instruction in thinking skills and content-area skills and knowledge is independent.

◆ **Dual-agenda approach.** Instruction in higher-order thinking is combined with instruction in another area of the curriculum. Instruction in both areas may be provided independently within the course, but the content-area learning tasks provide an opportunity for practicing thinking skills.

◆ **Authentic task approach.** This approach requires the application of higher-order thinking in performing activities that lead to the development of both thinking and content-area skills and knowledge. Rather than being developed independently, thinking skills are learned through the application within domain-appropriate activities.

The debate over which approach is best could be approached in a number of ways. One issue concerns whether it is reasonable to isolate and learn very general thinking skills so they can then be applied in many areas (Singly & Anderson, 1989) or whether it is necessary to learn thinking skills within the areas in which they are to be applied (Brown et al., 1989). You will encounter comments on this distinction as you continue, but we regard the issue as unresolved at this point. If it can be assumed that all three approaches have the potential to develop higher-order thinking skills, efficiency may also be an issue to consider. How many schools will be willing or able to offer a course dedicated to thinking skills? Is it reasonable to involve students in programming, a course that probably is not central to the standard curriculum, because it provides a good opportunity to practice higher-level thinking?

Table 3.3 summarizes some key points about the different approaches to developing higher-order thinking skills. At the bottom of the table we have

TABLE 3.3

Summary of Ways to Teach Higher-Order Thinking

	INSTRUCTIONAL STRATEGY		
	STAND ALONE	DUAL AGENDA	AUTHENTIC TASK
Focus	Higher-order thinking	Targeted higher-order thinking skills and content-area knowledge	Higher-order skills appropriate to content area and content-area knowledge
Instructional method	Independent course	Process skill instruction added to course	Content course activity selected to require content and thinking skills
Thinking skill/ content-area relationship	Potential to apply thinking skills in other courses	Thinking skill relevant to content tasks	Thinking skill essential to content tasks
Technology example	HOTS (Pogrow, 1996)	Programming and problem solving (e.g., Salomon & Perkins, 1987)	Use of data loggers in authentic student research (e.g., Albrecht & Firedrake, 1998)

The HOTS Project

provided an example of how technology has been used in implementing each instructional approach. The HOTS Project (Higher Order Thinking Skills; Pogrow, 1996) was created as a way to develop higher-order thinking skills in struggling upper-elementary students. It is a pull-out program in which a teacher assists a small number of students who need extra attention with instructional software applications that require critical thinking and problem solving. The computer experiences and the interactions with the teacher focus directly on the development of thinking skills. Programming and the use of technology in authentic research are examples of the dual-agenda and authentic task approaches. Our focus will be on these two instructional strategies.

PROGRAMMING AND THE DEVELOPMENT OF PROBLEM-SOLVING SKILLS

A nearly classic problem-solving activity

On the surface, the argument that students can learn general problem-solving skills from programming experiences seems logical. Programming is nearly a classic problem-solving activity. Descriptions of what experienced programmers do (Pea & Kurland, 1987b) are almost identical to more general descriptions of the problem-solving process (Bransford & Stein, 1984; Hayes & Simon, 1974). As the programmer attempts to accomplish a programming task, he or she must:

1. Understand the task.
2. Develop a plan for completing the task on the computer.
3. Convert the plan into programming code.

4. Evaluate the extent to which the program functions as desired and modify the program when necessary.

Do students learn to become better problem solvers because they have spent time learning to program? Providing a direct answer to this question is difficult. Various reviews of the research attempting to summarize this issue have not reached a unanimous conclusion (Keller, 1990; Pea & Kurland, 1987b; Salomon & Perkins, 1987).

Reasons for Conducting an Overview of the Research

Why consider the research?

The body of research about the relationship between programming and the development of problem-solving skills is important for several reasons:

◆ Becoming familiar with the research will help you when you are trying to make decisions about how to integrate technology effectively into your classroom. If you decide to provide your students with programming experiences, for example, you should attempt to determine whether programming benefits them and which approaches to teaching programming seem most productive.

◆ The research literature provides an example of the evolution of theory and related ideas about classroom applications. Consideration of this body of work demonstrates that the results of research studies can cause recommendations for practice to change.

◆ Because nearly all of the research on programming and problem solving was conducted in classroom settings, it provides insights into how teachers use LOGO. The impact of LOGO on student behavior is directly determined by the actual experiences of students, not by the potential experiences that are never realized.

◆ The studies seem to lead to recommendations for practice that mesh with many of the ideas developed in Chapter 2: cognitive apprenticeship, authentic tasks, and learning for transfer or application.

Early expectations of LOGO may have been overly optimistic. When new and promising educational ideas do not deliver as advertised, the educational community often drops the ideas and looks for the next innovation. We agree with those who caution against this reaction and suggest that educators treat the educational application of LOGO itself as a LOGO program that does not work as anticipated. Even an inexperienced programmer realizes that a complex program often does not run on the first attempt, and the appropriate response should be to evaluate the program and its assumptions carefully rather than abandon the work that has been completed.

Conditions for Low- and High-Road Transfer

The process by which specific skills and knowledge learned in one situation prove generally useful in a variety of new situations is referred to as **transfer**. When you think about it, transfer is what formal education is all about.

Unless what we teach and learn in our classrooms has some general value in other classrooms and outside the school setting, why bother acquiring the knowledge in the first place?

Low-road transfer

Transfer can occur in two ways, sometimes referred to as low- and high-road transfer (Salomon & Perkins, 1987). In *low-road transfer,* behavior is practiced extensively and in a variety of situations and learned to the point of **automatization**. Automatized behavior is behavior that a person has learned to the point at which he or she can complete a task without thinking about it. For example, if you drive or are a competent typist, you have practiced skills extensively and in a variety of situations and have likely automatized behaviors related to typing and driving. When you type the letter *q,* the fact that the little finger on your left hand moves straight up one row is probably not something you are aware of.

High-road transfer

In *high-road transfer,* skills must be deliberately transferred from one context to another. Two requirements must be met. First, the individual must be capable of re-representing the original skill at a level that will include a greater range of cases than was covered by the context in which the original skill was first acquired. For example, if a student both observes from experiences with programming and is capable of explaining that it is often useful to take a complex problem and identify individual tasks to be accomplished, the student has re-represented programming knowledge in an abstract and verbal fashion that would apply to many tasks. Second, the student must be willing to make a conscious effort to use past experiences to attack current problems. Such an approach requires both motivation and metacognitive skill.

Identifying whether studies met the requirement for either high- or low-road transfer turned out to be an accurate way to predict whether the studies were successful in demonstrating the transfer of problem-solving skills (Salomon & Perkins, 1987). To summarize, when students did not (1) spend enough time programming to develop a reasonable level of skill or accumulate enough diverse experiences, (2) consider and discuss how they solve problems when they program, and (3) consider how the problem-solving skills involved in programming might apply to other domains, the research studies were unlikely to demonstrate that students could transfer programming skills to other areas.

Issues in Implementing LOGO

The original philosophy of LOGO stressed the importance of personal discovery within a responsive exploratory environment. Many teachers appear to have interpreted the initial guidelines for working with LOGO as advocating little planning or intervention on their part (Keller, 1990). As a result, they typically introduced students only briefly to commands or techniques and then allowed them to explore on their own. Observation of students' behaviors under these circumstances indicated that they found the LOGO environment to be motivating. However, whatever the expectations, most younger

LOGO is motivating

students working in LOGO do not spontaneously engage in the general problem-solving skills thought to be prompted by programming environments. Without specific guidance, many students would find some set of commands that produced an interesting pattern and fiddle with this pattern by entering slightly different values for the key variables (Littlefield et al., 1988). They might continue variations on the same theme for several class periods using a trial-and-error approach. Researchers noted that students seemed highly motivated and intrigued with the interesting results their programs would produce, but that they were frequently unable to predict what a specific version of the program would do before they ran it or explain why particular results were produced. These observations suggest that many students engage in only weak problem-solving practices when they are allowed complete freedom to explore. In terms of the principles we discussed in Chapter 2, it seems that the external activity of programming within a discovery environment often does not engage internal processes thought to be important components of problem solving (see pages 60 through 61).

A Matter of Style

Even when students are task oriented, some educators believe they tend to work in a way that may be successful in the short run but does not lead to advanced problem-solving skills in the long run. Observation suggests that most young LOGO programmers use a style described as "product oriented," "brute force," and "linear" (Kurland, Clement, Mawby, & Pea, 1987). In this approach, the student has some desired screen effect in mind and generates a sequence of individual commands (linear approach) to achieve the desired effect (product oriented). The highly interactive nature of LOGO programming almost rewards this kind of behavior; the student can note bugs and insert or change individual commands very easily (by trial and error or brute force). A more disciplined approach would emphasize careful analysis of the problem to identify subproblems, the generation of procedures to solve the subproblems, and the construction of superprocedures to integrate the procedures. Some teachers require students to sketch out a plan on paper before working at the computer. This approach is an attempt to encourage students to think the task through before they begin to enter code, like asking students to construct an outline before writing.

MORE EFFECTIVE PROGRAMMING INSTRUCTION

These observations of students' programming have implications for teachers and schools that want to use LOGO or other languages to develop problem-solving skills.

First, the analysis suggests that educators take a more realistic look at what they expect LOGO to accomplish. At best, students in elementary and junior high school settings are likely to spend thirty to fifty hours in a year programming (Pea & Kurland, 1987b). Schools have many instructional responsibilities, and it may not be practical to assume that they can increase this time commitment substantially. Perhaps it is necessary to accept the reality that students will not become very proficient as programmers in thirty to fifty hours, especially when they use much of the time in self-directed discovery. The solution may be to switch away from pure discovery experiences. This is the approach taken by educators who advocate more structured and mediated (but not lock-step) approaches to LOGO instruction.

Structured approaches to LOGO

Second, it appears that the development of problem-solving skills requires guidance. Increasing the amount of structure in the learning environment seems to improve student knowledge of LOGO, but it does not appear to be sufficient to develop general problem-solving skills (Littlefield et al., 1988). It appears that more general skills can be developed when teachers employ **mediated instruction** (Keller, 1990; Littlefield et al., 1988). In a mediated instruction approach, the teacher works directly to develop the thinking skills or strategies associated with the academic task the student is performing. The teacher must take care to establish that he or she is as concerned with the development of important thinking processes as with more visible products. When the content taught by mediated instruction is programming, key thinking processes might include planning, breaking complex problems into smaller problems, and using a systematic approach to identify and fix bugs. In contrast, the products are the program code and the result of the program (a graphic design when using turtlegraphics).

What to explain to students

Students need to be told that planning and other cognitive activities are important, taught how to perform these skills, and monitored to make certain they use the skills. Because of the broad educational expectations associated with programming, it might also be useful to ascertain that students understand that the targeted cognitive behaviors may be processes involved in general problem solving.

Planning, breaking down complex problems, and debugging are useful processes in many arenas, but it appears that the transfer of these skills to general applications is not automatic. Thus, mediated instruction might also concern the conscious transfer of skills learned in one domain to other settings and other problems. Teachers might ask students to think about how planning or debugging skills emphasized in programming might apply to writing or preparing a speech. Students must understand that they are learning skills they will be expected to apply in a variety of areas.

Mediated instruction

Mediated instruction involves a number of techniques. First, the teacher makes critical strategies explicit. Then he or she can mention specific skills and demonstrate them through think-aloud techniques. The teacher can demonstrate how to debug a faulty program and discuss how to bridge thinking skills learned in programming to other areas. For example, Littlefield et al. (1988) discuss applying processes from programming to plan a class party: What are the components of the problem, and what has to be done to prepare for each component? Second, mediated instruction attempts to involve students in thinking about and analyzing their own thinking and behavior. This can be a very different process from telling students what to do or evaluating the product of what they have done. Teachers seem to communicate differently when teaching LOGO than when teaching other subject matter. They provide fewer instructions and ask more questions (Emihovich & Miller, 1988). The questions often are not requests for information but are intended to get the students to think about their own behavior. A sequence of such questions might include: What did you tell the turtle to do? What did you want it to do? How are you going to fix it? (Au, Horton, & Ryba, 1987; Clements & Gullo, 1984). The use of questions is also opportunistic; teachers must generate the appropriate questions in the appropriate situations. Guidelines that teachers might follow to involve students more actively appear in Focus: A Process-Oriented Checklist for LOGO.

PROGRAMMING TO LEARN IN OTHER CONTENT AREAS

Relationship between programming and other content areas

The relationship between programming and other content areas may not be intuitively obvious. The programming examples in this chapter may have involved concepts you recognize from other content areas. For example, you may relate the concept of variables to an algebra course. Papert (1980) saw the relationship as potentially much more general. To understand his view, it is useful to appreciate his vision of a computer microworld. A computer **microworld** provides an environment representing some discipline. The student can explore and manipulate this environment and experience systematic consequences as a result of actions taken. These consequences allow the student to construct an understanding of the environment through processes of assimilation and accommodation. Papert adopted the ideas of assimilation and accommodation from Jean Piaget. In **assimilation,** external experiences are interpreted as fitting with existing mental structures. In **accommodation,** mental structures are changed to fit experiences. These interacting processes describe the development of personal understanding by construction (see discussion of constructional theory in Chapter 2, pages 62 through 63).

Turtle Geometry

The LOGO turtle provides access to the microworld of turtle geometry. Papert (1980) argued that geometry is understood through action and that turtle geometry is just another style of "doing geometry." Euclid's style was logical, Descartes' style was algebraic, and the turtle's style is computational. If you find this a bit abstract, think about your own understanding of the concept "circle." You may represent a circle as a definition: a closed plane figure with all points equidistant from a common point. As an algebraic expression,

Focus

A Process-Oriented Checklist for LOGO

1. Resist the impulse to solve problems for students. Keep your hands off the students' keyboards!

2. Make certain you give students the opportunity for individual discussions. Walk around the room when students are working.

3. Ask that students explain their solution strategies in their own words.

4. Require that students apply general problem-solving processes to non-LOGO situations. Have them analyze and develop plans for other tasks, such as preparing for a field trip. Discuss how general problem-solving techniques apply.

5. Ask students to describe the problem they are working on in concrete terms (for example, ask, "What do you want the turtle to do?").

6. Encourage students to be flexible thinkers. Require that they write a different procedure to draw the same shape.

7. Ask follow-up questions when observing student work (for example, "Why do you think the turtle did that?").

8. Allow students to work on some problems in small groups. Have groups share their strategies for arriving at solutions.

Source: Selected from a larger list provided by Au et al., 1987.✳

a circle can be represented as $x^2 + y^2 = r^2$ (assuming the Cartesian center is 0, 0), with r representing the radius of the circle. If you fix the radius as 1, the unit circle can be defined as $x^2 + y^2 = 1$. A circle can also be represented as the product of a LOGO program. Most students willing to experiment with LOGO eventually come across the simple program REPEAT 360 FD 1 RT 1. For a more sophisticated method for generating a circle, consider the following procedure (based on Yoder, 1992):

```
to CIRCLE :RADIUS
    REPEAT 360
        FD :RADIUS
        WAIT 10
        PD
        FD 1
        PU
        BK 1
        BK :RADIUS
        WAIT 10
        RT 1
    END
```

If you have an opportunity, enter these commands and run the program. The program draws a circle with the radius you specify. The turtle moves forward the distance you have specified as the radius, puts the pen down, and moves forward one step. This creates a point. The turtle then puts the pen up and moves back to the center of the circle. Finally, the turtle turns one degree to the right. This sequence is repeated 360 times. If you watch the turtle repeatedly run out, make a mark, and then run back as it generates the circle (the WAIT commands have been inserted so that program execution slows down), you may understand what a circle is in a different way than you would if you just thought about "a closed plane figure with all points equidistant from a common point."

Certainly the computational method of defining shapes is the only method among those briefly presented here that defines geometry in terms of action (movements of the turtle). Young children intuitively understand spatial notions in terms of action and the LOGO approach (Battista & Clements, 1988). One experience cited in support of this claim is the frequently observed tendency of children (or adults) to "become the turtle" to solve LOGO problems. You can watch children moving their bodies as they think about a problem. Teachers often suggest that students become the turtle when students want help. Try it. Can you walk in a circle? Translate what you are doing into LOGO commands. Would your program read, "Move ahead a little, turn a little, ahead a little, turn a little, and so on"?

Becoming the turtle to solve LOGO problems

Although it is most frequently used with elementary or junior high school students, LOGO is not limited to understanding only the most basic features of geometry. Turtle geometry can be used to explore advanced topics in geometry as well (Abelson & diSessa, 1981; Yusuf, 1995).

LEGO-LOGO

An interesting extension of LOGO is LEGO-LOGO (Rosen, 1993; Shimabukuro, 1989). LEGO-LOGO allows the student to build simple machines and then uses the computer to control the machines through an interface box. The LEGO kit includes blocks, motors, gears, touch and photo sensors, and a counting mechanism. These extensions allow some new and interesting programming problems. New LOGO primitives (such as ON, OFF, REVERSE DIRECTION) are provided. In addition, the LEGO-LOGO microworld allows the exploration of certain topics in physics, engineering, and mathematics. Because the machines move and lift, physical properties such as force, work, weight, friction, speed, time, and distance come into play. The sensors can be used to gather data for analysis. For example, the photo sensor can detect when an object breaks a beam of light. The object could be the car a student has built, and detecting when the car passes a certain point can be used to determine how long it took the car to move a certain distance—from the start line to the finish line, for example. You can imagine the

Building simple machines

Understanding physical properties

potential for a LEGO-LOGO drag strip and a little friendly competition! However, the LEGO-LOGO microworld should also encourage the development of both programming skill and content-area knowledge. Could you write a program to determine the speed of the cars? What is speed, anyway?

Programming Microworlds: Learning with Stagecast Creator

There are two unique problems in learning to program. First, programming requires the learner to master an entirely new language. Second, programming languages are artificial rather than natural languages. Core concepts in the language—things like data structures and iterative algorithms—are based on the way computers and not people think. In a way, programming requires that you learn how a computer works. If this knowledge takes a considerable time to acquire and yet has little value for the learner, other potential benefits of the process of programming or the tasks that can be accomplished with programming skills may be ignored (Smith & Cypher, 1999).

Skills needed for programming

Various efforts are under way to develop programming methods that "move the computer closer to the learner" rather than to expect the learner to "move closer to the computer." One approach that seems particularly suited to the learning experiences we have decided to emphasize has been described as analogical programming (Smith & Cypher, 1999). In **analogical programming,** the programmer performs actions that are analogous to the effects to be produced by the program. Think of this as "programming by demonstration." To make this possible, developers must first create customized programming environments for a category of programming tasks. For a carefully defined set of tasks, programmers can then (1) identify a situation and (2) demonstrate what the programmer wants the computer to do when it encounters the designated situation.

Stagecast Creator (see Resources to Expand Your Knowledge Base at the end of this chapter for additional information), a customized programming environment developed for younger learners, allows analogical programming to be applied to the development of simulations, animated stories, or instructional tutorials and games. Activities using this programming environment could be integrated into many content areas and thus encourage the dual-agenda approach of developing content-area knowledge and higher-order thinking.

Stagecast Creator allows programming within an environment defined by these elements:

◆ A stage (background) divided into equal-size areas
◆ Characters (objects)
◆ Rules that define the actions of characters

These features all allow customization by the programmer. All of the features can be seen in Figure 3.5. The stage in this case is a solid color, although

FIGURE 3.5
Stagecast Creator Screen Showing Rule Maker

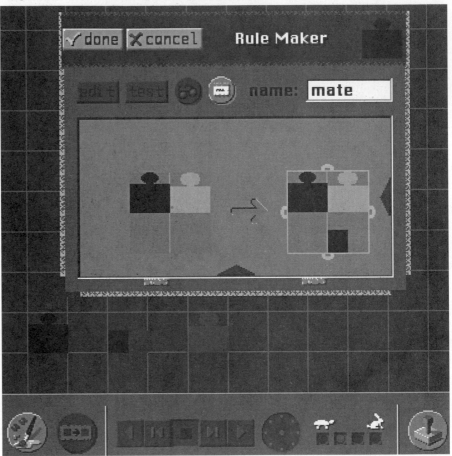

A customized programming environment

it could contain a scene suited to the application being developed. The grid structure that defines the discrete areas of the stage is visible only when a program is being developed. You see three characters on the stage. Again, the appearance of any object is limited only by the artistic skill of the programmer. The "Rule Maker" appears on the screen because the programmer is in the process of demonstrating what the program should do when a dark-colored object is located to the left of a light-colored object. What you see being developed is a simulation that attempts to demonstrate Mendelian genetics involving a hypothetical organism (the character) with a single gene. The gene has a recessive and a dominant trait. The homozygous organisms are dark (both dominant versions of the gene) or light (both recessive versions of the gene). The heterozygous organism (one dominant and one recessive gene) has a mixed appearance (actually the heterozygous organism would probably be dark, but this simulation shows two colors so heterozygous organisms are visible). The rule you see being established ("mate") tells the computer what to do when a dark character is positioned to the left of a light-colored character. The pair "gives birth" to a heterozygous character. The rule is created by demonstrating the "before" and "after" conditions and is attached to the dark colored character. Examine Figure 3.5 carefully to see how this is accomplished. Note that before the rule is implemented, the space below the character on the right is vacant. After the rule has been implemented, the same space contains a heterozygous organism. Computer scientists refer to the programming technique of attaching programming code to a defined object as **object-oriented programming** and this technique is a fundamental feature of many advanced programming languages.

If you remember a little about genetics and have begun to think about this simulation, you can probably anticipate some of the many tasks the programmer would have to accomplish. One of the most basic tasks is to program characters to move about in such a way that from time to time they bump into each other. The programmer can demonstrate how a character is to move. For example, the character can be shown that if the space to the right is vacant, move into that space. The same character can be shown that if the space down and to the right is vacant, move into that space. Creator offers the programmer the opportunity to develop what programmers would call subroutines. A *subroutine* is a combination of programming statements designed to accomplish a specific task. In Creator, a subroutine is established by putting multiple rules in a folder and then defining the relationship among the rules. For example, if we wanted to create a subroutine that would cause one of the characters to move about in an erratic fashion, we might put the two movement rules just described in a folder and specify the relationship among the rules as random. This movement folder would cause our object to move to the right—sometimes directly right and sometimes in a downward direction. Other subroutines allow multiple actions to be taken in response to a specific condition or allow a sequence of actions to be taken as long as the necessary conditions are met.

LEGO-LOGO and Creator provide examples that involve a form of programming and content-area learning. Both examples are still dual-agenda approaches.

DEVELOPING HIGHER-ORDER SKILLS IN OTHER WAYS

We conclude this chapter by describing a very different use of technology. Here, we discuss how technology can be used as a tool enabling students to record measurements related to various characteristics of their physical world. The design, implementation, and presentation of research based on these data provide an authentic way to investigate topics in several different content areas and also to develop higher-order thinking skills. In this case, higher-order thinking and content-area knowledge do not simply represent multiple domains that can be emphasized within the same course. Research requires an authentic integrating of content knowledge and higher-order thinking.

MEASURING CHARACTERISTICS OF THE PHYSICAL WORLD: GRABBING DATA TO ENCOURAGE HIGHER-ORDER THINKING

Practitioners in many fields are very data oriented. They seek answers to questions through the process of research, which requires the careful measurement of critical variables. Students can learn through authentic tasks when they are provided the means to model the activities of these practitioners.

Thinking like a scientist

Educators can now purchase devices that allow students to measure characteristics of the physical environment and store these data for analysis and graphical representation by calculators and computers. The cognitive processes involved in deciding how to collect data to provide answers to significant questions, interpreting the data once collected, and communicating what conclusions can be drawn based on this interpretation are the same processes required of scientists and sometimes mathematicians. They both involve higher-order thinking and allow students to take an authentic approach to the exploration of many content areas.

All data collection devices consist of at least two components. The first is a **sensor** that is sensitive to some aspect of the physical environment and an interface that allows the user to tell the sensor what to do, stores data the sensor generates, and transfers data to a computer or calculator for analysis. When the sensor can be connected to and disconnected from the interface, it is often called a **probe.** These two components are present in at least three identifiable types of devices:

- ◆ A **microcomputer-based laboratory** (MBL) provides a link between a computer and the sensor. Different sensors can be connected to the same interface device.
- ◆ A **calculator-based laboratory** (CBL) provides a link between a calculator and the sensor. Different sensors can be connected to the same interface device. Data stored by the calculator can usually also be uploaded to a computer.
- ◆ A **data logger** is a freestanding device that contains a sensor, an interface, and a battery. Because data loggers are designed as an integrated unit,

they cannot be adapted by attaching different types of sensors. The data logger is connected to a computer for programming and to upload data.

This categorization system actually simplifies some of the options that are available. Some MBLs and CBLs can be detached from the computer or calculator and taken into the field to gather data. Devices that are neither a calculator nor a full-featured computer (e.g., Palm Pilot, DreamWriter) and were designed specifically to provide portability also allow the use of data collection devices.

Types of probes available

To develop an appreciation for the variety of areas that student researchers might investigate, consider a partial list of the probes that schools might purchase. Each probe provides a unique type of data and is suited to a certain range of tasks. Probes are available for measuring pH, temperature, light intensity, humidity, heart rate, voltage, acceleration, dissolved oxygen, carbon dioxide, and a variety of other variables.

Because temperature is perhaps the most frequently measured characteristic of our physical environment and a familiar concept to nearly everyone, research involving temperature is a great way to begin exploring how educators

Students can use probes connected to a computer or calculator to gather information for a variety of problem-solving activities. (© Michael Zide)

might make use of data grabbers (Albrecht & Firedrake, 1999). For example, students can:

◆ Fill different-colored containers with water, place the containers in the sun, and measure how quickly the temperature changes in each container.
◆ Compare the speed with which a container of cold water placed in different types of insulated picnic coolers warms; compare the speed with which a container of warm sand placed inside different brands of sleeping bags changes on a cold day.
◆ Compare temperature variability in natural bodies of water (river, shallow pond, deep lake).
◆ Boil water and record temperature changes relative to time as the water cools; attempt to fit linear, quadratic, and exponential functions to these data.

Temperature is a key variable in many biological and physical reactions. Changes in temperature may increase or decrease enzyme activity (biology), influence the rate of diffusion in a solution (biology, chemistry), and influence the state of matter through freezing, melting, and evaporation (chemistry). Chemical reactions produce or require heat (endothermic or exothermic reactions). The chemical reactions in the breakdown of organic materials produce heat, and proper regulation of this heat is a key factor in successful composting (ecology). Representing the trends in data (exponential functions, asymptote), modeling the influence of several variables, and accounting for some inconsistency in measurements are involved in many types of research (mathematics, statistics).

One of the easiest ways for teachers to gain classroom experience with data collection projects is to purchase a data logger and interface software. The cost for a temperature logger and software should be less than $100. A data logger is a self-contained device that is designed to be left in a location to collect and store data. The type that we feel will be of interest to teachers is about the size of a book of matches (see Figure 3.6). The data logger contains a small battery that powers the device for a year. Data loggers need to be connected to a computer only for setup and then later to retrieve the data. The setup might tell the logger how frequently a measurement is to be taken.

A faculty member at the university where we work is interested in the factors that influence the nesting success of grebes, a bird found in wetland habitats. He studies one type of grebe that appears to leave the nest unattended under some circumstances, behavior that is detrimental to the hatch rate of the eggs. He needed a way to measure the frequency and duration the eggs were unattended, and a temperature data logger was the answer. The scientist painted a plastic colored egg to resemble a grebe egg, put a temperature logger inside the egg, and left the egg in an actual nest. Changes in temperature

Start-up costs are low.

FIGURE 3.6
HOBO Light Intensity Data Grabber. This is the device used by the middle-school students participating in the ice dusting project described in Chapter 1.

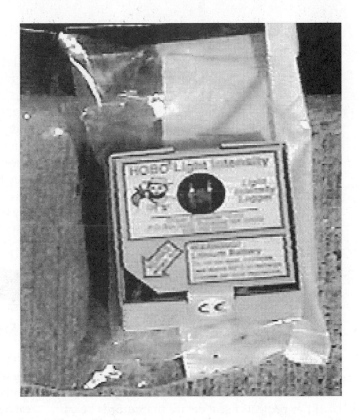

indicated how frequently and how long the eggs were left unattended. By gathering data from many different sites and carefully collecting other data about the sites (e.g., the population of predators), he could test hypotheses about nesting behavior.

Components of an
authentic project

Data logging is only one component of an authentic project, of course. The other activities that provide the context for this component are just as important in encouraging meaningful learning and the development of higher-order thinking skills. Research activities do not originate in a vacuum; scientists engage in research as a way to extend what they already know about a particular topic. Establishing or activating background knowledge and connecting the research task with this knowledge is important for creating productive content-area learning experiences. Thinking through the research methodology is an important opportunity for developing higher-order thinking skills. You have probably read articles in research journals as part of your own college experience, and you should recognize that each article carefully explains the method used to conduct the research. Most methods have weaknesses, and the goal in designing a research study is to develop a method that allows the strongest test of a particular hypothesis.

Once the data are collected, the scientist must find a way to create meaning from the numbers. Transforming numerical data into a graphic representation, a common method, allows the scientist to contemplate the data in a visual form. Statistical procedure may also be necessary to find what is a "typical" outcome based on multiple samples. For example, the biologist we have been describing studies several nests from several locations. Calculating a variable such as the average hatch rate from each location would likely be part of the process of attempting to understand differences across the locations. Students might use a spreadsheet (see Chapter 5) to create graphs or calculate statistics based on the data they have gathered.

Finally, the research process is not complete until scientists and student scientists communicate what they have discovered. For students, communication requires interpretation and the use of existing knowledge. Generating a prod-

Focus

Using a Data Logger to Measure Stress

Laurie Tweeton, a health and physical education teacher, engages her students in projects that require the collection and analysis of data. Some of her projects use a device that records heart rate data. The device, which consists of a strap worn around the chest and a data recorder worn like a wrist watch, allows complete freedom of activity. The data recorder holds more than 8 hours of information and is easily connected to a computer for data transfer.

One of Laurie's favorite projects involves the parents of her middle school students. She asks for three parent volunteers with three different occupations who are willing to wear the heart monitor during their workday. When they can remember, the volunteers are asked to push a button on the recorder when they change activities and to keep notes identifying the different activities. The data logger marks the time when these transitions occur. Students bring the heart monitor back to school, offload the data onto a computer, create a chart from the data, and enter labels on the chart corresponding to the activities that the parents report. Students then compare the heart rate patterns of each subject and discuss which activities seemed to create the greatest stress.

Having actual data to consider may help you understand the types of investigations that are possible. Laurie allowed us to use the heart rate monitor, and we tried to generate our own authentic investigation. Here is what we came up with. We recently purchased a hot tub (called a spa in some locations) and in reading the operating instructions noted some health warnings. Individuals with certain medical conditions are cautioned against using the hot tub. The heart rate monitor seemed a possible way to measure the stress generated by sitting in 104°F water. The design of our experiment was simple: Establish a 20-minute baseline, sit in the hot tub for 20 minutes, and conclude with a 20-minute cooling-off period.

FIGURE 3.7
Data Plotted by Heart Rate Monitor Software

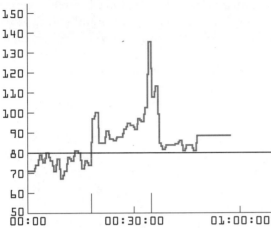

The data generated clearly demonstrate the stress heat imposes on the body (see Figure 3.7). Note the two marks on the *x*-axis. These marks indicate the transitions between stages of our experiment. The middle segment of the graph, the time during which Mark was in the hot water, demonstrates an elevated and accelerating heart rate. Note irregularities in the data appearing near the transitions between stages of the experiment. During these transi-tions, Mark was in his swimming suit working to remove and then reattach the hot tub cover with an air temperature of 20°F.

The computer can also store the raw heart rate data as a text file consisting of the numeri-cal values recorded by the data logger. Once this has been done, the text file can be opened with a spreadsheet (see Chapter 5), and the data can be manipulated and analyzed in various ways. For example, we selected data values for the first and second segments that did not include the irregularities associated with removing the hot tub cover. The spread-sheet *average* function was then applied to these two sets of numbers. The average heart rate before entering the hot water was 74 beats per minute, and the average heart rate after entering the hot water was 89 beats per minute. It appears that our hypothesis con-cerning the stress experienced because of heat has been supported. Many related ques-tions might follow. Why does the heart work harder when the body temperature is raised? Would you expect heart rate to be affected in the same way on a very warm day? Who should be cautioned against spending time in a hot tub?✳

uct requires that learners attempt to explain the concepts or phenomena they have studied. Students must think through what they have done, what they have observed, and what the data they have collected mean. Communication can take many forms, and several forms involving technology are considered in this book. Chapter 10 discusses options for authoring multimedia and on-line presentations. Multimedia presentations represent an exciting way for students to communicate the results of their research.

The Resources to Expand Your Knowledge Base section at the end of this chapter explains how you can learn more about data logging devices, sensors, and curriculum materials for using data loggers in science and mathematics classes.

SUMMARY

Higher-order thinking involves mental behaviors that are complex, effortful, self-regulated, and judgmental. Problem solving and critical thinking are two examples of higher-order thinking emphasized in educational settings and are involved in learning activities that emphasize information problem solving.

Programming is the process of instructing the computer to perform a desired action. Programmers communicate with the computer through specialized languages, each of which has a unique vocabulary and requires the use of a formalized syntax.

LOGO was developed as a programming language for the educational environment. An important characteristic of the LOGO language is the use of procedures—stored sets of instructions. Ideally, procedures are developed to perform one clearly defined task. Procedures can also be combined to perform more complex tasks.

Programming has been proposed as a way to develop student higher-order thinking skills. Educators can emphasize higher-order thinking in several ways: a stand-alone course, a dual-agenda approach combining instruction in higher-order thinking and content-area knowledge, and authentic tasks that require the use of higher-order thinking and the learning of content knowledge. LOGO programming is an example of a dual-agenda approach.

Although programming is a good example of problem solving, evaluations of the use of programming experiences as a way to teach problem solving are inconclusive. Careful examination of programming experiences provided for this purpose reveals some potential problems. Proposed solutions to these limitations include the development of more structured learning experiences and the use of mediational teaching methods, which focus on the cognitive processes used in performing particular skills. In general, the teacher attempts to make these internal processes more understandable to the student and influence the development of these skills.

Programming can also provide an active way to learn a content area. The LOGO turtlegraphics environment was developed as a geometry microworld. When operating in this setting, the student can engage in a computational style of representing geometric principles and concepts. LEGO-LOGO may provide a similar type of environment for learning principles of physics. Other ways to apply programming in content-area instruction are being developed.

Programming courses may not be educationally efficient. Projects provide an authentic way to investigate topics in content areas and also to develop higher-order thinking skills. Such projects would be included in existing content-area courses. Technology can be used as a tool enabling students to measure various characteristics of their physical world. The design, implementation, analysis, and presentation of research based on these data provide the basis for authentic projects.

REFLECTING ON CHAPTER 3

Activities

◆ Consider where in your own academic experiences you were purposefully taught higher-order thinking skills. Describe the learning experience, and classify the experience as stand-alone, dual agenda, or authentic task.

◆ Consider how to explain what programming is. Then develop an explanation of programming that you might present to (1) third-grade students and (2) eighth-grade students.

◆ High-road transfer requires that students be taught to transfer what they have learned. Provide an example of a nonprogramming learning task that might provide an opportunity to discuss transfer from programming experiences. How would you help students see the connections?

◆ Search the Internet for learning activities that make use of calculator-based laboratory, microcomputer-based laboratory, or data logger technology. Search for CBL, MBL, or data logger and a term such as *education* or *experiment*. Share interesting classroom activities you locate with your classmates.

Key Terms

accommodation   *(p. 98)*
analogical programming   *(p. 101)*
assimilation   *(p. 98)*
authentic task approach   *(p. 92)*
automatization   *(p. 95)*
binary   *(p. 83)*
bug   *(p. 88)*
calculator-based laboratory   *(p. 104)*
critical thinking   *(p. 81)*
data logger   *(p. 105)*
direct mode   *(p. 87)*
dual-agenda approach   *(p. 92)*
higher-order thinking   *(p. 91)*
icon   *(p. 83)*
indirect mode   *(p. 88)*
mediated instruction   *(p. 97)*
microcomputer-based laboratory (MBL)   *(p. 104)*
microworld   *(p. 98)*

object-oriented programming   *(p. 103)*
primitives   *(p. 86)*
probe   *(p. 104)*
problem solving   *(p. 81)*
procedure   *(p. 88)*
programming   *(p. 83)*
recursion   *(p. 91)*
sensor   *(p. 104)*
stand-alone approach   *(p. 92)*
subprocedure   *(p. 90)*
superprocedure   *(p. 90)*
syntax   *(p. 86)*
transfer   *(p. 94)*
turtlegraphics   *(p. 85)*
variables   *(p. 89)*

Resources to Expand Your Knowledge Base

Higher-Order Thinking Skills

Information about Pogrow's HOTS project is available at **http://www.hots. org.**
    The following books focus on higher-order thinking skills:

Driver, R. (1983). *The pupil as scientist?* Philadelphia: Open University Press.

Tishman, S., Perkins, D., & Jay, E. (1995). *The thinking classroom: Learning and teaching in a culture of thinking.* Boston: Allyn and Bacon.

Zorfass, J. (1998). *Teaching middle school students to be active researchers.* Alexandria, VA: Association for Supervision and Curriculum Development.

Books Exploring Programming as a General Learning Environment

Papert, S. (1980). *Mindstorms: Children, computers and powerful ideas.* New York: Basic Books.

Papert, S. (1993). *The children's machine: Rethinking school in the age of the computer.* New York: Basic Books.

Turkle, S. (1984). *The second self: Computers and the human spirit.* New York: Simon & Schuster.

Software

Stagecast Creator is available for Macintosh and Windows computers. (**http://www.stagecast.com**)

Resources for Teachers Interested in Using LOGO

The International Society for Technology in Education (ISTE), 1787 Agate Street, Eugene, OR 97403, has been helping teachers apply LOGO for years. ISTE is committed to demonstrating the cross-curricular versatility of LOGO.

Also consult these two books:

Muller, J. (1997). *The great LOGO adventure: Discovering LOGO on and off the computer.* Madison, AL: Doone Publications.

Yoder, S. (1996). *MicroWorlds-Hypermedia project development and Logo scripting.* Eugene, OR: International Society for Technology in Education, 1996.

Data Logging Resources

Learning and Leading with Technology carried a series of articles on classroom use of data gathering technologies:

Albrecht, B., & Firedrake, G. (1998). Grabbing data: What you need to log and use real-world data. *Learning and Leading with Technology, 26*(1), 36–40.

Albrecht, B., & Firedrake, G. (1998). Get moving. *Learning and Leading with Technology, 26*(3), 14–17.

Albrecht, B., & Firedrake, G. (1999). Blowin' hot and cold about my data. *Learning and Leading with Technology, 26*(5), 32–36.

Information about data loggers, calculator-based laboratories (CBLs), micro-computer-based laboratories (MBLs), and probes that attach to the CBLs and MBLs can be located on the Internet. Some of these sites also sell curriculum materials related to these products. Some sources follow.

HOBO data loggers are available from Onset Computer Corporation. (**http://www.onsetcomp.com**)

The Polar Heart Rate Monitor is available from Heartmind Heart Rate Monitors. Software associated with this product is available for both the Macintosh and Windows operating systems. (**http://www.heartmind.net/tempo. htm**)

Vernier sells sensors, kits of sensors suited to particular math and science courses, and lab manuals describing a variety of experiments that can be performed with the sensors. The Vernier site also identifies more companies that can use these probes, information that may be useful in extending the small list we provide here. (**http://www.vernier.com**)

ImagiWorks sells ImagiLab, a product that is designed to work with the Palm Pilot (**http://www.palm.com**) and various probes. The Palm Pilot, a hand-held device, is a simple computer called a personal data assistant (PDA). The data from the Palm can be sent to either a Windows or Mac platform computer for further analysis. ImagiProbe for Macintosh enables students to share data in real time over the Internet. Software that comes with the Palm interface allows annotations and sketches to be stored. ImagiWorks makes available suggested activities to get teachers started. (**http://www. imagiworks.com**)

Texas Instruments sells a calculator-based laboratory (CBL) for use with its popular calculators. This is a good site for learning about CBLs and the probes and activities that can be completed with CBLs. Data from a CBL can also be uploaded to a computer. (**http://www.ti.com/calc/docs/cbl.htm**)

The DreamWriter I.T. is a specialized computer developed for use in schools running the Windows CE operating system. A special data logger and probeware can be purchased to work with the computer. The DreamWriter is a product of NTS Computer Systems LTD. (**http://www.nts.dreamwriter. com**)

Chapter **4**

Using Instructional Software for Content-Area Learning

ORIENTATION

This chapter acquaints you with computer applications used in an instructional role. First, we consider what instruction is and look at how traditional instructional activities are being challenged. Then we present a system for categorizing instructional software. Once you understand this system, you should be able to classify new programs that you encounter and understand how each category of software engages learners. For example, you will learn how to determine whether software presents new ideas and develops new skills, helps students become more proficient with skills learned elsewhere, or both presents new skills and provides opportunities for practice. In short, you will learn how to evaluate software and how it is used.

As you read, look for answers to the following questions:

Focus Questions

- ◆ What are the four stages of a complete instructional experience? Which of the stages of instruction do computer-based tutorials, simulations, drill-and-practice software, educational games, and exploratory environments address?
- ◆ Why would teachers want students to experience a computer-based simulation rather than the "real thing"?
- ◆ How are simulation fidelity, speed of learning, and likelihood of transfer interrelated?
- ◆ When are drill-and-practice activities used inappropriately?
- ◆ What are the characteristics of an exploratory learning environment, and what role should teachers play to help students learn from exploratory environments?

◆ Is it possible to apply constructivist principles with instructional software?

◆ What factors might teachers consider in evaluating software for potential adoption?

An Example of Learning from the Computer

A teacher and an elementary school student work with an activity called the *Eco-Simulator*. The *Eco-Simulator* is an example of a simulation, one of several categories of instructional software you will encounter in this chapter. As you read this dialogue, consider how the simulation and the teacher involve the student. Does this experience qualify as what Chapter 2 describes as meaningful learning?

Teacher: What's an herbivore?

Student: [*no response*]

Teacher: What do herbivores eat?

Student: They eat herbs.

Teacher: Okay, what's a carnivore?

Student: It has something to do with cars.

Teacher: Do you know what a food chain is?

Student: It starts with something little and then something eats that. [*crouches to demonstrate*] Some little fish eat something that lives in the water—little plants or something. [*pretends to engulf small plants with two-hand overhand motion*] Then bigger fish eat the little fish. Then bigger fish still eat those fish. [*stands a little more out of crouch with increasing size of fish*] Then [*arm over head for fin, then begins two-arm scissors motion and* Jaws *theme—daaa-duh, daa-duh, da-duh, da-duh*] a shark eats them all!

Teacher: Is that the only kind of food chain?

Student: No, people can be in a food chain, too. We eat other animals and plants.

Teacher: Let me show you how to work with this computer program.

Student: It looks like you get to draw pictures or something.

Teacher: Well, in a way you do. First, you click on one of these small pictures to select a biome. What do you think this one is?

Student: It's kind of small. I don't know.

Teacher: What does it say here? [*points to field above picture*]

Student: "Salt water."

Teacher: Do you know what that means?

Student: Sure, it would be like the ocean.

Teacher: Do you remember telling me about the food chain? If I remember correctly, you told me about plants and fish that live in the ocean. Let me show you how to put plants and animals in the ocean. You just use the mouse to drag them into the picture. [*demonstrates how to use the mouse to drag object*] What would you put in the ocean?

Student: [*drags in algae, small fish, and a shark; see Figure 4.1*]

Teacher: How will this food chain work?

Student: The little fish will eat the plants, and the shark will eat the little fish.

Teacher: Let me show you something. Click on this button [*points to simulate button*] and watch these graphs. These graphs show how the number of plants and animals changes. Some of the plants and fish get eaten. Herbivores are fish or animals that eat plants. Carnivores are fish or animals that eat other fish or animals. The number of fish grows when they have

FIGURE 4.1
Screen Display from *Eco-Simulator*

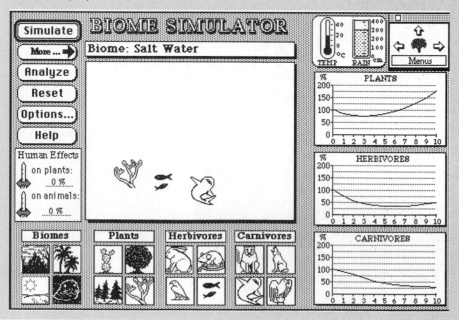

baby fish. New plants may also grow. If the line on the graph goes up, there are more. If the line goes down, there are less. Why does the line for the little fish go down?

Student: Sharks eat them.

Teacher: Why does the line for the sharks go down?

Student: [*pause*] Probably get killed by boats?

Teacher: What do you think happens when the sharks have few little fish left to eat?

Student: Oh, they die, too. The line would go down.

Teacher: Why would the line for the plants go up?

Student: Maybe it wasn't the right kind of plants for the fish to eat. Oh! There are less fish to eat them.

Teacher: How could you fix it so we end up with more sharks by the end of the graph?

Student: Put in more fish, but they'll need more plants to eat.
[*Now has a total of one shark, five sets of little fish, and five plants. Clicks simulate button to produce graphs marked B in Figure 4.2.*]

FIGURE 4.2
Screen Display Showing Graphs After Three Simulations in *Eco-Simulator*

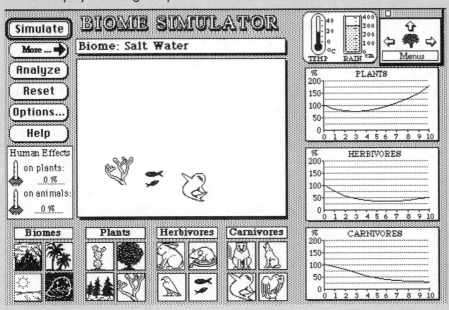

Teacher: What happened?

Student: It still didn't work right. The plants went down too fast. I'm going to take out some of the little fish. [*Removes two sets of little fish. Now has five plants, three sets of little fish, and one shark. Clicks simulate button to produce graphs marked C in Figure 4.2.*] There. Is that what you wanted me to do?

Teacher: Yes, there are more sharks at the end. [*points to graph*] Why do you have to start with more little fish than sharks?

Student: Because the shark could never live on just a few little fish. It's a lot bigger and it has to eat lots of little fish.

COMPUTER-BASED INSTRUCTION

CBI and CAI   ·

Applications of technology to instruction are often called **computer-based instruction** (**CBI**) or **computer-assisted instruction** (**CAI**). If we were to categorize these applications using the traditional tutor, tool, tutee model (Taylor, 1980) introduced in Chapter 1 (page 16), the applications we discuss here would best fit within the category of computer as tutor. You might remember that the terms *tutor, tool,* and *tutee* refer to the role played by the computer. As a tutor, the computer is directly responsible for instruction. As a tool, the computer makes academic tasks such as writing and calculating easier. In the role of tutee, the student instructs the computer by writing programs. We discussed programming in Chapter 3, and we will get to a discussion of computer tools in later chapters.

Technology in the role of tutor

In the role of tutor, technology exerts a high degree of control over the information to which students are exposed and over how students interact with this material. It is expected that students will acquire knowledge or skill directly from interacting with the activities provided by the computer. As a teacher or a student, you are no doubt familiar with such instructional activities. You have been exposed to them all of your academic life. The general characteristics of control we just described for technology-based activities could just as easily apply to textbooks, workbooks, and teachers' presentations. Each type of instruction presents information and engages students in specific activities to promote understanding, retention, or skill mastery.

This chapter presents the most traditional view of the purposes of education and the roles of educators and students. This traditional view argues that technology simply provides the means for educators and students to play their roles more effectively. Other advocates of instructional technology argue for drastic reform in both the purposes of education and how these purposes are accomplished; we discuss some of these views in greater detail in other chapters. From this latter perspective, the increasing availability of new and powerful technologies provides both the opportunity and the means to accomplish rather drastic changes in schools.

Instructionism and constructionism

Some of these changes have been captured in Papert's (1993) distinction between **instructionism** and **constructionism.** Instructivist approaches seek to convey knowledge and skill as effectively as possible and argue that the route to better learning is through the improvement of instruction. The constructionist position holds that students benefit most by finding and generating their own knowledge. The teacher's primary responsibility is to support students in these tasks. Whereas some (Papert, 1993) have urged educators to take a bold step and move strongly toward a more constructionist model of education, we think that a more productive approach, and the model more likely to be implemented in current school settings, will involve students in a combination of teacher-centered (here also used to mean instruction-oriented) and student-centered learning experiences. We believe that the distinction between learning activities seeking to instruct students and learning activities requiring students to take more responsibility for what and how they learn is not necessarily the same as the distinction between passive and active learning. High-quality technology-based learning experiences of any type should engage learners in the active cognitive behaviors we identified in Chapter 2.

A MODEL OF INSTRUCTION

A complete instructional experience takes students through four stages: (1) presentation of information or learning experiences, (2) initial guidance as the student struggles to understand the information or execute the skill to be learned, (3) extended practice to provide fluency or speed or to ensure retention, and (4) assessment of student learning (Alessi & Trollip, 1991). This model is intended as a general description of the components of instruction and not a model specific to instruction delivered with technology. If it can be accepted that all four stages should always be present in some form, awareness of the stages of instruction can serve several useful purposes. Here, we use an awareness of the four stages primarily to identify and differentiate the purposes of different categories of instructional software.

Four stages of instruction

Insight, from awareness of the four stages

Some of the more important insights you may gain from analyses of this type will be the recognition of important instructional experiences not provided by specific learning tasks. Some of the more common criticisms of instructional technology can be understood in this manner. For example, classroom teachers may make assumptions or take liberties that are inappropriate. A common mistake of this type is to use materials designed for the third, or practice, stage as an initial instructional activity. Practice activities provide feedback on the quality of student performance, but this feedback is often not adequate to teach new skills to students who have little understanding of the task. Simple feedback when basic principles are poorly understood is not very helpful.

CATEGORIES OF INSTRUCTIONAL SOFTWARE

In this section, you will learn the characteristics of five categories of instructional software: tutorials, simulations, drill-and-practice applications, educational games, and exploratory environments. You will become familiar with the stages of instruction that each type of software most frequently covers and see that some categories of learning activities offer students more control and flexibility than others. Once you have completed this section, you should be able to identify some of the strengths and weaknesses of each software category, in theory and in practice. When you reach the final section of this chapter, you can apply your understanding to selecting software to use in your classrooms.

TUTORIALS

Tutorials adapt instruction to individual students.

High-quality **tutorials** should present information and guide learning—the first two stages of the instructional model (Alessi & Trollip, 1991). We usually think of tutoring as a form of instruction involving a teacher and one or two students. The individual nature of the interaction between tutor and student is assumed to offer certain advantages. In comparison to group-based instruction, tutorials can more precisely tailor the rate of progress and the content of presentations to the needs of the individual student, immediate adaptations in instruction can be made, and students can interact with the tutor. The individual nature of the tutorial approach is frequently proposed as an advantage of computer-based tutorials.

How Tutorials Function

The human tutor usually begins by presenting a small segment of information or demonstrating a specific skill. Then the tutor requires some type of activity on the student's part. Depending on the content being taught, the tutor might ask the student to respond to a question or to demonstrate the skill just presented. The student's performance allows the tutor to judge how well the student has mastered the newly acquired content or skill. This appraisal allows the tutor to do two things: (1) provide motivational feedback ("You're doing very well" or "I think we need to work on this a little more") or (2) use the quality of the student's performance to determine what to do next. Perhaps the student is having no difficulty, in which case it makes sense to move on. Perhaps the student has misunderstood something, in which case the tutor needs to explain a specific concept again.

Students can take an active role in tutorials.

In a tutorial relationship, the student can take an active role by asking for clarification or requesting that the tutor repeat an explanation. Of course, the student can also just ask questions that come to mind. If the questions are relevant to the topic, the tutor can interact with the student to explore the topic, using the student's own curiosity and background knowledge.

High-quality computer tutorials are capable of imitating some of these elements of instruction. Even relatively inexpensive computers can present information using text, sound, animation, illustrations, and video. The powerful presentation capabilities of the computer, or the computer in combination with such devices as a CD-ROM or videodisc player, provide a fairly satisfactory solution to the requirements of the first stage of instruction. A CD or a videodisc offers tremendous storage capacity and can make a great deal of information available to the student. The more subtle and dynamic instructional elements present in guiding student learning are more difficult to mimic, however. Computers can certainly gather information about student understanding or skill mastery by frequently asking questions or requiring that students perform assigned tasks. However, computers' information-gathering and interpretation skills are crude in comparison to those of human tutors.

Linear tutorials and branching tutorials

Simply communicating to a student that he or she has missed key ideas in the lesson or has not developed important skills does not satisfy the expectations of guidance. Tutorials attempt to provide additional guidance through hints and remedial explanations. In **linear tutorials,** all students work their way through the same body of information. Students performing poorly may be cycled through a particular segment of instruction a second time. In **branching tutorials,** students having difficulty receive a different instructional approach rather than returning to material that has already proved difficult for them to understand. Branching decisions can also be made based on pretest information. Questions may reveal that some students already know some of the material a particular tutorial was designed to teach. Rather than sending these students through an unnecessary sequence of instruction, they can be routed to the material they need to learn. Branching programs are more complex than linear programs but allow for greater individualization of instruction.

Evaluating Tutorials

A fair question for you to ask when evaluating the instructional potential of computer-based tutorials is: What type of instruction represents a fair comparison? Although computer-based tutorials attempt to model some key behaviors of human tutors, they cannot duplicate all of these behaviors. The human tutor can evaluate student behavior in more sophisticated ways and can respond to student needs more flexibly. Classroom teachers, however, may often be unable to function as tutors because there are too many students and too many different responsibilities in classrooms. It is possible that there are some situations in which a less-than-perfect computer-based tutor can productively augment or provide an alternative to what the classroom teacher and traditional instructional materials are able to accomplish. It is neither necessary nor desirable to eliminate the teacher's involvement totally when some instructional functions are provided by technology. It may be possible for teachers to monitor student work as the student interacts with tutorials and to respond to student questions after the learning session. The most fundamental questions in evaluating tutorials concern the clarity, efficiency, and appeal with which important information is presented.

SIMULATIONS

Controlled learning environments

Simulations provide controlled learning environments that replicate key elements of real-world environments. A simulation's focus on a limited number of key elements provides a simplified version of the real world that allows the student to learn a topic or skill very efficiently. A simulation is designed so that the actions a student takes within the simulated environment produce

Teachers should continually monitor student activity when students work with simulations, tutorials, and other CAI tools. (© Charles Abel)

results similar to those that would occur in the actual environment. The student acts, and the simulated environment reacts.

Role playing is a kind of simulation

Simulations can be used to learn about properties of physical or biological objects or the principles by which a variety of physical, social, and biological phenomena function. You may already have some experiences with simulations. Role-playing experiences, for example, are a type of simulation. Before student teachers go into elementary or secondary schools to work with students, they commonly role-play such skills as leading a discussion, giving a short lecture, asking questions and providing feedback, and working with a misbehaving student. Instead of dealing with the complexities in an actual classroom, role-playing experiences tend to focus on a particular skill, such as leading a discussion. Computer-based simulations attempt to meet similar instructional objectives.

What can simulations be used for?

Simulations can be used before the formal presentation of new material to pique students' interest, activate what students already know about the topic, and provide a concrete example to relate to the more general discussion that follows. Simulations can also be used after students have been exposed to a new topic. In this approach, the simulation allows students to attempt to transfer what they have learned to an actual application and perhaps to reveal any misconceptions they may have. Research (Brant, Hooper, & Sugrue, 1991) suggests that using a simulation prior to formal instruction is particularly effective. Simulations can be used for all four stages of instruction: presentation, guidance, practice, and assessment (Alessi & Trollip, 1991). Although this does not mean that every simulation is intended to provide a stand-alone educational experience, it does imply that simulations are the most versatile of the different categories of computer-assisted instruction.

Operation: Frog—An Example of a Simulation

Do you remember dissecting a frog in high school biology? Do you remember your reaction and the reaction of some of your classmates when your teacher explained that before you could begin the dissection, you would have to "pith" your frog? (To pith a frog, you use a dissection needle to destroy the connection between the brain and body so that body organs such as the heart will still be functioning and can be observed during the dissection.) *Operation: Frog* is a computer program designed to allow students to simulate the dissection of a frog. And, no, you don't have to pith the frog before you begin! The program presents students with a set of dissection tools, a dissection tray complete with specimen, and an examination tray for organizing and examining organs removed from the frog (see Figure 4.3).

Informative text, labeled graphics (see Figure 4.4), and digitized photographs from an actual dissection are available for each organ. Occasional animations (for instance, of blood flow) or QuickTime movies are also provided. (QuickTime is a common format for presenting digital video on a variety of computers.)

FIGURE 4.3
Screen Display for *Operation: Frog*—Dissection Pan and Examination Tray

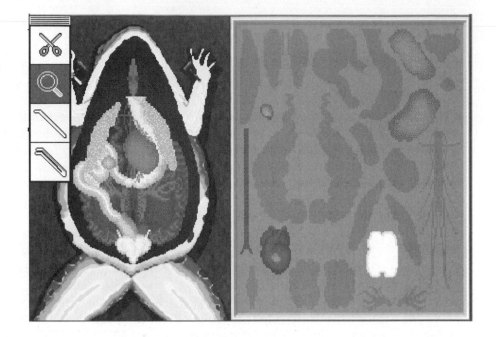

Operation: Frog exemplifies some of the features of simulations. Simulations tend to present a simplified version of the real thing and attempt to focus learners on key ideas, skills, or components. In contrast to the clumsiness and messiness that comes with dissecting a frog, work with the simulated frog uses simpler procedures and reveals simplified information. When simulated incisions are made at the proper locations, the skin magically disappears. Attempted incisions at other points are ignored. In fact, it is impossible to cut at

Learners focus on key ideas, skills, and components.

FIGURE 4.4
Exported Graphic from *Operation: Frog*

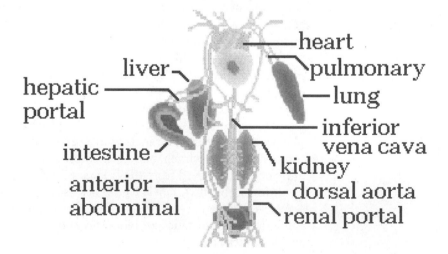

an inappropriate point or to move a body part that the simulation does not intend the student to move. Developing the physical dexterity necessary to use dissection instruments is not a target behavior, so there is no attempt to teach these skills. The organs to be removed at a particular stage of the simulation are designated by color to make them easier to find. There is no need to separate the skin from other tissues or to remove abdominal muscles. Learning about the frog's musculature is not an objective of the simulation, so the abdominal muscles are not present in the simulation. Based on the original description of *Operation: Frog*, you may be able to list several other ways in which the simulation has been simplified. The simulated dissection clearly focuses the student on the location of specific organs within the body of the frog.

Attributes of Simulations, Learning, and Transfer

The extent to which a simulation mimics reality is called **fidelity** (Alessi, 1988). When you make decisions about instruction or selecting instructional

Focus

Instructional Software on the World Wide Web

The better Web sites do a great job of presenting information, but typically do not engage learners in any other components of instruction. There are exceptions, of course, and a few Web sites do engage students in ways that are similar to the techniques used by the instructional software presented in this chapter (Kinzie, Larsen, Burch, & Boker, 1996). Why aren't many instructional applications available on the Web? A number of factors are probably involved. First, the speed of Internet connections available in many schools is slow and may make certain experiences too tedious. The transitions from one view of the frog to another that are nearly instantaneous in *Operation: Frog* may take 30 seconds or more in a Web-based dissection. Second, Web applications are very good at serving information on request, but are typically poor at accepting, in-

terpreting, and storing the many sources of information learners might provide as they work. Even the most basic tutorial programs keep a record of learner responses to provide feedback to the learner and to make decisions about when he or she should go on to new material. This would be an uncommon feature in a Web application. Finally, commercial uses of the Internet are emerging slowly. Instructional software is readily available because it can be sold to schools. Most examples of instructional applications on the Web are demonstration projects developed by a university or company.

Although the current offerings are limited, the long-term perspective is positive. Ways to overcome the limitations will likely emerge soon, and the Internet will become a source of powerful instructional applications.✱

materials, an important issue to consider is how fidelity relates to learning and application. When looked at beside an actual dissected frog, the various forms of simplification identified in *Operation: Frog* do result in lower fidelity. Your initial reaction might be that if it is practical, experience with the real thing is always best. But consider, for example, learning to fly an airplane. Would it be ideal to expose a novice to experiences in an actual plane? Even if the issues of cost and safety were ignored or somehow taken care of, the situation of highest fidelity is still not necessarily the best learning situation. The student would be too anxious and the situation too confusing to allow much learning (Alessi & Trollip, 1991). Similar situations may happen in classroom settings more familiar to you. In presenting new concepts or principles, most experienced instructors initially ignore the exceptions and complications that might just confuse and increase the anxiety of students. The initial presentation describes concepts and principles with less than perfect fidelity. It appears that a moderate degree of fidelity is best for initial learning.

Applying or transferring knowledge

Now consider the student's ability to apply or transfer what he or she has learned. (The relationship of learning, the context of learning, and transfer was discussed in Chapter 2.) Transfer depends on the degree of learning and the extent to which a student has contextualized what has been learned or related what has been learned to the situations in which the skills or knowledge are to be applied. Here we confront a dilemma: extremely high fidelity would appear to reduce learning but increase transfer. At the extremes, the problems of high and low fidelity are obvious. With no learning, there is nothing that can be transferred, no matter how similar the learning environment is to the eventual application environment. The example of the novice pilot in an actual airplane fits this case. It is also possible to represent situations at the other extreme. The problem of inert knowledge (see Chapter 2, page 66) describes situations in which learning has occurred but the experiences surrounding learning make it unlikely that the knowledge will be used. Under more moderate circumstances, learning and transfer occur but are both somewhat inefficient. A level of fidelity could very likely be identified that would confuse but not totally baffle the student. The realism of the learning environment increases the likelihood that the student, after an initial struggle to overcome the confusion, will be able to apply what has been learned.

Advantages of Simulations

Simulations have several potential advantages over allowing students to experience the real world. We have already considered how the simplification allowed by simulations can help learners focus on critical information or skills and make learning easier. Simulations can also allow students to observe phenomena that are not normally visible, control processes that are not normally controllable, or participate in activities that would normally be too expensive or too dangerous. Simulations make certain experiences practical and other experiences possible. There are other advantages too.

Concreteness. Consider first that many things that students study cannot really be observed. You probably learned about the relative positions of the planets revolving around the sun, how electrons flow in electrical circuits, the movement of glaciers, continental drift, economic principles of supply and demand, how a signal is passed along and between neurons, and the interrelatedness of populations in a food chain. Clearly certain phenomena are difficult or impossible to observe.

Putting objects and phenomena in observable form

Sometimes the object of study has to be made larger (the neuron) and sometimes smaller (the solar system or continents). Sometimes the phenomena have to be speeded up (movement of glaciers and continents; the passage of generations of plants and animals) and sometimes slowed down (movement of electrons within electrical circuits). Sometimes what you view in the real world has to be put in a different form for you to observe it at all. The biome simulation we used to introduce this chapter and simulations of different economic principles often represent the relationships among several factors graphically, as with the economic principles of supply and demand or the biological interdependence of predator and prey. Whether the technique involves making the object of study smaller or larger, the phenomena faster or slower, or just providing a way to visualize complex relationships, simulations give students concrete representations to ponder.

Control. A second valuable characteristic of simulations is the opportunity they provide for students to make decisions with logical consequences. Simulations put students in control of situations with which they would seldom be allowed to experiment under any other circumstance.

Students build their own explanations.

For example, a simple business simulation might be based on mathematical expressions that define the relationship among such variables as money spent on advertising, the price the customer has to pay for the product, the number of items sold, and profit. As they work with this simulation, students might try to maximize profit and control both the price and the cost of advertising. The computer would inform the student of the number of items sold and the profit earned. As advertising increases and price decreases, customers will buy more of the product. However, total profit will not necessarily increase because of increased expenses (advertising) and a lower profit on each item sold. The ideal solution to the simulation will depend on how the simulation's designers have weighted the value of spending a certain amount of money on advertising and how they have decided changes in price will influence the number of items sold.

Cost-Effectiveness. Sadly, educators have to be constantly aware of how much money educational experiences cost. This reality applies to decisions regarding the purchase of hardware and software, but it also applies to the experiences or materials that simulations might replace.

The components that physics students need to assemble electrical circuits are costly. Certain components, such as transistors, can easily be ruined if students make mistakes in the way they assemble circuits. A computer program allowing students to simulate the assembly of circuits does not require that additional components be purchased when students make errors. In certain situations, simulations provide quality experiences at a reasonable cost.

Safety.   There are some things that students should learn that would be dangerous for them to experience directly. Some experiments in chemistry or projects exploring how electrical devices work may be too dangerous for elementary or secondary school students. The use of simulators in pilot training is an example of the value of simulation in increasing the safety of training experiences.

DRILL AND PRACTICE

Learning basic skills

You probably take your ability to recognize and spell common words for granted. Of course, this was not always the case. Back in early elementary school, you spent a good deal of time becoming familiar with words. Do you remember what you did to learn basic word recognition skills? Obviously you spent time reading. You probably also spent time completing worksheets or some other type of activity that emphasized specific reading skills. The activities focused on specific skills could probably be classified as drills.

If you have not experienced computer-based drill, you may want to consider the following example. Word Scramble is one of several activities contained on the Letter Sounds CD from the Tenth Planet Explores Literacy Series. Word Scramble would qualify as a drill activity specifically designed to familiarize the learner with the consonant-vowel-consonant word pattern. Skills in letter-sound correspondence and letter patterns are important components contributing to word identification and spelling.

The *Word Scramble* program follows a simple repetitive pattern. It presents a picture and pronounces the word the picture represents. The program also presents the letters spelling the word in a scrambled order. The learner's task is to drag the individual letters from the box in which they appear to the word construction box (the lined stationery box in Figure 4.5) and arrange them to spell the target word. Clicking the arrow adds the correctly spelled word to the learner's word bank (see Figure 4.5). The word bank continues to grow as the learner works with the program. The word bank also serves as a mechanism connecting several of the learning activities found on the CD.

The designers of the Tenth Planet Explores Literacy Series recommend that fundamental skills be developed through a diversity of learning activities and suggest hands-on activities that can be coordinated with the computer experiences. The designers have given thought to other important issues as well. Evaluating student progress is an important part of any learning activity. The Letter-Sounds CD comes with a management system that stores data

FIGURE 4.5
Screen Display from *Word Scramble*

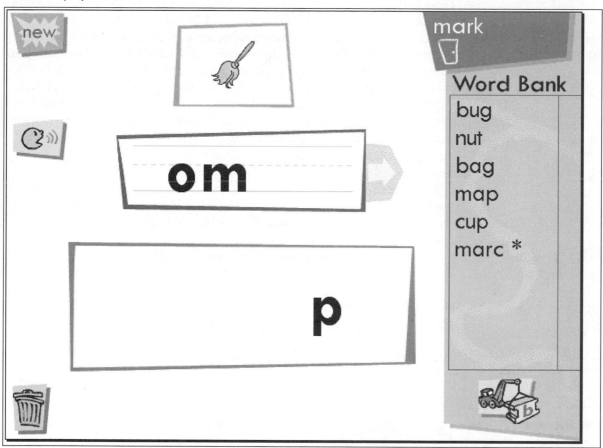

generated by student activity. One particular activity, the Word Building Tool (see the construction equipment image in the lower right corner of the *Word Scramble* screen in Figure 4.5), encourages students to try to spell words they know. The idea is that students will use the Word Building Tool to try out skills they have developed with the drill activities. Words generated with the Word Building Tool appear within the Word Bank marked with an asterisk to indicate they have been added by the learner and are stored along with entries generated by drill activities for the teacher to examine. As you might expect, words created with the Word Building Tool may not be spelled correctly. However, the teacher can glean a great deal of useful information from the student's efforts. What words did the student try to spell? Do the attempts at phonetic spelling indicate an understanding of letter-sound correspondence? Archiving some of these efforts over time provides portfolio entries documenting changes in student understanding.

Applications of Drill-and-Practice Software

Providing extended practice

Drill-and-practice software is developed to meet the needs of the third stage of instruction: extended practice. Students' initial exposure to academic facts or skills is seldom sufficient for an adequate level of mastery. Extended study is required before the facts or skills can be considered learned. The exact proficiency that students should develop varies with the type of content. For factual information (e.g., the product of 2 × 2, the capital of West Virginia), the expectation is that students will be able to retrieve the information from memory quickly, smoothly, and with few errors. Students are also expected to perform many tasks that require mastery of a routine (e.g., complete long division problems with accuracy, type 40 words per minute). You will typically hear drill-and-practice software discussed as if it were a single category. Actually, **drill** activities concern factual memorization, and **practice** concerns the development of skill fluency (Price, 1991). But we are not considering instructional software in great detail, so we follow the tradition of treating drill-and-practice software as a single category.

Drill and practice to develop typing skills

Consider an activity designed to develop skill fluency. *Microtype* (see Figure 4.6) is a popular practice activity for developing touch-typing skills. Students progress through a series of lessons. Each lesson begins with a review of skills from previous lessons and a brief tutorial introducing the skills or letters for the current lesson (such as *f* and *b*). The lesson begins with practice on the individual letters and simple letter combinations (*f b bf bf fib*), advances to simple phrases (to *fib* or *rob*), and then moves to timed lines (see Figure 4.6)

FIGURE 4.6
Screen Display from *Microtype* Practice Activity

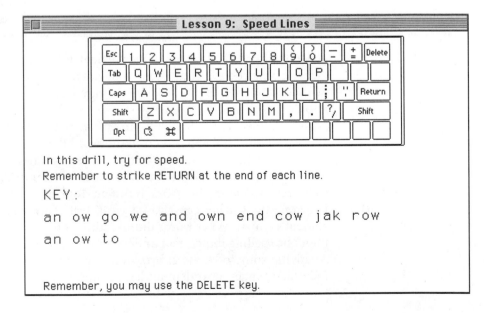

and timed paragraphs. Each lesson concludes with a simple game in which the student types lines of text to reveal parts of a picture.

Typing is a skill we want students to be able to perform accurately, swiftly, and automatically. **Automaticity** frees some of the limited capacity of short-term memory for other uses (see Chapter 2, pages 43 through 45). Usually it is desirable that students not think about their finger placement or the location of the letters as they type. Extended practice is about the only way to accomplish automaticity.

Focus of Drill and Practice

When should drill-and-practice software be used?

Whereas other types of instructional software may be used for several of the phases of instruction, drill-and-practice software has a more limited focus. It should not be used to introduce new areas because it has a narrow approach and is not suited to helping students understand new material. Drill-and-practice activities are appropriate after students have advanced past the guidance phase of instruction. Teachers need to be aware of this issue and emphasize drill and practice when fact availability and skill fluency are appropriate goals.

EDUCATIONAL GAMES

When are instructional activities categorized as games?

Instructional activities are categorized as **games** when the activities emphasize competition and entertainment. If the activity has a winner or a loser or focuses the student on competing against established records or standards, the activity has gamelike qualities. Games also employ fantasy, action, uncertainty, and similar features to make the activity interesting for the players. You will probably recognize that many of these same features were present in the activities already described as examples of other CAI categories. Commercial instructional software often combines elements of several different categories of software. If software is to be labeled, it is often necessary to determine subjectively the degree to which certain characteristics are present. Is some entertainment used to motivate learning, or does some learning result as a by-product of play? Some have begun describing some game activities as **edutainment.**

Examples of Educational Games

The Oregon Trail

Certain educational games have been popular for a long time and seem to embody characteristics teachers find of value. *The Oregon Trail* and *Where in the World Is Carmen Sandiego?* fall into this category. *The Oregon Trail* was first released in 1978 in a text-only format.

The Oregon Trail, now a CD-based multimedia product, takes the student on a covered wagon journey from Independence, Missouri, to Oregon in 1865. The game puts the student in the role of expedition leader, and the outcome of the journey depends to some degree on the decisions he or she makes along the way. What items should be purchased to outfit the wagon as the trip begins? How far should the wagon attempt to travel in a day? Should the wagon stop at a fort for supplies? Stops at landmarks, forts, and towns engage the leader in "conversations" that can be useful in revealing obstacles that are likely to be encountered and in suggesting ways to survive these difficulties. The leader may learn how to cross the river or when to hunt for food.

We categorize *The Oregon Trail* as a game rather than as an authentic simulation because of its emphasis on entertainment and the general nature of its historical experiences. The game does provide a sense of the experiences of the early pioneers and may be a useful way to generate interest in a unit about this time period. Educators have taken to supplementing the game activity in a number of ways. One approach is to have students keep notes as they play the game and then write diary entries compatible with their notes. *The Oregon Trail* is so popular that World Wide Web sites have been developed or located to accompany the game. Such sites may provide current scenes along the route of the trail, related historical information, or the perspective of Native Americans from the region.

The Carmen Sandiego series

The Carmen Sandiego series (*Where in the World Is Carmen Sandiego? Where in the USA Is Carmen Sandiego? Where in Time Is Carmen Sandiego?* and others) puts the student in the role of detective. A crime has been committed, and the thief is dashing from city to city or country to country (this aspect varies with the version of the game). As the detective, the student must attempt to trail Carmen or her partners, using the clues that are revealed (e.g., the kind of currency the villain is using, some characteristic of the city). Reference materials (*World Almanac Book of Facts* reference guide) supplied with the software help students interpret the clues. The newest CD-ROM version includes colorful graphics and allows the detective to question a witness, search the crime scene, compare notes with other detectives, log evidence in a database, and issue warrants. Students can play the game over and over again without encountering the same case. The game acquaints students with several aspects of geography (location of cities and countries, factual information about specific places), requires the use of reference materials, and encourages note taking.

SimLife

Now consider something a bit more exotic. *SimLife* gives a player the tools to create a world complete with oceans, mountains, and deserts; to populate this world with plants and animals; to mix in a few natural and man-made disasters; and, finally, to stand back and watch what happens. Which plants and animals will survive? Will the living organisms mutate, and what will the surviving species look like five hundred years after the artificial world was created? It is nearly impossible to describe the full scope of this activity. Players can manipulate nearly any imaginable characteristic of the world or the flora and fauna living within the artificial world. Temperature, soil quality, characteristics of the seasons, rainfall, and many other features can be precisely determined. For each animal or plant, the player can adjust sliders, buttons, and

FIGURE 4.7
Screen Display of
Genome Tool and
Sample World from
SimLife

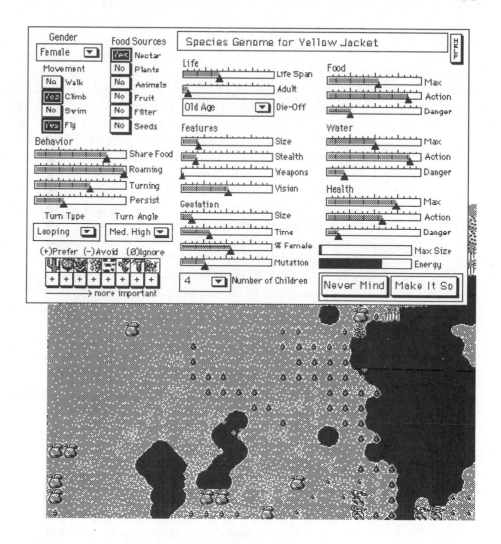

menus to set numerous characteristics (see Figure 4.7). A different set of controls allows characteristics such as intelligence, method of locomotion, and preferred habitat to be established.

How *SimLife* can be entertaining may be obvious, but it may not be apparent how it can be enjoyed as a game. Like so many other features of this activity, players create their own games. The complex data-acquisition features provide plenty of opportunities for scorekeeping or establishing standards of excellence. Perhaps the goal is to create a creature that can most quickly and extensively populate an unknown world or a world that will sustain the most species of plants and animals for five years. As soon as players can agree on a challenge, the game is afoot.

Classroom Uses of Games

Benefits of educational games

Teachers use educational games in several ways. Some, such as *The Oregon Trail* and *SimLife,* provide interesting ways to initiate related areas of study. Like simulations, carefully selected games may activate existing knowledge and pique student interest in the more traditional academic work that follows.

Although games are often equated with competition, they can also be used to enhance cooperation. In some games, the competition is with the computer, not with other students. The complexity of some games provides opportunities for teamwork. *SimLife,* for example, encourages extensive record keeping and planning. Students can share these tasks and benefit from opportunities to discuss strategy or evaluate game consequences. The Carmen Sandiego games make heavy use of travel guides and almanacs. Several students can work together to look up information.

Finally, teachers may also use educational games to reward hard work or achievement. There is nothing wrong with using technology in this way, but you should be aware of potential problems. Sometimes students who always get their work done first are the only students who get to spend time with the computer games. Teachers need to take care that computer games do not become an exclusive opportunity for certain categories of students. Teachers must also be aware of the proportion of precious computer and classroom time devoted to games. Game use must be kept in check, and care must be taken that time on the computer does not become play time.

EXPLORATORY ENVIRONMENTS

Computer-based worlds to explore and manipulate

Exploratory environments provide manageable and responsive computer-based worlds for students to explore and manipulate (Hsu, Chapelle, & Thompson, 1993; Joyce, 1988). These computer-based activities have also been described as intentional learning environments (Scardamalia, Bereiter, McLean, Swallow, & Woodruff, 1989) and interactive environments (Kozma, 1991). In a way, exploratory environments attempt to place the learner in a "real world" situation and require the learner to engage in tasks authentic to that situation.

An exploratory environment offers elements for students to work with and a setting in which the manipulation of these elements allows students to explore a cohesive body of information or a rule system (Hsu et al., 1993). The specific nature of the elements, information base, or rule system depends on the content area the environment was developed to represent. Exploratory environments present information, but they are not directive in the manner of tutorials. The material that students spend time examining or manipulating is largely self-selected. One difference among the types of exploratory environments mentioned here is in whether they contain a task, goal, or problem to be solved. One difficulty with these nondirective environments is that a rich database of information is not always enough to engage many students in active learning. So whether an assignment is embedded in the exploratory environment or suggested by a teacher, guided interaction with the environment appears to be most productive. This issue will be raised again after you have had an opportunity to become more familiar with exploratory environments.

Characteristics of Exploratory Environments

It is difficult to list an exact set of requirements for an exploratory environment. One consistent characteristic, though, is a high degree of *learner control*. Clearly, exploratory environments encourage and may actually require that students exercise control over their experiences. The environment is responsive to the student and tends to offer a great deal of flexibility in what might be done. *Flexibility* is a second characteristic of exploratory environments. Students can typically do many different things. They can even do the same thing in several different ways, revisiting the same concepts from different perspectives or using different approaches. Exploratory environments are designed to provide opportunities for active learning that are anchored in realistic situations, experiences, and goals.

Active learning anchored in realistic situations, experiences, and goals

Hypermedia and Interactive Videodisc Environments

Environments developed using hypermedia or interactive videodisc technology resemble simulations in many ways and allow the student to explore settings rich in information. Some environments of this type allow the student to exercise control only through movement. The student moves from setting to setting, and each setting reveals certain information or makes certain experiences available. Settings may reflect different physical locations (different regions of a state) or points in time (important dates in history). Other environments allow the student to select an action from among a specific set of actions. The student selects this action in a particular setting and then experiences the consequences of that action. Programs of this type are useful in representing social situations. For example, a brief scenario might describe a social dilemma such as a classroom disciplinary situation. The software might then present alternative courses of action the teacher might take. When the student using the software selects one of these alternatives, the social interaction moves to some kind of conclusion based on the alternative selected.

Exploring settings that are rich in information

If you are familiar with "choose your own adventure" books, you have some understanding of how one approach works. In a "choose your own adventure," the reader follows the text to a choice point and is presented several options. A page number accompanies each alternative, and the reader moves to the page number of the desired choice to follow the story. The computer can control videodisc presentations in a similar way. Choices allow students control, and greater control allows the creation of more complex exploratory environments.

The Adventures of Jasper Woodbury.   *The Adventures of Jasper Woodbury* is a series of learning activities based on a combination of video, text, and computer software. Originally developed by the Learning Technology Center of Vanderbilt University as a research program focused on contextualized learning, the videodisc adventures are now available commercially to schools.

The Jasper adventures present students with believable stories, each ending with a challenge. The challenge is a complex problem that includes several subproblems. The typical classroom approach is to have the entire class view one of the adventures and then have small groups of students work to propose solutions to the challenge at the end of the adventure. To solve the challenges, which require a problem-solving approach and focus on mathematical concepts, students have to examine the content of the videodisc carefully for data relevant to the problems. The developers of the series argue that this "embedded data design" improves the transfer value of skills that students develop.

A problem-solving approach

In *The Big Splash,* one of the Jasper adventures, a high school student decides to help the school fund the purchase of a video camera by setting up a "Dunk a Teacher" booth at the school carnival. Because the dunking booth will cost some money, the student approaches the principal for a loan. The principal agrees to provide the loan if the student can produce a business plan demonstrating the likelihood that the project will make a profit. To produce the business plan, the student must estimate the potential revenue and probable expenses. Surveying students to determine whether they would spend money to dunk a teacher and how much they would be willing to pay for the chance determine the potential revenue. Consideration of how to conduct a survey provides an opportunity for the exploration of research methodology and statistics.

The student eventually locates a dunking machine and a pool. Because the pool must be rented by the day, the time the pool is in the possession of the school is an issue. The dimensions of the pool, but not the capacity, are known. The amount of time required to fill and drain the pool poses another problem to take into account. Several methods for filling the pool are available and vary in cost and risk. The school hose is available but slow. A water truck is available, but it charges by the mile and has an added fee each time it is filled. The water truck also cannot carry enough water in one trip to fill the pool. The fire chief volunteers the local fire truck but warns that the truck will not be available if a fire should occur. This list should give you some idea of what would have to be considered in producing the business plan.

Analogous problems and other content areas

The Jasper adventures have also been developed to be extended to analogous problems and other content areas. The analogous problems modify the original story to create opportunities for students to transfer what they have learned. For example, students can consider whether a Jell-O slide would generate more income than the dunking pool. To extend the Jasper adventures into other content areas, teachers are given suggestions for further study following up on some issue raised in the adventure. For example, *The Big Splash* raises the issue of taking out a loan. Students might explore how to apply for a loan at a bank, how the bank makes money on the loan, what collateral is, and other concepts related to the lending of money.

Hypermedia Exploratory Environments: Exploring the Nardoo.

Hypermedia allows the integration of text, drawings, sounds, video, and animation in a common computer-accessible database, and the purposeful exploration of these information sources can provide effective learning experiences (Scardamalia et al., 1989). *Exploring the Nardoo* is an exploratory environment that allows students to conduct biological, geological, and chemical investigations of an imaginary Australian river. Problems and the information to suggest solutions to these problems are embedded within a complex hypermedia environment. This learning environment attempts to create authentic learning activities that are situated within a realistic setting (Brown et al., 1989). The software was developed by a team of instructional designers at Australia's University of Wollongong in collaboration with the New South Wales Department of Land and Water Conservation.

An authentic context for understanding nature

The logical place to begin our description is at the Water Research Centre (see Figure 4.8). Here the student meets three scientists who describe their own investigations and provide assistance. Most of the items visible in the Research Centre serve as links to information sources. For example, the River Investigations board at the rear of the room explains the details of thirteen investigations that are in progress. The filing cabinet (just visible in the lower right-hand corner) contains files of documents related to many of the issues raised by the embedded investigations. The clipboards (above the computer) provide access to radio and television programs and the office computer provides a way to search all of the embedded resources.

Tasks that encourage students to gather and analyze information

Explorations are not confined to the information sources located within the Water Research Centre office. Learners explore the river itself. They can visit four regions of the river as it flows from mountains to plains and can explore each region during four time periods covering sixty years. Learners are provided with a multipurpose tool, the personal digital assistant (PDA), which allows them to move about the hypermedia environment (e.g., between the river and Research Centre, among regions of the river), collect and organize data, and generate reports. In Figure 4.9, you can observe one use of the PDA. In this case, the PDA's data gathering tool (the eye dropper) is being used to gather two types of data (river flow rate and turbidity) from the middle of the river channel. These are two of the many measurements of stream quality that can be taken.

We have become interested in factors that influence flooding (see Chapter 1), and the river simulation allowed a test of a hypothesis that interests us

FIGURE 4.8
The Water Research Centre in *Exploring the Nardoo*

personally: that farming practices that reduce natural vegetation and encourage rapid drainage of water from the land increase the likelihood of flooding. One way to test this hypothesis within the Nardoo environment was to attempt to gather data on river rate and turbidity at approximately the same river location before and after the land was heavily farmed. In Figure 4.9, you will note that much of the vegetation has been cleared on the right-hand side of the river, and the data indicate greater turbidity and a more rapid flow of water than when these same measurements were taken at an earlier time period. The PDA shows these data recorded after visiting two eras in the history of the river. As expected, the rate at which the river flows and the turbidity are both greater after land along the river has been developed for farming. In reality, you cannot travel back in time, but time travel might be possible in an exploratory environment.

It is important to consider how students might use this rich, interactive information environment so that meaningful learning occurs. Without a task or problem to solve, students might simply move within the hypermedia environment, seeing what they can find and what tools do what. The richness and interactivity of the software are entertaining to explore, but do not guar-

FIGURE 4.9
Personal Digital Assistant Used to Measure River Flow and Turbidity in *Exploring the Nardoo*

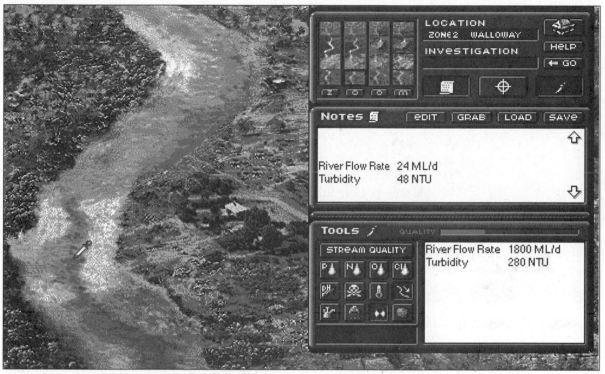

antee meaningful learning. Such behavior would be similar to the rote discovery behavior described in Chapter 2 (page 56). The investigations embedded within the hypermedia environment provide tasks for individual students or groups of students to accomplish. For example, in one task students are told, "A conference is being held dealing with the sustainability of current farming practices and the effect they have on the environment. Students from your school have been invited to make a multimedia presentation at the convention dealing with the impact of farming practices on the river environment. In your presentation you should provide a summary that shows the variety of farming types present in the Walloway region."

Activities that challenge students

The investigations that students are asked to complete are challenging in several ways. Students may lack the background to anticipate the types of data that may be relevant to the tasks they have been asked to accomplish. They may also be inexperienced in crafting the required product to summarize what they have learned. The hypermedia environment provides several mechanisms for supporting students in accomplishing these tasks (see the discussion of scaffolding on page 73). For example, the scientists from the Water

Resource Centre assigned to the investigations are available to offer advice. The software even provides scaffolding for the authoring tasks that students are to accomplish based on their explorations. Students can load genre templates that provide advice on how to structure presentations of various types (see Figure 4.10). *Exploring the Nardoo* was designed to engage students in demanding investigations, reflections, and communication tasks, but also to support student work in ways that allow them to take on these authentic challenges (Gordon, 1996).

Effectiveness of Exploratory Environments

With the exception of evaluations conducted with the Jasper Woodbury interactive video materials (Cognition and Technology Group, 1990, 1996; Goldman et al., 1996), exploratory environments and the learning tasks they enable have not been thoroughly evaluated. The focus on embedded authen-

FIGURE 4.10
Scaffolding to Support Student Authoring Tasks in *Exploring the Nardoo*

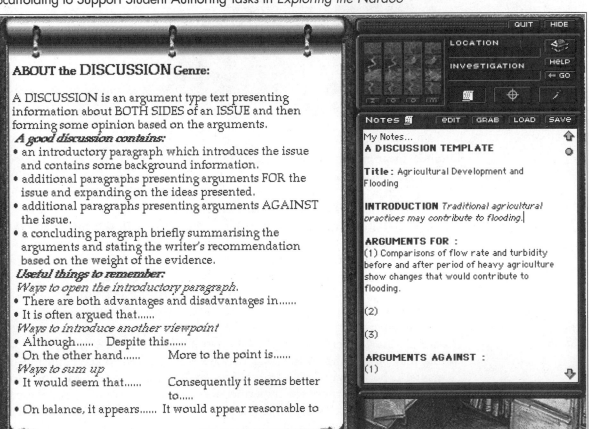

tic learning emphasizes skills not easily evaluated using traditional research methods (Greeno, 1998). The exploratory work conducted with the Jasper Woodbury adventures is encouraging. It appears that the realistic and dynamic experiences provided by video encourage students to develop mental models to account for the phenomena they have observed. Learning is described as being anchored in realistic problems and experiences provided through interactive video.

The importance of structuring tasks or problems

One element that experiences with the Jasper Woodbury adventures and with the hypermedia environment of *Exploring the Nardoo* have suggested is important is the presence of structuring tasks or problems. Experience has suggested that it should not be assumed that students will engage in the most desirable types of active exploration or generative thinking when exposed to exploratory environments (Gordon, 1996; Grabe, 1992; Hsu et al., 1993).

HOW TO EVALUATE AND USE COMPUTER-ASSISTED INSTRUCTION

A great deal of research has been conducted evaluating the effectiveness of computer tutorials and other forms of CAI. Over the past twenty-five years, well over two hundred studies have been completed (Lepper & Gurtner, 1989). Because of this huge volume of information, it is common to rely on reviews in evaluating the effectiveness of CAI (Fletcher-Flinn & Gravatt, 1995; Liao, 1992; Niemiec, Samson, Weinstein, & Walberg, 1989; Niemiec & Walberg, 1987; Thomas & Hooper, 1991). Tutorials and drill activities have been studied most extensively. These studies have found that technology seems to offer a moderate advantage over traditional instruction, with tutorials somewhat more effective than drill activities, particularly for younger and less able students (Lepper & Gurtner, 1989). The effect is labeled "moderate" because 66 percent of students taught using CAI performed better than the average for a group taught more traditionally. One of the more recent reviews compared more current CAI research with older studies and suggests that the advantage of CAI may be increasing. However, the general benefits are still described as moderate (Fletcher-Flinn & Gravatt, 1995). A review of the research evaluating simulations reached a similar conclusion (Thomas & Hooper, 1991). With the exception of LOGO (see Chapter 4) and the work done with the Jasper Woodbury interactive video materials, research evaluating exploratory learning environments is much less extensive.

A moderate advantage for CAI?

Even the moderate advantage for CAI instruction has been questioned, however. Critics point out that studies producing no advantage for CAI are less likely to be published, that many studies involving CAI do not control study time to make certain that students receiving CAI do not work longer, and that computers in many situations are so novel that students may respond to them more positively because of the uniqueness of learning with technology. Others accept the findings that CAI may offer an advantage but argue that CAI materials are often just more carefully developed and that there is no intrinsic advantage in the actual method of instruction (Clark, 1985; Fletcher-Flinn & Gravatt, 1995).

HELPING TEACHERS WITH CONTRADICTORY FINDINGS

Most teachers do not follow the research reports that appear in research journals; nevertheless, they should pay some attention to the general conclusions of educational researchers because these findings should eventually be translated into changes in classroom practice. The popular press (e.g., Healy, 1998; Oppenheimer, 1997) has also raised questions that educators need to consider. For example, educators advocating large investments to increase student access to technology are asked to defend these requests given the lack of research demonstrating consistent benefits to students.

So what should you make of these confusing research findings related to instructional applications? At present, teachers should not expect miracles from technology (or from any other approach to instruction, for that matter). However, when used thoughtfully and with common sense, many commercial products make learning opportunities available to students. The "big question"—Is it better?—is probably naive and very difficult to answer given the complexities of classroom learning. Researchers and educators might most productively focus instead on how best to use computers to support learning by asking general questions about what factors improve learning (Hannafin, Hannafin, Hooper, Rieber, & Kini, 1996):

General questions about how to improve learning

◆ How can learners be most effectively oriented to important lesson content?

◆ What are the most effective ways to use multimedia sources to encourage learning and understanding?

◆ How can learners be assisted in detecting and responding to errors in their understanding?

◆ How can the sequencing of content be best adapted to individual learner needs?

◆ How can learners develop the ability to apply what they know?

◆ What factors motivate learners?

Clearly, instructional software does not eliminate the need for teaching, nor does it eliminate the need for teacher supervision. Students will have questions in response to a learning activity presented by the computer just as they may have questions during a science laboratory or about a social studies

Keep the phases of instruction in mind.

reading assignment. Teachers need to take an active role in structuring the learning environment , and this includes the use of instructional applications.

We suggest that teachers keep the four phases of instruction in mind as they consider instructional software. Table 4.1 summarizes our comments regarding how different types of software benefit students. In general, the ratings indicate that instructional software provides positive but incomplete experiences. The summary also suggests that guiding students, especially in ways necessary to develop complex mental skills, is frequently beyond the current capabilities of technology. Recall from Chapter 2 that techniques such as cognitive apprenticeship attempt to model effective thinking and problem-solving behaviors and don't just help students identify problem areas. Teachers must continue to provide some of the guidance necessary for effective learning, which will often mean that teachers and students may want to interact together with the technology.

There may be some situations that lend themselves especially well to CAI (Alessi & Trollip, 1991). Many of the following suggestions appear throughout this chapter but are summarized here for emphasis. Technology is often of unique value when:

Summary of situations where CAI is of unique value

◆ Prolonged individual practice is necessary (math facts, typing).
◆ Traditional approaches fail to make the content exciting (history).
◆ Learning the skill presents a significant danger to the learner (flying an airplane).
◆ Concepts to be learned are difficult to visualize or conceptualize (calculus, physics).
◆ Students progress at significantly different rates and need to proceed at their own pace (any content area that builds heavily on prerequisite knowledge).

TABLE 4.1   Potential Software Effectiveness, by Stage of Instruction

		COMPONENTS OF INSTRUCTION			
		PRESENTATION	GUIDANCE	PRACTICE	ASSESSMENT
APPLICATIONS	Tutorial	* * *	*		
	Simulation	* *	*	* *	* *
	Drill-and-Practice			* * *	
	Educational game	*	*	* *	*
	Exploratory environments	* *	*	*	*

Note: We have ranked effectiveness on a scale of 0–3.

◆ Practical limits of time, space, or money make certain experiences impractical (genetics experiments).

Individual teachers might use this list as they think about the experiences that they want to provide their students.

CONSTRUCTIVISM AND INSTRUCTIONAL SOFTWARE

Using software in a constructionist classroom

Do the types of software we have described here allow a constructivist approach? This is a tricky question, and we think that the answer depends on how you define constructivism and which category of instructional software is being considered. It also depends on how software is used. Instructional software does not totally control the learning environment; the teacher can and should take responsibility for how instructional software will be used. In an interesting way of making this point, Squires (1999) proposes the phrase "subversive use." *Subversive use* refers to situations in which the teacher may imagine a creative use for a learning activity not considered or promoted by the original developers. The point is that a student's experience with instructional software does not define the total learning experience, and the teacher can incorporate the computer task into a broader activity. When we suggested that a student might be asked to create a diary based on his or her experience with *Oregon Trail*, we were suggesting a "subversive use" of *Oregon Trail*—that is, one not required by the software designers. After working individually with *Eco-Simulator*, students might be brought together and asked to discuss what they had discovered about food chains. How are organisms at the top and bottom of food chains different? Are humans part of food chains? Are humans always at the top of food chains? Instructional activities can be extended to create a more active learning experience.

Working on an instructional program with a partner represents one way to change the nature of the learning activity. In many situations, assigning two students to a computer is a matter of practicality, but it also represents a way to change the nature of the learning experience. Research suggests that cooperative learning seems to benefit students working with tutorials (but not drills) and that students should receive some training in how to learn cooperatively to benefit from cooperative experiences (Susman, 1998). These findings make sense if you make some assumptions about what might be happening in the learning environment. While drill tasks would provide little opportunity for meaningful interaction, students experienced in working together could use a tutorial as a way to promote discussion.

EVALUATING SOFTWARE

The process of selecting software is subjective. If you have the opportunity to serve on a curriculum committee charged with selecting software, you will soon discover that committee members often have very different opinions.

Nevertheless, a subjective decision should not be confused with an arbitrary one. The curriculum committee participants are likely to have plenty to say in support of their recommendations. Teachers have different styles, philosophies, and insights into how students learn, and they may value certain learning outcomes over others. These differences account for some of the variability in the classroom behaviors of teachers; they also explain why reactions to a particular piece of software can be so different. One teacher might value the methodical and organized way in which a particular tutorial presents information, and another teacher might feel that the same tutorial leaves too little room for student independence. Teachers will use techniques and materials that are consistent with their values and beliefs (Hannafin & Freeman, 1995).

Teachers consider many factors when selecting software. However, the discussion of things to think about and the lists of things "experts" suggest ought to be valued should not obscure one essential question that all teachers examining software must ask: Would I be able and willing to integrate this activity into my existing curriculum? Schools should purchase software that teachers are committed to using.

Formalized evaluation procedures

Formal evaluation procedures do have a place. These methods are of value when several people must collaborate in making software selections. These procedures provide a convenient framework for discussing strengths and weaknesses, as well as a way to retain information gathered through the review process for later consideration. Inexperienced teachers and inexperienced technology users may also benefit from a formal evaluation process and a checklist of desired features. The expectations raised by a checklist may make less experienced teachers think about issues they may not otherwise have considered. The benefits may be immediate, or the formal process may hasten the development of personal standards. Ring (1993) has demonstrated that a checklist increases the accuracy with which inexperienced teachers are able to predict how well they will like programs after extended use. If experience with a checklist would prevent inexperienced teachers from purchasing software they would not use, working with a checklist would be time well spent. For these reasons, we have included evaluation forms for teachers to use when selecting software.

EVALUATION FORMS

Evaluation forms can be found in many sources (Bitter, Camuse, & Durbin, 1993; Ring, 1993). The form shown in Figure 4.11 (pages 148 to 149) begins with open-ended questions requesting the reviewer's descriptive and subjective comments and follows with a checklist of important program characteristics. This is fairly typical. The program title, publishing company, cost, and other general information are included for archival purposes. Certain items are included to remind the reviewer to check system and hardware

Keeping Current

Locating Appropriate Software

A tremendous amount of commercial instructional software is available today. In purchasing software for your own classroom or for your school, you should develop an awareness of a reasonable sample of the products that are available and then proceed to gather more detailed information about the quality and curriculum appropriateness of specific products that seem most interesting. This process is probably more difficult than inexperienced individuals might anticipate. Unlike the tool applications discussed in other chapters, individual instructional software products target niche markets. Major tool applications such as word processing programs are used in homes, business settings, and schools. The marketing budgets for such products are huge, major computer magazines publish in-depth analyses and comparisons of the major products, local retailers are likely to have demonstration copies available, and it is probable that other computer users will be able to provide advice. Often these same sources are less useful in helping you locate quality instructional software. The companies producing most instructional software are relatively obscure in comparison to companies producing general-purpose computer tools, local retailers cannot afford to maintain an extensive inventory of instructional materials, and other technology-oriented teachers with whom you work may teach in other disciplines and not pay attention to products that might interest you.

So how do you become acquainted with the software you might purchase? Here are several suggestions:

◆ *Attend conferences and conventions.* State teachers' conventions frequently have ses-

sions on instructional technology, and many vendors' booths are devoted to product demonstrations. It is also possible there will be a conference in your region devoted specifically to educational computing. Such conferences provide an excellent opportunity to meet other teachers interested in technology and to see what vendors have to offer.

◆ *Take a class or workshop.* If you are using this book as part of a college course, you are already in a setting in which you are likely to work with a variety of software products. This experience will be valuable in developing your awareness of useful software. If you are an undergraduate student, many new products will be available by the time you are working in a school and in a position to recommend software for purchase. Many colleges and universities sponsor brief workshops for practicing teachers. Sometimes teachers gather for a special session at a local college, and sometimes people from the college go out to the schools. School districts able to fund a position for a computer coordinator may provide their own staff development activities. In most locations, workshops must cater to a cross-section of teachers to be cost-effective and will be unlikely to discuss a large number of individual instructional software products. Still, workshops are an effective way to develop a background about effective instructional software and refine your ideas.

◆ *Browse through magazines for educators.* A number of magazines are written specifically for computer-using educators (see a list in Resources to Expand Your Knowledge

Base at the end of the chapter). Teachers may subscribe to these publications themselves, schools may purchase the magazines and make them available through school libraries, or teachers may find them in a local college library. It is often informative to read reviews by many different authors, keeping in mind that they have biases just like anyone else. Reading several reviews will provide some balance in the information you gather.

◆ *Interact with other teachers using telecommunications.* The Internet and commercial network services allow teachers to interact with other teachers. The teachers participating have already self-selected themselves as computer users. It is common to see messages such as, "We have $4,000 to spend on software for the science department. Do you have any recommendations?" (You will find information on telecommunications in Chapter 6.)

◆ *Communicate directly with software companies.* Software companies have a vested interest in making sure that educators are aware of their products. However, these companies cannot be expected to provide an unbiased evaluation of their own products and are unlikely to offer information on the programs of other companies. Contacting a company can be especially useful if it is willing to provide a review copy. Usually the best way to obtain an examination copy is through an administrator or computer coordinator who approaches the company. Companies are quite concerned with the pirating of their products and seem more comfortable with an individual in an administrative capacity. Some companies provide sample programs that have been altered in some way from the originals. Often only some of the content of the program is included, and certain functions, such as saving or printing, have been disabled. Finally, companies are beginning to offer previews of their products—program descriptions and samples of what the student would see on the screen—on World Wide Web sites. ✳

requirements. Some packages require additional memory or add-on hardware items such as a speech synthesizer, or function only with the most recent operating system. It is all too easy to purchase software that will not run on existing equipment.

The remainder of the form asks the reviewer to consider how students might use the software and to comment on certain characteristics of the software that could influence how productive and valued student experiences might be. You will notice that the review form is designed so that the form itself does not identify how important any given characteristic or issue should be in the final decision. The form asks the reviewer to make such value judgments.

The reviewer makes value judgments.

On the checklist, the weight for the perceived importance of each characteristic and the rating of the extent to which the program satisfies the characteristic fall on a six-point scale (0 to 5). The product of the weight and the rating results in a score for each characteristic.

FIGURE 4.11

Software Evaluation Form with Open-Ended Questions and Weighted Checklist of Program Characteristics

Review Summary Sheet

General Information

Reviewer _____

Title _____

Publishing company _____

Publication date _____

List price _____

Availability of site license _____

Site license agreement _____

    Price _____

Hardware and Operating System Requirements

Host microcomputer _____

Operating system compatibility _____

Requires _____ K of memory

Is product network aware? _____

Storage _____ Hard drive _____ MB approximate capacity required

_____ CD-ROM player

Other hardware requirements _____

Program Format

_____ Drill Practice _____ Tutorial _____ Simulation _____

_____ Other (Describe:) _____

_____ Combination (Describe:) _____

Brief Description _____

_____

_____

Curriculum Compatibility

Subject area _____

Grade level _____

Specific topics _____

Reviewer Recommendation and Comments _____

_____

_____

Checklist

Rating: Extent to which the software successfully meets objective

Weight: Extent to which the objective is important to the rater

Total: Product of rating and weight

(Higher values are intended to indicate greater quality and importance.)

FIGURE 4.11 *(continued)*

EVALUATION CATEGORY	RATING (0–5)	WEIGHT (0–5)	TOTAL (0–25)
CONTENT			
Easily integrated with existing content	_____	_____	_____
Content presented accurately	_____	_____	_____
Content presented efficiently	_____	_____	_____
Content presented effectively	_____	_____	_____
Presentation approach is motivating	_____	_____	_____
Program encourages active thought	_____	_____	_____
Content avoids offensive representations	_____	_____	_____
Quality of content justifies cost	_____	_____	_____

Comments: _____

PROGRAM FUNCTIONS	RATING (0–5)	WEIGHT (0–5)	TOTAL (0–25)
Program is easy to operate	_____	_____	_____
Pace is appropriate	_____	_____	_____
Student can save work in progress	_____	_____	_____
Student can control rate of progress	_____	_____	_____
Student can change shift among activities	_____	_____	_____
Feedback is appropriate	_____	_____	_____
Saves data on student performance	_____	_____	_____

Comments: _____

SUPPLEMENTS	RATING (0–5)	WEIGHT (0–5)	TOTAL (0–25)
Quality of student supplemental materials	_____	_____	_____
Quality of instruction manual	_____	_____	_____
Useful suggestions for program use	_____	_____	_____
Useful followup ideas	_____	_____	_____

Comments: _____

Total score _____

We hope you will have an opportunity to apply this evaluation procedure to a number of software products and to discuss your conclusions with your classmates and instructor. This process should help you clarify what you will eventually look for when you find yourself in the position of purchasing software for your students' use.

SUMMARY

In contrast to other educational applications of technology, computer-based instruction (CBI) exerts greater control over the content to which students are exposed and how students are expected to interact with this content.

A complete instructional experience takes the student through four stages: (1) the presentation of information or learning experiences, (2) guidance as the student struggles to develop knowledge and master skills, (3) extended practice, and (4) assessment. Not all activities, computer or otherwise, should be expected to provide all four stages of instruction. Often lower-quality instruction occurs because it is assumed that an experience satisfies the expectations of all four stages, or because a task suited to one stage of instruction is used inappropriately to provide the experiences of a different stage.

Tutorials, simulations, drill and practice, games, and exploratory environments are categories of CAI. Commercial products seldom represent a pure example of any single category.

Tutorials are designed to present information and guide learning. Teachers must participate actively when students are working with tutorials.

Simulations attempt to replicate the key elements of an actual experience. Although it is unlikely that any one product will provide for all four stages of instruction, simulations can provide for all of them. Fidelity, the exactness of the match between a simulation and reality, influences both learning and transfer. The relationships between fidelity, learning, and transfer are complex, and the best situation for rapid learning is not always the best situation for effective transfer. Simulations offer potential solutions to a number of instructional problems and can make learning experiences more concrete, more controllable, less expensive, and safer.

Drill-and-practice activities have a bad reputation. Nevertheless, they are appropriate when information and skills need to be overlearned. Care must be taken not to emphasize memorization unless it is actually the intended objective of instruction.

Games put a premium on motivation, entertainment, and competition and can engage students with appropriate academic content. Educators might consider games as a way to introduce students to new topics or as ways to motivate. When a game is used to motivate work independent of the game itself, care must be taken for all students to have a realistic chance of receiving this reinforcement so that students do not view technology as only for play.

Exploratory environments allow a student-centered approach to learning in a specified domain. For best productivity, teachers need to remain involved as students work with this software.

Research evaluating the effectiveness of CAI has been extensive. In general, comparisons seem to demonstrate a moderate level of success. Teachers should not expect miracles of technology and must realize that thoughtful implementation is the key to providing students with valuable experiences.

Teachers determine how students will use CAI software. Even traditional presentation software can be incorporated into a broader learning task that encourages students to construct personal understanding.

Software selection is an important but subjective activity. In making purchasing decisions, teachers are encouraged to consider carefully their own instructional priorities and to determine how they would integrate the software into their curricula.

REFLECTING ON CHAPTER 4

Activities

- List simulations, computer or otherwise, that you have experienced. What principles or causal relationships was each simulation constructed to represent?
- Analyze several games, and list the specific characteristics you feel make each game enjoyable.
- Use Figure 4.11 to evaluate a commercial software product. Discuss your evaluation comments with your classmates.
- Locate one of the journals mentioned in Resources to Expand Your Knowledge Base as providing useful information for teachers. List the types of information you discovered in reviewing one issue. Share this information with your classmates.

Key Terms

automaticity *(p. 131)*

branching tutorial *(p. 121)*

computer-assisted instruction (CAI) *(p. 118)*

computer-based instruction (CBI) *(p. 118)*

constructionism *(p. 119)*

drill *(p. 130)*

edutainment *(p. 131)*

exploratory environment *(p. 134)*

fidelity *(p. 125)*

game *(p. 131)*

instructionism *(p. 119)*

linear tutorial *(p. 121)*

practice *(p. 130)*

simulation *(p. 122)*

tutorial *(p. 120)*

Resources to Expand Your Knowledge Base

Technology Journals

A number of journals are written to inform K–12 teachers about issues related to classroom applications of technology. These journals can be helpful in several ways. Teachers can learn about new developments in hardware and software and can also learn how other teachers are applying technology. These periodicals frequently carry critical reviews and side-by-side comparisons of hardware and software products. Information about the strengths and weaknesses of products can be very helpful when planning purchases.

Children's Software Review (**http://www.childrensoftware.com**)
Learning and Leading with Technology (formally *The Computing Teacher*)
    (**http://www.iste.org/L&L/index.html**)
Electronic Learning (**http://scholastic.com/EL/**)
Journal of Computers in Mathematics and Science Teaching
    (**http://www.aace.org/pubs/jcmst/index.html**)
Multimedia Schools (**http://www.infotoday.com/MMSchools/default.htm**)
NewMedia Magazine (**http://newmedia.com/**)
Technology and Learning (**http://www.techlearning.com/**)

World Wide Web Sources

Kinzie, M. (1994). *The interactive frog dissection: An on-line tutorial* [On-line]. Available: **http://curry.edschool.virginia.edu/go/frog** [March 2000].
Securities Industry Foundation for Economic Education (SIFEE). (1999). *The Stock Market Game* [On-line]. Available: **http://www.smg2000.org** [March 2000].
Lawrence Berkeley National Laboratory. (1998). *Virtual Frog Dissection Kit* [On-line]. Available: **http://www-itg.lbl.gov/vfrog/dissect.html** [March 2000].

Software

The Adventures of Jasper Woodbury. Jasper Woodbury was developed by the Learning Technology Center, Vanderbilt University. Six adventures were copyrighted in 1992 and are available through Optical Data Corporation. (**http://peabody.vanderbilt.edu/ctrs/ltc/**)

    Eco-Simulator. The *Eco-Simulator* is one program within a package called Ecology, produced by Earthquest, Inc., 125 University Ave., Palo Alto, CA 94301. *Exploring the Nardoo* is distributed in North America by Learning Team. The CD-based program is accompanied by an Instructor's Manual prepared by a team of teachers. The manual explains how tasks encouraged by *Exploring the Nardoo* meet specific science standards and provide activities that teachers can use to provide related learning experiences within the classroom and community. (**http://www.learningteam.org**)

    Operation: Frog. *Operation: Frog* is available in MS-DOS and Macintosh versions from Scholastic, Inc. (**http://www.scholastic.com/**).
The Oregon Trail. *The Oregon Trail,* from the Learning Company, exists in several formats for several different computers. The latest version is available on CD-ROM. (**http://www.mecc.com/**)

    SimLife. *SimLife* is a product of Maxis. Maxis also has produced *SimEarth, SimAnt,* and *SimCity* for Macintosh, MS-DOS, and Windows. (**http://www.simcity.com/home.shtml**)

Where in the World Is Carmen Sandiego? Where in the World Is Carmen Sandiego? (1992) and other games in the Carmen Sandiego series are products of Broderbund. Software is available for Apple, Macintosh, and MS-DOS machines. The latest versions of these products come in deluxe CD-ROM versions. (**http://www.broderbund.com/**)

Word Scramble is one activity from the Tenth Planet Explores Literacy Letter Sound CD. This product is available for both Macintosh and Windows Platform from Sunburst Communications, Inc. (**http://www.tenthplanet.com/**)

Chapter 5

Using Tools: Word Processors, Databases, and Spreadsheets

ORIENTATION

In this chapter you will read about word processing, spreadsheet, and database applications. Tools for using the Internet have generated so much recent interest and offer so much promise that we devote a separate chapter to them. These are the most common computer tools in educational use, and they play somewhat similar basic roles in influencing student behavior. Tools can increase students' productivity, help them become more active learners, and allow them to acquire knowledge and develop skills in unique ways. You will read about ways you can introduce these tools to your students and apply them in your classroom.

As you read, look for answers to the following questions:

Focus Questions

- ◆ What are three different levels on which students benefit from applying tool applications in content-area tasks?
- ◆ Why are the capabilities of word processing applications especially well suited to teaching writing using the writing process approach?
- ◆ What are some classroom word processing, spreadsheet, and database activities that lead to more active processing of course content?
- ◆ What are the general characteristics of tool activities that increase the probability of meaningful learning?

Mark Grabe's Use of Computer Tools

I am a typical college professor. A week for me is probably not that different from a week for many other teachers. Certain tasks, for example, are common:

◆ Preparing instructional materials for classroom presentations or distribution to students
◆ Preparing and scoring exams
◆ Recording data on student performance and calculating grades
◆ Communicating with students, colleagues, and a variety of other individuals, through several different mechanisms
◆ Writing for many purposes
◆ Gathering information to facilitate instruction and scholarly work

I use my computer and one or more common tool applications in each of these activities. Surveys of teachers' use of technology reveal that teachers make the most frequent use of word processing in their own work. I'm no exception; I generate all of my written material, including simple Web pages that I project during my large group classes and later make available on the Internet, with a word processing program. If I do anything out of the ordinary with word processing, it would probably be including more graphics, particularly scanned images and images captured from videotape, in the documents I produce. (We'll discuss some of these techniques in later chapters.)

A second way many teachers use a computer is to record grades. There are computer programs developed specifically as gradebooks, but like many other teachers, I prefer to use a spreadsheet program. Once mastered, a spreadsheet program is relatively easy to use, and I prefer to use one because I can adapt it to several atypical evaluation techniques I use in my classes. In the large lecture courses I teach, students are allowed to retake alternative versions of unit exams. This means that three different tests are available for each exam period, and students can decide to take one, two, or all three versions. The highest score is the score I count. The spreadsheet is useful because it offers the versatility I need to calculate final grades under these different circumstances. The discussion of spreadsheet applications in this chapter should provide enough information for you to understand how to create your own gradebook for most straightforward grading procedures.

Databases: Generating and Improving Tests

Like most other teachers, I devote a considerable amount of time and energy to evaluating my students' performances. Because some of my classes are large, I give tests that include one essay question and many multiple-choice items. Multiple-choice items are frequently criticized for being shallow, but I feel that the often-negative emphasis on factual knowledge in such tests occurs because items of this type are the easiest to write and the easiest to defend when students disagree with the answer. In any case, my approach is to write a substantial proportion of questions that require students to apply knowledge gained from the textbook and classroom presentations. Writing challenging questions takes a lot of time. My development of questions is a process that takes place across semesters. When I find items that seem to work well, I keep them. When I can identify flaws in items I've used, I modify the items and try them again. The evaluation procedure I use in my courses requires me to generate a very large number of test items. A database plays a significant role in the way I generate my tests. The approach I take may or may not end up saving time, but I think it improves the quality of the testing process for my students.

Rather than generating test items immediately before each exam, I write and store items continuously. I usually spend part of the hour before each class going over the material that I'm going to present. This is usually also a good time to write a few items. I find that I am more creative in preparing questions if I don't try to write all of the questions at once. Preparation time is also a good time to write questions because the content is fresh in my mind. I just turn from my notes to the computer and work on a question.

I store the questions in a HyperCard database. HyperCard is now considered old technology, but it still suits my personal needs. Because database applications are designed to assist the user in storing, organizing, and retrieving large amounts of information, a collection of one thousand test items represents an almost perfect application for this tool. In creating a database, the user establishes fields for the different types of data to be stored. (You might think of a field as a container established to hold a designated type of information.) A database developed to store my test questions contains individual fields for the chapter number, the answer, and the question and several fields allowing storage of data on student performance and dates of use. After I write new items, I always sort the database on the chapter field. This process reorganizes the database so that items from each chapter appear consecutively. I use a special field to designate the individual items to be used for a particular exam. When I click on this field, the computer automatically enters a check mark. To prepare an exam, I search the database for questions related to particular chapters, select the items I want to include from each chapter by checking the selection field, and then click on the "dump test" button, shown in Figure 5.1. The database then creates one output file containing the selected test items and a second file containing the test key (that is, the correct answers

FIGURE 5.1
Screen Display from Test Generation Database

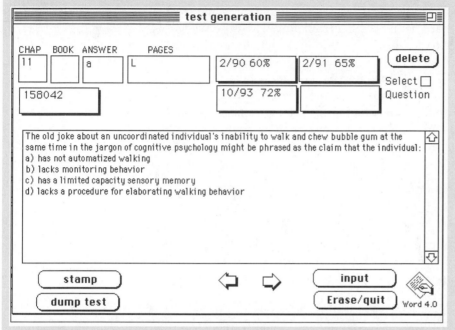

and a unique number designating each question). The output file containing the test items is edited with a word processing program and then printed.

Once the examination has been scored, I return to the test item database, search by identification number for items administered, and enter the date I used the item and the student performance on the item. I enter the date so that I won't use the question too frequently. I may want to remember that I've already used the item in a particular semester and shouldn't use it again on the final exam. The proportion of students answering the question correctly gives me an indication of how difficult the question is and how well students understood the material covered by the item. Entering these data also provides an opportunity to consider the quality of the item and possibly to modify the question.

I consider a number of sources of information in modifying questions. During or after taking the tests, students may raise issues or ask questions that let me know that something about the question needs to be fixed. For example, I used the word *gist* in a question, and a large number of students didn't know what this word meant. Students may argue that an alternate answer for a particular question should also be counted as correct because it is true in at least some cases. (You've probably raised similar questions with your own instructors.) Sometimes the students' logic makes me see a problem in the question that I hadn't considered before. The university test-scoring service also provides some statistical data that allow me to spot questions that seem particularly problematic. With these sources of information in mind, I can modify the database; that is, I can rework items. I can replace the word *gist* with the phrase "the main idea of the passage." And I can write new, less ambiguous answers. Generating tests isn't an easy process under any circumstances. However, the use of a database allows a systematic and efficient approach to item collection, test production, and item improvement.

Internet Tools: Accessing People, Interactive Services, and Communicating with Students

Although Internet tools are presented in the next chapter, allow me to complete this discussion of personal tool use with a brief description of some of the ways I use the Internet. Including the Internet activities will allow a more complete description of tool applications from the perspective of a teacher.

The computer on my desk is connected directly to the campus local area network (LAN) and the Internet. From my desk, I can connect to people and services across campus and around the world. The discussion of telecommunications in the next chapter is organized around communicating with people, interacting with remote services, and transferring resources. These three categories cover my own activities as well.

Electronic mail (e-mail) has been a valuable addition to the ways in which I can interact with others. I exchange e-mail with my students, administrators to whom I report, local teachers, colleagues around the country, the editor of this textbook, and my wife and coauthor. I am also on several mailing lists and receive thirty to forty messages a day from people with things to say or ask about computer software I use, computers in education, outdoor education, and the field of psychology. A mailing list is similar to the bulletin board in the teachers' lounge. You post a request or an idea and see if anyone responds. I respond to the mail sent directly to me, and I mostly read the mail generated by the mailing lists to keep up on topics that interest me. E-mail has become an integral part of the way I do my work.

I also use my office computer to access a number of remote computer services. Probably the most common application of this type involves doing literature searches. The college and university libraries in my state and the public library in my community allow a computerized search of library holdings. In other words, I can determine whether a book I want exists in a higher education library collection somewhere in the state or in my local public library. The library at my university also allows me to determine whether the book I want is on the shelf. When it is 20 degrees below zero, I want to take the cold walk across campus only if I know the book I want is there. Computerized library searches are available in many elementary and secondary schools. Students may also be able to conduct similar searches in local public libraries. Perhaps you've already made frequent use of the kind of search process I have described.

Another kind of search procedure allows an even more exploratory approach to finding library resources. Most students in colleges of education have made use of the Educational Resources Information Clearinghouse (ERIC) services. ERIC provides a directory of published resources in the field of education. The resources include articles in education journals and other materials, such as the print version of conference presentations, which have been stored in many libraries on microfilm.

We hope this description of how Mark Grabe uses computers in his teaching has begun to show you just how helpful computer tools can be. As you continue, you will learn more about the computer tools we have just described. You will acquire a greater awareness of how you and your students might apply these tools and gain a basic understanding of how they are used. We cannot take total responsibility for teaching you how to use computer tools; there is too much variability in the hardware and software you might encounter. Your instructor will be able to provide more specific information and may, we hope, provide you with some hands-on experiences. We hope we can get you excited about the potential of these applications and start you thinking about classroom uses.

Gaining awareness and understanding of using tools

A *tool*, by definition, is an object that allows the user to perform tasks with greater efficiency or quality. For example, a calculator allows a student to add a series of numbers more quickly and accurately than the student could add them with pencil and paper. The computer, in combination with different kinds of application software, can function as many different tools. The tool functions performed by the computer can improve the efficiency and quality with which the user manipulates information—much as the calculator does. Nearly everyone has some occasion to manipulate information every day. Certainly teachers and students are heavily involved with information and could benefit from tools that improve the efficiency or quality of their work. This chapter and the next will familiarize you with some of the basic computer tools that teachers and students might find useful. The specific

Computers can function as many different tools.

computer tools we consider in this chapter are word processing programs, spreadsheets, and databases. Other computer applications, such as graphics programs and computer tools used to explore and communicate using the Internet, also meet the general definition of a computer tool, but you will encounter these applications in later chapters. We want you to understand the type of tasks that computer tools allow the user to perform and to gain some insights into what the user does as he or she works with each type of tool.

Ways computer tools may benefit students

As you learn about computer tools, consider that working with them may benefit students on several levels (Perkins, 1985). As you have already seen, tools can help the user work more efficiently and effectively. In part, students learn to use computer tools because tools can help them perform schoolwork (such as writing papers) more effectively or perhaps provide them with valuable occupational skills. These skills are part of what constitutes computer literacy. There is the potential for more, though. Computer tools in content-area instruction may allow students to acquire knowledge and develop skills in unique and powerful ways. It appears that educational experiences with computer tools result in students' (1) learning to use the computer tools, (2) performing certain academic tasks more effectively and efficiently because of the tools, and (3) learning domain skills such as writing and problem solving or acquiring content-area knowledge through the application of computer tools to content-appropriate tasks. Others have noted and are attempting to help teachers make these same distinctions. Sometimes new descriptive terms can help bring new insights. For example, the functions we have just listed have also been described as *technology as tool* and *technology as intellectual partner* or **mindtool** (Jonassen, 1995). The notion that ordinary computer tools can be more than a means to boost efficiency is an intriguing possibility.

Results of educational experiences with computer tools

The broader role computers can play

In the material that follows, we consider all of the levels on which tool use might be beneficial. However, we continually emphasize that student mastery of how the computer can be used to perform basic tasks is not enough. We need to find ways to allow students to apply the skills they acquire and, we hope, to apply these skills in a variety of meaningful circumstances. As you encounter each computer tool in the presentations that follow, think carefully about potential applications of the tool in your area of interest and about the several levels on which students might benefit from experience with that tool.

WORD PROCESSING

Word processing programs may help students write more effectively.

Word processing, an application allowing the entry, manipulation, and storage of text, is the single most popular use of computer technology in schools, for several reasons (Ravitz, Wong, & Becker, 1999). First, word processing is the most widely used computer application in the work and home environments, and educators are sensitive to the development of skills valued in these settings. Second, writing is one of the fundamental skills taught in schools. Features of word processing programs may help students write more effectively and develop writing skills more quickly. Third, writing is a skill that may contribute to the generation and integration of personal knowledge in nearly all content areas. Writing forces students to externalize what they know as they attempt to put ideas on paper (or in this case on the computer screen) and requires an active use of knowledge. Remember from Chapter 2 that the active processing of information increases the likelihood of meaningful learning.

Word processing use

Surprisingly, although many students are exposed to word processing in courses that teach computer literacy, the extent to which they *use* word processing is not as high as you might expect. In a recent survey (Ravitz et al., 1999), teachers were asked if their students had made use of word processing in at least three lessons during the past year. The study indicated that 69 percent of elementary school classrooms and 60 percent of middle school and secondary English classrooms met this criterion. The use in other middle and high school subject areas was substantially lower: in science, 41 percent; in social studies, 38 percent; and in math, 15 percent. This situation may exist because schools do not have enough computer equipment and students have difficulty gaining immediate access to the technology that is available (see Emerging Technology: Inexpensive "Keyboard" Computers). However, it is clear that access is not the only issue. Teachers can increase the use of writing as a learning activity and can expect that students will accomplish this writing by using word processing applications. Because opportunities for writing exist in all content areas and because the necessary hardware and software for word processing are now more likely to be available, educators have a real opportunity to expand computer use in this area.

CHARACTERISTICS OF WORD PROCESSING PROGRAMS

Basic functions of word processing

Most word processing programs, even those designed for young students, allow users to accomplish nearly the same set of basic functions: text input, storage and retrieval, formatting, editing, and printing. Because many word processing programs also allow the integration of graphics, the storage and retrieval, formatting, editing, and printing functions potentially apply to the combination of text and graphics that the user creates.

Text Input

Word processing programs have some special features that optimize the writer's ability to input text from the keyboard. One feature that most computer users take for granted is word wrap. When working on a typewriter, writers have to pay attention to how close they are coming to the end of a line

Word Processing Activities for All Grade Levels

Word processing software can be used even with students in the primary grades. Young children can write stories with software that defaults to a large-size font and prints out on primary-style paper. This software still allows for the complete editing features of deleting, cutting, copying, and pasting. Young children can:

- Write stories using predictable patterns ("The House That Jack Built").
- Create alphabet books (the ABCs of space, winter ABCs).
- Keep a daily journal.
- Create lists of factual information from reference books and write reports with this information.
- Create a class book, with one page of personal information for each child.
- Create content-area class books, such as "Animals Where I Live" or "People in My Community."

In the intermediate grades, students can extend the word processing activities they started in the primary grades. They can:

- Write and revise factual reports using cut and paste and spell-checking.
- Create journal entries using the "insert date" feature.

- Use the thesaurus to expand vocabulary and eliminate redundancies.
- Write collaborative stories.
- Create cooperative reports, with each member of the group responsible for a different topic.
- Cut and paste to organize the report.
- Write poetry and publish it using center alignment or acrostic poems using a larger-size font for the first letter of each line.
- Write creative stories using different font styles to express emotions such as fear or shyness.
- Publish newspapers that might have been published in the past.

Middle-school and high school students can:

- Write scientific reports that include tables and graphs.
- Use outlining features to organize reports.
- Create questionnaires using tab set fills to draw the lines for answers (tab fills draw a solid or dotted line to the next tab that has been set).
- Create lists of information using the columnizing feature to align the list entries.
- Publish newsletters with columns and clip art. ✳

and decide when to press the return key to move to the beginning of the next line. With **word wrap,** the computer automatically moves to the beginning of the next line when the word being entered would extend beyond the right margin. Similarly, the computer program also breaks to the next page when the specified number of lines has been entered. Word processing programs also allow writers to insert a forced page break at any time.

Storage and Retrieval

Saving a copy to disk

Storage and retrieval involve the processes of saving a copy of the document to disk and loading a saved document from the disk back into the computer memory. These processes allow work done with a word processor to be extended over time. They have special significance for students who are learning to write with a word processor, because students can submit documents for evaluation and then rework them in response to the comments of peers or their teacher. Storage and retrieval of the original document allows the student to spend time addressing the specific areas of difficulty noted in the comments rather than wasting time regenerating parts of the document that didn't require additional attention.

Formatting

The physical appearance of a document

Formatting refers to the physical appearance of the document created with a word processor. Writers may apply formatting features at the level of the character, the paragraph, or the entire document.

The character level

At the character level, word processing programs usually allow the user to control font, style, and size. The **font** refers to the design of the character. All characters from the same font share certain design features. For example, this is Geneva, this is Palatino, this is New York, and this is Times. Font **style** alters a particular font in terms of slant or thickness. This is **bold**, and this is *italic*. <u>Underlining</u> is also a style. Characters can be displayed in a variety of sizes. A writer might want to control character formatting for several reasons. Think about the material you read and how character style is used. Newspapers use large, bold type for headlines and article titles. Textbooks use bold print, italicized type, and underlining to bring readers' attention to particular words or phrases. Text written with some variability in character appearance is more interesting and thus allows the author additional mechanisms for communication.

The paragraph level

At the paragraph level, formatting typically allows setting **tabs** and **margins,** text **justification,** and line spacing. Tabs, margins, and text justification control the alignment of text on the screen and the printed page. A few formatting features apply to the entire document. For example, some word processors allow the user to designate how many columns of text will appear on a page. Teachers or students who create newsletters may find this feature useful.

Editing

Editing involves modifying text at any time after it has been generated. Most writers composing at the computer notice and correct typing errors as they appear on the computer screen or immediately attempt to improve a sentence that does not sound quite right. Other changes occur much later in the writing process. Some methods of writing instruction require students to have their papers critiqued by the teacher or other students before they write a final draft. In this case, the original material is likely loaded from disk and re-worked in response to the comments generated by the original draft.

Standard editing features

There are some standard editing features in all word processing pro-grams, including the character-level functions of **insert** and delete and the block operations of delete, cut, copy, and paste. A change in the existing for-mat of a block of text (for example, making plain text bold) might also be considered editing.

Block editing

Block editing involves making a change to a designated segment of text. The first step in block editing is to **select,** or mark, the segment of text to which the change will apply by dragging the **cursor** over the text with the mouse. Once a block of text has been selected, the writer can execute such commands as delete, cut, paste, or copy. The **delete** function erases the se-lected text. The **cut** function removes the selected text and stores it temporar-ily in the computer's memory for insertion at a different location. The process of moving the text from the computer's memory back to the screen at a point designated by the cursor is called **pasting**. The **copy** function temporarily stores the selected text in the computer's memory but differs from the cut command in not removing the text from its original location. Text copied to memory can also be pasted. Writers can use block editing to make major changes in a document; it is particularly useful to reorganize larger docu-ments or to move segments of text from one document to another.

Special Tools

Tools to improve a writer's effectiveness

Word processing programs often come equipped with special tools to im-prove the writer's effectiveness. The most common tools are an outliner, a spell checker, and a thesaurus.

Outlining

Most students are familiar with outlining. Incorporating an outlining tool in a word processing program allows the writer to plan the structure of the document. Often the outline entries become headings within the docu-ment, and the writer can move back and forth between the outline view and the extended text as an aid to organizing a major project. This capability helps the writer to escape the detail level and regain a sense of the overall purpose and structure of the document.

Spell checkers

Spell checkers check text for spelling errors. Most spell checkers identify each word assumed to be misspelled, offer a list of possible alternative words, and then allow the writer to accept a word as originally spelled or to replace the misspelled word or all words in the document spelled in a similar manner with one of the alternatives by clicking the appropriate button. Spell checkers have shortcomings, however. Unique terminology and proper names are ini-tially reported as spelling errors. Spell-checking a list of references is difficult because the spell checker will find an "error" in nearly every line (e.g., authors' names are reported as spelling errors). Words that a writer knows are correct can be added to the dictionary to make the spell checker more efficient over time. But spell checkers also cannot detect typing errors that result in a different valid word (*then* instead of *the*, for example), so writers must always proofread their work. Spell checkers have some instructional value in that they point out words that are consistently misspelled. The awareness that you often misspell a certain word—a form of metacognition—can help you learn to spell the word correctly or prompt you to look it up.

An electronic thesaurus

An electronic thesaurus allows a writer to generate a list of words with roughly equivalent meanings. This list allows the writer to find a word with just the right shade of meaning for a specific situation or to search for a different word when the writer feels he or she has been using a particular word too frequently. For example, we considered the word *nuance* for the previous sentence, but the word seemed a bit too formal. The thesaurus recommended eight other words and phrases as potential equivalents, and *nuance* became *shade of meaning*.

Integrating Graphics

Pictures, diagrams, and charts

Word processors typically allow the integration of text and graphics, such as pictures, diagrams, and charts. Positioning graphics within text presents a somewhat different set of issues from those applying specifically to text and some challenges too. For example, once a graphic is inserted, does it remain at a fixed position on the page as new text is inserted above the graphic, or does the illustration slide down the page with the rest of the text? How does a particular word processing program allow text to flow around all sides of a graphic or position the graphic in the middle of a page, with text to the left and right? Mastering all of the options of word processing programs would take students a considerable amount of time, but most programs offer great power and flexibility.

The role of purpose and motivation

Why the concern over such features as fonts, styles, printing multiple columns on a page, and manipulating the position of graphics within text? One initial reaction might be that such features are frills having little to do with the message of the text or the educational benefits of creating the text. But a very different perspective is possible. Consider the importance of purpose and motivation in effective writing and in learning to write. Writers need to be engaged in tasks in which they have authentic opportunities to communicate what they know, want, or feel. Appearance can influence perceptions of authentic authoring and perceptions of importance. The value to young writers of creating a book that really looks like a book or a newspaper that really looks like a newspaper should not be underestimated.

WRITERS, WRITING, AND WORD PROCESSING

Writing has sometimes been regarded as a mysterious craft practiced by unusual characters with special talents. Some common educational expectations

Will word processing make better writers?

about word processing seem to leave these myths intact (Pea & Kurland, 1987a). Many people assume that writing with a word processing program will lead to better products and that making frequent use of word processing while learning to write will produce better writers. Perhaps this powerful machine can somehow magically transform all of us into competent authors.

The "opportunities get taken" hypothesis

In learning, as in other areas of life, you seldom get something for nothing. Still, a logical case has been proposed for how simply working with word processing for an extended period may improve writing skills and performance. Perkins (1985) calls this the "opportunities get taken" hypothesis. The proposal works like this. Writing by hand has a number of built-in limitations. Generating text this way is slow, and modifying what has been written comes at a substantial price. To produce a second or third draft with a pencil or typewriter requires the writer to spend a good deal of time reproducing text that was fine the first time, just to change a few things that might sound better if modified. Word processing, on the other hand, allows writers to revise at minimal cost. They can pursue an idea to see where it takes them and worry about fixing syntax and spelling later. Reworking documents from the level of fixing misspelled words to reordering the arguments in the entire presentation can be accomplished without crumpling up what has just been painstakingly written and starting over.

With word processing, writers can take risks and push their skills without worrying that they are wasting their time. The capacity to save and load text from disk makes it possible to revise earlier drafts with minimal effort. Writers can set aside what they have written to gain new perspectives, show friends a draft and ask for advice, or discuss an idea with the teacher after class, and use these experiences to improve what they wrote yesterday or last week. What we have described here are opportunities—opportunities to produce a better paper for tomorrow's class and, over time, opportunities to learn to communicate more effectively.

Do writers take the opportunities provided by word processing programs and produce better products? The research evaluating the benefits of word processing (Bangert-Drowns, 1993; Cochran-Smith, 1991; Perkins, 1985) is not easy to interpret. Much seems to depend on the experience of the writer as a writer and computer user and on what is meant by a "better" product. If the questions refer to younger students, it also seems to depend on the instructional strategies to which the students have been exposed. General summaries of the research literature (Bangert-Drowns, 1993) seem to indicate that students make more revisions, write longer documents, and produce documents containing fewer errors when word processing. However, the spelling, syntactical, and grammatical errors that students tend to address and the revision activities necessary to correct them are considered less important by many interested in effective writing than changes improving document

Focus

Learning Word Processing Features

Many word processing features can be introduced as needed. The teacher can demonstrate each new feature within the context of a learning activity that will take advantage of that feature. Teachers can also:

Create "how-to" posters that can be posted by the computer or small "how-to" cards that can be kept by the computer in an empty disk box.

Create text files purposely written to allow students to:

◆ Edit paragraphs with punctuation and capitalization errors.
◆ Delete unnecessary information.
◆ Sequence the events of a story or a set of directions using cut and paste.
◆ Use the thesaurus to find alternatives for underlined words.
◆ Add charts and graphs.
◆ Move and resize clip art.✳

content or document organization. Many writers bring their writing goals and old habits to the new medium. They revise in ways they already know to fix errors they are aware of. Beginning writers may thus not have the orientation or capabilities to use the full potential of word processing, and their classroom instruction may also emphasize the correction of more obvious surface errors. Thus, there are differences in the products generated when working with word processing tools, but the areas in which younger writers seem to improve are not regarded by many as involving some of the most important characteristics of effective communication: content, clarity, and organization.

Many of the potential educational advantages of word processing appear only as students acquire considerable experience writing with the aid of technology. Perkins's (1985) argument that writing with word processing programs will improve writing skills because word processing allows students to experiment with their writing makes sense only in situations in which students have written a great deal and experimented with expressing themselves in different ways. The fact that most research evaluating the benefits of word processing has examined performance over a short period of time, with students having limited word processing experience, thus represents a poor test of the potential of word processing (Owston, Murphy, & Wideman, 1992). Recent research based on a three-year study following elementary students as they learned to write with and without access to word processing opportunities has demonstrated a significant advantage for students with ready access to technology (Owston & Wideman, 1997). This study seems to indicate that the technology itself offers some advantages and is consistent with Perkins's proposal that a powerful tool may encourage learners to write in a different way. Although we think that access to technology by itself will seldom radically change student performance, it will be interesting to follow what new research shows about a generation of writers learning with the benefit of more powerful tools.

The importance of how teachers and students apply technology

The role of word processing in developing writing skills depends on the goals of the teacher and individual students, the social context provided for writing, and the amount of writing that students do with the assistance of word processing. Certain combinations of these factors appear to allow word processing to have a more profound impact on the development of writing skills (Cochran-Smith, 1991; Cochran-Smith, Paris, & Kahn, 1991; Owston et al., 1992; Snyder, 1993).

THE WRITING PROCESS APPROACH

The stages of the writing process

Features of word processing are particularly well suited to what is often called the **writing process approach,** which encompasses the stages of planning, drafting, editing/revising, and publishing (Graves, 1983). Process models are constructivist in orientation (see Chapter 2, pages 62 through 63), and the components in the composing process emphasize that the writer's tasks are to create and communicate meaning. The development of composition skills within this orientation often involves collaboration, and writers frequently receive help and feedback from classmates and their teacher during all of the stages. The purpose of feedback is to improve performance. Feedback is given during the stages of composition to help writers improve their work rather than at the conclusion of a writing assignment as a summary evaluation. Students are expected to revise, and they learn to critique their own work and the work of others. The publication step implies that student compositions are authentic products prepared to entertain or inform a real audience. The process approach is often described as operating within a writing community in which students write, rewrite, read what others have written, and discuss the activities of writing (Montague, 1990).

Word processing and editing/revising

Word processing fits with the writing process approach in a number of ways. The most obvious application is editing/revision. The recursive nature of process writing—that is, the expectation that ideas will be generated, written, considered, and rewritten several times—is ideally implemented within a system that allows written products to be saved, retrieved, and modified efficiently. Specific strategies for process writing encourage writers to do things like put what they have written aside for a day and then reread and revise it the next day; exchange papers with a writing partner and request ideas for improvement; or discuss what they have written and what they are trying to say

Students write, collaborate, and read each other's work. *(Michael Newman/ PhotoEdit)*

with a teacher, to generate some new ideas for improving their papers. These activities are likely to be perceived more positively if the revisions they lead to can be implemented efficiently.

Word processing and other stages of the writing process

Word processing can also contribute to the other writing process stages. For example, a variety of word processing activities can contribute to the planning phase. Students can develop an initial structure using the outlining tool available in many word processing programs or a tool designed specifically to encourage the exploration and organization of ideas (see Focus: Using *Inspiration* to Brainstorm). Pon (1988) proposes a variety of brainstorming techniques that take advantage of technology. With a single classroom computer, the teacher can request story ideas from students and record them in a single file. This list of ideas can be printed and distributed to all students. The teacher can generate a list of key questions that might help a student come up with ideas for a project. For a paper on friendship, students might be asked to list five qualities of a good friend, briefly describe their good friends (without providing names) and why they like them, and describe how they try to be a friend to others. These tasks could be saved in a file for each student, and each student could be asked to respond individually to the questions. Responses could be discussed in class before students go on to write about friendship.

The publishing stage

The publishing stage is important if classroom tasks are to be perceived as authentic. Younger children need to see their work displayed on the bulletin board or in the halls. They see their stories as more meaningful when they are compiled into a classroom book that students take home and read to parents.

Focus

Using *Inspiration* to Brainstorm

Brainstorming, as part of a problem-solving task, might be described as the nonjudgmental process of generating and organizing ideas. A tool suited to this process should make it easy to (1) record ideas as they are generated, (2) organize ideas that have been generated into some type of meaningful structure, (3) record additional comments related to individual ideas without creating a confusing display, and (4) allow easy modification of both content and structure.

Inspiration is a software program designed to encourage the production and organization of ideas. Ideas can be entered in outline or graphical mode (see Figure 5.2). Ideas and the structure of ideas can be treated indepen-

FIGURE 5.2
Inspiration Screen Image in Graphic Mode

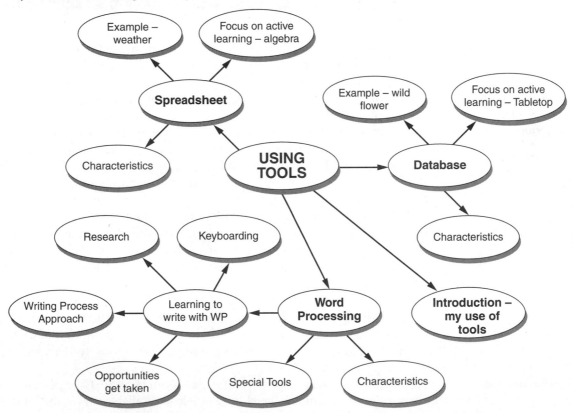

dently. That is, the ideas can first be generated and then linked in a hierarchical fashion. Once generated, both the idea elements and the structure of the elements can be altered. Text notations can be attached to individual ideas and can be hidden or displayed. Once completed, an *Inspiration* file can be used to generate a text file, a graphic file, or a web page.

Inspiration and other outlining tools can prove helpful to individual writers as they think through their goals and generate the structure of a future document. *Inspiration* in graphic mode can also be a very useful tool for group planning. In this case, members of a group might sit around a large screen or projected display and work to plan a project.✳

Older students can publish their work in school papers or occasionally send it to local newspapers. Students' informative writing or opinion papers can become required reading in subsequent classes covering similar topics.

Benefits of an authentic audience

The World Wide Web is also becoming a way for students to present their work (see Focus: Publication on the Internet on page 172). Having an authentic audience has some positive benefits. Material written to be communicated to peers through telecommunications has been found to be better organized, mechanically more correct, and more informative than papers on identical topics written to be graded by the teacher (Cohen & Riel, 1989). Having a peer audience seems to be more motivating than the red marks, gold stars, or grade the teacher might attach to the paper.

KEYBOARDING

A long-term controversy

One of the long-term controversies over computer use at the elementary school level concerns whether precious time should be devoted to the development of keyboarding skills. Those who favor making keyboarding part of the curriculum make two points. First, students must achieve some level of typing proficiency before writing at the computer can be very effective. Second, encouraging students to write at a computer without adequate training allows them to develop bad habits that will be more difficult to overcome when students do attempt to develop keyboarding skills. The opposition in this dispute is not really against the development of keyboarding skills, but against holding off access to writing on the computer until students achieve keyboarding proficiency. With the number of computers and the time each student can spend working at the computer each day so limited, some educators question whether allocating time to developing keyboarding proficiency makes sense. There may not be enough time to develop skill, and time might be more productively spent on other activities.

What level of proficiency is adequate?

How much training a student needs to become an adequate typist depends to some extent on what level of proficiency is considered adequate.

Focus

Publication on the Internet

The World Wide Web (see Chapter 6 for an extended discussion) provides a number of opportunities for student publication. The more formal outlets operate much like print publications. Potential authors submit manuscripts for consideration; an editorial board reviews these submissions. For example, MidLink publishes the work of ten- to fifteen-year-old students four times a year. Each edition has an announced theme, and published material is kept online for one year. The decision to include a particular manuscript is made by a student review board with teacher supervision. KidNews, set up as a wire service, takes a different and unique approach. Students are invited to submit news articles and to use the articles submitted by other students in local publications. Proper credit to author and source must accompany any article taken from KidNews and used in a school paper.

Be forewarned: Sites of this type seem to change host machines frequently and may cease to exist if the individuals responsible no longer have the time to maintain them. Sites that change locations can usually be found by searching the World Wide Web for the site name (e.g., KidNews).

The addresses for several student publication sites are provided at the end of this chapter. Contacting one of these sites is also a good way to learn about other opportunities for student publication.

There are other opportunities for publication on the Web that are much more immediate and less formal. Many schools sponsor their own Web sites and provide individuals, classes, and student organizations opportunities for publication.✳

Students in the upper elementary school grades write with a pencil at a rate of about ten words per minute (Wetzel, 1990). Without keyboard training, upper elementary school students will write at the keyboard at about half the rate they can achieve with a pencil. To equal the proficiency elementary students are able to achieve with a pencil requires approximately twenty to thirty hours of keyboard training. After that, students must use their keyboarding skills regularly, or they will regress to an unacceptable level of proficiency. Given what you know about the number of students in a typical classroom, the number of computers available, and the length of the elementary school day, you can see what a challenge this requirement represents. Teachers would have to devote a large portion of the time actually spent on computers to keyboarding instruction in order to make students proficient typists. Exposure to keyboarding software without close monitoring by the teacher and without teacher understanding of proper technique also is not likely to produce competent typists (Balajthy, 1988). Cochran-Smith et al. (1991) give a more optimistic view. They contend that two or three 20- to 30-minute sessions will be sufficient to get elementary school students familiar with the keyboard and basic computer functions (insertion, deletion, block moves) and into writing. They do recommend a more intensive style of adult-student interaction, called coaching, during writing time.

Resolving this dispute with the typical level of resources may not be possible. The development of keyboarding proficiency and the application of computers in content-area instruction represent different values, and student use of technology will require value-based decisions about how computers should be used. Access to computers is improving, and inexpensive alternatives to multimedia computers are available (see Emerging Technology: Inexpensive "Keyboard" Computers on page 174), but the question of how to spend valuable classroom time remains.

SPREADSHEETS

Storing and manipulating numerical data

Spreadsheets, a common computer application and an important reason for the microcomputer's rapid growth in popularity, are convenient for storing and manipulating numerical data and have long been useful to business-people. A **spreadsheet** allows an accountant or a small business owner to organize numerical information; perform calculations on these data; display the results of these calculations in informative ways (charts or graphs); and even ask hypothetical questions about the data, such as what would happen to total profits if three more cents were charged per unit.

The processing and interpretation of numerical data are more meaningful in some content areas than in others. Teachers and students recognize that manipulating numbers is part of mathematics. However, storing and interpreting numerical data and asking questions related to those data are also essential to political science, sociology, economics, geology, chemistry, physics, and biology. Consider the following diverse set of questions. What total electoral vote would have resulted if a particular presidential candidate had received 5 percent more votes in a specific block of southern states? How much would a 200-pound man weigh if he were transported to each of the other known planets? Is it colder in November in Fargo, North Dakota, or in Juneau, Alaska?

A spreadsheet (see Figure 5.3 on page 176) is a grid of columns (designated by letters) and rows (designated by numbers). The intersection of a column and a row is a **cell** (designated by a letter and number, such as A2). The spreadsheet user can do two very different things with any cell. The first is to place a data item in the cell. Although titles and labels can be entered in cells to make it possible to interpret the spreadsheet, numbers are the most frequently entered data in cells. Each cell contains one number. A cell entry may

Emerging Technology

Inexpensive "Keyboard" Computers

Immediate and unlimited access to computers is a distant goal for most schools. There simply is not enough equipment to allow every student to use a computer any time a computer might be useful. Several companies have recognized this reality and have developed simple computers that can take over some of the demand for computer time. The products look very much like the keyboard of a traditional computer and are designed to perform limited word processing applications. Positioned above the keys is a simple liquid crystal display (LCD) panel capable of presenting eight lines of eighty characters of text each (some models present four lines of forty characters). Again, depending on the model, these machines can store up to eight text documents, for a total of sixty-four pages. Simple editing is possible with all machines, and some are capable of underlining and bolding. Some also include a built-in dictionary and thesaurus. All connect to a computer so stored text can be uploaded for storage, editing, and printing. The machines are much lighter than notebook computers, have a much longer battery life (up to 100 hours), and are quieter. And the most important feature is that the least expensive of these machines, when purchased in bulk, costs approximately $200.

Naturally, the companies producing the machines recommend that schools purchase them in quantity. One company offers a package deal including a special security cabinet for storing and recharging forty machines. This storage area is positioned beneath the work space for a full-function computer and printer. This one piece of furniture can be rolled from classroom to classroom as needed and provides an instantaneous word processing lab.

The advantage of such equipment is that activities such as keyboarding or the early phases of writing can become much more familiar without monopolizing the computer lab or classroom computers. In addition, the size and cost of these machines make them transportable. Students can carry them to the library or to the laboratory to take notes, or even take them home because the risk of damage or loss doesn't carry the same financial burden as a regular computer. The companies claim these products are extremely easy to use and thus less threatening to technophobes.

Information on two of these products, AlphaSmart Pro and DreamWriter, is included at the end of this chapter.✴

also be the product of a formula. The attachment of a formula is the second action that can be applied to any cell. The formula defines what will be entered in a cell and how the data to be entered will be generated. Here is an example. The simple formula =C2+C3 defines the cell to which the formula is attached as containing the sum of the values from two other cells (C2 and C3).

Conventions built into spreadsheets and stored functions allow some very complex operations to be expressed simply. For instance, the expression

Spotlight on Assessment

Electronic Portfolios

A portfolio is a systematic and selective collection of student work that has been accumulated to demonstrate the student's motivation, academic growth, and level of achievement. Portfolio assessment is most commonly used in classes in which much of the work takes the form of written or artistic products, but depending on the content area, portfolios can also contain videotapes or audiotapes, computer programs, science laboratory reports, and virtually any other product that can serve to demonstrate learning.

To understand what a portfolio is, imagine a file folder for each student containing carefully selected work samples, the student's comments about these products, and various types of evaluation data contributed by the student, peers, and the teacher. What you have imagined is probably a collection consisting entirely of sheets of paper: written documents and reports, drawings, evaluation forms, and summary evaluation reports. This is a good starting place. Now extend this understanding to a broader set of materials: products generated with technology that can also be incorporated in a portfolio.

Suggestions for Creating and Using Portfolios

Several researchers have suggestions for creating and using portfolios (Paulson, Paulson, & Meyer, 1991; Porter & Cleland, 1995; Tierney, Carter, & Desai, 1991):

- The development of a portfolio should be a joint activity between teacher and student. Teachers might suggest certain categories such as, "the piece I am most proud of," "something I had to really struggle to learn," "my attempt to do something very different," and so on. Teachers should also require that certain standard items—for example, the major paper for the course—be included.
- Students should be encouraged to think carefully about the process and purpose of portfolio construction. For each item, students might be asked to write a brief explanation of why the item was selected, what was to be learned from the task, and the student's assessment of his or her success in meeting task objectives.
- Portfolios should allow the teacher and student to evaluate the whole learning process. For example, the portfolio should contain preparatory materials (notes), early drafts or works-in-progress, and the final product. The collection of similar examples over time allows student progress to be assessed.
- With the students' permission, keep sample portfolios that other students can use for ideas for their own collections.
- Attach evaluation instruments, such as checklists and rating scales, to individual items in the portfolio. Periodically enter comments summarizing across portfolio contents to evaluate student progress.

Portfolios and Technology

Certain applications of technology and portfolio assessment are ideally suited to each other. Products generated with technology, ranging from word processing documents to major student-created multimedia projects, can be components of a portfolio. As you think about the writing process, consider how easy it would be to collect and compare multiple drafts a student has generated. Students might be asked to reexamine these drafts and comment on how they worked to create a better final product.

Technology supports the practice of portfolio assessment in another way. Products are available to assist teachers and students in creating, organizing, and evaluating portfolios (Barrett, 1994). Some of these products are essentially electronic portfolios. Student work samples (text, scanned images of writing samples and artwork, audio generated from oral reading) are stored and then evaluated using one of several existing modifiable checklists. Students, teachers, and even parents can also attach comments to work samples. Commercial products of this type have focused on the early grades. However, some of the same ideas can be applied to all grade levels using existing multimedia tools (see Chapter 8) and other forms of technology, such as videotape (Barrett, 1994).✳

=average(C2..C200) will generate the average of all the numbers contained in cells C2 through C200 (C2, C3, C4, . . . C200) and place the result in the cell to which the expression has been attached. This simple expression combines the convention for identifying all of the values within a range of consecutive values and the stored function for calculating an average.

The functions that can be pasted into a cell allow students to perform a wide variety of calculations or manipulations. Some functions perform statistical calculations, such as the average or standard deviation. Other func-

FIGURE 5.3
Screen Showing Blank
Spreadsheet

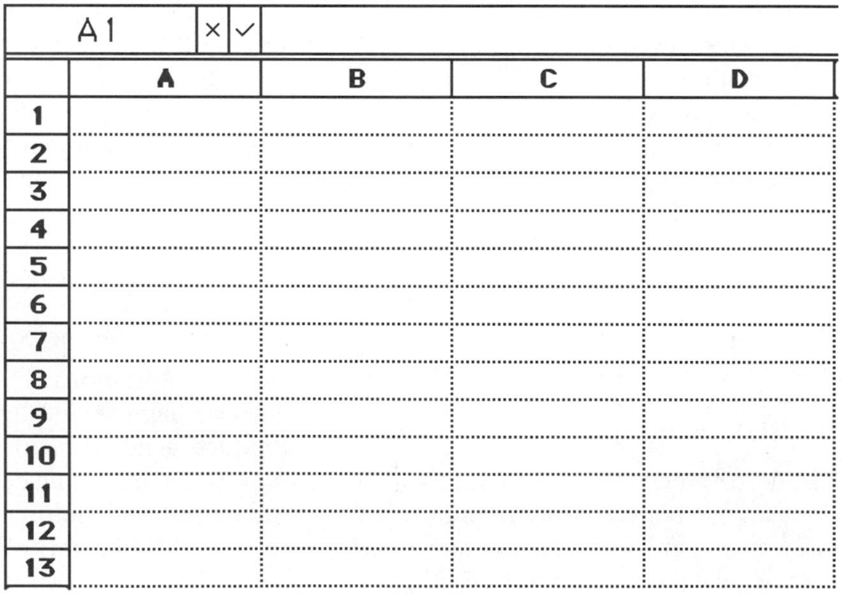

A1	×✓			
	A	**B**	**C**	**D**
1				
2				
3				
4				
5				
6				
7				
8				
9				
10				
11				
12				
13				

tions provide mathematical information familiar to secondary school math students, such as the logarithm of a number to base 10 or the tangent of an angle.

COMPARING WINTER TEMPERATURES: A SPREADSHEET PROJECT

Let's work through a quick classroom example to see how a spreadsheet works. Assume that a seventh-grade class has decided to compare the winter temperatures in various cities. The data here happen to be from cities in North Dakota and Alaska. For a class project, it is easy to examine data from many more cities—perhaps a city selected by each student in the class or a city from each state. (One method for obtaining these data is described in Chapter 6, pages 217 through 223.)

Each day at approximately the same time, students record the temperatures from the cities of interest. Entering these values in a spreadsheet is simple. A student selects the desired cell of the spreadsheet by clicking with the mouse or designating it with the arrow keys and enters the value. The same process is used to assign labels to the rows (the dates) and columns (city names). Students can attach a formula to a cell in a similar manner. In this example, the intent is to calculate the average temperature for each city. In the software program used for this example (AppleWorks spreadsheet), the = sign designates a formula. A cell entry beginning with the = sign is automatically understood by the spreadsheet program to be a formula and not data. The easiest way to calculate the average temperature for Juneau is to attach the formula =average(C3..C11) to cell C12 (see Figure 5.4). As soon as the

FIGURE 5.4
Spreadsheet Example:
Average Temperatures

E15	x ✓						
	A	**B**	**C**	**D**	**E**	**F**	
1							
2			Juneau	Anchorage	Bismarck	Fargo	
3		11/20	15	2	37	41	
4		11/21	15	12	18	20	
5		11/22	18	35	9	16	
6		11/23	30	33	3	21	
7		11/24	30	29	9	17	
8		11/25	30	22	10	27	
9		11/26	31	14	19	28	
10		11/27	30	21	20	11	
11		11/28	33	13	33	33	
12			25.77777777	20.11111111	17.55555555	23.77777777	
13							
14							

return or tab key is pressed to indicate that the formula has been entered, the result of the calculations appears in the designated cell.

One powerful feature of spreadsheets is that formulas are automatically adjusted when applied to different cells. For example, assume that the students decide to add the temperature for November 29 to this spreadsheet. The insert command allows a new row of data after row 11, and the average is now automatically calculated for rows 2 through 12 instead of rows 2 through 11. The formula developed to determine the average temperature for Juneau can also be copied and pasted to cell D12, and it now generates the average temperature for Anchorage. When copied to cell D12, the variables C2..C11 in the formula are automatically changed to the variables D2..D11, to produce the correct result. The capacity of a spreadsheet to make this kind of adjustment may not seem significant in this example, but consider the benefits if the example contained fifty cities and students wanted to compare average temperatures as new data were added each day for a month. Instead of entering fifty formulas each day, one formula could be entered one time and quickly copied to the columns for the other forty-nine cities; the formulas would adjust as the rows of data for each new day were added.

Most spreadsheet programs also allow numerical data to be represented in a variety of chart and graph formats (line graphs, pie charts, bar graphs), as in Figure 5.5. The opportunity to visualize numerical data may provide a useful perspective when students try to interpret the data. Students may also use the charts and graphs generated with a spreadsheet program in reports summarizing their research and analyses.

FIGURE 5.5
Bar Graph
Summarizing Average
November
Temperatures

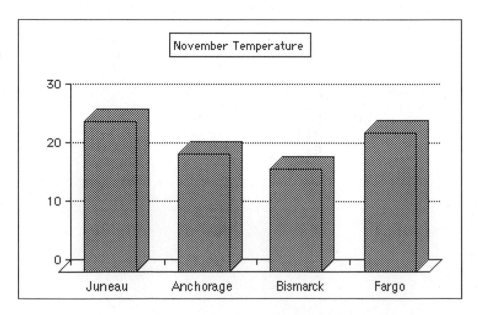

Working with charts and graphs provides opportunities for students to learn to interpret them. Because newspapers, magazines, and all types of educational materials communicate important data using charts and graphs, learning to interpret and critique them is an important educational objective.

DATABASES

What are databases used for?

Database programs are used to organize, store, and search for information. Although different software companies may describe their products using their own terminology, all databases are organized into three hierarchical levels: *fields*, *records*, and *files*.

Individual elements of information are stored in fields. Each **field** holds a user-designated category of information: flower pictures, last names, phone numbers, dates of birth, favorite baseball players, bird songs, or virtually any other category of information the user can imagine. Fields themselves are containers. In creating a field, the user establishes a field name, such as zip code, last name, or flower picture, and indicates the type of information that will appear in the field (a zip code would contain a number, a last name would contain text, and a flower picture would contain a graphic).

A **record** is a meaningful collection of fields and is really the defining feature of a database. Many computer applications allow the storage and retrieval of text, graphic, and numerical data, but the database requires the user to organize information so that the same set of fields is used consistently to describe the attributes of whatever happens to be the focus of the database.

Flexibility of databases

It is difficult to be much more specific about the purpose of a database, because a database can be prepared to organize categories of information on nearly any topic you might imagine. Commercial databases might be used to describe the attributes of the parts sold by an automotive supply store or the characteristics of potential customers a business might try to interest in its products. For the automotive parts database, fields might include part name, part number, a picture of the part, cost per item, number of items in a minimal order, and the name of the company manufacturing each part. The fields in a school's database might include student name, grade level, teacher, birthday, parents' or guardians' names, home phone number, parents' or guardians' work phone number, and emergency phone number. Students might use a database to investigate the characteristics of different countries (country name, population, size, form of government, primary language, capital city, gross national product, government leaders), or they might create a database for information they have gathered about the nutritional characteristics of different foods that adolescents consume. The total stored information about one automotive part, one customer, one student, one country, or one food represents a record within the appropriate database. The total collection of

Focus

Using a Spreadsheet to Help Understand the Solution to an Algebraic Equation

Solve the equation $4x - 14 = 4 - 2x$. We expect most of you still remember how to do this and end up with $x = 3$. How did you find the solution? You probably moved $-2x$ to the left side of the equation (reversing the sign) and -14 to the right side. Then you added and subtracted where possible to generate $6x = 18$. From there you divided each side by 6 and arrived at the answer: $x = 3$.

Now here is a different question: What does $x = 3$ symbolize? What have you found when you solve the equation $4x - 14 = 4 - 2x$? We suspect that many people who can solve the problem we have provided have no idea what the solution represents.

You may not understand what you have found when you solved the problem you were presented because you were able to arrive at an answer by relying on some well-learned rules. Collectively these rules represent an algorithm: a procedure that generates a correct solution if followed correctly. The math standards encourage that students learn to solve equations in different ways because of the problem we have just attempted to demonstrate: rote algorithmic procedures do not ensure understand-

ing (National Council of Teachers of Mathematics, 1989). A spreadsheet provides one alternative to the algorithmic approach you have learned to rely on.

Look carefully at Figure 5.6. In row 3, you see a sequence of numerical values: 1, 2, 3, and so on. These numbers will be used as values for the variable x. The cell entries in row 4 are calculated by substituting the value for x from row 3 in the expression $4x - 14$. Using the spreadsheet, cell C4 would be assigned to the value =4*c3 − 14. Once entered, this formula could be copied to the other cells of row 4 to generate the remaining values quickly. Cell c5 would be calculated as =4 − 2*c3. Again, the formula would be copied to the cells of row 5.

A spreadsheet (this happens to be Microsoft Excel) usually allows the generation of graphs as an alternative way to represent data. If rows 4 and 5 are transformed into a line graph, the display contained in Figure 5.6 is generated. If you look carefully, you should have a better understanding of what the solution to $4x - 14 = 4 - 2x$ represents. It is the x value at the intersection of the lines defined by $4x - 14$ and $4 - 2x$.

Source: Based on Niess, 1998.

records making up one of these databases is called a **file**. The file contains the entire collection of information about automotive parts, customers, students, countries, or foods.

DEVELOPING A DATABASE

Establishing the purpose of a database

The first and perhaps most important step in developing a database has nothing to do with the computer. The database developer needs to think carefully

FIGURE 5.6
Spreadsheet Used to Solve Algebra Equation

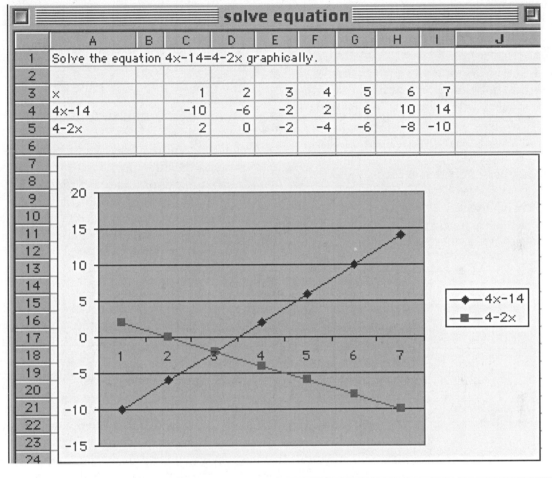

about the purpose of the database: who will use it, what kinds of backgrounds end users will have, and what questions they will want to ask of the database.

Consider the relatively popular suggestion of having elementary students develop a database of library books they have read. What would be the purpose of this database? The primary purpose might be either to provide information the teacher can use to evaluate student understanding or to provide a resource that other students can use to find an interesting book to read. This distinction would influence the categories of information included and what specific information students would provide in the database. If the purpose of the database is to interest other students in reading new books, it probably

Activities and Projects for Your Classroom

Spreadsheet Activities

Here are some ideas for spreadsheet projects:

- Take surveys on topics such as favorite foods, hobbies, sports, or pets. Graph the frequency with which the more popular alternatives were mentioned.
- Keep track of money earned from classroom projects or schoolwide fundraisers.
- Keep personal grade records.
- Keep records of calorie intake.
- Plan a budget.
- Calculate actual expenditures for different rate mortgages.

- Make conversion tables for weights and measures.
- Calculate age and weight on different planets.
- Plan a trip, and calculate distances for different routes.
- Collect litter for a week. Sort, weigh, and measure the litter. Use charts and graphs to motivate a campaign for recycling.
- Grow bean plants under different conditions (temperature, light), use a spreadsheet to keep track of data and represent the data with charts and graphs. ✳

should not provide a complete summary of the books, because this would diminish the excitement of reading mysteries and many other types of fiction. What categories or fields of information would be important to include? There are many possibilities, including author, illustrator, publication date, topic, genre, storage location of book, other books by the author, perceived difficulty, and perceived interest value.

Creating a template or layout

Once the database developer has established its purpose and scope, the second step is to use the database software to create a **template** (sometimes called a layout). In this process, the developer specifies the fields and, in some applications, positions them as they should appear on the computer screen. Many database applications allow the developer to establish attributes of fields. Depending on the program, it may be necessary to specify how much space (that is, how many characters) to set aside for each field and what type of information (text, number, date, picture) to include in each.

Specifying the type of information has a purpose you might not expect. In some programs, a field holding the information 06-09-00 could be identified to the program as containing text or a date (if this were to be recognized as a date, each program has a specific way in which the information would have to be entered, as in 06/09/00). One implication of establishing a field as containing a certain type of data relates to the types of searches that database users can conduct using that field. When databases grow very large, it is often most efficient to view only records having certain characteristics. How this is actually accomplished will be discussed in greater detail later. For now, imagine that the records in a database maintained by an automobile dealership contain information about all sales and that it becomes necessary to locate the owners of all cars sold between January 1999 and January 2000. If the field containing dates of sale contained information stored as a date, the appropriate records could be found. If the information had been stored as text, the program could locate only a specific match (say, 01/03/00), not all records falling in a range.

One final issue is important to consider. The usefulness of a database may depend on how closely the individuals entering and retrieving information follow conventions. In the example in the next section, you will see a database used to organize information about wildflowers encountered on a biology field trip. One characteristic of the flowers noted in this database was color. Different students using this database might have entered information in different ways: "white," "it was white," or "off-white," for example. It is helpful to know that the entry in this field should be a single word and perhaps that it should be one of a predetermined number of alternatives.

INVESTIGATING WILDFLOWERS: A DATABASE PROJECT

The wildflower database was the result of a summer biology field trip. The purpose of the database project was to give some structure to the field trip itself and to generate continuing activities that students could pursue once they had returned to the classroom. Before the trip, students decided on the layout, or template, for the database. The purpose of the information collected in the database was to help students investigate the relationship among location (open meadow, heavy woods, woods clearing), species of wildflowers identified, and physical characteristics (particularly height and color) of the flowers. The students also decided to record any other characteristics that students locating the flowers might find interesting. With these general goals in mind, the layout was to include fields allowing entry of common name, scientific name, location, habitat, observation date, flower color, and flower size. A general field was also included for extended comments, and a graphics field was included to hold an image of the flower. The layout for the wildflower project appears in Figure 5.7. The database application for this project was FileMaker Pro.

Students went into the field with a wildflower field guide, video camera, notebooks, and insect repellent. They worked in pairs to locate and identify as many wildflowers as possible and used the video camera to record an image of each flower that could later be digitized once they returned to school and inserted it in the database. Figure 5.8 shows a sample record from the completed database. You might wonder why we would use a video camera instead of simply collecting specimens. In part, this decision was made because of

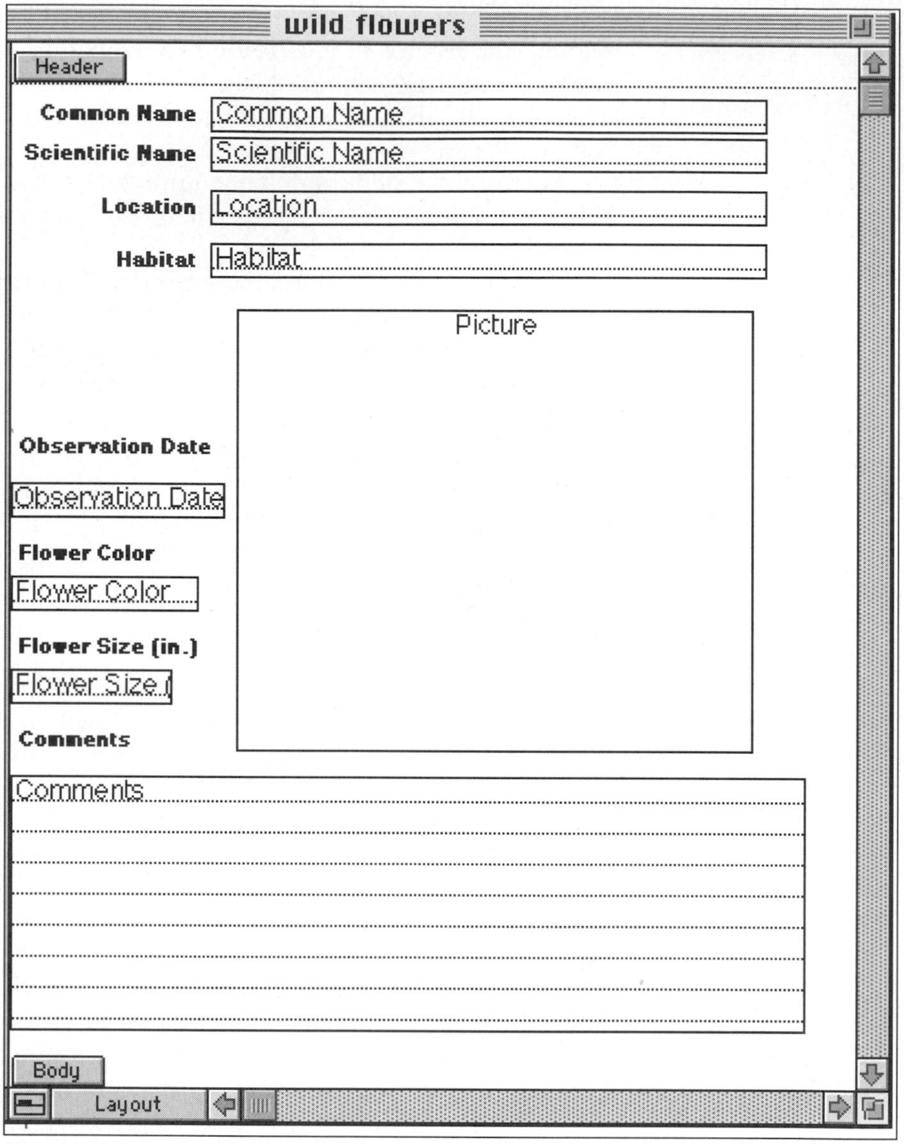

FIGURE 5.7
Wildflower Database
Template

interest in using the technology and because digitizing images from video allows schools to avoid the cost of developing film (see Chapter 9). The unnecessary collection of living materials is also an issue that students need to consider; in fact, some species of wildflowers, such as the lady's slipper, are protected by some state laws.

Once the records were complete, students applied sort and find functions to ask different questions of the database. Most database programs allow the

FIGURE 5.8
Record from
Wildflower Database

Common Name Dwarf Cornel Bunchberry
Scientific Name Cornus canadensis
Location Webb Lake, Wisconsin
Habitat Forest - Cross Country Ski Trail

Observation Date

06-09-99

Flower Color

White

Flower Size (in.)

6

Comments

This plant was found on a slope along the ski trail. The plant seems to grow in bunches. The white flower is not really a flower - the flower identification book says the white structures are bracts - the flowers are small green structures in the very middle. The book also says the flower grows in cold northern woods and has scarlet berries later in the season. Leaves occur in whorls of 6. The flower blooms May-June. The flower belongs to the dogwood family.

output from a sort or find operation to be described in a new version of the original layout. Often it is useful to create a layout containing a subset of the fields in the database and perhaps to organize this layout differently. For example, it is possible to create a two-column display sorted by habitat in which the first column contains the habitat (forest or meadow) and the second column displays the common plant name. In this display format, data from several records are displayed on the screen or printed page at the same time. If the records were sorted alphabetically on the habitat field, the initial rows of this report would list the plants found in the forest and the later rows would list plants found in meadows. This would allow students to discover which plants were unique to the forest and which plants were found in both habitats.

LEARNING WITH AND ABOUT SPREADSHEET AND DATABASE PROGRAMS

Both spreadsheet and database applications could certainly be used more frequently in classrooms. In a recent survey (Ravitz et al., 1999), teachers were asked if their students had made use of a database or a spreadsheet in at least three lessons during the past year. Only 8 percent of teachers working in elementary classrooms said their students met this criterion. Middle-school and secondary students made only slightly more use of these types of software. The study indicated that 17 percent of students in science classes, 13 percent in math classes, and 11 percent in social studies classes used a spreadsheet or database a total of three times. Although it has been argued that creating databases and working with spreadsheets can develop higher-level thinking skills and provide insights in course content (Hartson, 1993; Jonassen, Peck, & Wilson, 1999), researchers have paid little attention to evaluating the impact of experiences with these types of programs. Perhaps the lack of evaluation studies is a consequence of the relatively low level of classroom use.

A CONCLUDING GLIMPSE OF TOOL USE IN THE CLASSROOM

Data from classrooms indicate that tools are used less frequently than might be expected. When tools are used, much of the instructional time is focused on learning how to use the tools rather than on applying the tools to learning activities. In some cases, this situation can be explained by lack of time and equipment. Another important limitation is lack of teacher experience with tool applications and the ways that tools can be used in classroom activities. This chapter describes the characteristics of each tool application and provides an example to demonstrate how each is used. In addition, we have identified learning processes that teachers might encourage as students use these tools in projects. This discussion will continue as we consider telecommunication activities in the next chapter.

With the exception of the rather extensive work related to word processing, the educational potential of computer tools has not been carefully evaluated. The findings associated with word processing would likely generalize to the application of the other tools. The mere exposure of younger students to tool applications does not necessarily result in more meaningful learning. At

Focus

Tabletop: A Database Environment Developed for Educational Settings

For the most part, the tools we describe in this chapter were not created specifically for classroom use. They are commonly used in the offices of many businesses and organizations and also appear on many home computers. The "educational bundles" that schools purchase contain the standard software, but may also supply a manual describing classroom projects or files with either data or templates suited to educational tasks.

Tabletop is different in that it is an educational product with features assumed to enhance higher-order thinking and learning. Although it is certainly possible to accomplish similar ends with standard tool software, it may be easier to develop data analysis skills with a more focused product. *Tabletop* is built around the ability to explore flexibly the interaction among variables and represent these relationships visually in multiple ways. Our example extends our previous inquiry into regional differences in winter temperature. We first created a database of state and provincial capitals that included fields for (1) latitude, (2) average January temperature, and (3) location of the state or province relative to an ocean (inland or coastal) (and some other variables not relevant to this discussion). Some of the data entered into these fields are visible in Figure 5.9.

The special environment for exploring the database is called a Tabletop. We used an axis plot to analyze the relationship between temperature and latitude. This is one of several plot formats available and seemed most ap-propriate for exploring the relationship between two continuous variables. In Figure 5.9, you can see that winter temperature and latitude have a strong linear relationship. Our particular interest was in exploring deviations from this linear relationship (see the previous discussion of winter temperatures in North Dakota and Alaska on page 177). Because of the moderating effect of the nearby oceans, we hypothesized that cities in coastal states and provinces would be the most deviant from the general trend we had observed. In an attempt to test this hypothesis, we used a feature of *Tabletop* that allows a field entry to be displayed along with the plotted data points. If you look closely at the data points in Figure 5.9, you will see that all of the outliers above the general trend line are labeled with a "c" for coastal. Our hypothesis seems to be confirmed. Further exploration is possible by investigating individual cases. All of the information available for an individual data point can be displayed by clicking on that point. The most deviant case appears to be Juneau, Alaska.

We created this database to answer a particular question, and it probably is not really good for much else. You might consider what additional variables you would have added to allow some related questions to be investigated. We might have searched for July temperatures to contrast with winter temperatures in North America, for example. Are summer temperatures as strongly related to latitude as winter temperatures? ✳

FIGURE 5.9
Tabletop Database (rear) and *Tabletop* (front) Displays. The graphed data show the relationship between the latitude of state or provincial capitals and average January temperature.

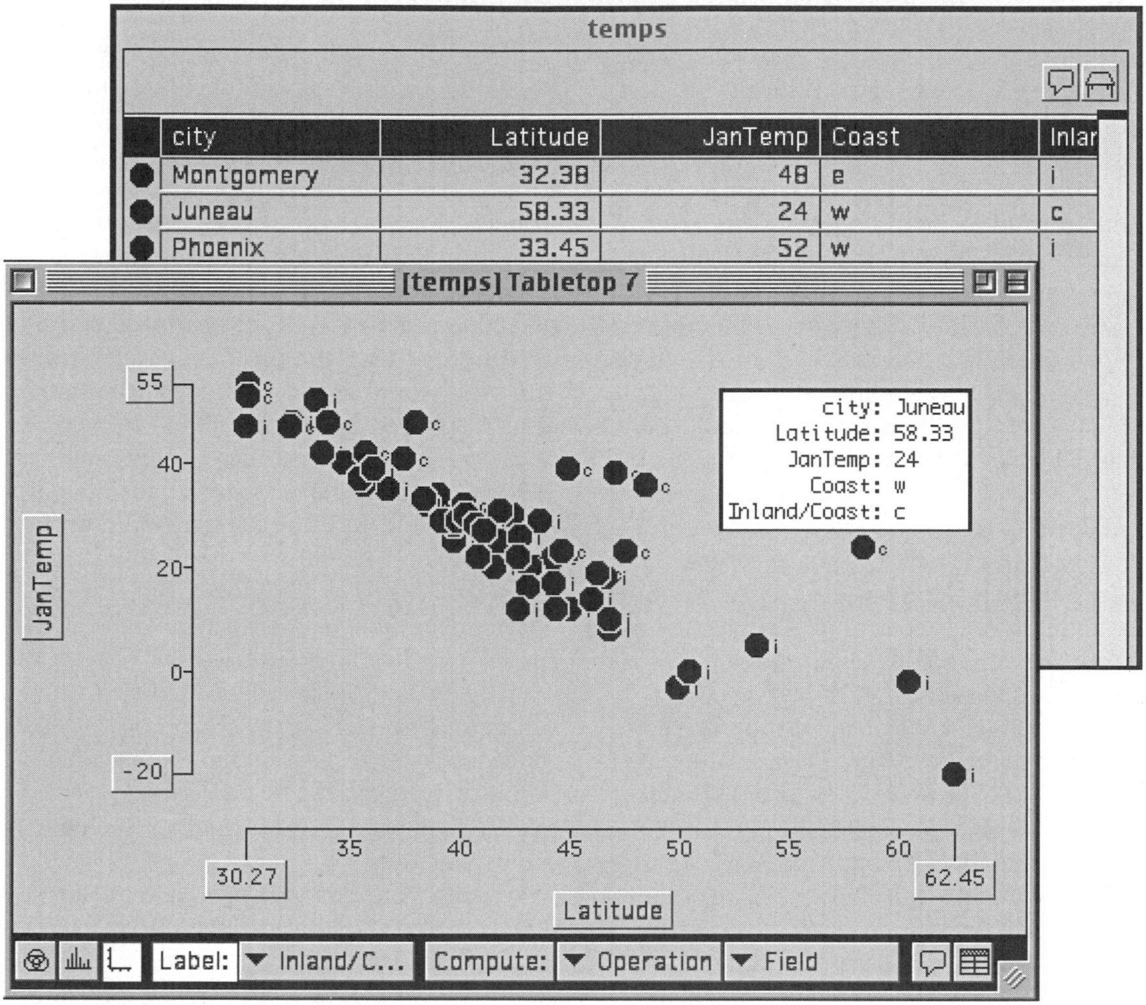

least with modest levels of experience, students will likely apply their traditional approaches to learning when using the tools. To be realized, the potential inherent in projects based on tool applications will require careful structuring, guidance, and modeling on the teacher's part.

SUMMARY

The most common computer tool applications are word processing, spreadsheets, databases, and telecommunications. In general, computer tools allow users to perform tasks with increased efficiency or quality. In addition, the most common computer tools can be applied in content areas in ways that give students a more active role in learning.

You might think of the difference in the purpose of word processing–based writing activities as the distinction between learning to write and writing to learn. Teachers are urged to consider word processing as one component of a writing environment. An effective environment for developing communication skills seems to emphasize coaching, authentic tasks, the writing community, and the writing process approach.

Spreadsheet and database applications are also described in terms of the power of these tools and the potential benefits of using them to explore content-area topics. Database programs are suited to the organization of factual information and the exploration of potential relationships within this information. Working with a completed database allows students to propose and test hypotheses about different relationships among the stored data. Spreadsheet programs allow many of the same opportunities in exploring quantitative data. Students can manipulate the data, evaluate hypotheses, and visually represent conclusions in the form of graphs and charts.

REFLECTING ON CHAPTER 5

Activities

◆ Create a paper layout for a database on an area of interest. What fields would be included? How would the fields be arranged? What questions should potential users be able to ask of the database?

◆ Evaluate the suitability of a particular word processing program for the type of general across-the-curriculum use described in this chapter. Consider such issues as ease of use, cost, formatting capabilities, and the ability to incorporate graphics. Describe to or demonstrate for your classmates what you have learned.

◆ Create a simple paper spreadsheet gradebook capable of determining the final percentage for two tests and two quizzes, each worth a different number of points. In your sketch of a spreadsheet, indicate the cells in which student name, test and quiz scores, and final percentage should appear. Write the formula for calculating the final percentage for two students, and indicate the cells to which each version of this formula should be attached. You should be able to complete this task using the sum function =sum(b2,c2,d2) and division =b4/a4. *Hint:* Use one row of your spreadsheet to keep track of the points possible on each test or quiz.

Key Terms

cell *(p. 173)*
copy *(p. 164)*
cursor *(p. 164)*
cut *(p. 164)*
database *(p. 179)*
delete *(p. 164)*
field *(p. 179)*
file *(p. 180)*
font *(p. 163)*
formatting *(p. 163)*
insert *(p. 164)*
justification *(p. 163)*
margin *(p. 163)*

mindtool *(p. 160)*
pasting *(p. 164)*
record *(p. 179)*
select *(p. 164)*
spell checker *(p. 164)*
spreadsheet *(p. 173)*
style *(p. 163)*
tab *(p. 163)*
template *(p. 182)*
word processing *(p. 160)*
word wrap *(p. 162)*
writing process approach *(p. 168)*

Resources to Expand Your Knowledge Base

Software

AppleWorks is available for the Macintosh operating system from Apple Computer. (**http://www.apple.com/education/k12/products/appleworks/**)

   Excel is available for the Macintosh and Windows operating systems from the Microsoft Corporation. (**http://www.microsoft.com/**)

   Inspiration is available for the Windows or Macintosh operating systems from Inspiration Software. (**http://www.inspiration.com/**)

   Tabletop and *Tabletop Jr.* were developed for both the Windows and Macintosh platforms from TERC Software and distributed by Broderbund. (**http://www.broder. com/**)

Word Processing, Database, and Spreadsheet Applications

Some companies and some enterprising authors have written books explaining how general software tools can be used in the classroom. These books provide general instruction in the use of the tools, as well as content-area ideas for teachers. Rather than making recommendations, we suggest that you search popular online booksellers for books making use of the tool software you have available. You might try:

   Barnes and Noble (**http://www.barnesandnoble.com/**)

   Borders (**http://www.borders.com/**)

   Amazon.Com (**http://www.amazon.com/**)

The companies selling tool software may also have Web sites focused on educational applications:

   AppleWorks (**http://www.apple.com/education/k12/products/appleworks/**)

   Microsoft Products (**http://www.microsoft.com/education/k12/classroom/**)

   Computer magazines for teachers often provide content-area ideas making use of tool software. One example consistent with the writing process approach is:

Pon, K. (1988, March). Process writing in the one-computer classroom. *Computing Teacher, 15* (6), 33–37.

Student Publication Sites on the World Wide Web

KidPub provides opportunities for both classes and individual students to present their work. (**http://www.kidpub.org/kidpub/**)

KidNews accepts news stories written by students with the understanding that the stories may then be taken from the Web site for use in local publications. Kid-News also encourages discussion about news gathering, writing, and computer applications in education. (**http://www.kidnews.com/**)

MidLink is an electronic magazine for students who are ten to fifteen years old. Theme issues are announced, and student submissions are evaluated for possible publication. (**http://longwood.cs.ucf.edu:80/~MidLink/**)

Global Show and Tell exhibits works in a variety of formats created by children up to age seventeen. When we visited the site, a drawing from a two-year-old was included. (**http://www.telenaut.com/gst**)

Keyboarding

Instructors interested in keyboarding issues can join a listserv at **http://www.onelist.com/subscribe/keystrokes.**

Some Web Sites That Provide Weather Data

The Weather Channel (**www.weather.com**)

The Weather Underground (**www.wunderground.com**)

USA Today Weather (**www.usatoday.com/weather**)

Keyboard Computers

The AlphaSmart Pro is available from Intelligent Peripheral Devices. Stored files can be transferred to either a Macintosh or a PC with Windows. The company manufacturing this product maintains a Web site at **http://www.alphasmart.com**.

The DreamWriter is available from NTS Computer Systems. Several models are available, some capable of connecting to the World Wide Web. Stored files can be transferred to either a Macintosh or a PC with Windows. The company manufacturing this product maintains a Web site at **http://www.dreamwriter.com**.

Computers and Writing Instruction

The role that computers play in teaching writing has generated so much interest that it now represents an area of research and practice complete with its own academic journals, professional organizations, annual conventions, college courses on how it should be done, Web sites, and listservs. There are some very practical issues to address, such as the level of keyboard competence necessary for effective writing, and some areas in which the field is pushing the boundaries of traditional writing, such as the rhetorical elements of Web authoring and idea processing software for authors.

Computers and Composition is a journal from Ablex Publishing (355 Chestnut St., Norwood, NJ 07648) developed for those with special interests in this area. The journal hosts a related Web site at **http://human.www.sunet.se/cc/index.html**.

The Alliance for Computer and Writing (ACW) is an organization offering support to K–12 and college faculty. The organization has affiliated regional and some state chapters. Its Web site is a great way to become familiar with the issues in the field, locate a variety of resources, and learn about other groups interested in related topics. The ACW Web site is located at **http://english.ttu.edu/acw/**.

Writing the Information Superhighway explores the relationship between writing and the Internet:

Condon, W., & Butler, W. (1997). *Writing the information superhighway.* Boston: Allyn and Bacon.

Chapter **6**

Learning with Internet Tools

ORIENTATION

In this chapter, you will read about various Internet tools that will allow you and your students to connect to other people, interactive services, and stored information in a variety of formats. We will explain how you can connect to these resources and use them in productive ways.

Focus Questions

- ◆ What are the different types of Internet tools available to teachers and students?
- ◆ What are some e-mail activities that can be adapted for the content area you plan to teach?
- ◆ How can course-relevant World Wide Web resources be found?
- ◆ With so many resources available on the World Wide Web, how can teachers structure Web projects to engage students in meaningful inquiry?

Meaningful Use of the Internet

We have several computers, lots of software, and a teenage daughter in our home, a combination that has provided some interesting opportunities to observe how young people use technology in unstructured and informal situations. Access to the Internet has long been an interest in our house. E-mail and online chats were entertaining for a while. In the mid-1990s, small groups of students would assemble in our home office after school, connect to a commercial online service, go to a chat room, and spend time talking with others about whatever it is young people talk about. At the time, we were connected through a service that charged us extra after we exceeded a monthly limit, and after a couple of large monthly bills, we decided to curb this activity. We now have an unlimited account, but interest in chat rooms seemed to have waned. The students all seem to have their own personal e-mail accounts using a free service.

When home access to the World Wide Web first became available, there were many new opportunities for exploration and fun. Our youngest daughter, Kim, was learning to play the guitar at the time. She found a place on the "Net" from which to download the words and chords to some of her favorite songs. Her instructor had been doing this for some time, and he has encouraged her to continue; apparently it's more fun to practice songs you hear on the radio than those in some dull old lesson book. Kim is also interested in whales and thinks she wants to be a marine biologist. North Dakota is about as far from an ocean as you can get, so her whale-watching opportunities are rare. Web sites dedicated to the observation and preservation of whales keep her interest alive.

Web use for Kim extends beyond hobbies. She searches for material for school reports and seeks information about issues that concern her. Recently she informed Cindy that she had found "three different places on the Net where it said you should go to the doctor when you start getting zits." This real problem in her life (we've all been teenagers) led her to search the Internet for information that might help her solve it. Cindy thought that the pimple on her forehead probably did not yet require a visit to the doctor, but she did agree that a visit would be helpful if acne became a serious problem. When I was that age, I too used to believe I had all kinds of serious conditions. I remember reading a book of medical advice my parents had, looking for answers. Perhaps all that has really changed is the information source.

Kim was recently appointed to a committee of young adults asked to make recommendations on technology access for the city of Grand Forks. This was a surprise to her and to us. Perhaps as a reaction to the stereotypes many people have attached to her parents, she takes great pains to distance herself from any visible sign that technology is interesting. Technology is not high on her list of personal causes. However, the point is that although our daughter and her friends are not particularly interested in learning about how computers work, they have become quite adept at using computers and the Internet to learn about the things that are important in their world. Not all of the time they spend using the Internet is productive. Sometimes it's just for fun, and once in a while, it gets a bit out of hand. However, the Internet is a useful tool, and they usually apply it in naturally productive ways.

Similar goals should be established for classroom applications. Students should have the opportunity to use the Internet to challenge themselves to address authentic tasks. As we discuss Internet resources available to students and educators, we will also explore how these resources can be used as part of content-area learning.

EDUCATIONAL ACCESS TO INTERNET RESOURCES

The Internet provides highly efficient access to a variety of helpful and stimulating resources. Visionaries see the Internet as offering new opportunities in many areas. Although our intent is to concentrate on current and future educational applications, we will not ignore other developments entirely. From the outset, it is important to recognize that the Internet is a shared resource that provides opportunities for commerce, entertainment, and education. No single entity is developing it, and certainly no single entity is paying for it. Educators must understand that they are tapping into a resource not designed specifically for their benefit. But it is a resource of unparalleled potential nonetheless.

The Internet serves many purposes.

The Clinton administration made an effort to establish a national commitment to connect schools to the Internet. In 1994, Vice President Al Gore proposed a vision for a "different kind of superhighway that can . . . give every American, young and old, the chance for the best education available to anyone, anywhere" (IITF/CAT, 1994). The goal was to have all classrooms and libraries connected to the Internet by the year 2000. The Telecommunications Act of 1996 was an attempt to make school connections more feasible by establishing the expectation that states, communities, and the Federal Communications Commission would work together to lower the cost of telecommunications services to schools. This act eventually resulted in a federal subsidy commonly referred to as the *e-rate*. Although it is available to all schools, the subsidy is more generous for rural schools and schools with larger proportions of low-income students. (The e-rate and other issues that are related to equity receive greater attention in Chapter 11.) As a nation, there has been a commitment to the educational potential of the Internet and to ensuring that all learners can take advantage of this potential.

Commitment to connect all students

THE INTERNET

The **Internet** is an international collection of computer networks with an estimated 215 million users worldwide—a number that continues to grow daily (Global Reach, 1999). To put this growth in perspective, the estimated number of Internet users was 40 million when we wrote the second edition of this book in 1998. Think of the Internet as a meta-network—that is, a network of networks. There are huge networks providing high-speed regional network backbones, and there are small networks within individual office buildings. One of these networks might be located at your university or local school district. By running the right software on one of the computers on any one of the networks, you become an active part of the entire system.

A network of networks

A unique characteristic of the Internet is that no one company or country really owns it. Members of the Internet community have made a commitment to share resources and to transfer information over the network in an agreed-on manner. This method of transferring information from computer to computer is called **transmission control protocol/Internet protocol (TCP/IP).** Each computer on the Internet has a unique identity or address called an **IP number.** Often the same computer also has a **domain name.** The difference between the two is that the IP number is expressed as a series of numbers and the domain name as an easier-to-remember series of abbreviated words. For example, the IP number for my desktop computer, 134.129.172.88, gets translated as grabe.psych.und.nodak.edu. The unique designation for each computer is important, ensuring that data sent over the Internet get to the right place. You don't have to understand how TCP/IP functions to appreciate what it allows users of the network to accomplish. Files can be quickly sent and received by different kinds of computers over great distances with great accuracy. Messages and files end up where they are supposed to, at a specific computer with a specific IP number. Once you get past the equipment, the software, and the mysteries of how it all works, the ability to communicate so easily with so many people, to share what you know and what you feel, is motivating.

Unique designation for each computer

Rapid growth

Investment in Internet connectivity has been increasing so quickly it is impossible to report accurate statistics. Even the common indicators used to demonstrate trends in school access to the Internet have changed. For example, when we wrote the second edition, the common indicator was the proportion of schools with Internet access. In 1996, about 50 percent of schools had Internet access. Now, with school access over 90 percent, the individual school is no longer a useful unit of measurement for understanding the rate of change. Changes in access are now quantified in terms of the proportion of classrooms with Internet access or even the proportion of classrooms with a certain number of computers (four seems to be the current standard) connected to the Internet. Approximately 40 percent of classrooms offer Internet access. Local area access, allowing multiple computers to be connected from a room, is present in approximately 18 percent of classrooms (Becker, 1999). We anticipate that this process of change will continue and suggest that you connect to the National Center for Educational Statistics (**http://nces.ed.gov**) for more current data.

Our discussion will focus on how teachers and students might take advantage of the resources that are available. Our primary focus will be on instructional strategies. Occasionally we will present some of the details of how a particular program used to access Internet resources works. However, we will not take the time to teach you everything you need to know to accomplish all of the activities described here. If you are interested in step-by-step instructions, you might consider one of the sources listed at the end of this chapter.

INTERNET RESOURCES

Access people, files, interactive hypermedia, and programs

One way to organize a discussion of the educational value of the Internet is to suggest that the Internet provides access to other people, to the multicomputer interactive hypermedia resource referred to as the World Wide Web, and to files or stores of information and programs that can be copied for personal use. We describe each of these resource categories, provide basic information about the computer tools and techniques needed to access each type of resource, and discuss ways to use these resources in classroom settings.

ACCESS TO PEOPLE

Putting people in touch

One of the most powerful uses of technology is putting people in touch with other people. Students and teachers can convey ideas and information nearly instantaneously over great distances, or the students or teachers at the other end of the conversation can have the freedom to respond at a convenient time, when they feel prepared.

There are other advantages to messages communicated using technology. Messages are automatically stored, so information collected in this way can be reviewed, integrated, and forwarded to other interested parties. If an interesting idea comes your way, it is relatively easy to forward a copy of it to others with whom you communicate. Obviously, communications should be stored and shared only when such activities are ethical.

Chat mode

Internet information exchanges among people fall into several categories. Real-time exchanges are possible. Sometimes this form of interaction is referred to as **chat mode.** "Keyboard conversations" might be a better description, since this kind of interaction is in the form of typed text. Commercial services such as America Online and CompuServe support a number of special interest groups, which often arrange specific times and topics for discussion. Internet portals such as Excite (**www.excite.com**) and the Microsoft Network (**www.msn.com**) also provide access to chat sessions. In some cases, a group will arrange for an expert to be available for a particular topic. All you need to do to participate in such a discussion is to log on to the service at the appropriate time and select the discussion you want from the various activities available. The comments in one of these discussions will appear on your screen as they are typed in by different people around the country. If you like, you may contribute your own thoughts when there is a pause. Commercial services often save transcripts of important discussions and make transcripts available as files. Chat opportunities are also available through **Internet relay chat (IRC).** An IRC works something like an international CB radio (for those of you who remember CBs) complete with "handles" (nicknames) and channels. A more conventional analogy is that of rooms. Groups organize themselves for discussion in different virtual rooms. Once you are connected, anything you type is relayed to the screen of everyone connected in your

Making the Connection

To understand how a computer on your desk can connect with the Internet and with resources on thousands of other computers throughout the world, it helps to think of the system as involving several components: the Internet service provider, the transfer line, the hardware device connecting your computer to the transfer line, and your computer and its software.

Internet Service Provider

An **Internet service provider** (**ISP**) is a company or organization that connects multiple users to the Internet backbone. Some of the largest ISPs are companies whose names you probably recognize (MCI and AT&T) and others whose names are less familiar (UUNET). A local ISP may be operated by your university or a small private company in your community (check the phone book under Internet). The connection to the Internet may also be provided through an online service provider such as America Online (AOL), Microsoft Network (MSN), or Prodigy. These companies offer propriety information resources, available only to members of the service, but they also connect members to the Internet at large.

Transfer Line

To get from your school or home to the ISP, digital information must travel over some kind of transfer line. This link may be a regular copper phone line—a setup often referred to as a *dial-up connection* or *dial-on-demand connection*. An **integrated services digital network** (**ISDN**) or **digital subscriber line** (**DSL**) connection provides a faster connection. Special requirements for ISDN and DSL connections limit the use of such systems to high population areas.

Leased fiber optic lines, sometimes called dedicated connections, come in different bandwidths. The *bandwidth* indicates the amount of information that can be moved in a fixed amount of time. Some common fiber optic lines transmit information at 56/64 Kbps (kilobytes per second). T1 lines (1.5 megabits per second) are also common. Schools sometimes lease part of a T1 line, known as a *fractional T1*. Many school districts using a leased line also use a service called frame relay, which allows multiple buildings to connect to a single leased line. Leased fiber optic lines are currently the most practical way to provide the bandwidth necessary to serve a large number of students.

Other options are available and may be used more heavily in the future. One approach makes use of the cable connections currently intended to bring a signal to your television set. A less common option relies on satellite technology. At one level, these various options are in competition, and it is hard to predict how much success the backers of these different approaches will have in popularizing their particular vision for the Internet.

Hardware Devices for Connecting to the Transfer Line

To send data through the transfer line, your computer needs a device to connect to that line. The type of device varies depending on the nature of your connection.

A **modem** is a hardware device connecting the computer to a copper phone line. A modem is necessary because a computer and a telephone communicate using different types of signals. A computer uses a digital signal and a telephone an analog signal. An **analog signal** is continuous, and the digital signal is discrete (either 1 or 0). An **analog modem,** the more popular type currently, functions by converting the computer's digital signal into an analog signal that can be sent over a standard phone line. The term *modem* stands for "modulate/demodulate," which represents the processes of changing a signal back and forth between the digital and analog forms.

Most analog modems today offer transfer rates of at least 28.8 Kbps. ISDN lines, which use an all-digital technology, are capable of transfer rates up to 128 Kbps, but they require a different type of modem and supporting hardware when the distance to the ISP is several miles.

For a still faster connection using fiber optic cable instead of standard phone lines, your computer must have a special hardware device called an *ethernet card,* which is installed in the computer itself. But it would be highly unusual for a single computer to be connected to one of these more expensive fiber optic lines. Usually several computers are first joined together in a **local area network** (**LAN**), and then the LAN is connected to the dedicated transfer line through a device called a *router*. The computers in a school lab or in different classrooms would likely be connected in this fashion.

The User's Computer and Its Software

Several different types of software must be installed on the computer you use to access the Internet. First, your computer must have TCP/IP software. This software allows each computer to conform to the common protocol that makes it possible for all computers to share resources over the Internet. Second, your computer must have application software appropriate to the type of work users want to do on the Internet. That is, if you want to send and receive e-mail, you need e-mail software. If you want to browse the World Wide Web, you need a web browser.

If you are connecting through a modem, the modem requires its own software. Most Internet applications operating over a modem require **serial line Internet protocol** (**SLIP**) or **point-to-point protocol** (**PPP**) software. A computer running SLIP or PPP effectively becomes part of the Internet. A more primitive type of connection would allow your personal computer to manipulate a remote computer on the Internet, but with this sort of connection, you could not use today's advanced applications, such as multimedia Web sites.

Not every school computer is adequate for Internet applications. Working with most of the applications described in this book requires a relatively fast central processing unit (CPU) and a significant amount of random access memory (RAM). We hesitate to say how fast or how much because new applications always seem to work best on machines of greater power. Suffice it to say that if the machine is greatly outdated, you are likely to experience some frustration in using Internet applications.✶

Personal connections with e-mail

group. Your nickname will appear, followed by your comment. If you like, you can select a private channel for discussion with a smaller group.

The most common format for interpersonal telecommunication is **electronic mail** or **e-mail.** A teacher or student using e-mail composes a message and then sends it to the address of another individual. When this individual logs on to his or her account and searches for mail, the message is detected and brought to the computer screen to be read. Exchanging e-mail messages sounds simple, and it is. And many creative projects based on the simple process of exchanging messages have demonstrated the educational potential of correspondence with other teachers, students, parents, scientists, the elderly, politicians, and potentially anyone else in the world with access to a computer, a modem, and a telephone connection. Among the more common e-mail projects are exchanges of correspondence with other students to learn about a different culture or to practice foreign language skills, projects that allow the collection and integration of data (for instance, on water quality) from many different locations, and projects that involve sharing student-generated literature or newsletters. Many students also seem to enjoy more informal opportunities to strike up friendships and correspond with a key pal. E-mail systems also allow a file to be attached to a message. Users with compatible systems can thus exchange whatever computer files they can create. Some Internet service providers (ISPs) do not allow this capability because of the storage space that must be set aside and because of the capacity required when users frequently send large files over slow connections.

Telecomputing Activity Structures

Communicating through e-mail provides the opportunity for many kinds of activities and projects. Frequently magazines written for computer-using educators (see Keeping Current in Chapter 4 on page 146) provide descriptions of classroom projects. Harris (1995) suggests that instead of looking for projects they can duplicate in their own classrooms, teachers should understand the properties of different kinds of projects—Harris calls them "activity structures"—and then apply these structures to the content being studied. Harris contends that this approach makes it more likely that classroom content will be emphasized. Similarly, we suggest that understanding these instructional strategies allows teachers to adapt the strategies to meet specific educational standards (see Chapter 2). Here is a brief review of the activity structures Harris identified:

Emphasize classroom content.

Interpersonal Exchanges. "Talk" among individuals, between an individual and a group, and among groups.

> **Key pals** Unstructured exchange among individuals or groups (e.g., exchanges to develop cultural awareness or language skills)

Using Chat in an Online Class

If you have not participated in an online chat, here is a brief description of what a chat session is like and one situation in which it might be used.

Part of my teaching responsibilities involves courses that are part of a graduate program in instructional design and technology. We have been experimenting with entirely online versions of a few of the classes that have traditionally been based on discussion, reading, and writing. Our logic has been that the methods of transferring information and communicating already used in classes of this type would be easiest to approximate online. Chat sessions were one substitute for what would normally be classroom discussions. Many of the tools discussed in this chapter (e-mail, Web pages, file transfer) were also used in the course.

A free chat tool, Instant Messenger from America Online (AIM), was used in a recent class. This tool offers two options: Instant Messenger and Chat. Instant Messenger is used to exchange messages with one other person. When you use Instant Messenger on a frequent basis, you develop what are called *buddy lists,* made up of names (often nicknames) for those individuals you frequently meet online. When you activate AIM, the program informs you of any members of your buddy list who are also online. The Instant Messenger allows you to send a message to any of these individuals, and their computer will tell them you are attempting to contact them.

The chat option works differently and requires that multiple individuals connect to a chat room. America Online offers chat rooms

or allows users to create a room for personal use. As a class, we agreed to call our chat room PSY501, the catalog abbreviation for our course, and at designated times, members of the class would connect to this room. Establishing a room with a unique name made it unlikely that the chat would be "crashed" by individuals not involved in the class. Chats were the primary form of interaction for the class and were intended to replace face-to-face class discussions. We scheduled three chat sessions a week at different times of day and required members of the class to participate in two of these sessions. The different times gave students some options, and many students participated in all sessions simply because they enjoyed the interaction.

Figure 6.1 shows the chat tool. Messages are entered in a window located near the bottom of the screen. As messages are sent, they appear in a common discussion area and continually roll up as more messages are received. Carrying on a discussion in this type of environment can become difficult when more than a few individuals are involved. It takes some time for students to enter their comments, and by the time the comment is actually submitted, the initial comment that triggered the student response may have rolled off the screen. As students begin to reply to comments submitted by other students, several slightly different topics begin to emerge with all of the different strands mixed together on the screen. If you try to follow the discussion shown in Figure 6.1, you will probably be able to imagine the nature of these challenges. AIM allows

FIGURE 6.1
Chat Tool from America Online Instant Messenger

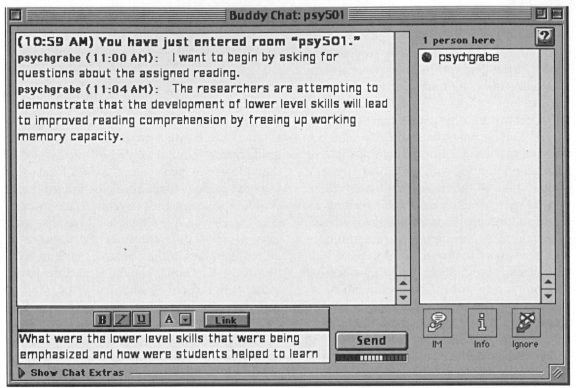

the transcript from a discussion to be saved, and we took advantage of this feature to save our chats and then make them available as Web pages for members of the class to review.

From our experience, I would think that online chats are somewhat less efficient than classroom discussion (we covered fewer topics in the same amount of time), are confusing with more than five or six students, and require that a chat leader take an active role to keep the chat focused on established goals. Although these insights all seem to focus on limitations, the students enjoyed the chat experience. The one situation that would be an exception to this positive reaction concerned class meetings that preceded course examinations. The slowness and confusion became irritants when the learning situation was more stressful. (These are personal observations based on a couple of online classes. A more formal evaluation of the limitations and advantages of online communication appears later in this chapter, on pages 206 through 208.)✳

E-mail project categories

Global classrooms Study a common topic and exchange accounts of what has been learned (e.g., themes in fairy tales)

Electronic appearances E-mail or chat interaction with a guest, perhaps after some preparation (e.g., a local engineer responds to questions from students in a physics class)

Electronic mentoring Ongoing interaction between an expert and a student on a specific topic (e.g., college education majors offer middle-school students advice on class projects)

Impersonations Participants interact "in character" (e.g., correspondence with graduate student impersonating Benjamin Franklin)

Information Collections. Working together to collect and compile information provided by participants.

Information exchanges Accumulation of information on some theme (e.g., favorite playground games, recycling practices)

Electronic publishing Publication of documents based on submission by group members (e.g., publication of a district literary magazine of short stories submitted by elementary students)

Tele-field trips Share observations made during local field trips (e.g., visits to local parks; a special case could be expeditions undertaken by experts, such as a bicycle trip through Central America)

Pooled data analysis Data collected from multiple sites are combined for analysis (e.g., cost comparison of gasoline)

Problem-Solving Projects. Focus of interaction involves solving problems.

Information searches Solve a problem based on clues and reference sources (identify state landmarks or cities in response to a progression of clues)

Electronic process writing Post written work for critiques before revision (e.g., composition students comment on classmates' papers)

Parallel problem solving Groups at different sites solve the same problem and then exchange and discuss methods and conclusions (e.g., compare ideas to improve school spirit)

Sequential creations Work on sequential components of an expressive piece (e.g., add a stanza to a poem about friendship)

Social action projects Groups take responsibility for solving an authentic problem and share reports of activities and consequences (e.g., cleaning up the environment, helping the homeless)

Mailing lists for discussions

Not all e-mail messages need to be addressed to a specific individual. In certain applications, users may send an open message to all interested readers.

This process is accomplished in several ways. With one approach, the user sends the message to a designated address, where it is relayed to a list of readers. Applications of this type are often called **mailing lists** or **listservs,** and the site from which the list originates is called the **list server.** There are many lists addressing both general and specific topics relevant to teachers. Members of active lists may receive several dozen messages a day. Some messages request assistance with problems a reader knows nothing about or has no time to provide. For example, a school recently connecting to the Internet might want to know what other schools have done to keep students from accessing inappropriate material. The reader also reads the responses of other members of the list to these requests. Many schools are interested in the issue of inappropriate material on the Internet, and of course you don't always have to be the person asking the question to learn something new. Some of the questions and messages sent through a list will be of little interest to you. These you can quickly scan and delete. A lot of information will come your way, and relevant messages may provide some useful piece of information or identify an individual to contact for further discussion.

Often discussions focus on a specific topic until the topic is exhausted and then move on to something new. This sequence of messages, called a **thread,** can be informative, and the discussion sometimes gets quite heated. A thread is created when a user "replies" to a previous message. A reply is an option allowed within most e-mail systems that keeps the **header** (a descriptive phrase) from the previous message. Archived files of list discussions allow you to a follow a thread and ignore unrelated messages.

Follow a discussion thread.

A different approach to the exchange of messages within a group does not result in a large number of messages being sent directly to you. Instead, the messages are "posted" to a network location, where users go to review the material electronically. To understand how this works, think of departmental bulletin boards in high schools that inform students of activities and news. Information on the upcoming orchestra concert, notice of band instruments for sale, and a notice of jazz band auditions would be found on the bulletin board near the music department. Other bulletin boards serving similar functions would be located throughout the school. High school students interested in different topics would peruse different bulletin boards.

Newsgroups like bulletin boards

The electronic equivalent of the bulletin board, called a **conference, forum,** or **newsgroup,** can hold hundreds of messages and can be read by people from all over the world. Often many conferences are available through the same electronic source. People who participate in conferences are encouraged to start relevant new discussions with a question or comment, respond to a posted comment, or just read the existing comments to glean whatever useful information might be available. Obviously the more participants there are, the more material will be available.

Focus

Joining a List Maintained by a Server

It is not difficult to join a list; following is a description of the process.

Electronic mailing lists usually have both a submission address and an administrative address. The submission address designates where to send messages you want included on the list. To subscribe to the list, you are usually asked to send a message to the administrative address. The message should have nothing in the portion of your message that asks for the subject of the message and should include the simple statement SUBSCRIBE LISTNAME FIRSTNAME LASTNAME as the main body of the message. Messages for members of the list are sent to the submission address.

When you first subscribe to a list, you may be sent a summary of the procedures that apply to that list. Often the procedures explain what to do if you are going to be away from your computer for a while and would rather your "e-mail box" not be filled with mail from the list, how to receive the individual messages as a digest (a single file instead of many individual messages), and how to remove yourself from the list (our explanation of this procedure follows).

One of the major problems is that users frequently forget the administrative address. Although they constantly receive e-mail messages, the messages come from the submission address, and the administrative address is not mentioned. Nevertheless, the administrative address is needed to implement any of the procedures, so save the instructions you receive when you first subscribe. Print them out and pin them to the bulletin board next to your computer, and save them as a file on that disk of very important documents. If you choose to ignore this advice, then you must be patient. The list administrator usually sends the list procedures out as a message every month or so.

It is sometimes difficult to tell if the list you subscribe to will be useful until you have tried it for a while. The purpose of the list may turn out to be something other than what you anticipated. You may also find, after subscribing to several lists, that the volume of mail is overwhelming. You can remove your name from a mailing list by sending a message to the administrative address (*not* the submission address). The message should read UNSUBSCRIBE LISTNAME (SIGN-OFF LISTNAME is also used in some cases). Sending an UNSUBSCRIBE message to the submission address rather than the administrative address is a common mistake; list readers often see messages from other members attempting to remove themselves from the list.

One more hint about using mailing lists: Often telecommunications services have an automatic reply feature, which allows you to send a message in response to one you have just received. When reading a message on a mailing list, remember that the immediate source of the message is the list server, not the person who actually wrote the message. Using the reply feature will send what you may intend to be a private message to all members on the list. More than one person has been embarrassed by such an error. The message author's address will appear somewhere in the message; this is the address to use when private correspondence is desired. ✷

Keeping Current

Finding Useful Mailing Lists

Most days we all have discussions that draw on the knowledge of our colleagues. Such casual conversations allow us to request help from experienced associates and to check out what others might think of our new ideas. Imagine having similar access to hundreds of experienced colleagues, and you can begin to appreciate the potential of mailing lists.

Here are a few mailing lists you may find helpful. Lists do change address or simply go out of service, but the ones listed here have been around a while. In addition, the Web site at **http://www.liszt.com** maintains a database of approximately 85,000 lists. Another useful directory is maintained at **http://www.tile .net/listserv/alphabetical.html.**

List Name	List Topic	Administrative Address
BGEDU-L	Forum on Educational Reform	listserv@lsv.uky.edu
EDTECH	Topics in Educational Technology	listserv@msu.edu
IECC	International Classroom Connect	iecc-request@stolaf.edu
INCLASS	Internet in the Classroom	listproc@schoolnet.carleton.ca
ITS	Integrating Technology in Schools	listserve@unm.edu
K12ADMIN	Educational Administration	listserv@suvm.syr.edu
MIDDLE-L	Middle-School Topics	listserv@postoffice.cso.uiuc.edu
SIGTEL-L	Telecommunications in Education	listserv@unmvma.unm.edu
WWWEDU	The Internet in Education	listproc@ready.cpb.org✱

Advantages and Disadvantages of Computer-Mediated Communication

The uses of the Internet we have described as providing access to people are sometimes referred to as **computer-mediated communication (CMC)**. As the opportunity to communicate by way of the Internet has become more practical, it has become important to understand the educational advantages and disadvantages of computer-mediated communication in contrast to face-to-face communication.

At first, you may not be able to imagine any possible educational advantage of interacting by way of the Internet when compared to meeting in the same classroom. However, if you take a broad view of education, some advantages of CMC are obvious. CMC is place independent—that is, individuals do not have to be in the same location to communicate. Some forms of

CMC, such as e-mail, are also time independent and do not require the participants to interact at the same point in time. For these reasons, CMC offers practical solutions to some very real educational problems relating to time and location. For example, consider the graduate course we described in our description of online chat. Some teachers in our state who want to take a course of this type live more than one hundred miles from the nearest university. They cannot drive to a class after they finish teaching for the day. We started teaching an Internet version of our course because this was the only practical option for some of our students.

Students in K–12 classrooms may also face challenges of time and place that CMC can help with. Consider some of the activity structures described on page 200. While we would encourage students to take advantage of the opportunity to spend time in other countries to learn a second language or experience another culture, the reality is that such experiences are rare. Key pal and global classroom activities take advantage of the place independence of CMC. A teacher we know is very interested in the Iditarod (the Alaskan sled dog race). She has brought mushers to her class, and her class has also communicated with mushers online. We would guess that fourth-grade students in Florida have few visits from mushers, but connecting to Iditarod Internet sites during the annual race and participating in online chats would still be possible.

The issues of time and place come into play in some other important ways. Class time is precious, especially time devoted to class discussion, and it turns out that CMC may have a significant positive impact in that area.

CMC's Impact on Discussion. The nature of classroom discussion has some startling characteristics. When classes are involved in what is defined as discussion, teachers speak between 40 and 80 percent of the time, and most communication is between the teacher and a student rather than among students (Dunkin & Biddle, 1974). Such discussions tend to draw in students who are good at developing quick responses and are able to gain the attention of the teacher and group within a time-dependent environment (Althaus, 1997). Quick responses are also rewarded because most teachers pause for less than 2 seconds after asking a question before speaking again to call on another student, rephrase the question, or provide an answer (Tobin, 1986, 1987).

Reviews of research with college students indicate that the properties of CMC change some of these patterns of interaction. It appears that online discussions encourage greater and more diverse participation. A higher proportion of students tend to be involved when given the opportunity to contribute comments by e-mail. One research group found that student comments in the classroom averaged 12 words, but contributions to an e-mail discussion averaged 106 words. Students obviously have more time to construct an e-mail message, so it is not surprising that the messages are longer. Also, e-mail messages are more complex than classroom comments and range over several topics. As you might expect, message complexity in chat sessions is more similar to that found in face-to-face classroom discussions (Althaus, 1997; Black, Levin, Mehan, & Quinn, 1983; Olaniran, Savage, & Sorenson, 1996; Quinn, Mehan, Levin, & Black, 1983). Two factors may contribute to these advantages. One is that in both chat and e-mail discussions, participating students can work on the preparation of their comments at the same time and can be assured that the comments will eventually be added to the discussion. The first student to click Send does not block out other participants. Also, CMC reduces a variety of classroom cues (sounds and visual information) that may inhibit some students. Even the visible presence of the teacher as authority figure may cause some students to take less initiative.

In summary, CMC may encourage more productive discussion by increasing the number of active student participants and extending the time available for discussion. It can help those who cannot think as quickly as others, may not be as proficient in using the language, or may be apprehensive of sharing when in the physical presence of peers (Althaus, 1997). Even for those who have no difficulty expressing themselves in class, the writing activities involved in e-mail allow the time for reflection not available in a fast-paced classroom discussion.

Potential Problems with CMC.   Despite the advantages of CMC, there are some difficulties that are important to recognize. Although some forms of CMC make use of interactive audio and video (see page 210), the forms of CMC we have mentioned here rely on keyboarding skills and are the most common. Keyboarding speed varies greatly. Participating in a chat can be frustrating even for those used to entering text at a keyboard, and students with poor keyboarding skills may even be challenged by course requirements that require the construction of e-mail.

Some difficulties of CMC derive from the same basic attributes that are also perceived as advantages. One of the most consistently recognized characteristics of text-based CMC is the reduced number and variety of visual and auditory cues that accompany the words. Some researchers think that fewer cues encourage greater student participation. But others think that the lack of cues can be associated with immature, insensitive, and unproductive behaviors. There is some indication that CMC results in more evaluative comments, including comments that are too critical (Smilowitz, Compton, & Flint, 1988). If you participate in mailing lists, you may have experienced this already. When we read the comments that some people post, we wonder if they act this way with the people they see at work. Anonymity can result in purposeful maliciousness. However, the nature of CMC may also result in unintentional problems. You should be aware that CMC messages can be misinterpreted, participants may be too blunt, and the result can be an escalating negativity. Students involved in CMC can be sensitized to these limitations, learning to become more careful in the construction of the messages they send.

THE WORLD WIDE WEB

The resources available on the Internet are disorganized because they have resulted from the efforts of many institutions and individuals operating independently and contributing whatever they think might be useful. Because the Internet lacks a central directory, it can be challenging for inexperienced users and time-consuming for anyone to pull together resources related to a specific topic.

World Wide Web is hypermedia

The **World Wide Web** (**WWW**) represents a significant improvement because it allows a variety of information sources to be interconnected through a special type of hypertext or hypermedia link (see the discussions of hypertext and hypermedia in Chapter 7). The information sources might be text documents, graphics, sounds, or even other Web sites. The major advantage to educators and students of individual Web sites is that someone else has already done the work of locating and organizing meaningful collections of Internet resources.

A Web site might be thought of as a special type of publication. In some cases, the Web author contributes the entire contents of an individual site. In other instances, a Web site consists of some material developed by the Web author and connections to other resources found on computers throughout the Internet. A Web user does not have to keep track of who authored what. The user simply follows links embedded within the content of Web pages from one topic of interest to another.

Browser software

Special software, called a **browser,** is required to connect to and interpret the protocol used by Web servers. A browser provides a graphic interface (see Figure 6.8 on page 236) and interactive involvement with the full range of hypermedia—text, pictures, sounds, and movies. You can follow links from resource to resource in a variety of ways, including using the mouse to click on specially marked pictures or words that serve as links to other resources.

First encounter is home page

The **home page** is what you encounter when you first connect to a specific Web address. On this page are links that can be clicked with the mouse. The links can be words or pictures and are usually differentiated in some way. Picture links are identified by a color border. Text links are underlined and appear in a color different from the other text on the page. (The color is not apparent here because of the need to reproduce these images in grayscale.)

Figure 6.3 shows part of the home page from the VolcanoWorld Web site operated at the University of North Dakota by Dr. Charles Wood. VolcanoWorld is located at the Web address **http://volcano.und. nodak.edu** (see Focus: Internet Addresses on page 214 for an explanation of Web addresses). As you can probably guess, VolcanoWorld was developed to provide

Emerging Technology

Videoconferencing with Microsoft NetMeeting

Videoconferencing is synchronous video and audio communication; that is, participants send and receive video and audio simultaneously. NetMeeting, free software developed by Microsoft Corporation for computers running the Windows operating system, allows educators who have an Internet connection, a computer equipped with video and audio digitizing hardware, a camera, and a microphone to participate in videoconferencing (see Figure 6.2). Special video cameras, specifically designed for the single purpose of feeding a video signal into computers, can be obtained for less than $100. A high-speed connection to the Internet is likely to be the most common barrier. A 28.8 Kbps modem connection is required for minimal quality participation. However, faster connections (see Focus: Making the Connection) increase the number of video frames sent per second and make it less likely the audio will break up.

Videoconferencing is one tool from a suite of communication options available through NetMeeting. The software also allows users to chat, exchange files, and share a white board—a graphic space on which multiple participants can draw and paste information from other applications. The NetMeeting videoconferencing tool is designed for **point-to-point** communication. A point-to-point application connects one computer with one other computer and might be contrasted with an application such as chat, in which many computers are able to send messages to many computers. There are some situations in which a teacher might want all members of a class to participate in the same conversation. For example, a common opportunity of this type would en-

gage the class in a conversation with a subject expert. The video and audio from the expert would not be sent to every computer in the classroom or lab, but would be sent to one computer and then might be displayed on a large screen or projected on a screen using a video projection system. Students wanting to ask the expert a question would have to move to the connected computer so the microphone on that computer would pick up the question. An alternative approach would allow students to ask questions through the chat tool, and the expert could then pick questions and offer a live response.

Finding ways to use NetMeeting and other videoconferencing tools (see Resources to Expand Your Knowledge Base at the end of this chapter for additional information) requires teachers and students with a sense of adventure. Classroom videoconferencing is unlike tuning into either a television news program or the interactive television you may have experienced in a college class. Sometimes the sound is garbled beyond recognition. The visual image can also be lost or change so slowly that parts of two images appear simultaneously. Still, videoconferencing is functional, and it allows some very interesting opportunities.

Connecting two computers with a videoconferencing system is easy: turn on the computer, start the software, and enter the IP number of the other computer to open a connection. The most difficult part may be determining the IP number of your own computer (ask a technician for help). Videoconferencing can be used effectively in any situation in which a visual or auditory signal would add to the authenticity of an online project. Many of the telecomputing activity structures that Harris (1995) recommended could be implemented using this technology. The companies selling or promoting videoconferencing technology recognize the opportunities for their products in the field of education and offer ideas through their Web sites.✳

FIGURE 6.2
Mark Grabe and Colleague Using NetMeeting. In this configuration, the image being sent appears as a small inset.

information about volcanoes. We can show only a very small portion of this resource here, but it should be sufficient to give you an idea of what a hypermedia Web site looks like and how such a site works. Clicking on the text "What is VolcanoWorld?" (on the home page) displays another page, part of which is shown in Figure 6.4.

Web browsers provided the first practical applications for viewing images as they are sent across the Internet. The images appear on the computer screen rather than being saved as a file for later viewing. (Browsers can also be

FIGURE 6.3
VolcanoWorld Home Page

used to save the information that is received.) Figure 6.5 on page 215 is an example of a graphic from VolcanoWorld: a satellite view of Mount St. Helens.

used to save the information that is received.) Figure 6.5 on page 215 is an example of a graphic from VolcanoWorld: a satellite view of Mount St. Helens.

The World Wide Web has incorporated many earlier uses of the Internet,
and the newer browsers allowing users to navigate the Web are incorporating
many functions of programs needed to use the Internet. A Web browser can
be used to send and receive mail, **download** files, and visit newsgroup sites.
The Internet continues to exist apart from the Web and software applications
for using the Internet still exist, but there is no real need for most users to

FIGURE 6.4
Sample Page from VolcanoWorld Web Site

What is VolcanoWorld ?

Volcanoes are one of the most dramatic phenomena in nature, attracting millions of visitors each year to US national parks, and fascinating millions more children in school science courses. We will greatly enrich the learning experiences of these targeted groups by delivering high quality remote sensing images, other data, and interactive experiments that add depth, variety and currency to existing volcano information sources.

VolcanoWorld brings modern and near real time volcano information to specific target audiences and other users of the Internet. VolcanoWorld draws extensively on remote sensing images (AVHRR, Landsat TM, Magellan, Gloria, etc.) and other data collections. We add value to these data by relating each image to geologic processes, and by encouraging users to analyze images with provided algorithms. VolcanoWorld has a very easy to use, Hypercard-like interface which will ultimately have these options:

1. Update on volcanic activity
2. Volcanic regions
3. How volcanoes work
4. Historical eruptions
5. Submarine volcanoes
6. Planetary volcanoes
7. How to become a volcanologist
8. Ask a volcanologist
9. Volcano contests
10. Further explorations
11. About this volcano

Currently, some information is available for items 1, 2, 7, 8, and 10. Check us out frequently, because we add new information - and answer your questions - every day!

learn the intricacies of other ways to locate and interact with Internet resources.

Web Browsers

Web browser assembles pieces of information

The exciting multimedia displays you encounter when exploring the Web are sent to you in pieces and then assembled by your Web browser. The one essential piece among the assortment of file types is a simple file containing plain text. This file has no large headline-sized fonts, no centered headings, and not even mandatory paragraph breaks. There certainly are no integrated pictures of the sort you encountered when you read about word processing (see Chapter 5). This simple text document has one unique characteristic.

Focus

Internet Addresses

You may have noticed that throughout this book, we include Internet addresses for your use. Most look something like this: **http://ndwild.psych.und.nodak.edu/book/default.html**. This address, called a **universal resource locator (URL)**, provides a program that is running on your computer the ability to request a specific file from a specific remote computer located on the Internet. This remote computer you have asked to send you a file or files is called a *server*. This address consists of three components:

♦ The **protocol,** which defines how the file will be sent
♦ The name of the server making the file available
♦ The location of the file on the server

For our example, the protocol is **hypertext transfer protocol (http)**, which identifies the information requested as a Web page. You may encounter other protocols, such as **file transfer protocol (FTP)**, when using the Internet for other tasks (see page 225). The server name in our example is *ndwild.psych.und.nodak.edu,* and the file on the server is located in the directory named *book* and has the name *default.html.*

To visit the Web sites we mention throughout this book, you will have to enter the URLs in the field located near the top of the Web browser (the area in which you enter this information is labeled "Address" for Internet Explorer and "Netsite" for Netscape Navigator). You will not have to enter long URLs repeatedly. Luckily, browsers have the capacity to store a list of URLs when users believe they may want to visit these sites again. This list of stored URLs is referred to as *favorites* (Internet Explorer) or *bookmarks* (Netscape Navigator) and can be accessed from a menu that appears near the top of the browser (see Figure 6.8 on page 236).✳

Embedded within the text are the special tags making up the **hypertext markup language (HTML).** The tag <BR> tells the browser to break and start a new line of text. The tag set <I></I> surrounding text would cause that text to appear italicized. The IMG tag causes an image to be transferred and displayed (e.g., <IMG SRC="mark.gif">). You can view samples of HTML by asking that your browser show the **source** code for a Web page. Look for the source option under one of the browser menus. (You will learn more about HTML and how to construct Web pages in Chapter 10.) A Web browser interprets—or, more accurately, tries to interpret—the HTML tags and builds the Web page before your eyes. Because different browsers may do this work in different ways, the appearance of a Web page will depend on the browser you use. HTML is also constantly evolving, and there are differences of opinion over which functions should be included. If your browser is out of date or

FIGURE 6.5
Sample Graphic from VolcanoWorld Web Site

Mount St. Helens, WA on 10/16/94 from STS-64

(STS064-51-025)

When Mount St. Helens erupted on 18 May 80, the top 1300 ft. disappeared within minutes. The blast area covered an area of more than 150 sq. miles and sent thousands of tons of ash into the upper atmosphere.

is not designed to implement one of these new functions, some feature that the Web page author included will not be displayed.

Expanding variety of formats

The variety of formats available over the Web is constantly expanding. We have already mentioned text, pictures, movies, and sounds. New additions include three-dimensional virtual experiences (based on **virtual reality modeling language—VRML),** streaming video and audio, and small programs (**applets**) that are transferred to your computer and run within your browser (e.g., Java applets). With so many formats constantly emerging, it is difficult to predict which will take hold and become standards. We think that online video and audio offer some exciting educational possibilities, and streaming technologies may make these formats practical. The great volume of data required to present digital video makes transferring, storing, and then displaying lengthy video segments impractical. Instead of saving a large data file, the approach used in streaming continuously *caches* (temporarily stores) part of an audio or video segment for presentation on your computer. The computer needs only to store enough data to keep ahead of what is being presented at the moment. The quality of this format is improving rapidly, and extended "video on demand" would seem to have many educational applications. We will discuss new video formats in greater detail in Chapter 9.

Helper applications and plug-ins

This variety of formats is available because of special applications software that works as a companion to the browser. Usually developers first create what are called **helper applications,** which function like a second program. The browser downloads a file (e.g., a QuickTime movie), and the helper application presents it—in this case, the movie. Browsers incorporate what are called plug-ins. A **plug-in** is a special type of software developed to function within another software application. Many helper applications have been converted to plug-ins. Plug-ins perform their roles within the browser— for example, by presenting a movie within the browser window rather than in a separate window. As newer versions of browsers are developed, the more popular functions once provided by helper applications and plug-ins are sometimes incorporated into the browser.

Plug-ins and helper applications must be obtained independent of the browser. This usually means they must be downloaded from a different Internet source, which can often be accomplished using the browser. You connect to the Web site sponsored by the company responsible for the additional software and select an option that will send the software to your computer over the Internet. Plug-ins and helper applications are almost always free and are made available to increase sales of the software used to create and serve new formats of Internet content. Sometimes when a Web author uses an uncommon multimedia element (e.g., a VRML scene), the author will also point you to a Web site where the player for that element can be obtained.

Get a free browser.

Browsers are free. You simply connect to the host site of the company that developed the browser and download it. How do you get started if you don't have an old browser with which to download a new one? Most computers now come with at least one browser already loaded. Another possibility is to purchase a book about the World Wide Web for educators because many books come with software. Another suggestion is to get a copy from an educator who already uses the Web. Addresses for obtaining copies of the most popular browsers (Netscape Navigator, Microsoft Internet Explorer) are provided at the end of the chapter.

Keeping track of valuable sites

All browsers have the capability to store the location and perhaps even a brief description of Web pages you have visited and may want to find again. Depending on the browser, this list of important URLs may be referred to as *bookmarks* (the term we will use) or *favorites*. Adding a bookmark to the stored list is as simple as selecting the Add Bookmark option from one of the browser menus. Browsers all have some system for categorizing the list of stored URLs. A common system is to allow the user to create and name file folders and then to move individual URLs into the appropriate folders. An organized system becomes helpful when you have located hundreds of sites you want to remember. One final option may be helpful to teachers. It is possible to export or save a list of bookmarks as an HTML document (authoring HTML documents is discussed in Chapter 10). A student can open this document with a browser, click on one of the options from your list, and visit that Web site.

LOCATING INFORMATION ON THE WEB: BROWSING VERSUS SEARCHING

Before the Web can be a useful resource, teachers and students must become familiar with the tools for locating information within its vastness. Online services offer users two basic approaches to locating resources: browsing and searching.

Browsing to explore a topic

Browsing, is based on a Web index or directory consisting of a hierarchical system of subject headings and subheadings. As you move down through this hierarchical system, you reach a level at which links to specific sites are provided. The links have terse but descriptive titles and are sometimes accompanied by a sentence of additional information. This system is useful when you are exploring a topic and trying to gain an understanding of its ramifications.

Searching, the second approach, is based on the use of a **search engine,** an online database that contains information about a large number of Web sites. A search engine accepts a user's request or **query** and searches through its body of stored information to identify potentially useful Web sites. Then a list of these addresses and brief content descriptions are returned to the user.

Searching with a goal in mind

Searching is most useful when you begin with a specific goal in mind and generate a query targeted fairly precisely to this goal.

Online services cannot be neatly divided into those offering browsing and those offering search engines. Because the online services are competing to attract as many users as possible, many commercial sites now offer a combination of methods. Let's look at some examples both for browsing and for searching.

An Example of Browsing

For a demonstration of how you might browse a directory to solve an information problem, we can use Yahoo!, one of the most popular Web directories. Assume you want to research the topic you are now reading about: locating information on the Web.

The Yahoo! home page offers fourteen basic subject categories that are very broad: "Health," "Science," "Society & Culture," and so on. For our topic, the category "Computers and the Internet" is obviously the most relevant. This link leads to a new page containing approximately thirty new subject headings, several of them potentially useful: "Information," "Internet," and "World Wide Web." As this example shows, it is sometimes difficult to know *Trying different options* which subject to select. You will sometimes have to try several different options. Let's assume we choose the category "World Wide Web."

Selecting this link brings us to a list of thirty new subject headings. Among them is the promising topic "Searching the Web." Selecting this subject reveals three subheadings: "How to Search the Web," "Indices to Web," and "Search Engines." Each of these options finally produces a long list of links to individual Web pages. The links are the titles from the Web pages. Sometimes an additional sentence is added to provide a better hint about the site's contents. Sometimes, though, the title is not very helpful, and you have to look to see if the site will be useful.

Our browsing has taken us through four levels of subject headings, and we have ended up with three groups of links to Web pages. To put what we have accomplished into perspective, Yahoo! is subdivided into approximately 25,000 categories that link to slightly over 500,000 Web sites. The procedure we described did not require a great deal of time, and it located a large number of informative Web sites appropriate to our initial question.

As you can see, browsing in a well-organized system can be quite productive, and we encourage you to try the process on your own. The Web address for Yahoo!, as well as those for the search services described in the following section, is listed in Resources to Expand Your Knowledge Base at the end of the chapter.

Types of Search Services

Commercial search engines There are many search engines bidding for your attention. Universities maintain a few experimental ones as part of research projects, but most are commercial. This does not mean that you have to pay to use them. As soon as you connect to a commercial search engine, you will realize that it is supported by advertising dollars. You have to maneuver around the colorful product displays to get your work done.

The major services all offer some form of searchable database, but they differ in how sites are added to the database and what information about each site is stored in the database. New servers and new Web pages may become known to the online service through nominations received from the public (mostly from people who are themselves page authors). Alternatively, the service can identify new sites by using a software *robot* (also called a *bot, spider,* or *crawler*) that continually roams the Internet looking for new servers and new pages.

Web librarians—people who examine Web documents and classify material they think might be useful—can generate the information stored in the database. Or, as an alternative, the service can use indexing software that automatically examines designated parts of Web pages and identifies keywords. Some indexing software generates keywords by examining a limited amount of information, such as the page title and the first hundred words of text. Other indexing software reads and processes *all* of the text found on each Web page.

Differences among search services

The indexing process is especially important, and it accounts for some noticeable differences among the search services. For example, computerized indexing methods are less expensive than Web librarians and generate larger databases. Also, indexing methods that use the entire Web page link more descriptive terms with each page. Therefore, searching with a service that has built its database from computerized searches of entire Web pages tends to generate a longer list of sites to examine. In some cases, this may be an advantage. In other cases, however, you may find it much more useful to examine a list of ten quality sites rather than a list of a hundred sites that vary greatly in quality.

Because of such differences among search services, you will want to become familiar with several of them. The following sections offer some guidance.

Search Engine and Directory Combinations.   Several search services are based on a cataloging system very much like that maintained by conventional libraries. Human editors examine Web material and organize content within what they consider to be a useful classification system. You can browse the classification system or search the cataloged material using key terms.

Combining browsing and searching

You can also use a combination of browsing and searching to improve the quality of your search, a unique advantage of this type of service. Let's say you want to learn more about the type of spider that wanders about the Web searching for new Web pages. If you were to connect to Yahoo! and search for "spider" from the home page, you would find about 600 sites, including pages that address a cartoon character, a type of car, eight-legged arthropods, as well as the Internet search robot. However, if you first select the Yahoo! subject heading "Computers and Internet" and then perform the same search, the return would be approximately twenty-five links, nearly all of them appropriate to the topic of interest.

This type of search system provides access to less of the Web than do search services that rely on a computer-generated database, but it might be argued that the overall quality of material is a little higher. Examples of this type of search service are Yahoo! and Magellan.

Index Search Engines.   Index search engines rely on a computer-generated index of the contents of Web sites. Thankfully, the techniques used are more sophisticated than a simple list of all the Web pages containing a specific word. Some form of proprietary artificial intelligence system is used to determine which Web pages are most relevant to your query. For example, search engines that index entire Web pages use variables such as how many times keywords are mentioned in an article and how close to the top of a document a keyword appears. When the search engine responds to your query with a list of sites, the ones deemed most relevant appear at the top of the list.

Index search engines tend to provide access to huge numbers of Web pages. HotBot, the search engine with perhaps the largest database at the time this text was written, found over 200,000 sites for the search term "spider." Other examples of this type of search service are AltaVista and Northern Light.

Meta-Index Searches.   Some search tools activate and cross-reference the results from several search engines. These meta-index searches take a little longer because various individual searches must be initiated, the results integrated, and duplicates eliminated. However, a meta-index search does not accumulate *all* the sites generated by all of the search engines. To keep things more manageable, the search tool takes only the top ten to fifty sites generated by each search engine.

You might suppose a meta-index search would always be the most productive. However, as you'll see later in this chapter, search engines offer certain advanced search methods that can help you in many situations, and these methods differ from one engine to another. For this reason, meta-index search tools can use only basic search procedures, consisting of combinations of keywords. Examples of this type of search service are MetaCrawler and SavvySearch.

Which Type of Search Engine Should I Use?   Every experienced user of the Web seems to have an opinion about which search engine is most useful. From time to time, articles in computer magazines compare the different search engines on a standard set of search tasks. Despite authors' recommendations based on these analyses, examination of the actual search data shows that search engine effectiveness differs between assignments. If anything, reading such articles has caused us to try different search engines than we might normally employ.

Explore several search engines

We suggest that you too take the time to explore several search engines to gain some familiarity to make your own decisions. At the end of the chapter, we provide the addresses for the search tools we have mentioned.

Whenever the results from your favorite search engine are disappointing, it is worth trying both a different engine and a different combination of search terms.

How effective are search engines?

You might wonder if you can really search the entire Web using any of these search engines. The questions of how effective search engines are in providing access to the vast amount of information available and just how large the Web really is are not easily answered and have become the basis for some interesting research. Lawrence and Giles (1998, 1999) have developed a technique in which they submit the same search requests to multiple search engines and then examine the overlap among the lists of hits the search engines produce. They conclude that all search engines miss a large proportion of the available Web sites. In fact, the research indicated that the best search engines found only 16 percent of the sites available. Because the companies maintaining these search engines know how many sites they have referenced, the proportion of the Web accessible from specific search engines can be used to estimate the size of the Web. The researchers estimate the size of the searchable Web (this would not include subscription services or online databases) at 800 million pages (Lawrence & Giles, 1999). In the time between the two analyses that were conducted (about one year), the estimated size of the Web climbed from 320 million to 800 million pages, and the proportion that had been indexed by any single search engine fell from 35 percent to 16 percent. Providing access to more of the Web has become a challenge to the companies providing search services, and some have claimed that they will soon drastically improve the proportion of the Web that will be searchable through their site. What do some of these findings mean to you? First, the resources of the Web are immense and increasing at a rapid rate. Second, if a comprehensive search is your goal, it may be necessary to use several search engines or a meta-search engine.

Conducting a Search

Web search engines usually present users with a very simple and easy-to-use interface. An unfortunate consequence is that many users never really learn to take advantage of the powerful search features that are available. It is so easy just to type something into the little text field, click Submit, and see what you get. For serious research, however, it is important to learn at least some of the rules that govern searches.

The rules that govern searches

For example, consider the type of search students might conduct in a high school history course. When we submitted a request for information on Civil War battles, we generated more than 600,000 sites—far too large a number for anyone to examine productively. But when we changed the request to "civil war battles" (that is, with the phrase enclosed in quotations), the search generated slightly more than 1,300 entries, still a large number but much more manageable.

Why did this happen? The search engine interpreted our two requests in very different ways. In the first situation, the search process located all Web pages containing the word *civil,* the word *war,* or the word *battles.* Thus, we might have found pages about battles between Athenians and Spartans, or between spiders and wasps. In the second situation, the search engine found only those pages containing the entire phrase *civil war battles.* Actually, the situation is a little more complicated. Since the search engine we used lists documents containing several of the targeted terms before documents containing fewer of the terms, some of the links near the tops of the two lists were similar. Still, the difference between 1,300 and 600,000 was well worth the effort of typing in quotation marks.

Search engines are usually capable of conducting what are called **Boolean searches.** You probably learned the basics of Boolean logic in a high school math class. Boolean operators, such as AND, NOT, and OR, define ways in which sets are combined. Let's see what you remember. What could we accomplish with the following search request?

bat NOT baseball NOT computer

The answer is that we would generate a list of Web resources about bats—the furry flying kind. You can probably guess the purpose of "NOT baseball." This excludes the large number of Web pages containing information about baseball players who *bat* right- or left-handed, pages devoted to collecting baseball *bats,* and other pages focused on the game of baseball. The request to exclude pages about computers may stump you, but it has a similar explanation. Some older computers use *bat files,* which list special instructions the computer is to follow, and various Web pages contain information about such files. At any rate, excluding Web pages about baseball and computers generates a list of resources containing a much higher proportion of sites on the topic we really want to review.

Specifying search techniques

As the Web evolves, search engines are changing to make it easier for users to conduct more complicated searches. Instead of requiring that users learn Boolean operators, several search engines now offer a form in which you can specify certain search techniques. After entering your keywords in a text field, you choose from menus the operators to be applied to these words, as shown in Figure 6.6 on page 224. Typical choices include "all of the words," "any of the words," "exact phrase," "must contain," and "must not contain"—terms that users can understand without a lot of training. HotBot, the search engine displayed in Figure 6.6, also allows users to define a search based on publication date, location of the server (by country or type of organization), and how deep within the Web site the search is to be conducted. For example, on the topic of deformed frogs, a search of this type produced a list of eighteen Web pages established within the past twelve months on K–12 servers in the state of Minnesota. Learning to apply techniques of this type can greatly improve the efficiency of your searches.

Focus

Tips for Successful Searches

Here are some suggestions that should help you conduct more powerful searches with most search engines. To learn the unique techniques that apply with a particular search engine, look for a "Help" link somewhere on the search engine home page.

◆ *Use quotation marks when searching for a multiword phrase.* Quotation marks tell the search engine to return only those sites containing all the target words in the exact order, for instance, "acceptable use policy" but not "policy use" or "acceptable policy."

◆ *Use Boolean operators to require certain combinations of words.* The operator AND (in capitals) or the plus sign (+) will produce pages containing more than one targeted word. For instance, to find pages on spider monkeys, you could link the word *spider* and the word *monkey* with an AND or with a plus sign:

spider AND monkey

spider +monkey

In the second instance, there is a space before the + but no space between the + and the second word.

Similarly, using OR between search terms will return documents containing at least one of the words: monkey OR ape. Using AND NOT or the minus sign (−) will locate documents containing one word but not the other:

spider AND NOT monkey

spider −monkey

You can create more complicated expressions by using parentheses with the Boolean operators. For example, a search for

basketball AND (bulls OR jazz)

should produce Web sites about either of two basketball teams, the Chicago Bulls or the Utah Jazz.

◆ *Use a capital letter only when you really want words that contain a capital letter.* A lowercase request will find both lower- and uppercase matches. An uppercase request will find *only* uppercase matches:

mark → mark or Mark
Mark → Mark
maRK → (no matches at all!)

◆ *Take advantage of HTML tags to locate certain kinds of material.* You can use some HTML tags to search for words contained within the tags. This works with the tags "image," "title," and "text." You join the full word for the tag and the target word with a colon. The most useful application of this tip is probably in searching for images. For instance, by typing image:frog, you tell the search engine to look for pages that contain images labeled "frog." The HTML tag "IMG" identifies an image file (see Chapter 10) within the statement that causes an image file (e.g., tree_frog.GIF) to be loaded when you connect to a Web page. The databases generated by some search services store the names of image files that have been located. Submitting the search descriptor image:frog would possibly locate a Web page containing the image tree_frog.gif.✳

FIGURE 6.6

Some Search Options Available from the HotBot Advanced Form

HotBot® is a registered trademark and/or service mark of Wired Ventures, Inc., a Lycos Company. All rights reserved.

ACCESS TO FILES

Types of free material available

Various commercial, public, and government institutions maintain archives of files that users can copy, or download, to their personal computers. These files can be text documents, graphic images, sounds, or programs. If the archive has been developed specifically for educators or students or just happens to provide material that would be useful in classrooms, the files might be lesson plans for hands-on science activities, information about the latest space shuttle mission, the text of *Moby Dick,* a data set providing multiple air quality variables from different regions of the country, pictures of U.S. presidents or views from the Hubble telescope, or a virus protection program for your computer (a source for FTP sites is provided in the Resources to Expand Your Knowledge Base at the end of the chapter).

You may initially think that access to all of this material is just too good to be true. It is important to understand and appreciate the various commitments individuals have made to providing these resources. The resources to which you have access through the Internet are provided with different expectations. One term with which you should be familiar is shareware. A **shareware** product is distributed for evaluation, but the author has copyrighted the material and expects to receive payment if use extends beyond the initial evaluation. Some users of commercial services assume that the fees they pay for the service somehow cover the cost of the shareware products they download. This is not the case; software and other resources designated as shareware come with the expectation that the author will eventually receive some compensation. You will learn more about shareware and other copyright issues in Chapter 11.

Files of computer data are transferred using the FTP, which allows users to upload and download files from a server. The files could be any data (text, image, video, etc.) or program file used by your computer. With the development of more sophisticated e-mail and Web systems, the average user is less likely to use a program providing only FTP functions. File transfer options have been incorporated into mail (i.e., attachments) and Web browsers. You have probably used FTP through your Web browser and perhaps not known it. You did not have to enter FTP as part of a URL (see page 214) because you followed a link available from a Web page. The URL beginning with FTP was part of the HTML that you did not see. One very common use of FTP from within a Web browser occurs when users download an upgrade to the browser they are already using. If you own a computer and use the Internet, you have probably done this. It is now also fairly common to purchase and then download software over the Internet. You find the program you want, provide your credit card number, and download the software right to your hard drive. Other common uses of FTP in schools include downloading the file of information that allows a virus detection program to detect new viruses (see Chapter 11) and uploading Web pages and related images to the school Web server (see Chapter 10).

There are some specialized programs for FTP, including Fetch for the Macintosh and WS_FTP (Winsock FTP) for the Windows Platform. These programs are now used less commonly in schools because FTP downloads can be accomplished with a Web browser. However, a browser does not allow files to be uploaded (sent). Educators or students who create Web pages need to upload this content to a Web server so it can be made available on the Internet. The specialized FTP software is designed to both download and upload files. Software that is involved in the preparation of material for the Internet (i.e., Web publishing tools; see Chapter 10) now frequently has FTP tools built in so that material can be transferred to a web server without having to start another program.

CATEGORIES OF WEB RESOURCES

The Internet—particularly the large body of information available through the World Wide Web—is a tremendous educational resource. The quantity and breadth of what can be explored is impressive, and educators should be excited by the potential. However, using Internet resources in the classroom does present some challenges. Because there are so few restrictions on who can publish in this forum, educators are becoming all too familiar with content that is potentially biased, in poor taste, or even dangerous. Educators do need to be aware of issues related to inappropriate Internet content, and we will discuss this issue in some detail in Chapter 11. Without discounting the existence of inappropriate content or suggesting that parents and educators should feel comfortable in allowing unsupervised or unprotected Internet access, we do feel comfortable in promoting classroom use of Internet resources.

To help you think through some of the different approaches to instruction that might be taken, we propose the simple category system shown in Table 6.1 that identifies types of educational resources that can be found on the Internet. Our purpose in recognizing these categories is to create a point of departure for discussing how teacher and student activities might vary when learning from different types of resources.

Think of the categories as points along a continuum differentiated in terms of the amount and type of involvement expected of the classroom teacher. The online equivalent of a computer-based tutorial, an **online tutor-**

Using the Internet presents challenges.

TABLE 6.1

Categories of Instructional Resources Found on the Internet and Related Teacher Responsibilities

	ONLINE TUTORIAL	**INSTRUCTIONAL RESOURCE**	**PRIMARY SOURCE**
Description	Resource takes responsibility for instruction.	Resource outlines activity but does not provide instruction.	Resource provides raw materials on which learning activity might be based.
Teacher role	Teacher trouble-shoots when student encounters problem.	Teacher responsible for facilitating and evaluating learning.	Teacher locates source, creates related activity, facilitates and evaluates learning.
Example	Online tutorial; online class.	Online curriculum activities.	Teacher created WebQuest based on general-purpose Web pages.

ial, would be located at one extreme end of the continuum. The Internet now makes complete courses—even complete degrees—available. While K–12 students in our state are taking specialty courses online and such experiences will likely become more common everywhere, our intent in this chapter is to focus your attention on learning activities rather than courses. Online tutorials are designed for independent learning with well-integrated learning sources, explanatory segments, and evaluation activities. Most activities of this type are likely to be available through subscription services—companies that provide educational resources as a business. Like computer-based tutorials (see Chapter 4), any educational use of technology may shortchange learners on at least one of the components of instruction (presentation, guidance, extended practice, and evaluation). This is why we suggest that the classroom teacher should be involved when students are using online tutorials.

What we define as **instructional resources** are positioned at the midpoint of our continuum. Here the Internet provides the components of a learning activity, but the teacher is responsible for implementation and evaluation. Someone else has identified the lesson goals, located and developed the information resources, proposed learning tasks related to lesson goals, and in some cases arranged online experiences to support the classroom learning activities and provided possible evaluation rubrics (evaluation guidelines). The teacher clearly is not starting from scratch, nor is the teacher turning control of the learning experience over to the organization responsible for the resources.

Primary sources

Our emphasis in this chapter is really on the end of our continuum labeled primary sources because this final resource category provides the opportunity to take advantage of a tremendous amount of Internet content and because working with this content engages learners in unique and authentic information processing activities. **Primary sources** are raw information sources not necessarily developed to meet educational needs or even to provide a fair or unbiased treatment of a particular issue. Many sources of information we encounter daily fall into this category. Newsmagazine articles (*Newsweek, Time*), newspaper articles (*New York Times*), and encyclopedia entries qualify, and so do interviews that students might conduct with members of their community. Most library books—even some of the ones in school libraries—are not specifically packaged to meet educational goals. The online equivalents of commercial news sources are becoming more and more common in school libraries (see Keeping Current: Subscription Information Services). Then, of course, there are the millions of free World Wide Web pages and downloadable files that the first part of this chapter was intended to help you learn to search and access. Such raw information sources are typically developed independent of any curriculum standards and often not with the K–12 age group in mind.

Teachers orchestrate how students in their classes will use Web resources. They might require that students "study" specific Web resources (for example,

Keeping Current

Subscription Information Services

Online commercial information services are becoming more and more common. These services range from providers offering the on-line equivalent of a library (full-text versions of many books, magazines, and newspapers) to the online version of a single source, such as a major newspaper.

Schools purchase access to such services because of the quantity and selection of materials, the search tools, and the reasonable cost. The quantity of information available is impressive. The resources available from each of the general services vary, but it is common to have access to the full-text version of hundreds of magazines and newspapers, maps, and photo collections. Some sites provide access to news wire services. The resources are selected to meet the information needs of educational institutions, and the search features give students important aids in finding the information they need. Although schools must pay for access, the cost is typically less than that of subscribing to several newspapers and magazines.

You can find a list of several commercial services and related Web addresses in the Resources to Expand Your Knowledge Base at the end of this chapter. The Web sites allow you to peek at the information sources that are available. ✳

Incremental versus transformational advantage

visit specific URLs). Working with the Web in this way might provide an **incremental advantage** over existing practices in that students have access to many more resources and can access these resources more efficiently than is now the case, but they do not offer a **transformational advantage.** Student experiences would still emphasize similar classroom activities and the same cognitive skills, even without the Internet. The transformational advantage of Internet activities would be realized if students were engaged in different learning activities emphasizing cognitive skills that have some unique value. These skills might be unique in emphasizing new areas, such as information literacy, or in finding ways to target skills effectively that have always been valued but are difficult to develop in some content areas, such as critical thinking and problem solving.

Our discussion of the Big Six Research Process in Chapter 1 (page 21) identified information processing skills as essential to productivity in the Information Age. In our view, in order to develop the search, inquiry, and critical thinking skills necessary to solve the information-related problems we encounter in both school and daily life, students need more opportunities to work with information in challenging ways. To this end, we think students would benefit from more tasks requiring that they use primary sources rather than prepackaged instructional resources and that information from primary sources be applied to the solution of authentic information problems.

To accomplish these goals, teachers will need strategies that engage students with Web resources in ways that are productive. A popular and fairly accurate description of what many Internet users do is "surf the Net." The user drifts from resource to resource as first one link and then another attracts a click of the mouse. As we have emphasized repeatedly, exposure to information is not the same as meaningful learning. Exposure does not necessarily result in the depth of thought necessary to discount biased or inaccurate information. Nor does it guarantee the mental activity necessary to construct personal meaning. What we want students to experience is the use of the Web to solve authentic information processing problems. The Web can provide factual answers to simple objective questions, but it can also provide information that students can use in trying to resolve complex problems and questions with no definitive answers. Using primary sources in the investigation of complex problems is a good way to integrate the use of technology into nearly any content area and a way to take on authentic challenges that students can attack collaboratively. Giving students the opportunity to use knowledge and skills in ways that are authentic to the discipline provides valuable opportunities for assessment.

USING THE WEB FOR ACTIVE LEARNING

The intuitive nature of browsers and the power of search engines allow students to find information easily on almost any topic imaginable. The quantity and breadth of what can be explored is impressive, and educators should be excited by the potential. Students can visit museums around the world; access the same satellite images and meteorological data available to local weather forecasters; and tag along as adventurers climb mountain peaks, explore the depths of the oceans, or bicycle through parts of the world most of us will never see—all without leaving the classroom. The Internet presents educators and learners with tremendous opportunities. The resources alone, however, are not enough.

Creating an authentic learning environment

Here is a somewhat different way to think about how you might want to use Web resources. Consider how Web access might contribute to providing an active and authentic learning environment. Using Web resources in the investigation of complex problems is a good way to integrate the use of technology into nearly any content area and a way to take on challenges that students can attack collaboratively. Giving students the opportunity to use knowledge and skills in ways that are authentic to the discipline provide valuable opportunities for assessment.

The World Wide Web provides access to a tremendous number of different information resources. Here students use the World Wide Web as part of a collaborative project. *(© Michael Zide)*

OBTAINING CURRENT WEATHER DATA: AN INTERNET PROJECT

Here is an example of a project that uses the Web as a source of authentic scientific data. Working with data allows students the opportunity to use knowledge and skills in ways that are appropriate to a particular subject matter domain (see the discussion of authentic activities in Chapter 2, page 65). The teacher's role in this example is critical. He or she must help students propose questions that are interesting and appropriate to their backgrounds and abilities. The teacher's involvement as the project unfolds is also essential in challenging students to think deeply about what they are doing and what they are discovering.

The Weather Underground has provided current weather data on the Internet for several years. The system makes use of the World Wide Web and is easy to learn.

Simple data can address complex issues.

Consider a project based on the question, "Are winter temperatures in Alaska colder than winter temperatures in North Dakota?" This question might seem relatively simple, but determining a valid way to find the answer requires some careful thought. Are there places in Alaska that are colder than places in North Dakota? Are there places in North Dakota that are colder than places in Alaska? Is Alaska the coldest state? What would be a reasonable way to summarize winter temperature as a single variable? Why might people hold stereotypes about what particular places they have not actually experienced are like?

One way to begin is to explore to determine what information is available. The Weather Underground provides current weather conditions for designated cities. After examining the city list for each state, as in Figure 6.7, students know that they can obtain weather information for ten Alaska cities and four North Dakota cities. It might occur to them that to provide a complete answer to the question, they may need to gather information related to more than one location in each state. How many cities and which to include are important questions. Perhaps it would be enough simply to select every other one on each list. Perhaps it might be useful to examine a map and select cities from different parts of each state or cities reflecting different geographic characteristics. To continue this example, assume that students have selected Fargo and Bismarck in North Dakota and Anchorage and Juneau in Alaska.

The data gathered from a single day in mid-December indicate that the current temperatures were Bismarck, 21; Fargo, 17; Anchorage, 26; and Juneau, 30. At this point, students might want to determine whether they can now answer the original question. There are always abnormally warm and cold days during the winter. Perhaps the data are not representative of typical winter temperatures. Perhaps Juneau is having an unusually warm spell. A more

FIGURE 6.7
Weather Underground Information for Alaska

City	Temp. (F)	Humidity	Pressure (in)	Conditions
Anchorage	26°	44%	30.36	blowing snow
Barrow	-15°	77%	30.64	Clear
Fairbanks	-9°	77%	N/A	light snow
Juneau	30°	100%	N/A	Clear
Ketchikan	35°	89%	29.66	Clear
Kodiak	32°	45%	N/A	Clear
McGrath	-22°	74%	30.85	Mostly Cloudy
Nome	19°	87%	30.54	light snow
Valdez	38°	28%	30.16	Mostly Cloudy
Yakutat	26°	100%	29.91	Mostly Cloudy

Use Web with other computer tools.

scientific approach might be to gather data over several weeks and then to calculate an average to determine the typical temperature. Having easy access to data and thoughtful guidance from a teacher can help students learn some of the skills of thoughtful inquiry. Students could use a spreadsheet to record the data from several cities over several days and calculate an average temperature for each city (see the spreadsheet and graph from the study in Chapter 5, pages 177 through 179). Some parts of Alaska are warmer and others are colder than the typical winter temperatures in North Dakota. The teacher and students might want to know why this is the case. Finding out why will require that students go to the library or the Internet and do more research.

SCAFFOLDING WEB EXPLORATION

How do we help students use the Web effectively, particularly when we want to encourage them to use Web resources in ways that are likely to be unfamiliar? One approach is based on cognitive apprenticeship, scaffolding, and some of the other concepts you first encountered in Chapter 2. The basic idea is to ease students gradually into what are likely to be challenging tasks by creating a supportive structure to guide their work. In other words, as the teacher, you would initially do some of the work for students.

Here is how the process would work and how you might create a scaffold to support novice students. Assume that you would like your students to write a position paper on a controversial topic. If the student were working independently, he or she would have to find resources related to the topic, examine a number of the resources in an attempt to determine both the opposing positions and the basic arguments for and against each position, select a position to defend, find particularly good sources related to that position, carefully review the sources to obtain key data and develop sound arguments, and

Why students need help

then write the paper. Consider just a couple of areas that might cause difficulty. Students may lack the experience to use a Web browser in a sophisticated way, such as to conduct a sophisticated search or bookmark potentially relevant resources. Students might be unable or unmotivated to find truly good sources among the many that are available, or they might lack the reading or inquiry skills necessary to identify different positions or the arguments for and against these positions.

Guidance from the teacher

Now consider how the teacher might participate to assist the student. The teacher might conduct an initial Web search, generate a list of potential sites, and then designate three helpful sites students must review. For each of these sites, the teacher might offer guiding comments, such as, "This resource presents a good description of the general problem and outlines positions A and B," or "This site provides some very persuasive arguments for position B." The teacher might also deal with some computer skill issues by authoring a simple Web page that presents this background material to the students and directly linking students to the more productive sites (Chapter 10 discusses Web authoring). If the students have even the most basic competence in using a browser, this Web page would allow them to connect directly to the suggested resources. The cognitive apprenticeship model assumes that students will gradually take on more and more of these skills. Perhaps the process might begin by having students search for their own resources to augment those provided by the teacher or by having students review key resources without suggesting specific things they should try to learn from each resource.

The WebQuest

Bernie Dodge (1995) has proposed that educators provide scaffolding through what he describes as WebQuests. A WebQuest is a document (usually prepared as a WWW page) consisting of (1) a brief introduction to a topic, (2) the description of an inquiry task related to that topic, (3) a set of primary Web resources students can use in performing the task, and (4) suggestions for how students might use the Web resources in performing the task.

Because the structure of a WebQuest is simple and relatively easy to describe, it has been useful for helping teachers understand how they might create learning tasks based on Internet content. However, the WebQuest is probably also an example of an instructional strategy that appears to be very simple but yet requires experience and careful preparation to achieve optimal results. To develop a learning activity that promotes information problem solving and requires more than the location of factual information, the teacher needs to identify an interesting and appropriate topic, define a task that requires information problem solving and reflection, and locate Web resources that provide information for processing rather than preprocessed conclusions. It is not our intent to make the preparation of a quality Web-Quest appear to be tremendously difficult, but we do mean to suggest that using Web resources to locate specific factual information to answer specific factual questions is not the intended goal of this activity.

The Snow Goose Crisis: A WebQuest Example

Here is an example of a WebQuest and a description of the process we followed in developing this activity. To help you understand why we think this WebQuest involves inquiry and information problem solving, we will also explain a little about the content area the WebQuest addresses. This project originated in a magazine article that described how a rapid increase in the population of snow geese was threatening the fragile ecology of the Arctic tundra. The article went on to consider whether this was a situation that biologists should attempt to address and, if intervention was appropriate, what possible actions might be taken. This seemed an interesting problem for a middle-school or high school WebQuest, and because we live in the middle of a goose migration route, it was also an authentic issue for students in the schools we work with to address. Students could be asked to examine information related to the snow goose crisis and to propose what, if anything, should be done. The problem seemed complex enough that students might realistically argue for several different courses of action.

Background. To understand the situation, students would need background information. Because of the extreme climate, tundra vegetation grows very slowly. Geese use the tundra as a breeding ground, and the parents and young rip plants out by the roots as they feed around the nesting areas. Once an area has been destroyed in this manner, geese, other wildlife that feed on the vegetation, and animals that feed on the plant eaters will not be able to inhabit the area for many years. There is a very real threat of a population crash in which many birds and animals will die from malnutrition and related diseases.

One of the most basic issues in such a situation is whether humans should intervene to alter a process of nature. Noninterventionists argue that nature will find a solution even though the process may be harsh. In contrast, biologists favoring active management of natural resources assume that intervention can avoid extreme swings in populations. Those favoring intervention also argue that some of the causes for the existing situation are the result of human actions. For the snow geese, these human causes include changes in farming practices that leave a great deal of waste grain on the ground following harvest, making it easy for birds to feed during the fall and winter, and the development of a system of protected areas that allow geese to avoid hunters and predators during the fall and spring migrations.

If biologists choose to intervene, there are many possible, but untested, approaches. One interesting question is whether economic benefits should be considered. For example, a solution that extends the hunting season and increases the bag limit (the number of birds that can be shot each day) may attract more hunters and money to certain areas of the United States and Canada. Reducing food and habitat in areas in which geese overwinter would also reduce the population, but with no economic benefits. There is also the matter of expense and who pays for the intervention (taxpayers, nature lovers, hunters). Finally, there is a question of personal values regarding such issues as intervention and killing wildlife for sport.

Instructional Tasks. A major part of creating a structured inquiry task of this type is locating task-appropriate Internet resources. The teacher takes responsibility for this job. But why not just make the assignment, you may ask, and allow students to find their own resources?

Assume that this activity is being developed for middle-school students. Students familiar with Web searching might reasonably conduct a search on the phrase *snow goose*. We did our own search of this type and received over 4,200 hits. Listed among the first four sites were the titles "Snow Goose with White Wine," "Snow Goose Hunting in Nebraska," and "Snow Goose Inn." Yes, you may say, but why not use Boolean search techniques (see page 223)? Well, a search on the Boolean expression *"snow goose" +population* returned

427 hits, and a search on *"snow goose" +crisis* returned 115 hits. Even if middle-school students were experienced enough to generate these Boolean searches, the amount of material to examine would be formidable and would require a great amount of their time.

Thus, although students do need to learn to conduct their own Web searches, you might decide in this case to locate useful sites in advance so that your students could concentrate on the problem-solving process. You might also want to locate task-appropriate Web resources simply to save the students time and because certain resources would lend themselves to thinking through different positions.

In general, WebQuests are described as scaffolded because the teacher assists the student in ways that allow the student to address challenging problems with an acceptable level of effort and a reasonable opportunity for success. This is particularly important for younger students. As a teacher, you can set the stage for your students, allowing them to focus on key issues and encouraging them in their critical thinking and problem solving.

WebQuest Presentation.   Figure 6.8 shows most of the finished WebQuest prepared as a Web page. The WebQuest Introduction, which is intended to establish a background for the activity and generate student interest, contains a photograph showing the devastation caused by the feeding habits of snow geese (note the difference between the fenced and unfenced areas) and explains that snow geese and other Arctic species are in serious jeopardy. The task, which is to generate a multimedia presentation, requires the student to propose and defend a course of action federal and state biologists might take in responding to overpopulation of snow geese. In preparation for this task, students are directed to some specific Web sites (only two are visible) that offer information relevant to the assigned task. You will note from Figure 6.8 that these links have been annotated so that students know what they might attend to most closely when studying a particular site. What does not appear in the figure is the list of secondary resources. In addition to the Web pages we wanted every student to visit, we provided a list of supplemental sites that contained additional information some students might find helpful.

There is no reason the WebQuest has to take this exact format. Some WebQuests provide multiple tasks and offer students a choice. In some of our own work, we have looked at the WebQuest as a method for extending traditional classroom experiences through information problem solving and have tried to focus on primary sources (see page 67) as a way to define information problem solving. It has been helpful to think in terms of Internet-based, school-based, and community-based primary sources and perhaps committing to the design of activities involving information resources from all three areas. For example, a history activity focused on the different experiences of male and female teachers in one-room schools included online primary sources from the Library of Congress *American Memory Collection,* an article

FIGURE 6.8
Snow Goose WebQuest Presented as a Web Page

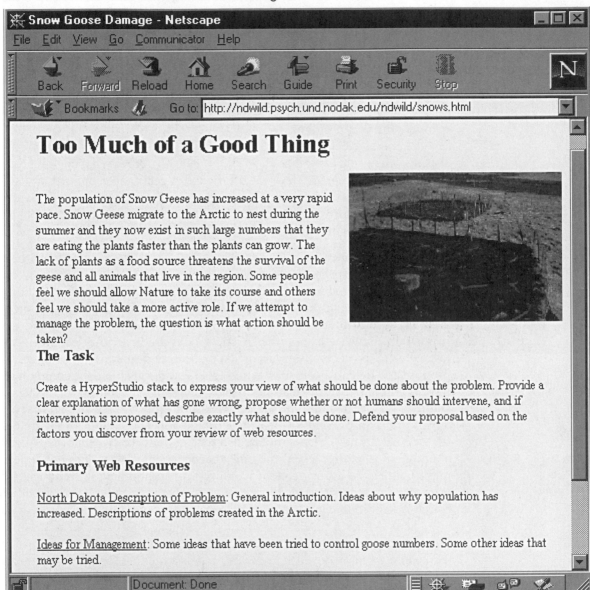

from an edited collection published by the State Humanities Council and found in the school library, and interviews with older citizens from the community who had taught in or attended one-room schools. We believe that once teachers understand some of the basic principles exemplified by the WebQuest model, they will be able to extend the model in a variety of ways.

HOW ARE TEACHERS USING THE INTERNET IN THEIR CLASSROOMS?

Access to the Internet has reached such a level that we should begin taking a serious look at how students have been influenced. We do not mean to imply that access is not an issue. In 1999, 65 percent of students had Internet access in either their classroom or a school computer lab (Becker, 1999). Thus, many students have no access, and the access available to the remainder may not be available frequently enough to allow meaningful work to be accomplished. Keeping such limitations in mind, let us see what students are actually doing.

The most frequent classroom use of the Internet is information gathering. Searching for Web resources is the third most common use of technology after word processing and working with CDs. Data indicate that approximately 30 percent of K–12 students have used the Web for research. This rate is low partly because some students have no access at all or very few

Focus

Citing Internet Sources

Research is one of the most common reasons that secondary and elementary students use the Internet. Students need to learn to provide citations for Internet resources just as they cite the sources of other information. Some believe that citing Internet sources is especially important because the nature of the Internet makes it so easy to copy and paste material. Providing accurate citations makes students aware of their responsibilities and provides teachers a way to follow up on the resources students have used (Li, 1996).

Here is the basic citation format:

Author/editor. (Year). *Title* (edition), [Type of medium]. Producer (optional). Available: Protocol (e.g., FTP, HTTP): Site/Path/File [Access date].

Sample WWW Resource

Li, X. (1996). *Electronic sources: APA style of citation* [On-line]. Available: http://www.uvm.edu/~xli/reference /apa .html [1996, June 22].

opportunities to connect because there are few connections and the computers capable of connecting are located at a distance from the classroom. If students have some form of access in their classroom, nearly 50 percent have used the Web. If students have access to the Internet through a high-speed connection, 30 percent of K–12 students have used the Web for educational purposes on at least ten occasions.

Use of the Internet for communication, collaborative projects, or Web publishing is much lower. Data from the Becker (1999) survey indicate that 7 percent of students have used e-mail in three lessons, 6 percent of students have used the Internet to participate in a project with another class, and 4 percent of students have published work on the Web.

Part of this same study sought to understand the factors that determine student experience. Several possible predictors were compared to assess their relative impact on two categories of student use: (1) using the Web for research and (2) participating in collaborative projects or publishing on the Web. The three best predictors, in order of importance, were (1) the degree of classroom connectivity, (2) the extent to which the teacher holds constructivist beliefs, and (3) the computer expertise of the classroom teacher. The classroom access variable accounted for the greatest variability in student experience. The other two important predictors, teacher expertise and teacher constructivist beliefs, were roughly equivalent in the extent to which they influenced student use. The importance of teacher expertise, which consisted of self-ratings of general computer competencies, is not surprising. Teachers are unlikely to assign tasks they feel unprepared to supervise. The importance of teacher beliefs may have been the most interesting finding from the study. Differences in teacher beliefs were determined by asking the teachers to indicate their support for certain values (e.g., multiple classroom activities rather than a common activity for all students) and their commitment to specific instructional practices (e.g., working on projects that take a week or more). The beliefs and practices were not described in terms of the application of technology. Becker (1999) concluded that teachers' beliefs and practices related to how relevant they felt Internet resources and related activities were for their teaching.

We cannot hope to have an impact on the resources you will have available in your classroom, but we do believe that the course you are taking will develop your expertise and expose you to values and practices consistent with the constructivist perspective. Preparation of the type you are receiving should make a difference in the extent to which K–12 students will learn from Internet experiences.

SUMMARY

The Internet, the vast web of interconnected computers that spans the globe, has been growing at a phenomenal rate. Educational interest in the resources of the Internet has heightened too. Approximately 90 percent of schools have some form of access to the Internet, and 40 percent of classrooms are now connected. Access is improving rapidly.

The Internet provides access to other people, files that can be downloaded for personal use, and the interactive hypermedia environment called the World Wide Web (hypermedia will be explained in the next chapter). Teachers and students can communicate directly with others through e-mail or take part in discussions by sending comments to a list server that will relay those comments to all members who subscribe to the list.

Under the older system for transferring stored information across the Internet, the user connected to a remote computer and transferred a file to the local computer. The user could then choose the appropriate software to examine the information (for example, a text file with a word processor) or, if the transferred file was a program, use the program. An alternative approach now provides this capability and some exciting new features. This system, called the World Wide Web, transfers information from a remote computer to the host computer in somewhat the same manner as the older system, but allows a more interactive approach because the same software used to access the remote computer presents the information. In addition, those preparing resources for access by World Wide Web browsers are able to present multimedia content and include links users can follow to other resources found on other servers.

Whether students communicate with other people or explore information resources, access alone is not sufficient for meaningful learning. Teachers need to give serious thought to how they will help students use the vast resources of the Internet to learn and solve authentic problems more effectively. One approach recognizes that much of what exists on the Internet should be regarded as primary source material rather than material prepared specifically as instructional resources. This chapter suggested a number of introductory activities that require students to work with the information the Internet makes available.

REFLECTING ON CHAPTER 6

Activities

- ◆ Subscribe to one of the listservs described in this chapter or in another resource for educators (make sure you take note of the procedure for unsubscribing). After one week, summarize the topics discussed on the list, and evaluate how helpful you feel the list would be to educators.

◆ Compare the productivity of several Web search engines. Select a search engine from each of the categories described on pages 232 and 237 and submit an identical search request (e.g., WebQuest) to each. What do you note about the results you generate? Does the search topic seem to make a difference?

◆ Design the "paper equivalent" of a WebQuest for a topic that interests you. Describe a problem, propose inquiry questions, and identify key Web resources as described on pages 232 through 237.

Key Terms

analog modem   *(p. 199)*
analog signal   *(p. 199)*
applets   *(p. 215)*
Boolean searches   *(p. 222)*
browser   *(p. 209)*
chat mode   *(p. 197)*
computer-mediated communication
    (CMC)   *(p. 206)*
conference   *(p. 204)*
digital subscriber line (DSL)   *(p. 198)*
domain name   *(p. 196)*
download   *(p. 212)*
electronic mail (e-mail)   *(p. 200)*
file transfer protocol (FTP)   *(p. 214)*
forum   *(p. 204)*
header   *(p. 204)*
helper application   *(p. 216)*
home page   *(p. 209)*
hypertext markup language (HTML)
    (p. 214)
hypertext transfer protocol (http)
    (p. 214)
incremental advantage   *(p. 228)*
instructional resource   *(p. 229)*
Internet   *(p. 195)*
Internet relay chat (IRC)   *(p. 197)*
Internet service provider (ISP)
    (p. 198)
integrated services digital network
    (ISDN)   *(p. 198)*

IP number   *(p. 196)*
listserv   *(p. 204)*
list server   *(p. 204)*
local area network (LAN)   *(p. 199)*
mailing lists   *(p. 204)*
modem   *(p. 198)*
newsgroup   *(p. 204)*
online tutorial   *(p. 226)*
plug-in   *(p. 216)*
point-to-point   *(p. 210)*
point-to-point protocol (PPP)
    (p. 199)
primary source   *(p. 227)*
protocol   *(p. 214)*
query   *(p. 217)*
search engine   *(p. 217)*
serial line Internet protocol (SLIP)
    (p. 199)
shareware   *(p. 225)*
source   *(p. 214)*
thread   *(p. 204)*
transformational advantage
    (p. 228)
transmission control protocol/Internet
    protocol (TCP/IP)   *(p. 196)*
universal resource locator (URL)
    (p. 214)
virtual reality modeling language
    (VRML)   *(p. 215)*
World Wide Web (WWW)   *(p. 209)*

Resources to Expand Your Knowledge Base

Any good bookstore is likely to carry a number of publications describing the Internet and providing detailed explanations for using different World Wide Web browsers. We have found the following more specialized publications for teachers to be useful.

Classroom Connect Staff. (1999). *Educator's Internet companion.* Lancaster, PA: Wentworth.

Benson, A., & Fodemski, L. (1999). *Connecting kids and the Internet: A handbook for librarians, teachers, and parents.* New York: Neal-Schuman.

Technology journals for teachers carry features and regular columns dealing with Internet activities. In 1992, *Computing Teacher* (now *Learning and Leading with Technology*) initiated a column called "Mining the Internet." ISTE, 1787 Agate St., Eugene, OR 97403.

Classroom Connect, Wentworth Worldwide Media, Inc., P.O. Box 10488, Lancaster, PA 17605-0488, is a monthly publication providing information on using the Internet and commercial telecommunications services. It also offers a series of instructional booklets and books on Internet topics. These materials are written for both teachers and K–12 students. (**http:// www.classroomconnect.com**)

Locating the Software and Services Mentioned in Chapter 6

America Online Instant Messenger is available to AOL users from the AOL site (**http://www.aol.com**), and it can be downloaded from the Netscape site. (**http://www.netscape.com/computing/download/**)

NetMeeting is a videoconferencing tool developed by Microsoft and available free of charge for the Windows operating system. Information and the opportunity to download the software are available online. (**http://www. microsoft.com/windows/ netmeeting/**)

CUSeeMe is one of several videoconferencing tools available from White Pine Software, Inc., for the Windows and Macintosh operating systems. (**http:// www.wpine. com/**)

The Web browsers described in this chapter can all be downloaded for educational use:

Microsoft Internet Explorer (**http://www.microsoft.com/ie/iedl.htm**)

Netscape Communications Navigator (**www.netscape.com/comprod/mirror/ client_download.html**)

Fetch is an FTP client for the Macintosh operating system developed at Dartmouth College. *WS-FTP* is an FTP client for the Windows operating system. The most recent version is available from Ipswitch Inc. *Fetch* and *WS-FTP* can be downloaded from **http://www.shareware.com**.

Search Engines

The number of search engines is continually expanding as both commercial and experimental services are added. Here are addresses for the search services mentioned in this chapter:

AltaVista: **http://www.altavista.com/**

HotBot: **http://www.hotbot.com/**

Magellan: **http://magellan.excite.com/**

MetaCrawler: **http://www.go2net.com/search.html**

Northern Light: **http://www.northernlight.com/**

SavvySearch: **http://www.savvysearch.com/**

Yahoo!: **http://www.yahoo.com/**

Internet Resources

FTP sites can be loaded through the directories maintained by Tile.NET (**http://tile.net/ftp-list/**) or the University of Illinois (**http://hoohoo.ncsa .uiuc.edu/ftp/**)

The weather project used the University of Michigan's Weather Underground. This Web site provides current weather data, maps, satellite images, and curriculum guides for teachers. (**http://www.wunderground.com**)

Sources for Structured Internet Activities

Global Grocery List, an ongoing e-mail project, especially good for Internet beginners, asks students to visit their local grocery stores and record the prices of items on the grocery list. Through sharing this information, data are collected from students all over the world. No fee for participation. (**http:// www.landmark-project. com/ggl.html**)

GlobaLearn conducts expeditions twice a year to places such as Turkey, Black Sea Nations, Brazil, and Africa, and facilitates classroom experiences related to these expeditions. The Web site shares the discoveries of the explorers and organizes resources for teachers and students. Fee for participation. (**http:// www.globalearn. org/**)

JASON Project sponsors an annual scientific expedition to engage students in science and technology and to provide professional development for teachers in grades 4 through 8. Classes can participate individually or receive further services through statewide-sponsored networks. Fee for participation. (**http:// www.jasonproject. org/**)

KidChronicles encourages students to produce their own newspaper based on the news articles submitted to *Newsday* by student reporters all over the world. No fee; two projects a year. (**http://www.gsn.org/project/newsday/ index.html**)

North American Quilt is an interactive online project designed to bring an interdisciplinary approach to the study of geography. Students study their local geography and share their research on the World Wide Web Sponsored by Online Class; fee for participation. (**http://www.onlineclass.com/NAQ/ NAQhome.html**)

One Sky, Many Voices provides the opportunity for K–12 students to use technology tools to investigate environmental themes related to weather. Projects run from four to eight weeks. Nominal fee for participation. (**http://onesky .engin.umich.edu/**)

Online Interactive Projects, sponsored by NASA, allows students to share in some of the excitement of authentic scientific explorations, such as high-altitude astronomy, Antarctic biology, and robotics. Resources include television broadcasts and videotapes, printed workbooks, and online interaction. No fee for participation. (**http://quest.arc.nasa.gov/interactive.html**)

The Journey North is a yearly adventure that engages students in a global study of wildlife migration and seasonal change. No fee for participation; a charge for associated curriculum materials. (**http://www.learner.org/jnorth/**)

ThinkQuest is an annual contest that challenges students and teachers to create Web projects that harness the power of the Internet. The archives create a library of Internet educational materials for use in the classroom or at home. Project competitions include an international division for students ages twelve through nineteen, a junior division for U.S. students in grades 4–6, and a teacher division for U.S. teachers. No fee to participate and contestants compete for cash prizes. (**http://io.advanced.org/ThinkQuest/**)

Subscription Services That Provide Information Resources

General Information Services

EBSCO Information Services: **http://www.ebsco.com/**

The Electric Library: **http://www.elibrary.com**

Encarta OnLine Library: **http://www.encarta.msn.com/library/intro.asp**

ProQuest Direct: **http://www.umi.com/proquest/**

SIRS Researcher on the Web: **http://www.sirs.com/**

News Services

Washington Post and *Los Angeles Times:* **http://www.newsservice.com/**

Wall Street Journal: **http://www.wsj.com/**

New York Times: **http://www.nytimes.com/**

Chapter 7

Introducing Multimedia Applications for Classroom Learning

ORIENTATION

The goal of this chapter is to identify ways students can use multimedia tools to explore, think about, and involve themselves with course content in personally meaningful ways. First, we look at ways multimedia can be used as a delivery system for the computer-assisted instruction (CAI) you read about in Chapter 4. Then we look at other types of multimedia software, such as talking books, that are not CAI materials. Finally, we examine the educational advantages of multimedia and hypermedia as applications that present information in a variety of ways. As you read, look for answers to the following questions:

Focus Questions

◆ What changes might multimedia tools bring about in the functioning of schools?

◆ In what ways can multimedia and hypermedia support verbal instruction?

◆ What kinds of content can multimedia present to students in particularly powerful ways?

◆ What are some of the unique advantages offered by multimedia environments?

◆ How do multimedia applications support students' meaningful learning?

◆ What are some concerns related to multimedia applications that classroom teachers need to recognize?

WHAT ARE MULTIMEDIA, HYPERMEDIA, AND HYPERTEXT?

The terms describe different combinations of media and communication methods.

Official definitions of *multimedia, hypermedia,* and *hypertext* don't really exist. There are no industry standards, and different people use the terms differently. Educators sometimes use the terms interchangeably, even though they are intended to describe different combinations of media and communication methods. We have developed the definitions offered here based on product characteristics, and our system seems in agreement with the distinctions others have drawn in efforts to differentiate the terms (e.g., Tolhurst, 1995). A product is whatever the developer gives to the consumer to communicate information, experience, and emotion. This book is a product that you and we are using to share information, experiences, and some feelings.

If a product uses more than one modality (say, visual and auditory), at least two symbol systems within a modality (words and pictures), or at least two genres within a symbol system (prose and poetry, a still image and video), the product includes multiple media—that is, multimedia. *Multimedia* thus translates as "many formats." By this definition, a child's story illustrated with drawings or a series of slides with musical accompaniment is multimedia.

The term *multimedia* has been around since the early 1970s. Instructional media courses used to refer to slide-and-sound or filmstrip-and-sound presentations as multimedia. You may remember filmstrip and tape combinations in which a beep from the tape recorder told someone to advance the filmstrip.

This book concentrates on forms of multimedia in which a computer is involved. The computer either presents information directly or controls the presentation of information from some other source, such as CD-ROM or videodisc. Some would prefer that the term *multimedia* (as well as *hypermedia*) refer to the entire system, including hardware, software, and document, used to communicate with the system user (Marchionini, 1988). The term *document* here refers to the actual data file or files storing the text, graphics, and sounds. The combination of hardware, application software, and document is probably what most educators now understand multimedia to be. This definition would exclude a textbook with pictures, for example. **Multimedia** is a communication format that integrates several media—text, audio, video, and animation—most commonly implemented with a computer.

Multimedia and hypermedia defined

Hypermedia allows multimedia to be experienced in a nonlinear fashion. In this format, units of information, such as individual words, segments of text, segments of audio, pictures, animations, and video clips, are connected to each other in multiple ways. Hypermedia environments are often described as *interactive* because the hypermedia user must direct the software and hardware environment to present the next unit of information to be experienced. Because control is vested in the user, different individuals potentially have very different experiences as they work in hypermedia environments. When the information in hypermedia consists entirely of text, the term **hypertext** is sometimes used. Hypertext was actually the first form of hypermedia, but now this format rarely exists in educational settings.

The idea of an organized yet nonlinear system might be a bit confusing. Here's a comparison that might help explain how hypermedia works. Traditional books are organized in a linear fashion. As you read, you encounter a series of ideas. An author orders the ideas in this series based on his or her opinion of the structure that will make the information most interesting, most persuasive, or easiest to understand. If you were to read a section of a chapter a second time, you would obviously encounter the same series of ideas in the same order.

What is nonlinear organization?

Now consider how a book, perhaps a science textbook, might be presented in a hypermedia format. From a particular segment of text describing scientific discoveries, the reader might be able to access the definition of any term appearing in boldface print, view a picture of the famous scientist responsible for each discovery, read a short biographical sketch of the scientist, and review the scientific principles on which scientific breakthroughs were based. Some scientists and some scientific principles might be associated with several different discoveries. Different students might explore this environment in different ways. Some might just review the scientific discoveries. Some might read all the biographies of the scientists. Some might take each discovery in turn and learn about the discovery, the scientist, and the principles associated with that discovery. Some might review everything available about a famous scientist's work. In contrast to the predictable pattern of readers' working with a textbook, the exploration of a hypermedia environment offers much more variety.

Although multimedia and hypermedia are distinct, a separate discussion of each would be unnecessarily complicated. In this book, we use the term *multimedia* to discuss issues that apply to both multimedia and hypermedia. We use the term *hypermedia* only when an issue relates exclusively to hypermedia.

WHAT ARE VIDEODISC, CD-ROM, AND DVD?

Discussions of multimedia and hypermedia always seem to include some reference to videodiscs, CD-ROMs, and DVDs. There is a practical reason for this association: these storage systems offer the capacity necessary to hold a lot of information and, in particular, information that takes a great deal of disk space (e.g., video). Multimedia and hypermedia require access to tremendous amounts of information. The connection between the applications and the storage media is thus a very logical and necessary one. Some basic information about videodiscs, CD-ROMs, and DVDs should help you understand how they work and when they can be of particular value in classrooms.

Unlike the blank diskettes you might buy to store data from a word processing program or other computer tool, CD-ROMs, videodiscs, and DVDs are usually purchased already loaded with data. **CD-ROM** stands for *compact disc–read only memory*. In other words, information stored on a CD-ROM can be read from the disc. (Notice that optical discs are spelled with a *c* and magnetic disks are spelled with a *k*.) into the memory of the computer but cannot be erased or modified. Until recently, this also meant that compact discs were used only for distributing commercial products and that consumers could not take advantage of compact discs' large capacity to store their own information. The same has been true for **digital video disc (DVD)**, a fairly recent innovation. Because of our experience with music CDs, this is probably a limitation we take for granted. However, recordable CD and DVD technology is now available to consumers. As you will read in the material that follows, recordable CDs and DVDs will likely become very common because of their great storage capacity provided at very low cost.

Recordable CD and DVD technology

VIDEODISC TECHNOLOGY

The **videodisc** is the oldest of the three formats as a popular commercial product. A videodisc is about the size of a 33-rpm record and silver in color. It requires a special videodisc player, which spins the videodisc at a very high speed while a laser beam is bounced off the disc's surface. Microscopic pits in the surface of the disc cause variations in the way the laser beam is reflected back to a pickup device and allow the pickup device to read information from the disc. Since nothing touches the surface of the disc, there is no wear, and discs should last indefinitely. Videodiscs are sometimes called **laserdiscs** because of this method of reading information from the disc. A videodisc is capable of storing both video and stereo audio. Instead of stereo, the two auditory channels are sometimes used to store two auditory sources—perhaps descriptive information in two different languages or a computer program.

Videodiscs store visual information as a series of frames or pictures. This is also true of videotape. The videodisc or videotape player sends these images to the screen at the rate of thirty frames per second, giving the illusion of motion. There is an important difference in the way a videodisc and a videotape store these individual images. A videotape stores the images in a series. A videodisc stores the images as concentric circles on the disc. With at least one type of videodisc, the same circle of information can be read over and over to

The storage capacity of videodiscs

provide a stationary image of very high quality. Because there are 54,000 frames on each side of this type of videodisc (most commercial videodiscs use only one side) and individual frames can be accessed very quickly, a tremendous number of high-quality images are nearly instantly available with videodisc technology. To appreciate this storage capacity, translate this as the equivalent of 54,000 photographic slides that can be accessed at will, and you will begin to imagine how much information can be stored on one of these platters. In contrast, videotape is unable to provide practical access to individual images in a reasonable amount of time.

Videodisc Formats

The videodiscs themselves come in two formats: **constant linear velocity (CLV)** and **constant angular velocity (CAV).** A CLV videodisc can hold about one hour of video but is really useful only for showing continuous video. A CAV videodisc holds only thirty minutes of continuous video but offers several useful advantages. CAV discs allow the display of individual frames and also allow the user to step through a sequence of video one frame at a time and to play video segments at different speeds, both forward and reverse. The instructional advantage of examining individual frames and precisely controlling the display of specific segments is well worth the difference in storage capacity.

Accessing videodisc images

Most educational videodiscs contain images to be displayed as individual frames, short video segments, and audio. The images can be accessed manually from the control panel on the front of the player, a remote device similar in appearance to the device you use to change channels on your television or control your videotape player, a bar code reader, or a computer connected to the videodisc player. When a computer controls the videodisc player, the images from the videodisc are often displayed on a separate screen. In this case, the student could watch both the computer screen and the screen attached to the videodisc player. Images can also be viewed through the computer screen. Depending on the type of computer, watching video through the computer screen may require that special hardware be added to the computer (Barron, Breit, Boulware, & Bullock, 1994).

Video and sound are stored on a videodisc in **analog format**. This format provides high quality and efficient storage, but does not allow the computer to manipulate the information without first capturing and digitizing the information. The information is not stored on the videodisc in the **digital format** used directly by your computer. One way to understand the difference between analog and digital is to think of the difference between a traditional and a digital clock. The time is expressed discretely by the digital clock. With a traditional clock, the expression of time is continuous and always changing. Computers need information represented in a discrete fashion.

Types of Videodiscs

Videodiscs are controlled in several different ways. Some are controlled with a hand-held device that allows the user to display a segment of video or advance to a specific frame. This device functions something like the remote you might use to control a videotape player.

Using the bar code reader

The bar code reader uses the technology you know from grocery store checkout lines. The bar codes indicate commands (forward, reverse), frame numbers, or the beginning and ending frames of a video segment and are often printed in the teacher's resource materials. Along with the videodisc, the teacher might receive a looseleaf notebook containing sample lesson plans and bar codes. As the teacher moves through the lesson with the class, the bar code reader is swiped across the bar code at the appropriate time to present an image or video segment on the monitor.

Software is also available (Videodiscovery MediaMAX) to create your own bar codes, like those shown in Figure 7.1. These bar codes can be printed by themselves or inserted in computer-generated text documents or graphics. A teacher or students can do some very interesting things with this kind of program. A teacher can create and print a list of bar codes representing the images he or she might want to display during a presentation. During the presentation, simply running the bar code reader over the appropriate bar code displays the desired image on a monitor attached to the videodisc player. Students might prepare presentations of their own or create bar codes and stick them on maps, a globe, diagrams, or even a skeleton. Running the bar code reader over the bar code would present whatever image the student wanted the viewer to see (Barron et al., 1994).

FIGURE 7.1
Sample Bar Codes Produced with MediaMax

18516 (President Kennedy)

18516

19522 (Berlin Wall)

19522

A computer can also control the videodisc player. In some cases, the program running on the computer simply makes the selection of frames or segments easier for the viewer. A menu might appear on the computer screen, and the viewer then selects the segment to be displayed on the screen. A teacher might use this menu to present images as part of a classroom presentation. In the other main application, the video frames or segments displayed are a component of the instructional program with which a student is interacting. Here, the student is involved in computer-assisted instruction of one form or another, and the videodisc is used to supply video and auditory information. The computer presents text, accepts student responses from the keyboard or some other input device, and makes decisions or offers choices in order to control how the instruction should proceed.

CD-ROM TECHNOLOGY

A CD-ROM holds about 600 **megabytes** (1 million bytes) of information on a disc that costs about $2 to produce. You are probably familiar with the appearance of CD-ROMs because they have nearly replaced records and tapes as the format of choice for music. With computer programs becoming larger and larger, CD-ROMs have become the most common format in which commercial software is made available. New computers usually come with a CD-ROM player already installed, and on some computers, the CD-ROM is the only storage device other than the computer's hard drive.

The advantage of digital format

CD-ROMs store information in digital form. This means that they can store not only music and pictures as data files but also computer programs. The advantage of the digital format is that the computer user can bring data of this type into the memory of the computer and work directly with the information. A picture from a CD-ROM can be modified using a graphics program or can be inserted in a word processing document.

It is now possible for schools to purchase, for a reasonable price, the equipment to generate their own CDs. The technology is a little different from the approach used to produce commercial CDs. The commercial process generates a master expensively and stamps individual CDs cheaply. The alternative approach is to burn information into a special CD blank (CD-R). This process is much less expensive for producing individual CDs, but very expensive and slow if you want to create thousands. An individual blank for this process is currently under $3.

Surprisingly, CD-ROMS do not offer enough capacity for some applications. High-quality images may easily require 10 megabytes of space, so a CD cannot store as many images as a videodisc. However, it is the interest in extended video that really taxes the capacity of CDs. The interest in long segments of full-screen video requires that users move to DVD.

Emerging Technology

The Evolution of Multimedia Encyclopedias

It is difficult to appreciate what can be stored on a single CD-ROM. Here is the list of contents from Microsoft's Encarta, an electronic multimedia encyclopedia (Gates, 1995).

- 9 million words of text on 26,000 topics
- 8 hours of sound
- 7,000 images
- 800 maps
- 250 interactive charts
- 100 animations and video clips

Multimedia encyclopedias are becoming much more than just encyclopedias on a disc. The companies creating computer-based reference tools have always had vast stores of information to draw on, but competition and consumer interest have led to products that are both more powerful and augmented by activities and tools intended to involve students with information in a more active manner. The "old-style" encyclopedia on a disc made limited use of powerful search features or true hypermedia. Now encyclopedias offer more sophisticated searches (i.e., Boolean searches) and embed links to related articles, images, interactive activities, and even games within articles. Companies may also develop thematic approaches that present a topic at a more general level or a historical approach based on a time line and then provide links to a number of individual encyclopedia articles.

No matter how sophisticated disc-based reference materials become, they have one inherent weakness true of all reference materials: once published, they are immediately at least partially out of date. New discoveries that may negate long-held beliefs and important events occur daily. Companies developing multimedia encyclopedias are making use of the Internet to keep the content they offer as current as possible. One approach uses the Internet to provide online access to the encyclopedia (e.g., *Grolier Multimedia Encyclopedia Online*). The delivery system uses the Internet rather than a CD and is similar to the subscription services described in Chapter 6. Companies suggest that the online version is an advantage when many students might want to use the encyclopedia at the same time. The content offered would also be the most current available.

The other approaches rely on what have been described as hybrid strategies: various combinations of the CD and the Internet. For example, Grolier links articles from its *Year 2000 Grolier Multimedia Encyclopedia* with carefully selected World Wide Web sites through a special interface called the Internet Index. A staff continues to add hundreds of new sites a month in an effort to expand the basic reference tool and provide the most current examples possible. A feature called "Article Update" also allows owners of the CD to access new articles written for the encyclopedia.

Microsoft has taken this approach even further in establishing the Web-based Encarta Schoolhouse. The Encarta Schoolhouse provides Internet links based on a series of themes. Each theme, covering a topic such as the Civil War, life in the ocean, or earthquakes, is supported by suggested activities and links to some of the best related Internet content. Encarta has also developed the Yearbook Builder, which makes use of the Internet to download a monthly review of that month's most important events and new articles that are linked to existing Encarta content. What is especially impressive about the approach that has been developed is that not only is it possible to examine the new material and then find related articles on the original CD, but it is also possible to click the update icon while working with the CD to search for any updated material that has been downloaded. The idea is to simulate the experience of working with an integrated product released within the past month.

The resources described here should provide teachers with some powerful opportunities to engage students in meaningful learning. The theme-based activities would provide great opportunities to develop WebQuests, as described in Chapter 6 (page 233). Teachers would need only to review some of the Internet resources and establish scaffolding activities. The links established between current events and more standard encyclopedia content offer a different kind of opportunity. In that case, students could use experiences that are more immediate and specific to understand issues and content that are likely to be more remote and abstract.

The Internet addresses for the two products described here and several similar products are provided at the end of the chapter. ✳

DVD TECHNOLOGY

DVDs store more information than CDs.

A DVD looks very much like a standard CD, but the DVD player uses a more sophisticated laser system that allows the disc to contain more tracks and more densely packed pits, and to spin faster. In addition, a DVD potentially allows two layers of information to be stored on both sides of the disc (a CD has one layer of information on one side). These differences allow a great deal more information to be stored. The lowest-capacity DVD holds several gigabytes and the high-end DVD holds 17 gigabytes. The most obvious benefit of this amount of storage will be in the delivery of high-quality video for entertainment or educational purposes. A standard movie of the type you are used to renting on videotape will fit comfortably on the lowest-capacity DVD, and the high-end disc will hold 8 hours of video. The opportunity to integrate extended high-quality video segments into educational multimedia will provide experiences that are not now possible with standard CD technology.

Applications of DVD technology have probably not emerged as quickly as some had hoped. The one exception seems to be in the area of DVD players that connect to your television (sometimes called DVD-video). This type of DVD is used mainly for entertainment and has made some headway in the home entertainment market. The version of DVD (DVD-ROM) that holds computer data has received less attention even though combination CD/DVD drives are available for most new computers. One exception might be in the area of reference materials such as products offering a combination of an encyclopedia, atlas, fact book, and so on (see the discussion of multimedia encyclopedias in Emerging Technology: The Evolution of Multimedia Encyclopedias on the previous page). A newer application, **DVD-RAM** (or

DVD-RW), allows rewritable storage with a capacity of at least 2.5 gigabytes at a cost of under $30 for each disc. This low-cost storage or backup capacity can be very useful in an educational setting and will encourage the increased use of the DVD format.

Those who are used to storing projects on 2-megabyte disks may not be able to imagine how they would ever make use of several 2.5-gigabyte DVDs; each DVD would offer as much capacity as 1,200 disks. First, consider that computer hard drives are fallible, and backing up the contents of a personal computer is a wise practice. Copying the contents of a hard drive to a DVD-RAM is convenient, quicker, and even less expensive than backing up a several-gigabyte hard drive in some other manner. Second, certain types of projects require large amounts of storage. For example, we work with students who do video editing on a computer (see Chapter 9). They edit together segments of video to create a documentary about their field trip, a memento of season highlights for members of the basketball team, or perhaps a tour of the school building for new students (see pages 337 to 340). The amount of disk space required for such projects can strain the capacity of a hard drive, and for a while the stored material had to be erased once the videotape had been created and the project was over. The large capacity of DVD-RAM allows the digital information to be stored in case there is some reason to work with some elements of the project again.

EDUCATIONAL APPLICATIONS USING MULTIMEDIA AND HYPERMEDIA

Multimedia and computer-assisted instruction

Multimedia can be used as a delivery system for the CAI activities described in Chapter 4. Often a multimedia environment will combine a number of different CAI activities. For example, *Animal Pathfinders* combines access to videodisc frames and video segments with various computer-based CAI activities to present a number of lessons about animal behavior. One lesson, "Bee Dances," explains how bees communicate the location of a food source. The capabilities of the videodisc and computer simulations are important in helping students grasp animal behaviors and many other phenomena that would be difficult to describe adequately with other techniques. The observation of an actual event in any content area is nearly always a highly desirable option, and students should not have to rely on simple diagrams or written accounts. The use of video segments can also give students a richer context for understanding animal behavior. (You might want to review the discussion of authentic tasks in Chapter 2, page 65.)

Establishing a richer context for student understanding

Students learn about biological phenomena in order to understand the natural world better. The key is whether students will form these associations when confronted with information separated from the actual phenomena the information seeks to explain. Some students will, and some will not. For some, the concepts will be learned but will remain inert, instead of useful outside the classroom situation in which the information was encountered. Video segments depicting the inside of a beehive or bees searching for flowers may allow students to connect with experiences not found in the classroom.

Among other examples, the *Animal Pathfinders* videodisc shows how a scout bee uses the "waggle dance" to communicate the location of a food source to other bees in the hive. The dance consists of a pair of looping movements separated by a running motion. The direction of the run explains the direction of the food relative to the position of the sun, and the duration of buzzing during the run indicates the distance to the food source. Probably the most difficult part of this phenomenon to understand is the way both the direction of the bee's run and the position of the sun must be used to determine the direction of flowers. It may also be difficult for students to imagine what a bee's dance might look like. Perhaps our definition of two loops surrounding a running motion has not been sufficient for you to visualize a bee performing this dance. Does the bee lead with its left foot or its right? Viewing a short video clip quickly solves the problem of recognizing the dance, but viewing the video clip cannot by itself do much to solve the more complex problem of understanding the relationship of the dance, the position of the sun, and the location of the flowers.

Combining a tutorial, a simulation, and a game

The developers of "Bee Dances" combine a tutorial, a simulation, and a game to present information, assist students in achieving understanding, provide extended practice, and evaluate understanding (the four stages of instruction; see Chapter 4). The tutorial uses text, a few simple diagrams, and images from the videodisc to explain the communication techniques of the honeybee. One simulation provides an opportunity to learn the geometric relationship of the dance, sun, and flowers. One simulation lets the student become a bee and attempt to find flowers.

OTHER FORMS OF MULTIMEDIA FOUND IN CLASSROOMS

There are some unique types of multimedia software that are not really CAI materials. This section presents some of these applications—talking books, reference materials, and cooperative problem-solving activities—and the classroom situations in which you might choose to use them. If you have the opportunity to work with products of the type described here, you may find that some include several forms of CAI and several of the applications listed in this section. We isolate these applications here primarily to make it easier to describe and discuss each type of software.

Talking Books

The storage capacity of CD-ROMs has made possible the creation of talking books. These products are most commonly based on popular and award-

Dances with Bees

Teacher: What does *communicate* mean?

Student: It means to talk—kind of. It means to tell someone what you are thinking.

Teacher: Are animals able to communicate?

Student: Sure, my dog tells me when he wants to go outside. [*Laughter*]

Teacher: How does your dog tell you he wants to go outside?

Student: He gives a few yips and moves toward the door.

Teacher: Okay. Do you think insects communicate? [*Silence*] How about honeybees? Do you think they communicate? How would they communicate, and what would they have to say?

Student: They would buzz, I suppose.

Teacher: What would they want to tell each other? [*Silence. Starts the "Bee Dances" tutorial. Plays initial video segment.*] So tell me what you observed.

Student: The bees were flying to the flowers. They took nectar from the purple flowers and flew back to their hive. They put the nectar in the honeycomb. Eggs are laid in those holes in the honeycomb too.

Teacher: Did you see the eggs?

Student: No. I just know they do that.

Teacher: Did you see any dances? Watch this again. [*Points to dancing bee.*]

Student: Oh, that one wiggling its butt is dancing. [*Imitates; everyone laughs.*]

Teacher: I guess we'll have to call this lesson "Dances with Bees." Why don't you work on this program on your own. Click on the arrow keys when you're ready to go to the next page. Watch for buttons telling you there's some special demonstration to look at. Sometimes you will watch more video on the monitor, and sometimes you will see something special on the computer screen. [*Steps back to watch.*]

[*One student controls the keyboard, and the other watches. The initial part of the tutorial explains that dances are used to direct other bees to sources of food that have been discovered. When the flowers are close to the hive, the bee performs a round dance to inform other bees that the flowers are close. Bees then use their olfactory sense to find flowers.*]

Student: What does *olfactory* mean?

Teacher: It means the bees can find the flowers by smell.

[*The student continues with the tutorial and now learns about the "waggle dance." The waggle dance consists of two loops connected by a running movement. The orientation of the run explains the position of the flowers relative to the position of the sun. The combs are positioned vertically in the hive. If the run is toward the top of the comb, the dance means the flowers are toward the sun. Straight down means they are away from the sun. Movements that depart from the vertical indicate that the flowers are located at an angle away from the sun. The duration of the waggle indicates the distance from the hive. The students move from the tutorial to a simulation that allows either the flowers or the sun to be moved. Clicking on the hive indicates the direction of the dance that would indicate this relationship between sun and flowers (see Figure 7.2). Students spend some time working with the simulation.*]

Teacher: Do you understand that [*refers to simulation*]?

Student: It is like the direction of the run in the hive shows how far you have to turn away from the sun to find the flowers. [*Students are having some difficulty orienting the bee dance to the picture of the hive, flowers, and sun.*] It would be easier to see if you could move this part [*points to part of*

FIGURE 7.2
"Bee Dances" Simulation Allowing Student to Experiment with Position of Food and Sun

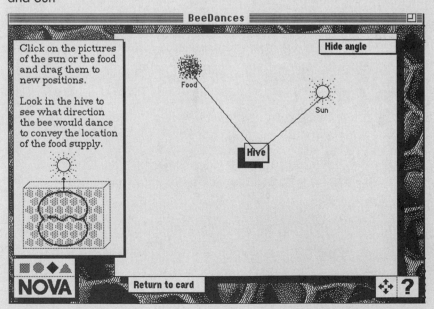

simulation showing the orientation of the dance]. You should be able to point the top of the hive at the sun.

Teacher: I don't think the bees are allowed to do that.

[*Student works a while longer and then moves to final activity—a game called "You Be the Bee" (see Figure 7.3). In this activity, the student clicks on the hive and views a dancing bee. The run of the dancing bee (see Figure 7.4—the dancing bee appears near the middle of the picture) is oriented at an angle of about 100 degrees relative to the top of the picture. (The student attempts to interpret the dance and clicks on a potential food source; refer to Figure 7.3.) The program then displays the flight of the bee from the bee's perspective. As the bee flies through the meadow, the student experiences moving through the meadow. If directed properly, the bee finds the flowers. If misdirected, the bee ends up at a bush.*]

Student: I knew it was this one. It's the only one turned to the right from the sun this much [*points to computer screen and the angle displayed*]. Click on "New" and let's do another one.

FIGURE 7.3
Screen from "Bee Dances" Allowing Student to Select Position of Flowers

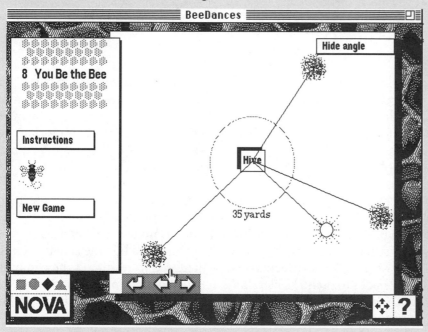

FIGURE 7.4
Image of Dancing Bee from "Bee Dances"

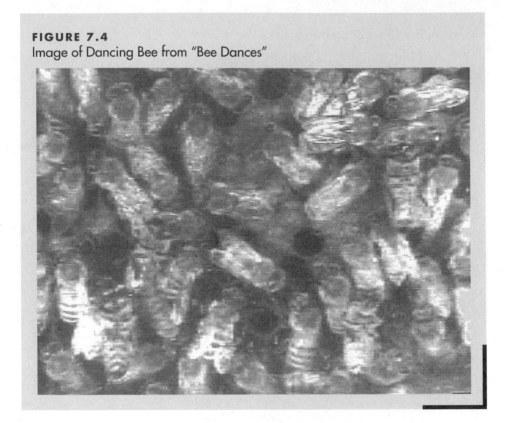

winning children's literature and are characterized by colorful artwork, optional access to narrators who read the story "in character," access to pronunciation and definitions by clicking on words, and objects within the artwork that perform simple actions when clicked. The CD-ROM is important because it provides the capacity necessary for the high-quality sound, graphics, and simple animations hidden in the artwork. As you can see in Figure 7.5, these products purposely mimic the appearance of books.

Teachers can often appreciate how this use of technology, the high-quality narration, and the fun of looking for the hidden treasures in the artwork might intrigue young students. The questions teachers often ask are, "Is it worth spending this much money when you could buy the actual book for much less?" and "Will students be less interested in reading if the computer will read books to them?" The value in talking books is in helping children develop a relationship with books and in building excitement about reading (Chomsky, 1990).

Content-area reading materials for young readers have also been developed using the talking book approach (*National Geographic Wonders of*

Helping children develop a relationship with books

FIGURE 7.5
Screen Display from *Scary Poems for Rotten Kids*

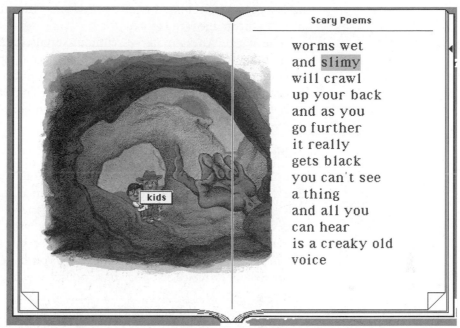

Learning CD-ROM Library). Instead of presenting children's literature, this software explores topics such as "The World of Plants" and other topics from science, nature, and geography. Like the previous example of children's literature, the content-area reading materials appear as a colorful book on the computer screen. *Scary Poems for Rotten Kids* and the *National Geographic Wonders of Learning Collection* were both developed by Discis Knowledge Research, Inc. This particular collection allows the user to select from a number of features in addition to basic narration. Individual words can be pronounced and explained in context, in either English or Spanish. The Spanish-language option is intended to assist students learning English as a second language.

The talking book concept has also been developed into a system for language arts instruction. WiggleWorks is based on a series of lavishly illustrated stories and nonfiction works published by Scholastic for young children. The students have the option of reading the "books" to themselves or having the computer read the books to them. Each student's oral reading can be recorded, played back, and contrasted with the narrated version. The materials take an approach that emphasizes the connections between reading and writing. In one option available for each selection, students are presented a "coloring book" version of the original book. This coloring book version can be modified in a variety of ways with several different types of tools. The text from a particular page can be retained, and paint tools and image stamps appropriate to the theme of the story can be used to create a new illustration. Or the image can be retained and "colored" and the student can add new text suited to the image (see Figure 7.6).

The WiggleWorks materials contain sophisticated management and assessment tools. The computer keeps track of what students do with each text selection (listen, read, write) and saves any products that the student creates (written samples, recordings of oral readings). The teacher can review this information, add notes for archival purposes, and export any of this information for inclusion in a student portfolio.

Multimedia References

School libraries, and to a lesser extent individual classrooms, make certain reference sources available to students. Reference materials such as encyclopedias, almanacs, globes, and atlases have general value in many content areas. Some books and magazines are also purchased because of their value as reference material. Most schools have a subscription to the *National Geographic Magazine* and possibly to the more youth-oriented *National Graphic World*. School libraries also may have books that might be described as mul-

FIGURE 7.6
Sample Screen from WiggleWorks "Coloring Book" Activity

timedia collections—for example, *Birds of North America, Wildflowers of the Northern Plains,* or images from World War II. Alternatives to all of these examples are available on CD-ROM and sometimes on videodisc. Similar products are emerging on DVD.

Advantages of technology-based multimedia references

Technology-based multimedia reference material offers several advantages. In some cases, the CD-ROM version is less expensive. All volumes of *National Geographic* (more than 110 years) are available on CD for approximately $160. CD-ROM versions of popular encyclopedias cost approximately $50 (see Emerging Technology: The Evolution of Multimedia Encyclopedias). Multimedia resources offer a second advantage in making information available in multiple formats. Some information sources cannot be presented in text format, and some information sources that could be presented as text are more motivating when presented in other ways. For example, reading about the cry of a loon is not the same as hearing it. Reading the words of President John F. Kennedy's inaugural address is less moving than hearing the speech in his own voice.

Search and exploration options

Multimedia encyclopedias allow powerful search features. CD-based encyclopedias have hypertext links among articles that allow powerful searches using individual terms or various combinations of terms. Searches using multiple terms are often called Boolean searches. Boolean searches refer to the logic involved in defining when certain conditions have been met. Searches are usually classified as AND or OR searches (see Chapter 6, page 222).

Finally, references often allow a **copy-and-paste** capability. These two procedures allow material to be copied from the reference and then pasted into another application. This is sometimes described as cut and paste in manuals accompanying reference software, but this description is inaccurate because nothing is actually removed, or "cut," from the original source. The availability of copy and paste allows students to use pictures, maps, and tables from other sources in their own documents. You may be concerned that this option encourages students to copy when they are usually asked to summarize and organize the material they take from references. However, because copying is so obvious in this case, it actually gives teachers a convenient opportunity to explain students' responsibilities in using information from other sources.

Cooperative Problem Solving

Group-based learning activities

Learning activities involving groups of students or even entire classes have practical advantages. The equipment necessary for using multimedia may not be available in abundance, and group-based approaches can use available equipment more efficiently. Student groups provide an ideal setting for exploring ideas through discussion. Both preparing for a discussion and testing personal ideas against the scrutiny that a discussion provides can be valuable learning opportunities. With the exception of methods for group-based information presentation, applications of technology are seldom designed with the group context in mind.

Cooperative problem solving involves groups of students with information in a nontraditional manner: students work in groups to solve problems posed through text and video. In the tasks developed by Tom Snyder Productions (*Great Ocean Rescue*, *Great Solar System Rescue*, the *Decisions, Decisions* series), several subproblems are set within a single scenario, and students work through these subproblems to resolve the central problem. The activities follow a carefully structured approach to ensure efficiency, make managing the classroom easier, and scaffold the students' approach to solving the complex problems that are presented.

In the *Decisions, Decisions* series, groups of students take on a hypothetical role and make a series of decisions. Each decision has consequences that create the situation for a new decision. For example, in *Decisions, Decisions: The Environment*, students put themselves in the role of a mayor who must deal with a pollution problem during a reelection campaign. The mayor must confront the complex public policy issues that can occur as a consequence of the conflicting agendas of low taxes, cost-effective manufacturing, and the desire for clean air and water. The mayor must decide whether to clean up a local pond (the immediate problem but not the long-term solution), change practices at a local dump (the real problem, but an expensive task and an issue for local manufacturers that use the dump as a disposal site), or study the problem further. The stages in each decision require students to:

◆ Analyze the situation.
◆ Set priorities.
◆ Consider options.
◆ Make a decision.
◆ Evaluate consequences.

Students are given individual responsibilities for developing knowledge relevant to decisions, and this collective knowledge is then called on in the problem-solving process. As the group integrates the information, they are often required to reach consensus on the next step. The need to come to an agreement generates a great deal of class discussion.

Here is a more detailed description to help you understand how one of these cooperative problem-solving tasks might work in a classroom setting. In the following example, "Grief on the Reef" (pages 265 to 266), the central problem is to find an explanation for the widespread death of marine life on an ocean reef. To solve this problem, students first have to locate the reef and then decide which biological tests might provide useful information. Using the information from the tests, students then attempt to identify the reason for the reef's decline. The students go through a sequence of three subproblems to reach a final decision.

Video resources available on videodisc or videotape can play a valuable role in many classroom activities. *(© Michael Zide)*

Types of group interdependencies

The cooperative nature of these activities is based on several types of group interdependencies (Johnson, Johnson, & Holubec, 1991). Students working with these problem-solving activities experience **reward interdependence,** because the point system allowing teams to compete against each other is based on the money that whole groups must pay each time they make a choice regarding location, request that a test be administered, or suggest a reason for the problem (see the description that follows). Because the group must make such requests as a group and must spend as little money as possible in competing against other groups, the team, and not the individuals, wins or loses.

Each member of a team is given a specific role and provided unique access to information related to that role. Thus, these activities also involve resource interdependence. **Resource interdependence** exists when each group member has a portion of the resources necessary for a task to be completed and must combine these resources with those of others to complete the task. In this case, the resources are the information each student must master. This type of cooperative learning is sometimes described as **jigsaw cooperation** because each member of the group has a piece of the puzzle the group must assemble for success.

EVALUATING MULTIMEDIA AND HYPERMEDIA

New and readily available innovations such as multimedia and hypermedia often capture educators' imaginations. There is a certain excitement in promising new ideas and powerful innovations that allow students and teachers opportunities that were not previously available. However, there is also reason for caution. There is some vulnerability present in the excitement connected with new opportunities. Merchandisers can play on this excitement to market products urging well-intentioned educators and school boards to take advantage of the newest resources for the benefit of their students. Although such situations may occasionally result from opportunism, there is also the real possibility that the potential of new products and new approaches has yet to be fully understood.

A number of reviews have summarized studies comparing traditional instruction with various types of videodisc or interactive multimedia presentations. Although the classroom research attempting to establish general benefits of multimedia should be regarded as inconclusive, research activity does provide reasons to be optimistic about multimedia (Dillon & Gabbard, 1998; Moore, Burton, & Myers, 1996). Basic research provides support for the practice of presenting information in multiple formats, particularly when the presentation method allows the multiple formats to be experienced simultaneously (e.g., narrated comments on a diagram). There is also research demonstrating the educational value of learning experiences that anchor these experiences within more complex and authentic environments. Multimedia offer some unique practical advantages in providing these complex learning environments. These advantages will be explored in greater detail in the discussion of specific strengths and concerns associated with the use of multimedia.

Be an aware decision maker

As you make decisions, the best advice is to combine awareness of the general strengths and concerns expressed by experienced users and developers, the conclusions generated by the available research, and the qualities of a particular product with your particular instructional goals. Do these sources of information and values converge to recommend that a particular product and learning activity be made available to your students?

Grief on the Reef: A Group-Based Interactive Videodisc

Cully Gause is a life science and earth science teacher at South Junior High School in Grand Forks, North Dakota. We asked him to describe his experiences working with group-based interactive videodiscs.

Cully: Interactive video can work great with a group if you remember to do one important thing. You need to find a way to get everyone involved, make everyone accountable for something. I have used several of the Tom Snyder videodiscs. They were designed for group work and have good ideas for giving all students something to do. The tasks and worksheets are all set up and ready to go. I find most of the suggestions and activities work pretty well, so I haven't had to prepare new activities.

Here's what it's like to use *The Great Ocean Rescue*. This videodisc contains four "missions." A mission is really a problem the group is supposed to solve. I remember one of the missions was "Grief on the Reef," and the group had to determine why the sea life on a coral reef was dying. A student group is supposed to be made up of four people, with each student assigned a role: an environmental scientist, a geologist, an oceanographer, and a marine biologist. When students take a role, they take responsibility for learning certain information and being able to answer certain kinds of questions. The materials support these responsibilities, because students in different roles are given different materials to study. All students view some common video sequences and read some common material from booklets. Each student also reads some material no other student in the group sees.

All students read from a booklet. They read some general information and some information specific to their own roles. Actually, each expert's manual is about thirty pages long, so each student is responsible for a lot of information. The same information is used for all four ocean missions. By reading this information, the experts acquire ideas that might be helpful in solving the problems they will be asked to solve, and they learn something about what people in their role do. They need to have some idea of what kind of things they should look for.

When the video begins, students see a scene of a beautiful reef with lots of fish and living things. Then they see a reef that is dead. Information that is potentially useful for making future decisions is provided, so most students take notes. They can use the worksheet to write down any information they think might be important. They generally seem to want to contribute so they won't let the group down.

The first task each group is given is to locate the reef. The screen displays four different locations, and students have to use the information they've gathered to make a selection. Each student tries to determine how the information at his or her disposal would argue for or against each location. The group talks it over, considers what each person knows, and comes to some conclusion.

After the reef has been located, the next step is to select a test that will determine what is responsible for the problem at the reef. Again, four tests are available. Taking a water sample provides information about the presence of any unusual chemicals. An inspection of the coral indicates whether certain diseases are present. Inspecting the fish tells you what fish are present, if there have been any changes in the fish population, and if the fish are healthy. Checking the coast tells you if anything happening on land might be causing damage to the reef. The way this activity works is that any choice costs money. The idea is to come up with the right answer quickly and spend the least amount of money.

After the tests are completed, each group needs to give a reason for the problem and offer a recommendation. Each group writes out the recommended action on the worksheet. Again, picking a reason costs money. Once the choices are in, I allow the videodisc to evaluate each answer. If neither group is correct, I let them pick again.

I've used this activity three times. You do learn some things that work well, but each group is also different, so what worked last time may not work so well this time.

Interviewer: *Do you have students who are reluctant to participate?*

Cully: Some of my students do very little in class anyway. They just don't seem to care. These group activities have been helpful in getting junior high students to respond. The group activity may exert the kind of pressure or create the kind of interest to which some of these students will respond. I sometimes put a student in a key role, so that person will have to do something. Maybe the student is the person to make and announce a particular choice for the group. It's kind of a gut feeling how each student will react to this.

Interviewer: *How did you evaluate these activities?*

Cully: The students came up with their own grading system. Since the activity is a competition focused on points, the team spending the least money gets 100 percent, and the groups spending more money get 90 percent. Everyone does well if he or she participates. I collect the worksheets to make sure students have filled in the information: notes, choices, and reasons. Students must complete the worksheet to get full credit for the points their team has earned.

STRENGTHS AND WEAKNESSES OF MULTIMEDIA AND HYPERMEDIA

Experts have identified both strengths and weaknesses in multimedia learning resources. Here is our summary of these issues.

Advantages of Multiple Formats and Alternative Perspectives

Multimedia and hypermedia expand the number of ways in which a **courseware** (instructional software) designer can present information, and these alternative formats offer possible advantages. Understanding these advantages will help classroom teachers recognize when multimedia applications are most useful.

Presenting information to students effectively

Practical Delivery Systems for Effective Learning Experiences.   Multimedia and hypermedia provide an efficient and cost-effective way to deliver effective learning experiences. The advantage over traditional methods of instruction is the likelihood that students will have the opportunity to have certain productive experiences.

The availability of text, sound, animation, video, and still images for presenting information and the easy transitions among these formats can increase the clarity of explanations. Different methods of representation are potentially suited to explaining or demonstrating different concepts or skills, and multimedia and hypermedia make it easy to give students these different experiences. For example, it is more effective to give a basic explanation of mitosis and then step through a time-lapse video of cell division than to struggle through a verbal analysis of how the chromosomes align themselves along the equatorial plate or how the spindle fibers pull the chromatids toward the centrioles. A teacher can easily point out these phenomena in the images displayed on a screen. The teacher might first talk the students through the stages of mitosis by advancing the videodisc a few frames at a time, describing changes and pointing to interesting developments as they appear. Then the teacher might run the entire sequence so students will have an opportunity to appreciate how the process unfolds.

Multimedia can support verbal instruction in other ways. Consider the challenge of helping students understand the form of musical composition called a fugue. It is easy to give a verbal definition, but will terms like *theme, imitation,* and *counterpoint* mean much to students? Of even greater importance, would students be able to identify a fugue if they heard one? Again, the teacher's definition or the definition in a tutorial could be supported by listening to a musical selection, such as an appropriate passage from *Beethoven's Ninth Symphony.* The teacher might play a few seconds of music, pause to ask if the students are able to hear different voices imitating each other at different pitches, maybe hum a few bars to identify the imitation, and then play the brief selection again. The appropriate CD and related software (such as *Analysis of Beethoven Symphony #9*) make this type of demonstration easy to implement.

Content multimedia presents in powerful ways.

There are other kinds of content that multimedia can present in particularly powerful ways. Kozma (1991) argues that multimedia, particularly combinations involving video, are very useful when the content has to do with social situations, interpersonal problem solving, foreign language training, or moral decision making. Multimedia can encourage students to think about complex issues. Kozma uses the example of *A Right to Die? The Case of Dax Cowart* (Covey, 1990). This social documentary examines the actual experience of a young person who had been burned over 60 percent of his body and lost his sight. He would always be disabled but could survive if willing to submit to a long and painful treatment. The patient found the treatments unbearable and wanted to have them stopped. The video provides actual comments from the patient, mother, doctor, nurse, and lawyer. As the student works with this material, he or she is asked to make decisions. The student's decision making and the presentation of opposing perspectives, in the words and images of real people, provide a depth of experience that would be impossible without interactive multimedia.

Presenting authentic learning tasks

A similar argument has been made in support of providing authentic learning tasks anchored in realistic settings (Bransford, Sherwood, Hasselbring, Kinzer, & Williams, 1990). The video format provides experiences that are both more complex and more like situations outside the classroom, exposing students to realistic experiences they may not have encountered directly. Video provides more information to sort through and think about, and video material can often be examined from multiple points of view (see previous discussion of *Decisions, Decisions,* page 262). Working to process such a rich information source is one way to engage students in more active learning. Learning experiences that combine extended video segments and other resources and activities allow students to anchor what they learn in realistic goals, activities, and situations. (The ideas of active learning, anchored instruction, and situated cognition were presented in Chapter 2. An example of anchored instruction relying heavily on videodisc-based video, *The Adventures of Jasper Woodbury*, was presented in Chapter 4, pages 136 through 137.)

In summary, multimedia and hypermedia offer several advantages because students are provided efficient access to information presented in different ways. It can be argued that certain ideas or procedures are easier for students to understand when experienced in other than a text-based format, multimedia can provide experiences that cannot be provided by an instructor or conventional instructional materials, and extended video segments or other more complex learning resources allow students to anchor what they learn in more complex and realistic experiences.

Dual-Coding Theory.   The capability of efficiently offering related experiences in different forms may have other advantages. Paivio's (1986) **dual-coding theory** is often cited as support for exposing students to both pictures and verbal information. Dual-coding theory argues that imagery and verbal

Helping students retain information

information are stored in different ways. You might recall that we distinguished different types of memory codes in Chapter 2 and that imagery represented a distinct memory code. Experiencing something verbally and through imagery offers advantages because the experiences may result in two memory codes instead of one. Students exposed to pictures or video and verbal input may store and retrieve information more effectively than students who do not have these multiple inputs; the multiple representations allow students more direct retrieval options and more indirect retrieval options because of connections with other memory units.

It is possible to be even more explicit about the conditions under which multiple formats are advantageous (Mayer & Anderson, 1991; Moreno & Mayer, 1999). When you are explaining relatively complex phenomena, dual codes are most beneficial when students are able to interrelate the codes. For example, a computer animation with narration was found to lead to better understanding of how a bicycle pump works than allowing students first to hear the narration and then to watch the animation. Access to both sources of information also resulted in an advantage over access to only one source of information. In this example, hearing the narration while watching the animation resulted in greater integration of the two inputs. Students were less able to use two codes to support each other when the two codes were presented sequentially.

Multimedia and hypermedia frequently allow sequential rather than integrated experiences with multiple media. Often a student working with multimedia or hypermedia is allowed to access a video segment or an animation voluntarily when he or she feels that an additional form of input would be helpful. In many such situations, text and sometimes simple diagrams are used initially to present information. The information sources might be separated because of cost factors or because it was considered desirable to offer the student a choice of one or both sources of information. When multiple forms for conveying the same idea are presented sequentially, the student must work more actively to integrate the information sources.

Allowing students to control information they experience

Meeting Individual Needs.   Both interactive multimedia and hypermedia offer students some degree of control over the information they experience. Students can get help when they need it. When they have difficulties, they can get supplementary information or experience information in a different format.

Other needs are also important. Sometimes a student understands the information but wants to know more. Imagine a learning environment in which a student can quickly ask for more depth, greater detail, or additional examples when encountering something of great personal interest. The control allows students working in responsive environments to meet their own needs.

You may recall from the previous discussion of talking books (pages 254 through 260) that these CD-based products allow readers to click on

*Responding to diversity
needs in classrooms*

unfamiliar words to have words pronounced and defined. Students struggling with English can even listen in Spanish. The frequency with which these options are used and the individual words with which students need assistance vary greatly. Multimedia and certainly hypermedia programs often leave the decision to display a video segment, diagram, or supplemental text to the student. In theory, students who need access to a different type of explanation or are likely to find a visual representation helpful have opportunities to customize their learning environment.

The point to note in both examples is that multimedia offers more variety than traditional materials. Individual students can take advantage of this variety to find ways to solve individual difficulties. As multimedia and hypermedia environments become more sophisticated, options for students will become even more varied.

Multimedia and Hypermedia Are Motivating. Finally, the variety of formats that multimedia and hypermedia offer is motivating. For many students, seeing a human take the first steps on the moon or hearing Dr. Martin Luther King's "I Have a Dream" speech results in very different affective reactions than simply reading about the lunar landing or reading Dr. King's speech. Emotion is part of school learning and part of what makes learning exciting.

Concerns About Multimedia in Classrooms

Experts have raised a number of concerns related to the multimedia and hypermedia programs that are currently available and to some of the assumed benefits of multimedia and hypermedia. We want you to have a realistic sense of how multimedia applications are used in classrooms and to understand that there are potential problems. Such awareness will help you recognize classroom situations in which problems might develop and help you make more informed decisions about how to use multimedia with your students.

*Making informed
decisions about
multimedia in your
classroom*

Duplication of Existing Instructional Materials. Talking children's books and CD-based atlases, encyclopedias, and almanacs are clearly similar to the books already common in classrooms. Images of artwork, plants, whales, and other collections of photographs on a CD or a videodisc are similar to slide collections. Is this redundancy necessary? Or is there nothing wrong with duplication? Certainly there is nothing wrong with taking a good idea and making it available in a different form. Computer-based resources are sometimes less expensive than printed ones, have greater durability, and may be perceived as more interesting by students. Counterarguments can be offered, however. Computer-based resources are not always less expensive. And a CD may be a cost-effective replacement for an encyclopedia, but is it a cost-effective replacement for a children's book?

*Cost-effectiveness is an
issue.*

Another issue concerns how educators should use a valuable limited resource. If a limited number of computers or videodisc and CD players are available, why not make certain these resources are used for unique purposes? Perhaps the emphasis should be on using technology in ways that offer students experiences they do not have now.

Inadequate Student Skills.   Learning from any information source requires that students have skills suitable to both the format and the particular method in which information is made available. Young children are capable of learning by observing and listening before they are able to learn by reading. They have the necessary skills. They acquire strategies for learning from textbooks and from teacher presentations as they move through school and experience these types of learning experiences. Sometimes the strategies are taught formally. Somewhere during late elementary or junior high school, a teacher may talk with students about taking notes. Often, however, students develop their own study and learning strategies through trial and error.

Developing new learning skills

Multimedia and hypermedia are new learning environments. It makes sense that if they offer an alternative to learning from traditional sources, these new formats will also require the development of new learning skills. For example, it has been demonstrated that approaches combining text with extensive video can sometimes result in poorer learning. In one informative study, junior high earth science students worked with multimedia containing interesting video from the Great Quake of 1989 (Levin, 1991). When presented with text only, students seemed to be in a familiar element. When presented with text and the opportunity to watch interesting video, the students appeared to become distracted by the video and retained less essential information. By the way, this is not really a new phenomenon. It has been known for some time that pictures in books can interfere with the performance of young readers (Schallert, 1980). This early work with traditional reading material offers some additional insights. Pictures in any medium must serve a purpose. Pictures interfere when they do not convey useful information. As readers gain experience, they seem to learn to ignore pointless graphics. As students become experienced users of multimedia, they may adopt similar strategies. We can only hope that multimedia designers will use graphics and video effectively, and that students will have a reason for giving these sources of information careful consideration.

Moving freely among ideas and information sources

The choices available in hypermedia offer another challenge to learning skills. Hypermedia allows students to move freely among ideas and information sources. There may be some ways in which the richness of resources and the freedom of exploration allowed by hypermedia are problematic. For example, it is not well established that students can make effective decisions regarding their own learning. Given what is known about general metacognitive competence and students' control of their learning with technology (see Chapter 2), inconsistency in taking advantage of potentially helpful learning experiences is not surprising.

Categories of learners   Research that has studied the approach learners take as they explore hypermedia has identified several categories of learners (Lawless & Brown, 1997; Locatis, Letourneau, & Banvard, 1990):

- ◆ *Knowledge seekers:* Learners who use a strategic approach concentrating on the examination of material consistent with an assigned goal
- ◆ *Feature explorers:* Learners who seem captivated by special effects and gravitate toward options such as movies and sound files
- ◆ *Apathetic users:* Learners who spend very limited time interacting with instructional material, moving through what is available in a rapid and linear fashion

These categories suggest that when learners use hypermedia ineffectively, it may be for a variety of reasons. They may wander off, get lost, or simply lose interest.

When learners do have unproductive experiences with hypermedia, is the problem in the learning environment or in the learner? Both learners and software design may be at fault.

It appears that experience plays an important role in determining how effectively learners use a hypermedia environment. With poor background knowledge, learners have little insight into what might be important to examine carefully. They may be unaware of holes in the understanding they are creating. Learner control (see Chapter 2) is ineffective if learners are unable to make wise decisions. Learners with poor background seem to be more easily distracted by attractive but nonessential features and to face greater danger of becoming lost and frustrated (Dillon & Gabbard, 1998; Gay, 1986; Lawless & Brown, 1997).

There are clearly also better and poorer ways to design learning environments so that learners appreciate the structure of information and examine it systematically (Jonassen & Grabinger, 1990). Effective hypermedia provides an easy-to-use navigation system and convenient ways for learners to return to key landmarks in the instructional content.

SUMMARY

Definitions of *multimedia* and *hypermedia* can be confusing because the terms are used inconsistently. In this book, *multimedia* describes a communication format implemented with a computer and integrating several media, such as text, audio, video, still images, sound, and animations. *Hypermedia* is an interactive nonlinear form of multimedia in which the units of information are connected to each other in multiple ways. The hypermedia user has considerable freedom to choose which links to pursue and in what order.

Because information in the form of sound, high-quality pictures, or video requires large amounts of storage space, multimedia and hypermedia often make use of the large storage capacity of videodiscs, CD-ROMs, or DVDs.

Multimedia can be incorporated into traditional computer-based instructional activities such as tutorials, drills, and simulations. Other educational applications of multimedia and hypermedia include talking books, reference sources, and cooperative problem-solving activities.

Although research provides some evidence that learning from multimedia is slightly more productive than learning from traditional materials, more impressive claims that multimedia and hypermedia may herald the restructuring of traditional education and result in experiences of greater personal relevance are still largely without strong empirical support.

Intuitively, however, multimedia and hypermedia offer several advantages. Multiple presentation formats allow students more diverse experiences. Some ideas may be easier to understand when portrayed in a realistic video, when heard, or when carefully outlined in text. Dual-coding theory holds that the redundancy present in multiple formats can allow more effective storage in and retrieval from memory. Multimedia also allows experiences that are more like the rich and motivating contexts found outside the classroom. To the extent that students have some flexibility in controlling what they encounter or the form in which information is presented, students may also be able to adapt learning experiences to their individual needs.

Concerns about multimedia and hypermedia do exist. Critics often lament the lack of imagination in many commercial products and observe that many products do not really offer alternatives to existing traditional instructional materials. Why offer more expensive alternatives to existing products? Finally, students may not have the academic skills necessary to be responsible for their own learning. Students may be distracted by superfluous sounds or graphics and learn less efficiently. Some students may even have difficulty navigating quality information sources when they have to make their own decisions about which information source to consider next. New forms of instructional materials require some new learning skills and continued teacher guidance.

REFLECTING ON CHAPTER 7

Activities

◆ Locate a review (try *Electronic Learning, Learning and Leading with Technology,* or one of the other technology sources listed at the end of Chapter 4) of a multimedia product relevant to your content-area specialty. Write a summary of the review.

◆ Compare a paper and a CD-based encyclopedia (preferably from the same publisher, such as Grolier or Encarta). Look up the same topics in each source, and write a summary of what you observe.

◆ Review the description of WiggleWorks presented on pages 259 to 260. What examples of scaffolding (structured support for learning) do you detect?

◆ Learn to use a videodisc player. You should be capable of connecting the player to a computer and monitor. You should also be able to locate and play designated video segments using a hand-held controller, a bar code reader, and appropriate computer software. Demonstrate these capabilities for classmates using a videodisc appropriate to your content-area specialty.

Key Terms		

analog format   *(p. 248)*   DVD-RAM   *(p. 253)*

compact disc–read only memory   hypermedia   *(p. 245)*
   (CD-ROM)   *(p. 247)*   hypertext   *(p. 246)*

constant angular velocity (CAV)   *(p. 248)*   jigsaw cooperation   *(p. 264)*

constant linear velocity (CLV)   *(p. 248)*   laserdiscs   *(p. 247)*

copy-and-paste   *(p. 261)*   megabytes   *(p. 250)*

courseware   *(p. 267)*   multimedia   *(p. 245)*

digital format   *(p. 248)*   resource interdependence   *(p. 263)*

digital video disc (DVD)   *(p. 247)*   reward interdependence   *(p. 263)*

dual-coding theory   *(p. 268)*   videodisc   *(p. 247)*

Resources to Expand Your Knowledge Base	

For a fuller discussion of videodisc and CD-ROM applications and resources try the following sources:

The Videodisc Compendium for Education and Training. Available from Emerging Technology Consultants. (**http://www .emergingtechnology.com/noframes/compendium.html**)

Perhaps the best way to keep up with new developments is to review some of the technology magazines for educators. A list of these publications appears in Chapter 4.

Videodiscs

A good source for educational videodiscs is Videodiscovery. (**http://www. videodiscovery.com**)

Here are some software examples:

Analysis of Beethoven Symphony #9 (R. Winter, 1991) is one in a series of companion products offered by the Voyager Company. Each product consists of a CD containing a major musical work and related software. The software controls the CD and allows specific segments of music to be played. (**http://voyager.learntech.com/ cdrom/**)

Animal Pathfinders. Videodisc and software from Apple Computer and WGBH Education Foundation. Distributed by Scholastic Software (**http://www.scholastic. com/**).

MediaMAX. Videodiscovery program for creating presentations from multimedia resources, with bar codes to reference videodisc images or segments. (**http://www. videodiscovery.com**)

Talking Books

Scary Poems for Rotten Kids. Original book written by Sean O'Huigin. Discis Knowledge Research, Inc. (**http://www.discis.com**)

WiggleWorks: The Scholastic Beginning Literacy System is a K–2 language arts system available on CD-ROM for Windows and Macintosh from Scholastic New Media. (**http://www.scholastic.com/wiggleworks/**)

Scholastic Inc. and the Center for Applied Special Technology (CAST) maintain a Web site for Teaching with WiggleWorks. The site allows teachers who use WiggleWorks programs and CAST staff to exchange ideas. (**http://www.cast.org/wiggleworks**)

A World of Plants. One CD-ROM from the National Geographic Wonders of Learning CD-ROM Library developed by the National Geographic Society and Discis Knowledge Research, Inc. (**http://www.discis.com**)

Multimedia References

The *Complete National Geographic: 109 Years of National Geographic Magazine* on DVD-ROM or CD-ROM is available from the National Geographic Society. (**http://www.nationalgeographic.com/**)

Encarta Encyclopedia for Macintosh and Windows is available from Microsoft Corporation. (**http://encarta.msn.com/EncartaHome.asp**)

The WWW address for the Encarta Schoolhouse is **http://www.msn.com/encarta /sch/default.htm.**

Grolier Multimedia Encyclopedia (CD-ROM and DVD) for Macintosh and Windows computers is available from Grolier Interactive. (**http://www .grolier.com/**)

World Book Millennium 2000 multimedia encyclopedia for Windows and Macintosh is available from World Book, Inc. Links to World Book Online can be found on this site. (**http://www.worldbook.com/**)

Cooperative Problem Solving

The Great Solar System Rescue, The Great Ocean Rescue, and *Decisions, Decisions* are group problem-solving activities available on videodisc (not including *Decisions, Decisions*) and CD-ROM from Tom Snyder Productions. The online version of *Decisions, Decisions,* which is focused on current events, is free to the public and available from this same address. (**www.tomsnyder.com**)

Chapter 8

Using Multimedia Tools

ORIENTATION

This chapter has two broad goals: (1) to develop a simple system for classifying student multimedia projects and (2) to describe some of the software authoring tools students can use to produce multimedia projects. You have read about multimedia tools in other chapters, but here we present these tools more systematically and describe their capabilities more completely. After reading this chapter, you will know about and be able to recommend several specific software tools that students can use to generate each category of multimedia project. In addition to reviewing multimedia tools, this chapter introduces the concept of multimedia authoring environments. As you read, look for answers to the following questions:

Focus Questions

◆ What is an embellished document, and what are some examples that students could create for a content-area course?

◆ What is a linear presentation or slide show? What are some examples of assignments that could result in a student-created slide show?

◆ What is interactive hypermedia?

◆ What options and issues do you need to consider when you choose authoring software?

◆ How do students' multimedia projects encourage meaningful learning?

Multimedia in a Ninth-Grade Classroom

As you know, we believe that student projects often encourage meaningful learning. Students engage in active learning and thinking as they work to complete projects appropriate to the content they are studying. Let's start this chapter by looking at an actual multimedia project.

Monte Hahn teaches a ninth-grade word processing course at Schroeder Junior High School in Grand Forks, North Dakota. If you have preconceived notions of what goes on in a word processing course, put your assumptions on hold for a bit. Teacher creativity presents surprising and wide-ranging options for working with the content of any course. We asked Monte about hers.

Grabes: *So how did you get started doing multimedia projects in your class?*

Hahn: We were working on a service-learning activity at a home for the elderly around Christmastime [service learning merges an educational activity with community service]. Our original plan was to play board games like Trivial Pursuit with the people at the home in order to get better acquainted. Following this session, each student paired up with an elderly person and took dictation of a Christmas letter for that person to send. The students videotaped each resident so that an image could be captured as part of the letter. It was the first time we had worked with capturing images from videotape and using the images in computer applications.

The students really enjoyed this project, and we started talking about other things we might try. Somehow the idea of a tour of the school came up. The school counselor had been talking about doing a program that would inform parents and new students about our school. This sounded like a useful project.

Grabes: *Had your students worked in cooperative groups before?*

Hahn: At the beginning of the year, we had a leadership training week and learned about roles within cooperative groups. As a class, we developed lists of ways to be a good leader and things to avoid. We did the winter survival exercise from the Johnson book [Johnson et al., 1991, is referenced and discussed in Chapter 7]. This is a simulation that puts a group in the northern woods in the dead of winter and has the group make decisions about what they need to do to survive. I'm convinced that this type of training is important. Group projects have gone better when we've taken the time to train group skills than when we've just started in on the projects.

Grabes: *How were group skills applied in the multimedia project?*

Hahn: Each group had a designated leader, an encourager, and a recorder [so there was someone responsible for keeping the group moving toward goals, someone making certain that each individual was recognized for his or her contributions, and someone creating a record of the ideas and decisions that were made]. The groups began by talking about what new students need to know. They brainstormed by trying to remember what had

FIGURE 8.1
Captured Image Used in the Schroeder Slide Show

confused or scared them when they were new to the school. I wanted the students to develop a formal plan, so they were required to use an outlining program to structure their presentation. The major headings were the major topics they wanted to cover, such as school activities, class schedules and options, administration, faculty, student council, library, and special events. Sometimes I suggested topics that the students had overlooked but that I knew should be covered—for example, building entrances and access times, and lunchroom rules. Then the students tried to think of images we could use for each category and added these suggestions under the appropriate headings.

One of the headings in our outline was "Student Council." The student council has sponsored several special events, and we wanted to show some of these activities. The student council had just completed a contest in which classes had decorated their classroom doors with class names. They came up with names like "The Weasel Easels" for the art teacher. My room was "Hahn's Hall of Famers." The students tried to decide which door decorations would be most interesting. They did the same kind of thing for the other categories. When we were finished, we had an organized list of the images we wanted to include in our project.

We used the completed outline as a way to keep the members of the group accountable. Students were assigned to provide each image. We were working with one video camera and one multimedia station for processing the images from videotape. Students signed up for the video camera, and we crossed images off the list as they were stored on the computer. Originally, all the students wanted to make sure they had their turn working with the video camera. After a while, the novelty wore off. Sometimes the pictures weren't that good, and the process had to be repeated. Then students started helping each other out; someone who had a free period might be sent back to get a better picture.

Grabes: *So you started with a project outline and then generated a series of pictures based on the outline. What did you do next?*

Hahn: We created a series of screens using the slide show option in Claris-Works (now AppleWorks). [We discuss this procedure in the section on slide show tools on pages 288 through 290.] Sometimes several images were combined in making one slide. We added text to some slides, but this was kept to a minimum because we didn't think it would be that easy to read information from the screen [see Figure 8.1]. Each slide show ended up with about thirty-five different slides.

We made a decision to display each slide for ten seconds, which seemed a reasonable amount of time. Students then began to write the narration. Background music was selected, and the students tried to use some of the lyrics in the narration. Because we'd decided to display the slides at a fixed rate, developing the matching script was a challenge for the students. The script had to conform to the time a certain category of pictures was being shown, which took a good deal of trial and error and rewriting. One student was designated to do the final narration. This student practiced several times, trying to keep pace with the slide show program. Finally, the student recorded the narration on audiotape.

The district had just purchased some AV Macintoshes, and we used one of these computers to produce the videotape. The AV computers can output a signal directly to a video recorder. You just connect the computer and tape recorder to the video recorder. You start the slide show on the computer and play the audiotape, and both sources are recorded. It may take a few tries to coordinate the two sources. If you don't like the recording, you just rewind the videotape and try it again.

Grabes: *Any final comments on doing this kind of project?*

Hahn: As a teacher you have to be flexible and able to tolerate a little bit of chaos. Because of our equipment limitations, some students had down time. Students may need to have other activities to work on. Students need to mill around, look at each other's work, and talk with each other. We were also learning a lot as we went along. Neither the students nor I had much experience when we started, but that made the project kind of fun. When you try something new, there has to be a time when you don't know exactly how everything works.

There were some unique benefits. Some students just aren't book-and-paper-type people, yet some of these students emerged as leaders. It was interesting to see some of these students spending time after school and working harder at the project than many of the others. Even parents talked about how interested their children were. I couldn't have gotten the same reaction by having the students type nine letters. This project seemed to give them an important sense of ownership.

Other word processing teachers may not understand this project. I think I see the purpose of this class a little differently. Computer applications will soon encompass much more than writing letters and constructing tables. The students now have a sense of how the computer can be used to communicate, and they're excited about what they've learned. I think you have to involve students in projects that challenge them to try something new. One of my college professors told me something I've always remembered. He said, "Don't be a textbook wired for sound."

A SYSTEM FOR CLASSIFYING STUDENT MULTIMEDIA PROJECTS

We emphasize and differentiate three types of multimedia projects in this chapter: (1) embellished documents, (2) linear multimedia presentations (often called slide shows), and (3) hypermedia. (Video, because it integrates visual and auditory information, might also be considered multimedia. We delay a discussion of video projects until Chapter 9 so we can focus on the techniques in greater detail.) Knowing about the different categories of multimedia projects should help you think about multimedia projects to use in your teaching. Figure 8.2 contains visual representations of these different project types.

EMBELLISHED DOCUMENTS

Kinds of embellishments

An **embellished document** is a text document that has been enhanced with other multimedia elements. Student authors might add pictures, sounds, or video segments to text because information in these alternative formats seems more informative or more interesting than text alone. Students can prepare some form of embellished document with nearly every word processing program and with other tools such as paint programs (see Chapter 9) and Web authoring programs (see Chapter 10).

Examples of embellished documents

If an embellished document is to include sound or video, the audience will have to view the document using a computer. The author does not have to be present or use his or her own computer to show this kind of document to a reader. It is as easy to send someone a word processing file on disk as it is to send a letter, and embellished documents can usually be sent as an attachment to an e-mail message. Students in other classrooms or schools can easily view the document containing sound and video that you or your students have created. If the document contains text and still graphics, students can print and distribute it. Common examples of embellished documents are student-authored newsletters, reports, and instructional manuals. A single Web page might also be considered an embellished document.

LINEAR MULTIMEDIA PRESENTATIONS OR SLIDE SHOWS

A **slide show** is a **linear multimedia presentation** that might be used as a self-contained presentation or may accompany a speech or lecture. The defining attribute of this format is the linear nature of the presentation. Slide shows can be viewed on the computer screen or by using a projection system, recorded on videotape for presentation, printed to produce a series of overhead transparencies, or made available on the Web. Like all the other projects discussed in this chapter, a slide show can incorporate text, several types of graphics, and sound. You may have experienced presentations of this type as a college student. It is fairly common for college instructors to use what is frequently referred to as *presentation software* to prepare and present multimedia material as support for their lectures. Students can also use the same software to prepare their own presentations (see pages 292–296). See Activities and Projects for Your Classroom: Slide Show Activities (page 284) for more suggestions for student-authored slide shows.

Use of presentation software

FIGURE 8.2
Categories of Student-Authored Multimedia

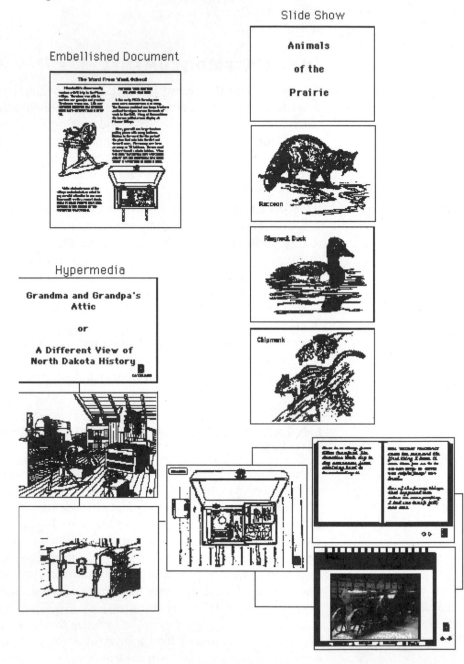

Some programs students may use to create embellished documents allow them to incorporate video and sound. (© Michael Zide)

HYPERMEDIA

A **hypermedia** project differs from embellished documents and linear multimedia in the complexity of the pathways that are available through the information and the degree of control that users can exercise in navigating those pathways. As you discovered in Chapter 7, authors segment information into meaningful units and create pathways among the units. In creating the units of information and establishing the links, authors attempt to anticipate the types of information different users might find helpful and provide convenient ways for these users to explore. Users decide which of the options provided by the author they want or need to experience.

Meaningful units of information

THINKING BEYOND WHAT YOUR PROJECTS WILL LOOK LIKE

How might we sum up all of this information? Clearly, the three formats we have described differ in complexity. Embellished documents or slide shows can be used in any situation in which reports are used to develop communication skills and encourage students to think about course content. Nearly all classes require students to write reports or research papers or to give oral

Activities and Projects for Your Classroom

Slide Show Activities

Many classroom activities traditionally done with paper, pencils, and crayons can easily be converted to slide shows incorporating text, color graphics, and sound. Slide shows can be either a whole class activity, in which each student is responsible for one or two slides, or an individual or small group activity, in which the individual or group is responsible for the entire presentation. The following examples should get you thinking about the many opportunities for using slide shows in your classroom.

Here are some examples of whole class slide shows:

Getting to Know You

◆ A parents' night introduction of class members

Theme-Based Alphabet Books

◆ *The ABC Book of Space*, for example, or *The ABC Book of Birds*

Recycling Posters

◆ Student-created slides to encourage recycling

Parade of States

◆ Student-created slides depicting important facts about states

Seasonal Poetry

Our Favorite Books

◆ Student-created slides depicting favorite books could be kept in the library and viewed by other students.

Memories of Junior High

◆ Created by current students as an orientation for future students

Here are examples of individual or small group slide shows:

◆ Book reports
◆ Creative stories
◆ Modern fairy tales
◆ Autobiographies
◆ Historical portraits
◆ Geographic travelogues
◆ Cartoons
◆ Animal reports
◆ Stages of meiosis or mitosis
◆ Stages in the development of a thunderstorm
◆ Chronology of world events, such as the breakup of the Soviet Union
◆ Differing viewpoints on controversial issues such as welfare✳

presentations of some type. Incorporating a few graphics or a short video segment takes a little additional time and new skills (see the discussion of techniques in Chapter 9), but developing embellished documents or using a slide show to improve an oral presentation would not call for a serious deviation from existing activities. On the other hand, creating an interactive hypermedia project does involve committing a significant amount of time to developing some new skills in using technology and developing the project itself. In deciding to embark on involving students in developing hypermedia, you need to be committed to something that is currently quite out of the ordinary.

Thinking about developing valuable skills

One of the greatest challenges in introducing student-authored multimedia projects is to get teachers thinking beyond what finished projects will look like. We want teachers to think about the skills that students will develop and draw on in completing the projects. Think about the following questions too:

◆ Why would you have students spend their time developing these projects?
◆ How will students gather and transform information as they prepare to create their multimedia project?
◆ How will you encourage active student involvement with the central course ideas that you want to emphasize in a particular project?
◆ How will you assess student projects?

Projects stimulate valued mental activities.

We hope that we can help you interconnect all these issues. Unfortunately, the linear format of a textbook does not allow us to interweave these ideas very effectively. It would be nice if we could insert buttons that would let you instantly return to Chapter 2 to review how external activities, such as projects, can stimulate valued mental behaviors or just as instantly glance ahead to later chapters, where we make the point that many important behaviors in project development have nothing to do with the computer. But because a textbook is not hypermedia, the best alternative seems to be to remind you constantly of why projects are valuable activities that encourage your students to think and how to integrate projects within the social setting and curriculum of your present or future classrooms.

SOFTWARE TOOLS FOR CREATING MULTIMEDIA PROJECTS

A basic set of software tools can be used to construct the entire range of project types, and the project types can be applied to a variety of content areas, at many levels of sophistication, by students at all grade levels. The time that students spend learning how to use the software tools and design each category of multimedia will be spent efficiently if they continue to use similar software tools to design similar projects. Whether students will eventually communicate with multimedia the way many adults now communicate with text remains to be seen, but it is reasonable to predict that multimedia—very possibly student-authored multimedia—will play an increasingly important role in academic settings.

GETTING STARTED AUTHORING MULTIMEDIA

Students can create multimedia projects in a number of ways. In many cases, no specialized software is required, because many of the most widely used software tools have built-in multimedia capabilities. You have already read about some of these tools in previous chapters, but we will revisit them to discuss their specific multimedia applications. Keep in mind that multimedia capabilities are not found only in sophisticated application programs. General-purpose tools such as word processing and paint programs targeting the K–12 market also emphasize integrating graphics, sound, and video segments. Creating the categories of multimedia outlined here usually does not require that schools purchase a great deal of expensive new software.

Creating multimedia is financially realistic.

We also consider specialized multimedia tools. Specialization implies that a software tool was developed to accomplish a well-defined set of tasks. A word processing program is a general tool. A tool designed specifically to link a number of pictures together into a slide show is a specialized tool. Specialized multimedia tools often offer more powerful options and may make similar functions easier to implement than general tools. Teachers will have to balance this additional power and ease of use against the added cost and training time needed for their students to create projects with more specialized tools.

Helping students develop their projects

The purpose of discussing multimedia tools in some detail is to help you link specific software tools with each type of multimedia project. It is important for you to feel confident that you would know where to begin in helping students develop their own projects. After you complete this section, you should be able to suggest several specific programs that could be used to author each category of multimedia project. You should also be able to describe in general terms what the author does in working with each type of software.

CREATING EMBELLISHED DOCUMENTS WITH WORD PROCESSING PROGRAMS

Most word processing programs are capable of producing multimedia. Some not only allow a combination of text and graphics but also allow users to integrate video segments and digitized sound. These more flexible programs are used mainly to produce printed documents, but they have the potential of creating a file containing information stored in the other formats. This file can be shared with others who own the same program.

A small embellished document appears in Figure 8.3. This simple document consists of three elements: a title, an explanatory text segment, and an

FIGURE 8.3
Simple Embellished Document Created with a Word Processing Program

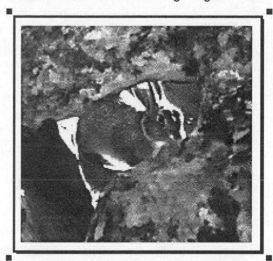

Rabbit in the Rock

You never know what you will find when you spend time walking outdoors. When we were on our field trip, I noticed a strange looking rock beside the trail. The rock was different because it was hollow. When I looked inside, this is what I saw. Have you ever seen a rabbit in a rock?

image. The image was digitized from a videotape (we describe the specific technique in Chapter 9). The document shown in Figure 8.3 was prepared using the type of word processing program likely to be available in most schools (in this case AppleWorks). Short QuickTime segments (audio or video) can also be incorporated into embellished documents prepared with standard word processing programs.

Computer applications capable of integrating text and graphics, using different text styles, and arranging text in columns are often described as **desktop publishing** programs. Historically, word processing programs and desktop publishing programs were distinct, but now they are much less clearly differentiated. Basic publishing features are included in many word processing programs. These features can do a great deal to increase student pride in authorship.

Some of the most fundamental desktop publishing capabilities are the integration and positioning of text and graphics. Desktop publishing programs allow the author to lay out pages exactly as they are to appear to the intended audience. Many word processing programs provide some of the basic

Publishing features in word processing programs

Integrating and positioning text and graphics

capabilities (see Figure 8.3). The author should be able to view on the computer screen what the printed page will look like and experiment until the desired appearance is achieved. The full range of text editing features described in Chapter 5 should also be available (see pages 163 through 164). In addition, the author should be able to treat segments of text and graphic images as objects and edit these objects. Think of a **text object** as a rectangular frame containing text. The sides of the frame are usually not visible. Any time you work with a word processing program, you are actually entering text into a frame of a sort. The frame is established by the left and right margins, and the text frame changes if you decide to change the margins. In desktop publishing, one text object does not cover the entire page, and there are likely to be several text objects on each page. The author can position text and graphic objects on the page and move these objects around to determine which arrangement is most effective. Programs differ a great deal in the capacity to edit at this level.

If a teacher wants to emphasize multimedia applications, it may not be enough for him or her simply to know that a particular program is capable of desktop publishing applications. Often a decision will have to be made about trade-offs among ease of use, the desktop publishing functions available, and price. There are a number of very useful products available, but teachers should have their own objectives and budgets in mind when making a decision.

CREATING MULTIMEDIA SLIDE SHOWS

Multimedia slide shows can be created using either general multimedia authoring tools or tools designed specifically for linear multimedia presentations. We will present good examples of tools that teachers and students have used to do some interesting things, but we are not claiming that they are the best. Your instructor and your own investigations may lead you to other applications that you prefer. Nevertheless, these examples should get you started thinking about this category of multimedia tools and give you a better understanding of how students use a slide show tool to create a project based on a class topic. As you read, try to develop your own examples of slide show projects for your content areas.

Developing your own project examples

AppleWorks

Monte Hahn's students created their slide show project using ClarisWorks (now called AppleWorks), a single product that integrates a number of the most commonly used computer tools. The applications described in Chapter 5 (word processing, spreadsheet, database, communications), as well as tools for creating and manipulating graphics (see Chapter 9), are all available within this integrated package. Schools often consider integrated packages as a way to make tools available to students because so many basic functions come in a single purchase.

The slide show option is available when using several of the AppleWorks tools (word processing, drawing, painting), but the draw tool is probably the best option. A slide show is developed by creating a multipage document. Think of a multipage document as a number of sheets of paper joined to each other at the top and bottom edges. Each page within the multipage document will eventually become a separate slide in the slide show. The draw tool allows the author to combine and precisely position different types of information on each page. You can enter text from the keyboard or import text from a stored file, load a color picture created with some other application, draw using the tools available within AppleWorks, import charts from the spreadsheet, or add sound or a QuickTime movie. Once the elements are available on the page, you can move them around to create an effective display.

Multipage draw documents as slide shows

The presentation of a multipage draw document as a slide show is accomplished by selecting the slide show option from the View menu. Selecting this option produces the **dialog box**, or selection of options, shown in Figure 8.4. From this dialog box you can present the slide show or add some final touches and refinements. If you like, you can change the order of the pages.

Selecting whether a page is presented as opaque, transparent, or hidden controls how the images will appear when you display them. When pages are presented as opaque, one page is experienced as replacing the previous page.

FIGURE 8.4
AppleWorks Slide Show Options

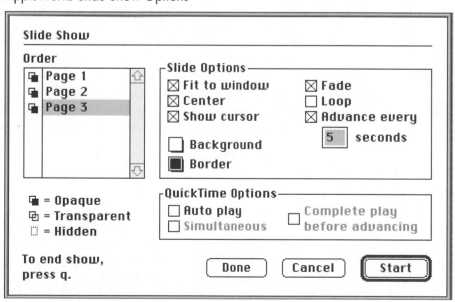

When pages are presented as transparent, the image on one page is added to whatever appeared on the previous page. Transparent images are used when you want to build an image stage by stage. You have probably seen presentations in which the speaker wanted the audience to view a building list of points, with each new idea added at the time it was presented. To create this effect, the author of a multimedia slide show develops a series of slides with text positioned at the appropriate location on the pages and then presents the series of pages in transparent mode. The same thing can be done with pictures. Single images can be accumulated until the desired composite is achieved. This procedure is useful when an author wants to demonstrate stages, such as those in the metamorphosis of a butterfly, or to call attention to individual parts of a whole, such as the parts of a frontier fort. Once the series of cumulative images is complete, a page presented in opaque mode gives the viewer the impression of moving on to a different slide. Designating an image as hidden allows an image to remain part of the multipage document and not be displayed. This option might be used when the author wants to create and save a set of images, but perhaps use only some of them for a particular presentation.

Ways of running slide shows

A slide show can be set to run automatically or to operate under manual control. The distinction is established by selecting or deselecting the box next to the "Advance every" option. (The term **deselecting** means that selecting, or clicking on, an option that has already been selected will cause the option not to be applied. If an author uses the mouse to click on a selection box containing an X, the X will disappear, and the option will no longer be applied.) When functioning automatically, the slide show will run from beginning to end on its own. If the "Loop" option is also selected, the slide show will run continuously. When the slide show is functioning manually, the next slide is displayed when the user clicks the mouse. If a slide show is developed to accompany a presentation, it makes sense to allow the speaker or presenter to control the slides manually. If the slides are complex, it also makes sense to allow individual viewers to advance to the next slide when they are ready. If users are likely to be inexperienced, authors should include a message on the slide, such as "Click anywhere to continue," as a prompt.

Kid Pix Slideshow

Kid Pix Slideshow was designed specifically to generate slide shows. As its name implies, it is a feature of Kid Pix, a popular and inexpensive paint program designed for younger children (we discuss Kid Pix in more detail in Chapter 9) and is also included as part of Kid Pix Studio. Kid Pix allows a multimedia author to create color pictures, include text with the picture, and record sound. Each screen image is saved as a separate file. Kid Pix Slideshow allows several Kid Pix sound and picture files or graphics files created with other software tools to be organized into a slide show.

This system of creating and then integrating separate files works well for school projects. In a fairly common application, individual students or student teams are assigned to create one slide in a series. Each student or student group might provide information about one butterfly, one fish, one classmate, or one low-fat food to become part of an integrated series dealing with biological organisms, the class, or nutrition. As the project develops, students may work simultaneously on several different computers to develop their contributions to the final product. When the individual files have been completed, Kid Pix Slideshow allows the teacher or the students to integrate and organize the individual files.

Kid Pix Slideshow is an easy product for students to work with. If you look carefully at Figure 8.5, you will notice three buttons below each miniature picture. When the first, or picture, button is clicked, a dialog box appears listing the graphics files available. The author selects the desired file, and a miniature of the picture appears. If you keep looking carefully at Figure 8.5, you will notice that a graphic has yet to be selected for slide 12. When the

FIGURE 8.5
Kid Pix Slideshow Assembly Area

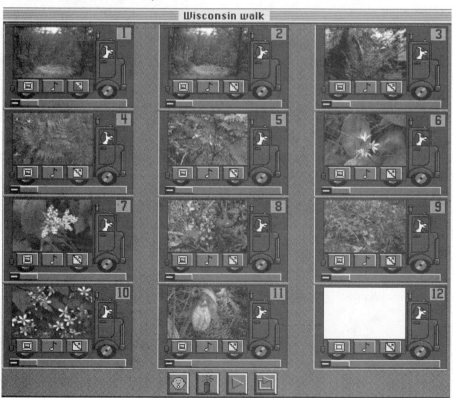

middle, or sound, button is clicked, the author is given the opportunity to record a segment of sound that will be played when the picture is displayed. Sounds previously recorded with Kid Pix will be attached automatically. The final, or transition, button allows the author to specify the visual transition that will be used between the displayed slide and the next slide to be displayed. Transitions show how one image appears to replace another on the computer screen. One image may appear to slide over the image on the screen, emerge and expand out of the middle of the existing image, or replace it in a number of other possible ways. Authors may use transitions to convey the relationship between the two images, such as whether the information on the new slide continues the presentation on the same level or provides greater depth about what was presented on the previous slide. Transitions are also useful to keep the presentation a little more interesting. Inexperienced authors often take the potential for creating a more interesting presentation too far and use so many different transitions that the variety of changes becomes distracting. Young students often employ transitions haphazardly, and teachers have to decide whether to encourage a more systematic approach.

Transitions convey information.

The miniature pictures in Figure 8.5 show spring wildflowers. This slide show was prepared to chronicle observations that students made during a hike down a forest trail. Narration accompanying the images describes the surroundings and identifies the flowers. Kid Pix Slideshow is perfectly suited to this kind of project. Once the images have been isolated and stored as individual files (techniques are described in Chapter 9), it takes just a few minutes to bring the individual images into Kid Pix Slideshow. High school students can quickly learn all they need to know to work with the program and can spend their class or homework time developing the comments to accompany the images.

Slide shows to chronicle observations

Presentation Software and Multimedia Slide Shows

The multimedia slide show is a common format because this category includes the type of multimedia material that speakers frequently use to support their presentations. The category of software that has been developed to support this type of application is described as **presentation software** (see Chapter 5).

Presentation software provides a set of tools specialized for the purpose of helping communicate information to others in a way that is structured, forceful, and transitory. The word *helping* is critical to this definition. Presentation software is seldom totally responsible for delivering information by itself and is intended to support the efforts of a speaker. Presentation tools produce and present the computer-based equivalent of overhead transparencies or 35-mm slides. Although presentation tools can be used to create slides and transparencies, the more popular method of delivery is probably with a **video projector** or a large monitor. Presentation tools are designed to help

Helps communicate information

users perform three tasks: organize the ideas for a presentation, generate the visual materials, and deliver the presentation. Often presentations are initially created with an outlining tool. An outliner allows the user to get ideas down quickly and to cluster and reorganize ideas efficiently. Projected presentations place a premium on the expression of ideas in a succinct fashion. An outliner provides a good way to prepare and organize precise statements.

The visual components of presentation images—think of them as projected slides—consist of text, multimedia elements (images, video and sound segments), and a background. A presentation tool allows these components to be combined into the composite images the audience will eventually view. Text must be displayed in a large font so it can be read easily. The carefully crafted text statements are often presented as **bulleted charts** for easy reading. Often the presenter uses a technique called a **build** and reveals bulleted items one at a time against a fixed background so the significance of each idea can be stressed as it is revealed. Projected visuals are often displayed against a white screen. So that the presentation is easy to view, the text and graphics are typically placed on some type of colored background. It is easier to read white lettering against a colored background than vice versa. A single background color and perhaps simple graphic elements (e.g., a project title) may remain across the entire presentation. Most presentation programs allow the preparation of a **master slide** that contains all elements common to all slides, a technique that greatly increases preparation efficiency. Only the text and some graphics change from slide to slide. Many presentation tools provide templates to make the creation of the master slide even easier.

Finally, presentation tools are used to deliver presentations. While this primarily means controlling the projection of each slide, it is usually also possible to print out miniature images of the slides. Copies can be distributed to the audience so that they can follow along, read the slides if they don't happen to have a good view of the screen, and take notes. Most presentation tools allow the presenter a method for coordinating a set of more detailed notes to use while presenting and that can be made available to the audience.

The type of presentations likely to be given by teachers or students could be prepared and delivered in many different ways. HyperStudio, AppleWorks, web authoring tools (see Chapter 10), and many other general-purpose multimedia tools could be used to create effective presentations. In contrast, the tools described in this section are more specialized and include products developed for individuals who make frequent presentations as part of their work (e.g., Corel Presenter, PowerPoint) and products designed specifically for student presentations. We differentiate the presentation tools designed for students and tools designed for a broader group of users, although we recognize that such a distinction is somewhat arbitrary. The student presentation tool we will describe is quite sophisticated and is capable of generating and delivering nearly all of the professional presentations we have ever observed (see Focus: MPExpress—A Presentation Tool for Students). On the other hand, many educators are having students create classroom presentations with the same tools that professionals use. The more powerful software is often readily available because it comes as part of a suite of software products that the school has purchased (PowerPoint is one component of Microsoft Office and Corel Presenter is part of the WordPerfect Suite).

Presentations can be created with a variety of tools. HyperStudio, Apple-Works, and many other multimedia products discussed in this book can be used to create effective presentations. In contrast, the tools described in this section are more sophisticated and designed for those who give important presentations as part of their work or specifically for student presentations. As with many other tools, we come to what might be described as the cost/time/benefit question. Is the cost to purchase and time to master a unique tool worth the benefit? It is certainly worth becoming acquainted with high-end presentation tools to answer this question for yourself (we list several of the more popular products at the end of the chapter). Is it worth purchasing a presentation tool developed specifically for students when presentations could also be prepared with existing software? Our focus on student projects causes us to emphasize general-purpose tools, but some teachers may find it worthwhile to become skilled in the use of presentation tools for their own use and to have students use them as well.

Consider costs, time, and benefits

Here is an example of the classroom use of presentation software. A recent controversy in our community focused on the decision of whether to construct a large events center. This building, named the Aurora, is now being constructed and will be used for college football games, concerts, and other events that draw large crowds. When constructed by a small city, a building of this size is very expensive, and the decision to fund such a project with local money was not an easy one. The issue of whether to build the Aurora was put to a vote several times before the necessary citizen commitment was achieved.

The Aurora controversy created an opportunity to follow local politics and consider the various issues presented for and against an issue of local importance. A classroom teacher might take advantage of this situation by dividing the class into small groups, asking individual groups to adopt a pro-Aurora or anti-Aurora position, and then assigning each group the task of preparing a presentation in support of its position for a public forum. While public meetings would probably be much too heated for student presentations, presenting to classmates would be realistic enough to generate enthusiastic discussions. Arguments would have to be well thought out because claims for or against the project would be vigorously challenged.

Presentation software would be useful for this type of classroom activity. While a verbal presentation is the assigned activity, the use of a presentation tool can focus students on the creation of an organized product and encour-

Focus

MPExpress—A Presentation Tool for Students

MPExpress was designed to make it easy for students, even those in the elementary grades, to create impressive presentations. It offers many of the same features as more powerful presentation software:

◆ **Slide templates**. Presentation tool users do not have to create each screen image from scratch. Templates provide authors a starting point for entering and formatting text

and multimedia elements. MPExpress has the following template options:

Title page. Presents title and author information.

Points page. Presents a series of related ideas, such as bulleted points. The presentation of ideas is cumulative, and points appear one at a time as the speaker presses the space bar. Figure 8.6 is an example created with the points page template.

FIGURE 8.6
Page Created with MPExpress Points Page Template

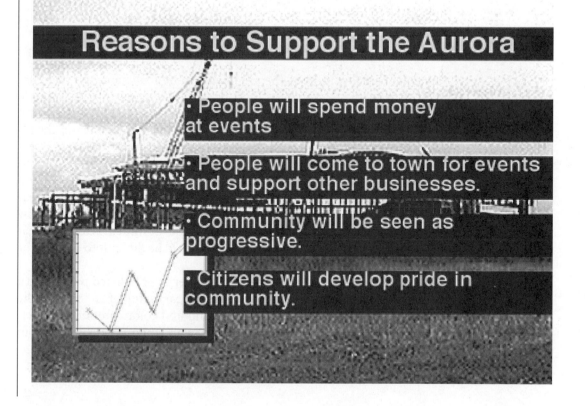

All-purpose page. Allows the greatest flexibility in integrating multimedia or displaying text. The page has one area for text and allows other multimedia elements to be positioned more creatively. The page is used when students want to display video.

Credit page. Used to summarize credits for the presentation. When a credit page slide is displayed, the credits automatically roll up the screen.

◆ **Color schemes**. Users can select from preset color combinations and related design considerations such as whether the text will appear against a solid background or without a background. They do not have to rely on their own sense of which color combinations are effective. Color schemes can be applied to the entire presentation, to all slides based on a type of slide template, or to individual slides.

◆ **Integration of multimedia**. MPExpress is capable of presenting text, images stored in a variety of formats, audio, and video. It contains the tools necessary to record and mix audio and the tools for resizing images.

◆ **Transitions**. Transitions concern the appearance of how one slide changes to the next. For example, slides can be made to appear as if one slide dissolves into the next or to slide over the previous slide.

◆ **Notes**. It is possible to store notes associated with each slide. These notes are not displayed, but can be used to assist the presenter or distributed as a resource for the audience.✳

age a careful consideration of the arguments to be made and the structure that would make these arguments most persuasive. Figure 8.6 is an example of a typical presentation tool slide. The slide presents a set of reasons that a new events center would be valuable to the community. This slide was the result of the time spent gathering and interpreting information to identify persuasive arguments favoring the construction of the Aurora. It is important to remember that presentation tools are intended to support a speaker and do not necessarily provide everything the speaker wants to convey. The information available from the slide provides a structure that allows listeners to follow the speaker more effectively. Slides can also provide multimedia elements that allow the speaker to present information that would be difficult to describe or less interesting if presented orally.

The sample slide in Figure 8.6 consists of a series of bulleted points and a small image (the line graph). These elements appear on top of an image of the Aurora used as a background. The background and color combination (yellow letters against a dark blue background if you could view this image in color) remain consistent throughout the presentation. The points page template controls the appearance and positioning of the text elements in this slide.

MULTIMEDIA AUTHORING ENVIRONMENTS FOR HYPERMEDIA

A multimedia authoring environment often achieves the following results:

◆ Integrates a variety of tools frequently used to produce multimedia products.

◆ Allows basic multimedia functions to be included in products without requiring the author to engage in detailed programming

◆ Allows the author to produce specialized products through programming or inclusion of small specialized programs that others have produced

Support and power for student and teacher multimedia authors

The combination of these characteristics gives teacher or student multimedia authors a great deal of support and power.

Let's look at what each of the characteristics of a multimedia authoring environment contributes. Remember that at a basic level, multimedia is a combination of text, graphics, and sound. A multimedia authoring environment provides tools for manipulating and perhaps creating all of these types of information. It should be possible to enter and edit text, import or create graphics and video segments, and import or record sound. Once the basic resources are available, the authoring environment should allow you to integrate and rearrange the different types of information easily. For example, the multimedia authoring environment should allow you to combine text and graphics and position these elements of information exactly as you would like to have them appear on the computer screen. Finally, the component that most clearly distinguishes multimedia authoring environments from the other applications we have discussed is the ability to create the means by which users will interact with the multimedia content. The author may create presentation methods that range from giving the users no control over what or when anything is experienced to allowing the users always to select what is to be experienced next.

Multimedia authoring environments can generate embellished documents, linear presentations, and interactive multimedia, but it is the production of interactive hypermedia projects that most clearly demonstrates the full capabilities of authoring environments.

A number of multimedia authoring environments are appropriate for teachers and students, and even more products of this type are likely to appear in the near future. We will review several of these products so that you will have some idea of what authoring environments are like and what can be done with them. *Do not worry at this point if you think that you are not learning enough to develop multimedia materials on your own. You will learn more in the chapters that follow.* There are also many how-to manuals available to help

*Creative application of
basic computer skills*

teachers learn both the basics and advanced techniques (we list several appropriate references at the end of this chapter in Resources to Expand Your Knowledge Base). However, you will also see that you do not need a lot of know-how to start experimenting with simple projects. Keep in mind from the beginning that if your intent is to use a multimedia project to involve students in meaningful content-area learning, they should not have to spend a long time developing computer skills. The creative application of a reasonable number of simple skills should give them powerful experiences. Such experiences are available through HyperStudio, one of the most popular multimedia environments in school settings.

HYPERSTUDIO

Like other multimedia authoring environments, HyperStudio might be described as a multimedia construction set. It contains elements that might be seen as multimedia building blocks and others that provide the tools to work with these building blocks.

Most HyperStudio tools are available directly from the menu bar. When you click on a heading in the menu bar, a menu drops down. For this reason, you might hear this type of user interface called a *drop-down menu bar*. Several of the drop-down menus in HyperStudio are actually **tear-off palettes**, which can be detached from the menu bar and then remain available wherever you place them on the screen (normally, a menu disappears when the mouse button is released). The top part of Figure 8.7 shows the drop-down Objects menu, the tools palette, and the patterns and colors palette for the paint tools. The individual tools from the tools palette are also labeled in the lower portion of Figure 8.7.

Using just the tools displayed in Figure 8.7, the author can (1) create some HyperStudio elements (button, field, graphic, sound, text), (2) access these elements to move and modify them (button, field, graphic, sound, and text tools), and (3) create and modify the appearance of what appears on the screen using the painting tools. As we proceed, we will provide additional information on how these tools (and others that are not displayed in Figure 8.7) perform their functions. The important point here is that HyperStudio and other multimedia authoring environments provide the author with convenient access to a variety of powerful tools for manipulating and integrating both the building blocks of multimedia and the actual information sources from which multimedia products are assembled.

Elements of the HyperStudio System

HyperStudio products are assembled from the following elements. They are listed in a somewhat hierarchical order; stacks are made up of cards, and cards hold backgrounds, buttons, fields, scripts/NBAs, and other objects. The dis-

FIGURE 8.7
Tools and Actions Available from HyperStudio Menu Bar

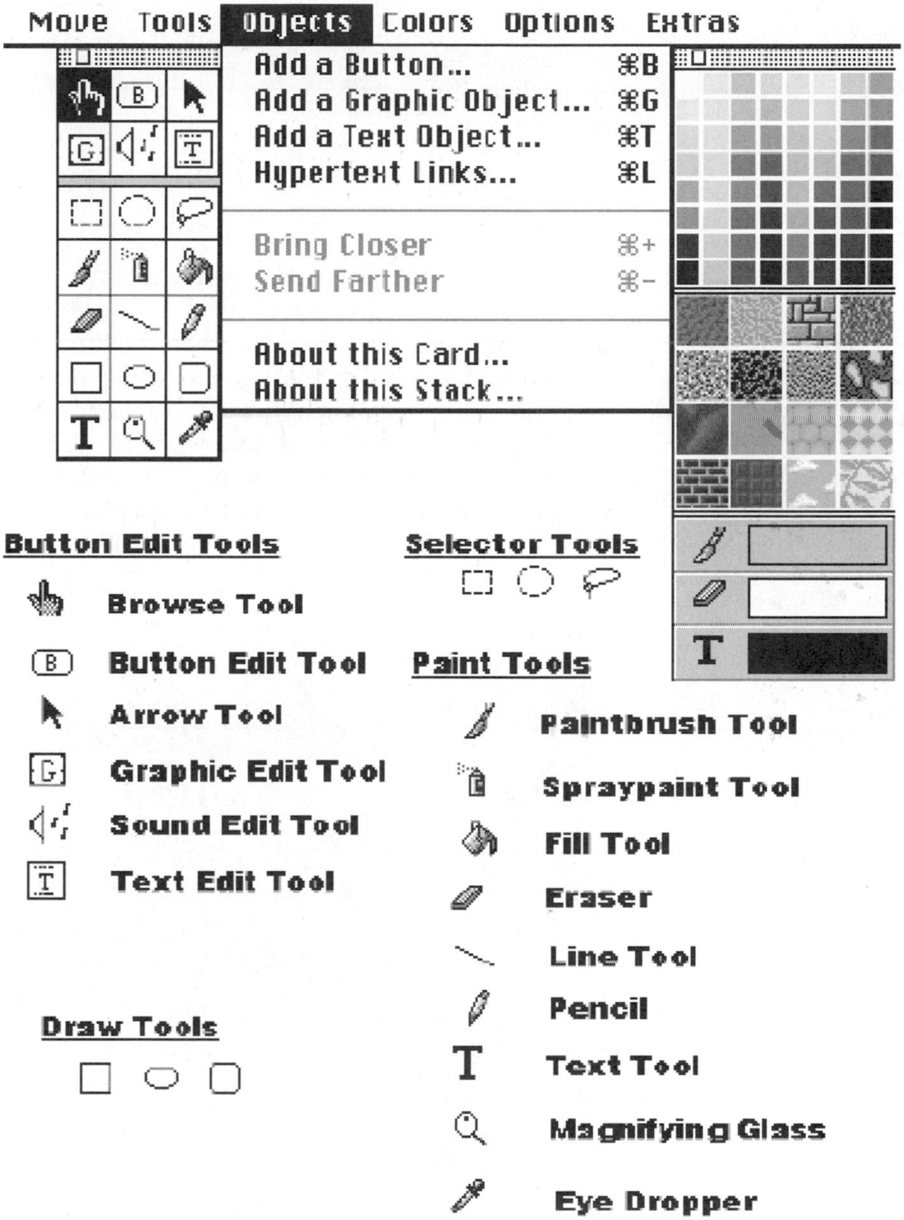

| Move | Tools | **Objects** | Colors | Options | Extras |

Add a Button...	⌘B
Add a Graphic Object...	⌘G
Add a Text Object...	⌘T
Hypertext Links...	⌘L
Bring Closer	⌘+
Send Farther	⌘-
About this Card...	
About this Stack...	

Button Edit Tools

👆 **Browse Tool**

Ⓑ **Button Edit Tool**

▶ **Arrow Tool**

Ⓖ **Graphic Edit Tool**

◀┊ **Sound Edit Tool**

T̄ **Text Edit Tool**

Draw Tools

☐ ⬭ ▢

Selector Tools

☐ ◯ ♡

Paint Tools

🖌 **Paintbrush Tool**

🔫 **Spraypaint Tool**

🪣 **Fill Tool**

◢ **Eraser**

╲ **Line Tool**

✎ **Pencil**

T **Text Tool**

🔍 **Magnifying Glass**

🖊 **Eye Dropper**

cussion, however, follows another order, because it is easier to understand what a stack is made of if you understand what a card is first.

◆ Stack
◆ Card
◆ Background
◆ Button
◆ Field
◆ Script/NBA
◆ Other objects

Card.   The **card** is the fundamental unit of the HyperStudio system. You can usually think of a card as equivalent to what you see on the computer screen at any one time. What users see when examining a card are sources of information such as text, graphics, video, and some of the other elements of the HyperStudio system. Figure 8.8 shows a card containing a graphic, text within two fields, and buttons providing access to other cards and to a sound.

With HyperStudio, it is useful to differentiate between the surface of the card, called the **background**, and objects placed on the card. The background may be painted with color or a pattern, an image, or text. If the author wants

FIGURE 8.8
HyperStudio Card

several cards to share the background, a new card can be created with the background of an existing card. Objects are layered on top of the card. HyperStudio offers a variety of object types including graphics, text fields, and buttons. You will learn about objects later.

Stack.   A HyperStudio file is called a **stack** and consists of a series of cards. You might find it helpful to imagine a stack as a pile of note cards like those you would use to prepare a speech or study for a test. You can easily shuffle through the cards in a stack in sequential order using keyboard commands. Moving from card to card brings into view the information that each card contains.

Imagine a stack as a pile of note cards.

Cards in a stack do not necessarily contain exactly the same categories of information. This is the case only when using hypermedia strictly as a database. Again, HyperStudio is a multimedia authoring environment, and it can take on whatever form the author desires. If the author wants each card in a stack to have a unique appearance and to contain a unique combination of information types, then the stack can just as easily be put together in this format.

Fields.   A multimedia author can enter text directly on the card background or within a text field. The advantage of entering text in a **field** is that it allows the author or a later user of a stack to take advantage of word processing capabilities built into the multimedia authoring environment.

When you enter text directly on the card, you sacrifice many capabilities. For example, if you decide to return and edit work that you've already completed—perhaps to enter text in a different font size or to insert or remove words—you'll have a lot of work to do. Text entered directly on a card is "painted" on the card, and you must remove it before you can add new text. Attempting to insert text does not work because existing text does not move aside to provide space for the new words. Similarly, when text is deleted, the remaining words do not slide back together. In most cases you must erase the work that you have completed and start again.

When you enter text in a text field, most of the editing features of a typical word processor are available (see characteristics of word processing programs in Chapter 5). You can easily make font changes; delete and insert text; and cut, copy, and paste between fields or between applications. Keep in mind, however, that there are a few situations in which you might find it useful to enter text directly on the card. Painting text on a card can be useful when creating special effects, with text arranged in an unusual configuration; perhaps you don't want your text in a straight line, or you want to use a font that may not be available on user machines.

Sometimes it is useful to enter text directly on a card.

Adding a text field to a card is easy. The command "Add a Text Object" appears under the Objects menu. When you select this command, a field appears in the middle of the card. You may drag this field to the position you want it to occupy on the card and then drag the field by the edges to make it the size you want.

Other characteristics of the field can be modified using a dialog box, as shown in Figure 8.9. The dialog box appears when the area outside the field is clicked. You can also return to edit a field by selecting the Text Tool (Tools menu).

Several characteristics of the text field can be determined using the dialog box. It is possible to set both the color of the text and the field background. "Draw Frame" will determine whether the text will be enclosed within a visible frame. For some purposes, it may be preferable to have the text appear without a frame. Using unframed text is often preferable to entering text directly on the card (because editing capabilities are available), and the result will appear the same to the user.

The scrolling option is useful when the amount of text to be placed in a field exceeds the card space available. A field can contain approximately 32,000 characters—obviously many pages of text. Using scrolling fields containing a great deal of information is a controversial technique. Many experts believe that presenting such large units of information defeats the whole purpose of hypermedia authoring. This is another one of the design guidelines that individual teachers may or may not endorse.

Finally, authors may want to consider setting the "Read only" property of a field (see Figure 8.9). Setting a field to "**Read only**" prevents users from al-

FIGURE 8.9
HyperStudio Text Appearance Dialog Box

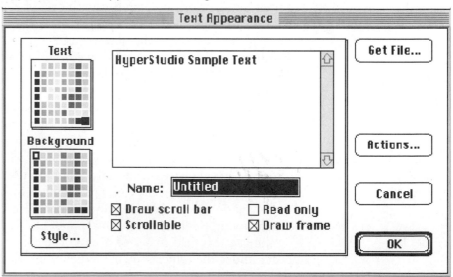

tering what the author has entered in it. There are times when the user is expected to contribute to a field and times when the author just wants the user to read what is written. If many users will be viewing a stack, the authors may not want the first users to alter the stack before later users have had a chance to work with it. Although unlocking a "Read only" field is relatively easy for an experienced user, the danger is minimized because such a user will realize that the author did not intend for the text entered in a locked field to be altered.

Optional actions with buttons

Buttons.   **Buttons** allow the HyperStudio author to prepare optional actions for the eventual user of the stack—for example, moving to other cards, revealing and hiding color pictures and QuickTime movies, playing sounds, manipulating a videodisc player, or revealing a hidden text message.

Adding a button to a stack is similar to adding a field. The "Add a button" option from the Objects menu opens the dialog box shown in Figure 8.10. There are several options to note in the button dialog box. First, you can attach a name to each button. It is particularly useful for the button's name to describe its purpose. A button labeled "Song" near a bird picture, for example, suggests to most users that the button will provide that bird's song. The button name may be visible or invisible depending on whether the "Show Name" option is selected.

Button style allows the shape and general appearance of the button to be set. A very important style option is transparent. The capability of creating a

FIGURE 8.10
Button Appearance Dialog Box

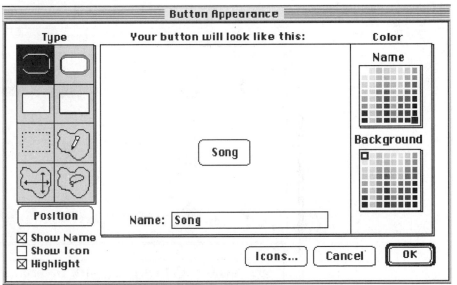

button that the user cannot see may at first seem confusing. The advantage in using invisible buttons—usually several different buttons—is to cover different objects or parts of an object. Sometimes an invisible button is used to cover the entire card. Clicking anywhere on the card will initiate any action attached to the button. Often the object to be covered is a graphic. By carefully positioning invisible buttons over critical features of the graphic, a software author might allow users to reveal text describing each selected feature or to move to another card with a larger, more detailed image of the selected part of the original image. Or, instead of using buttons to present information, invisible buttons can be used as part of a method for evaluating understanding. Buttons can be used to program test-like events ("Click on the carburetor," for example, or "Click on the part of the weather map showing the cold front") and to provide feedback.

Icons represent functions.

From the dialog box, the author can choose the Icons button to move to a collection of button shapes that can be incorporated into any new project (see Figure 8.11). **Icons** are pictures that are intended to represent functions. The icon's appearance should suggest the action that clicking the button will produce. Icons can save authors a lot of work, and using standard icons consistently can make stacks easier to use. Often authors combine the icon with a meaningful button name to make certain that users understand the button's function—for example, naming a forward arrow "Next Card."

The purpose of buttons is to allow the user to take some action designated by the author. HyperStudio offers several ways to assign actions to but-

FIGURE 8.11
Button Icons

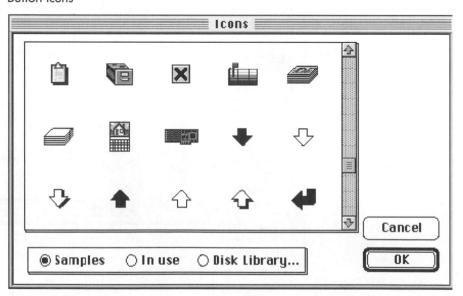

FIGURE 8.12
HyperStudio Button Actions

```
╔══════════════════════ Actions ══════════════════════╗
║                                                      ║
║  ┌─ Places to Go: ──────┐  ┌─ Things to Do: ──────┐ ║
║  │  ○ Another card...    │  │  ☐ Play a sound...    │ ║
║  │  ○ Next card          │  │  ☐ Play a movie or video... │ ║
║  │  ○ Previous card      │  │  ☐ New Button Actions... │ ║
║  │  ○ Back               │  │  ☐ Play frame animation... │ ║
║  │  ○ Home stack         │  │  ☐ Automatic timer... │ ║
║  │  ○ Last marked card   │  │  ☐ Use HyperLogo...   │ ║
║  │  ○ Another stack...   │  │  ☐ Testing functions... │ ║
║  │  ○ Another program... │  └──────────────────────┘ ║
║  │  ● None of the above  │                           ║
║  └──────────────────────┘    ┌─ Cancel ─┐ ┌─ Done ─┐ ║
║                                                      ║
╚══════════════════════════════════════════════════════╝
```

NBAs assign actions.

tons. Some actions are simply assigned by selecting the desired action from the options provided on the button dialog box (see Figure 8.12). Additional button actions can be obtained by selecting the New Button Actions (NBAs) option from the dialog box. (Focus: New Button Actions on page 307 describes several interesting NBAs and an example of how each might be used.) Finally, you can program buttons to initiate actions of your choice using HyperLogo (the programming language available in HyperStudio). Perhaps because HyperStudio comes with many preprogrammed actions, we have seen few examples of students programming button actions.

One of the most useful functions that authors can make available with buttons is the transition from one card to another. Think of this as moving from one source of information to another. The purpose of adding a button to provide this function may be as simple as giving users the opportunity to control when they proceed to new material. At the most basic level, having this ability to move from one source of information to another is like turning the pages in a book. When an option is intended to move to another card, a special dialog box appears on the screen (see Figure 8.13).

Using the "Move To . . ." dialog box is a simple matter. Once this dialog box appears on the screen, you use the arrows to move to the desired destination for the link. The box then remains on the screen during these transitions. When the destination card has been reached, click the OK button in the special dialog box. The link will automatically be established, and the author will be returned to the location of the button. When the button is clicked, the user will move from the location of the button to the destination that was selected.

FIGURE 8.13
HyperStudio "Move To . . ." Dialog Box

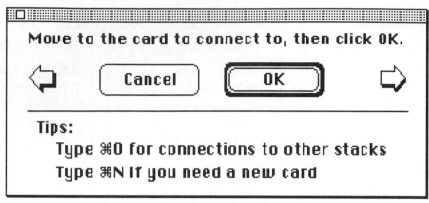

HyperStudio also allows users to assign visual effects to buttons. Visual effects can give the user the feeling of movement when moving from card to card. Perhaps it is desirable for the user to have the impression of turning the pages in a book. The visual effect involved in turning pages is sometimes called *binding*. Most textbooks have left binding. Some notebooks have top binding. The effects *left to right* and *right to left* are used to simulate left binding. The effects *top to bottom* and *bottom to top* are used to simulate top binding. *Iris open* is used to indicate movement to a deeper level of detail, and *iris close* is used to return to a higher detail level. In all, twenty-seven different visual effects can be assigned.

Multiple buttons provide multiple options.

Multiple buttons can also provide users with multiple options. For example, individual buttons covering each state on a U.S. map might allow the user to move to a larger map of a given state. Such buttons can give users the opportunity to choose the information they will encounter next. A key application of buttons is to give users a way to move to different places, such as different rooms in a house, parts of the body, buildings in a city, classrooms in a school, or exhibits in a museum. Buttons allow users to initiate the desired transitions. Learning to use buttons greatly expands the diversity of projects student authors can develop.

Features that accommodate Internet links

HyperStudio's developers have added two interesting features to accommodate the tremendous interest in the Internet: a "button action" that will launch a Web browser and ask the browser to load a designated URL and a browser plug-in that will play HyperStudio stacks within the browser window. This means that students can create a project in HyperStudio and then load it on a school server. A link within a Web page can request that this file, the HyperStudio stack, be sent to a browser. If the browser has the necessary **plug-in** (which can be downloaded at no cost; see Resources to Expand Your

New Button Actions (NBAs)

An important factor contributing to the success of HyperStudio in school settings has been the relatively powerful techniques available to novice users. Although these techniques may be available in more expensive hypermedia authoring environments or in less expensive environments through author-generated programming, HyperStudio is not expensive and allows many options without programming. HyperStudio allows hyperauthors to assign New Button Actions (NBAs) to stacks, cards, and any object. NBAs are essentially small programs that have already been written. The user never actually sees the language of the program, but may be allowed to set certain parameters controlling how the program will work. Following are examples of NBAs and how they might be used:

- **Animator.** The button moves a user-designated graphic along a path that the author has established. *Example:* A dog appears to move around the card.
- **Blabbermouth.** The computer speaks text designated by the author. *Example:* A message that the user enters is read back to the user.
- **HideShow.** The button hides or shows a screen object. *Example:* Show a hidden text field to explain image on a card.
- **Netpage.** The button opens Netscape (a World Wide Web browser; see Chapter 6) and goes to a Web site that the author has selected. *Example:* Connects user to a Web site providing information to supplement HyperStudio presentation.
- **SlideShow.** The button shows all cards in a stack at speed and with transitions designated by the author.✳

Knowledge Base at the end of the chapter), the stack appears within the browser and is fully functional. These two enhancements can be combined to produce some interesting and impressive presentations. A stack capable of card-to-card transitions, sound, animations, video, and many other interactive features—still difficult to produce over the Internet—can operate within a browser and also provide links to other Web content.

The one negative factor we see in this approach is the issue of file size and transfer speed. Even relatively small HyperStudio stacks can be over 1 megabyte in size, and transferring this much information over the Internet, even with a direct connection, can take a considerable amount of time. It may be worth the wait. Once the stack is on your machine, you can work with it intensively without additional waiting.

If your students have considerable experience with HyperStudio, it may be wise to take advantage of this experience rather than spending time developing the students' Web authoring skills. The combination of a very basic Web page and HyperStudio may offer an efficient way to generate a high-quality Web product and encourage active learning.

OTHER MULTIMEDIA AUTHORING ENVIRONMENTS

Multimedia authoring systems for other operating systems

We have concentrated our attention on HyperStudio because it is available for both Windows and Macintosh platforms. Several other high-quality authoring environments appropriate for student projects have been developed, and more appear to be on the way. We list several notable examples at the end of this chapter and their Web addresses. Most of these Web sites also give curriculum-related ideas and examples of student projects. Even if you do not intend to purchase a particular product, it is worth examining the Web site for suggestions you might adapt to your content-area interests and choice of hypermedia authoring tools. Remember that Web sites come and go, and you can always use the Web to search for information by name.

SUMMARY

Student multimedia projects can be classified as embellished documents, linear multimedia presentations or slide shows, or interactive hypermedia. An embellished document is a text document that has been enhanced with images, video, or sound. A classroom newsletter printed and sent home to parents or shared with other students is a common example of an embellished document.

A slide show is a linear multimedia presentation. Using elements of text, sound, still images, and video, the author prepares a series of multimedia slides to inform and entertain an audience.

Interactive hypermedia, the most complex of the multimedia formats, offers users choices instead of binding them to a single type of experience. The user has greater control over which sources of information to consider and perhaps the formats in which information will be encountered. Developing hypermedia is complex because the author has to prepare a much more extensive body of information to explore.

Teachers have many options available when selecting software tools that students might use to create multimedia projects: both general and common software tools such as word processing programs, more specialized multimedia tools designed to create slide shows, and powerful hypermedia authoring environments, or a combination of all of these.

The authoring environments offer project developers a variety of tools for creating and linking information resources. When teachers consider the various ways in which multimedia projects can be created, they might think about a number of issues. How is the project intended to encourage thorough consideration of information? Does the project include additional objectives, such as the development of interpersonal skills, problem-solving skills, or communication skills? Finally, teachers might want to consider whether students are likely to use the same software to create other projects in the future.

REFLECTING ON CHAPTER 8

Activities

◆ Consider the unique advantages and disadvantages of slide show and hypermedia applications. Describe a classroom project most appropriately presented as a slide show and one most appropriately presented as interactive hypermedia.

◆ Familiarize yourself with a word processing program capable of integrating text and graphics. Demonstrate the capabilities of this program to your classmates.

◆ Familiarize yourself with a slide show application. Demonstrate the capabilities of this program to your classmates.

Key Terms

background   *(p. 300)*
build   *(p. 293)*
bulleted charts   *(p. 293)*
buttons   *(p. 303)*
card   *(p. 300)*
deselecting   *(p. 290)*
desktop publishing   *(p. 287)*
dialog box   *(p. 289)*
embellished document   *(p. 281)*
field   *(p. 301)*
hypermedia   *(p. 283)*

icons   *(p. 304)*
linear multimedia presentation   *(p. 281)*
master slide   *(p. 293)*
plug-in   *(p. 306)*
presentation software   *(p. 292)*
"Read only"   *(p. 302)*
slide show   *(p. 281)*
stack   *(p. 301)*
tear-off palettes   *(p. 298)*
text object   *(p. 288)*
video projector   *(p. 292)*

Resources to Expand Your Knowledge Base

Software Resources

AppleWorks (formerly ClarisWorks) is available for Macintosh and Windows computers. Apple Computer Corporation. (**www.apple.com/appleworks/**)

Kid Pix products (Kid Pix Studio Deluxe, Kid Pix, Kid Pix Activity Kits) are available for Macintosh and Windows computers. Broderbund Software. (**www.broderbund.com**)

Hypermedia Authoring Environments

HyperStudio: Available for both Macintosh and Windows. Roger Wagner Publishing. (**www.hyperstudio.com**)

Digital Chisel: Digital Chisel 2.1 is available for the Macintosh and Digital Chisel 3 is available for Windows. Pierian Spring Software. (**www.pierian.com**)

MicroWorlds Pro: Available for Windows. Logo Computer Systems Inc. (**www .microworlds.com**)

Presentation Tools

PowerPoint: Available for both Macintosh and Windows. Microsoft Corporation. (**www.microsoft.com/office/powerpoint/**)

Corel Presenter: Available for both Macintosh and Windows. Corel Corporation. (**www.corel.com/office2000/**)

MPExpress: Available for both Macintosh and Windows. Bytes of Learning. (**www.bytesoflearning.com**)

Learning to Use Software and Ideas for the Classroom

Most of the company Web sites associated with products we have described include basic instruction and also ideas for the classroom. Use the Web addresses provided to connect. The following books are also helpful:

Adams, P., Pressley, S., & Davis, J. (1999). *PowerPoint97 for teachers.* Charlotte, NC: CPI Training Solutions.

Cochran, D., & Staats, R. (1999). *HyperStudio Express 3.1.* New York: Glencoe/ McGraw-Hill.

Lifter, M., Kessler, S., Adams, M., & Patterson, J. (1998). *Multimedia projects for Kid Pix.* Bloomington, IL: Family Time Computing.

Chapter 9

Learning to Work with Images, Sound, and Video

ORIENTATION

This chapter explores some of the tools and basic techniques that allow students and teachers to produce the kinds of images, sounds, and video segments described in multimedia applications throughout this book. After reading this chapter, you should understand how these information resources are represented digitally and the function of sample software and hardware used to create these representations. As always, actually working with the applications is likely to provide a much fuller understanding. We encourage you to supplement your reading with hands-on experiences. As you read, look for answers to the following questions:

Focus Questions

- ◆ What distinguishes paint programs from draw programs, and what are some educational applications of each?
- ◆ Why must teachers pay attention to the file format used to store graphic images and sounds?
- ◆ How can teachers and students capture images for use in their own projects?
- ◆ How can teachers and students combine video segments and other multimedia formats into an integrated video production?
- ◆ Where might teachers find prepared images to use with computers?
- ◆ How do students benefit from the collection and manipulation of sounds and graphics?

The Case of the Missing Gerbil

Cully Gause, a science teacher at South Middle School in Grand Forks, North Dakota, wanted to provide his students a laboratory experience involving electrophoresis, a procedure in which a small electrical current is used to carry molecules through a special gel. The size of the molecule determines how quickly the molecule moves. Over time, differences in the speed with which molecules travel separate the different molecules from an unknown substance into distinctive bands. Comparing the pattern of bands produced by a known and an unknown substance (e.g., a blood sample) is the basis for DNA fingerprinting and other techniques in which it is necessary to separate protein or other molecular fragments. Cully realized that his students had some awareness of this procedure through television shows and would be interested in the procedure if he could present it in the right way. Lecturing about electrophoresis was probably not going to be an effective approach. But he was not able to purchase enough materials to allow many small groups of students the opportunity to perform a hands-on experiment.

Faced with this dilemma, Cully decided to create a movie based on a crime investigation. The movie chronicles the adventures of Cully and his assistant (the student teacher) as they investigate the disappearance of a classroom gerbil. As the movie begins, the investigative team is exploring the crime scene. Soon Cully is off to interrogate various school personnel who give both logical and illogical reasons that they could not possibly be the gerbil snatcher. During a more thorough investigation of the crime scene, Cully's assistant locates some drops of what appears to be blood. Perhaps the culprit was cut dragging the gerbil from its cage or perhaps the gerbil bit the abductor before being subdued! Cully is soon off to collect samples from his prime suspects. Were teachers really willing to donate blood for "the cause"? No; that would have been asking a bit much of even the most dedicated teacher. The samples were actually the demonstration solutions that came with the electrophoresis kit.

This complex scenario was established purely to create a background for the demonstration of the electrophoresis technique. With the exception of labeling the comparison samples with the names of the suspects, the demonstration proceeds pretty much as described in the laboratory manual. At the conclusion of the demonstration, the students are shown the gel slab (see Figure 9.1) and asked to identify the culprit.

Students knew the video was a spoof, but it still engaged them in a way a scientific documentary would not. The use of their own school as the set-

FIGURE 9.1
Images from the Missing Gerbil Movie

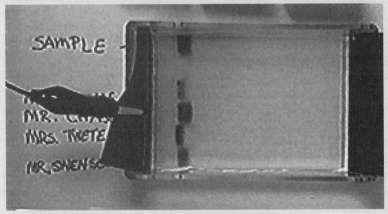

ting allowed students to recognize and hypothesize about the crime scene. The suspects in the video were familiar school personnel, and watching their teachers and others they knew behave in rather uncharacteristic ways seemed to maintain the attention of these middle-school students. Cully was also able to mix in a lot of humor. After asking the head cook if she could account for her whereabouts during the hours before school began, he asked her if there were any unusual meat entrees on the day's lunch menu.

We normally emphasize student use of technology in this book. We made an exception in this case because we felt this was a highly creative application that took advantage of available technology resources to engage students. Cully's video production put what might have been a standard teacher demonstration into a much more interesting and thought-provoking context. Creating your own video is quite feasible, and you may be surprised at what can now be accomplished with a camcorder, multimedia computer, and some ingenuity. Video production is one of the topics we discuss in this chapter.

TOOLS FOR CREATING, CAPTURING, AND MANIPULATING IMAGES

Differentiating created and captured images

Images can be brought into the computer environment in a variety of ways. To differentiate those applications in which images are *created* using technology from those in which images are *captured* using technology, think of the more familiar examples of an artist using paints and canvas to create a painting and a photographer using a camera to capture a photograph. Both processes require creativity and technique. The same is true in the application of technology. In the discussion that follows, we describe paint and draw programs as tools for creating and manipulating images and scanners and video digitizers as tools to capture images.

PAINT AND DRAW PROGRAMS

Student access to a graphics program is essential to the multimedia project approach frequently mentioned in this book. Graphics programs are traditionally differentiated as paint or draw programs. Paint programs store images as records of the individual dots of color, and draw programs represent what appears in an image mathematically. We will consider this distinction in greater detail at a later point. Paint programs are generally more useful for multimedia projects. In order to function successfully in this role, a paint program should allow students to do the following:

◆ Create graphics from scratch.
◆ Modify graphics from other sources.
◆ Save images in the format required for other application programs.

Creating Original Images

Can technology enhance talent?

All paint programs allow users to produce original artwork. The quality of what they create depends on their talent and the tools the paint program makes available. The question of whether technology can enhance existing artistic talent is complicated. People who are accustomed to creating art with a pencil or paintbrush may find their initial attempts to draw or paint using a computer program and a peripheral device such as a mouse frustrating and unsatisfactory. It helps to keep in mind that with experience, artists do learn to work with the tools of technology to produce some remarkable products.

Although not all students can create impressive illustrations even with technology, students with limited artistic skill and experience nevertheless can generate informative displays using the tools of a paint program.

Modifying Existing Images

Sources of high-quality images

Much of this chapter deals with ways technology can be used to capture images from sources external to the computer environment (see the sections on scanners and video digitizers). We also provide some suggestions for locating graphic resources that are already converted into a format suitable for computer use. Both sources supply images that are likely to be of much higher quality than those that students could create themselves and are most likely the equivalent of a photograph rather than a drawing or crude painting.

The opportunity to capture or acquire images without having to draw or paint them does not eliminate the need for access to graphics tool software, however. Existing images may not be suited to the exact purpose or presentation style that students or teachers have in mind for their projects, so they will frequently want the means to make modifications. Providing opportunities to rework images is important for another reason. Working with images allows students to engage with the ideas and processes those images represent. Appropriate tools can more actively involve students.

There are three most frequently used tool capabilities:

Loading graphics files

◆ Loading, or opening, existing graphics files. Although this may seem obvious, not all graphics programs were developed for the purpose of modifying graphics files created by other programs or methods. Files can be stored in many formats (see the discussion of file formats on page 328), and programs differ in how many different file types they can access.

Copying and pasting

◆ Copying and pasting parts of images. Frequently students want to use part of an existing picture to create a new display. Students may want to take parts of several individual images and combine them into a new, composite image to demonstrate stages in some process or to make various comparisons. Perhaps they want to show the stages in a butterfly's development: egg, caterpillar, chrysalis, butterfly. Or they may want to contrast the painted lady butterfly with the monarch.

Composite images

◆ Enhancing an existing image using a variety of tools. They may want to use the text tool to label parts of an image or create a composite image of several small color pictures and a line drawing they have created themselves.

Saving Images That Can Be Used by Application Programs

When developing projects, students use a paint or draw program at an intermediary stage rather than as the final host program for the images that have been created. The images are being prepared to be viewed using other computer software and might eventually appear in a multimedia presentation, be included on a Web page, be used as part of a record in a database, or be printed as part of a word processing document. The programs representing the final destination for the images are likely to have much less powerful tools for modifying images, so the ability to generate the exact images desired is a valuable feature of the graphics program.

Compatibility issues

Compatibility issues can be important. The paint or draw program should be able to save images of the type required by the intended authoring or presentation program. Some graphics programs and some multimedia authoring environments are versatile in the file formats they allow, and some are not. Teachers may want to consider the issue of compatibility before beginning to work on projects. However, they should also be assured that there is usually some way to make the necessary adjustments if compatibility problems arise. Programs are available to convert graphics files from one format to another. (We discuss screen capture and file conversion, techniques that can be very helpful when compatibility problems arise, later in this chapter.) Often the exact image desired can be temporarily copied to the memory of the computer and then pasted into a file opened by a different application program. In this way, the second application program does not actually have to open a file saved by the first program. Finally, a more powerful graphics program can be used to make necessary adjustments when students' programs cannot generate exactly the final product they need.

Comparing Paint and Draw Programs

Graphics programs used in school environments tend to fall into two general categories: paint programs, producing bit-mapped images, and draw programs, producing object-oriented images. Each category has advantages and disadvantages.

Bit-mapped images

Paint programs are used to create and manipulate **bit-mapped** images. With such bit-mapped programs, an image is created on a "page" that contains a set number of visual elements. You might think of visual elements as the individual points or dots that make up the image and background. A bit-mapped image is "painted" on the background by changing the color of these individual dots. In many early applications, the individual points making up the screen display—the **pixels**—would be either black or white. Images made up of only black or white pixels are called **line art**. With the proper equipment and software, individual pixels can also be defined in terms of many colors or shades of gray. Working at the level of individual pixels offers the greatest flexibility in creating an image, but paint programs also have some disadvantages

Screen Capture

Screen capture is the process of saving the screen image or part of the screen image (even if the screen contains text as a graphics file). The process is very much like taking a picture of the screen. Screen capture capabilities are built into newer versions of the Macintosh and Windows operating systems. In Windows, the keyboard command is Alt-Print Screen. A copy of the screen is saved to the **clipboard,** a computer memory buffer from which it can be loaded into a paint program such as Windows' own Paintbrush. The Macintosh equivalent is Command-Shift-3. Executing this command should result in the reassuring sound of a camera shutter click that lets the user know the computer has taken the requested action. Screen capture for the Macintosh saves the screen image as a file on the computer's hard drive. A paint program can then be used to load and work with the captured image.

That both Windows and the Macintosh require a multiple key command to capture a screen image sometimes confuses novices when they first encounter a description of this type. An effective way to explain multiple key commands is to compare them with the method for producing a capital letter with a word processor or typewriter: depress the shift key, and then depress the letter to be capitalized. For screen capture on the Macintosh, depress the command key and the shift key, and then press the 3.

It is also possible to purchase (often as shareware) small programs (sometimes called *utilities*) that extend the basic screen capture techniques. For example, such utilities usually allow the user to select and then capture any part of the image that appears on the entire screen and then to print or save the designated segment.

Screen captures can be used for many different purposes. One important use is capturing screens from application programs to use in material that explains to others how to use those programs. Many images in this textbook were captured from the screen for this purpose. Teachers may have opportunities to use this technique to prepare instructional materials for their students. If you wanted to prepare handouts explaining to students how to use a new program, this would be a useful way to display what the computer screen would look like at certain critical points.✳

---

when modifying, storing, and printing images. There are problems in effectively adjusting the size of images, and the images tend to take up more disk space than images created by draw programs.

Programs used to create and manipulate **object-oriented images** are commonly called **draw programs**. Object-oriented programs define the elements (points, lines, circles) making up these images in terms of mathematical equations. When an object-oriented image is saved to disk, it is this mathematical information, *not* a record of the color of individual pixels, that

Object-oriented images

is saved. This does not mean that a young student working with a draw program needs to know the equation for defining a circle and locating the circle at a particular spot on the computer screen. The program takes care of the mathematics.

Creating an image from individually defined objects can be useful when great precision is required. Special versions of draw programs using **computer-assisted design (CAD)** are commonly used to create engineering or architectural drawings and may be used in specialized secondary school classes. Because object-oriented programs are composed of individual objects and these objects can be isolated and modified, certain editing functions are much easier with draw programs.

Draw programs store images efficiently.

Draw programs also tend to store images much more efficiently and display images with higher quality than paint programs do. The display quality of an image in a draw program is limited only by the quality of the computer screen or printer used to produce the display. At issue is how much information—that is, **dots per inch (dpi)**—the screen or printer is capable of presenting. The mathematical formula defining draw objects can be used to produce basically the amount of information that the display device is capable of representing. The quality of bit-mapped images is defined when the images are created and thus may be lower than the quality of image that the display device can present.

Students will often capture images for projects.

We emphasize bit-mapped images and the programs and hardware used to create them because the images that students use in content-area applications often are captured from other sources rather than developed as original student artwork. It turns out that the methods used to capture such images work by capturing bit-mapped information. You have already read about techniques for capturing images from the computer screen. Later, you will encounter procedures for capturing images from live sources, student-recorded videotape, and paper sources. It is these capture techniques and the information resources that these techniques make available to students that make so many student projects practical to implement. Many of the images students will have access to using these techniques will be complex, and any student editing will be minimal. Students may want to cut the picture of, say, a wildflower, a deer, or a classmate from some source and display it in another application. The emphasis here is on capturing and displaying realistic images rather than on reconstruction or drastic alteration. Actions of this type are easier in the bit-mapped paint format than in the object-oriented draw format.

AppleWorks.   One effective way to demonstrate some of the differences between draw and paint programs is to consider an application such as AppleWorks (formerly ClarisWorks) that makes both types of tools available. You will notice in Figure 9.2 that the paintbrush, pencil, paint can, airbrush, and eraser are available as paint tools but not as draw tools. Paint tools allow the

FIGURE 9.2
Paint and Draw Palettes from AppleWorks

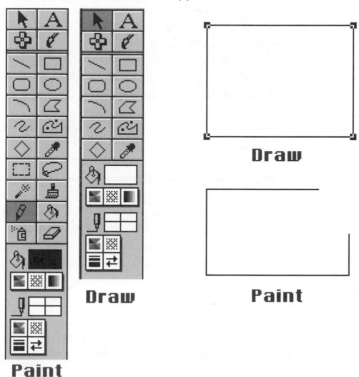

manipulation of individual pixels with great flexibility. The pencil tool provides a good example of this flexibility. A pencil can be used to sketch or to scribble. The complexity of either of these images would be difficult to represent efficiently in a mathematical equation. All of the other tools that are unique to the paint format can be applied with the same flexibility.

You will note from Figure 9.2 that both paint and draw palettes offer tools for creating basic shapes, such as rectangles, lines, and polygons. Even when draw and paint tools are used to create identical images, the properties of the images are still very different. Compare the two rectangles on the right side of Figure 9.2. The rectangle created with the draw tool is a single unit. If the user decides to remove it from the computer screen, it will be deleted as a unit. The small, dark squares appearing at the corners of the rectangle are handles the user can drag (click with the mouse and move with the mouse held) to change the shape of the rectangle. These handles can also be used to modify the rectangle to create a square. The handles disappear as soon as the user selects another tool or begins work on another part of the computer screen. The rectangle created with the paint tool is not a single unit; it is actually made up of pixels that can be manipulated independently. To demonstrate the difference

Comparing draw and paint images

between rectangles created with draw and paint tools, the eraser tool has been used to eliminate a corner of the painted rectangle in Figure 9.2. A set of pixels has been removed, and the rest of the rectangle remains. The eraser is not available when working on draw objects because they must be treated as whole units. Similarly, because the painted rectangle is not one unit, it cannot easily be reshaped into a square.

Distortion with enlarged paint images

One other unique problem that users of paint programs encounter is the distortion that occurs when the size of an image is changed. The individual pixels that make up an image are like tiny blocks. When an image is enlarged, these blocks are simply magnified. In some cases, particularly with diagonal lines, this magnification results in a distortion that is often called **jaggies** (see Figure 9.3).

Do schools need both draw and paint applications? There are some very useful applications for object-oriented images in the fields of design and engineering, and educational experiences related to these areas offer opportunities for draw applications. However, these applications are relatively infrequent in comparison to the opportunities to use paint programs. The flexibility of bit-mapped graphics is extremely important for the general computer tool approach we advocate here.

Paint programs especially for younger students

Kid Pix Studio—A Paint Program.   Kid Pix is one of the best examples of a paint program developed specifically for younger users. This inexpensive program combines a set of functional graphics tools, an interface intended to make the program more intuitive for young users, and some quirky tools and features just for fun.

The Kid Pix interface was designed to make the program's options apparent even to inexperienced users. The idea is to use icons that visibly suggest what can be done with each tool so that the user does not have to learn or remember complicated procedures. Although most users have to experiment a bit to become familiar with what some of the options actually do, this **graphic user interface (GUI)** makes it easy to learn and remember how to use the program.

FIGURE 9.3
Bit-Mapped Line Magnified Four Times

Icons represent tools.

If you have had little previous experience with computer paint programs, the structure of the Kid Pix interface might serve as a convenient model for understanding more complicated programs. As you examine a monitor displaying Kid Pix (see Figure 9.4), you will see a column of icons down the left side of the screen and a row of icons across the bottom of the screen. These icons represent *paint tools*, *color options*, and *tool options*. Although not all paint programs make these choices visible simultaneously to the user, other paint programs work in approximately the same way. The user selects a paint tool to work with; when applicable, the color the paint tool is to apply; and an option for the specific effect the tool will have. The tool options are presented in a particularly useful way with Kid Pix. When a tool is selected, the tool options available for that tool appear automatically. The young user does not have to remember the options that are available or how to implement them. In some cases, all of the available options cannot fit in a single row. When this is the case, a numbered arrow at the end of the row informs the user that more options are available. The user can view the additional options by clicking on the up or down arrow.

FIGURE 9.4
Kid Pix Monitor Display

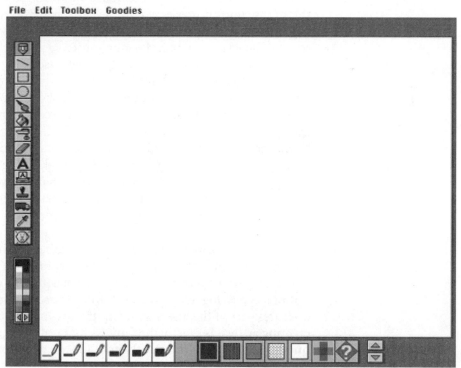

USING GRAPHICS TOOLS IN A WRITING ASSIGNMENT

How are the various graphics tools used to construct a picture? The following description takes you step by step through the process of creating a simple image, which was the cover for a writing assignment, "My Pet," by our daughter Kim. (The finished image is provided in Figure 9.6 on page 324.) This image combines the picture of a dog, captured using a video digitizing technique, with simple line art and text created in Kid Pix.

For detailed work, magnify images.

The process begins with the original picture of a dog sitting under a kitchen table. To get just the part of the image that is needed, the area around the dog is carefully erased. One useful approach when doing very detailed work is to magnify an image several times. Working on an enlarged image calls for much less delicate control of a tool such as the eraser. It would be very easy to slip and erase a paw if it were necessary to work on a same-size image. Kid Pix does not allow image size to be easily manipulated, so the detailed work needed to isolate the picture of the dog must be done in a more sophisticated program.

Once the file containing the picture of the dog is opened in Kid Pix, the moving van tool is used to move the picture to the bottom of the screen, out of the way. One of the options available with this tool allows an area of the screen to be selected using the mouse and then relocated by dragging. When the mouse button is released, the selected material remains in the new location. Having the picture of the dog present on the screen gave Kim a better sense of how large to make the doghouse.

The first step in constructing the doghouse is to generate a large rectangle using the rectangle tool. After it is selected, the tool is positioned in what is intended to be one of the corners of the finished shape. The mouse button is then depressed, and the rectangle tool is moved toward the opposite corner of the intended shape. If the user starts in the upper-left corner, the mouse can be moved on a downward diagonal or over and then down (see Figure 9.5). As long as the mouse button remains depressed, the rectangle tool will draw a rectangle between the initial point and the point to which the tool is moved. When the mouse is released, the size of the rectangle is fixed. If the image does not meet the user's expectations, it can be removed with the undo tool and redrawn.

When you examine Figure 9.6, the fact that you no longer see a complete rectangle may at first confuse you. The oval tool was used to generate a large oval on top of the rectangle. Because the opaque tool was selected from the fill options appearing across the bottom of the screen (see Figure 9.4), the oval obscures part of the line making up the original rectangle. The technique for creating an oval is exactly the same as for creating a rectangle. Start at a point on one boundary and move the tool toward the corresponding point on the

FIGURE 9.5
Technique for Using Paint Rectangle Tool

Starting Point

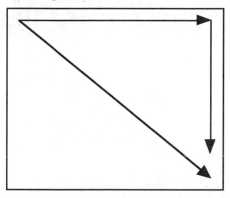

Ending Point

opposite side of the figure. With a little practice, users learn to create ovals of different shapes. Of course, you also do not see a complete oval in Figure 9.6. The bottom part of the oval was erased using the erase tool, beginning at the points where the oval intersected the rectangle. The result is the entrance to the doghouse.

Kim created the roof by using the line tool to draw three lines and the paint bucket to fill the enclosed area with a pattern selected from the available options. It is important when using a fill procedure to make certain there are no gaps in the boundary of the area to be filled. If an opening is present, the fill color or pattern will leak out across any open area of the picture. If this should happen (and it happens to everyone, because breaks in lines are not always easy to see), the key is not to panic. Simply use the undo tool to delete the last action taken. It is also good practice to save your work every few minutes, so that you will never be in the position of losing work that has taken a long time to create.

Undo deletes the last action.

To finish the picture, text is added using the text tool, and the student's signature is added using the pencil tool. The image of the dog is then moved, using the moving van, to the side of the doghouse. Because Kid Pix moves only rectangular areas, some of the lines on the doghouse were covered up with the "white" space that surrounded the picture of the dog. These lines had to be redrawn. Obviously, some of the mechanical techniques used in computer graphics are a little different from those used with pencil, crayons, and paper. Learning these techniques is just a matter of awareness and practice.

It is difficult to describe the process of creating a picture with a paint program. Some processes are best learned by experience; if you have the

FIGURE 9.6
Sample Kid Pix Picture

opportunity, you should certainly take the time to acquaint yourself with at least one paint program. Paint programs can be used to good effect by individuals with some artistic talent.

Kid Pix was one of the first purchases made for the elementary school computers in our community, and some interesting products surfaced very quickly. Teachers were allowed to take a classroom computer home for the summer to become acquainted with it and the software tools that had been purchased. Soon after taking a computer home, one of the teachers returned with the picture shown in Figure 9.7. Her son, Joel Quamme, a high school sophomore, created it. This is the kind of product one might expect from a more expensive draw or CAD program in the hands of an experienced user. Would you be able to create an image of this quality? If you have little artistic

FIGURE 9.7
Joel Quamme's Mondo Castle

talent or experience, probably not. This student has an obvious appreciation of scale, shading, and depth perspective over and above his computer skills.

In some ways, it might be argued that creating art on the computer is more difficult than creating art with paper and pencil. As an input device, the mouse is probably more difficult to manipulate than a pencil. In some ways, though, creating art on the computer is easier than using paper and pencil. Lines and shapes can be drawn with great precision, and areas can easily be filled with colors or patterns. There are a number of sources for computer graphics projects. Make sure you take a look at Resources to Expand Your Knowledge Space at the end of this chapter.

It should not be assumed that schools will need only a basic graphics program like Kid Pix. Because of the cost and intended users, Kid Pix does not have some of the tools or tool options that are available in full-featured graphics programs and does not meet all the needs of educational settings. There are a number of limitations that are important to recognize. Kid Pix opens only certain types of image files. Schools may want to work with graphic images stored in other formats. In addition, all Kid Pix images appear on the same size canvas. Not all portions of larger images can be viewed, and small images will be surrounded with a great deal of white space. This lack of versatility makes for a number of limitations. For example, if the paint program is being used to prepare graphics files to be opened by other programs, it is often desirable to save images of different sizes. Kid Pix also lacks the capability to modify image size—that is, to shrink or enlarge an image, transform images from color to gray scale, or modify such image characteristics as brightness or contrast. High-end graphics programs also perform certain adjustments automatically or offer some optional images and let you pick the option that looks the best. Factors like these can come into play when schools work heavily with graphic images for multimedia applications. It is not necessary to invest in many copies of a higher-end program with these capabilities, but at least one workstation with additional tools and features should be available so that students and teachers can perform more sophisticated functions.

Benefits of a workstation with additional tools and features

UNDERSTANDING GRAPHICS FILE FORMATS

Why is there a variety of graphics file formats?

When a graphics program stores a graphic image, the resulting file has a characteristic format. Users may encounter a bewildering variety of graphics file formats. This situation exists for several reasons. First, certain file types are associated with different hardware platforms. For example, BMP is a common format on computers running the Windows operating system, and PICT is a common Macintosh format. Second, certain file types were designed to accomplish certain tasks. The TIFF format was developed for scanned images, for example, and the GIF format was designed for exchanging graphics through the Internet. Finally, many graphics programs have a *native format.* This means that programs of this type save graphics files in a format that is intended to be loaded only by the same program. In most cases, however, programs offering a native format also allow files to be saved in other formats.

Why should teachers using computers in their classrooms bother to become aware of the various graphics file formats? Here are some situations you might encounter:

◆ An elementary school teacher wants to scan some line art from a coloring book and then have his students paint the images using Kid Pix. The school's older scanner saves the scanned images as TIFF files. (Scanners are discussed later.) Kid Pix cannot load this file format. What should the teacher do?

◆ A high school science teacher finds some breathtaking photographs on the Internet from a recent space mission. The photographs are in GIF format. The school has Macintosh equipment. Should the teacher download the files?

◆ You have a great collection of free clip art stored on a Macintosh CD. A teacher friend of yours has ideas for using some of the images in a classroom newsletter, but the teacher uses a Windows machine. Is there some way to make the images available to her?

There are several ways to deal with the various file formats you might encounter. If you are lucky, you will be able to ignore them. Many programs

Spotlight on Assessment

Using Peer Comments

Educational accomplishments take time and effort. Our understanding or the projects through which we demonstrate our understanding are seldom perfect immediately; they evolve as we work. Feedback can be very important in improving the efficiency of learning and constructive processes. Although we must learn to evaluate our own efforts (review our discussion of metacognition in Chapter 2), it is often very helpful to have input from others. We often think of teachers as providing this type of information. However, other students may also represent a very valuable resource. Here are two things to consider:

◆ Providing enough individual attention for an entire class may be too much to expect of one person. Student reactions to the work of their peers can increase the amount of feedback available.

◆ Students may benefit from evaluating the work of others. Examining work that is less familiar allows students to practice their evaluation skills.

As students work to complete a classroom project, it can be useful to set up a system in which they receive feedback from peers before presenting the project to the teacher for more formal evaluation (Tierney, Carter, & Desai, 1991). Student work in progress can be distributed to peers along with a request for spe-

cific feedback. Students can contemplate these comments as they make final revisions. Consider questions that we might ask fifth-grade students to guide their comments about a cover page they have all been asked to generate:

◆ Does the cover page make me want to read this report? What might be changed to make the cover more interesting?

◆ Does the cover page help me understand what the report is about? What might be changed so that the cover is more closely related to the report?

◆ Does the title provide a good summary of the report?

◆ Is the picture on the cover a good choice? Is it clear and of appropriate size? What might be improved?

◆ Are the picture and the drawing put together attractively? What might be improved?

Because students could be asked to consider many different aspects of the report and the cover page, the comments you request students to provide should be related to the characteristics you will evaluate in the more finished product. The issues you raise will determine the informativeness of peer comments and will also help students think about their own work.✳

have built-in **translators**—small utilities that allow the program to accept a variety of file formats. Programs of this type can also be used as an intermediary. For example, Kid Pix accepts PICT files. Photoshop is a much more powerful and flexible program that allows files to be opened and saved in a variety of formats. If it were necessary to get a TIFF image into Kid Pix, Photoshop could be used to open the image in TIFF format and save the image in PICT format. Kid Pix could then work with the image. This is one of the reasons we recommend that schools invest in a more powerful graphics program even if students would only rarely use such a program. There are also utility programs that are designed primarily to convert files from one format to another.

Here is a brief glossary of graphics file formats you may encounter; they are better known by their abbreviations in parentheses:

> **bitmap (BMP) format.** Common bit-map formats for the Windows platform.
>
> **encapsulated PostScript (EPS).** A format commonly used for storing object-oriented graphics files.
>
> **graphics interchange format (GIF).** A format created by CompuServe for efficient transfer of bit-mapped images to and from commercial telecommunications services. The GIF format continues to be popular for this purpose. Several Macintosh and DOS/Windows application programs support this format.
>
> **Joint Photographic Experts Group (JPEG).** A "lossy" compression format that produces high-quality images while drastically reducing file size. **Lossy** implies a form of compression in which data, and thus some quality, are lost during the compression process.
>
> **PICT, PICT2.** A generic file format for the Macintosh that allows a mixture of bit-mapped and object-oriented graphics. PICT and PICT2 files are often not differentiated, but PICT2 technically allows more color options. (Note that "PICT" and "PICT2" are not acronyms.)
>
> **tag image file format (TIFF).** The most flexible format for bit-mapped (not object-oriented) graphics and often the standard output file for scanning. Can be used to cross Macintosh and DOS/Windows hardware platforms.

CAPTURING IMAGES

Scanners and video digitizers

Students can use reasonably priced technology to transfer existing images from paper into a form computers can use and manipulate, or to capture images from their surroundings, much as they would capture images with a camera. Flatbed scanners are used for capturing images from paper sources or

Focus

Graphics for the Web

Preparing images for presentation on Web pages presents two challenges:

- Images that are part of Web pages are viewed using different browser software used on a variety of hardware platforms.
- Transfer speed across the Internet can be a problem, particularly when users are connecting by modem. It is important to keep the file size of images as small as possible.

The current solution to these challenges is to use file formats that are **cross-platform**—meaning that the format is accepted by different types of computers—and to take advantage of techniques that minimize file size. Nearly all Web graphics are sent over the Internet in one of two file formats: GIF or JPEG format. Anyone wanting to include graphics on their Web pages needs to know how to convert existing images to these two formats and to understand the strengths and weaknesses of each format type.

Large graphic files can be a problem because users become impatient when files take a long time to transfer over slow Internet connections. One way to control the size of graphic files is to restrict the number of colors that are used. For example, GIF files rely on 256 or fewer colors rather than the thousands or millions of colors allowed in JPEG files. When the **color palette** (the set of colors available on a particular computer; also called the **color lookup table,** or CLUT) is restricted to 256 colors, the options available for each pixel can be represented in 8 bits (2 to the eighth power). The difference in disk space required

to store 8 bits in contrast to 16 or 24 bits per pixel is substantial.

There are two problems in representing images in 256 colors. These problems become evident when an original image contains colors not included among the designated 256 or when the 256 colors available on a particular hardware platform do not match the 256 colors used in creating the image file. Unfortunately, the palettes for the Macintosh and Windows systems rely on slightly different sets of colors; only 216 of the 256 colors are the same. This means there may be distortion in converting an original to the 256-color palette available on a particular computer and distortion because of the lack of commonality in this palette across computers. When a computer is unable to generate a match for a requested color, it resorts to **dithering**—trying to simulate the color by mixing pixels of other colors. On close examination, dithered images appear spotty. If you have spent much time on the Web, you probably have encountered this problem.

The JPEG format allows many more colors and so is better suited to saving images when the specific colors cannot be controlled. But JPEG uses a lossy compression technique to keep file size manageable and this creates a different problem. A lossy compression technique introduces a small amount of error, or *visual noise*, into an image; that is, the stored image is not an exact replica of the original. When the image is complex (with lots of colors and a complex pattern), the noise is difficult to detect. But when the image has large solid areas and a simple pattern, the distortions are noticeable.

Understanding these difficulties allows Web designers to match the file format to the task. Although there are other issues to consider, the most basic advice is to use JPEG when presenting photographic-like images that have been captured (scanning, digital capture, digital photography) and use GIF when presenting simple illustrations you have created (e.g., original work generated with a paint program).✳

from photographic slides and transforming these images into a bit-mapped digital format that the computer can store. **Video digitizers** are used to create graphics files from video sources such as camcorders, VCRs, video cameras, and laserdisc players. Digital cameras offer a third option and store information in a digital form that can then be transferred to a computer. We discuss digital cameras on page 333.

Scanners and video digitizers working in combination with a computer were developed to convert an external image into a digitized graphics file. This means that existing images, such as a crayon line drawing created by a young student, a secondary school student's original pencil illustration, the view through a microscope, or virtually any other image that might now be captured with a photocopier, camera, or camcorder, can be converted into the kind of digital information that a computer can use. Information in the form of a graphics file can be saved to disk, loaded back into the computer later, displayed on the computer monitor, or printed. Once an image is present in a form the computer can manipulate, tool software can be used to cut sections from a larger image to form smaller images; integrate images from several sources to form a new composite image; add text to label parts of an image; add color to black-and-white drawings; and modify, combine, and manipulate the stored images in many other ways. Once brought into the computer with a scanner or video digitizer, and perhaps enhanced with graphics software tools, images captured from an external source can become part of the multimedia products discussed in several other chapters of this book.

Flatbed Scanners

Flatbed scanners operate in a way similar to photocopiers.

If you have ever copied documents with a photocopying machine, you are well on your way to being able to operate a flatbed **scanner.** You begin by lifting the lid of the scanner and placing the sheet of paper with the image you want to scan face down on the glass. When the scanning process begins, you will notice the familiar light source moving along the length of the image beneath the glass plate. In a scanner, a lens or mirror system beneath the glass plate focuses the light reflected from the original image into the

charge-coupled device (CCD). The output from this device is translated within the scanner into the digital form acceptable as input to a computer.

Video Digitizers

Scanners can be used to capture images from only a narrow range of sources. With the exception of specialized scanners designed to capture images from photographic slides, these would be the same sources suitable for photocopying. You cannot directly capture the images of a classmate or a zoo animal with a scanner. Video digitizers make other sources of images available. Among the additional possibilities, you or your students might use this type of equipment to bring into the computer environment the images from sources you might pursue with a camera. Two methods are available for digitizing video input: video digitizing boards and digital cameras.

Video digitizing boards convert the analog video signal generated by a videocassette player, a camcorder, a television tuner, or a videodisc player into a digital signal. Without going into great detail, an **analog signal** is continuous, and a digital signal is discrete. The cable between the "video out" connection of your videocassette player and the "video in" connection of your television carries an analog signal, that is, a signal capable of being represented by continuous values. This same cable can be connected directly to a video digitizing board to convert the analog signal to a digital signal and save still frames or video segments as graphics files.

Ask questions when your school makes a purchase.

This description of a board (sometimes called a *card*) is purposefully vague. Some computers, perhaps described as multimedia or audiovisual computers, may have this capability built in. If this is the kind of computer you want, you should ask specific questions when making a purchase to be certain the desired capabilities are present. The ability to create or display multimedia should not be confused with the capability to capture graphic images from an analog source. Many school computers can also be used to digitize video input but require additional hardware to make this capability available. There are several commercial hardware products that can add the capability to digitize an analog signal. Now, instead of being actual cards that are inserted within the computer, these devices are also available as external add-ons (peripherals) that attach to a port on the computer and connect the computer to the camcorder. Rather than just a cable of some type, this connection runs the input signal through a small box containing the hardware necessary to feed the video to the computer. Whether the capability comes built in or must be added, a hardware device integrated with the other hardware components of the computer accomplishes the transformation from analog to digital signal.

Video capture is accomplished by first activating a software program that accesses input from the video digitizing card. The active image from a

The camcorder lets students capture images in the field and allows them to continue learning from unique experiences even when they return to the classrooms. *(© Michael Zide)*

camcorder, video camera, videocassette player, or some other input device appears in a window on the screen. This window can serve as a rather expensive and very small television. The exact method for capturing images varies with the hardware and software that are used. The example in Figure 9.8 shows the video digitizing feature built into HyperStudio. You watch the video in a small window. When you find an image you would like to capture, you click the freeze button. At this stage, the image has not been saved. If the still image that results is what you want, you click the OK button, and new tools are made available for selecting the exact part of the image you want to use and placing the image on a card. If your reactions are a little slow and you miss what you wanted to capture, click at the location of the freeze button, and you are back watching live video. You might have to rewind the videotape and try several times to get the exact image you want.

Image size   Digitizing boards differ in the size of the image they generate when capturing images from a recorded source. This is one situation in which the cost of the product will come into play. Larger digital images require more memory and more time to generate. Less expensive boards digitize an image from several successive frames sent from the videocassette player. Video is commonly recorded at thirty frames per second, and the speed at which some

FIGURE 9.8
HyperStudio Image Dialog Box

boards convert the signal to a digital form requires that several frames be combined to produce the image, a process that can reduce the quality of the image.

Digital Cameras

It may surprise many to learn that digital cameras have been around for some time. These devices may appear similar to traditional cameras, but instead of capturing images on film, digital cameras use a charge-coupled device like that used in a camcorder. The older versions kept images on a special video floppy disk, and the method of storage was similar to that of videotape. These images were not digitized. The images stored on this type of disk still have to be converted to a digital format with a video digitizing card before they can be used in multimedia applications. The digital cameras available over the past few years store images in a digital format. The quality of the images available from these cameras and the price have improved dramatically, and digital cameras are being purchased by many schools.

Image quality

There are several things to keep in mind when purchasing a digital camera for school use. The quality of the captured images is a big issue. Currently, the more you are willing to pay, the higher-quality images you will be able to store. Probably the most significant factor in image quality is the density of pixels the CCD is able to capture; the more tightly packed the dots of color are, the higher quality the image is. Pixel density is typically described as a pair of numbers—for example, 640 × 480 (this was the typical density of older cameras)—representing the number of pixels in the width and height of an image. Newer cameras, sometimes referred to as megapixel cameras, are capable of storing 1 million or even 2 million pixel images. The industry typically identifies a camera as meeting the megapixel standard if one of the file dimensions exceeds 1,000 pixels—for example, 1,024 × 768. (If you do the math, you will note that this is less than 1 million pixels, but who is counting?) The more pixels used to represent the same area, the higher the quality of the image.

There are some other factors that determine image quality. Such factors include the quality of the lens system and the algorithm used to process the image for storage. Lens systems differ in quality and also in whether the lens allows the photographer to zoom in and out. If a zoom feature is available, it may be either an electronic zoom or a true optical zoom. With the electronic zoom, the digital image is simply magnified, much like the action you might use to increase image size with a paint program. This type of magnification causes some distortion. The true optical zoom produces images of much better quality. Some storage methods use a lossy method to allow more images to be stored (see page 329), and this results in images of somewhat lower quality. Camera manufacturers are willing to degrade the quality of images because of the practical limits of storage. A camera that can hold eight images and then needs to transfer the images to a computer does present some practical challenges when working in the field.

Storage methods

The storage method and the related issue of how you transfer the images to a computer for student use are important issues to consider. Storage mechanisms include RAM (memory chips much like those contained in a computer), **flash memory** (a kind of removable memory cartridge), and even floppy disks. There are advantages and disadvantages to each. For example, RAM memory is the least expensive but requires that the camera be frequently linked to a computer to offload pictures.

For those familiar with traditional cameras, working with a digital camera takes a little adjustment. One thing you will notice is the delay. The camera does not record the image the instant you attempt to activate the shutter. It takes a couple of seconds, and this makes photographing moving images or pictures that require a quick reaction difficult. It also takes a little while for the camera to process and store the image. You cannot click away as you can with traditional 35-mm cameras.

As you can see, purchasing and using a digital camera requires that a number of issues be considered. It is important to determine how the camera will be used and what features are necessary for that type of use. You can purchase a camera capable of taking digital pictures that rival what you could generate by taking photographs with a traditional camera and then scanning the developed pictures for under $1,000. It is also possible to purchase ten cameras capable of storing eight 640×480 resolution pictures for the same total amount of money. Which would be the better choice for the situation in which you will use technology? Some suggestions for learning about digital cameras are included at the end of this chapter.

Recording Video Segments

Incorporating video segments in class projects

As you have seen in earlier chapters, many class projects can incorporate video segments. Students and teachers can create their own video segments using the hardware and software described here. It is important to realize from the beginning, however, that a video segment recorded on school

Activities and Projects for Your Classroom

Images to Capture

Once you understand the basics, generating a list of the types of images students might capture is easy. The opportunities to provide examples, demonstrate something, or just liven up your writing are limitless. Here are a few ideas to get you started. Videocapture techniques could be used to generate images that:

- Contrast proper and improper weightlifting techniques.
- Reveal geometric shapes in your environment.
- Personalize a language board (a device used to communicate by pointing at pictures) for a seriously language-impaired student.

- Recall experiences from field trips to a farm, factory, museum, lake shore, or local business.
- Show the birds that have visited your bird feeder.
- Expose instances of local pollution.
- Exemplify merchandise displays you consider interesting and effective.
- Show the many ways computer technology is used in the workplace.
- Illustrate some of the things that make you happy.✶

equipment will probably have nowhere near the quality of the original motion sequences captured with a camcorder. Some of the reasons for the limitations are informative and worth considering.

First, there is the matter of speed. Most of us are used to video displayed at the rate of thirty frames per second. At this display rate, we are unable to distinguish individual images from continuous motion. To create a digitized video segment, a computer has to be capable of both digitizing and displaying many frames at a very rapid rate. Because of the large amount of data that must be manipulated and moved, these are not trivial matters. Display speed can also be limited by how quickly image files can be read from the disk. As you can probably guess from the previous discussion of capturing individual images, most computers cannot achieve the rate of capture and display needed to achieve the rate we have grown to expect from our experience with television, movies, and home videos.

Images can take up 1 megabyte of memory.

The other difficulty is capacity—both storage capacity and computer memory capacity. Quality full-screen images can require 1 megabyte of memory each to store. Imagine the problem of trying to store thirty such images for each second of video. This is one of the reasons that the digitized video you see is likely to use rather small images and that commercial applications of digitized video make the storage capacity of a CD nearly mandatory. This is also one of the reasons that digitized video is likely to be recorded and presented at a much lower rate of frames per second: twelve frames per second is an achievable speed. Finally, capacity problems have led to the development of compression techniques. Compression techniques such as JPEG (see page 329) sacrifice only a small amount of image quality in order to save a large amount of disk space. Compression rates of ten to one are possible with reasonable quality.

The QuickTime format is often used for storing video segments and presenting them as part of Web pages. **QuickTime,** a software capability that can be purchased and added to a computer, provides the compression methods and timing mechanisms necessary to keep video presentations synchronized. For example, different machines will not be able to display the same number of frames per second. With slower machines, some of the frames will automatically be dropped so that the sequence will run at the proper speed and remain coordinated with any accompanying sound.

Digital Video Camcorders

We are writing this book at what appears to be a transition point in the camcorder industry. It is now possible to purchase digital video camcorders; the video is stored on the tape or sometimes on another form of storage media in a digital format. As the price of these camcorders falls, digital video will become the standard.

VIDEO PRODUCTION

The generation of a polished video product might be described as video production, a process that encompasses far more than taking some footage with a camcorder. When it is done as a learning task, the other steps in the process contribute to making the experience active and authentic.

The process of video production is typically accomplished through a sequence of three steps. We will use educational terminology in describing these steps, but the activities are roughly equivalent whether engaged in for commercial or educational reasons.

Planning Phase

Video projects typically begin with a planning phase. Planning establishes goals for the project and identifies the resources that will be needed.

Collecting Primary Sources and Generating Interpretive Products

Video productions are constructed from both raw materials—primary sources—and interpretive products generated to explain or integrate these raw materials. What qualifies as raw material and interpretive product varies with the type of video production. If a class decides to create a drama depicting the initial meeting of the explorers Lewis and Clark with Sacajawea and her husband, Toussaint Charbonneau, at the Knife River Village, the students would have to use online and library resources to research the Lewis and Clark expedition. From these primary sources, the students would write a script and then tape a short play. The script and the video production would represent their interpretive products.

If students have decided to create a documentary focused on their community's recycling efforts, primary sources would include the raw audio and video resources collected on location. Additional information might be extracted from books, newspapers, interviews, and other sources. This information may be directly included in the video product or may be used in making decisions about whether other resources will be included. Other resources may also have to be created or collected. For example, video productions often include still images such as photographs and charts to illustrate specific positions. This type of production would likely require that a narrative script be written to integrate the various information sources. This script would serve to interpret the multiple primary sources.

Video Editing

Video editing is the process of integrating multimedia elements (text, audio, video, images) into a video production and making changes to these elements or the integrated product in order to improve quality.

Focus

Resources Necessary for Classroom Video Authoring

Video cameras, sometimes referred to as camcorders, are commonly available in schools. Most athletic events are taped, as are theater and musical programs. Although video authoring projects can be completed using only a camera, some additional resources can greatly expand the quality and variety of projects that can be completed. Here is a more complete list of desirable resources:

◆ *Camcorder.* The video camera is the most essential feature for video projects. Cameras range in price (from $300 up) and format (VHS, VHS-C, 8-millimeter, Hi-8, digital).

◆ *Camcorder accessories.* Certain accessories improve the quality of what can be captured with a camcorder. Our suggested accessories are a good tripod, light source, and remote microphone.

◆ *High-end computer with large storage capacity and videocapture capabilities.* A powerful computer is needed to convert the input from a camcorder to digital format and to edit digital information. The computer must have a fast processor and large amounts of RAM to work with the real-time processing of video and audio. Video also requires large storage capacity, so a multigigabyte hard disk is a necessity. The conversion of an analog input into digital audio and video requires special hardware (see videocapture on page 331).

◆ *External storage.* No matter what the capacity of the computer hard drive, it will be necessary to consider some form of external storage for archiving video products. One of the easiest solutions is to send any finished products back out to videotape. Another solution is to store video products on CD.

◆ *Videocapture and video editing software.* Unless students or teachers have access to a digital camcorder, the "primary source" video from the camcorder will have to be converted to a digital format (usually QuickTime). Then the video editing software is used to combine the video and audio segments with other information sources. Although video editing software ranges greatly in cost and power, it is possible to create high-quality productions with software costing less than $100. Several video editing programs are included in Resources to Expand Your Knowledge Base at the end of this chapter.

Baecker and Posner (1999) contend that classroom digital authoring will be successful when hardware and software are available that make the editing process efficient enough to generate short video projects with a few hours of labor, schools can afford the necessary equipment and software, and educators can create a learning environment in which open-minded criticism, cooperation, and hard work are valued.✳

Video editing environments should provide the capacity to accept different types of media (video, audio, images), edit existing media (add text, delete unneeded portions of video or audio), create some basic resources (record narration), add video and audio transitions (fades between video segments, fade audio in and out), and create an integrated final product. MovieWorks, an easy-to-use and inexpensive example of a video editing environment appropriate to the classroom, provides all of these capabilities.

Putting a movie together

MovieWorks uses individual tools for capturing video, creating paint documents, recording audio, and creating animations. Multimedia elements created in other ways can also be used. The main MovieWorks program is used to combine and sequence multimedia elements. The key components of this program are visible in Figure 9.9. Putting a movie together can be fairly easy. First, the window size for the project is established. The window size you see in Figure 9.9 is very small because the project being developed was ultimately intended for presentation on the Internet. An easy way to add multimedia elements is to use the mouse to drag the file into this window (**drag and drop**). This operation automatically opens the file in the window and adds the multimedia element to the sequencer. The sequencer tool is used to order the appearance of multimedia elements, control the time allotted to individual elements, and add transitions (the sequencer appears at the bottom of Figure 9.9). The movie being developed includes an initial title image (Text-1), a video segment (distantpond) of approximately 8 seconds overlaid with a short narration (Sound-1), and a final video segment (cattail).

Once completed, the movie can be incorporated as a component of a multimedia product. Short video segments can be added to many types of multimedia projects (see Chapter 8). Video segments can be included as part of an embellished document (e.g., AppleWorks and many other popular word processing programs), a multimedia slide show generated and displayed by a presentation tool (e.g., PowerPoint), or a hypermedia project (e.g., HyperStudio). The movie can also be viewed as a self-contained product. Movies of longer length are often created to stand alone. This is the format in which we encounter the commercial material we view for entertainment or educational purposes. The equipment and editing software we have just described allow teachers and students to create their own movies.

Presenting a movie

There are several options for presenting self-contained movies. In one approach, the movie is stored in digital format and displayed using a computer. An interesting option for digital movies is Internet delivery. In this case, the digital information, often in a compressed format, is downloaded from a server before it is displayed by the client computer (see Chapter 6).

Digital movies can also be sent out to a VCR or camcorder to be recorded in the conventional analog format. Most computers capable of generating digital video have both video-in and video-out capabilities. Once stored on tape, the movie can be played on the traditional video equipment available in

FIGURE 9.9
MovieWorks Sequencer and Project Window

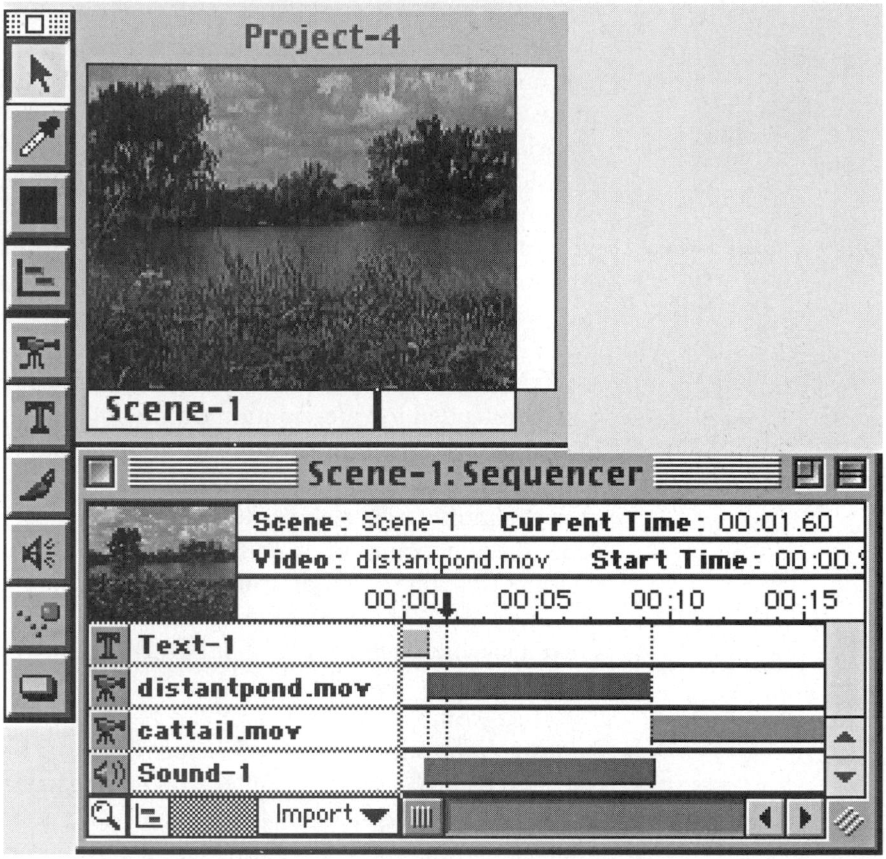

most schools. Digital movies take a considerable amount of disk space, and long-term storage of the products that are produced is an issue. Archiving finished products on videotape is a convenient solution.

LOCATING ALTERNATIVE IMAGE SOURCES

Searching for multimedia resources will take you into new territory. It has led us to carry our camcorder down wooded trails and into county historical museums. We have become acquainted with student artists at all educational levels. We have scoured bargain bookstores and museum and zoo gift shops in search of unusual coloring books, as well as the backs of computer magazines for the ads of small companies offering collections of sounds, video clips, and pictures.

Activities and Projects for Your Classroom

Video Productions

Here are some ideas to get you started thinking about classroom video projects.

Training tapes. Create a videotape explaining to the next class how your class did something (e.g., using the computer to create T-shirt iron-on transfers).

Video storytelling. Create a video with no words, and then have students make up stories to go with the video.

Regional news broadcasts. Create news segments that summarize school or local events. Language classes might use this activity as a way to make practical use of the language skills they are learning.

Conversational language situations. Have students prepare videos to demonstrate conversational German, Spanish, or another language through meeting the family of a friend, ordering in a restaurant, buying a bus ticket, or asking directions to a local historical site.

Extending classroom resources or opportunities. Bring an experience to students that would not be possible for them to experience directly, as Cully Gause did in the Case of the Missing Gerbil (see page 312).

Interviews with local experts. Arrange to video local people who have specific expertise.

Portfolios. Accumulate segments of oral reading over the course of a year.

Documentaries. Present a local issue, and examine both sides of it.

Video autobiographies. Students present themselves including comments from significant people in their lives.

Public service announcements. Create appeals for community action or awareness on such issues as alcohol abuse or household recycling.

Time-lapse studies. Record the process of a major local construction project or the development of a butterfly, for example.

Critique performances. Record musical, theater, or athletic events for later analysis and evaluation.

Video yearbook. Publish a video version of the yearbook.

Extracurricular highlights. Provide a summary of the experiences of an athletic team, the group responsible for a play, or a senior trip.✳

Huge range of multimedia resources

Increasingly resources are becoming easier to find. The market for multimedia resources has started to expand, and inexpensive collections are now available in every educational supplies catalog. Nevertheless, we urge teachers not to rely completely on such material and to make project-by-project decisions about how best to gather resources. The convenience of providing students access to commercial multimedia collections should be balanced against the fun and educational value of searching for your own resources.

Camcorder Tips

Students of all ages can use a camcorder effectively, but that does not mean that teachers should take their camcorder skills for granted. Some opportunities, such as a major field trip, might come only once a year, and scant experience can mean that students return from such a trip with little in the way of a permanent record. If we were to offer only one suggestion, it would be to allow the students to practice using the camcorder before they attempt to record an important event. Give students some fun and simple recording assignments, such as a favorite cook in action, the school's messiest locker, plants on the school grounds, or close-ups of the contents of a pocket, and then take the time to critique their work.

There are many books that explain basic camera techniques to hobbyists, and you will find it worthwhile to thumb through one. If you intend to use the video primarily to capture individual images for computer projects, here are some additional suggestions to consider:

◆ Show students how to identify what is informative or interesting and get a tight shot of it. Students seem to capture video images that are too distant and too general. There is nothing wrong with capturing images from a variety of distances, but generally the close views are most useful.

◆ Do not pan a scene and assume you will be able to capture later what is useful. Capturing still images from video works best when you have a still image to work with. Pause for ten to fifteen seconds when recording individual scenes you expect to be useful.

◆ For the best shots, students should set the camera to extreme wide angle and move it toward the object until they get the image they want. Most students intuitively take the wrong approach to capturing close-ups. They tend to stand at a comfortable distance from the object and then zoom in with the telephoto. Getting close to an object with a wide-angle setting will increase the amount of the image that will be in focus. The students may find themselves on their hands and knees in the dirt, with the camera two inches from a wildflower, but the picture will be great.

◆ Always carry an extra battery.

◆ Read the instruction manual so you know, among other things, how to stop the camera from stamping the time and date on the recording. ✳

Because scanners are used to capture images that already appear on paper and because teachers tend to be familiar with many sources of this type, it may be most productive to comment on a few resources teachers may overlook.

Coloring Books

Coloring books provide images that are nearly ideal for scanning. Because the images are drawn simply, emphasizing only the essential details, the quality of the captured images tends to be very high even when they are scanned with inexpensive equipment. Also, the images are already drawn in line mode, so images captured from coloring books can be saved in files that do not take up very much disk or memory space. Coloring book images also lend themselves to a more active role for students. Students can label, color, and incorporate parts of the images into their own artwork.

Theme coloring books are published for a variety of audiences. College students enrolled in human anatomy or neuroanatomy, for example, frequently use specialized coloring books to study the subject matter of these courses. The students are asked to use colored pencils to indicate certain structures or differentiate organ systems in a complex line drawing. Other coloring books emphasize specific topics, such as butterflies, mammals, plants and animals of Rocky Mountain National Park, or natives of the northern plains. Coloring books are frequently published by organizations such as state historical societies, groups with an interest in wildlife management or preservation, the national park system, and major museums. These coloring books are most easily found by visiting shops run by the organizations. Several publishing companies also offer a variety of publications in coloring book form. These resources are most likely to be found in large bookstores. Often bookstores have only some of the coloring books available and may need to special order the ones you are interested in.

Those producing or sponsoring coloring books have different motives. In many cases, their intent is to make money, and scanning images from the books would be regarded as copyright infringement. Teachers might be surprised to learn that companies have different policies on this matter. A careful reading of the copyright information, which is usually located on the inside of the front cover, may yield the requisite information. Many companies deny access to the entire contents of the coloring book. Others allow a specific number of images to be used for projects. It is also sometimes worth the time to write to the organizations that sponsor coloring books you are interested in using; some allow images to be used for educational purposes. (We discuss this topic in more depth in Chapter 11.)

World Wide Web

You know the Web provides access to hypermedia and is rich in high-quality images. Although Web browsers allow you to save any image that strikes your fancy, actually doing so is a questionable practice (which we discuss in Chapter 11). If you see an image you would like to use, you should contact the owner of the Web page before taking it.

Search for free clip art

The Web offers an alternative you might consider. Several sites specialize in organizing collections of images for public use. Try using a search engine and the word "clip art" to get started (see the search engines in Chapter 6, page 217).

Student Art

Another scanning resource to consider is student artwork. Students can draw or paint images relevant to a particular topic, and these creations can be scanned for inclusion in projects.

Creating multidisciplinary linkages

Two factors particularly recommend this source. First, working with student art provides an opportunity to create a unique multidisciplinary linkage. Art can contribute to other content areas, and the work in content areas can provide opportunities for artistic expression. This relationship may be informal, simply by extending the typical content of a science or history course, or it may involve a more formal cooperation between two classes and two instructors.

Engaging student artists actively

Second, drawing on student artistic talent showcases the unique abilities of some students who may otherwise receive little attention in a science or history classroom. Artistic talent is far from perfectly correlated with the other academic talents teachers encounter. Providing artistic students an opportunity to contribute may also engage them more actively with the course content.

Clip Art and Sound Clip Collections

Images and sounds can be purchased from a variety of sources. Commercial photos have long been available to those who are willing or able to pay. Advertising agencies or publishers may deal with vendors of **stock photos** (collections of images to use for a fee) rather than attempt to generate their own pictures. If an agency wants a photograph of an Alaskan fishing village, for example, it is certainly less expensive to purchase an image than to send a photographer to Alaska.

Collections of images are available to computer users. These collections have generally been targeted at desktop publishers, but the collections about places, cultures, land formations, historical events, or biological organisms also have relevance for classrooms. It is possible to purchase CDs containing 100 butterflies, mammals, scenes from Germany, and many similar collections for about $20. CDs containing over one thousand PICT images are available from another vendor. These resources are often advertised as royalty free. Owning a collection of royalty-free clips allows the use of these resources for classroom projects without concern for copyright restrictions. Collections of sound clips—often sound effects and background music—are also available. Personal computer catalogs are a good source for these CDs.

Finding the educational applications

These resources are not always marketed in ways that emphasize educational applications. Products of this type will eventually become more prevalent for the education market, however, and will be offered through outlets familiar to teachers. A few specific suggestions for locating these resources are included at the end of this chapter.

Emerging Technology

Background Music

Students often have a strong interest in using music to embellish their multimedia projects. Music can create an emotional background for presentations, and the message in carefully selected popular songs often seems a way to emphasize the intended message. However effective in accomplishing student goals, unrestricted use of music violates copyright restrictions. The restrictions are most extreme when the multimedia project is to be presented on the Internet. Specific copyright issues are addressed in Chapter 11.

It is possible to purchase soundtracks in much the same way as it is possible to purchase clip art. You will not be able to locate tunes from the most recent Top 40, but you will be able to find tracks that will serve as an effective background for presentations.

SmartSound from Sonic Desktop Software takes a unique approach. The Maestro component of this software allows the user to select from a series of options to locate an appropriate musical selection. The basic CD allows the

user to indicate how the music will be used—for example, as an opener, to accompany action, or as a background. The user then indicates how long a segment is desired. After several more choices (including style and instrumentation), the program offers and opens the proposed composition in the editor. If the composition is satisfactory, the editor allows the music to be exported in several different audio formats (see audio file formats, page 348).

The editor also provides another very interesting opportunity. The musical compositions are made up of many small individual segments—musical phrases. The user can work directly with these segments to modify the existing composition or create an entirely new composition from scratch. It is something like having your own musical construction set. This basic approach can be expanded by purchasing additional CDs that focus on specific themes (e.g., holidays, drama and documentary, classical masters). ✳

CAPTURING SOUND

How sounds are captured

The process of capturing sound bears many similarities to the process of capturing a graphic image. The process in both cases requires that an analog signal be converted into a digital signal, which, in both cases, is accomplished using specialized hardware. The hardware may come built into the computer or may require a special board. A microphone or other source of audio input connected to this hardware brings an audio signal into the computer. The specialized hardware then converts the analog signal into a digital signal that can be stored and used in computer applications. As with the conversion of the analog graphics signal, several variables come into play in converting an analog sound signal.

The first variable concerns the accuracy with which the analog signal is converted to a digital signal. Analog sound is represented as a continuous sound wave. The conversion to a digital form is accomplished by representing this continuous wave in discrete steps. The more steps there are, the more accurately the original information can be represented. A digital representation allowing 16-bit sound divides the sound wave into 65,536 steps. Hardware allowing 8-bit sound allows 256 steps in the sound wave to be differentiated and to have a lower level of accuracy. This difference is noticeable, but for most applications is not of great importance. As with graphics, the bit depth of the representation influences the size of the file that ends up being stored.

The other variable associated with sound digitizing is the **sampling frequency**, which is the number of times per second that a digital representation of the analog signal is produced. Sampling frequency is usually described in thousands of samples per second, or kilohertz (kHz). A typical sampling frequency is 22 kHz. For storage, sounds are often stored at 11 kHz. Both the bit depth and the sampling frequency influence quality and storage requirements. The CD-recorded music that you listen to is probably stored at a bit depth of 16 and a sampling frequency of 44.1 kHz. The sound recorded in the applications described in this chapter would more likely be recorded at a bit depth of 8 and a sampling frequency of 11 kHz. The difference in sound quality is noticeable but acceptable for most purposes. A 10-second sound recorded at the lower-quality settings would require about 115 kilobytes of disk space.

The method for recording sounds can be fairly simple. For example, many newer Macintosh computers have sound capabilities built in and do not require an extra board. Applications that support sound usually open an audio palette when the user selects the menu bar option allowing sound to be recorded. Figure 9.10 shows the audio palette from HyperStudio.

Using a sound palette

The operation of the sound palette is straightforward. The user clicks the record button with the mouse, speaks into the attached microphone, and clicks the stop button when finished. The play button allows the recorded sound to be played back. A name for the sound is entered in the selection field. When the save button is clicked, the sound is attached to the stack. A sound can be attached to a button (to be played when the button is pushed) or a card (to be played when the card appears).

It is easy to become so enamored of sounds that you clutter a presentation with a lot of useless noise. The skillful use of sound is another of those design-related matters for which there are probably no hard-and-fast rules. Our approach is a little different. Although student projects should be tasteful, our priority is the kinds of experiences that motivate students and help them work with information actively. Putting together a thirty-second speech about a butterfly or a fish can be a useful experience for a second grader. Agreeing to record a short poem that an elementary school student writes to

Increasing your students' motivation

FIGURE 9.10
HyperStudio Audio Palette

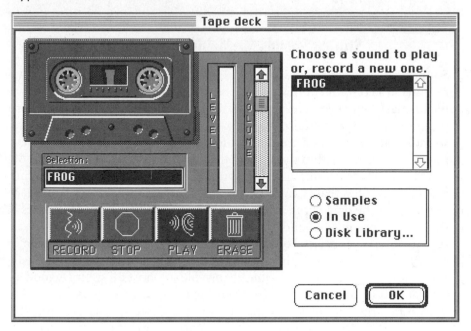

accompany a drawing can increase her motivation to write the poem. As a teacher, you will need to consider specific situations and determine when working with sound would meet the criteria of increased motivation or more active involvement with information.

LEARNING WITH SOUND AND GRAPHICS TOOLS

Sounds, pictures, and content knowledge

Up to this point, the discussion in this chapter has focused mainly on techniques of getting sound and pictures into the computer and manipulating these sources of information once they have been transformed into digital form. These are obviously very practical skills for anyone who wants to work with multimedia. What may not be obvious, though, is what these skills have to do with learning more traditional content knowledge. We hope that the background from other chapters has provided some insights into how these skills may facilitate the active manipulation of information. It may also be useful to take a more direct approach and list some of the ways in which working with sound and graphics can contribute to traditional learning.

Storing Sounds for Multimedia Productions

Sounds can be stored as independent files or as resources (a component that is part of a mixed file format). When you create a multimedia program with HyperStudio or Kid Pix, any sounds that are included are usually incorporated as resources within the stack or the multimedia file. Applications also store sounds as independent files; that is, the file contains nothing but the data necessary to reproduce a sound. Like graphics, sounds can be stored in several different formats. HyperStudio can store a sound as an SND (the native Macintosh sound format) file. The audio interchange file format (AIFF) is used by many software applications that produce files to be loaded by other programs and other hardware platforms. Windows sound applications frequently use the WAV format. There are even generic formats intended to be shared through the World Wide Web. For example, the AU format is commonly used as a component of Web pages because it can be interpreted by Web software running on several different hardware platforms.

We offer educators advice regarding sound file formats similar to that mentioned concerning graphics file formats. First, relevant educational packages that can handle multiple formats are an advantage. For example, HyperStudio can load AIFF, SND, WAV (Waveform Audio Format), AU (mu-law, the most common Internet format), MOD (music files), and QuickTime sound files (Latess, 1995). This versatility provides HyperStudio users with an advantage when the interest is in incorporating sounds not originally recorded with the host program. A good example is loading and using sounds recorded within Kid Pix or sounds shared through the Web. Second, it is useful to acquire a utility capable of converting sound files from one format to another (e.g., SoundConverter). This option requires several steps and greater experience. However, a conversion program does increase what you can accomplish when your existing software applications are limited in the file formats they can handle.✷

Two important proposals in Chapter 2 were that (1) certain external tasks or activities increase the probability that students will engage in desirable cognitive behaviors and (2) those external activities can provide a purpose and meaningful context for important thinking and learning behaviors. To illustrate these possible links, let's identify some of the actions required when students use sound and graphics tools in projects.

Projects can require that students search for sounds or graphics that exemplify a particular principle or justify a particular argument. Images that students have captured and labeled are more realistic than schematic drawings and are more meaningful because students themselves have collected the examples. To find appropriate examples, they must thoroughly understand the principle or argument to be demonstrated and evaluate alternative sources of information to find an appropriate illustration. What pictures could be collected at a zoo to provide examples of carnivores, and which would illustrate herbivores? Which poem demonstrates the rhythm of iambic pentameter?

Teachers may also require that students identify the features present in visual or auditory information. Students may be required to find the esophagus in a dissected frog or the point at which the oboe begins to play in a piece of music. When a student is asked to use computer tools to label images or mark the point at which a specific sound is present, identification skills are likely to be engaged.

Images and sounds lend themselves to comparisons and contrasts of many type—for example:

◆ Illustrate the difference between a moth and a butterfly.
◆ Illustrate the difference between a cocoon and a chrysalis.
◆ Compare the sounds of an oboe and a bassoon.
◆ Discriminate among major thirds, minor thirds, major sevenths, and minor sevenths (musical chords).

Sound and graphics tools and meaningful learning

As we noted at the beginning of this chapter, education presents students with information in the form of sounds and graphic images, but students often do not have opportunities to manipulate information in these formats. Students are inundated with graphics and sounds, but they seldom act on this information directly. Sound and graphics tools provide opportunities for manipulation and exploration.

SUMMARY

Students normally play a receptive role when relating to information represented in the form of images or sounds. Tools for manipulating images and sounds allow students to relate to these forms of information more actively.

Technology allows users to create original images or capture representations of existing images. Software applications that allow images to be created and modified can be categorized as paint and draw programs. These applications differ in their representation of images.

Because a paint program allows the manipulation of images at the individual pixel level, it is probably the most general educational application. Draw programs are used to create and manipulate graphic objects rather than individual pixels. Draw programs may be of special value when precision illustrations are required.

Paint programs differ widely in cost; more expensive programs tend to offer more tools. If a school decides to purchase many copies of a less expensive program, it should also consider making a small number of copies of a more expensive program available. One useful feature of more expensive programs is the ability to open and save files in different file formats. Unfortunately, different kinds of computers and different software programs store graphic images in different ways. It is sometimes necessary to convert an image stored in one format to a different format so that other computers or programs can access the image.

Image capture can be accomplished with a scanner or video digitizer. Scanning is used to capture images that already appear on paper. Video digitizers transform the analog signal generated by a camcorder, videocassette player, or television tuner into digital data that can be saved as a graphics file. Short video segments can also be captured using the input from some of these same devices. Combining video segments into video productions is now a real possibility using inexpensive video editing software and a powerful multimedia computer.

Sound capture is similar to video capture. Software and hardware are used to convert an analog signal to a digital signal. The quality of sound resources and the capacity required to store them are influenced by the bit depth and sampling frequency used in the conversion process.

To contemplate the role of graphics and sound tools in content-area instruction, it may be useful to consider the actions these tools allow students to exercise.

Activities

REFLECTING ON CHAPTER 9

◆ Locate an example of a commercial image collection you might use. Describe the properties of this collection, the tools you would use to work with the images, and some projects that might incorporate these images.

◆ Construct a list of criteria to use in evaluating a graphics tool designed for younger students.

◆ If your students had access to videocapture equipment, what types of graphics collections would you have them compile?

◆ Propose a three-minute video you would like to make. What primary sources would be involved?

◆ Familiarize yourself with a paint program. Demonstrate the program's capabilities to your classmates.

Key Terms

analog signal   *(p. 331)*
bit-mapped   *(p. 316)*
charge-coupled device (CCD)   *(p. 331)*
clipboard   *(p. 317)*
color lookup table (CLUT)   *(p. 329)*
color palette   *(p. 329)*
computer-assisted design (CAD)   *(p. 318)*
cross-platform   *(p. 329)*
dithering   *(p. 329)*
dots per inch (dpi)   *(p. 318)*
drag and drop   *(p. 339)*
draw programs   *(p. 317)*
flash memory   *(p. 334)*
graphic user interface (GUI)   *(p. 320)*

jaggies   *(p. 320)*
line art   *(p. 316)*
lossy   *(p. 328)*
object-oriented image   *(p. 317)*
paint programs   *(p. 316)*
pixels   *(p. 316)*
QuickTime   *(p. 336)*
sampling frequency   *(p. 346)*
scanner   *(p. 330)*
screen capture   *(p. 317)*
stock photos   *(p. 344)*
translators   *(p. 328)*
video digitizers   *(p. 330)*

*Resources to
Expand Your
Knowledge Base*

Books

Herrell, A., & Fowler, J. (1998). *Camcorder in the classroom: Using the videocamera to enliven curriculum.* Upper Saddle River, NJ: Prentice Hall.

Hardware Resources

Audio Board

Sound Blaster: An audio board for DOS/Windows platforms available from Creative Labs, Inc. (**http://www.soundblaster.com/home.html**)

Digital Cameras

JamCam: An inexpensive digital camera capable of 640 × 480 resolution from KidBoard. The camera, computer interface, and software cost less than $100. (**http://www.gojamcam.com/**)

SONY Mavica camera: Stores images and thirty-second video segments on standard floppy disks. From SONY Electronics Corporation. (**http://www.sony.com/mavica**)

There is a great deal of information about digital cameras on the Internet. Use any search engine to search for digital cameras.

Image Editing Software and Image Collection

Kid Pix: Is available for Macintosh and DOS computers from the Learning Company (**http://www.learningco.com/**). Information about Kid Pix products can be found at **http://www.kidpix.com**.

Photoshop: A high-end graphics editing program available for both the Macintosh and Windows operation systems. From Adobe Systems. (**http://www.adobe.com**)

SoundConverter: A shareware utility designed to convert sounds stored in one file format to other file formats. The best way to locate SoundConverter is with a World Wide Web search engine.

Audio and Photo Collections

Corel distributes a large number of CDs containing royalty-free, photographic-quality images stored in the Kodak Photo-CD format. Software on the CD allows the images to be exported to either Macintosh or Windows machines. (**http://www.corel.ca/products/clipartandphotos/index.htm**)

Many programs likely to be used in school settings (word processing programs, Web authoring programs, multimedia authoring programs) come with clip art collections.

Video Editing Software

Low-End Products

Avid Cinema from Avid Technology, available for both Macintosh and Windows platforms. (**http://www.avid.com**)

IMovie from Apple Computer, available for the Macintosh platform. (**http://www.apple.com/imovie**)

MovieWorks from Interactive Solutions, available for the Macintosh platform. (**http://www.movieworks.com**)

High-End Products

Adobe Premiere from Adobe Systems, available for both Macintosh and Windows platforms. (**http://www.adobe.com/premiere**)

Final Cut Pro from Apple Computer, available for the Macintosh platform. (**http://www.apple.com/finalcutpro**)

Audio Software

SmartSound from Sonic Desktop, available for Windows and Macintosh platforms. (**http://www.sonicdesktop.com**)

Chapter **10**

Learning from Student Projects: Knowledge as Design and the Design of Hypermedia

ORIENTATION

In this chapter we explore a major concept in both hypermedia and learning: design. It is typical to think of design as the process by which professionals construct useful products. Architects design buildings, for example, engineers design bridges or cars, and educational software developers design software. It also seems that motivated and active students design their own meaningful representations of their experiences. Design is thus a general concept that recognizes the importance of skilled behavior applied to the accomplishment of a meaningful goal.

The product of a design process is also called a design. A bridge is a design resulting from a design process. So are buildings, computer programs, and knowledge. Our focus here is on student-designed hypermedia and the learning opportunities when students participate in such projects. As you read, look for answers to the following questions:

Focus Questions

◆ What organizational, graphic, text, and interface design principles should students be aware of as they develop hypermedia projects?
◆ What student and teacher activities are typical of the various stages in a cooperative group project?
◆ How can the design of hypermedia facilitate the design of knowledge?
◆ How does the teacher interact with students to make the creation of projects valuable learning experiences?

353

Discovering the Painted Lady: A Second-Grade Adventure in Learning

Two second-grade girls sit in the front of the room working on a computer. From there you can hear one student ask the other, "But how do I change the font?"

"You need to click in the field and then choose Text Style under Edit."

Near the side of the classroom, two boys are looking at a butterfly distribution chart that has been taped along the length of the chalkboard.

"Do you think the painted lady butterfly lives in places that the monarch butterfly doesn't?"

"You find the monarch on the chart, and I'll find the painted lady, and we'll compare. Look, the monarch doesn't live here. What state do you think this is?"

A butterfly garden has been established in the corner of the classroom. Some butterflies have already hatched, and others have not emerged from their chrysalises. Pam Carlson, the teacher, is operating the video camera.

"Mrs. Carlson, this would be a good time to get a picture of the butterfly while it rests. See how the wings are straight up?"

In the back of the classroom is a large bookshelf covered with resource books about butterflies.

"Let's see if we can find out what that red liquid is called that's dripping from their wings. Do you think it's blood?"

Two students are standing at a chart reading over the questions: How much does the caterpillar weigh? What does the caterpillar eat? How does the caterpillar move? Will the caterpillar form a chrysalis or a cocoon? How long will it take for the butterfly to hatch out of the chrysalis?

These behaviors are atypical of most second-grade classrooms. These students are answering science questions that they themselves have posed. You will see shortly that what they do with their answers is even more unusual. Let's follow the project from the beginning.

The Project Begins

In the fall, one of the students brought in a monarch caterpillar, and the second-grade class observed its development. The excitement of this event led the teacher to explore other avenues to extend and enhance the experience. She was aware that live caterpillars could be purchased for each student to monitor the development of a larva. She had also experimented with classroom applications of technology and had involved several of her previous classes in the development of simple hypermedia projects. Most recently, she had seen examples of how graphics captured with a video camera could be used in computer applications. Her students could record the development of butterflies on videotape and capture the images for a cooperative class science project.

One morning in April, a box from the scientific supply company arrived. The teacher had decided that the students would not be given any information about the larvae. It would be their job to observe and try to identify which butterfly would emerge. The video camera was readied to capture the experience as each student put some food into a vial and then carefully placed the caterpillar in its new home.

The research began. The students pored over charts and books from the library, hunting for information that might yield the butterfly's identity. They weighed and measured the larvae, all captured on videotape. Each day, the teacher wrote a clue on the board that might help the students identify the larvae. One of the clues stated that this caterpillar ate the malva plant. Two boys approached the teacher.

"We think it's the painted lady butterfly, but we have one more thing to look up. This book says that the painted lady eats thistles. We need to find out if the malva plant is a thistle."

With the help of the clues and the information gathered from resource books, the class agreed that the developing larvae would hatch into painted lady butterflies. The video camera captured their development as the days progressed. As the students observed the process, they generated a list of questions to help in the research process.

The Hypermedia Project

The students had previously used the computer to write reports and create slide shows, so the teacher decided these skills would allow the class to create a project that would explain the butterfly unit to their parents. A question-and-answer format based on the students' research questions was chosen as the design model for the project. Each student would choose a question and be responsible for creating two cards. On the first card would be a field with the research question, a sound button with the student's recording of the question, and a button that would take the user to the second card. The second card would have a field with the answer to the question, a sound button with a recording of the answer, a button to go back to the question, a button to go to the next stack, and, when possible, a captured picture illustrating the answer.

The students already knew about fonts, font sizes, and styles from their experience with word processing. They were familiar with paint tools and the recording palette from using Kid Pix. So the teacher gave a general introduction to hypermedia authoring, focusing on the new elements of cards, buttons, and fields, and how to navigate through a stack. She then worked through the individual elements of building the two-card stack with one student. She created the first card in the stack, and the student created the second card minus the captured picture window. After the first stack was created, the experienced student became the teacher for the next student, again modeling the first card and monitoring the creation of the second card. This process continued until all students had created a two-card stack. The students then viewed the videotape and decided on images that would best represent the answers to their questions. Each image was captured and placed on the appropriate card.

Chris decided to find out what the caterpillar eats. In Figure 10.1 you see his answer: "It eats from the Malva plant."

"We think it's some kind of thistle," says Chris.

The completed project provided a chronology of the observed development of the painted lady and consisted of twenty-three two-card stacks connected with buttons and incorporating pictures and full-motion video.

FIGURE 10.1
Chris's Answer to the Question, "What does the caterpillar eat?"

THE PAINTED LADY PROJECT AND MEANINGFUL LEARNING

What is going on in this classroom? You probably realize from earlier chapters that these students are working on a hypermedia project as part of a science unit. Why should teachers add hypermedia projects to the more traditional experiences they provide students? How does involvement in such projects help students learn in a generative way? How do students go about putting a project together? In this chapter we provide some answers to these questions by exploring the topic of knowledge as design, discussing the process and basic principles of multimedia design, and describing several multimedia projects. We will return to Pam's classroom to follow her and her second-grade class as they develop several new projects. One of these projects will be presented in considerable detail so you will have a thorough understanding of what teacher and students do over the course of developing a theme-based project. You will learn how active learning, student collaboration, and technology come together as students prepare for and craft their project.

Active learning, collaboration, and technology

Useful knowledge

As we describe how students can design projects relevant to many content areas, we will try to instill one important perspective: meaningful learning as the result of a student's personal cognitive process of design. Useful knowledge can be considered a design (Perkins, 1986). Understanding and developing learning experiences around the concept that useful knowledge is purposefully generated by learners could have important implications for your classroom. The more traditional concept of design may also be important. One way to involve students is by challenging them with a design project. Designing a tangible product appears to facilitate the design of personal knowledge. As we proceed, we will explore both the design of products and the design of knowledge, as well as connections between these two types of tasks.

KNOWLEDGE AS DESIGN

Knowledge as information

How we think about knowledge can strongly influence our behavior as teachers and learners (Perkins, 1986). At least two perspectives are possible. The first views knowledge as information. Information is basically factual knowledge—ideas that are accumulated from various academic and life experiences and are known for the sake of knowing. Information is stored with the assumption that it will eventually prove useful. The perspective of knowledge as information is consistent with the metaphor of learning as transmission. A more knowledgeable person passes knowledge on to a less knowledgeable person.

Knowledge as design, learning as construction

In contrast, **knowledge as design** is knowledge adapted to a purpose. In the context of the model of active learning used throughout this book, knowledge as design is a probable product of meaningful learning. It is information generated by a student as a tool to accomplish some purpose. The perspective of knowledge as design is consistent with the metaphor of learning as construction. The learner with a purpose takes advantage of the information available to build personal understanding. A more knowledgeable person may facilitate the process of knowledge construction in a less knowledgeable person, but the person doing the learning must perform the acts of knowledge construction.

It is important to understand that the distinction between knowledge as information and knowledge as design is inherent not in the raw facts and experiences that learners encounter, but *in what the learner does with these raw materials*. You can test this position by considering content that most people would regard as basic factual information. What about those names and dates we all attempted to learn in history classes? What is the purpose of knowing that Columbus reached the New World in 1492? If you asked a middle-school student this question, you would likely hear that the purpose in knowing this date is to get a question right on the next exam. We might smile at the naiveté of this response, but do we have anything better to offer? Perkins (1986) proposes that even historical dates can represent a design. To understand how this works, think about the work of professional historians and how they might use landmark dates. For the historian, dates become tools of organization. A date can be a way to connect several simultaneous events, perhaps as a precursor to exploring possible cause-and-effect relationships. Dates can also serve to sequence events over time. Students can use dates the same way, but they are more likely to think like the middle-school students described here and not like apprentice historians. It is unfair, though, to place the blame totally on the student. The teacher may be as focused on the upcoming test as the student is.

A **design** is a tool developed to accomplish a purpose. Both concrete designs and knowledge as design fit this framework. What is significant here is that a purpose exists and is recognized from the outset. One of Perkins's (1986) favorite examples of a tool is a screwdriver. He suggests the absurdity of someone fashioning an object and then wondering what might be done with it. "Oh, this might be useful for mixing cookie dough. No, I think I'll use it to turn screws." Strange? Yet school learning often proceeds in just this way. A student often learns or memorizes information, thinking that this fact or idea should be useful for something, but at the time the student is often not exactly certain what. In contrast, the introductory example from Pam Carlson's classroom provides some good examples of purpose. The two girls in the example are trying to learn about the features of a computer program because they want to include some different text styles in the product they are working on. Two of the boys are studying the habitats of the painted lady and monarch butterflies because this information may provide a clue to the iden-

Purposes of learning facts

A design is a tool.

Immediate applications

tity of the mystery caterpillar that they are raising. In these situations, there is an immediate application for what students learn.

These experiences could have been very different. Pam might have asked her class to memorize the names of fifteen different butterflies. Students would probably have said they were learning because their teacher asked them to learn or because they were preparing for a test. In a way, students always learn with some purpose in mind; even storing information for a test might be considered a purpose. However, storing information has less long-term utility than generating personal knowledge and accumulating at least some experiences in how this knowledge can be used.

Active, purposeful learning

Emphasizing knowledge as design implies that students should spend a good part of their school time in active, purposeful learning. Some activities work particularly well to provide design experiences. For example, what if students designed useful products instead of studying them? What if they were able to play the roles of engineers, biologists, or historians and had to design a new piece of playground equipment, evaluate the pollution of a local pond, or develop a historical account of a past event? What if students designed software—in particular, instructional software?

LOOKING AT STUDENT-AUTHORED HYPERMEDIA

This chapter emphasizes student-authored hypermedia. Design projects could also be based on the development of databases, projects requiring the analysis of data with a spreadsheet, and various kinds of writing activities. (The idea of learning through design is versatile and does not require technology, but our focus in this book, of course, is on technology projects and on suggesting productive ways that teachers and students can use technology.)

Many possibilities for projects

Possibilities for hypermedia projects abound. Imagine that on the 125th anniversary of their state, an eighth-grade history class decides to design a World Wide Web account of important aspects of their state's history and contribute this project to the school and the state by posting this material on the school's server to be viewed during the year-long celebration. Imagine that as a science project, a second-grade class rears painted lady butterflies. The class decides to study different aspects of the butterfly life cycle (form and size at different stages, food consumed at different stages) and presents their observations to their parents as a hypermedia document. As you may have already guessed, this is exactly what was happening in Pam Carlson's classroom.

FOCUSING ON THE DESIGN OF HYPERMEDIA

Now that you have been introduced to the concept of knowledge as design, let's shift focus to the design of hypermedia. We begin with some guidelines for the development of hypermedia projects and then return to the topic of meaningful learning as design, emphasizing the opportunities for meaningful learning inherent in hypermedia projects.

PRINCIPLES OF HYPERMEDIA DESIGN: THE PROCESS OF DEVELOPING SOFTWARE

Hypermedia design is the purposeful process of developing a hypermedia product that is informative, interesting, and easy to use and understand. The production of truly professional and high-quality products that meet these standards is both science and art. Certain concrete skills can be learned. There are some standard questions developers should ask of themselves and guidelines that novice developers should follow. In this section, we concentrate on some basic guidelines that apply to HyperStudio creations and other simple development environments likely to be available to students: content organization, graphic design, text presentation, and development of the user interface (Apple Computer, 1989). The intent is to cover some of the basic principles that might be immediately useful in student-generated projects. Many of the principles described here are also relevant if students have the opportunity to author hypermedia materials for the World Wide Web.

CONTENT ORGANIZATION

An author in any medium exercises a fairly substantial degree of control over the sequence in which the reader or user encounters the various elements of information. For example, in a typical textbook, the author creates a structure so that the reader encounters ideas in a certain order and interrelates them in a certain way. From the textbook author's perspective, ideas flow into each other in a logical way, and the author's intention is to communicate this logical sequence to the reader. In a book, illustrations are placed close to text ideas that they explain or exemplify. Access to ideas or illustrations in other chapters or even earlier in the same chapter can be somewhat cumbersome for the reader. The reader can override the structure imposed by the author, but the reader will then have to search about blindly (thumbing back through a chapter to reread a section) or use a general guide (table of contents) or a specific guide (index) to find related material. The extent to which the author has planned for these alternate ways to interrelate ideas is likely to have been very limited. It is usually not assumed to be the author's responsibility to encourage or expedite nonsequential reading of the book. Books must be organized in a linear style, and the author must commit to a single organizational structure to accommodate this limitation.

Linear organization of books

Experiencing Content in a Variety of Ways

Nodes are units of information.

One of the advantages (and, some might say, curses) of hypermedia is that it allows the author to present content that users can experience in a variety of ways. The medium does not impose the limits. The user could theoretically move from any unit of information (called a **node**) to any other unit of information. The connections between nodes are called **links** (see Chapter 2).

Multiple linkages among ideas

Although it is a bit of an exaggeration to claim that all nodes in most hypermedia applications are interconnected, it is fair to claim that multiple linkages among ideas are available. To maximize the effectiveness of the presentation, the hypermedia author designs a structure by allowing some subset of all possible links. The structure the author imposes on the information shapes the environment in which the user can explore. The structure of linkages should be based on the author's analysis of the purpose of the software product and the possible logical connections the content expert sees in the material. The extent to which the user is allowed to control access is closely related to the product's intended purpose.

Organizational Structure

Organizational structure concerns the pattern in which nodes are linked (Jonassen & Grabinger, 1990). Here we examine three common structures: sequential design, hierarchical design, and web design. (They are shown in Figure 10.2.) Teachers wishing to help students develop hypermedia products might start with an understanding of these three basic structures. These models describe pure forms. In practice, the structure of hypermedia is often some variation on or integration of these structures.

Sequential Design.   The most basic way to present information is with a **sequential design,** in which each element leads directly to the next in logical sequence, with no other options for the user. You are already familiar with this structure because it is typically used in print media to present short descriptions or explanations. Television programs and educational videotapes also use this organizational structure.

Simplicity as an advantage

The major advantage of a sequential design is simplicity. Users are familiar with this format, and it is also relatively easy for the designers because there is no need to set up a complicated navigation system. The designer can concentrate on communicating a specific message logically, informatively, and interestingly. This may be the best structure for younger or beginning hypermedia designers. The sequential structure is especially useful when the purpose is to train the viewer in a specific skill.

Hierarchical Design.   A **hierarchical design,** as you can see in Figure 10.2, organizes content as a system of categories and subcategories. A user interacts with information of this type by moving through a series of choice

FIGURE 10.2
Common Organizational Structures for Hypermedia Projects

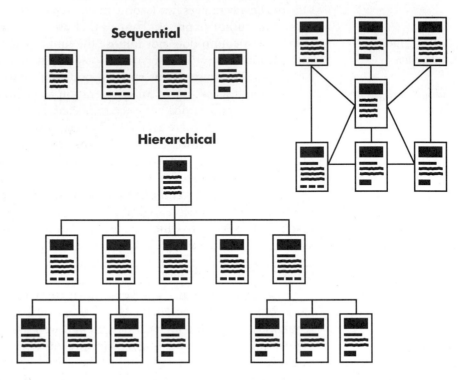

points—that is, **branches.** Each branch narrows the user's immediate focus in some way.

The Yahoo! Web directory, described in Chapter 6, is a good example of an extensive Web project organized in this manner. One purpose of a hierarchical structure is to organize information so users can find what they need without inspecting all the available information. A hierarchical structure also allows users to reorient themselves if they become lost. When they get disoriented, it is a simple matter to move back up the hierarchy and gain a sense of the structure for the entire site.

Organizing information   Structure is important in a second way. Even if the user is intended to process all of the information provided, the structure of the hypermedia can help the user organize what is learned. For example, certain systems for classifying biological organisms (remember phylum, class, order, family, genus, and species from high school biology) have a theoretical rationale. The student may develop an appreciation for such a classification system while navigating the structure to explore individual animals. The biologist's design for classification is integrated into the design of the hypermedia.

Web Design. A **web design,** as Figure 10.2 illustrates, takes fuller advantage of the potential of hypermedia by creating a complex set of connections among nodes. The intent is to provide users as much freedom as possible to follow links that address their interests and needs.

Advantages of network structures

A network structure allows the user the greatest flexibility in examining the content provided, and it allows the hyperauthor the related opportunity to create more open-ended, exploratory information environments. The World Wide Web is a good example of the power and problems of a network structure. Because the Web has been created by thousands of different authors who do not have to commit to a single design model and link to other resources as they see fit, the structure of the Web is freeform and complex. The practical value of flexibility depends to some extent on the user's ability to navigate the content effectively. It is quite possible for the user to become lost within the network because the richness of the many interconnections and the lack of a simple organizational structure can be confusing. Even when working within a hypermedia application intended for use on a single computer, the user may be able to move among definitions of key words, alternate documents making a similar point, illustrations, other illustrations providing greater detail of segments of earlier illustrations, selections from speeches or music, and short video pieces. Each of these items might be considered a node, and when it is understood that the user can enter and leave many nodes using different links, the difficulty some users might have in using the network becomes apparent. A user who gets sidetracked can have difficulty picking up the initial theme again. The human factors issue of how to assist the user in navigating complex hypermedia systems has become an interesting area of inquiry. You might recall that we discussed how some learners had difficulty with hypermedia in Chapter 7 (page 271).

GRAPHIC DESIGN

Appearance and content of material

Graphic design concerns the appearance and content of the material appearing on the computer screen. The purpose of careful graphic design is to make this displayed information as informative, easy to understand, and interesting as possible. This section provides an overview of selected topics likely to be applicable to student developers. While these are sound principles that can guide the graphic design process, truly outstanding products also arise from experience and creative talent.

Screen Layout

Facilitating use

Objects—buttons, pictures, or text fields—should be placed and grouped in a way that facilitates the user's activities. One way to develop a strategy for screens of a certain type is to make use of a **grid:** a pattern of lines that organizes the placement of objects and maintains consistency across similar screens (see Figure 10.3). A grid does not have to be complicated to be effective; it may be

FIGURE 10.3
Layout Grid

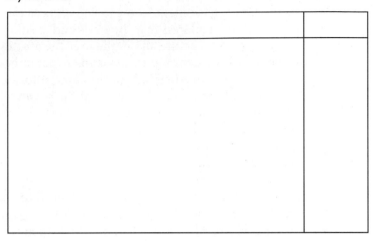

merely a line dividing the screen into two main areas. The layout used in Figure 10.3 might be used to present a series of illustrations. As you can see in the figure, the lines designating key areas of the screen do not have to appear on the screen.

Here are some guidelines for screen layout:

◆ Buttons (see pages 303 through 308) should usually appear along the edges of the screen. Make an exception when a button has an impact on just part of the screen. This might be the case when the button would reveal some hidden information such as labels for a diagram. The button should then appear adjacent to the object or area it influences.

◆ Group buttons together that serve similar functions. Buttons that appear on all cards should also be separated from buttons that are card specific.

◆ Use size to control the user's attention. Allocate the most grid space to the most important elements.

◆ Do not abandon the grid concept just because the screen displays only text. A screen of solid text is dull and hard to read. Organizing text elements on the screen can increase both readability and interest (see the next section on design principles for text; Apple Computer, 1989).

Try evaluating the principles of screen layout as they apply to the example in Figure 10.4:

◆ Could you sketch the grid that was used to organize this screen?

◆ Would you organize a set of screens containing a picture, text information, navigation buttons, and buttons establishing topical links in any other way?

◆ Have the general guidelines for screen layout been followed?

TEXT PRESENTATION AND WRITING STYLE

Communication, legibility, motivation

Principles for using text in hypermedia emphasize clear communication, legibility, and motivation. In general, hypermedia will not present the user screen after screen of continuous text, for several reasons. First, screens of solid text are difficult to read, so designers are encouraged to present text in

FIGURE 10.4
Sample Screen Layout

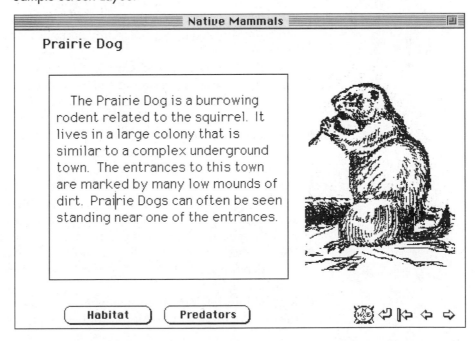

chunks surrounded by space for greater legibility. Second, hypermedia is based on the notion of connecting specific idea units in complex ways. Small blocks of text rather than continuous screens of text are best suited to constructing these connections. Usually the text component of hypermedia prepared for younger readers will read differently from extended text.

Placement and appearance of text on screen

Text layout goes beyond writing style and statement length to encompass the placement of text on the screen and the appearance of the text itself. Briefly summarized, the text on the screen should be easy to read, and special embellishments (special fonts, bold type, size) should be limited to situations in which it is important to draw the user's attention to something unique and specific. Teachers introducing any kind of program allowing text display (word processing, a paint program, HyperStudio) are likely to find that students will manipulate text characteristics unnecessarily at first. It is great fun to experiment with the many elements of text appearance, and this process of experimentation is one way for student designers to become familiar with the possibilities. However, at some point, the student as designer needs to consider how these different options might be used most productively to communicate with the user. Following are some general guidelines for designers of text (Apple Computer, 1989):

◆ Text messages should be concise. When it is important to communicate complex ideas or large amounts of information, consider identifying the important ideas and presenting them as separate but linked nodes. Avoid the use of scrolling fields except for special circumstances. (Scrolling fields allow the user to control the display of a large document using a mouse or the keyboard. The text scrolls, or moves up and down on the screen, as directed by the user. Only part of the total document is visible at any one time.)

◆ Text should be easy to read. Consider issues such as font size, line spacing, and margins. Lines should be neither too long nor too short. They should not stretch from one edge of the screen to the other, nor should they be so narrow that they consist of only a couple of words.

◆ Consider presenting text in several different fields within the same screen display. A title or heading can be separated from the main body of text, or distinct ideas can be separated from each other.

◆ Do not overuse multiple fonts, font sizes, or font styles. Use larger fonts, bolding, or underlining to bring attention to titles, important ideas, or key terms. When techniques for distinguishing text are used too frequently, specially designated text is no longer special.

◆ Use special fonts sparingly. For example, script is comparatively difficult to read, but it might be used to designate entries from a special source such as a diary.

◆ Keep in mind that the user of a hypermedia document may interact with the document on a different machine from that on which the document was created. If a particular font is not available on the user's machine, unexpected results may occur. For example, the default font may be larger than the intended font and, as a result, part of the intended message may no longer be visible.

It is probably fair to argue that the hypermedia author typically does some preprocessing of information for the user. Unless the user is expected to develop an appreciation for original documents or gain experience in working with primary sources, the author provides a service by identifying and summarizing important ideas, isolating individual ideas as nodes, and providing some appreciation for the structure of the content area through the links among the nodes. Those situations in which the user might be linked to original documents (historic documents, diaries, scientific reports, legal opinions, poems) represent special cases in which the user is expected to gain some unique benefit from interacting with primary sources.

Educational benefits warrant ignoring design guidelines.

Design principles emphasize using text in a controlled fashion—for example, keeping text segments short and simple. Teachers may want students to write more extensively. Thus, in some situations, the goals of learning from the project and of meeting ideal design guidelines may be in conflict. One solution to this dilemma is to realize that the hypermedia product does not need to contain all of the writing the student has done related to the project.

USER INTERFACE AND NAVIGATION

The hypermedia author must give considerable thought to the practical mechanisms by which the potential user will interact with the information provided. Collectively, these mechanisms represent the **user interface**. Careful development of the interface is especially important if the structure of the hypermedia is to allow the user to make choices about what will be experienced. If the user is to exercise a substantial degree of control over interaction with the material, he or she must have some idea what the hypermedia product is about and how the material is organized. At any point, the user must know what actions are possible and what the consequence of each action is likely to be. The user must also have some idea of where he or she is within the total body of information and how to get from one location to another. Finally, it is ideal if the mechanisms by which these goals are accomplished are either intuitively obvious or require very little learning time. The goal is to allow the user to think about the material, not about what must be done to interact with it.

Thinking about the material

Menus and Maps

Identifying topics in hypermedia

It is often helpful to provide a main screen that identifies the major topics covered by a hypermedia product. With World Wide Web projects, this is a common way to use the home page. By identifying the topics, the author gives the user a sense of the scope of the material available and a way to identify what has and has not been covered. A **menu** provides a list of the topics. This list might be presented using text or perhaps some form of graphical representation. In contrast, a **map** identifies the components of the presentation, as well as the main links among the components (see Figure 10.5). Maps are of particular value when the hypermedia product has a complex structure and allows the user many choices.

Buttons

In most forms of hypermedia, user actions are usually initiated by clicking a button. **Buttons** are areas of the screen that respond to commands issued by the user, such as clicking with a mouse, touching the screen, or pressing a designated key. Buttons offer an intuitive method of taking action. This is why buttons and the touch-sensitive screen are used in situations when instruction must be minimal and inexperienced users are many (as at kiosks in a museum or shopping mall). Buttons also provide a useful way for both the hypermedia author and the user to exercise control. By programming the allowable actions as buttons, the author can offer the user a specified set of alternative actions and allow the user to control when an action will be initiated and which action will be taken.

Buttons allow students to control actions.

FIGURE 10.5
Graphical Menu Developed by a Middle-School Student

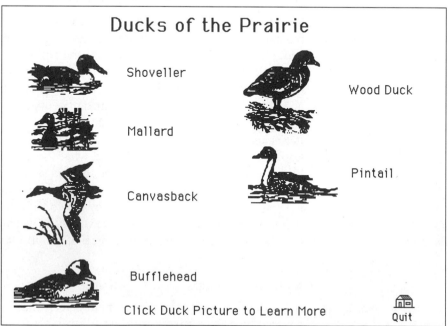

Ducks of the Prairie

Shoveller

Wood Duck

Mallard

Canvasback

Pintail

Bufflehead

Click Duck Picture to Learn More

Quit

Standard Buttons.   Authors working in a popular format (e.g., card-based hypermedia systems, Web pages) have developed certain conventions. Some button icons are used consistently to mean certain things. Although using buttons in unconventional ways is perfectly acceptable to the computer, this practice can confuse users and will clearly label the hypermedia author as a novice. For example, novice developers often use the "home icon" (a picture of a house) to return users to an initial menu. Although this might make some sense, experienced HyperStudio users expect the application they are using to be exited when the home button is clicked. A little experience with public domain or commercial hypermedia should be sufficient to pick up how standard button icons are used. The intended use of a button can also be communicated through an informative label (e.g., Next Card).

Project design and learning opportunities

These guidelines should acquaint you with basic principles that can guide the creation of hypermedia. Obviously, the guidelines are more concerned with the quality of the hypermedia product than with the learning experience students might have in creating such products. Nevertheless, teachers must be sensitive to areas in which product design and learning opportunities may be in conflict and to the amount of time necessary to develop high-quality hypermedia products.

In the next sections, we integrate the theoretical ideas of learning through the process of design and concrete suggestions for how to accomplish one type of design project—hypermedia—in classroom applications. For reasons related to practical matters of teacher time and resources and to the design of learning environments likely to encourage active learning, these classroom applications often require that students work together in cooperative groups. We like to think of these groups as design teams. We start with a short general discussion of cooperative learning and eventually move to an example of cross-grade hypermedia design.

STUDENT COOPERATION: FUNDAMENTALS FOR DESIGN TEAMS

You have encountered cooperative learning a number of times in this book. We have presented cooperative learning as (1) an essential component in many plans for restructuring the mission and methods of schools; (2) a way to make learning active and meaningful; (3) a partial solution when technological resources are in short supply; and (4) a productive way to implement multimedia projects. You will also learn that cooperative learning provides a meaningful way to involve students with varying levels of skill and with special needs. Cooperative methods can play a highly important role in learning with technology. We feel it is worthwhile to explore cooperative learning more directly. Here we want you to consider the basic principles of cooperative learning and acquire some concrete ideas for using cooperative approaches to student projects. This material should acquaint you with conditions that are essential to productive cooperative environments and leave you with the sense that you would know where to start should you decide to use cooperative methods.

Basic principles of cooperative learning

Cooperative learning techniques are hardly new. In elementary school, you probably took turns quizzing a classmate with flash cards. You may have encountered situations in your college experience in which an education instructor divided your class into groups and asked you to discuss a topic, generate possible solutions to a teaching problem, or practice a specific teaching skill. You probably participated in these experiences with little training and with mixed results.

What has changed is that more formal cooperative learning methods have been proposed and carefully evaluated at different grade levels and in different content areas. Details can be important. Not every situation in which one student interacts with another is effective. What has come from this research are some concrete and practical learning methods and an understanding of key components that influence student learning. We cannot review this entire body of work or present all of the many successful strategies that have been developed, but if the ideas presented here appeal to you, there are some very helpful sources you might consult to learn more (Johnson,

Computer-based projects provide many different opportunities for cross-age interaction.
(© Michael Zide)

Johnson, & Holubec, 1991; Slavin, 1991, 1995). See Resources to Expand Your Knowledge Base at the end of the chapter.

At the most basic level, **cooperative learning** refers to a classroom situation in which students work together to help each other learn. The idea is to create an environment in which students want each other to succeed and work to motivate and teach each other, to accomplish this goal. Typically, cooperative groups consist of two to five students and are often purposely made heterogeneous, that is, mixed with respect to ability, gender, and ethnic group. Cooperative groups provide a way to include students with special needs.

Team rewards and individual accountability

Research indicates that *team rewards* and *individual accountability* are especially important for success. **Team rewards** are some form of recognition for team success. These rewards can take many different forms: certificates, posting pictures of outstanding teams, and special activities, for example. **Individual accountability** means that team success is based on the individual accomplishments of all team members. For example, each team member may be expected to take a test on the content covered, and team performance is based on all of the scores earned. Sometimes scores are compared with past performance so that each team member has an equal opportunity to contribute to team success (Slavin, 1991).

Considering different learning goals

In considering specific cooperative methods, it is important to recognize that different methods are best suited to different learning goals. Some cooperative methods were designed to help students master content typified by single right answers, and other methods focus on more open-ended problems requiring data acquisition, analysis, and synthesis. Some methods retain a fairly typical role for the teacher; that is, the teacher presents the content. Other methods require the teacher to focus on facilitating the learning process and to allow students to take more responsibility for the content.

GOING BEYOND FACTUAL INFORMATION

The cooperative methods of greatest relevance here are those that have been developed to involve students in group tasks requiring both the acquisition and the application of knowledge and skill. These approaches, referred to as **task specialization methods** (Slavin, 1995), require that individual students contribute in unique ways to the accomplishment of a group task. Task specialization methods require individual accountability and team rewards. In task specialization methods, the quality with which the task is completed determines the team's reward. Individual accountability is accomplished through task specialization. Each student must accept unique responsibility for some aspect of the assigned task, and the group's performance thus depends to some extent on the contribution of every group member. The Tom Snyder products described in Chapter 7 (Cooperative Problem Solving, pages 261 through 264) use this approach.

Group investigation is a task specialization method that results in the production of group projects associated with a general theme proposed by the teacher (Sharan & Sharan, 1992). There are several reasons to consider this approach.

Guidelines for classroom projects

First, concrete strategies for group investigations have been worked out in detail, and some very useful guidelines have been established to help teachers implement group projects in their classrooms. Second, the group investigation model can be easily adapted to technology-based projects. Group investigations are intended to result in an informative summary report and presentation, and a multimedia project can serve as the summary report or support the group's presentation to the entire class. Finally, the effectiveness of the group investigation method has been carefully studied. Because the research base in support of technology-based group projects is limited, demonstrations that projects of a similar nature result in effective learning experiences are reassuring. Research demonstrates that group investigations result in significantly better performance than traditional learning activities (Slavin, 1995).

The group investigation model has been worked out in detail (Sharan & Shachar, 1988; Slavin, 1995), and you will probably stick close to this model when you implement group projects for the first time. With experience, you will discover what works in your classroom. Substituting a multimedia project for the final report may require some alterations. The system may also require some tweaking to meet the needs of your students, fit your teaching style, and be feasible within the amount of time you can allot. When you decide to approach a topic using group investigation, you do not have to limit student learning opportunities to those provided through cooperative group experiences. You might decide to initiate the unit of study in a traditional way. Perhaps students will work with a textbook and whole group instruction at first. These experiences might be used to establish background and develop some of the issues that might then be pursued through group investigation. Or you might decide to jump right in and initiate the study of a new unit with the group investigation process. Then as you think about the topics students have selected, you may feel the need to provide supplemental experiences. As the class moves through the time period allowed for the unit, it is appropriate to mix in other learning experiences and assignments. The group investigation process does not have to be the sole learning experience you use.

HYPERCOMPOSITION DESIGN MODEL

The hypercomposition design model (Lehrer, 1993; Lehrer, Erickson, & Connell, 1994) provides a concrete way to integrate many of the themes we have developed throughout this book. It deals specifically with hypermedia

Activities and Projects for Your Classroom

Planets

Students study the planets at many grade levels. Let's take a look at how the six stages of group investigation could be applied to this unit using HyperStudio as the presentation tool for the final project.

Stage 1: Identify the Topic and Form Student Groups   After viewing an introductory video on the planets, have students submit the name of the planet they would be interested in studying in greater depth. Divide the class into groups based on their choices.

Stage 2: Team Planning   Once the groups have been formed, the members of each one must decide on a plan for how their group will function. Will each member choose a special area to research, such as the planet's geology or its weather? Or will the team members gather information, come back to the group to share what they have learned, and then divide responsibilities?

Stage 3: Team Members Conduct Inquiry As the group members gather resources, ongoing decisions must be made as to what information should be included in the project. In this phase, it is important that students take detailed notes they will be able to share with group members. They should also keep in mind visual images that might help illustrate the concepts being summarized. For example, students might connect to the Tom Snyder laserdisc "The Great Solar System Rescue" and show clips that give graphical representations of the sizes of the planets.

Stage 4: Prepare the Final Report   The students in each group must now map out the project. Each group member can take on a specific role, such as being responsible for the graphics, entering the text, connecting the visuals, or developing the navigation system. Or each student can take responsibility for one planet feature, such as the makeup of the atmosphere, and be responsible for organizing all of the information sources related to that feature. When each group has its planet report put together, the class as a whole can decide how to integrate the different team projects. In what order should the planets be presented? What kind and how many introductory screens are needed? How will the project end?

Stage 5: Present the Final Report   The students in the class can view the finished project and question group members about information that may not be clear or that seems of special interest. The project can then be shared with other classes or parents. The project could be recorded on a videotape and saved in the library for future classes to use as a resource.

Stage 6: Evaluation   Although we call this the last step, it is important to realize that assessment comes into play throughout the project. The teacher should meet periodically with the groups and discuss what is happening. What kind of resources have been gathered? How was the information organized? How were decisions made as to what information should be included? Who took responsibility for what? What difficulties have been encountered, and how have group members attempted to solve problems? What suggestions do the group members have to improve future projects?✶

projects as content-area learning experiences and comfortably incorporates meaningful learning, cooperative learning, knowledge as design, and many other themes we have emphasized. The model is intended to guide teachers in the implementation of hypermedia projects. Although we feel it is important to offer concrete ideas that teachers can relate to, we are not suggesting that teachers must implement projects exactly as we have described them. Examples and models should provide you with principles, strategies, and ideas. Your own experiences will determine how you integrate these elements into classroom practice.

General framework based on the writing process

The hypercomposition design model was developed by observing and interviewing students as they completed hypermedia projects. The observations were then incorporated into a general framework to help other teachers facilitate hypermedia projects. The general framework for the model was based on a widely accepted model of the writing process (Flower & Hayes, 1981; Hayes & Flower, 1980) and shares many features with the model for group investigations you have just encountered. To create guidelines for hypermedia design, Lehrer (1993) extended the writing process approach (see writing process, Chapter 5, page 168) to include the generation of knowledge (it is not assumed that hypermedia authors have already learned what they will eventually present), attention to the special features of hypermedia, and the requirements of collaborative authorship. Note that hypermedia design is not proposed as a strictly linear process. In general, authors do work from the beginning to the end of a project, but a good deal of looping back occurs as work at later stages reveals the weaknesses of work completed at earlier stages. The model proposes that projects incorporate the major elements of planning, transforming, translating, and evaluating and revising.

PLANNING

The topics teachers propose to guide their students' hypermedia projects are usually broad. The intent is to allow the members of student groups to explore a bit and then concentrate on what interests them. In the initial planning stage, group members should attempt to define major topics, establish the basic format of the presentation, and work out how the group will function.

It is very possible that students will be so inexperienced with the general topic or with group processes that the group will be unable to make effective decisions. In this case, the teacher must offer advice. You may tell students to do some initial research and give them some sample sources of information. More specific decisions about topics and responsibilities may result from this initial investigation. This would be a great opportunity to propose a Web-Quest (see Chapter 6, page 232).

Students also might not function effectively in a group setting. Some students may dominate the decision making and leave others out. Others may not know how to listen, criticize, or accept criticism. The teacher might need to establish some guidelines for group functioning and monitor performance in this area.

The general tasks in planning the group project require the group to do the following:

1. Develop major goals.
2. Propose topics and the relationships among topics.
3. Propose a presentation format to fit this organizational scheme.
4. Establish team member responsibilities.

TRANSFORMING AND TRANSLATING

The transformation and translation phase consists of two general processes: collecting information and generating knowledge.

Collecting Information

Search strategies

To collect information relevant to project goals, students must identify potentially relevant sources through the use of effective search strategies, locate the information relevant to project goals, and employ some process to retain the information for later use. Search strategies could encompass methods as diverse as electronic searches of the card catalog in the school or local library, use of the index in books covering the general area of interest, and asking questions of people who might know something about the topic. Once good sources are located, students might use photocopying, note taking, audio recording, or video recording to collect the information. These skills could be novel, and some training might be necessary. Not all students know how to operate a camcorder, for instance. Students might also need to learn effective note-taking skills.

Creating information

The potential for creating information should not be overlooked. Students can conduct original experiments or replicate established procedures to gather original data, develop questionnaires to give to students from their school or local residents, or conduct structured interviews.

You will probably want to review samples of student work (notes, sources selected) to provide feedback and offer suggestions. One advantage of a project approach is the opportunity to help students learn to learn. Projects put more responsibility in the hands of students and require them to engage in diverse self-guided activities. Projects provide great opportunities, but students need guidance to profit from these opportunities. Students are likely to have the most experience processing information that a textbook author or a

Spotlight on Assessment

Evaluating Projects

For authentic tasks to achieve their potential benefits, student performance must be evaluated in ways that students both find informative and perceive as fair. Here we look at two assessment devices you might use to communicate expectations to students, guide your evaluation of projects, and communicate feedback to students. The specific components of these assessment devices (some authors have used terms such as *assessment rubrics* and *analysis guides* in a similar way) will vary with the nature of the project and with what you want to emphasize. What you want to emphasize might also be worked out in the project planning stage through negotiation with your students.

To provide a context for this discussion, let's propose a sample project:

> *Task:* Create a HyperStudio stack that presents your team's analysis and recommendation regarding beverage container recycling. This stack will be viewed by the general public in the city library and will urge the public to support the recycling plan you propose.

We will gloss over all of the activities required of you to facilitate this project and get right to how you might create useful assessment devices.

Continua of Descriptors

Generating continua of descriptors allows you to specify the competence areas to be used in the assessment process and to define specific levels of accomplishment within each competence area (Tierney, Carter, & Desai, 1991). The intent of the continua is to help the evaluator and those being evaluated identify levels of quality in prescribed areas. In implementing this approach, it is useful to create a form to present the assessment guidelines and communicate areas of strength and weakness clearly. The form might take the following general structure.

Project Title

Strong Performance		Needs Improvement
Competency 1		
Descriptor 1A	Descriptor 1B	Descriptor 1C
Competency 2		
Descriptor 2A	Descriptor 2B	Descriptor 2C
Competency 3		
Descriptor 3A	Descriptor 3B	Descriptor 3C

. . .

Because one of the goals in creating this type of form is to present information concisely, you might feel it is necessary to add material in which the descriptors are laid out in more detail.

Now let's develop continua of descriptors for our sample project. Again, in practice, we would urge you to develop assessment devices in collaboration with your students.

The project example might require evaluation in several general areas: domain knowledge and procedural skills, design skills, and team skills. Specific competencies could involve content coverage, argument communication, screen layout, graphics, user interface, involvement level of team members, and team support. Each area of competency would then be defined in terms of concrete levels of accomplishment. For example, for content coverage, the following categories might be used:

> *Exhaustive* coverage of multiple issues bearing on local recycling situation
>
> *Adequate* presentation of main recycling issues
>
> *Incomplete* coverage of important issues

The form built from these continua might look something like this.

Beverage Container Recycling Project

Strong Performance   **Needs Improvement**

Content Coverage

Exhaustive coverage of multiple issues	Adequate coverage of issues	Incomplete coverage of essential issues

Argument Communication

Persuasive use of logic and data	Adequate presentation of position	Unpersuasive or unclear argument

Screen Layout

Interesting display with proper and predictable placement of buttons and graphics; text attractive and easy to read	Understandable positioning of buttons and graphics; text readable	Confusing or disorganized placement of screen elements; text difficult to read

Graphics

Informative and interesting, with proper placement	Adequate information value	Graphics often unrelated to message or improperly placed

User Interface

Easy to understand; functions without error	Error free	Confusing or occasionally fails

Team Involvement Level

All students contribute in meaningful way	All students active	Some students uninvolved

Team Support

Exceptional praise and assistance	Adequate praise for teammates	Inadequate support; bickering

Holistic Scoring Guide

The holistic scoring method differs from the continua technique in the assignment of each project to a summary category. In making a holistic judgment, the evaluator could consider the same competency areas used in the continua method, but the descriptive statements associated with the competency areas have been organized to reflect different holistic levels of accomplishment. The evaluator has to determine which cluster of descriptors best describes the project and the process generating the project. The labels assigned to the categories are intended to reflect the nature of the holistic evaluation. Sets of terms—*beginning, intermediate, advanced; exceptional, adequate, marginal*—that seem suited to the nature of the project and to the type of feedback intended are used as category labels (Tierney et al., 1991).

A form is useful in guiding evaluators and providing expectations and feedback to students. A holistic guide for the beverage container recycling project might look something like this:

Beverage Container Recycling Project
Marginal Project

Projects may be classified as marginal because of the quality of the project or the process producing it. Marginal projects might be incomplete or inaccurate or might not function as they should. The process associated with a marginal project might not involve all team members, or team members might treat each other poorly. Specific characteristics might include:

Project does not establish sufficient background describing general problem of waste disposal and specific problems associated with the disposal of beverage containers.

The proposed recycling plan is sketchy and difficult to understand.

The arguments supporting the recycling plan are not persuasive.

Placement of buttons is haphazard.

Text segments ramble and make key points difficult to identify.

Message of graphics is frequently unclear.

Unfamiliar user would find it difficult to use this product.

Buttons strand user without a way to move on or do not work at all.

Project was completed by only some of the team members.

Comments of team members were frequently critical or did not provide constructive advice.

Adequate Project

Projects are described as adequate when they indicate a reasonable understanding of the problem and propose a logical solution. The entire team should make some contribution to the completion of the project. Specific characteristics might include:

The project presents an overview of the problem of waste disposal and provides specific information on difficulties created by beverage container disposal.

A reasonable plan for beverage container recycling is proposed.

Buttons controlling the presentation appear in a consistent screen location.

Text segments are concise and informative.

Graphics contribute to the message of the presentation.

Use of the project requires little instruction.

Buttons and other control devices function as intended.

All students make a unique contribution to the completion of the project.

Team members are positive in remarks made to other team members.

Exceptional Project

Projects are described as exceptional when the information provided is extensive, the arguments advanced are particularly persuasive, and the proposed problem solution is insightful. The project should be interesting for viewers and exhibit exemplary design principles. Team members should work to bring out the best in each other team member. Specific characteristics might include:

The project provides an extensive overview of the problem of waste disposal and specific information on difficulties created by beverage container disposal. An effort has been made to provide information that defines the problem at the local level. The presentation is well organized and interesting.

Multiple suggestions are provided for recycling beverage containers. The argument for recycling is persuasive.

Buttons controlling the presentation appear in a consistent screen location.

Text segments are concise and informative.

Graphics are informative and interesting.

Graphics are used to increase the impact of the basic message.

Use of the project requires little instruction.

Buttons and other control devices function as intended.

All students make a unique contribution to the completion of the project.

Team members go out of their way to encourage and assist each other.

Team members teach each other needed skills.

✳

teacher has already organized and thought through for them. Be careful that students are not left to drift aimlessly as they encounter new expectations.

Generating Knowledge

Organizing, summarizing, interpreting

Once they have gathered the raw information, students will need to organize, summarize, and interpret it. Some specific academic skills could be introduced at this point. Students might benefit from learning to outline, generate concept maps, or write summaries (Day, 1986). Also, some basic statistical procedures might be applied to quantifiable data. Statistical procedures can be as basic as determining the frequency of an event or finding the average of multiple measurements. Perhaps these data can be graphed in informative ways. This might be an opportunity to introduce students to spreadsheets and related data visualization capabilities. Students need to interpret what they have discovered. What are the major ideas? What are the causal factors that appear to be present? What alternative interpretations might be possible?

The other major task of knowledge generation involves the publication of what has been learned. One decision is determining the format for publication. Desktop publishing, electronic slide shows, and hypermedia have been discussed previously and represent alternative formats. The decision you and your students make will depend on the type of information to be conveyed, the equipment and time available, and the students' skills.

To summarize, the stage of transforming and translating includes processes involved in the collection of information and the generation of knowledge. Students working on projects would:

◆ Search and collect information.
◆ Develop new information.
◆ Select and interpret information.
◆ Segment information.
◆ Link information.

EVALUATING AND REVISING

Understanding and fixing problems

Authoring is not a one-pass process. Sometimes the product does not meet expectations. A variety of difficulties can occur within the product itself or in the way the product conveys information to users. In some cases, a problem is obvious as soon as a button does not take the user to the intended destination. In other cases, problems can be more subtle or even hidden from the author. For example, the author may assume an unrealistic level of background knowledge on the user's part and thus present new information too rapidly or briefly.

Evaluation is the process of searching for all of these difficulties and many more. It is really impossible to list all of the things that might go wrong; even experienced developers continually encounter new problems. We are always amazed when we attend technology demonstrations to see just how frequently experts encounter difficulties demonstrating the products they have created and worked with for hundreds of hours. We have found ourselves in the same situation several times. Because problems seem unavoidable, here are some suggestions for how to make the problems surface so that you or your students can understand and fix them. Note that we use the term *problems* to refer to problems in both the software and the content that the software was developed to present:

◆ *Software developers can learn to test systematically all planned and unplanned actions within programs that have been created.* It is sometimes users' unintended actions that cause problems. A developer can easily become focused on what he or she thinks should happen and forget that the eventual user does not have this same insight. When confused or without the benefit of knowing exactly what to do, users may do something that was not intended and cause a problem. So test a product for the unanticipated. For example, if the user is asked to type a number into a box, try typing "one" and not just "1." If you developed this product, you probably assumed the user would use a digit and not a word to represent a number.

Trying out products

◆ *Developers can ask naive users to try out products and carefully observe what happens.* Do naive users try to do things that were not intended? Do they become confused or say that they cannot understand the ideas presented? Listen carefully to what they have to say. You probably do the same kind of thing with papers you write for college classes. You ask a classmate or a friend to read your paper and tell you what he or she thinks. Consider a hypermedia product as another way to inform or communicate, and ask others what they think.

◆ *Test out products on different equipment* (preferably the exact equipment your target audience will use). Different equipment is the cause of most difficulties that experts encounter in novel situations. Programs have a nasty habit of not working exactly the same way on different machines or on machines using different versions of the operating system. Often the equipment used to develop software is more powerful (more memory, larger monitor) than the machines software users work on. A variation of this recommendation for Web page authors is to test the Web pages with different browsers.

Asking experts' opinions ◆ *Ask a content-area expert to review the product.* Commercial developers of educational software do this all the time. For example, if the product is in the area of history, history teachers and historians not associated with the project are asked to review it. As a classroom teacher, you might end up serving as the content-area expert responsible for this type of review. It might be useful to have several teachers participate in the review of hypermedia projects. One teacher might evaluate how effectively the product meets standards of effective communication (organization, clarity, grammar), and another might evaluate the factual accuracy and logic of arguments. Each of these procedures might identify limitations that the design group will want to take into account in upgrading the product's quality.

THE TEACHER'S ROLE IN THE DESIGN PROCESS

Now that you are familiar with some basic design principles, some of the fundamental ideas of cooperative learning, and at least one general model for student hypermedia projects, let's look at some of the implications of bringing such projects into your classroom. You may have already generated your own implications after considering some of the sample projects.

WORKS OF MIND

When teachers incorporate projects, many will need to adjust what they do and, in some cases, what they teach. Perkins (1986), who advocates the concept of learning as design, justifies the need to engage students in a different type of learning activity this way. His concern is that schools seldom allow students to do "works of mind" (original projects or investigations that are largely the responsibility of the learner). Schools teach students about math-

Focus

Experimenting with Different Structures and Linking Systems

Because students will likely have little experience in browsing or authoring hypermedia, teachers might want to consider the following suggestions for introducing the ideas of nodes and links. It is best to allow students to experiment with ways of partitioning and linking information before investing too much time in software development. Professional instructional designers use a process called **storyboarding,** in which they rough out the sequence of displays and activities to be incorporated in the software (an example of a storyboard appears in Figure 10.10 on page 399).

Students can do the same thing. They can represent nodes with sketches or brief statements entered on note cards. Each node might be thought of as the information the eventual user will view or hear at one time. These note cards can be tacked to a bulletin board and linked with lengths of yarn. It shouldn't be too difficult to imagine representing the different organizational structures presented earlier in this chapter in this manner. One interesting variation is to use sticky notes instead of note cards. These notes can be easily positioned on a blackboard and connected with chalk lines.✳

Learning by doing

ematics, history, and biology but do not allow students to do mathematics, history, or biology. One of the few exceptions Perkins notes to the principle of "learning about rather than doing" is in art. Students at most grade levels do works of art. Why? As educators, we recognize that a design like a picture can exist at a very elementary level. Even kindergarten students draw, paint, and sculpt objects from various materials. But most other content areas seem different. We often cannot think of what an elementary design in biology or history would look like. One reason is the assumption that an accumulation of information is required before a work of some form is possible. In many cases, however, the nature of the problem is scalable, and background knowledge can be acquired. Students can design a history of their own families or study the ecology of their classroom aquarium. If second-grade students need to know about the malva plant and the identity of marconium (the red liquid that Pam Carlson's students observed dripping from the wings of the butterfly emerging from the chrysalis) to understand their observations of butterfly metamorphosis, this information can be acquired and used in the designs they construct to account for their observations.

Lehrer and his associates (Carver et al., 1992; Erikson & Lehrer, 1999; Lehrer, 1993; Lehrer et al., 1994), as well as others (Brown, 1992; Harel, 1991; Harel & Papert, 1990; Pearlman, 1991; Resnick, Bruckman, & Martin, 1999; Toomey & Ketterer, 1995), have proposed that projects in which groups of students attempt to explain or teach with technology qualify as works of

Coaching small groups of students

mind. In a typical classroom activity of this type, the teacher coaches small groups of students as they pursue projects that fall within some general domain. The general domain refers to the topic designated for study by the curriculum: the Civil War, the life cycle of the butterfly, and so on. Individual projects prepared by different groups pursue the general topic in different ways or emphasize different aspects of the overall theme, depending on the interests and abilities of group members and the information that students encounter as they research the general topic. To maintain a student focus, teachers should intervene to redirect students only after careful consideration. Instead of direct intervention, teachers would be more likely to influence students by asking leading questions such as, "Why do we have historians? What do they do?" Carver et al. (1992) use Sheingold's (1991) phrase "adventurous teaching" to describe the tolerance teachers must exhibit to allow students the necessary freedom to construct knowledge. Students cannot truly function as junior biologists, historians, writers, or political advocates if teachers make key decisions for them.

Constructing knowledge

APPRENTICESHIP METHOD

If teachers do not transmit information and do not tightly control student activity, what do they do? It is useful to view the teacher's function as initiating students into the community of scholars appropriate to the area or areas being investigated (Lehrer, 1993). To develop domain-appropriate learning and thinking processes, students are engaged in tasks authentic to the domain within an apprenticeship relationship with the teacher and perhaps with other domain experts (people within the community). Students, as a result, experience activities as authentic tasks that might confront domain experts, and they acquire knowledge and problem-solving skills associated with these tasks. For example, a historian uses primary sources (original maps, diaries, letters, newspaper accounts, legal documents, pictures, personal interviews) to describe past events and explain past behaviors. The historian must locate sources, analyze the material for important information, integrate ideas into a logical account of behavior, and communicate an effective description and explanation of past events to others. Students can take on similar tasks using similar sources and engaging the same cognitive processes. The issues could resemble the topics covered in traditional textbooks (battles of the Civil War) or could be more unusual or local in orientation (for example, early education in your community—the first teacher, building, student characteristics). Often activities are multidisciplinary because scholarship of this type frequently does not confine itself to a single traditional content area, such as reading, mathematics, or science.

Authentic tasks

Multidisciplinary activities

Developing cognitive skills

We discussed cognitive apprenticeship in Chapter 2. To review briefly, it concerns not the transmission of factual information but the development of cognitive skills. In developing cognitive skills, the role of the teacher shifts over time from demonstrating (modeling), to coaching the student through early efforts, to a more passive role in which the teacher may observe and intervene only occasionally. The coaching stage is especially critical. A key component of coaching is the provision of support devices, such as reminders, conventions (common techniques or strategies for performing expected tasks), or constraints, that help the apprentice to approximate the complex behavior of the expert. When the skills to be learned are cognitive, it is also important to find some way to externalize these behaviors so that the internal cognitive behaviors can be observed and discussed. Often the expert must attempt to explain what he or she is thinking to provide the novice some awareness of internal behavior.

PROJECT QUALITY

Pride in software products

Realistic classroom goals

The quality that should be expected of student-generated products is the subject of some debate. Some contend that students should develop only prototypes and not strive to produce products of high quality (D'Ignazio, 1990). This position might imply that students should learn only the most basic software design techniques and not spend time on embellishments or refinements. In some respects, it is clear that there is a diminishing return on time spent in polishing a presentation. However, there is also a somewhat different perspective. Much of our rationale for student projects includes the idea of involving students in authentic activities. A student's sense of scholarship and authorship comes with producing something of which he or she can be proud. Students know what a real newspaper, a real video production, and authentic computer software look like. Student designers want to develop projects others would use and appreciate. A realistic classroom goal is probably to familiarize students with some fundamental principles of design that apply to their particular project. These fundamental principles will vary with the nature of the project, the age and experience of the students, whether the project is an individual or a cooperative venture, and the teacher's goals.

STUDENT PROJECTS, STANDARDS, AND RESTRUCTURING

Changing roles for teachers and students

Advocates of engaging students in sophisticated design projects often slip into arguments for restructuring schools (Lehrer et al., 1994; Thomas & Knezek, 1991). When educators talk about restructuring, they are in part proposing changes in the curriculum, the roles played by teachers, and the learning activities provided for students (Thomas & Knezek, 1991). Our discussion of reform and educational standards in Chapter 2 (pages 34 through 42) recognized the growing pressure for valuing a wider range of domain-appropriate performance skills. Certainly design projects engage teachers and students in unique activities, have them play somewhat different roles than they did in the past, and use school time in different ways. Hypermedia design projects change the teacher's role from dispenser to facilitator. In many cases, students are expected to find information themselves and then construct knowledge from it. Students may encounter situations and discover information that teachers have not experienced directly. They may try to do things that their teachers have not done. The information they use will not always be found in traditional textbooks or even in the school library. Often it will be found outside the traditional school setting—in the community, biological habitats, work settings, and other nontraditional but content-appropriate settings. The activities of the student focus on gathering, assessing, integrating, and using this information. Projects based on these activities take schools into relatively unfamiliar terrain. More activities will be group based. Activities will have to be graded in different ways. Spending fifty minutes each day in the classroom may not provide the optimal setting for many activities. Traditional school practices are difficult to change, but some exciting proposals seem to be emerging.

Technology-based projects require flexibility.

Using technology-based projects to explore content you might normally teach in a traditional manner will require flexibility on your part. You cannot expect to approach a project with the same high degree of structure possible with textbook-related instructional materials. Even a project that echoes an activity already implemented by another teacher or replicates a project you did with last year's class is an adventure in learning. You will likely find that some uncertainty is desirable and that a degree of flexibility creates a more active learning environment. Uncertainty provides opportunities for students to make decisions and allows you the opportunity to model problem-solving skills. Some spontaneity is necessary. If students run into an idea that fascinates them, they should be encouraged to pursue this opportunity and find a way to integrate their experiences into the project.

Modeling problem-solving skills

Encouraging more active involvement with content

You have had an opportunity to encounter various aspects of project implementation in this textbook. At one point or another, you have been asked to consider how project activities might encourage more active involvement with content, familiarize yourself with various software and hardware tools that might be used in project activities, learn basic principles of design relevant to multimedia projects, and consider planned social processes that might be useful in implementing cooperative projects. As you have progressed through the various topics in this textbook, new ideas may have caused you to recall and reconsider projects you first encountered some time ago. You may have found yourself recalling projects from earlier chapters when we discussed techniques such as scanning, video digitizing, and sound capture or when hypermedia and paint tools were presented. Now you have a better understanding of how those projects were created. The discussions of cooperative learning or design principles may also have encouraged you to reconsider some of these projects. You may already have judged some of the projects against basic standards of design or thought about more effective ways that groups of students might have studied the same content areas. Examples represent raw information; we hope you have taken the opportunity to work mentally with these examples to create personal knowledge.

STUDENT MULTIMEDIA PROJECTS

We have devoted the rest of this chapter to some of the practical issues involved in implementing classroom projects. We first discuss the development of World Wide Web pages as an option for student projects. We then look at an extended example of a hypermedia project.

STUDENT PROJECTS ON THE WEB

The Web offers an alternative outlet for multimedia projects. Most of the projects we have described throughout this book could have been implemented in some form as Web pages. Web projects also offer some powerful and unique opportunities. The capacity to link your multimedia projects with other Internet resources can be useful. The process of searching the Internet for good resources serves as a way to involve students actively with content. The Web also allows an efficient means for collaboration with students from other locations.

Mastery of Web basics builds confidence

We would like teachers to concentrate on developing stimulating Web projects and the classroom skills necessary to use such projects to engage students in active learning. These goals are unlikely to be achieved until teachers feel confident they can help their students develop Web materials and get these materials on a Web server. An understanding of some Web basics and the mastery of a couple of basic tools should provide this confidence. Acquiring such knowledge is productive for both teachers and students. As we have suggested in our discussion of other forms of multimedia, the skills necessary to produce Web-based multimedia can be learned in a reasonable amount of time and can be used repeatedly as an efficient and creative way to explore and process course content.

In the pages that follow we describe Web materials and the mechanics of Web authoring simply but accurately. The capabilities of the Web are expanding daily, and some functions are quite complex. We cannot hope to help you grasp the entire potential of authoring for the Web, but we will give you the background necessary to do useful work. We propose that you adopt a minimalist approach to Web multimedia (D'Ignazio, 1996), learning as few new software tools and as few new technology skills as possible. If this experience is productive and exciting, there will be plenty of related techniques and ideas you can explore.

Components of Web pages

Think of Web pages as consisting of a combination of (1) multimedia elements (text, graphics, sounds, movies, and such), (2) a special command language called **hypertext markup language (HTML)** that informs the browser how to organize these multimedia elements for display, and (3) links allowing access to other pages. You already have considerable knowledge of multimedia elements from previous chapters. You have also learned that an Internet link can be expressed in the form of a URL (see Chapter 6, page 214). The element of Web authoring you have yet to experience is HTML.

You have already used one type of markup language, perhaps without realizing it. If you have word processing experience, you have probably underlined and bolded text, centered and enlarged a segment of text to serve as the title for a paper, and perhaps inserted a picture at a specific location in your document. You did not type any commands to make text bold (the HTML commands would be <B> text </B>) or to position a graphic (the HTML commands might be <CENTER><IMG SRC="name.GIF" WIDTH="261" HEIGHT="110" ALIGN=bottom NATURALSIZEFLAG="3"><CENTER>), but you did ask the word processing program to perform that function. For example, you probably selected a segment of text and then used a keyboard command (Command-b or Control-b depending on the operating system) or the equivalent menu option to bold text. The commands to create bold text on the screen and on the final printed version of your document were inserted in the word processing file you created. Although the commands are not visible, the results are.

You can now create Web documents in exactly the same way. As you will see, certain Web authoring programs allow you to control the appearance of a Web page by positioning multimedia elements on a blank page and manipulating various aspects of their appearance (e.g., size, justification, and text appearance). The markup language that creates this appearance is not visible on the screen; it is saved in the file that is eventually sent to the machine that serves your Web pages. These commands that are not visible to the user but are interpreted by the browser are called **tags**. You could also create the same file by entering all of the markup tags and the text content of the Web page directly from the computer keyboard. There are some reasons you might want to do this (more options become available or control of screen appearance is more precise), but the time required to learn the unique tags necessary to perform these unique functions is not worthwhile for most individuals.

Basic Features and Skills

One way to help you understand the possibilities and demands of authoring for the Web is to outline some of the fundamental skills student authors should have. Think of these as the building blocks of Web pages. When students combine these components in different ways, they will be able to create a wide variety of projects. Following is a list of actions and a brief description of how each action is implemented. Several Web authoring programs are listed at the end of this chapter. All of the programs we have included (and several more we did not) are capable of doing the following actions without requiring the user to enter HTML tags:

◆ Set background color. Select the menu option, and then select the color from a palette to control page color.

◆ Add text to the page. Type or open a text-only file created by some other application.

◆ Set the size of headings. Select the text with the mouse, and then select heading size from the menu to create bold page headings of different sizes.

◆ Create lists. Select lines of text, and then select a menu option to create hierarchical lists.

◆ Add graphic, sounds, and movies to the page. Drag the image file (sound file or QuickTime movie file) to the page, and drop or open the file using the menu bar option.

◆ Link the text or a graphic to other pages. Select the text or graphic; then use the menu option, and select the file for a link. For pages at other sites, select the text or graphic, and then use the menu option to type in a URL for the link.

◆ Horizontal rule. Use the menu option to draw a horizontal line to separate areas of the page.

◆ Table. Use the menu option to add a table of cells to the page. The boundaries of the cells can be manually adjusted using the mouse to create cells of different size. Tables provide a convenient way to define a Web page template (see Figure 10.8 on page 394).

Many of the techniques described here were used to create the page in Figure 10.6 from two graphics files and a text file. (The logo at the top of the page is a graphic image created in another program.) Some comments have been added to the figure to point out noteworthy features. All underlined text and the smaller graphic serve as links to other Web pages. When the Web authoring program saves the page, the resulting HTML file consists of the text, the HTML tags, and information that will allow a browser to load and position the graphics and follow a link to another location. To make this information available to users, the HTML file and the two graphics files would have to be loaded to a server. We won't explain what is necessary to operate a server or how to load files to the server; operating the server requires some computer experience and is usually left to someone with special training (for a different point of view, see Emerging Technology: Personal Web Servers). Loading files is not difficult, but the technique will vary with the kind of server a school uses.

FIGURE 10.6
Sample Web Page Showing Common Elements

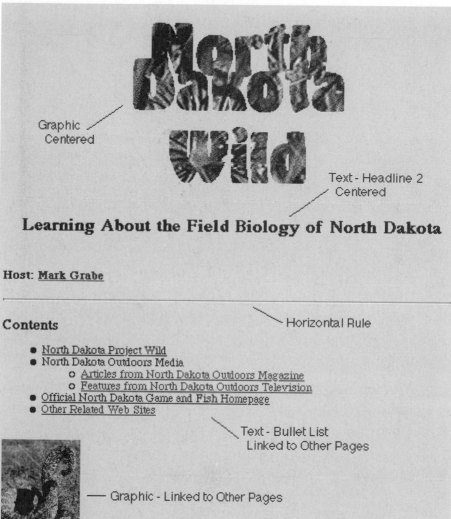

The raw HTML document responsible for what you see in Figure 10.6 looks like this:

```
<HTML>
<HEAD>
    <TITLE>North Dakota Wild</TITLE>
</HEAD>
<BODY>
<CENTER><IMG SRC="pics/ID.GIF"</CENTER>
<BR>
<H1><CENTER>Learning About the Field Biology of North Dakota </CEN-
TER></H1>
<BR>
Host: <A HREF="/dept/grabe">Mark Grabe</A>
<BR>
<HR>
<H3>Contents</H3>
<UL>
<LI><A HREF="instmat.html">North Dakota Project Wild</A>
<LI>North Dakota Outdoors Media
    <UL>
    <LI><A HREF="media.html#anchor37399">Articles from North Dakota Out-
doors Magazine</A>
    <LI><A HREF="media.html#anchor38708">Features from North Dakota Out-
doors Television</A>
    </UL>
<LI><A HREF="http://www.state.nd.us/gnf/">Official North Dakota Game and Fish
Homepage</A>
<LI><A HREF="others.html">Other Related Web Sites</A>
</UL>
<BR>
<A HREF="keyhead.html"><IMG SRC="pics/rattleS.GIF">North Dakota Reptile and
Amphibian Identification Project</A><BR>
<BR>
<BR>
<A HREF="http://ndwild.psych.und.nodak.edu/owlshome.html">Outdoor Wildlife
Learning Sites (OWLS)</A> - The newest NDWild project focuses on the development
of habitats as service and learning projects. Learn about this opportunity. This resource
is in the early phases of development, but you are certainly welcome to take a
look.<BR>
</BODY>
</HTML>
```

Alternative Ways to Construct Web Pages

As a Web page author, you can choose to work with HTML or ignore it. It exists in either case. No matter how you choose to develop Web content, it is helpful to understand the basics of what HTML does and to recognize that with the exception of text, multimedia elements presented by Web pages are not actually part of the HTML file. Just these insights can be helpful. For example, one of the most common problems beginning Web authors encounter is having pages they have designed on a classroom machine fail to present graphics when loaded to a server. The problem occurs because the graphic files cannot be located. Perhaps the author has loaded the HTML file but forgotten to load the graphics files to the server. Perhaps the files have been loaded but have been stored in the wrong place. "Disappearing images" are a common problem, but a little understanding of how HTML functions goes a long way toward knowing what to look for in finding a solution.

Using authoring software

In most educational settings, Web projects are developed using some type of authoring software. As the author, you concentrate on what should appear on the page and where the elements of your page should be placed. The authoring software generates the necessary HTML codes. Here are some authoring software options:

Word Processing Programs. The same word processing program you use to write term papers probably has the capability to create Web pages (a partial list of such programs is included at the end of the chapter). Some functions are performed automatically, and all you have to do is indicate that you want to save the document as HTML. To do this, select Save As instead of Save from the menu bar of the word processor program, and determine if HTML is one of the options you are given. (It is always a good strategy to save the document first as a traditional word processing document. If the Web page does not come out looking like you had hoped, it will be easier to make adjustments to the word processor file than to the HTML file.)

When you save a word processor document as HTML, the program recognizes certain features in your document and attempts to duplicate these features in HTML. For example, images embedded in the document will be converted and saved as JPEG files, and text that appears in bold type will be saved in the HTML document surrounded by the <B> </B> tags. Some important features of Web pages, such as links to other pages, are not created automatically. Instead, the word processing program will offer you a method for creating these features directly. For example, a link is usually created by selecting a phrase of text and then selecting a menu option that allows a Web address to be associated with that phrase. When the word processor document is saved as HTML, the selected phrase becomes a link.

Take a careful look at the capabilities of the word processing programs available to you. If you are interested in creating simple Web pages, you probably already have the software you need to complete the task.

Web Authoring Software for Students.   Software companies, taking note of the potential for student Web page authoring, have created products that attempt to simplify and focus the process of creating Web pages.

SiteCentral is a recent example of this type of program. This Web authoring program can be used in several different ways. In one approach intended to assist less experienced authors, the user selects a function (e.g., Background, Template, Text, Sounds), and the program then displays options related to this function. In Figure 10.7, you see the options for adding text to the Web page. The Web author can determine the font; control text color and size and justification; and apply styles such as bold and underlining by selecting from the options. More experienced Web authors are not limited to selecting

FIGURE 10.7
Screen Image of SiteCentral. Note the functions and options available for the text function.

from the menu of options and can create Web pages more directly. When used in this fashion, SiteCentral is similar to a general-purpose Web authoring program.

General-Purpose Web Authoring Software. Instead of purchasing Web authoring software developed specifically for educational settings and younger learners, most educators rely on general-purpose Web authoring software. This software is readily available through retail outlets or catalogs and in some cases can be obtained at no cost. As Web publishing proliferates, it is clear that products can be sorted into varying levels, and as you might expect, the more sophisticated software demands a significantly higher price. In most cases, software with basic features is sufficient for student projects. A list of some of the less expensive software is included at the end of this chapter.

Design Tips for Web Pages

Student Web projects have become so common that we here highlight some of the specific design guidelines educators should consider as their students create Web pages. Here are general design categories that apply to Web projects and some specific issues associated with each category.

Navigation System. The navigation system defines the way users can move about within the Web site. The basic mechanism allowing navigation is the collection of links the designer embeds within the pages making up the site. Creating a navigation system that allows users to orient themselves easily and return to main choice points (see Content Organization, page 360) can be very helpful. Links to these choice points might consistently appear as in a cell along the left margin of pages or at the bottom of pages. At the very least, users should have frequent access to a link allowing them to return to the last major choice point they encountered.

Page Layout. Objects on a Web page should be grouped in a way that facilitates the user's activities. An object could be a segment of text, a picture, links serving a specific purpose, or any multimedia element that can be presented on a Web page. In general, the placement of objects should be predictable, and objects important to the purpose of the page should appear in prominent locations. One way to develop a strategy for pages of a certain type is to create a template. This is very similar to the idea of a layout grid (page 363). The template shown in Figure 10.8 was developed for a project in which individual teams would develop a single page for incorporating into a class project. (Figure 10.9 shows a finished Web page based on the template.) Our sample template incorporates a navigation system and identifies the common elements that students are to provide. Its organization is based on two tables, each made up of three cells. We strongly suggest that teachers wanting to help students create Web pages learn how to structure the pages using the table tool, which is available in most Web page authoring programs. Tables offer a convenient way to create a page template.

Creating a template

FIGURE 10.8

Example of a Web Page Template. This template consists of two tables, each made up of three cells. The areas identified as title, image, and narrative are not actually defined within the HTML but are suggested components to be included for this example.

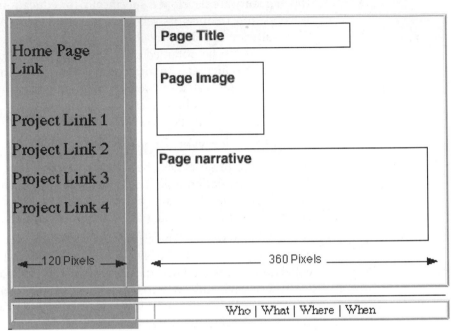

Use of Graphics. A high proportion of Web pages include graphics. There are several issues to consider when incorporating images on your Web page.

The size of Web images should be a consideration. The text and individual images that make up a Web page are sent over the Internet as separate files (see page 388), and the browser integrated the files to form the page you see on the computer screen. Image files tend to be much larger than the HTML (text) file and take longer to transfer. With a slow connection, the wait for several images to load can be significant. Web designers wanting to make heavy use of graphics often try to offer alternatives for users without a high-speed connection. One approach makes use of thumbnails rather than large images. A **thumbnail** is a small version of a large image. The small image provides an idea of what the larger image looks like and serves as a link to a page containing the full-size image. Following the link to the page containing the full-size image results from a conscious decision and allows users with slow access to spend the additional time only when they think that viewing the full-size image is essential.

Using thumbnails instead of large images

FIGURE 10.9

Example of a Finished Web Page Based on the Template in Figure 10.8

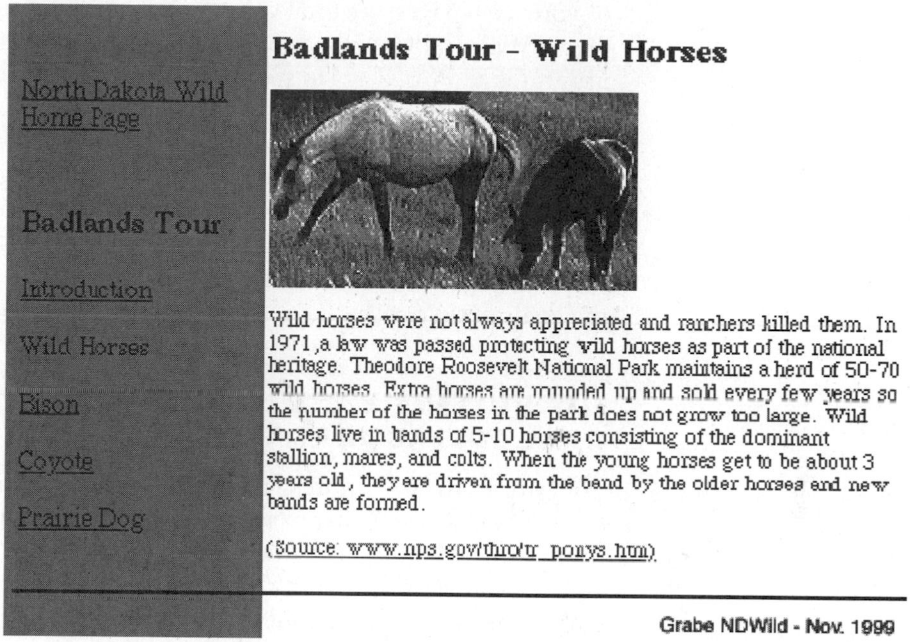

Badlands Tour - Wild Horses

North Dakota Wild Home Page

Badlands Tour

Introduction

Wild Horses

Bison

Coyote

Prairie Dog

Wild horses were not always appreciated and ranchers killed them. In 1971, a law was passed protecting wild horses as part of the national heritage. Theodore Roosevelt National Park maintains a herd of 50-70 wild horses. Extra horses are rounded up and sold every few years so the number of the horses in the park does not grow too large. Wild horses live in bands of 5-10 horses consisting of the dominant stallion, mares, and colts. When the young horses get to be about 3 years old, they are driven from the band by the older horses and new bands are formed.

(Source: www.nps.gov/thro/tr_ponys.htm)

Grabe NDWild - Nov. 1999

For the best quality, remember the advantages and disadvantages of GIF and JPEG images. Use JPEG with complex images such as photographs that have many colors in a complex pattern. Use GIF for images containing large areas of solid color, as might be the case in logos, simple illustrations, or large decorative text.

When you are preparing graphics for the Web, always save your original image file when creating new images of a different size or a different file type. If you decide to change your mind, starting over with the original image will result in a better final product than trying to work backward from an altered image.

Text Presentation. Although long segments of text are difficult to read from a computer screen, there are situations in which the content to be presented consists mainly of text. The solution is not to ask users to move through many Web pages containing small segments of text. The usual recommendation is to present Web pages containing at least three pages of text. You can break up the extended text in a variety of ways: blocking text messages and surrounding them with space, using headings to organize and separate blocks of text, and reworking text information in the form of numbered or bulleted lists.

Breaking up long text passages

Remember that many users will print longer segments of text rather than read the material from the screen. If you use tables to control the appearance of your Web pages, the total width of your table should be approximately 500 pixels. Wider tables will not print properly on standard paper. Web authoring programs allow authors to specify the height and width of the cells that make up a table.

Although we suggest that educators make the effort to learn some design fundamentals, it is also important to remember that student Web projects may sometimes require different priorities from those emphasized by design experts. For example, educators might encourage students to use extended text or many images when such information sources would be consistent with the goals of the project.

THE BUTTERFLY COLLECTION: AN EXTENDED EXAMPLE OF A COLLABORATIVE STUDENT DESIGN PROJECT

We want to use one more classroom example to bring together many of the themes we have considered separately. Implementation of a successful classroom project requires consideration of many issues. We have used several examples from Pam Carlson's classroom to show you how one experienced and creative teacher thinks about integrating technology. This project was one of many activities contributing to a multidisciplinary unit, this time developed around the theme of butterflies. At the elementary school level, a theme like this allows the teacher to involve students with a variety of language arts activities, music, visual arts, science activities, problem-solving activities, and social experiences.

Getting the Project Started

Pam Carlson introduced the class to the idea of a multimedia project by showing them projects that previous classes had completed. This year the class was studying butterflies, but maybe they could think of a way to create a similar project. Pam promised to bring in lots of books from the library and find a videotape the class could watch. They would do many different activities, not all of them on the computer. They would read a lot, write stories, and draw pictures. Pam said she even knew some songs they could learn. Maybe the class would be able to come up with some ideas of their own. What did they want to know about butterflies? One student did bring in a monarch caterpillar that the class kept in a glass jar and watched as it spun a chrysalis.

To get the class started on their multimedia project, Pam provided scanned pictures. Students were asked to choose a butterfly to work on and learn about. Pam told the students they could color the pictures using Kid Pix and then write something interesting about each butterfly. The students were given the names of the butterfly pictures and then used the resources available

Emerging Technology

Personal Web Servers

Once you or your students have authored Web pages, the final task is to make the pages available to users of the Internet, which requires access to a Web server. It is possible that your district has direct access to the Internet but not be operating a server. It is also possible that a server is available, but creating accounts for individual classrooms is something the Internet administrator does not regard as a high priority. Actually, most individuals responsible for a school's Internet server would probably be very interested in helping you make class projects available. However, there may be something even better than taking advantage of this sophisticated equipment and the expert's willingness to help: running your own server right in your classroom. If you have a dedicated connection to the Internet running into your classroom, a personal Web server would give you and your class this capability.

Personal Web servers share several attributes:

- *Low cost.* Personal servers are free or very inexpensive (see the examples provided at the end of this chapter).
- *Limited hardware requirements.* Personal Web servers are designed to run in the background on a normally configured computer. The computer can be used for routine applications and will serve Web pages when sufficient memory resources are available.

- *Limited output.* Personal Web servers respond more slowly and can service fewer users. Some of the more sophisticated data processing options available with dedicated servers and more sophisticated software may not be available.

Personal Web servers were developed for small business applications, often for internal communication within a company (sometimes called an **intranet**). A personal Web server could be used in exactly the same way within a school building. However, if a machine has a permanent Internet address (a dedicated connection), that machine is part of the Internet, and anyone with a browser can access it. The same machine you use to write tests and send notes home to parents can make projects that your students have created available over the Internet. As technology evolves and the Internet becomes even more pervasive, it is likely that most computers connected to the Internet will also function as servers.

This would seem to be the type of application that will find many uses within educational settings. Imagine the potential of posting assignments, displaying student work, and offering a list of your favorite Web sites from your desktop. It is likely that the basic operating systems for the computers of the future will come with this capability built in. If you can't wait, we list several existing products at the conclusion of the chapter.✳

in the classroom to find a colored picture and learn what they could about each butterfly.

Keep in mind that these are second-grade students, and research skills at this grade level are quite basic. Students mostly accumulate a list of facts they find interesting. Pam tried to communicate to the students that they were to try not to copy and instead write as much as they could using their own words. She reports an interesting strategy some students used to try to meet her expectations: The students would read a little bit and then close the book while they wrote so they would be less tempted to copy.

While the Project Is Underway

The butterfly project was based on a cooperative approach in which each student contributed information on one butterfly to a class hypermedia project. As students investigated individual butterflies and discussed the information they were finding, they made some decisions about what each butterfly report would contain: a color image of the butterfly, a brief written summary of student research about the butterfly, and a map showing the butterfly's normal range. Students seemed interested in seeing whether different butterflies might be found where they lived, and including range maps was a way to provide this information. Working with maps added another dimension to the learning experience. Students created their butterfly images by coloring scanned images in Kid Pix. The individual reports were then integrated in a final product. One card was used to display the butterfly, and a second card to present the text information and the range map (see Figure 10.10).

When most of the butterfly reports were finished and students had completed the other activities associated with the butterfly unit, it was time to work on the final project. Pam talked with the students about what they had learned about butterflies and what they would like to present to their parents. Obviously the final project would incorporate the individual butterfly reports.

One major component that students had studied was the series of stages in the process by which a butterfly developed. They had even learned a song to help them remember the stages. Thinking about the song gave them an idea. The students could record the song on the computer and show pictures of the different stages of metamorphosis at the same time. They could draw pictures of the egg, caterpillar, chrysalis, and butterfly and then show the pictures using the song as background.

One final question remained: How could they create an interesting system allowing users of the class project to view individual butterflies? The answer came from another experience that had been part of the unit: an insect collection. Pam's father is a scientist and trains science teachers at the local university. He brought an insect collection to show the class. Scientists who study insects, entomologists, often mount insects on pins and place the mounted and labeled insects in glass-covered boxes. Later the idea emerged to

FIGURE 10.10
Butterfly Information and Range Map

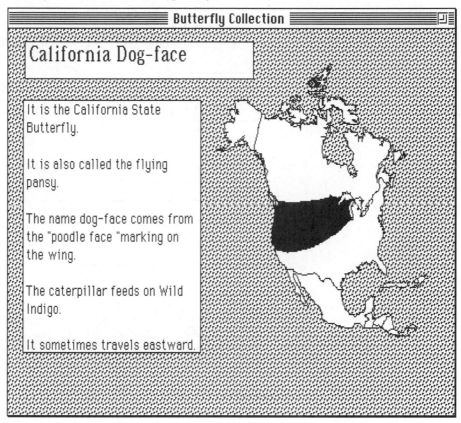

use an insect collection as a menu allowing access to the individual butterflies in the project. A screen display could be developed that looked like an insect collection, and users could select a butterfly by clicking on the insect.

Now the task was to work these various elements into a presentation. When putting together a presentation, it is often useful to draw a rough sketch of a project to work out the details of how the parts will fit together and what the individual elements will look like. You will recall that this process is called storyboarding. The storyboard in Figure 10.11 includes sketches and notes that define critical features of the final Butterfly Project.

The Butterfly Project begins with an introductory screen and a digitized copy of the class picture. The introductory images are followed immediately by individual colored pictures of an egg, caterpillar, chrysalis, and butterfly accompanied by the butterfly song. These pictures were scanned from a student drawing and painted with Kid Pix. The composite drawing appears in Figure 10.12.

FIGURE 10.11
Butterfly Project Storyboard

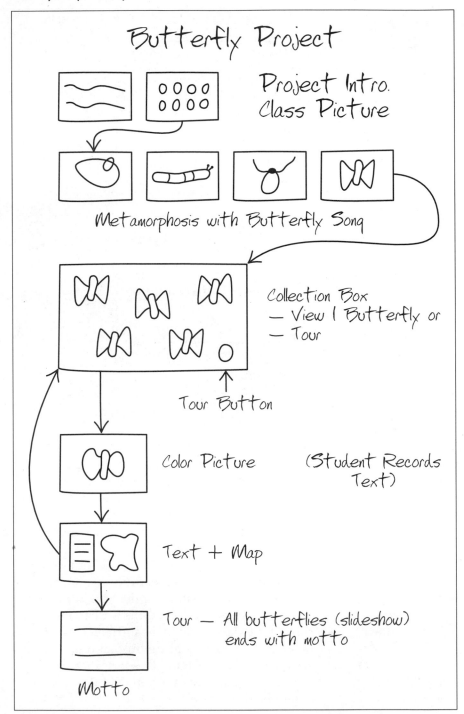

FIGURE 10.12
Student Drawing of Metamorphosis Stages

The insect collection box shown in Figure 10.13 serves as a convenient organizational system for users. The butterfly collection can be viewed as a narrated slide show by clicking on the "tour button" (lower right), or the material describing individual butterflies can be viewed by clicking on the small image of a particular butterfly. The small image of each butterfly is covered by an invisible button (see Chapter 8, page 304), and that button is linked (see Chapter 8, page 305) to the other cards providing information about the butterfly.

The slide show version of the butterfly tour concludes with a project motto (Figure 10.14) that provides a good message for students of any age: Learning never ends!

SUMMARY

This chapter integrates two views of design: design of products and design of personal knowledge. Design involves constructing or structuring a product for a purpose. For computer software, the purpose might be to help the user

FIGURE 10.13
User Interface Based on Butterfly Collection Box

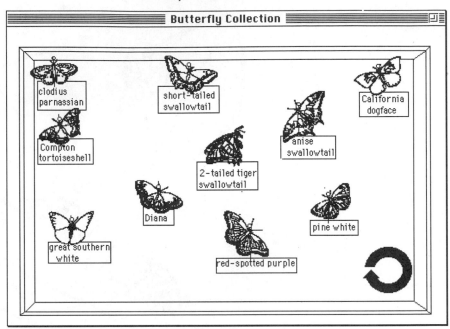

FIGURE 10.14
Class Motto and Project Conclusion

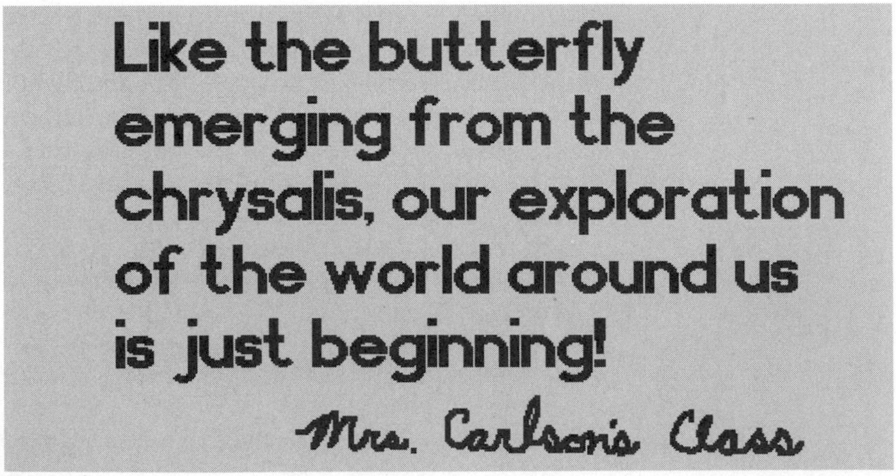

Like the butterfly emerging from the chrysalis, our exploration of the world around us is just beginning!

Mrs. Carlson's Class

accomplish some task more efficiently, learn something, or have an entertaining experience. The design of knowledge also stresses the connection between structure and function. Knowledge as design helps the learner do something. Without purpose, learning becomes focused on the accumulation of information, not its application.

Student-authored hypermedia represents a concrete integration of the design of knowledge and the design of a public product. In this unique situation, students are designing knowledge in order to generate a product. The hypermedia product provides a purpose for the hypermedia author's construction of personal knowledge.

To create products that are informative, interesting, and easy to use and understand, hypermedia authors should attend to the organization of content, basic principles of graphic design, clear writing, and the development of an effective user interface.

Hypermedia design projects might be considered a special application of a cooperative learning model called group investigation. In a group investigation, students identify aspects of a general theme that interest them and then join teams to study these individual topics. The teams are expected to determine how they will gather, analyze, and summarize information relevant to their topic. Individual students are expected to assume some independence in contributing to this process. Each team identifies the essence of what the members have learned and presents this information to the entire group.

Hypermedia design uses a complex set of processes that can involve young hypermedia authors in the construction of personal knowledge. Learning is situated in a task that provides a purpose for student activities. The design model presented here bears a strong resemblance to a popular model for the writing process. Identifiable components of this model include planning, information collection, knowledge generation, and evaluation and revision.

Within this model, the teacher involves the student as an apprentice and takes responsibility for coaching both the knowledge design and the hypermedia design skills. In the early stages of a project and especially when working with inexperienced designers, the teacher may be required to provide some direct instruction, demonstrate procedural skills, model cognitive processes by externalizing thinking behavior, and stimulate cognitive behavior with leading questions. As students become more experienced and the project takes shape, teachers will play a less direct role. Students will take on a great deal of responsibility for their own learning.

REFLECTING ON CHAPTER 10

Activities

♦ Consider the content and skills you intend to teach as they might be used by "practitioners." Identify who might be considered practitioners, and propose tasks appropriate to the capabilities of students that would put these students in the roles of these practitioners.

◆ Briefly outline a potential hypermedia project. Develop a holistic scoring guide and continua of descriptors appropriate to assessing the project and important project-related skills.

◆ Develop a storyboard for a simple hypermedia project appropriate to a content area that interests you.

◆ Determine if the word processing program you usually use is capable of generating HTML. If so, transform a document you have already created into HTML to see what the product looks like.

Key Terms

branch *(p. 362)*	link *(p. 361)*
button *(p. 368)*	map *(p. 368)*
cooperative learning *(p. 371)*	menu *(p. 368)*
design *(p. 358)*	node *(p. 361)*
graphic design *(p. 363)*	sequential design *(p. 361)*
grid *(p. 363)*	storyboarding *(p. 382)*
group investigation *(p. 372)*	tag *(p. 387)*
hierarchical design *(p. 361)*	task specialization methods
hypertext markup language (HTML) *(p. 387)*	*(p. 371)*
	team rewards *(p. 371)*
individual accountability *(p. 371)*	thumbnail *(p. 395)*
intranet *(p. 397)*	user interface *(p. 367)*
knowledge as design *(p. 357)*	web design *(p. 363)*

Resources to Expand Your Knowledge Base

Hypermedia Design Principles

Apple Computer. (1989). *Hypercard stack design guidelines.* Reading, MA: Addison-Wesley. This source offers concrete advice on all aspects of hypermedia design. The principles are of value no matter what authoring environment you use.

Web Design Principles

Lynch, P., & Horton, S. (1999). *Web style guide: Basic design principles for creating web pages.* New Haven: Yale University Press. (**http://info.med.yale.edu/caim/manual/**)

Williams, R., & Tollett, J. (1998). *The non-designers web book.* Berkeley, CA: Peachpit Press.

Resources for Cooperative Learning

Bonk, C., & King, S. (1998). *Electronic collaboration.* Hillsdale, NJ: Erlbaum.

Johnson, D., Johnson, R., & Holubec, E. (1991). *Cooperation in the classroom* (rev. ed.). Edina, MN: Interaction Book Company.

Putnam, J. (Ed.). (1993). *Cooperative learning and strategies for inclusion: Celebrating diversity in the classroom.* Baltimore, MD: Brookes Publishing.

Sharan, Y., & Sharan, S. (1992). *Expanding cooperative learning through group investigation* (3rd ed.). New York: Teachers College Press.

Slavin, R. (1991). *Student team learning: A practical guide to cooperative learning* (3rd ed.). Washington, DC: National Education Association.

Thematic Instruction, the Project Approach, and Project Ideas

Fredericks, A., Meinbach, A., & Rothlein, L. (1993). *Thematic units: An integrated approach to teaching science and social studies.* New York: HarperCollins.

Handler, M., Dana, A., & Moore, J. (1995). *Hypermedia as a student tool.* Englewood, CO: Teachers Idea Press.

Harel, I. (1991). *Children as designers.* Norwood, NJ: Ablex.

Katz, L., & Chard, S. (1989). *Engaging children's minds: The project approach.* Norwood, NJ: Ablex.

Perkins, D. (1986). *Knowledge as design.* Hillsdale, NJ: Erlbaum.

Teachers might review recent copies of the journals *Electronic Learning* and *Learning and Leading with Technology* for examples of student-generated hypermedia projects.

Web Authoring Software

Word Processing Software Capable of Generating HTML Documents
AppleWorks (formerly ClarisWorks) from Apple Computer, available for the Macintosh and Windows operating systems. (**http://www.apple.com/appleworks**)

Microsoft Word from Microsoft, available for the Macintosh and Windows operating systems. (**http://www.microsoft.com/office**)

WordPerfect from Corel Corporation, available for the Macintosh and Windows operating systems. (**http://www.wordperfect.com**)

Software Developed Specifically for Educational Settings
SiteCentral from Roger Wagner Publishing, available for Macintosh and Windows operating systems. (**http://www.sitecentral.com**)

Web Workshop, for young learners, from Sunburst Communication, available for Macintosh and Windows operating systems. (**http://www.sunburst.com**)

General-Purpose Web Authoring Software
Adobe PageMill from Adobe Systems, available for the Macintosh. (**http://www.adobe.com**)

Filemaker HomePage (formerly Claris HomePage), from Filemaker, available for the Macintosh and Windows operating systems. (**http://www.filemaker.com**)

Microsoft Frontpage, from Microsoft, available for the Macintosh and Windows operating systems. (**http://www.microsoft.com/frontpage**)

Netscape Composer from Netscape, available for the Macintosh and Windows operating systems. (**http://www.netscape.com**)

Personal Servers
Microsoft Personal Web Server, for the Windows operating system. This product can be downloaded at no charge from the Microsoft Web site (use the search feature to locate it). (**http://www.microsoft.com**)

Personal Web Sharing from Apple Computer Corporation for Macintosh computers. Personal Web Sharing has been included as part of the system software since version 8.0. Information about Personal Web Sharing can be obtained from the Apple Web site. (**http://www.apple.com**)

PART THREE

Looking at Issues and Looking Ahead

In Part Three, *we look at issues and concerns related to using technology responsibility. These issues include equity, protecting students from inappropriate content and personal harassment or harm, and computer viruses. Problems can arise in these areas, and you will explore ways to create solutions to them. Classroom applications of technology will not be supported by parents and the community unless these important issues can be addressed.*

Chapter 11

Responsible Use of Technology

ORIENTATION

This chapter discusses three topics related to responsible use of technology: equity, copyright law, and the protection of students from inappropriate content and experiences. After you have completed your study of this chapter, you should be able to explain important issues associated with each of these areas and list some concrete ways that teachers and schools might use to ensure that students will use technology in a responsible manner. The areas of responsible use that we discuss in this chapter represent challenges that must be met in order for technology to find broad success in classrooms. We must find ways for *all* students to take advantage of the learning opportunities technology offers, provide appropriate recognition and copyright protection for those who create these resources, and make certain that students have experiences that are safe and productive. As you read, look for answers to the following questions:

Focus Questions

- ◆ What inequities exist in student access to technology and in the learning activities students experience? What factors appear responsible for these inequities?
- ◆ What adaptations can be implemented for students with special needs?
- ◆ What is copyright law designed to protect? What resources can be used in student and instructor multimedia projects? What are key guidelines that determine what can be taken from the Internet and what can be placed on the Internet?
- ◆ What are some safety guidelines that all Internet users should know?
- ◆ What are some options schools might use to protect students from inappropriate Internet content?

Effects on students' future lives

EQUITY OF EDUCATIONAL OPPORTUNITY

We believe that technology already plays an important role in K–12 education and that it will play an increasingly important role in the future. Clearly technology has become an indispensable part of the way we live and work, and our educational system must accept some responsibility to prepare students for this reality. Students who move through the educational system without having access to technology not only are limited in the ways they can approach traditional academic subjects; they are also missing out on experiences that would enhance their future ability to work and learn in a world more and more dependent on technology.

To gain some perspective on equity issues, think of the technology trends of the past two decades. During the 1980s, schools became involved for the first time with computers and various computer peripherals. The 1990s served a similar function for the Internet. Early in each decade, funding the newer forms of technology was fairly experimental, and some districts moved ahead more quickly than others. As computer or Internet applications became more commonplace, not having access to these opportunities became regarded as a deficit. Lack of access was viewed with particular alarm when it perpetuated or exacerbated existing inequities.

A number of descriptive studies have attempted to identify inequities in technology access. They examine whether variables such as student-to-computer ratios, classroom Internet access, or what students do with technology can be associated with factors like gender or differences in student ability. Some focus on links with low **socioeconomic status (SES)**, a measure based on income, education, and occupation. We will offer some numbers generated by these studies, but we will focus more on trends than on the numbers themselves. Variables such as student-to-computer ratios and classroom Internet access change quickly; the overall trends are of much more lasting significance.

EQUITY AND SES

A number of resources must be present before students are likely to experience the uses of technology we have described in this book. The schools these students attend have to invest in the necessary hardware and software, connect computers to the Internet, and provide teachers with the background and support necessary to provide students meaningful learning experiences. These areas of emphasis have not been developed in a coordinated manner. Schools have been spending money on computers for years. More recently, attention has shifted to providing Internet access. Teacher support and training have traditionally lagged behind.

Inequities in speed of progress

One simple way to describe equity issues is to suggest that schools with a higher proportion of advantaged students seem to have progressed through this list—from computers to Internet access to teacher training and support—at a more rapid pace. Here are some findings that support this notion:

◆ Access to computers in schools, usually measured as the ratio of students per computer, once showed sizable differences when schools with high proportions of students from low-income families were compared with schools with low proportions of such students. These differences have now narrowed substantially (Jerald & Orlofsky, 1999; Wenglinsky, 1998).

◆ Schools with a low proportion of low-income students (defined as less than 11 percent receiving free or reduced-price school lunch) have greater access to the Internet than schools with a high proportion of low-income students (defined as more than 70 percent receiving free or reduced-price school lunch). The ratio of students to Internet-connected computers is 1:10 in the most affluent schools and 1:17 in the least affluent schools (Jerald & Orlofsky, 1999).

◆ Schools with a low proportion of low-income students are more likely to have a full-time computer coordinator. Using the same designations based on the proportion of reduced-cost lunches, the difference for the two most extreme groups is 39 percent versus 19 percent (Jerald & Orlofsky, 1999). Socioeconomic status differences in schools were also a predictor of whether teachers reported receiving professional development in the use of computers in the past five years (Wenglinsky, 1998).

Inequities in home resources

Technology access in school is not the only issue of concern. The resources available outside school influence the skills students bring to school and the academic work they can do on their own. Here the trend is more discouraging, and SES differences seem to be increasing as technology becomes important in more higher-income occupations. Students from homes with a family income in excess of $75,000 are likely to have access to a computer in the home (80 percent) and to the Internet (45 percent). In homes with a family income of $25,000, approximately 25 percent of students have a computer and 10 percent have Internet access. The phrase *digital divide* has become a popular way to describe this disparity, and the recognition of this problem has led to an interest in developing **community access centers** to ensure all citizens access to technology and the Internet. Because schools have often already made the investment in technology and Internet access, programs are being developed to make these resources available to students and members of the community after traditional school hours. In some cases, students not only learn in these centers, but also serve as mentors to community members needing to learn about technology or accomplish such concrete tasks as visiting an Internet site describing employment opportunities (National Telecommunications and Information Administration, 1999).

Are these SES differences important? We think so. Students with fewer technology-related experiences would seem less prepared to use technology in future work and learning settings. Lack of experience may also narrow a student's range of vocational aspirations. Of course, we also assume that lack of access will affect student academic performance. Is there more to offer on this subject than logical arguments? A recent major study provides an interesting perspective on some of the equity issues that we have just outlined.

Educational Testing Service (ETS) Mathematics Study

Relating standardized test scores to technological access

The ETS mathematics study (Wenglinsky, 1998) was based on data gathered from fourth- and eighth-grade students who took the 1996 National Assessment of Educational Progress (NAEP) exams in mathematics. This research is unusual because it relates achievement data gathered using a major standardized test and a national sample of students to variables providing information about the students' schools and the students' uses of technology. The students and their schools provided the following information:

◆ How frequently technology was used in the study of mathematics
◆ Student access to technology

Student beliefs about personal abilities and vocational opportunities will influence interest in technology. Students must assume that technology will be an important part of their future. (© Michael Zide)

- The professional development of teachers
- What students did with technology that was relevant to the study of mathematics
- The social environment of the school

Interpreting the study results

Several of these variables (access, student use, professional development, and social environment) are similar to ones we have already emphasized. The ETS study identifies equity differences similar to those mentioned earlier; more important, the study provides some possible connections between these equity issues and student achievement. The fundamental conclusion was that the most significant inequities did not lie in how frequently computers were used but in what students did when they used the computers:

- Mathematics achievement benefited when eighth graders used computers to work on content-area–appropriate simulations and applications. Mathematics achievement was lower when students used computers to work on drill-and-practice activities.
- Students in schools with a higher proportion of less affluent students or more minority students were more likely to use computers to work on drill activities.
- Teachers in schools with a higher proportion of less affluent students had received fewer professional development experiences with technology.
- Teachers with fewer professional development experiences were more likely to emphasize drill and practice.

The fact that several variables are interrelated does not necessarily demonstrate a causal relationship among them. Even when we take this caution into account, however, one way of interpreting the ETS mathematics data is clear: Some students do not do as well in mathematics because teachers engage them in less powerful uses of technology, and one reason that teachers are likely to use less powerful methods is the lack of appropriate professional development experiences. This lack of teacher preparation is a greater problem in schools with higher levels of low-income and minority students. These data also suggest that what students do with the technology available to them is a more serious equity issue than differences in how much time students spend using technology.

Role of Educators' Perceptions

Other studies have also found that what students are asked to do with technology is related to student economic background (George, Malcolm, & Jeffers, 1993; Sutton, 1991). However, teacher preparation is not the only explanation provided for why student experiences differ. A second interpretation focuses on educator perceptions of the type of learning experiences that would be most helpful to students. According to this view, educators working with large numbers of students from less affluent backgrounds assume that

A focus on remediation

these students lack basic skills and fundamental knowledge. Therefore, the educators conclude, the most productive use of school time and resources is to focus on the remediation of such fundamentals. The assumption is that the opportunity to apply knowledge and skills, problem solving, and authentic student projects must build on basic skills and will not be productive until students have first developed an adequate background.

It is indeed possible that this view is held by many educators and that it may explain the classroom activities they emphasize. Yet this hierarchical view of classroom tasks is not universally accepted. Many educators believe that even for students lacking certain basic skills, a more productive approach is to embed the practice of these skills within activities that students find to be personally meaningful. As you have seen throughout this book, using technology to facilitate activity-centered projects in content-area instruction is one way to provide such experiences. Students can be inspired by the opportunity to use technology in interesting and challenging ways, and it would be unfair to limit the involvement of any student who would profit from this source of motivation (Laboratory of Comparative Human Cognition, 1989).

A focus on meaningful activities

Equity and the Classroom Teacher

Not all studies have found the SES differences identified in the ETS study. For example, a survey of schools participating in the National School Network, a group of schools committed to Internet use, indicated that, if anything, schools with a higher proportion of students from low-SES families were more involved in activities such as collaborative online projects and student Web authoring (Becker & Ravitz, 1998). How can these studies come to such different conclusions? First, the schools participating in each study were not selected in the same fashion. Moreover, the schools and teachers involved in the National School Network may view the role of technology differently.

Think about the possible connections among such variables as student background, teacher training, teacher beliefs about what is best for students, variations in access to technology, and variations in how students use technology. All of these may affect your students and the way you teach in your classroom.

For classroom teachers, two issues particularly concern us. First, learning experiences of the type we have described in this book—inquiry and construction experiences in which students use technology to go beyond passive reception of information—may be less frequently available to some students because their teachers do not have the training and support necessary to guide them. One solution might be to provide practicing teachers with ongoing opportunities for professional development, perhaps through interaction with a full-time computer coordinator. Unfortunately, without external support, this is just the resource that is least likely to be available in school districts in low-income areas. Perhaps our observation that investments need to move from computers to Internet access and then to professional development will hold true, and eventually the support for staff development will be improved.

Our second concern is that teachers will focus disadvantaged students exclusively on the accumulation of information. The solution to this challenge is not financial; it is something you can address. Throughout this book we have encouraged you to consider applications that lead students to evaluate information thoughtfully and to use it to address personally meaningful problems. The matter is in your hands as a teacher. We hope the activities outlined in this book will provide you with some ideas.

GENDER EQUITY

Gender differences in choices and experiences

There are other inequities that cannot be explained in terms of differences in access or teacher preparation. Males and females have different experiences with technology, and these differences in experience may limit future academic or vocational opportunities (Weinman & Haag, 1999). Here is a sample of the type of indicators that concern some educators:

◆ Differences exist in the technology-related courses that males and females select. Females dominate courses focused on clerical skills, which are regarded as being associated with careers that are less technologically advanced.

◆ A very small proportion of high school females take the computer science Advanced Placement examination.

◆ Only about 25 percent of college undergraduate computer science degrees are awarded to women.

◆ Females rate themselves as having lower computer abilities than males and are less likely to believe that computer skills help them do better in school (American Association of University Women Educational Foundation, 1998).

Possible explanations

Why might males and females have different experiences, and why might they feel differently about themselves as potential users of powerful applications of technology? Several factors frequently appear as explanations:

◆ Stereotypes of computer use and computer users are perpetuated in popular media. Males are commonly represented as "power users," or those who use computers for more sophisticated tasks.

◆ Recreational software that may interest users in computers is strongly slanted toward males.

◆ The computer is viewed as a tool for math, science, and programming—subjects that, sadly, may be of less interest to many females.

◆ The more aggressive nature of young males may offer an advantage in gaining access to computers or the Internet when there is not enough equipment for everyone.

Focus

The E-rate as a Solution for Disadvantaged Schools

The **e-rate,** a subsidy for the costs of providing Internet connection to schools and libraries, was established by the Telecommunications Act of 1996. The more general purpose of this law is to ensure "universal telecommunication and information services" to all citizens of the country regardless of income or location. Elementary and secondary schools, health care providers, and libraries are specifically targeted within this legislation for access to "advanced telecommunications services" (Federal Communications Commission, 1997).

The e-rate is funded by charges to the telecommunications industry. Some argue that this charge represents a "back-door tax" levied without providing citizens the opportunity to approve the tax or control how the money is spent. Supporters argue that the intent was not to have the telecommunications industry pass on the cost to consumers, but to have the industry absorb these additional costs out of the savings allowed by regulatory changes that reduced access charges previously paid by long-distance companies. Thus, the funding mechanism for the e-rate is controversial, and the future of the program is somewhat uncertain (Department of Education, 1998).

The e-rate is intended to provide discounts on hardware and services essential to the transmission of information:

- Telephone connections
- Wiring for ethernet connections
- Internet access charges through dial-up or leased line connections

- Hardware required for Internet connections—routers, hubs, and computers used as servers

Schools are eligible for subsidies ranging from 20 percent to 90 percent, depending on the proportion of low-income students attending the school. Schools receiving the lowest reduction (20 percent) have less than 1 percent of the student body eligible for reduced-price lunches. Those schools eligible for the 90 percent reduction must have more than 75 percent of the students eligible for reduced-price lunches. Rural schools are eligible for slightly higher discounts because their telecommunication costs tend to be higher. Through February 1999, $1.1 billion had been awarded to 16,000 schools (Anderson & Ronnkvist, 1999).

The e-rate is administered for the Federal Communication Commission by the Universal Service Administration Commission. This organization receives applications and decides how the available money will be awarded. Applying for e-rate money is not a trivial exercise. Schools need to file a technology plan that explains how the e-rate money will be used to improve educational services. This plan must also include an assessment of communications needs, provisions for staff development, and a strategy and budget for maintenance. A school must also take steps to show that eligible vendors will have an opportunity to compete to provide the services that the school is requesting (Department of Education, 1998).✴

◆ Computer activities such as programming and competitive gaming emphasize mastery rather than social motives and may be more likely to appeal to males (Sanders & McGinnis, 1991; Weinman & Haag, 1999).

In contrast to past classroom applications of technology, it seems reasonable that the project approach we recommend offers some advantages in involving students with technology in a more equitable fashion. Female students feel equally competent in the use of computer tools (Gallup Organization, 1997), and focusing on applications rather than technology may encourage gender equity. Tool applications exist for all disciplines, offer the opportunity to engage all students, and can offer opportunities for collaboration and social interaction as well as opportunities for independence and competition. Moreover, the development of skills associated with tool applications can lead students toward vocational opportunities.

EQUITY AND STUDENT ABILITY

A number of studies have demonstrated that more and less able students have different experiences with technology. Less able students use computers less frequently, have fewer Internet experiences, and tend to spend a greater proportion of their time in drill-and-practice activities (Becker & Ravitz, 1999; Sutton, 1991). These differences may exist because more able students are assumed to be more trustworthy and capable of independent activity (Becker & Ravitz, 1999) or because the academic needs of less able students are assumed to require remediation focused on the development of basic skills and knowledge (Laboratory of Comparative Human Cognition, 1989).

Provide meaningful activities for all

However, a strict bottom-up model of instruction has been challenged because it cannot be assumed that the isolation and practice of lower-level skills is the most productive way to teach (e.g., Laboratory of Comparative Human Cognition, 1989). The alternative is to embed the practice of individual skills within more meaningful activities. Activity-centered projects offer this opportunity and also frequently take advantage of cooperative groups that involve students of various levels of ability. In addition, students can be inspired by the opportunity to use technology in interesting and challenging ways, and it would seem unnecessary to limit the technology-based experiences of less able students to drill and computer tutorials.

ADAPTING TECHNOLOGY FOR EQUAL ACCESS

This book is based on the premise that technology can provide meaningful learning experiences for the benefit of *all* students. However, more than 50 million Americans have some type of disability that requires that adaptations be made to take advantage of what technology has to offer.

Impairments that may affect technology use

These individuals may have mobility impairments that make it difficult to operate a mouse or use the keyboard. They may have visual impairments that make the computer screen useless as a device for presenting information or serving as the interface for user input. Learners may have auditory impairments or learning disabilities that present challenges. The computer and Internet can provide great independence and compensate for many traditional obstacles. However, without meaningful access, technology can also impose new barriers.

Adaptations for Mobility Impairments

Mobility impairments make it difficult for learners to interact with technology. The problem may be difficulty in manipulating input devices (keyboard, mouse) or even basic physical tasks associated with operating a computer or peripheral device (e.g., turning on the computer, inserting a diskette or CD). Here are some ways to respond to mobility impairments:

◆ A power strip, which can be used to turn all equipment on and off with a single switch
◆ Alternative keyboards, which position the keys farther apart and disable repeat keys so that users with slower and less precise movements have less difficulty
◆ Special software, which causes the cursor to scan across a screen representation or across program choice buttons, allowing individuals with the capacity to control a switch (using a knee, the mouth, or the head) to make selections

Adaptations for Visual Impairments

Visual impairment should not hinder learners from taking advantage of technology. Some of the following adaptations can be made:

◆ Blind individuals can use a standard keyboard. Braille key labels may be helpful to some of these students.
◆ Special **screen reader software** "reads" the screen to the learner (earphones can be used to reduce the distraction to others). Basic speech synthesis from text is fairly standard, but screen reader software can also "describe" menus, windows, and screen icons.
◆ Special software can allow magnification of the screen image for learners with limited vision. Some programs allow screen content to be enlarged sixteen-fold.

Adaptive Web Page Design

The adaptations we have described so far address the general use of computers, and they certainly apply to helping students make use of the Internet. In practice, though, challenges and solutions are often unique to a particular combination of learning limitation and computer application. The use of the Web by blind students offers a good example.

For blind students to use the Web, the adaptations we have already discussed, such as screen reader software, are essential. However, there are some other challenges that cannot be met through modifications in software or hardware. The way that Web pages themselves are designed is important.

Consider the issue from the perspective of the designer. Most Web designers recognize the need to accommodate limitations such as older versions of browsers and relatively slow modems. But designers often forget that some Internet users face very different challenges. Visually impaired students cannot read a Web page or scrutinize images and illustrations. Less obviously, these students cannot use the mouse to point at a text link or click on an image map hot spot. The hot spots of an image represent the areas of the image designated to serve as links. The browser usually takes different actions according to which hot spot is clicked.

A basic design suggestion

Some basic design suggestions can make a big difference, and Web designers of any age can implement many of these features (Adaptive Computer Technology Centre, 1998; World Wide Web Consortium, 1999). Often it is helpful to begin with the question: Could the Web page be interpreted totally by listening? This question does not imply that the author must create an audio version of each Web page; rather, the page design should allow the user's special software to "read" the screen to the user. Here are some principles to follow:

◆ If some page information is not presented as text—for example, if important content information is contained in images, illustrations, or video—consider offering alternative sources of information. An image map should be accompanied by text links that can be used as alternatives to the map's hot spots. A link to a separate page containing a text segment can be offered as an alternative to an explanatory illustration. Video can be supplemented with an audio track to provide descriptive information.

◆ Take advantage of the built-in opportunities to provide redundant information. HTML provides opportunities to include supplemental information, but designers frequently ignore these opportunities. Imagine, for example, that a Web page uses a graphic forward arrow as a link to the next page in a sequence. Many visually impaired students, who have no use for graphics, set their browsers to avoid loading graphic images. The designer can use the ALT attribute to specify text that will appear as a replacement for an image. In this case, specifying ALT="Next Page" would allow the text phrase "Next Page" to appear in place of the arrow. This kind of supplemental information is very easy to add when using a Web authoring program.

◆ Information presented in tables or multiple columns can be confusing when "read" by older screen reader programs, because the reader attempts to follow the text horizontally across the entire page. We do advocate the use of tables as a way to construct Web pages, but tables with side-by-side columns of lengthy text are especially problematic for users dependent on a screen reader. The best solution may be to insert a link at

Emerging Technology

Adaptations for Visually Impaired Web Users

To comprehend Web content and make effective use of the navigational and interactive elements built into Web pages, visually impaired users need more than a spoken version of Web page text. They need to hear a description of other elements appearing on a page, they need to know when text segments serve as links, and they need access to some of the alternative descriptive information that may not be automatically displayed. If the page author has done a conscientious job, all of this information is embedded in one way or another within the raw HTML; what is required is a different way of interpreting the HTML and presenting information to the user. A different type of browser or an enhancement for existing browsers could allow HTML to be interpreted and the embedded information presented in a different way.

Home Page Reader is an example of a program that extracts and presents supplemental information. This product:

- Reads text in a male voice and text links in a female voice.
- Reads ALT text and HTML 4.0 (a more advanced version of HTML with an expanded set of capabilities) information provided by Web page authors.
- Describes tables, frames, and forms.
- Summarizes page links and allows the selection of links using the number keypad.
- Allows visually impaired users to create "readable" bookmarks.

Advances in HTML, hardware, and software are coming together to allow visually impaired users to benefit from Web resources. ✳

the top of the page providing access to a single-column, alternative version of the page.
- Remember to use punctuation. Screen readers identify punctuation marks, and these can be critical for a user's understanding of the content. On many Web pages, items in lists do not end with punctuation marks, and this lack of punctuation can make them more difficult to interpret.

COPYRIGHT LAW AND RESPECT FOR INTELLECTUAL PROPERTY

All teachers need to be aware of their personal obligations regarding copyrighted materials, and they need to teach their students to respect the intellectual property of others. It may be helpful to think of these responsibilities as interrelated. A powerful way to develop any behavior in your students is to model this behavior yourself.

EDUCATION AND COPYRIGHT: ISSUES AND PROBLEMS

Importance of copyright questions in education

Copyright is such an important issue in education because the process of education relies heavily on instructional materials (including textbooks, films, and computer programs) and other resources that can serve an educational purpose (newspapers, television programs, videotapes, music CDs, reference books). We now must add Internet resources as a new option for both instructional material and general information. These essential information resources were purposefully created through the intellectual efforts of others—often as a way for these individuals to make a living. If we want creative individuals to spend their time preparing instructional materials, they must be compensated when their materials are used.

Examples of copyright violations

Educators can violate copyright law in various ways—for example:

◆ The music teacher may copy orchestra sheet music so each child can take a copy home to practice.
◆ The biology teacher may develop a personal collection of informative television programs for use in class.
◆ The English teacher who has purchased a new word processing program may copy it to all three computers in his room.
◆ A college professor may print out an article from a subscription Internet information service, make copies, and distribute them to her students.

Because teachers are not, as a rule, prone to breaking the law, why do they sometimes violate copyright law? Some may want to help students but lack the resources they think are necessary to do so. A second reason may result from a combination of easy access to the means for making copies and sketchy knowledge of when copying is appropriate. Nearly every teacher has access to a photocopier, tape recorder, video recorder, scanner, and computer with blank disks. These are available in schools and in most public libraries. Most users of the Internet probably realize that if you hold down the mouse button while clicking on a Web page image (or click with the right button when working on a Windows machine), the browser will ask you if you would like to save a copy of the image. If it were illegal to copy documents, TV programs, computer programs, Web images, and the like, would the methods and equipment for doing so be so readily accessible?

The answer is yes. The methods and materials are available even though some of the copying they are used for is illegal. Of course, schools, libraries, and the companies creating products that enable copying are not advocating theft of intellectual property. These organizations assume that those who use their products and resources understand when copying is appropriate and when it is not. When violations occur, it is sometimes because teachers or students assume that the opportunity to copy something implies more than it does. In this situation, teachers and students need a thorough understanding of what is appropriate.

False assumptions about Internet materials

For the Internet in particular, one final problem may be caused by a different set of false assumptions. Access to a tremendous amount of Internet material is free, and often there are no obvious indicators such as a copyright symbol or a statement that the material is protected. Can you steal something that has no posted price and that no one has openly spoken for? Yes, for these reasons:

◆ The assumption that you are not taking revenue away from an author by copying content from a Web page may be wrong. The individual responsible for the Web content may be paid by others—advertisers, for example—when the information on the page is accessed. If your behavior prevents others (such as your students) from visiting a Web page, it is possible you are limiting the income of the Web site author.

◆ The intent to make money is not necessary for intellectual property to be protected. The author has the right to control who displays what he or she has created.

◆ The absence of a copyright statement is not an indication that the author has given up his or her rights.

Again, teachers and students may simply need a better understanding of what is appropriate. Our goal in the following sections is to make you aware of some of the general issues regarding copyright and then to take a more specific look at issues pertaining to the Internet.

THE COPYRIGHT LAW

The government's authority to develop copyright law is established in the U.S. Constitution in Article I, section 8, which grants Congress the authority "to promote the progress of science and useful arts, by securing for limited times to authors and inventors the exclusive right to their respective writings and discoveries." This section of the Constitution is responsible for what we know as copyrights and patents.

The current copyright law was written in 1976 and has since been amended to make the law more specific. Congress has also formed committees to offer suggestions on such topics as copying from books and periodicals, copying of music, off-air videotaping, and, more recently, multimedia. This collected body of information does not address every possible situation, but the original law was written to be very open-ended and defines as copyrightable "original works of authorship fixed in any tangible medium of expression, now known or later developed" (Copyright Act of 1976, Title 17 of the U.S. Code, Section 102, included in Salpeter, 1992). Nearly any type of instructional material you can think of is probably included: print materials, software, pictures, recorded music, musical scores, television broadcasts, works of art, and Internet Web pages.

It is easy for educators to see only one side of copyright law: as telling teachers what they *cannot* do. However, if you read and think carefully about the statement from the Constitution authorizing copyright laws, you may gain a different perspective. Copyright law is intended to encourage "the progress of science and useful arts." In other words, if educators expect others to create and improve instructional materials, educators should also expect that mechanisms must be put in place to allow these individuals to make a fair profit on their work. For example, if subscription-based Web services become perceived as a market prone to frequent copyright violations, commercial developers will not put effort into creating high-quality products for that market.

Copyright encourages scientific and intellectual progress.

Establishing a Copyright

How exactly does a work's creator establish copyright under the current law? In fact, the creator does not need to take any specific steps to claim copyright because *any author's work is automatically protected from the time it is created.* This principle applies not only to written works but also to music, photographs, artwork, and so on.

An author can provide notice of copyright with a notation in the following form: © year name—for example, © 2000 Cindy Grabe. The word *copyright* can also be used in place of the copyright symbol. You are probably aware that there is a U.S. Copyright Office and that authors can register their works with this office. But the fact that a work has not been registered or even that it does not carry a notice of copyright should not be interpreted as a waiver of copyright.

Rights, Licenses, and Permissions

Copyright law grants authors or owners five basic rights:

1. *The right to make copies.* If you are the creator of the work, you can make as many copies as you want.
2. *The right to create derivations.* A derivation is an adaptation of the original. For example, a painter might create prints from an original painting, or an author might create a movie script based on a book.
3. *The right to sell or distribute copies.* The author can make a profit by copying and selling works to others.
4. *The right to perform a work in public.* Generally the author of a work controls the presentation of the work to the public. The performance right covers, for instance, live performances of music and the presentation of a play.
5. *The right to display a work in public.* This right covers situations like the display of a painting or the presentation of original artwork on the Internet.

Transfer of rights

The author or creator of a work can transfer some or all of these rights to others. If the copyright itself is assigned to someone else, that means that all rights are transferred. For example, a large software company may pay an independent developer a large sum of money to be assigned the copyright for a computer program the developer has written. From that point on, the company can do whatever it wants with the program. In an alternative arrangement, the granting of a **license,** only the rights specified in the agreement are transferred (Fritz, 1992). Although the term *license* may not always be used, this is a common type of agreement, and it may or may not involve money.

License agreements

Examples of license agreements in education are common. You may have heard of a software **site license,** which allows a school or other organization to make copies of software it has purchased. The license may limit the number of copies, or it may allow unlimited copying as long as the software is used on a machine that the school owns. A license of this type does not allow the school to distribute copies outside the site. A site license offers some advantages to both parties. The school is allowed to purchase the software for less than the standard price per copy, and the company selling the software usually saves on packaging and manuals.

When you ask a copyright holder for permission to copy a work in a specific way for a certain context, you are in effect applying for a mini-license. For example, you may ask an artist for permission to scan a painting or drawing to include it in a classroom project. In instances of this sort, only very specific and limited rights are granted. For advice on acquiring permission, see Focus: Obtaining Permission to Copy.

Copying Computer Software

The copyright law was amended in 1980 to address the copying of computer software (section 117). Illegal copying of computer software, often called **software piracy,** is rampant; estimates are that software authors lose $3 billion annually in U.S. sales (Business Software Alliance, 1998). Section 117 of the copyright law states that legitimate owners of software can copy the software in two situations. First, they can copy the software when making a copy that is essential in allowing the software to run on their own computers. This usually means that the owner of the software will have a copy of the program on the disks or CD he or she purchased and also on the hard drive of a computer. Section 117 also allows the individual purchasing the software to make a backup or archival copy. The backup is a safeguard against the loss or corruption of the original program. The backup legally should not be used on a second computer while the original is still in use.

When is it permissible to copy software?

The owners of a software copyright can also grant a license allowing software to be copied under an agreement called a site license. This agreement allows the purchaser to make a specified number of copies or to allow a

Obtaining Permission to Copy

The first step in obtaining permission is to determine who owns the copyright. With books, journals, and documents, the copyright notice usually appears near the front of the publication. Also check the acknowledgments page. Pay special attention to information about multiple copyrights. With music, the lyrics and musical score may be protected separately. This is also frequently the case with the text and illustrations in documents. Web sites may include a "terms and conditions" statement that explains the author's position on the use of site contents.

A list of items to include in your request for permission follows. This list assumes that you want to copy material from a document, and some of these items may need to be modified slightly if another type of material is involved. Circumstances may also require that the form of the letter or e-mail message be modified. Be sure to include the following elements:

- The full name of the author or artist responsible for the work you propose to copy.
- The exact reference for the source material.
- Page number(s) or the URL (for Web content) for the material you want to copy.
- The number of copies you propose to make.
- A full description of how the copied material will be used, including:
  —The nature of the project.

—Whether the material will be used alone or combined with materials to be obtained from other companies.
—Who will assemble the project.
—Who will view the finished project.
—How long the materials will be kept and what will happen to the project after the intended academic task has been completed.
- A description of the course in which the material is to be used.
- Your name, position, institutional affiliation, full address, and telephone number.

Some companies may expect you to pay a royalty fee for using their material. You may feel it is appropriate to acknowledge that this is a possibility and ask what the fee will be. For example, you might say, "If a royalty fee applies to copying the material that has been described, please notify me so that I can determine if funds are available."

It is important to allow several weeks for your request to be considered. It may take a month to process your request, and you will want to allow time to develop an alternate plan in case your request is denied.

Remember to be courteous. What you are requesting is a privilege.

Source: Based on suggestions provided by Long, Risher, & Shapiro (1997). We have added other suggestions based on our own experiences.✶

specified number of copies to be active on a **local area network (LAN)** of interconnected computers. Copying software to multiple machines (multiple loading) and allowing several users to use a program simultaneously over a network without a site license are violations of copyright law. Sometimes violations of this type are quite purposeful, as when a business purchases one copy of a spreadsheet and loads it on every employee's computer. In other cases, violations are more innocent. A teacher may purchase a program for her home computer and then decide to take the program to school so that her students can use it. If there is only one original, two individuals should not be using a program at the same time.

Fair Use

Libraries provide easy access to photocopiers, so it is very easy for anyone to copy material from books, journals, and magazines. This does *not* mean that all types of copying are legal; yet because libraries do not want to promote copyright violations, there must be some situations in which material can be copied without seeking permission from the author or creator.

In fact, you are allowed to make photocopies in the library because of a provision called **fair use,** defined in section 107 of the copyright law. The guidelines governing fair use can be confusing, and it is important for you as a teacher to understand what they mean. Essentially, section 107 provides some exceptions to the general principle that the creator of the work holds exclusive rights to copy and distribute it.

For purposes like teaching, scholarship, and research, section 107 specifies four "factors to be considered" in determining whether a particular act of copying represents fair use:

◆ *Purpose of the use.* Generally, copying is more acceptable if it is for nonprofit purposes than if it is done for profit.

◆ *Nature of the copyrighted work.* The copying of factual material, such as a summary of historical events, is more likely to be fair use than the copying of original poetry or fiction.

◆ *Amount and substantiality of the portion used.* Copying a small part of the original is more likely to be tolerated than copying the entire work.

◆ *Impact on commercial value.* Copying should not harm the commercial value of the original or deprive the creator or publisher of permission fees. For instance, copying of workbooks is not considered fair use because workbooks are intended to be purchased and used only once. A related consideration for many kinds of material is the number of copies made; obviously a large number of copies would have a greater impact on a work's commercial value than a small number.

These four factors were intended to be balanced against one another in particular cases. The overall intent was to create a law that is flexible and applicable to many situations, reflecting the great variety of copyrighted material and the equally great variety of possible uses. For many educators and other professionals, however, the result has been uncertainty about what they can and cannot do.

*Meaning of fair use
varies with the medium*

To make matters even more complicated, the meaning of *fair* in *fair use* sometimes varies with the medium (Major, 1998; Martin, 1994; Salpeter, 1992). For example, video is a common way of delivering educational content, and video players are common in most schools. Specific guidelines have been developed to guide the taping of television programs for classroom use. Television programs offered free of charge for viewing by the general public can be recorded and used for nonprofit instructional purposes. A number of conditions must be met:

◆ Recorded material must be used within the first ten school days of the forty-five calendar days following the actual broadcast. Material recorded in June, for example, could not be used in October because the time period extends beyond forty-five calendar days. A program recorded on December 27 might legally be used with a class on January 12 because consecutive school days do not include weekends or holidays. Recordings are to be erased by the end of the forty-five-day period.

◆ Schools cannot record a variety of programs and then make them available to teachers. Recordings can be made only by or at the request of an individual teacher, to be used by that teacher. A teacher cannot request that the same program be re-recorded no matter how many times the program is broadcast.

◆ Teachers do not have to show entire programs, but the content of the programs as broadcast is not to be altered. For example, combining small segments from several programs is not allowed. Any copy of a broadcast program must contain the broadcast copyright notice.

◆ Educational institutions are to accept responsibility for implementing adequate control measures to see that recorded material is used within the established guidelines. Schools allowing teachers to use recorded television programs in their classrooms are expected to take an active role in guaranteeing compliance with copyright law.

The companies responsible for some television programs have adopted a more lenient set of guidelines related to instructional use of the programs. See the description of Cable in the Classroom in Resources to Expand Your Knowledge Base at the conclusion of this chapter.

Fair Use as Applied to Multimedia and the Internet.   There are many areas for which specific fair use guidelines such as those just described for the use of content from television programs do not exist. Multimedia and Web page authoring, two areas emphasized in this book, are examples. We think there are some important areas in which teachers need guidance:

◆ Can students and teachers take resources from Web sites for use in learning and instructional activities?

◆ Can students and teachers use the material developed by others on their own Web pages?

◆ Can teachers post student work on the Web?

◆ What should teachers do if they want to protect online resources they have developed?

Without specific guidelines in these areas, the reasonable approach is probably a conservative one, drawing on existing policies that apply to other media.

Because of the matters left unresolved by the copyright law, there have been various attempts to bring interested parties together to negotiate more specific guidelines. One of the earliest such negotiations focused on the issue of photocopying of printed works, and a set of guidelines was worked out specifically for that medium. Let's look at what those rules entail. A key point to remember is this: *The guidelines that apply to copying material for your own professional use differ from the guidelines for preparing multiple copies for your students.*

Copying for Your Own Use. In general, as an individual, you are allowed to copy rather extensively in preparing for your classes or conducting scholarly work. For example, your college or university library will likely allow you to copy an entire journal article or book chapter as part of your research for a paper. The same is true when you are doing research to prepare for teaching a class. Fair use guidelines for individual scholarship are fairly liberal.

This does not mean, however, that there are no limits. For example, when Mark Grabe's university library honors his request to copy a chapter from a book, the library records his name and the book title. The library will not allow him to copy a second chapter from the same book. This is the point at which the library feels copying might be perceived as a substitute for purchasing the book.

Making Multiple Copies for Classroom Use. Guidelines for making multiple copies for class use are much more conservative than those controlling personal use. For books and periodicals, the multiple-copy fair use guidelines include these points:

◆ *Brevity.* A teacher is allowed to excerpt and distribute 1,000 words or 10 percent, whichever is less, from a written document. Similar guidelines have been set for other media, as we describe in the next section.

◆ *Spontaneity.* Copying a particular work must be the "inspiration" of the teacher who wants to use the work. For example, a librarian is not supposed to collect material for a teacher. The decision to use the work must occur so close in time to its actual use that it would not be practical to obtain permission.

◆ *Cumulative effect.* Material is to be copied for a single course, and the time period during which the material may continue to be used is restricted. To control the cumulative effect of the copying, limits are placed on how many items may be taken from the works of a single author or artist.

These are the guidelines that were developed to contend with the technological innovation called the photocopier. Now let's consider what headway has been made in dealing with more recent advances in multimedia and distance education.

Guidelines for Creating Multimedia and for Distance Education.   In recent years, individuals from various parties with a vested interest in fair use (such as the U.S. government, publishing companies, the Software Publishing Association, and the Association for Educational Communications and Technology) have met to propose guidelines for technological applications in educational contexts. These meetings evolved into the **Conference on Fair Use** (commonly referred to as **CONFU**). After two years of work, CONFU's suggestions for teacher- or student-created multimedia and for distance education were finalized in 1997. The full text of the documents prepared by this committee is available on the Internet (CONFU, 1997a, 1997b), and the preamble to each document includes a good discussion of fair use in general.

The CONFU guidelines still do not provide the focus on Internet resources or issues that we would prefer. When the CONFU meetings occurred, only a few colleges and schools were beginning to explore uses of the World Wide Web for teaching their students. Another attempt to deal with emerging copyright issues, the Digital Millennium Copyright Act, became law in late 1998. This law includes a provision (section 403) directing the Copyright Office to work with educators, nonprofit libraries, and publishers to submit a proposal to Congress concerning distance education and digital technology. This report has now been submitted (U.S. Copyright Office, 1999), but further action has yet to be taken at the time this book was written. For the moment, the CONFU guidelines are the most applicable ones, and they are worth examining in more detail.

Among the guidelines for distance learning and educational multimedia offered by CONFU, the multimedia guidelines have received widespread acceptance whereas the ones for distance education have prompted much disagreement. It is important to understand that all of these guidelines, however, are not legally binding; rather, they are in the nature of proposals.

Guidelines for distance learning

The suggestions for distance learning apply to telecommunications applications, such as teaching a class via videoconferencing. Generally they allow a teacher to read, display, or perform copyrighted works in a distance education setting in the same way that the teacher might in face-to-face instruction. The teacher can read a poem aloud, for example. But an entire work or "a large portion thereof" can be transmitted only once for a particular course. The transmission must be over a secure system so that only eligible students have access to it. Although the institution that receives the transmission can record or copy it, the recording can be saved for only fifteen consecutive class days without obtaining permission.

Guidelines for multimedia

The guidelines for multimedia may be more relevant to most of the applications described in this book. CONFU's multimedia guidelines address student use of copyrighted work as part of course-related multimedia projects and teacher use of copyrighted work in the creation of "noncommercial" multimedia for instructional purposes. CONFU attempts to suggest the applications, time frame, portion, copying, and distribution limits that would comply with established fair use standards.

Application

◆ *Students*. Students may create and present multimedia projects containing copyrighted material for educational purposes within the course for which they were created, and they may save these projects as examples of their academic work for future job or academic interviews.
◆ *Teachers*. Teachers may use multimedia including copyrighted material conforming to fair use for purposes of (1) face-to-face instruction, (2) student self-study, (3) remote instruction to enrolled students on a network providing controlled access, or (4) evaluations of teaching performance or job interviews.

Time, Copying, and Distribution Limits

◆ *Time*. Teacher-created multimedia may be used in instruction for up to two years. (If the teacher cannot prevent duplication of copyrighted material, the material can remain available for only fifteen days.)
◆ *Copying and distribution*. It is suggested that only two copies, the original and a backup, should be created. Only one copy should be available to users, and students should not be allowed to make personal copies. When the product has been the result of a collaborative effort, each participant may keep a copy for archival purposes.

Portion Limits

The portion limitation defines the amount of material that may be taken from a copyrighted work. These limits apply cumulatively to projects created by students or teachers. For example, a teacher who creates multimedia resources to be used in conjunction with daily lectures must consider the total material used in all lectures in determining what resources may be taken from a given source.

- ◆ *Video.* Users are allowed to use up to 10 percent or 3 minutes, whichever is less, of material from a video work.
- ◆ *Text material.* Users are allowed to use up to 10 percent or 1,000 words, whichever is less, from a copyrighted work. Poetry represents a special category. A poem of 250 words or less may be used in total, but no more than three poems by one poet or five poems from a published anthology may be used.
- ◆ *Music.* Users may use 10 percent or 30 seconds, whichever is less, from an individual musical work.
- ◆ *Photographs and other illustrations.* No more than five images by an artist or photographer may be used. For images from a collection (such as a book), the limit is 10 percent or 15 images, whichever is less.

Additional guidelines

There are some additional expectations. Students and educators are required to cite all sources carefully when using copyrighted material. Providing credit includes listing a full citation for the original work and any copyright notices displayed in the original source. With the exception of copyright information related to images, this information may be consolidated in a single section within the multimedia product (for instance, it may appear as a list at the end). For images, however, information about the source and copyright should accompany each individual image. Finally, students and teachers should include in the introduction to their multimedia product a statement indicating that material is incorporated in this product under the fair use exemption of the U.S. copyright law and is restricted from further use.

Unresolved questions

Gaps in the Guidelines.   As you can see, both the existing law and the guidelines developed by CONFU have gaps where teachers want answers. For example, the CONFU participants provided suggestions for what teachers can use in their classrooms and with locally based students, but they stated clearly that these guidelines do not apply to students involved in distance education. Nor do the separate guidelines for distance education answer many Internet-related questions that teachers will have. We certainly cannot assume that teachers are free to do online the same things they can do with in-class multimedia. The gap in the guidelines remains even when the teacher can guarantee that access is limited by a password protection system.

Another important uncertainty concerns the use of Web resources in the creation of student or teacher multimedia. For example, the CONFU guidelines make clear suggestions about the use of images from a book or part of a song from a CD. But there is no clear statement about using an image or part of a song copied from a Web page.

You can probably see other gaps in the guidelines that may apply to your own classroom situations. Within a few years the copyright rules for Internet educational uses should become clearer, through new laws or negotiated policies. For example, the U.S. Copyright Office report (1999) urges that on-site and distance education be regarded as equivalent, and if access to online material can be limited to students enrolled in classes (e.g., using passwords, screening for IP addresses), fair use guidelines should apply consistently. In the meantime a conservative approach is advisable.

USING STUDENT WORK ON WEB SITES

Students' possible rights as authors

Before we sum up our outlook on copyright issues, there is one more area we want to address. It is common to view student work on school Web sites. Do students have rights as authors? Copyright law is clear on the issue of ownership. Unless a student has been hired to create material and is operating under a formalized work-for-hire agreement, a student owns any work he or she has created.

Does this mean that the teacher cannot keep or make copies of a student's work? According to one opinion (Burke, 1993), a teacher may have an implicit license to make copies to be used as an example for later classes. For example, teachers sometimes save outstanding research papers so that students in later classes can see what the teachers expect. However, the instructor would not have the right to use student material in a derivative work—something like a book authored by the teacher in which the student work appears as an example. Because placing work on a Web site can clearly be considered a form of distribution, Web publication of a student's work raises similar concerns. Therefore, we make this recommendation: *The best policy is to treat student work in the same way you would treat the work of any other artist or author; that is, request signed permission to use the work.*

Permission from both students and parents

Note that because most K–12 students are minors, certain situations may also require permission from a parent or legal guardian. Often the best option is to work out the publication arrangements at the beginning of a project, obtaining the necessary consent from both students and parents.

Recognizing student work in this manner helps the student understand the concept of authorship. It also develops an appreciation for the rights accorded those who produce intellectual and creative works.

RULES OF THUMB: SUGGESTED ANSWERS FOR THE COPYRIGHT QUESTION

We have told you as much as we can about how copyright and fair use apply to the Internet. Obviously these are complex topics without definitive answers. Still, educators do want guidance, and if definitive answers are not available, they need rules of thumb. Returning to the four fundamental questions that we posed at the beginning of this discussion, here are our suggested answers:

◆ *Can students and teachers take resources from Web sites for use in learning and instructional activities?*

Check the Web site itself for terms and conditions governing usage. In the absence of guidelines on the site itself, a convenient way to think about fair use has been provided by Georgia Harper (1997), who recommends that educators follow the suggestion of "small parts, limited time, and limited access." The CONFU guidelines may provide a way to interpret this suggestion.

◆ *Can students and teachers use the material developed by others on their own Web pages?*

We believe that the use of copyrighted resources on Web pages without permission is questionable and should be avoided. Certainly the activities we have emphasized in this book do not require this type of material. The Golden Rule provides a useful way to think about this issue. As a teacher, would you want other teachers to "borrow" some of your best lesson plans or classroom materials without at least asking?

◆ *Can teachers post student work on the Web?*

We encourage schools to use the Web to present student work, but to do so in a way that recognizes the creative talents of the student. In any decision to publish student work, the students and parents should be involved.

◆ *What should teachers do if they want to protect online resources they have developed?*

There is no guaranteed way to protect your work once it is online. What you can do is to indicate that you regard your work as copyrighted and that it should not be used without your permission. (Be aware, however, that in some cases, the institution you work for, such as your school or school district, may believe that it owns the rights. You may want to check your district's policies.) If your work is intended for a specific audience such as students involved in a distance education experience, you can limit access through the use of password protection.

PROTECTING STUDENTS FROM INAPPROPRIATE MATERIAL AND EXPERIENCES

The Internet compared to other media

Educators must recognize that the Internet does not exist specifically to support educational goals. In this regard, the Internet is similar to other information systems we encounter in our daily lives. Cable television has the capacity to bring sporting events, congressional testimony, educational programming, and sexually explicit content into our living rooms. The telephone can be used to chat with grandma about Thanksgiving dinner or with a psychic about your future. For adults, all are acceptable forms of "information."

Digital Cheating

Recent anonymous surveys of students indicate that cheating is rampant in K–12 and college institutions. Even a high proportion of the most academically able students admit to cheating (e.g., Bushweller, 1999a). While academic cheating takes many forms, our interest is in **plagiarism**—representing someone else's work as your own. Plagiarism is certainly not dependent on technology, but technology makes the mechanical act of copying another's work easier.

Plagiarism takes many forms. Students may cut and paste from Web sites or CD-based encyclopedias. In some cases such plagiarism is unintentional and results from the inappropriate assumptions that "borrowing" small amounts of material is allowed. Some students, for example, assume that adding a citation allows copying paragraph-length excerpts. Most students know better and "borrow" material recognizing that it would be extremely unlikely their teachers would ever be able to locate the original source. The vastness and informality of Internet resources probably reinforce this perception.

The most blatant form of digital plagiarism involves the purchase of complete essays or term papers from a commercial online provider (Bushweller, 1999b). While many of these sites include disclaimers encouraging students to use the downloaded material for "research purposes only," the general tone of the sites and even site names (several contain the word *cheat*) suggest a very different purpose.

What can teachers do about this problem? Some urge the use of more effective methods of detecting plagiarism. Plagiarism.org offers a detection service to college instructors. Student papers are submitted online, and each is compared against a database of manuscripts. Segments of text identified as possibly copied are highlighted for the instructor to investigate.

Part of the solution is to establish clear guidelines and possibly make the generation of scholarly works a more interactive process. Students should learn how to cite their sources accurately (see page 237) and how to personalize and interpret primary sources in creating their own products. Students can begin to learn these skills at an early age. One second-grade teacher we know helps her students learn to take notes in their own words by having the students close the reference book before they write down any information. Writing can be made a more interactive process by asking students to submit intermediate products (e.g., notes, printouts of Web pages they intend to focus on) or by asking students to discuss their projects before or after the paper has been submitted for grading.✳

If we want to benefit from powerful communication systems, we must both recognize and find ways to adjust to the multiple purposes and audiences the Internet serves.

It is true that there are risks in allowing students to use the Internet. Both educators and students must recognize these risks so that protective measures can be taken. In this section we explore the dangers and outline what we consider reasonable responses to them.

POTENTIAL DANGERS AND REASONABLE PROTECTION

Possible risks from Internet access

What are the possible risks of Internet access? Students may encounter the following (Magid, 1998):

◆ Inappropriate content. Students using the World Wide Web may encounter material displaying sexual acts and violence, promoting the hatred of specific groups, or encouraging dangerous or unlawful activities.

◆ Physical molestation. Students using e-mail or chat areas may encounter individuals who wish to do them harm, such as pedophiles. Some individuals, often representing themselves deceptively, use Internet communication tools to become acquainted with students and eventually attempt to arrange a meeting.

◆ Harassment. Students using e-mail or chat areas may be subjected to harassment, becoming the target of demeaning or threatening messages.

◆ Legal and financial threats. Students may knowingly or unknowingly become involved in situations with legal or financial consequences. For example, an attempt may be made to deceive students into providing a credit card number.

Balancing Freedom and Protection

Putting the dangers in context

In the light of these potential dangers, the general public and educators are justifiably concerned about abuses of the Internet. However, proper caution and paranoia are two different reactions. There is some level of potential danger involved in openness to any means of communication. Pornography, hate literature, descriptions of how to create explosive devices, and the open discussion of drug use certainly exist, and educators cannot guarantee that students won't find such material on the Internet. But educators also cannot guarantee that such materials are not being stashed in some student's locker and passed around during school. Similarly, a small number of individuals seek to take advantage of young people through Internet conversations, but such individuals may also hang out near play areas after school.

One issue that educators face in trying to regulate students' Internet access is a clash between the democratic ideal of a right to personal expression and the desire of parents and educators to protect young people from harmful experiences. At least at an abstract level, most people would agree that both personal expression and individual safety are fundamental rights. The challenge is to create an Internet environment that does not impose censorship and yet allows adults to control what minors in their care experience.

An example and a compromise solution

Conflicts of this type are often resolved without major difficulty in other situations. For example, local grocery stores and gas stations carry magazines containing nudity. Publishers have a right to sell this material, and adults have a right to purchase it. The solution is for the magazines to be enclosed in a plastic envelope that cannot be opened until the magazine has been purchased, and the business establishments will not sell the magazines to minors. In this situation, reasonable measures have been taken to satisfy the conflicting values.

In the case of Internet use, how can educators provide a similar balance between freedom and protection? What would constitute reasonable measures? To answer this question, consider a parallel situation.

We, the authors of this book, have always allowed our children to answer the telephone even when we are not at home. The telephone is a valuable communication tool, and we recognize that our children have friends they want to talk to. We certainly want them to answer when we're calling them. On the other hand, we do recognize that there are possible dangers. We cope with these dangers in the following ways:

◆ Technology. One of our responses is technological: we have caller ID and voice mail. Our children can see who is calling or allow the caller to record a message. If we are calling from a phone that is not recognized by caller ID, our daughter may pick up the phone when she hears us talking to the voice mail system.

◆ Instruction. We supplement the technology with instructions we have given our children. For example, if a strange caller asks for one of us, our daughter is not supposed to say that her parents are not home. Instead, she says that they can't come to the phone right now and asks that the caller leave a message or call back in a little while.

The Internet presents a different set of challenges, but the goals are basically the same, and a similar combination of measures can be used. Educators can (1) direct students toward safe areas of the Internet, (2) take advantage of filtering systems that screen Internet content, and (3) directly intervene with students through supervision, instruction in safety guidelines, and the administration of an acceptable use policy. We believe that educators need to consider these methods rather than assuming that a single approach will be sufficient.

SAFE AREAS OF THE INTERNET

Internet sites that have been screened and operate under supervision may be thought of as "safe areas." We have mentioned several of these areas throughout this book, and we will attempt to organize and summarize them here. Additional information about the resources mentioned here is provided at the end of the chapter.

Here are some ideas for identifying and using safe areas:

◆ Search for Web sites using a directory that rates Web sites and that will allow searches to be limited to sites approved for students and younger users. A good example of a directory of this type is Yahooligans, an offshoot of Yahoo! The searchable Yahooligans database provides links only to sites appropriate for student exploration. Magellan takes a different approach, allowing "safe sites" to be set as one of the search criteria.

◆ Focus most student Web experiences on well-tested curriculum projects. For example, Pacific Bell sponsors Blue Web'n, a very large, annotated, online database of educational Web sites.

◆ Use chat services that provide supervision. For example, Kidlink, a service that establishes communication opportunities among students, sponsors supervised chat areas.

◆ Emphasize e-mail or videoconferencing projects that are organized through other teachers.

FILTERING

Filtering helps control what Internet users are able to access. Filtering is accomplished in different ways, but the basic idea is to block access to material and activities that have been judged to be inappropriate or dangerous. We will describe three approaches schools might consider: a firewall, commercial stand-alone filtering software, and filtering tools built into the most recent versions of the Netscape and Microsoft browsers.

Firewall

A firewall is basically a computer and sophisticated software that control the flow of data between two networks. A firewall might be used to separate the Internet and the network connecting the computers within a school district. In such a situation, the barrier created by a firewall could serve two functions: (1) protect the information maintained by the district's computers from being damaged or accessed from any computer external to the district network or (2) determine what someone within the district could request from the Internet.

Data flow across a firewall can be filtered on the basis of either IP address or protocol. This means that students can be prevented from downloading information from certain designated Web sites (identified by IP address) or from using specific services such as Internet relay chat or e-mail (identified by protocol). A firewall is also capable of gathering information on attempted external breaches of the security system or keeping a record of the Web pages requested by each computer in the district. An individual with advanced technical skills would manage a district firewall.

Stand-Alone Filtering Software

Commercial stand-alone software has been around for several years and is popular for both schools and homes. This software works primarily by refusing to accept material sent from certain targeted sites. The companies selling these products continually update their lists of sites that provide offensive material and make these lists available to those who own copies of the software.

These systems do not offer perfect protection. Offensive material can be added to an existing site at any time, and new servers are always being connected to the Internet. However, this software does provide a reasonable means of protection from established sites that offer material not appropriate in a school environment.

Filtering programs offer some other interesting strategies for controlling access. Several companies offer those who purchase their filtering software lists of disapproved and approved sites. Using a list of approved sites would offer protection against inappropriate material contained on new servers. Some filtering programs can also keep track of which sites students have visited. The intent is not so much to punish those students who ignore school policies (actually, it is the identity of the computer that is stored, not that of the user), but to make school personnel aware of which sites have been visited. If necessary, the school can use this information to add sites to the disapproved list.

One filtering program, Cyber Patrol, offers some protection against another concern: young people's revealing personal information to strangers during chat sessions. School personnel or parents can enter protected words (names, phone numbers, addresses, credit card numbers) into a file. If a student types one of the protected words during a chat conversation, a series of Xs will be substituted. While it would not be appropriate or practical to store all of these items of information on school computers, a subset of the items might be entered.

Public concern has encouraged the continued development of filtering software. Local and nationwide Internet service providers, such as America Online and WebTV, often offer filtering software free or at a nominal cost to their customers. A list of the more popular commercial filtering programs is included at the end of the chapter.

Browser Filtering

Recent versions of the two major browsers have built-in filtering options. These filters are possible because the World Wide Web Consortium (W3C), an oversight committee that attempts to guide the technical development of the Internet, created a protocol referred to as the Platform for Internet Content Selection (PICS).

You may encounter references to PICS-formatted ratings or PICS-compatible browsers. Just think of PICS as allowing an extension of HTML. A special tag, inserted at the top of a Web page, contains information about the type of information and images contained on that page. When a browser that has been prepared to receive PICS information encounters this tag, it checks the information carried by the tag against settings established by the person responsible for the browser. The rest of the page is displayed only if the comparison indicates the content is allowable.

There are several different rating schemes based on the PICS protocol (see Resources to Expand Your Knowledge Base at the end of the chapter). The simplest one, the Recreational Software Advisory Council on the Internet (RSACi) system, will serve as our example. The RSACi system is based on four categories: nudity, sex, language, and violence. Each category is assigned a rating based on guidelines from 0 to 4. For example, a level 0 nudity rating indicates that the Web site contains no nudity. A level 4 rating indicates the site contains provocative frontal nudity. Web authors who want to have their sites carry RSACi ratings connect to the RSACi Web site and provide information about their sites (see Focus: Self-Rating a Web Site). The process of self-rating does concern some people, who wonder whether it provides adequate safeguards; but self-rating does represent one way to address the clash between personal freedoms and the need to protect young people from inappropriate content.

In the Netscape browser (Navigator 4.5), the special tool for setting and modifying filtering categories is called Netwatch. Microsoft Internet Explorer 4.0 enables screening from the Ratings preference option. The terms and methods associated with setting filtering preferences may vary in future versions of the software. At this point, however, the process of setting up a browser to screen requested Web sites is fundamentally the same for both browsers; it requires that the person responsible for the browser do the following:

1. Enable (turn on) the filtering function.
2. Select the level of material that will be allowed in several different categories (see Figure 11.1).
3. Indicate whether Web sites that do not carry a rating will be allowed.
4. Enter a password.

How the procedure works

Consider how this procedure might be used for computers in a school library. The school computer coordinator might take responsibility for setting the screening categories according to established school policy. Students then would be shielded from most objectionable sites. Most likely, however, the password would be made available to the librarian because there would be

Focus

Self-Rating a Web Site

Both the Recreational Software Advisory Council on the Internet (RSACi) and the SafeSurf rating systems are based on labels provided by Web publishers. With RSACi, the system works like this:

A Web publisher visits the RSACi web site (**http://www.rsac.org**) and completes a form that includes the site URL and basic information about the publisher (name, address, phone, e-mail address). The publisher then goes through a series of descriptive phrases relevant to each of the four RSACi categories and provides a response indicating the most extreme behavior that may be present on the site. Ultimately the publisher receives a RSACi rating that ranges from 0 to 4, with 4 representing the greatest potential danger to a user.

Earlier in the book we used the North Dakota Project Wild site (NDWild) as an example (see Figure 10.6 on page 389). This site, sponsored by the North Dakota Game and Fish Department, promotes the educational exploration of the North Dakota outdoors. The RSACi standards were applied to this site. As you might expect, the site does not depict nudity or sexual acts, so in those categories it received a 0, the most inoffensive score. It also received a 0 in the language category. But one option in the RSACi violence category contains the phrase "death of non-human beings resulting from natural acts," and this seemed a possible way to describe hunting or fishing. So the NDWild site received a rating of 1 for violence.

Once the necessary information has been entered in the RSACi forms, the site records the information and generates an HTML code (a special META tag). The web publisher must insert this code in the heading section of site pages. The information in the tag is used by the web browser to determine if the site is acceptable on the basis of the standards stored within the browser software. Here is the HTML code for the NDWild site:

> <META http-equiv="PICS-Label"
> content='(PICS-1.1 "http://www.rsac.org/
> ratingsv01.html" l gen true comment
> "RSACi North America Server" for
> "http://www.und.nodak.edu/org/ndwild"
> on "1999.01.15T14:46-0800" r
> (n 0 s 0 v 1 l 0))'>✳

circumstances when the screening system would need to be disabled. For example, a teacher might want her class to examine a particular Web site although the author of that site had not taken the trouble to enroll with a screening service. Using the password, the librarian could temporarily disable screening, and the students would be able to view the site.

The success of browser screening assumes that Web authors will support this approach and make the effort to label their material accurately. This approach has been endorsed as a reasonable approach protecting the needs of most citizens (Center for Democracy and Technology, 1997).

FIGURE 11.1
Netscape Netwatch System for Assigning Content Ratings

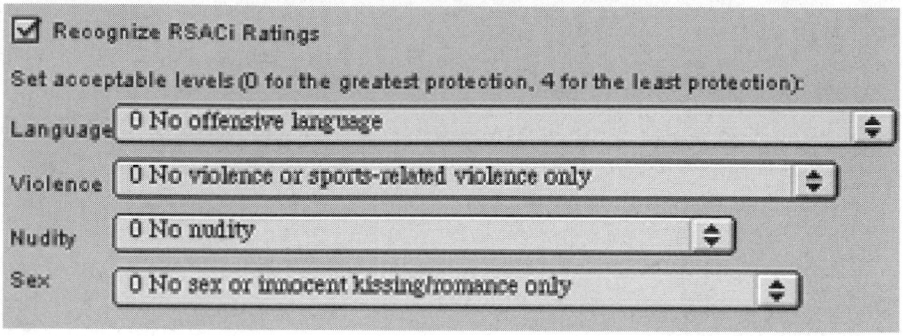

SAFETY GUIDELINES, ACCEPTABLE USE POLICIES, AND SUPERVISION

Because technological mechanisms are not foolproof, schools cannot rely totally on them to control how students will use the Internet. Preparing students to be responsible users of the Internet also involves helping them learn what is safe and appropriate behavior.

Safety Rules

Students need to know that inappropriate material exists on the Internet and that it is possible someone might attempt to exploit them through Internet conversations. They need to know what content and situations they are to avoid. It is especially important that younger students be informed in concrete terms of behaviors they should avoid.

For a summary of some common rules as they might be presented to younger students, see Focus: Rules for the Safe and Appropriate Use of the Internet. Classroom teachers should take the time to present and explain guidelines of this sort. In addition, it is helpful to post them in a visible location.

Acceptable-Use Policies

Schools need to establish clear standards that go beyond a simple list of rules. It is useful to formalize such guidelines in a written document, often called an acceptable-use policy (AUP).

An AUP typically establishes expectations for how students and sometimes faculty will use school resources, procedures they are expected to follow, and consequences when expectations and procedures are violated. If you are a student, we suggest you search through your room to find your institution's guidelines for student behavior. This document may be referred to as the "Code of Student Life" or some similar title. Somewhere within this doc-

Rules for the Safe and Appropriate Use of the Internet

Following are some sample rules for Internet use, worded as they might be presented to students. The wording could be adjusted depending on the age of the students.

1. I will not reveal personal information in e-mail or chat messages. Personal information includes:

   ◆ My home address
   ◆ My home phone number
   ◆ The names of my parents, my teacher, and other students in my class
   ◆ The name and address of my school

   [Note: Schools may also decide that students should not reveal their own names, perhaps using only a first name and last initial, such as "Cindy G."]

   If I am asked for any item of personal information, I will ask my teacher what I should do.

2. I will never agree to talk on the telephone or meet in person with anyone I met through chat or e-mail without first talking with my teacher.

3. I will tell my teacher if I find any information that I should not see or that makes me feel uncomfortable.

4. I will not share my e-mail password with anyone, including my best friends.

5. I will not make fun of other students in e-mail messages. If anyone sends me an e-mail message that makes me feel uncomfortable or angry, I will not respond. I will report e-mail messages that make me feel uncomfortable to my teacher.

6. I will not visit Web sites that are inappropriate for school use. If I accidentally load this kind of site, I will leave it immediately. If I have questions about whether I should be looking at certain Web sites, I will ask my teacher or librarian. I understand that viewing inappropriate sites may result in the loss of Internet privileges.

Source: Based on Magid (1998).✴

ument you will find policies relating to the use of computer and Internet resources and a general explanation of various actions the institution can take against you for violating these and other stated policies.

An AUP for a K–12 institution accomplishes similar goals, but with these differences:

◆ It is likely to exist as an independent document.
◆ It will emphasize instructional as well as regulatory goals.
◆ It will recognize that K–12 students are minors.

Issues that AUPs address   Rather than reproducing a complete AUP, we will outline some of the issues that typical AUPs address. Finding real examples of AUPs is easy: they are commonly included as Web pages within school Web sites. Use any search engine and request "Acceptable Use Policy," and you will find many examples.

AUPs usually address the general use of technology in schools. Here we will focus just on issues concerning the Internet. Typical AUPs treat the following subjects:

◆ Purpose. Student learning is the reason the school provides access to technology. Many AUPs begin by explaining that access to the World Wide Web, e-mail, and other Internet tools is provided to help students learn. This statement of purpose establishes boundaries that can then be used to set priorities or exclude certain activities. Playing online games, for instance, may be perfectly good fun, but such behavior is outside the established priorities. After connecting Internet resources with valued educational experiences, the statement of purpose often continues by explaining that certain rules and regulations are necessary to ensure that learning occurs in a safe and productive environment.

◆ Access to services. Most AUPs explain the services the district provides and what is necessary for students to use these services. For example, the school may make the Web available to all students, but students in the elementary grades may have access to e-mail only through a common class account. Middle-school and high school students might be given individual e-mail accounts provided the student and parents sign a user agreement form.

◆ Unacceptable behaviors. After making the point that many uses of technology are a privilege and not a right, most AUPs list behaviors that are not allowed and indicate sanctions that may be applied if students engage in unacceptable behavior. The common areas of concern include personal safety; violations of system security or purposeful attempts to damage system functions or online content; academic violations such as plagiarism; purposeful efforts to view online materials identified as inappropriate; and harassment of other people. Sanctions typically involve loss of access privileges; in severe cases they may include more severe punishment, such as suspension or even criminal prosecution.

◆ Position on privacy. Will school officials examine student or faculty e-mail, monitor Web sites that have been visited from a particular computer, or open data files saved in student accounts? If such practices are regarded as necessary, the AUP should state clearly that all accounts are considered school property and may be examined to ensure safe and responsible use.

Supervision

Monitoring as a function of active participation

The clear statement of rules and careful documentation of policies are not enough. Classroom teachers, librarians, and other school staff members need to be willing to monitor students' use of computers and the Internet. Teachers should participate actively when students work with technology. Supervision is yet another reason to remain involved, not sit at a desk while students under your charge do their work.

This combination of honest concern, clear standards, and appropriate supervision is how schools customarily teach and maintain appropriate behavior. Although absolute protection cannot be guaranteed, these measures do seem a reasonable response to the potential dangers.

SUMMARY

This chapter examines several issues under the general heading of the responsible use of technology. Accepting responsibility is a matter of acknowledging, understanding, and meeting obligations to the laws of our society, to parents and students, and to our colleagues.

Educational equity defines responsibilities educators have in providing fair and equal experiences for all students. Not all students have equal opportunities to use technology. Schools with a large number of less affluent students do not allow equal access to the Internet and engage students in different technology-supported learning experiences. Federal programs are beginning to address the issue of access, but access alone will not provide equal experiences. Teacher preparation and support and assumptions regarding what type of experiences students from less affluent homes require appear to be at the root of differences in what students experience. Concern also exists regarding differences in how males and females are involved with technology in educational settings. The communication, inquiry, and construction tasks the Internet allows may contribute to an improvement in female interest in technology. Students with physical, sensory, or cognitive limitations may also be at a disadvantage in taking advantage of Internet resources and experiences. In many cases, adaptations in hardware and software can provide improved access and opportunity. A more thoughtful approach to Web design can also be helpful.

Responsible Internet users respect copyright law. Both teachers and students need to know what resources they can take from online sources or present online as part of instructional or learning activities. Understanding what are called fair use guidelines is not always easy, and the familiarity with general principles and a willingness to ask permission are what must be expected of a responsible user.

Recognizing the potential dangers of Internet access and experiences and taking steps to protect students against such dangers is another responsibility educators must accept. Educators can direct students toward safe areas of the Internet, employ filtering systems that provide some barriers to the display of inappropriate materials, and directly intervene with students through supervision and instruction in safety guidelines.

REFLECTING ON CHAPTER 11

Activities

- ◆ Write a "Responsible User" contract that students and parents must sign before the student will be allowed an e-mail account.
- ◆ Try the following as a simulation of what visually impaired students experience when they use the Internet. First, modify the browser so that it does not display images. Second, use only the keyboard to explore the Web (use a Windows machine and the tab and return keys to select and follow links). Did you encounter pages that you could not comprehend? Were there situations in which you were unable to navigate?
- ◆ Several software products are sold for the purpose of downloading individual pages or entire Web sites. On the basis of your interpretation of fair use, argue for or against the legality of using this software to collect resources for (1) personal scholarship, (2) access by your class within your classroom, and (3) worldwide access from a server located in your school.

Key Terms

community access center   *(p. 410)*

Conference on Fair Use (CONFU)   *(p. 428)*

e-rate   *(p. 415)*

fair use   *(p. 425)*

license   *(p. 423)*

local area network (LAN)   *(p. 423)*

plagiarism   *(p. 433)*

screen reader software   *(p. 417)*

site license   *(p. 423)*

socioeconomic status (SES)
   (p. 409)

software piracy   *(p. 423)*

Resources to Expand Your Knowledge Base

Safe Areas of the Internet

Directories

Magellan's search service allows users to search for key words within what are designated as "green sites" (containing no objectionable content). (**http://www.mckinley.com/**)

Yahooligans was created by Yahoo! as a specialized and separate directory of sites for younger Web users. (**http://www.yahooligans.com/**)

Educational Content Databases and Content Lists

Blue Web'n, a database of "blue-ribbon" educational learning sites sponsored by Pacific Bell, provides access to reviewed, high-quality educational sites. (**http://www.kn.pacbell.com/wired/bluewebn/**)

Supervised Chat Environments

The Kidlink organization matches students from all over the world for e-mail and chat. The chat rooms are supervised. (**http://www.kidlink.org**)

Filtering Internet Content

Explanation of Filtering Tools

Center for Democracy and Technology (1997). Internet family empowerment white paper: How filtering tools enable responsible parents to protect their children on-line [On-Line]. Available: **http:www.cdt.org/speech/empower.html**.

Internet Filtering and Control Products

Cyber Patrol, from Microsystems Software, available for Windows and Macintosh platforms. (**http://www.cyberpatrol.com**)

CYBERsitter, from Solid Oak Software, available for the Windows platform. (**http://www.cybersitter.com**)

NetNanny, from NetNanny Software International, available for the Windows platform. (**http://www.netnanny.com**)

Surfwatch, from Spyglass, available for the Windows and Macintosh platforms. (**http://www.surfwatch.com**)

Platform for Internet Content Selection (PICS) and PICS Rating Systems

The World Wide Web Consortium (W3C) was responsible for developing the PICS protocol. (**http://www.w3.org/PICS/**)

The Recreational Software Advisory Council on the Internet (RSACi) is a nonprofit organization that promotes the rating of Internet resources using the PICS protocol. The RSACi rating system can be implemented in newer Netscape and Microsoft browsers. (**http://www.rsac.org/**)

The SafeSurf Rating Service is provided by SafeSurf Wave and applies a rating system using the PICS protocol. The SafeSurf rating system can be implemented in newer Netscape and Microsoft browsers. (**http://www.safesurf.com**)

Acceptable-Use Policies

Science and Math Initiative. (1998). Acceptable use policies and the BVSD Internet use contracts [On-Line]. Available: **http://www.learner.org/sami/contract.shtml** (January 1999).

Adaptive Software

JAWS, a screen reader for the Windows operating system ml, available from Henter-Joyce, is one of the most popular products for personal computers. (**http://www.hj.com/Index.html**)

Home Page Reader, a screen reader with special capabilities for Internet tasks, is available for the Windows operating system from IBM. (**http://www.austin.ibm.com/sns/hpr.html**)

Guidelines for Accessible Web Pages

World Wide Web Consortium. (1999). Techniques for Web accessibility initiative page author guidelines [On-Line]. Available: **http://www.w3.org/TR/WD-WAI-PAGEAUTH** [1999, February 10].

Gender Equity

The American Association of University Women promotes education for gender equity. (**www.aauw.org**)

SES Equity

The U.S. government has a Web site devoted to the "Digital Divide." (**http://www.digitaldivide.gov**)

Copyright Issues

The National Association of College Bookstores has placed the document "Questions and Answers on Copyright for the Campus Community" online. (**http://www.nacs.org/info/copyright/**)

The Association of American Publishers offers information about copyright issues. (**http://www.publishers.org/home/issues/index.htm#copyright**)

Copying Television Programs for Classroom Use

Cable in the Classroom is a massive public service venture supported by a large number of national cable companies. This organization provides information on cable programming with educational relevance, supplemental materials to accompany selected programs, and information on programming made available with liberalized provisions for copying. Cable in the Classroom has an informative Web site. (**http://www.ciconline.com**)

Plagiarism

Plagiarism.com is a Web-based site that allows instructors to compare a student paper against a database of papers available through the Internet. (**http://www.plagiarism.com**)

Teacher's Handy Reference

Useful Internet Resources

The following is a compilation of most of the Internet resources appearing in the "Extending Your Knowledge" sections of this book. Links to Web pages describing specific software applications have been included only when the company responsible for these programs makes an extended description available. For further ideas and updates, check our Web site for this book at **http://college.hmco.com** (and select "Education") or at **http://ndwild.psych.und.nodak.edu/book**.

Name | Internet Address

Online Curriculum Materials and Student Projects

Name	Internet Address
AppleWorks (Chapter 5)	http://www.apple.com/education/k12/products/appleworks/
American Memory Collection—Library of Congress (Chapter 6)	http://lcweb2.loc.gov/amhome.html
Blue Web'n (Chapter 11)	http://www.kn.pacbell.com/wired/bluewebn/
Classroom Connect (Chapter 6)	http://www.classroomconnect.com/
Encarta Schoolhouse (Chapter 7)	http://encarta.msn.com/schoolhouse/default.asp
Decisions, Decisions Online (Chapter 7)	http://www.teachtsp2.com/ddonline/
Global Show and Tell (Chapter 5)	http://www.telenaut.com/gst/
Globalearn.com (Chapter 6)	http://www.globalearn.org/
Inspiration (Chapter 5)	http://www.inspiration.com
Interactive Frog Dissection (Chapter 4)	http://curry.edschool.virginia.edu/go/frog/
Jason Project (Chapter 6)	http://www.jasonproject.org/
Journey North (Chapter 6)	http://www.learner.org/jnorth/
Kidlink (Chapter 11)	http://www.kidlink.org/
KidNews (Chapter 5)	http://www.kidnews.com/
KidPub (Chapter 5)	http://www.kidpub.org/kidpub/
Microsoft (Chapter 5)	http://www.microsoft.com/education/instruction/default.asp
MidLink Magazine (Chapter 5)	http://longwood.cs.ucf.edu:80/~MidLink/
Newsday Project (Kid Chronicles) (Chapter 6)	http://www.gsn.org/project/newsday/index.html
NASA Quest (Chapter 6)	http://quest.arc.nasa.gov/interactive/index.html
North American Quilt (Chapter 6)	http://www.onlineclass.com/NAQ/NAQhome.html
OneSky, Many Voices (Chapter 6)	http://onesky.engin.umich.edu/
Stock Market Game (Chapter 4)	http://www.smg2000.org/
ThinkQuest (Chapter 6)	http://www.thinkquest.org/
USA Today Weather (Chapter 5)	http://www.usatoday.com/weather/
Virtual Frog Dissection Kit (Chapter 4)	http://www-itg.lbl.gov/vfrog/dissect.html
Weather Channel (Chapter 5)	http://www.weather.com/
Weather Underground (Chapter 5)	http://www.wunderground.com/

Name   Internet Address

Internet Tools/Services

Name	Internet Address
AltaVista Search (Chapter 6)	http://www.altavista.com/
HotBot (Chapter 6)	http://hotbot.lycos.com/
Liszt Mailing List Directory (Chapter 6)	http://www.liszt.com/
Magellan Internet Guide (Chapter 6)	http://magellan.excite.com/
MetaCrawler (Chapter 6)	http://www.metacrawler.com/
Northern Light Search (Chapter 6)	http://www.northernlight.com/
SavvySearch (Chapter 6)	http://www.savvysearch.com/
Tile.Net/FTP (Chapter 6)	http://tile.net/ftp-list/
Tile.Net/Lists (Chapter 6)	http://www.tile.net/listserv/alphabetical.html
Yahoo! (Chapter 6)	http://www.yahoo.com/
Yahooligans (Chapter 11)	http://www.yahooligans.com/

Online Information Services

Name	Internet Address
EBSCO Information Services (Chapter 6)	http://www.ebsco.com/home/
Electric Library (Chapter 6)	http://www.elibrary.com/
Encarta Online (Chapter 6)	http://www.encarta.msn.com/
Grolier Multimedia Encyclopedia (Chapter 7)	http://my.grolier.com/
National Geographic (Chapter 7)	http://www.nationalgeographic.com/
New York Times (Chapter 6)	http://www.nytimes.com/
ProQuest Direct (Chapter 6)	http://www.umi.com:8090/proquest/
SIRS Researcher (Chapter 6)	http://www.sirs.com
Wall Street Journal (Chapter 6)	http://www.wsj.com/
Washington Post and Los Angeles Times (Chapter 6)	http://www.newsservice.com/
World Book Online (Chapter 7)	http://www.worldbook.com/

Software

Instructional Software

Name	Internet Address
Exploring the Nardoo (Chapter 4)	http://www.learningTeam.org/nardoo.html
SimLife/SimCity (Chapter 4)	http://www.simcity.com/home.shtml
Stagecast Creator (Chapter 3)	http://www.stagecast.com/
Tabletop (Chapter 5)	http://www.broder.com/education/programs/tabletop/
WiggleWorks (Chapter 7)	http://www.cast.org/wiggleworks/

Tool Software

Name	Internet Address
America Online Instant Messenger (AIM) (Chapter 6)	http://www.aol.com/
AppleWorks (Chapter 5, Chapter 10)	http://www.apple.com/education/k12/products/appleworks/
Avid Cinema (Chapter 9)	http://www.avidcinema.com/
CU-SeeMe (Chapter 6)	http://www.wpine.com/
Cyber Patrol (Chapter 11)	http://www.cyberpatrol.com/
CYBERsitter (Chapter 11)	http://www.cybersitter.com/
Excel (Chapter 5)	http://www.microsoft.com/office/excel/default.htm
Final Cut Pro (Chapter 9)	http://www.apple.com/finalcutpro/
FrontPage (Chapter 10)	http://www.microsoft.com/frontpage/
Internet Explorer (Chapter 6)	http://www.microsoft.com/ie
Home Page Reader (Chapter 11)	http://www.austin.ibm.com/sns/hpr.html

Name

Internet Address

Software

Tool Software

HomePage (Chapter 10)	http://www.filemaker.com/products/hp_home.html
HyperStudio (Chapter 8)	http://www.hyperstudio.com/
IMovie (Chapter 9)	http://www.apple.com/imovie/
JAWS (Chapter 11)	http://www.hj.com/
Microsoft Word (Chapter 10)	http://www.microsoft.com/office/word/
MicroWorlds Pro (Chapter 8)	http://www.microworlds.com/
MovieWorks (Chapter 9)	http://www.movieworks.com/
MPExpress (Chapter 8)	http://www.bytesoflearning.com/express.html
Net Nanny (Chapter 11)	http://www.netnanny.com/
Netmeeting (Chapter 6)	http://www.microsoft.com/windows/netmeeting/
Netscape Navigator (Chapter 6)	http://www.netscape.com
Inspiration (Chapter 5)	http://www.inspiration.com/
PageMill (Chapter 10)	http://www.adobe.com/products/pagemill/main.html
Personal Web Server (Chapter 10)	http://www.microsoft.com/windows/ie/pws/default.htm
PowerPoint (Chapter 8)	http://www.microsoft.com/office/powerpoint/
Premiere (Chapter 9)	http://www.adobe.com/products/premiere/main.html
SiteCentral (Chapter 10)	http://www.sitecentral.com/
SmartSound (Chapter 9)	http://www.sonicdesktop.com/
Surfwatch (Chapter 11)	http://www1.surfwatch.com/
Word Perfect (Chapter 10)	http://www.corel.com/Office2000/

Hardware

General

AlphaSmart (Chapter 5)	http://www.alphasmart.com/
Dreamwriter (Chapter 3, Chapter 5)	http://www.nts.dreamwriter.com/
Palm Computing (Chapter 3)	http://www.palm.com/

Probes and External Devices

HOBO Data Loggers (Chapter 3)	http://www.onsetcomp.com/
ImagiLab (Chapter 3)	http://www.imagiworks.com/prod_ed/index.html
JamCam (Chapter 9)	http://www.gojamcam.com/
Polar Heart Monitor (Chapter 3)	http://www.heartmind.net/tempo.htm
Sony Mavica Camera (Chapter 9)	http://www.sony.com/mavica
Vernier Probes (Chapter 3)	http://www.vernier.com/

Professional Issues and Resources

General

Alliance for Computers and Writing (Chapter 5)	http://english.ttu.edu/acw/
Association of American Publishers (Copyright) (Chapter 11)	http://www.publishers.org/home/issues/index.htm#copyright
Cable in the Classroom (Chapter 11)	http://www.ciconline.com/
Classroom Connect (Chapter 6)	http://www.classroomconnect.com/
Digital Divide (Chapter 11)	http://www.digitaldivide.gov/

Name

Internet Address

Professional Issues and Resources

General

Glatt Plagiarism Services (Chapter 11)	http://www.plagiarism.com/
International Society for Technology in Education (ISTE) Technology Standards for Students (Standards for K–12 students) (Chapter 2)	http://cnets.iste.org/
National Council for Accreditation of Teacher Education Professional Program Area Standards (NCATE Standards for Teacher Preparation) (Chapter 2)	http://www.ncate.org/standards/programstds.htm
Recreational Software Advisory Council (Chapter 11)	http://www.rsac.org/homepage.asp
Web Accessibility Guidelines (Chapter 11)	http://www.w3.org/WAI/
World Wide Web Platform for Internet Content Selection (Chapter 11)	http://www.w3.org/PICS/

Periodicals

Journal of Computers in Mathematics and Science Teaching (Chapter 4)	http://www.aace.org/pubs/jcmst/
Learning and Leading with Technology (Chapter 4)	http://www.iste.org/L&L/index.html
MultiMedia Schools (Chapter 4)	http://www.infotoday.com/MMSchools/
NewMedia Magazine (Chapter 4)	http://newmedia.com/newmedia/newmedia.html
Technology and Learning (Chapter 4)	http://www.techlearning.com/index1.html

Glossary

accommodation   Modification of existing strategies or existing knowledge as a result of a new experience.

alignment   The process of using standards to create consistency in what is emphasized in learning resources, instruction, and evaluation.

analog format   Variations in a signal represented as continuous; a sweep second hand in contrast to a digital clock.

analogical programming   Programming by demonstrating the desired actions the computer is to accomplish.

analog modem   A device that transforms a digital signal into an analog signal for transmission via telephone wires.

analog signal   A signal having the capability of being represented by continuous values. For example, there is no set number of colors in the visible spectrum. One shade blends gradually into the next.

applet   A small program that operates within a browser.

assimilation   Using existing strategies or existing knowledge to relate to a new experience.

authentic activities   The activities of people in their daily lives.

authentic task approach   A course in which higher-order thinking and content knowledge are learned through the process of completing authentic tasks.

automaticity   Process by which well-learned skills are executed with minimal mental effort.

automatization   Mastery of a behavior to such a high degree that the behavior can function without detracting from other behaviors occurring at the same time.

background   The surface of a HyperStudio card.

backup   Copy of a file as a safeguard against loss.

benchmarks   Carefully selected examples of student performance that characterize specific levels of achievement. They are often used to exemplify what would be expected of students in meeting a standard at different grade levels (for example, fourth or eighth), but may also be used to establish other points along a scale of accomplishment.

binary   Communication in which information must be coded as 1's and 0's.

bit-mapped   Representation of an image as rows and columns of pixels in which each pixel is represented by a number to indicate color or shade.

Boolean search   Search based on Boolean logic. In an AND search, all search terms must be located for a successful search. In an OR search, locating any one of the search terms results in a successful search.

branch   A choice point that narrows and focuses the information available to the user.

branching tutorial   Tutorial in which the sequence of content a learner encounters is determined by the quality of performance on the previous step.

browser   Software used to connect to Web servers and to display information on the local (client) computer.

bug   Error in a computer program.

build   A presentation technique in which related items are revealed in succession to emphasize the significance of each idea.

bulleted chart   A series of text statements often preceded by a bullet (·) for easy reading.

button   A card "hot spot" that initiates an action when clicked.

calculator-based laboratory (CBL)   An interface allowing a calculator to record data from probes.

card   The basic unit of information within HyperStudio and HyperCard. A card consists of the set of text, graphics, sounds, and buttons meant to be presented simultaneously.

cell   Intersection of a row and column in a spreadsheet; the point at which a number or formula is entered in the spreadsheet.

charge-coupled device (CCD)   An arrangement of tightly packed photoelectric cells, each of which produces a voltage in proportion to the amount of light received. In scanners these voltages are converted to digital values to generate the information a computer saves as a graphics file.

chat mode Form of telecommunications in which messages are exchanged in real time rather than stored for later reading.

clipboard Computer memory buffer that can hold images and other information for convenient exchange among programs.

cognitive apprenticeship Learning within a relationship with a more expert practitioner of the skill to be learned.

color lookup table (CLUT) The set of colors available within a particular computer system; same as *palette.*

color palette The set of colors a software application will use in attempting to display images.

community access center A facility providing public access to computers, software, and the Internet (e.g., a library).

compact disc–read only memory (CD-ROM) While the method used to store data on a CD uses a different technology, the data stored on a CD-ROM are in digital form and can be brought into the computer much like data stored on a floppy disk or hard drive.

computer-assisted design (CAD) Technique for creating engineering drawings and similar images on a computer.

computer-assisted instruction (CAI) Computer program intended to provide instructional experiences directly to the student.

computer-based instruction (CBI) *See* computer-assisted instruction (CAI).

computer-mediated communication (CMC) A form of communication that requires the exchange of information by computer, usually through the Internet.

Conference on Fair Use (CONFU) A series of meetings on copyright issues that produced guidelines in 1997 for teacher- or student-created multimedia and for distance education.

conference Online discussion group.

constant angular velocity (CAV) Videodisc format in which each frame takes exactly one track.

constant linear velocity (CLV) Videodisc format in which each track may contain parts of several frames. Each track is read at a constant speed.

constructionism Papert's proposal that students learn most effectively by finding and generating their own knowledge and that teachers should find ways to assist students in these activities.

constructivism Theory proposing that students create a personal understanding (construct their own knowledge) by interpreting their experiences.

content standard A definition of what a student is expected to learn.

cooperative learning Situation in which students work together to accomplish an instructional goal.

copy To copy data from the active document to be temporarily stored in computer memory.

copy and paste Process available within an application program allowing data to be copied to the memory of the computer and then inserted at another location in the present document or in a different document. In many cases data can also be transferred across application programs.

courseware Generic term for instructional software.

critical thinking Solving problems by gathering and interpreting information; as an instructional approach, it emphasizes the development of analytical skills that can be applied to a wide range of subject matter.

cross-platform Capable of functioning on computers with different operating systems, for instance, Windows and Macintosh computers.

cursor Symbol, usually a line or square, displayed on the computer screen indicating where the next symbol entered will appear.

cut To remove data from the active document for temporary storage in computer memory.

database Application program allowing the organization, storage, and search of information.

data logger A self-contained device containing a sensor, interface, and battery.

declarative knowledge Stored verbal information and facts.

delete (in word processing) To remove text at the location of the cursor.

deselecting Clicking on a selected option, often a box associated with the description of an option to be applied, causing the option not to be applied.

design A tool developed to accomplish a purpose.

desktop publishing Programs that facilitate the entry and positioning of text and graphics to control precisely the appearance of printed documents.

dialog box A program event in which a box appears on top of the information already appearing on the screen and requests the user to provide input by entering text or clicking on a button.

digital format Recording format in which information is stored as a series of numbers, allowing exact duplication of the original information.

digital subscriber line (DSL) A digital technology for moving large amounts of digital information through existing copper phone lines. An emerging alternative to the use of traditional modems, which send an analog signal over phone lines.

digital video disc (DVD)   A storage method capable of putting from 4.7 GB to 17 GB of information on a disc the size of a CD-ROM. DVD is referred to as digital versatile disc in some sources to indicate the capacity to store any type of digital information.

direct mode   Programming commands are executed as soon as they are entered.

discovery learning   Students discover important principles on their own.

dithering   A process by which a computer tries to simulate a color by mixing pixels of other colors.

domain name   A name that indicates a computer's address on the Internet; an easier-to-remember equivalent of the IP number.

dots per inch (dpi)   Term describing the resolution of printers, monitors, and scanners. The use of the term *dot* can be confusing because the smallest elements a scanner can detect or a monitor can display are called pixels.

download   To transfer a file from a remote computer to your computer.

drag and drop   A feature of a software application that allows functions to be performed by dragging objects to locations on the screen. For example, it may be possible to select an image in a paint program and then drag the image into the work area of a word processing program.

draw program   A graphics program using object-oriented images rather than bit maps. Mathematical descriptions are used to represent these objects.

drill   Computer application designed to facilitate factual memorization.

dual-agenda approach   A course in which higher-order thinking skills and content area knowledge are both taught.

dual-coding theory   Theory proposing that imagery and verbal information are stored in different ways and that information stored in both forms will be easier to retrieve.

DVD-RAM   A rewriteable DVD format available to computer users.

edutainment   Term for game-like software that offers educational benefits.

electronic mail (e-mail)   Personal message sent by the user of one computer to the user of another.

embellished document   A text document enhanced with graphics, video segments, or sound.

endorsement   Official recognition that an individual has satisfied a designated set of requirements.

episodic memory   Memory for an event usually connected with a specific time and place.

e-rate   A subsidy for the costs of providing Internet connections to schools and libraries, established by the Telecommunications Act of 1996.

exploratory environments   Setting providing elements for the learner to manipulate and learn as the result of this manipulation.

fair use   Guidelines describing the conditions under which the copying of intellectual property is appropriate.

fidelity   Extent to which a simulation mimics reality.

field (database)   Category defined by the user of a database to contain a specified type of information, such as age, name, zip code.

field (HyperCard)   A container into which you type text.

file (database)   Complete collection of related database records.

file transfer protocol (FTP)   Standards allowing the transfer of files to and from a host computer.

flash memory   A memory storage device that retains information over an extended period of time in special memory chips.

font   Standardized design of characters that determines the appearance of text (e.g., Helvetica, Geneva).

formatting   Determining the physical appearance of a document.

forum   Online discussion group in which participants contribute comments to be read by all participants; *see also* conference.

framework   A document organizing standards, benchmarks, and instructional practices.

game   Program that emphasizes competition and enjoyment. Certain games have educational benefits as well.

generative learning   A theory emphasizing the student's active search for meaning through the integration of new experiences with existing knowledge structures or the generation of inferences.

graphic design   Concerns issues of the appearance of information on the computer screen as appearance is related to informativeness, interpretability, and interest.

graphic user interface (GUI)   System for interacting with a computer based on the manipulation of icons rather than the input of typed commands.

grid   Method for organizing the computer screen using patterns of lines.

group investigation   Cooperative learning method in which group members develop a project related to a general theme proposed by the teacher.

header In an e-mail message, the top portion that contains, at a minimum, the address for the sender, the address for the receiver, and a topic for the e-mail.

helper application An application that processes files that cannot be processed by a browser.

hierarchical design A form of web site design in which the content is organized as a system of categories and subcategories.

higher-order thinking Thinking that is complex, effortful, self-regulated, and judgmental.

home page Initial display when connecting to a World Wide Web site.

hypermedia Multimedia that a user can examine in a flexible, nonlinear fashion. The user can typically move from one information source to several others and can control which of these options to take.

hypertext Text that can be examined in a nonlinear manner. The user can typically move from one segment of text to several others by responding to options made available by the computer program controlling the text presentation.

hypertext markup language (HTML) The special codes and tags inserted in an HTML document that inform a Web browser how to display hypermedia elements (e.g., text, graphics) and how to take specific actions (e.g., branch to another WWW document).

hypertext transfer protocol (http) The protocol used by the World Wide Web for transmitting pages; abbreviated as "http" at the beginning of a web site address.

icon A small image often used consistently to represent a specific program action or category of information.

incremental advantage Improvement due to increased efficiency.

indirect mode Programming commands are first stored and then executed at a later time.

individual accountability Requirement of cooperative learning demanding that individuals must achieve for the team to achieve.

inert knowledge Knowledge that students have acquired but fail to use.

insert (in word processing) To enter text at the position of the cursor.

instructional resource Information resource that has been prepared specifically for an instructional purpose.

instructionism Orientation emphasizing the improvement of student performance through the development of better instructional methods.

integrated services digital network (ISDN) A digital technology for moving large amounts of digital information through existing copper phone lines. An emerging alternative to the use of traditional modems, which send an analog signal over phone lines.

Internet International web of computer networks.

Internet service provider Company providing individuals with modem access to the Internet.

Intranet A web designed for use within an institution rather than for general access.

IP number For every computer with a permanent connection to the Internet, the number designating its precise Internet address.

jaggies Staircase effect in the production of lines that are not perfectly horizontal or vertical. Jaggies appear when the individual units used to construct lines are large enough to be visible.

jigsaw cooperation Form of cooperative learning in which each member of the cooperative group makes a unique and essential contribution to the accomplishment of the group task.

justification (of text) Alignment of lines of text against the left margin (left-justified), against the right margin (right-justified), or centered on the page.

knowledge as design Knowledge that has been applied or adapted to a purpose.

laserdisc Term sometimes used to refer to a videodisc.

LCD projection panel A special liquid crystal display panel that connects to a computer and sits on an overhead projector to project an image onto a display screen.

license An agreement that grants specific rights concerning the copying or reproduction of copyrighted material.

lifelong learning Learning continuously throughout one's life span as life presents new challenges; an idea promoted by those who believe that learners in the contemporary world will be unable to limit their learning to a designated period.

line art Images in which the individual pixels are either black or white. Files of this type are the smallest in size because only two values are needed to describe each pixel. This is called a 1-bit image.

linear multimedia presentation Multimedia information presented in a standard sequence; a slide show.

linear tutorial Form of instruction in which all learners go through the same material in the same sequence.

link Connection between nodes.

listserv An alternative term for a mailing list.

list server Computer server hosting a mailing list.

local area network (LAN) Interconnected computers in one location, such as a school building or office.

long-term memory (LTM) Memory store allowing virtually permanent storage.

lossy Implies a form of compression in which data and thus some quality are lost during the compression process.

mailing lists (*see also* list server) Telecommunications process in which an e-mail message is sent to a designated address and then resent to every member subscribing to receive messages from that address.

map Device that identifies the components of a hypermedia presentation and shows the main links among components.

margin Distance between the edge of text and the edge of the paper.

master slide The common color and visual elements held constant across all slides of a presentation.

meaningful learning Learning in which new experiences are linked with information already stored in long-term memory.

mediated instruction Instructional approach in which the teacher works to directly assist the student in acquiring the underlying cognitive skills associated with performing a complex behavior. The teacher's efforts are directed not just at the ability of the student to generate appropriate outcomes or products, but at the thinking and reasoning processes leading to these products.

megabytes Approximately one million bytes. The capacity of a high-density floppy disk is between 1 and 1.5 megabytes.

menu List of available options.

metacognition Knowledge about your own thinking and learning.

metacognitive control functions Behaviors involved in planning, regulating, and evaluating mental behaviors.

metacognitive knowledge Knowledge about how tasks are performed, what makes tasks easy or difficult, and personal skills and limitations.

microcomputer-based laboratory (MBL) An interface allowing a computer to record data from probes.

microworld Learning environment allowing the exploration of an academic domain in an experiential way.

mindtool The idea that the use of powerful computer tools may encourage problem solving and learning by freeing the learner from tasks that require attention or significant storage capacity.

modem Computer peripheral device allowing information to be exchanged over a telephone line between computers.

multimedia Communication format integrating several media (text, audio, visual), most commonly implemented with a computer.

network model A model of human memory representing the contexts of memory as interconnected nodes of information.

newsgroup Topical discussion group supported by the Usenet system for collecting and forwarding messages among subscriber sites. Presently over 4,000 topics are available. Messages are searched and read with a special reader.

node Unit of information; an idea, picture, or sound.

object-oriented image Image in which objects are represented using mathematical equations rather than as maps of pixel colors.

object-oriented programming Programming technique in which objects are isolated and programming code is associated with individual objects.

online tutorial An Internet-based activity intended to deliver direct instruction mostly through the presentation of information and simple methods for the evaluation of understanding.

paint program Computer program designed to create and manipulate graphic information.

paste To insert data stored in the memory of the computer into an active document.

performance standard A definition that defines an acceptable level of achievement.

pixel The smallest element a scanner can detect or a monitor can display.

plagiarism Representing someone else's work as your own.

plug-in An application that works within a browser to process certain types of files.

point-to-point A pattern of communication involving information sent between two computers rather than among many computers.

point-to-point protocol (PPP) One of the standard protocols used for modem transmissions over the Internet.

practice Computer application designed to facilitate the development of skill fluency.

presentation software A form of tool software intended for use in creating and delivering formal group presentations.

primary source A general information source prepared without consideration for student needs.

primitive Individual command built into a programming language.

probe Device built to measure variations in a specific variable (e.g., temperature, pH).

problem solving Thinking processes involved in overcoming an obstacle to reach a goal.

procedural knowledge Memory for how to do something.

procedure Section of code, defined and named by the programmer, capable of accomplishing a specific task.

programming Process of instructing a computer to perform some desired action.

protocol A set of rules and conventions governing how devices on a network exchange information.

query A request made to a search engine.

QuickTime Format allowing digital movies and sounds to be compressed, edited, and played on a computer.

read only A property of a text field set to prevent users from modifying the text appearing in the field.

reception learning Concepts, principles, and rules to be learned are presented directly to the students.

record Meaningful collection of database fields representing one unit of storage.

recursion Process or procedure that contains itself as a subprocess.

resource interdependence Situation in which members of a cooperative group must combine resources to achieve success.

reward interdependence Situation in which the success or failure experienced by all members of a cooperative group depends on the cumulative accomplishments of all members of the group.

rote learning Learning with little attention to meaning.

sampling frequency Number of times per second, in kilohertz (kHz), that digitized sound is produced. Frequencies used in microcomputer applications are likely to be in the 7- to 22-kHz range. More frequent sampling provides more realistic reproduction of original sound.

scaffolding External support for learning or problem solving.

scanner A device that captures a bit-mapped representation of an image.

screen capture The process of saving the image appearing on the computer monitor as a graphics file.

screen-reader software Software that reads the text and other screen information (e.g., menu options) for visually impaired users.

script The HyperCard program attached to a HyperCard object.

search engine A program, used by a search service, that checks a user's request against the database of web pages maintained by the service and returns a list of matches.

select To identify material to which some action (such as underlining or deletion) is to be applied.

self-regulated learning Strategic student behavior involving planning, evaluation, and appropriate adjustment of learning.

sensor A device capable of measuring a specific characteristic of the physical environment.

sequential design A form of web site design in which the content is organized so that each element leads directly to the next in logical sequence.

shareware Software available on "try it before you buy it" basis. If you continue to use the software, you are expected to pay the author.

short-term memory (STM) The limited capacity and duration store containing the thoughts, ideas, and images of which a person is aware; *see also* working memory.

simulation Computer program that imitates the key elements of realistic experiences.

site license License offering certain privileges to users at a designated site; for instance, allowing a school district to make a number of copies of software from a single original.

slide show Linear multimedia; a fixed sequence of images, text segments, sounds, or video segments.

socioeconomic status (SES) A measure of prestige based on income, education, and occupation.

software piracy Copying software to avoid payment or without the appropriate approval.

source code The programming statements or commands generated by the program author.

spell checker Word processing feature that checks for spelling errors.

spreadsheet Application program resembling a ledger sheet, allowing numerical data to be entered into cells arranged as rows and columns. Calculations can be performed on these data by attaching formulas to cells.

stack A collection of cards; a complete HyperCard document.

stand-alone approach A course focused exclusively on the development of higher-order thinking.

standards Expectations for knowledge, performance capabilities, or the availability of resources.

stock photos Collections of images that are available for purchase and use.

storyboarding Process of roughing out the sequence of displays and activities to be incorporated into new instructional software.

style (of characters) Standardized modification in the appearance of text, such as underlining or italicizing.

subprocedure Procedure representing a component process of the main program.

superprocedure Main program; perhaps organizing several subprocedures.

syntax Rules for combining commands, punctuation, and arguments to produce valid program statements.

tabs Predefined insertion point established in word processing. Setting a tab stop allows the user to move the insertion point to a specified column.

tag An HTML command.

task specialization methods Cooperative learning method in which the goal is cooperative accomplishment of a task requiring the application of what group members have learned.

TCP/IP (Transmission control protocol/Internet protocol) standards that allow different computers to transfer data over the Internet.

team rewards Requirement of cooperative learning that demands the team achievement result in some form of team recognition.

tear-off palette A set of icons allowing the selection of options (for example, tools or colors), that can be positioned anywhere on the screen the user desires.

template Organizational plan for a database or spreadsheet.

text object A framed segment of text treated as a unit by certain functions of word processing or desktop publishing programs.

thread A series of linked messages consisting of replies to previous messages.

thumbnail A small version of a larger image, often used on the Web as a link to a page containing the full-size image.

transfer Application of skills or knowledge learned in one situation to a different situation.

transformational advantage Improvement due to a qualitatively superior method.

translator A small utility added to an application that allows the conversion of files created with another program for use in the host application.

turtlegraphics Graphics mode in which drawings are created by executing commands that move a shape around the screen. This approach is emphasized in LOGO but is also available in other languages.

tutorial A learning activity in which the computer primarily presents new information to the student and provides opportunities for the student to become proficient with this information.

universal resource locator (URL) An address for an FTP or WWW file on the Internet.

user interface Methods by which the user interacts with the contents of a computer application.

variable Labeled storage container in a program, set aside to hold data on a temporary basis.

video digitizer Device used to convert an analog video signal to a digital representation of that signal.

videodisc Medium for storing analog video and audio on a disc in a form that is read by bouncing a laser beam off the disc's surface.

video projector Special hardware that projects a screen image onto a large screen.

virtual learning community An online learning community; a cooperative learning group that uses the Internet for communication among members.

virtual reality modeling The simulation of an environment that can be experienced visually as having width, height, and depth and in some cases can allow interaction or manipulation.

web design A form of web site design that establishes a complex set of connections among web pages.

word processing Application program allowing the entry, manipulation, and storage of text and sometimes graphics.

word wrap Characteristic of word processing programs allowing text that would extend beyond the right margin of a page to automatically move to the beginning of a new line.

working memory *See* short-term memory.

World Wide Web (WWW) System providing access to Internet resources based on hypertextlike documents.

writing process approach Method of writing instruction emphasizing planning, drafting, editing, revising, and publishing. This method emphasizes rewriting with guidance from the teacher and peers.

zone of proximal development Skills an individual can perform with some assistance.

References

Abelson, H., & diSessa, A. (1981). *Turtle geometry: The computer as a medium for exploring mathematics.* Cambridge, MA: MIT Press.

Adaptive Computer Technology Centre. (1998). *Accessible Web page design* [On-line]. Available: http://www.igs.net/~starling/acc/

Albrecht, B., & Firedrake, G. (1998). Grabbing data: What you need to log and use real-world data. *Learning and Leading with Technology, 26*(1), 36–40.

Albrecht, B., & Firedrake, G. (1999). Blowin' hot and cold about my data. *Learning and Leading with Technology, 26*(5), 32–36.

Alessi, S. (1988). Fidelity in the design of instructional simulations. *Journal of Computer-Based Instruction, 15*(2), 40–47.

Alessi, S., & Trollip, S. (1991). *Computer-based instruction: Methods and development* (2nd ed.). Englewood Cliffs, NJ: Prentice-Hall.

Althaus, S. (1997). Computer-mediated communication in the university classroom: An experiment with on-line discussions. *Communication Education, 46*(3), 158–174.

American Association of University Women Educational Foundation. (1998). *Gender gaps: Where schools still fail our children.* Washington, DC: Author.

American Psychological Association Board of Educational Affairs (APA/BEA). (1995). *Learner-centered psychological principles: A framework for school redesign and reform.* Washington, DC: American Psychological Association.

Anderson, J. (1976). *Language, memory, and thought.* Hillsdale, NJ: Erlbaum.

Anderson, J. (1983). *The architecture of cognition.* Cambridge, MA: Harvard University Press.

Anderson, R., & Ronnkvist, A. (1999). *The presence of computers in American schools: Teaching, learning, and computer national survey* [On-line]. Available: http://www.crito.uci.edu/tlc/findings/Internet-Use/startpage.htm

Apple Computer. (1989). *Hypercard stack design guidelines.* Reading, MA: Addison-Wesley.

Au, W., Horton, J., & Ryba, K. (1987). Logo, teacher intervention, and the development of thinking skills. *Computing Teacher, 15*(3), 12–15.

Ausubel, D. (1963). *The psychology of meaningful learning.* New York: Grune and Stratton.

Baecker, R., & Posner, I. (1999). Children as digital motion picture authors. In A. Druin (Ed.), *The design of children's technology* (pp. 169–200). San Mateo, CA: Kaufmann.

Baker, L. (1985). Differences in the standards used by college students to evaluate their comprehension of expository prose. *Reading Research Quarterly, 20,* 297–313.

Balajthy, E. (1988). Keyboarding, language arts, and the elementary school child. *Computing Teacher, 15*(5), 40–43.

Bangert-Drowns, R. (1993). The word processor as an instructional tool: A meta-analysis of word processing in writing instruction. *Review of Educational Research, 63*(1), 69–93.

Barksdale, J. (1996). Why schools of education are still sending you staff you'll have to train in technology. *Electronic Learning, 15*(5), 39–45.

Barrett, H. (1994). Technology-supported assessment portfolios. *Computing Teacher, 21*(6), 9–12.

Barron, A., Breit, F., Boulware, A., & Bullock, J. (1994). *Videodiscs in education: Overview, evaluation, activities* (2nd ed.). Tampa, FL: University of South Florida.

Bartz, W., & Singer, M. (1996). The programmatic implications of foreign language standards. In R. Lafayette (Ed.), *National standards: A catalyst for reform* (pp. 139–168). Lincolnwood, IL: National Textbook Company.

Battista, M., & Clements, D. (1988). Logo-based elementary school geometry curriculum. *Arithmetic Teacher, 36*(3), 11–17.

Becker, H. (1999). *Internet use by teachers: Conditions of professional use and teacher-directed student use* [On-line].

Available: http://www.crito.uci.edu/TLC/findings/ Internet-Use/startpage.htm

Becker, H., & Ravitz, J. (1998). The equity threat of promising innovation: Pioneering Internet-connected schools. *Journal of Educational Computing Research, 19*(1), 1–26.

Bernhard, J., & Siegel, L. (1994). Increasing internal locus of control for a disadvantaged group: A computer intervention. *Computers in the Schools, 11*(1), 59–77.

Bitter, G., Camuse, R., & Durbin, V. (1993). *Using a microcomputer in the classroom* (3rd ed.). Boston: Allyn & Bacon.

Black, S., Levin, J., Mehan, H., & Quinn, C. (1983). Real and non-real time interaction: Unraveling multiple threads of discourse. *Discourse Processes, 6*, 59–75.

Bransford, J., & Stein, B. (1984). *The IDEAL problem solver.* New York: Freeman.

Bransford, J., Sherwood, R., Hasselbring, T., Kinzer, C., & Williams, S. (1990). Anchored instruction: Why we need it and how technology can help. In D. Nix & R. Spiro (Eds.), *Cognition, education and multimedia: Exploring ideas in high technology* (pp. 115–141). Hillsdale, NJ: Erlbaum.

Brant, G., Hooper, E., & Sugrue, B. (1991). Which comes first—the simulation or the lecture? *Journal of Educational Computing Research, 7*(4), 469–481.

Brown, A. (1981). Metacognition: The development of selective attention strategies for learning from texts. In M. Kamil (Ed.), *Directions in reading: Research and instruction* (pp. 21–43). Washington, DC: National Reading Conference.

Brown, A. (1987). Metacognition, executive control, self-rejection and other more mysterious mechanisms. In F. Weinert & R. Kluwe (Eds.), *Metacognition, motivation, and understanding* (pp. 65–116). Hillsdale, NJ: Erlbaum.

Brown, A. (1992). Design experiments: Theoretical and methodological challenges in creating complex interventions in classroom settings. *Journal of the Learning Sciences, 2*(2), 141–178.

Brown, J., Collins, A., & Duguid, P. (1989). Situated cognition and the culture of learning. *Educational Researcher, 18*, 32–42.

Bruning, R., Schraw, G., & Ronning, R. (1999). *Cognitive psychology and instruction.* Columbus, OH: Merrill.

Burke, E. (1993). Copyright catechism. *Educom Review, 28*(5), 46–49.

Bushweller, K. (1999a). Generation of cheaters. *American School Board Journal, 186*(4), 24–30.

Bushweller, K. (1999b, March). Digital deception. *Electronic School* [On-line]. Available: http://www.electronic-school.com/199903/0399f2.html

Business Software Alliance. (1998). *1998 Global Software Piracy Report* [On-line]. Available: http://www.bsa.org/statistics/GSPR98/

Carver, S., Lehrer, R., Connell, T., & Erickson, J. (1992). Learning by hypermedia design: Issues of assessment and implementation. *Educational Psychologist, 27*(3), 385–404.

Center for Democracy and Technology. (1997). *Internet family empowerment white paper: How filtering tools enable responsible parents to protect their children on-line* [On-line]. Available: http://www.cdt.org/speech/empower.html

Champagne, A., Gunstone, F., & Klopfer, L. (1985). Instructional consequences of students' knowledge about physical phenomena. In L. West & A. Pines (Eds.), *Cognitive structure and conceptual change* (pp. 163–188). Orlando, FL: Academic Press.

Champagne, A., Klopfer, L., & Anderson, J. (1980). Factors influencing the learning of classical mechanics. *American Journal of Physics, 48*, 1074–1079.

Chomsky, C. (1990). Books on videodisc: Computers, video, and reading aloud to children. In D. Nix & R. Spiro (Eds.), *Cognition, education and multimedia: Exploring ideas in high technology* (pp. 31–47). Hillsdale, NJ: Erlbaum.

Christmann, E., Badgett, J., & Lucking, R. (1997). Progressive comparison of the effects of computer-assisted instruction on the academic achievement of secondary students. *Journal of Research on Computing in Education, 29*, 325–336.

Clark, R. (1985). Confounding in educational computing research. *Journal of Educational Computing Research, 1*, 137–148.

Clement, J. (1983). A conceptual model discussed by Galileo and used intuitively by physics students. In D. Gentner & A. Stevens (Eds.), *Mental models* (pp. 206–251). Hillsdale, NJ: Erlbaum.

Clements, D., & Gullo, D. (1984). Effects of computer programming on young children's cognition. *Journal of Educational Psychology, 76*, 1051–1058.

Cochran-Smith, M. (1991). Word processing and writing in elementary classrooms: A critical review of related literature. *Review of Educational Research, 61*(1), 107–155.

Cochran-Smith, M., Paris, C., & Kahn, J. (1991). *Learning to write differently: Beginning writers and word processing.* Norwood, NJ: Ablex.

Cognition and Technology Group. (1990). Anchored instruction and its relationship to situated cognition. *Educational Researcher, 19*(6), 2–10.

Cognition and Technology Group. (1992). The Jasper Series as an example of anchored instruction: Theory, program description and assessment data. *Educational Psychologist, 27*(3), 291–315.

Cognition and Technology Group. (1996). Multimedia environments for enhanced learning in mathematics. In S. Vosniadou, E. De Corte, & R. Glaser (Eds.), *International perspectives on the design of technology supported learning environments* (pp. 285–305). Hillsdale, NJ: Erlbaum.

Cohen, M., & Riel, M. (1989). The effect of distant audiences on students' writing. *American Educational Research Journal, 26*(2), 143–150.

Collins, A., & Quillian, M. (1969). Retrieval time from semantic memory. *Journal of Verbal Learning and Verbal Behavior, 8,* 240–247.

CONFU. (1997a). *Educational fair use proposals for distance learning* [On-line]. Available: http://www-ninch.cni.org/ ISSUES/COPYRIGHT/FAIR_USE_EDUCATION/ CONFU/DistanceLearning.html

CONFU. (1997b). *Fair use guidelines for educational multimedia* [On-line]. Available: http://www-ninch.cni.org/ ISSUES/COPYRIGHT/FAIR_USE_EDUCATION/ CONFU/Multimedia.html

Covey, P. (1990). *A right to die? The case of Dax Cowart.* Paper presented at the annual meeting of the AERA, Boston, MA.

Crooks, T. (1988). The impact of classroom evaluation practices on students. *Review of Educational Research, 58,* 438–481.

Daiute, C. (1983). The computer as stylus and audience. *College Composition and Communication, 34,* 134–145.

Daiute, C., & Taylor, R. (1981). Computers and the improvement of writing. *Association for Computing Machinery Proceedings* (pp. 83–88).

Day, J. (1986). Teaching summarization skills. *Cognition and Instruction, 3,* 193–210.

Department of Education. (1998). *Discounted telecommunication services for schools and libraries* [On-line]. Available: http://www.ed.gov/Technology/comm-mit.html

Digital Millennium Copyright Act. (1999). [On-line]. Available: http://lcweb.loc.gov/copyright

D'Ignazio, F. (1990). Restructuring knowledge: Opportunities for classroom learning in the 1990s. *Computing Teacher, 18*(1), 22–25.

D'Ignazio, F. (1996). Minimalist multimedia: Authoring on the World Wide Web. *Learning and Leading with Technology, 23*(8), 49–51.

Dillon, A., & Gabbard, R. (1998). Hypermedia as an educational technology: A review of the quantitative research literature on learner comprehension, control, and style. *Review of Educational Research, 68*(3), 322–349.

Dodge, B. (1995). *Some thoughts about WebQuests.* Available: http://edweb.sdsu.edu/courses/edtec596/about_ webquests.html

Duffy, T., & Bednar, A. (1991, September). Attempting to come to grips with alternative perspectives. *Educational Technology, 32,* 12–15.

Dunkin, M., & Biddle, B. (1974). *The study of teaching.* New York: Holt, Rinehart & Winston.

Eisenberg, M., & Berkowitz, R. (1990). *Information problem-solving: The big six skills approach to library and information skills instruction.* Norwood, NJ: Ablex.

Elton, L., & Laurillard, D. (1979). Trends in research on student learning. *Studies in Higher Education, 4,* 87–102.

Emihovich, C., & Miller, G. (1988). Talking to the turtle: A discourse analysis of Logo instruction. *Discourse Processes, 11,* 183–201.

Erikson, J., & Lehrer, R. (1998). The evolution of critical standards as students design hypermedia documents. *Journal of the Learning Sciences,* 351–386.

Fatemi, E. (1999). Building the digital curriculum. *Education Week, 19*(4), 5–8.

Fay, A., & Mayer, R. (1988). Learning LOGO: A cognitive analysis. In R. Mayer (Ed.), *Teaching and learning computer programming* (pp. 55–74). Hillsdale, NJ: Erlbaum.

Federal Communications Commission (FCC). (1997). Report and order in the matter of Federal-State Joint Board on Universal Service [On-line]. Available: http://www .fcc.gov/ccb/universal_service/fcc97157/97157.html

Flavell, J. (1987). Speculations about the nature and development of metacognition. In F. Weinert & R. Kluwe (Eds.), *Metacognition, motivation, and understanding* (pp. 21–30). Hillsdale, NJ: Erlbaum.

Fletcher-Flinn, C., & Gravatt, B. (1995). The efficacy of computer-assisted instruction (CAI): A meta-analysis. *Journal of Educational Computing Research, 12*(3), 219–242.

Flower, L., & Hayes, J. (1981). A cognitive process theory of writing. *College Composition and Communication, 32,* 365–387.

Fritz, M. (1992). Be juris-prudent. *CBT Directions, 5*(2), 6, 8–10.

Gagne, E. (1985). *The cognitive psychology of school learning.* Boston: Little, Brown.

Gagne, E., Yekovich, C., & Yekovich, F. (1993). *The cognitive psychology of school learning* (2nd ed.). New York: HarperCollins.

Gagne, R., & Glaser, R. (1987). Foundations in learning research. In R. Gagne (Ed.), *Instructional technology: Foundations* (pp. 49–83). Hillsdale, NJ: Erlbaum.

Gallup Organization. (1997). *U.S. teens and technology* [On-line]. Available: http://www.nsf.gov/od/lpa/nstw/teenov.htm

Garner, R. (1987). M*etacognition and reading comprehension.* Norwood, NJ: Ablex.

Gates, B. (1995). *The road ahead.* New York: Viking Books.

Gay, G. (1986). Interaction of learner control and prior understanding in computer-assisted video-instruction. *Journal of Educational Psychology, 78*(3), 225–227.

George, Y., Malcolm, S., & Jeffers, L. (1993). Computer equity for the future. *Communications of the ACM, 36*(5), 78–81.

Global Reach. (1999). *Global Internet statistics: By language* [On-line]. Available: http://www.euromktg.com/globstats/

Goldman, S., Petrosino, A., Sherwood, R., Garrison, S., Hickey, D., Bransford, J., & Pellegrino, J. (1996). Anchored science instruction in multimedia learning. In S. Vosniadou, E. De Corte, & R. Glaser (Eds.), *International perspectives on the design of technology supported learning environments* (pp. 257–284). Hillsdale, NJ: Erlbaum.

Gordin, D., Gomez, L., Pea, R., & Fishman, B. (1997). Using the World Wide Web to build learning communities in K–12. Available: http://www.covis.nwu.edu/Papers/k12web.html

Gordon, J. (1996). Tracks for learning: Metacognition and learning technologies. *Australian Journal of Educational Technology, 12*(1), 46–55.

Grabe, M. (1992). Learning in technology enriched study environments: Will students study effectively? *Reading and Writing Quarterly, 8,* 321–336.

Graves, D. (1983). *Writing: Teachers and children at work.* Exeter, NH: Heinemann.

Greeno, J. (1998). The situativity of knowing, learning, and research. *American Psychologist, 52*(12), 5–26.

Hannafin, M., Hannafin, K., Hooper, S., Rieber, L., & Kini, A. (1996). Research on and research with emerging technologies. In D. Jonassen (Ed.), *Handbook of research for educational communications and technology* (pp. 378–402). New York: Simon & Schuster.

Hannafin, R., & Freeman, D. (1995). An exploratory study of teachers' view of knowledge acquisition. *Educational Technology, 35*(1), 49–56.

Harel, I. (1991). *Children as designers.* Norwood, NJ: Ablex.

Harel, I., & Papert, S. (1990). Software design as a learning environment. *Interactive Learning Environments, 1,* 1–32.

Harley, S. (1996). Situated learning and classroom instruction. In H. McLellan (Ed.), *Situated learning perspectives* (pp. 113–122). Englewood Cliffs, NJ: Educational Technology Publications.

Harper, G. (1997). *Copyright law and electronic reserves* [On-line]. Available: http://www.utsystem.edu/ogc/intellectualproperty/ereserve.htm

Harris, J. (1995). Curricularly infused telecomputing: A structural approach to activity design. *Computers in the Schools, 11*(3), 49–59.

Hartson, T. (1993). Kid-appeal science projects. *Computers in Education, 20*(6), 33–36.

Hayes, J., & Flower, L. (1980). Writing as problem solving. *Visible Language, 14,* 388–399.

Hayes, J., & Simon, H. (1974). Understanding written problem instructions. In L. Gregg (Ed.), *Knowledge and cognition.* Hillsdale, NJ: Erlbaum.

Healy, J. (1998). *Failure to connect: Why computers are damaging our children's minds.* New York: Simon & Schuster.

Hirsch, E. (1988). *Cultural literacy: What every American needs to know.* New York: Vantage Books.

House of Representatives. (1994). *Goals 2000: Educate America Act* [On-line]. Available: http://www.ed.gov/legislation/GOALS2000/TheAct/intro.html

Howe, M. (1972). *Understanding school learning.* New York: Harper & Row.

Hsu, J., Chapelle, C., & Thompson, A. (1993). Exploratory learning environments: What are they and do students explore? *Journal of Educational Computing Research, 9*(1), 1–15.

Hutchinson, E., & Whalen, M. (1994–95). Female students and LEGO TC logo. *Computing Teacher, 22*(4), 22–25.

IITF/CAT (Information Infrastructure Task Force Committee on Applications and Technology). (1994). *A transformation of learning: Use of the NII for education and lifelong learning.* Report of the Information Infrastructure Task Force Committee on Applications and Technology, National Institute of Standards and Technology Special Publication No. 857, U.S. Department of Commerce, Washington, DC: Government Printing Office.

International Society for Technology in Education. (1997). *NCATE program standards for educational computing and technology* [On-line]. Available: http://www.ncate.org/inst_rel/folios/iste.pdf

International Society for Technology in Education. (1998). *National educational technology standards for students* [On-line]. Available: http://cnets.iste.org/

Jansen, B., & Culpepper, S. (1996). Using the big six research process. *Multimedia Schools, 3*(5), 32–38.

Jerald, C., & Orlofsky, G. (1999). Raising the bar on school technology. *Education Week, 19*(4), 58–69.

Johnson, D., & Johnson, R. (1989). Social skills for successful group work. *Educational Leadership, 47*(4), 29–33.

Johnson, D., & Johnson, R. (1999). *Learning together and along* (5th ed.). Boston: Allyn & Bacon.

Johnson, D., Johnson, R., & Holubec, E. (1991). *Cooperation in the classroom* (rev. ed.). Edina, MN: Interaction Book Company.

Jonassen, D. (1986). Hypertext principles for text and courseware design. *Educational Psychologist, 21,* 269–292.

Jonassen, D. (1991, September). Evaluating constructivistic learning. *Educational Technology, 32,* 28–33.

Jonassen, D. (1995). Supporting communities of learners with technology: A vision for integrating technology with learning in schools. *Educational Technology, 35*(4), 60–63.

Jonassen, D. (1996). *Computers in the classroom: Mindtools for critical thinking.* Englewood, NJ: Prentice-Hall.

Jonassen, D., & Grabinger, R. (1990). Problems and issues in designing hypertext/hypermedia for learning. In D. Jonassen & H. Mandl (Eds.), *Designing hypermedia for learning* (pp. 3–25). New York: Springer-Verlag.

Jonassen, D., Peck, K., & Wilson, B. (1999). *Learning with technology: A constructivist perspective.* Upper Saddle River, NJ: Merrill.

Joyce, J. (1988, November). Siren shapes: Exploratory and constructive hypertexts. *Academic Computing, 3*(4), 10–14, 37–42.

Katz, L., & Chard, S. (1989). *Engaging children's minds: The project approach.* Norwood, NJ: Ablex.

Keller, J. (1990). Characteristics of Logo instruction promoting transfer of learning: A research review. *Journal of Research on Computing in Education, 23,* 55–71.

Kendall, J., & Marzano, R. (1996). *Content knowledge: A compendium of standards and benchmarks for K–12 education.* Aurora, CO: Mid-Continent Regional Educational Laboratory.

Kinzie, M., Larsen, V., Burch, J., & Boker, S. (1996). Frog dissection via the World-Wide Web: Implications for the widespread delivery of instruction. *Educational Technology Research and Development, 44,* 59–69.

Knapp, L., & Glenn, A. (1996). *Restructuring schools with technology.* Boston: Allyn & Bacon.

Kozma, R. (1991). Learning with media. *Review of Educational Research, 61*(2), 179-211.

Kulik, C., & Kulik, J. (1991). Effectiveness of computer-based instruction: An updated analysis. *Computers in Human Behavior, 7,* 75–94.

Kurland, D., Clement, C., Mawby, R., & Pea, R. (1987). Mapping the cognitive demands of learning to program. In R. Pea & K. Sheingold (Eds.), *Mirrors of minds: Patterns of experience in educational computer* (pp. 103–127). Norwood, NJ: Ablex.

Laboratory of Comparative Human Cognition. (1989). Kids and computers: A positive vision of the future. *Harvard Educational Review, 59,* 73–86.

Laboratory Network Program Frameworks Task Force. (1998). *Summary of analyzed state curriculum frameworks* [On-line]. Available: http://www.mcrel.org/hpc/sum-cur-fram/

Lafer, S., & Markert, A. (1994). Authentic learning situations and the potential of Lego TC Logo. *Computers in the Schools, 11*(1), 79–93.

Latess, T. (1995). *HyperStudio reference guide.* El Cajon, CA: Roger Wagner Publishing Company.

Lawless, K., & Brown, S. (1997). Multimedia learning environments: Issues of learner control and navigation. *Instructional Science, 25*(2), 117–131.

Lawrence, S., & Giles, C. (1998). Searching the World Wide Web. *Science, 280*(3), 98–100.

Lawrence, S., & Giles, C. (1999). Accessibility of information on the Web. *Nature, 400,* 107–109.

Lehrer, R. (1993). Authors of knowledge: Patterns of hypermedia design. In S. Lajoie & S. Derry (Eds.), *Computers as cognitive tools* (pp. 197–227). Hillsdale, NJ: Erlbaum.

Lehrer, R., Erickson, J., & Connell, T. (1994). Learning by designing hypermedia documents. *Computers in the Schools, 10*(1/2), 227–254.

Lepper, M., & Gurtner, J. (1989). Children and computers: Approaching the twenty first century. *American Psychologist, 44*(2), 170–178.

Levin, S. (1991). The effects of interactive video enhanced earthquake lessons on achievement of seventh grade earth science students. *Journal of Computer Based Instruction, 18*(4), 125-129.

Li, X. (1996). *Electronic sources: APA style of citation* [On-line]. Available: http://www.uvm.edu/~xli/reference/apa.html

Liao, Y. (1992). Effects of computer-assisted instruction on cognitive outcomes: A meta-analysis. *Journal of Research on Computing in Education, 24*(3), 367–380.

Littlefield, J., Delclos, V., Lever, S., Clayton, K., Bransford, J., & Franks, J. (1988). Learning LOGO: Method of teaching, transfer of general skill, and attitudes toward school and computers. In R. Mayer (Ed.), *Teaching and learning computer programming* (pp. 111–135). Hillsdale, NJ: Erlbaum.

Locatis, C., Letourneau, G., & Banvard, R. (1990). Hypermedia and instruction. *Educational Technology, Research and Development, 37*(4), 65–77.

Long, D., Risher, C., & Shapiro, G. (1997). *Questions and answers on copyright for the campus community.* Oberlin, OH: National Association of College Stores.

Loving, C. (1997). From the summit of truth to its slippery slopes: Science education's journey through positivist-postmodern territory. *American Educational Research Journal, 34*(3), 421–452.

Magid, L. (1998). *Child safety on the Information Highway* [On-line]. Available: http://www.safekids.com/child_safety.htm

Major, A. (1998). Copyright law tackles yet another challenge: The electronic frontier of the World Wide Web.

Rutgers Computer and Technology Law Journal, 24(1), 75–105.

Marchionini, G. (1988). Hypermedia and learning: Freedom and chaos. *Educational Technology, 28*(11), 8–12.

Market Data Retrieval. (1999a). *New teachers and technology.* Shelton, CT: Author.

Market Data Retrieval. (1999b). *Technology in education 1999.* Shelton, CT: Author.

Markman, E., & Gorin, L. (1981). Children's ability to adjust their standards for evaluating comprehension. *Journal of Educational Psychology, 73,* 320–325.

Martin, J. (1994). Are you breaking the law? *MacWorld, 11*(5), 125–129.

Mayer, R., & Anderson, R. (1991). Animations need narrations: An experimental test of a dual-coding hypothesis. *Journal of Educational Psychology, 83*(4), 484–490.

McCloskey, M. (1983). Naive theories of motion. In D. Gentner & A. Stevens (Eds.), *Mental models* (pp. 71–94). Hillsdale, NJ: Erlbaum.

McLellan, H. (1996). Situated learning: Multiple perspectives. In H. McLellan (Ed.), *Situated learning perspectives* (pp. 5–17). Englewood Cliffs, NJ: Educational Technology Publications.

McLuhan, M. (1964). *Understanding media: The extensions of man.* New York: McGraw-Hill.

Means, B., Blando, J., Olson, K., Middleton, T., Morocco, C., Remz, A., & Zorfass, J. (1993). *Using technology to support education reform.* Washington, DC: Office of Educational Research and Improvement.

Milheim, W., & Martin, B. (1991). Theoretical bases for the use of learner control: Three different perspectives. *Journal of Computer-Based Instruction, 18,* 99–105.

Montague, M. (1990). Computers and writing process instruction. *Computers in the Schools, 7*(3), 5–20.

Moore, D., Burton, J., & Myers, R. (1996). Multiple-channel communication: The theoretical and research foundation for multimedia. In D. Jonassen (Ed.), *Handbook of research for educational communication and technology* (pp. 851–875). New York: Macmillan.

Moreno, R., & Mayer, R. (1999). Cognitive principles of multimedia learning: The role of modality and contiguity. *Journal of Educational Psychology, 91*(2), 358–368.

Moursund, D., & Bielefeldt, T. (1999). *Will new teachers be prepared to teach in a digital age?* [On-line]. Available: http://www.milkenexchange.org/project/iste/ME154.pdf

Muller, J. (1997). *The great LOGO adventure: Discovering LOGO on and off the computer.* Madison, AL: Doone Publications.

Murie, M. (1993). *Macintosh multimedia workshop.* Carmel, IN: Hayden Books.

Naisbitt, J. (1984). *Megatrends: Ten new directions transforming our lives.* New York: Warner Books.

National Commission on Excellence in Education. (1983). *A nation at risk.* Washington, DC: U.S. Department of Education.

National Council of Teachers of Mathematics. (1989). *Curriculum and evaluation standards for school mathematics.* Reston, VA: National Council of Teachers of Mathematics.

National Telecommunications and Information Administration (NTIA). (1999). *Falling through the cracks: Defining the digital divide* [On-line]. Available: http://www.ntia.doc.gov/ntiahome/fttn99/contents.html

Nielsen, M., & Hoffman, E. (1996). Technology, reform, and foreign language standards. In R. Lafayette (Ed.), *National standards: A catalyst for reform* (pp. 119–137). Lincolnwood, IL: National Textbook Company.

Niemiec, R., Samson, G., Weinstein, T., & Walberg, H. (1989). The effect of computer-based instruction in elementary school: A quantitative synthesis. *Journal of Research on Computing in Education, 20,* 85–103.

Niemiec, R., & Walberg, H. (1987). Comparative effects of computer-assisted instruction: A synthesis of reviews. *Journal of Educational Computing Research, 3*(1), 19–37.

Niess, M. (1998). Using computer spreadsheets to solve equations. *Learning and Leading with Technology, 26*(3), 22–27.

Office of Technology Assessment. (1992). *Testing in American schools: Asking the right questions.* Washington, DC: U.S. Government Printing Office.

Olaniran, B., Savage, G., & Sorenson, R. (1996). Experimental and experiential approaches to teaching face-to-face and computer-mediated group discussion. *Communication Education, 45*(3), 244–259.

Oppenheimer, T. (1997). The computer delusion. *Atlantic Monthly, 280*(1), 45–62.

Owston, R., Murphy, S., & Wideman, H. (1992). The effects of word processing on students' writing quality and revision strategies. *Research in the Teaching of English, 26*(3), 249–276.

Owston, R., & Wideman, H. (1997). Word processors and children's writing in a high-computer-access setting. *Journal of Research on Computing in Education, 30*(2), 202–220.

Paivio, A. (1986). *Mental representations: A dual coding approach.* New York: Oxford University Press.

Palincsar, A., & Brown, A. (1984). Reciprocal teaching of comprehension-fostering and comprehension-monitoring activities. *Cognition and Instruction, 1,* 117–175.

Panel on Educational Technology, President's Committee of Advisors on Science and Technology. (1997). *Report to the president on the use of technology to strengthen K–12 education in the United States* [On-line]. Available: http://www1.whitehouse.gov/WH/EOP/OSTP/NSTC/PCAST/k-12ed.html

Papert, S. (1980). *Mindstorms: Children, computers and powerful ideas.* New York: Basic Books.

Papert, S. (1993). *The children's machine: Rethinking school in the age of the computer.* New York: Basic Books.

Paris, S., & Lindauer, B. (1982). The development of cognitive skills during childhood. In B. Wolman (Ed.), *Handbook of developmental psychology* (pp. 333–349). Englewood Cliffs, NJ: Prentice-Hall.

Paris, S., & Winograd, P. (1990). How metacognition can promote academic learning and instruction. In B. Jones & L. Idol (Eds.), *Dimensions of thinking and cognitive instruction* (pp. 15–51). Hillsdale, NJ: Erlbaum.

Paulson, F., Paulson, P., & Meyer, C. (1991). What makes a portfolio a portfolio? *Educational Leadership, 48*(5), 60–63.

Pea, R., & Kurland, D. (1987a). Cognitive technologies in writing. In E. Rothkopf (Ed.), *Review of research in education #14* (pp. 277–326). Washington, DC: American Educational Research Association.

Pearlman, R. (1991, January). Restructuring with technology: A tour of schools where it's happening. *Technology and Learning,* 30–37.

Perkins, D. (1985). The fingertip effect: How information-processing technology shapes thinking. *Educational Researcher, 14,* 11–17.

Perkins, D. (1986). *Knowledge as design.* Hillsdale, NJ: Erlbaum.

Pogrow, S. (1996). HOTS: Helping low achievers in grades 4–7. *Principal, 76*(2), 34–35.

Pon, K. (1988). Process writing in the one-computer classroom. *Computing Teacher, 15*(6), 33–37.

Porter, C., & Cleland, J. (1995). *The portfolio as a learning strategy.* Portsmouth, NH: Heinemann.

Pressley, M., Snyder, B., Levin, J., Murray, H., & Ghatala, E. (1987). Perceived readiness for examination performance (PREP) produced by initial reading of text and text containing adjunct questions. *Reading Research Quarterly, 22,* 219–236.

Price, R. (1991). *Computer-aided instruction: A guide for authors.* Pacific Grove, CA: Brooks/Cole Publishing.

Quality Educational Data. (1996). *Quality Educational Data national education database* [On-line]. Available: http://www.qeddata.com

Quinn, C., Mehan, H., Levin, J., & Black, S. (1983). Real education in non-real time: The use of electronic message systems for instruction. *Instructional Science, 11,* 313–327.

Raizen, S. (1998). Standards for science education. *Teachers College Record, 100*(1), 66–121.

Ravitz, J., Wong, Y., & Becker, H. (1999a). *Report to the participants: Teaching, learning, and technology national survey* [On-line]. Available: http://www.crito.uci.edu/tlc/findings/special_report/body_index.htm

Ravitz, J., Wong, Y., & Becker, H. (1999b). *Teaching, learning, and computing: 1998—Report to participants* [On-line]. Available: http://www.crito.uci.edu/tlc/findings/special_report/

Read, J., & Barnsley, R. (1977). Remember Dick and Jane. *Canadian Journal of Behavioral Science, 9,* 361–370.

Resnick, L. (1987). *Education and learning to think.* Washington, DC: National Academy Press.

Resnick, M., Bruckman, A., & Martin, F. (1999). Constructional design. In A. Druin (Ed.), *The design of children's technology* (pp. 149–168). San Mateo, CA: Kaufmann.

Riel, M. (1997). *The Internet: A land to settle rather than an ocean to surf and a new "place" for school reform through community development* [On-line]. Available: http://www.gsn.org/teach/articles/netasplace.html

Ring, G. (1993). The effects of instruction in courseware preview methodology on the predictive validity of teacher preview ratings. *Journal of Educational Computing Research, 9*(2), 197–218.

Rosen, M. (1993). Lego meets LOGO. In T. Cannings & L. Finkel (Eds.), *The technology age classroom* (pp. 226–230). Wilsonville, OR: Franklin, Beedle & Associates.

Salpeter, J. (1992). Are you obeying copyright law? *Technology and Learning, 12*(8), 14–23.

Sanders, J., & McGinnis, M. (1991). *Computer equity in math and science: A trainer's workshop guide.* Metuchen, NJ: Scarecrow Press.

Scardamalia, B., Bereiter, C., McLean, R., Swallow, J., & Woodruff, E. (1989). Computer-supported intentional learning environments. *Journal of Educational Computing Research, 5*(1), 51–68.

Schallert, D. (1980). The role of illustrations in reading comprehension. In R. Spiro, B. Bruce, & W. Brewer (Eds.), *Theoretical issues in reading comprehension* (pp. 503–524). Hillsdale, NJ: Erlbaum.

Sharan, Y., & Sharan, S. (1992). *Expanding cooperative learning through group investigation.* New York: Teachers College Press.

Sheingold, K. (1991, September). Restructuring for learning with technology: The potential for synergy. *Phi Delta Kappan,* 28–36.

Shimabukuro, G. (1989). A class act: Junior high students, LEGO and LOGO. *Computing Teacher, 16*(5), 37–39.

Shipstone, D. (1988). Pupils' understanding of simple electrical circuits. *Physics Education, 23,* 92–96.

Singly, M., & Anderson, J. (1989). *The transfer of cognitive skill.* Cambridge, MA: Harvard University Press.

Slavin, R. (1991). *Student team learning: A practical guide to cooperative learning* (3rd ed.). Washington, DC: National Education Association.

Slavin, R. (1995). *Cooperative learning: Theory, research, and practice* (2nd ed.). New York: Merrill.

Slavin, R. (1996). Research on cooperative learning and achievement. *Contemporary Educational Psychology, 21*(1), 43–69.

Smagorinsky, P. (1995). Constructing meaning in the disciplines: Reconceptualizing writing across the curriculum as composing across the curriculum. *American Journal of Education, 103,* 160–184.

Smilowitz, M., Compton, D., & Flint, L. (1988). The effects of computer mediated communication on an individual judgment. *Computers in Human Behavior, 14,* 311–321.

Smith, D., & Cypher, A. (1999). Making programming easier for children. In A. Druin (Ed.), *The design of children's technology* (pp. 201–221). San Mateo, CA: Kaufmann.

Snyder, B. (1971). *The hidden curriculum.* Cambridge, MA: MIT Press.

Snyder, I. (1993). Writing with word processors: A research overview. *Educational Research, 35*(1), 49–68.

Squires, D. (1999). Educational software for constructivist learning environments: Subversive use and volatile design. *Educational Technology, 39*(3), 48–53.

Steinberg, S. (1989). Cognition and learner control: A literature review, 1977–1988. *Journal of Computer-Based Instruction, 16,* 117–121.

Susman, E. (1998). Cooperative learning: A review of factors that increase the effectiveness of cooperative computer-based instruction. *Journal of Educational Computing Research, 18*(4), 303–322.

Sutton, R. (1991). Equity and computers in schools: A decade of research. *Review of Educational Research, 61*(4), 475-503.

Taylor, R. (1980). *The computer in the school: Tutor, tool, tutee.* New York: Teachers College Press.

Tennyson, R. (1980). Instructional control strategies and content structure as design variables in concept acquisition using computer-assisted instruction. *Journal of Educational Psychology, 72,* 525–532.

Tennyson, R., & Buttrey, T. (1980). Advisement and management strategies as design variables in computer-assisted instruction. *Educational Communication and Technology Journal, 28,* 169–176.

Thomas, J., & Rohwer, W. (1986). Academic studying: The role of learning strategies. *Educational Psychologist, 21,* 19–41.

Thomas, L., & Knezek, D. (1991). Facilitating restructured learning experiences with technology. *Computing Teacher, 18*(6), 49–53.

Thomas, R., & Hooper, E. (1991). Simulation: An opportunity we are missing. *Journal of Research on Computing in Education, 23*(4), 497–513.

Tierney, R., Carter, M., & Desai, L. (1991). *Portfolio assessment in the reading-writing classroom.* Norwood, MA: Christopher-Gordon Publishers.

Tobin, K. (1986). Effects of wait time on discourse characteristics in mathematics and language arts classes. *American Educational Research Journal, 23,* 191–200.

Tobin, K. (1987). The role of wait time in higher cognitive level learning. *Review of Educational Research, 57,* 69–95.

Toffler, A. (1980). *The third wave.* New York: Morrow.

Tolhurst, D. (1995). Hypertext, hypermedia, multimedia defined. *Educational Technology, 35*(2), 21–26.

Toomey, R., & Ketterer, K. (1995). Using multimedia as a cognitive tool. *Journal of Research on Computing in Education, 27*(4), 472–482.

Tulving, E. (1972). Episodic and semantic memory. In E. Tulving & W. Donaldson (Eds.), *Organization of memory.* New York: Academic Press.

Turkle, S. (1984). *The second self: Computers and the human spirit.* New York: Simon & Schuster.

U.S. Copyright Office. (1999). *Report on copyright and digital distance education* [On-line]. Available: http://www.loc.gov/copyright/cpypub/de_rprt.pdf

Vygotsky, L. (1978). *Mind in society: The development of higher mental processes.* Cambridge, MA: Harvard University Press.

Wakefield, J. (1996). *Educational psychology: Learning to be a problem-solver.* Boston: Houghton Mifflin.

Weinman, J., & Haag, P. (1999). Gender equity in cyberspace. *Educational Leadership, 56*(5), 44–49.

Wenglinsky, H. (1998). *Does it compute: The relationship between educational technology and student achievement in mathematics* [On-line]. Available: http://www.ets.org/research/pic/dic/techtoc.html

Wetzel, K. (1990). Keyboarding. In S. Franklin (Ed.), *The best of the writing notebook* (2nd ed., pp. 46–48). Eugene, OR: Writing Notebook.

Wheatley, G. (1991). Constructivist perspectives on science and mathematics learning. *Science Education, 75,* 9–21.

Whitehead, A. (1929). *The aims of education.* Cambridge, UK: Cambridge University Press.

Wittrock, M. (1974a). A generative model of mathematics learning. *Journal for Research in Mathematics Education, 5,* 181–197.

Wittrock, M. (1974b). Learning as a generative process. *Educational Psychologist, 11,* 87–95.

Wittrock, M. (1989). Generative processes of comprehension. *Educational Psychologist, 24,* 345–376.

Wittrock, M. (1992). Generative learning processes of the brain. *Educational Psychologist, 27,* 531–541.

World Wide Web Consortium. (1999). *Web Accessibility Initiative page author guidelines* [On-line]. Available: http://www.w3.org/TR/WD-WAI-PAGEAUTH/

Yoder, S. (1992, March). 1/3+1/3+1/3=1 . . . Right? *Computing Teacher,* 38–40.

Yusuf, M. (1995). The effects of LOGO-based instruction. *Journal of Educational Computing Research, 12*(4), 335–362.

Zinsser, W. (1988). *Writing to learn.* New York: Harper & Row.

Index

THE HOUGHTON
LIBRARY
10905 BAKKER

The emphasis in this book is on learner's meaningful use of technology. The special features listed here support and help activate key learning goals.

THE NORTHERN COLLEGE
LIBRARY
10295 BARNSLEY

Spotlight on Assessment

Explorations of ways to try to broaden awareness of assessment alternatives.

- Relating Learning and Assessment
- Performance Assessment
- Electronic Portfolios
- Using Peer Comments
- Evaluating Projects

Activities and Projects for Your Classroom

Content-area or age-specific variations of applications described in the text.

- Ideas for Content-Area Projects
- Word Processing Activities for All Grade Levels
- Spreadsheet Activities
- Slide Show Activities
- Images to Capture
- Video Productions
- Planets

Keeping Current

Sources of information that address educational issues and provide reviews of software, hardware, and applications.

- Locating Appropriate Software
- Finding Useful Mailing Lists
- Subscription Information Services

Emerging Technology

- Inexpensive "Keyboard" Computers
- Videoconferencing with Microsoft NetMeeting
- The Evolution of Multimedia Encyclopedias
- Background Music
- Personal Web Servers
- Adaptations for Visually Impaired Web Users

Focus

Extended discussions of important people, instructional issues, and instructional strategies.

- The Big Six Research Process
- The Emerging Importance of the Computer Coordinator
- ISTE Technology Standards
- How Standards May Be Shaping What You Learn About the Application of Technology
- Are We Abandoning Truth?
- Using the Internet for Authentic Activities
- Lev Vygotsky
- Seymour Papert and LOGO
- The Original Bug
- A Process-Oriented Checklist for LOGO
- Using a Data Logger to Measure Stress
- Instructional Software on the World Wide Web
- Learning Word Processing Features
- Using *Inspiration* to Brainstorm
- Publication on the Internet
- Using a Spreadsheet to Help Understand the Solution to an Algebraic Equation
- *Tabletop:* A Database Environment Developed for Educational Settings
- Making the Connection
- Using Chat in an Online Class
- Joining a List Maintained by a Server
- Internet Addresses
- Tips for Successful Searches
- Citing Internet Sources
- MPExpress—A Presentation Tool for Students
- New Button Actions (NBAs)
- Screen Capture
- Graphics for the Web
- Resources Necessary for Classroom Video Authoring
- Camcorder Tips
- Storing Sounds for Multimedia Productions
- Experimenting with Different Structures and Linking Systems
- The E-rate as a Solution for Disadvantaged Schools
- Obtaining Permission to Copy
- Digital Cheating
- Self-Rating a Web Site
- Rules for the Safe and Appropriate Use of the Internet

ECONOMICS

FIFTH EDITION

OCR, IB, WJEC, CCEA, SQA, HE

ALAIN ANDERTON

Tower Hamlets College
Learning Centre

116174

THE LIBRARY
HAMLETS COLLEGE
HIGH STREET
N E14 0AF

7763

Credits

Original cover design by Susan and Andrew Allen, fifth edition by Tim Button

Cover drawing by Pete Turner, provided by Getty images

Cartoons by Brick

Graphics by Kevin O'Brien and Caroline Waring-Collins

Photography by Andrew Allen and Dave Gray

Edited by Dave Gray

Proofreading by Mike Kidson, Heather Doyle, Sue Oliver.

Acknowledgements

The author and publishers wish to thank the following for permission to reproduce photographs and copyright material. Other copyright material is acknowledged at source.

Corel pp 3(t), 21, 347, 394, 697, Digital Stock 299(c), Digital Vision pp 2, 3(b), 7, 16(b), 67(t), 87, 92, 266, 271, 295, 311, 391, 404, 405, 407, 417, 420(c), 424, 570, Image100 156, 407, 420(b), 437, Photobiz p 390, Photodisc pp 9, 29, 65, 96(bc,br), 110, 120, 244, 264, 270, 298(b), 309, 343, 385, 387, 389, 420(t), 427, 431(b), 524, 538, 568(t), 643, Rex Features pp 12, 107, 112, 151, 290(t), 429, 455, 458, Shutterstock pp 25(t,b), 89, 95, 116, 122, 126, 127, 128, 132, 141, 157, 158 (l,r), 160, 168, 175, 183, 184, 196(t), 205, 206, 208, 259, 265, 279, 281, 285, 290(b), 301, 318, 321, 324, 325, 335, 340, 341, 356, 366, 368, 397, 398, 399, 400, 462, 467, 468, 471, 472, 484, 485, 491, 492, 497, 498, 503, 504, 505, 506, 509, 510, 512, 565, 566, 597, 623, 627, 632, 634, 635, 650, 656, 672, 674, 677, 696, 713, 714, 718, 723, Stockbyte pp 175, 431(t), 454, Stockdisc pp 143, 337(t). 521, 572, Topfoto pp 96(bl), 178, 473.

Office for National Statistics material is Crown Copyright, reproduced with the permission of the Controller of Her Majesty's Stationery Office.

Every effort has been made to locate the copyright owners of material used in this book. Any omissions brought to the notice of the publisher are regretted and will be credited in subsequent printings.

British Library Cataloguing in Publication Data.

A catalogue record for this book is available from the British Library.

ISBN 978 1 4058 9235 3

Pearson Education, Edinburgh Gate, Harlow, Essex, CM20 2JE
Contribution © Alain Anderton
Published 1991 (reprinted 3 times)
Second edition 1995 (reprinted 4 times)
Third edition 2000 (reprinted 4 times)
Fourth edition 2006 (reprinted twice)
Fifth edition 2008

Typesetting by Caroline Waring-Collins (Waring Collins Limited), Ormskirk, L39 2YT.
Printed and bound by Graficas Estella, Navarra, Spain.

Order No:
Class: 330 AND
Accession No: 116174
Type: 3 WK.